ISLAMIC JIHAD

A Legacy of Forced Conversion, Imperialism and Slavery

M. A. Khan

ISBN: 978-1-926800-04-2

felibri

Felibri.com

Printed in the U.S.A. by Felibri.com 2011

Based on meticulous investigation of the Quran, the author has abundantly demonstrated that Islam—more specifically, its doctrine of Jihad or holy war—unequivocally calls for forced conversion and enslavement of non-Muslims and for the establishment of an imperial Islamic rule globally. Thereafter, based on extensive study of the original biographies and traditions of the Prophet, he demonstrates how these commands of the Islamic God, of eternal relevance, were scrupulously applied by Prophet Muhammad: he engaged in forced conversion and enslavement, and established the first imperial Islamic state in Arabia. Through rich historical documentation, this book further demonstrates how Muslims have expanded and perpetuated these paradigmatic models of Jihad over vast parts of the world throughout history to this day. The author predicts that Islamic Jihad, in all likelihood, will intensify over coming decades with serious consequences for humankind, for the infidel and Western world in particular.

This book, I believe, will be a very important contribution for making a thorough understanding of the rising challenges both Muslim and non-Muslim world faces from Islamic extremists.

– Ibn Warraq, Author of *Why I Am Not a Muslim*

This is a must read book, very important and eloquently written, that sheds light on the violent imperialist nature of jihad: a main doctrine in Islam that can only be accomplished at the expense of violating human rights of non-Muslims as well as Muslims... It is one of the best that I read on Islam.

– Nonie Darwish, Author of *Now They Call Me Infidel*

I read this book and found it fascinating. "Islamic Jihad" is a comprehensive reference, which entails in detail lots of facts about Islam and its prophet, in historical and current times. It is very well documented. All that makes it a must read to all of those, who want to understand the driving force behind Jihad and terror.

– Sami Al Raba, Author of *Veiled Atrocities*

I would call "Islamic Jihad" a masterpiece and a great contribution to humanity. Like a spellbound man, I have gone through this book. I will call it a mighty weapon against Islam.

– Shamsuzzoha Manik, Scholar and author of Islam

"Islamic Jihad" is of huge magnitude, in depth and has a great scope. Much of the historical material is largely unknown and greatly needed. It has done a remarkable job on slavery. This work is a blessing to humanity.

– Bill Warner, Scholar and author on Islam; Director of *Center for the Study of Political Islam*

"Islamic Jihad" is so incredibly documented that it leaves little room to criticize the book for the accuracy of the Islamic exposé. So do not tackle this book for reading enjoyment, rather engulf the book to educate your self on the actual nature of Islam's past to understand its present and predict its future.

– Slant Right Blog

This book had me reading it intently from the very start. I enjoyed the chapters on Islam in India... The history of Islam and its adherents throughout history is discussed thoroughly, and fairly, taking into account all sides of the argument. A MUST read. This book is all the more important in the world with what's happening today.

– Goddess 101 (in amzon.co.uk)

At times, the book can be quite disturbing when reading about the misfortunes and massacres of the conquered and enslaved peoples. There is much writing that needs to be comprehended by the reader in order to understand the mind of the Jihadist and the bloody wars fought in the name of Allah. Mr. Khan writes a compelling book that is very detailed, backing it up with extensive footnotes, bibliography, and index. It is a book that should be kept as a reference source for anyone and everyone who is interested in understanding the bloody history of Islamic Jihad and all the consequences that have emerged from it.

– Steven B. Simpson, Writer

Khan's work stands out from the field, [it's] a goldmine. With Khan's book, you will have solid amateur knowledge not only of Islamic history, but Islamic theology as well. For that reason, it is a threat to those who try to keep us blinkered about the reality of Jihad. And to open eyes was Khan's intention. He has succeeded magnificently... Khan depicts the life of Muhammad as a microcosm of Islamic doctrine and history, and he does so brilliantly. I cannot recommend this book highly enough. Read it and learn.

– C. C. Chrappa (on Amazon.com)

"Islamic Jihad" is well researched and scholarly written. Its strength is in its style, rich insight, depth of analysis and the fact that it is well-sourced from Islam's own literature, including the Quran... The book also presents powerful arguments and critical examination of the teachings of Islam and its sanctioning of jihad. It brings to light the reality of jihad and the horrors of surrendering to its evil known as dhimmitude. This book is an essential reading for all those, who are interested in understanding the menace of jihad.

– Mumin Salih, Scolar of Islam and writer

"The book, "Islamic Jihad: A Legacy of Forced Conversion, Imperialism and Slavery", is M. A. Khan's gift to mankind. It is an essential read for all of us, for it depicts the true nature of Islam and the serious threat it poses to the safety and well-being of non-Muslims. I thank the author for giving us such a precious gift."

– Mohammad Asghar, author of *Muhammad & His Quran*

"Islamic Jihad" is very scholarly, persuasive and cogent. The language is simple, easy to understand, and engaging. Once started reading, readers would feel an urge to finish the book. No serious readers of Islam should ignore this book. Read this book and you will grasp why the Islamic Jihadis are doing what they are doing. Readers of the subcontinent (India, Pakistan, Bangladesh), especially Muslims, will be shocked at the suffering their ancestors suffered at the hands of Muslim invaders from the Middle East and Central Asia. The compelling account of many invasions and subsequent incursions will force them to eagerly search their roots. Readers from elsewhere in the Muslims world, and even Europe and America, would also be able make a connection as to how Islam impacted lives of their ancestors.

This book is also a must read for today's political leaders—both Muslim and non-Muslim—to shake off their apathy towards the mortal danger of ascendant Islamic radicalism.

– Abul Kasem, Scholar and author of Islam

*"M. A. Khan's book, **Islamic Jihad: A Legacy of Forced Conversion, Imperialism and Slavery**, is a meticulously researched masterpiece on the subject of the history of Jihad that is a must reading for anyone interested in this topic."* – Jeffry King, Author of *Free Speech* (upcoming)

Preface

I was born and brought up in a conservative Muslim society. After graduating in India, I moved to the West for furthering my education. Despite my conservative Muslim background, I grew up with a liberal outlook. In my school and university days, my closest friends were Hindus and Sikhs: I felt more comfortable with them as they were more liberal, easy-going and humble with fewer religious scruples. I had wholly given up religious rituals by the time I completed my university studies: they just didn't attract me.

When the 9/11 attacks occurred in the U.S., I had lived in a liberal society for over a decade. I had become consciously convinced that religious rituals—prayers, fasting, pilgrimage—were all meaningless. I should be rewarded, I felt, for working hard, and intelligently, not for aping some wasteful rituals, which brings good to nobody. Non-Muslims were my best friends; shocking my Muslim peers, I ate *haraam* (prohibited) foods, drank alcohol (in moderation).

Despite the kind of a liberal person I had become, let me be honest that I was not excluded from those Muslims who felt that the 9/11 attacks were justified, although I felt that those perished in it died undeserving deaths. Muslim societies universally portray America as a mortal enemy of Islam, particularly for its stance on the Israel-Palestine conflict. America's mindless support for Israel has been causing terrible oppression and untold sufferings to Palestinian Muslims. There was, undoubtedly, an overriding sense of justification for the 9/11 attacks amongst Muslims; it gave the unjust superpower a bloody nose: I, so little a Muslim, thought that way too.

Weird as it may sound, I still believed in Islam. I thought that the terrorists, who are acting in the name of Islam, were misguided. After 9/11, I slowly started reading about Islam: the Quran, *Sunnah* and Prophet Muhammad's biographies; I hadn't read them in the thirty-five years of my life. I was shocked. I had been told all my life that Prophet Muhammad was the ideal human being: most merciful and just; that Islam is the most peaceful religion; and I believed it. But the Quran reads like a manifesto of open-ended war against non-Muslims for converting them to Islam, or for subjugating them into horribly degraded *dhimmi* subjects. In his prophetic career, especially during the critical last ten years, Prophet Muhammad was anything but what a peace-loving, merciful and just person stands for.

My curiosity grew. Over the past years, I have done extensive research on Islamic theology as well as on Islamic history: from Prophet Muhammad to modern times. It has been a harrowing tale of forced conversion, brutal imperialism and devastating slavery. It's a saga of great human tragedy—all in the name of Islamic holy war or Jihad, the foundational creed of Islam. This tragic tale is the subject of this book.

M. A. Khan

Acknowledgment

First, I must acknowledge my wife's encouragement and patient sacrifice in the course of this work; without her support, this book would not have been possible.

This work has been based on the works of human and superhuman scholars and authors; and most of the credit should go to them. Prominent mention must be made of Allah, the author of the Quran, of al-Bukhari, Abu Muslim, and Abu Dawud, the compliers of prophetic traditions, of Ibn Ishaq and al-Tabari, the authors of prophetic biographies, and of Muhammad Ferishtah, Ibn Battutah, HM Elliot and J Dawson, Jawaharlal Nehru, KS Lal, Giles Milton, Bernard Lewis, VS Naipaul, GD Khosla, PK Hitti, M Umaruddin, Andrew Bostom, RM Eaton, *Baharistan-i-Shahi* and *Aberuni's India* amongst others.

I am also no less indebted to my friends, namely Abul Kasem, Mohammad Asghar, Syed Kamran Mirza, Sher Khan, Mumin Salih, C Lee, Warner Mackenzie and many others, who have given me tremendous encouragement in the course of this work. Many of them have given me valuable feedbacks and suggestions. Special thanks go to C Lee for sharing his large collection of books with me, which has been very helpful to my research.

The topics discussed in this work are of universal interest but the historical data presented more extensively from India mainly for two reasons: firstly, a good body of historical information on India is available from the works of contemporaneous scholars; secondly, not to make the book too voluminous. While reading it, readers should bear in mind that the treatment of non-Muslims by Muslim rulers was the mildest in India; elsewhere, it was worse except rare instances (Spain).

There will remain some linguistic errors in this book, which, I hope, will not be too distracting to readers.

M. A. Khan
15 Oct. 2008

Contents

Chapter I

Jihad: The Controversies

'...one must go on Jihad at least once a year... One may use a catapult against them when they are in a fortress, even if among them are women and children. One may set fire on them and/or drown them.'

-- Imam al-Ghazzali, the second greatest scholar of Islam after Muhammad

'In the Muslim community, the holy war is a religious duty, because of the universalism of the (Muslim) mission and (the obligation to) convert everybody to Islam either by persuasion or by force.'

-- Ibn Khaldun, *The Muqaddimah*, New York, p. 473

The tragic 9/11 attacks in the United States have dramatically changed the world—a change that will persist for a long time to come. Indiscriminate violence worldwide by al-Qaeda and like-minded Muslim groups in the name of "Jihad" or Islamic "holy war" against the infidels (non-Muslims) has plunged both the Islamic and non-Islamic world into a crisis of security and stability. There is also an ascending tide of puritanical Islamic revivalism among the wider Muslim populace globally. Both these trends pose an unprecedented threat to future security of the secular-democratic nations, both in the West and elsewhere. The violent Jihadi groups that are aiming to establish puritanical Islamic rule globally, governed by the Islamic holy law (Sharia) seek to destroy the modernist, secular-democratic and progressive world-order through indiscriminate violence, death, and destruction. The nonviolent puritanical Islamic revivalism, which has a wider appeal amongst Muslims, seek to achieve the same goal, albeit through different means: through ever-growing demand for the legislation of Sharia and for the gradual suppression of practices and social behaviours in Western societies—freedom of speech, mixing of opposite sexes, and homosexuality etc.—deemed offensive to Islam.

A poll in 2006 found some 40 percent of British Muslims wanted to be governed by Sharia laws, while some 60 percent of them wanted to see Sharia courts operate for the mediation of Muslim affairs. A recent study by the Center for Social Cohesion in the U.K. found some 4 percent of Muslim students in British Universities support killing to "promote and preserve" Islam; 32 percent thought that killing was justified in the defence of Islam; 40 percent support the introduction of Sharia law for Muslims in Britain and 37 percent oppose it. Some 33 percent of them support the creation of a worldwide Muslim caliphate, with only 25 percent opposed to the idea.[1] The study also found that extremism is on the rise amongst Muslims and

---

1. Gardham D, *Muslim students back killing in the name of Islam*, Telegraph (UK), 27 July 2008

1

young Muslims are religiously more radical than their parents' generation. Although Muslims currently constitute only about 3.5 percent of the British population, many aspects of Sharia law are unofficially practised widely in the Muslim community.

Under these circumstances, Rowan Williams, the Archbishop of Canterbury, said in February 2008 that the introduction of Sharia law in the U.K. was "unavoidable" and urged the government to consider its legal introduction.[2] The British government has obliged to the popular demand of Muslims by making the ruling of a Sharia court legally binding in Britain in matters of divorce, financial disputes and even domestic violence. The Court, wrote the *Daily Mail*, claimed '*to have dealt with more than 100 cases since last summer, including six involving domestic violence, which is a criminal rather than civil offence, and said they hoped to take over growing numbers of 'smaller' criminal cases in future.*'[3] This is a step toward establishing Sharia laws in the U.K.

The Islamic "Jihad" or "holy war" stands for *Fighting in the Cause of Allah*, which Allah has introduced into the Islamic doctrine through a long list of verses in the Quran, such as verse 2:190.[4] There are more than 200 divine verses of Jihad in the Quran. Osama bin Laden, the famous protagonist of violent Jihad in our times, defines his Jihadi campaigns against the infidels in religious terms as follows:[5]

> As to the relationship between Muslims and infidels, this is summarized by the Most High's (God's) Word: '*We renounce you. Enmity and hate shall forever reign between us—till you believe in Allah alone.*' So there is an enmity, evidenced by fierce hostility from the heart. And this fierce hostility—that is, battle—ceases only if the infidel submits to the authority of Islam, or if his blood is forbidden from being shed, or if Muslims are at that point in time weak and incapable. But if the hate at any time extinguishes from the heart, this is great apostasy! Allah Almighty's Word to his Prophet recounts in summation the true relationship: '*O Prophet! Wage war against the infidels and hypocrites and be ruthless. Their abode is hell—an evil fate!*' Such, then, is the basis and foundation of the relationship between the infidel and the Muslim. Battle, animosity, and hatred—directed from the Muslim to the infidel—are the foundation of our religion. And we consider this a justice and kindness to them.

Others have disputed this Muslim-to-infidel unidirectional and unrestrained hostility as the theological foundation of Jihad. Many moderate Muslims and scholars of Islam argue that the acts of indiscriminate violence as perpetrated by al-Qaeda and like-minded Islamist groups must not be called Jihad. Jihad, they claim, stands for a peaceful spiritual struggle, totally disconnected from violence. Like President Bush, they argue that *Islam is a religion of peace* and that violence has no place in it. It is also widely claimed, including by many non-Muslim scholars of Islam, that the hallmarks of Islamic history were those of tolerance, peace and equality, which Christianity failed to offer to its Muslim (e.g., in Spain) and other non-Christian subjects (e.g., the Pagans and Jews in Europe and Americas).

Speakers at a *Counter Terrorism Conference* (February 19–21, 2008), organized by the East West Institute at Brussels, repeatedly argued that the term "Jihad" must be dissociated from violence of al-Qaeda because, for most Muslims, Jihad '*originally means a spiritual struggle and they don't want it hijacked anymore.*' Iraqi scholar Sheikh Mohammed Ali told the conference that "*Jihad is the struggle against all evil things in your soul... There is no jihadi terrorism in Islam.*" Emphasizing that Jihad can be a struggle *for elimination of poverty*, *for education* or *for something very, very positive in life*, General Ehsan Ul Haq, the

---

2. *Sharia law in UK is 'unavoidable'*, BBC News, 7 February 2008

3. Matthew Hickley, *Islamic sharia courts in Britain are now 'legally binding'*, 15 September 2008

4. Quran 2.190: *Fight in the cause of Allah those who fight you, but do not transgress limits; for Allah loveth not transgressors* (trs. Yusuf Ali).

5. Raymond Ibrahim, *The Two Faces of Al Qaeda*, Chronicle Review, 21 September 2007

former chairman of Pakistan's joint chiefs of staff, asserted that calling the terrorists Jihadists is either reflective of a *"lack of understanding of Islam"* or unfortunately *"an intended misuse."*[6]

Since the 9/11 attacks, orchestrated by al-Qaeda in the name of Jihad, Muslims as well as many non-Muslim scholars and academics, have come out in force to defend this nonviolent notion of Jihad. Daniel Pipes has quoted several examples of the positive portrayals of the meaning of Jihad, which are summarized below.[7]

Zayed Yasin, president of the Harvard Islamic Society, in a speech, entitled *My American Jihad*, at the University's 2002 commencement ceremony, said: *"Jihad, in its truest and purest form, the form to which all Muslims aspire, is the determination to do right, to do justice even against your own interest. It is an individual struggle for personal moral behavior..."* Harvard dean Michael Shinagel, probably with no knowledge of Islamic theology, gave an emphatic endorsement of Yasin's definition of Jihad as a personal struggle for promoting *"justice and understanding in ourselves and society."* Professor David Mitten, advisor to the Harvard Islamic Society, defined *true Jihad* as *"the constant struggle of Muslims to conquer their inner base instincts, to follow the path to God, and to do good in society."*

There are many in the U.S. academia propagating this view on Jihad. Professor Joe Elder of the University of Wisconsin sees Jihad as a *"religious struggle, which more closely reflects the inner, personal struggles of the religion."* To Professor Roxanne Euben of Wellesley College, *"Jihad means to resist temptation and become a better person,"* while Professor John Parcels of Georgia Southern University sees Jihad as a struggle *"over the appetites and your own will."* To Professor Ned Rinalducci at Armstrong Atlantic University, Jihad's goal is: *"Internally, to be good Muslim. Externally, to create a just society."* For Professor Farid Eseck at New York University, Jihad amounts to *"resisting apartheid and working for women's rights."* To Bruce Lawrence, eminent professor of Islamic studies at Duke University, Jihad may amount to *"being a better student, a better colleague, a better business partner. Above all, to control one's anger."* To him, even non-Muslims should inculcate the worthy virtue of Jihad; the United States, for example, can emulate the virtue of Jihad by reviewing her foreign policies for promoting justice for all in an unjust world.

Against this nonviolent and anything-good-one-does notion of Jihad, al-Qaeda and numerous radical Islamist groups triumphantly claim that their act of violence against the infidels, particularly the West and West-leaning/allied Muslim individuals, groups and governments, is Jihad. They often justify their claim with references from the Quran and examples from the life of Prophet Muhammad. Obviously, there is a great deal of disagreement or denial about this extremist discourse of Jihad.

It is undeniable that, out of misconception or not, the violent Islamist groups—with their unquestioned belief that they are *fighting in the cause of Allah*—will continue unleashing violence and terrorism against innocent men, women and children in the years and decades to come, causing incalculable damage and destruction to human life and society. Indisputably, Muslims are now a substantial and established group in almost every nation in the world. Due to high birth-rates amongst Muslims, their continued influx from the overpopulated Islamic world and decline of the native population, they may become, according to current demographic trends, the dominant religious group in many Western countries by the middle of this century. If the current tide of ascendant violent radicalism continues to thrive amongst Muslims, the stability of the tolerant, civilized world may face peril in the not-too-distant future. To secure the stability of the modernist, secular-democratic and progressive future of the world, nations must work unitedly for countering the ideology and activities of these radical Islamist groups, using both military and ideological means.

---

6. *What is jihad? Language still hinders terror fight*, Reuters, 20 Feb, 2008

7. Pipes D (2003) *Militant Islam Reaches America*, WW Norton, New York, p. 258–68

2-

As violent Islamists wreak havoc around the world, more so in Islamic countries, understanding the "true meaning" of Jihad, their central cause, is of central importance for both Muslims and non-Muslims in order to devise effective counter-measures against them. Without understanding *what Jihad truly means*, it is impossible for authorities and the people to devise effective remedies against the growing violent trend in the name of Jihad amongst Muslims.

This book is a small effort to give readers an idea of what Jihad truly means. It goes through the life of Prophet Muhammad as he progressively received revelation from the Islamic God (Allah) as contained in the Muslim holy book, the Quran. It will examine when and under what circumstances, Allah introduced the concept of Jihad into Islamic doctrines. It will demonstrate—based on the Quran, authentic prophetic traditions, and original biographies of Prophet Muhammad—how the Prophet of Islam had applied the doctrine of Jihad as he founded the Islamic creed during the last twenty-three years of his life (610–632 CE). Having thus made a sense of the religious foundation and prophetic model of Jihad, it will examine how this prototypical model of Jihad was perpetuated by Muslims through the ages of Islamic domination.

It is worth noting beforehand that, in putting Allah's doctrine of Jihad into practice at the birth of Islam, Prophet Muhammad had established three major models of Jihadi actions:

1. Use of violence for the propagation of Islam,
2. Islamic imperialism,
3. Islamic slavery

The historical accounts of these legacies of Jihad will be discussed in separate chapters in this book.

Chapter II

Basic Beliefs in Islam

An overview of the basic Muslim beliefs as summarised below will be helpful in a better and easy understanding of the content of this book.

Muslims believe that Islam is the final monotheistic religion of the Abrahamic School. Allah, the Islamic God—claimed by Muslims to be the same God as that of the Jews and Christians—had sent 124,000 prophets in succession to preach His guidance to humankind since the creation of Adam and Eve. Adam was the first and Muhammad was the last in this succession of prophets. Muhammad was the final prophet and the best of them all. He was the highest perfection of human life for all time. The final and best prophet also brought God's perfected, final divine revelation, the Quran and founded God's finalized religion, Islam. The earlier revelations and creeds sent by God, such as the Jewish and Christian scriptures and religions, are imperfect and inferior to the final one. Allah Himself asserts in the Quran that He sent Islam to abrogate and replace all other religions: '*He (Allah) has sent His Apostle (Muhammad) with the guidance and the (only) true religion that He may make it prevail over all the religions*' [Quran 48:28].[8]

Islam asserts that the Jewish scripture has been perverted or changed by the Jews over time [Quran 2:59]. Hence, it is canceled and must be abandoned. The Christian scripture gets a better evaluation in that, although considered inferior to Islam, it is still valid. The Quran asserts that Christians have forgotten some parts of their original scripture [Quran 5:14] and that they have misunderstood their teachings and wrongly consider Jesus as the son of God [Quran 5:72; 112:2; 19:34–35; 4:171]. It also asserts that Christians wrongly attribute Jesus as one of the Three—i.e., one of the three Gods or the Trinity [Quran 5:73; 4:171]. Although Christians practice their religion wrongly, Allah did not cancel Christianity altogether, but hopes that it would eventually be superseded by Islam [Quran 48:28]. Strangely, instead of sending Prophet Muhammad to explain how Jews had corrupted the Torah (Old Testament) or how Christians have forgotten and misunderstood the Bible (New Testament) and to correct those elements and sections, God chose to send down an entirely different religion with Prophet Muhammad at its head.

---

8. The Quranic reference has been included in the parenthesis within the text. Quran 48:28 stands for Quranic Chapter 48, Verse 28. One of the three most acceptable translations of the Quran, hosted by the University of Southern California (http://www.usc.edu/dept/MSA/quran/), has chosen for linguistic clarity.

Islam is based on two foundational components: first, the divine revelation, contained in the Quran and second, the prophetic traditions, also called *ahadith* or *Sunnah*. The divine revelation is God's message to mankind in His own words contained unaltered in the Arabic Quran. During Muhammad's career of preaching and propagating Islam between 610 and 632, Allah passed His revelations in bits and pieces to Muhammad through His messenger, angel Gabriel. Muhammad was possibly an illiterate man. Every time Gabriel came down with God's verses, he pronounced it to Muhammad until the latter memorized it word by word. Muhammad then got it written down by his literate disciples in order to keep them exactly as God's word. He also got it memorized by a group of his favourite disciples. These revelations, after Prophet Muhammad's death, were compiled into what is known as the Quran. The contents of the Quran, therefore, are exact words of the Islamic God intended for guiding human life in this world exactly in the way He wants. Such a life would enable believers to gain access to Allah's Paradise after death and reap His endless bounties therein.

The second element, indeed, the other half of the Islamic creed, is the prophetic traditions: the sayings, deeds and actions of Prophet Muhammad, collectively called the *Sunnah* or *ahadith*. Since Muhammad was the best amongst God's numerous prophets and the embodiment of the highest perfection of human life ever to walk on the earth—the only way for Muslims, indeed for all human beings, to live a perfect human life for achieving Allah's bounties in Paradise is to walk in the footsteps of the Prophet.

In Islamic belief, Muslims who live their life as perfectly as that of Prophet Muhammad will enter Paradise without ever serving any time in hell. But it is almost impossible for a Muslim to emulate Muhammad's sinless life. Therefore, most Muslims will first serve some period of time, being roasted in the horrifying fire of Islamic hell. The length of their residence in hell will be determined by the quantum of sins they commit in this life. They will, thereafter, enter Paradise to live there for eternity.

The only other group of Muslims who will enter Paradise, bypassing the roasting in hellfire, are those who would die as martyrs while *fighting in the cause of Allah*, e.g, while engaging in Jihad or holy war [Quran 9:111] (see more in Chapter III). Therefore, those hundreds of Muslims, who died while fighting in the wars commanded and/or directed by Prophet Muhammad in his lifetime as well as those hundreds of thousands, who died in Islamic holy wars over the subsequent centuries and those dying at present and will die in future, will directly land in the Islamic Paradise. Other Muslims, who die a normal death, will have to wait until the *Judgement Day* after the end of the world for Allah to judge how much time they will have to spend in hell before they can enter Paradise.

Therefore, it remains a universal desire amongst Muslims to emulate the life of Prophet Muhammad, namely his actions, deeds and sayings, in minute details. The other desirable outcome of the Muslim life is to become a martyr fighting in Islamic holy war against the infidels, particularly for expanding the domain of Islam by wrestling territories under non-Muslim control. The fledgling early community of Muslims, under the guidance of Prophet Muhammad in Medina, had wholly dedicated themselves in the profession of fighting Jihad and lived on the plunder, the divinely-sanctioned booty, obtained from those wars (see Chapter III).

During the twenty-two years of his prophetic career, Muhammad was in close contact with Allah. Allah was guiding him almost in every step of his life under all circumstances—be it the difficulties in war, dealing with prisoners, solving family disputes, and so on. Allah kept a constant vigilance over the actions and deeds of the Prophet. Whenever Muhammad made a mistake, Allah was there to admonish, correct or guide him. Hence, every saying or deed of Muhammad during his prophetic career was divinely guided or of divine nature. Accordingly, Abdul Hamid Siddiqi, erudite scholar and translator of *Sahih Muslim* (a collection of prophetic traditions), asserts that the *Sunnah* is of divine origin: '*...the teachings of the Qur'an and the Sunnah are derived from no human agency and are all inspired by God, and therefore transcend all material* *or worldly considerations...*'[9] Hence, the *Sunnah* of the Prophet constitutes an extrascriptural and semi-divine constituent of the Islamic creed, which Muslims must meticulously follow.

The desire for Muslims to emulate the life of Prophet Muhammad is not simply a theoretical deduction. Instead, Allah frequently commands Muslims to follow the Prophet alongside the instructions of the Quran. The Quran repeatedly says: *Obey Allah* (i.e., the *Quran*) *and His Apostle* (i.e., the *Sunnah*) [Quran 3:32; 4:13,59,69; 5:92; 8:1,20,46; 9:71; 24:47,51–52,54,56; 33:33; 47:33; 49:14; 58:13; 64:12]. The commands and precepts of the Quran and the *Sunnah*, therefore, constitute two almost equally important halves of the Islamic creed. However, some modern apologists of Islam, either out of defiance or ignorance of Allah's repeated reminders, seek to dissociate the *Sunnah* from Islam because some of its contents are unacceptable in modern conscience. They want to make the Quran the sole constitution of Islam. However, the *Sunnah*, compiled by outstanding Islamic scholars over 200 years after Prophet Muhammad's death, are overwhelmingly in agreement with the messages of the Quran and have been accepted by the religious doctors of Islam (*Ulema*) over the centuries.

The Sharia or the Islamic holy laws is another indispensable component of Islam. Sharia laws are not a separate constituent but derivations from the Quran and the *Sunnah*.

Although Muhammad had written down God's verses in bits and pieces and also had them memorized by a number of his disciples, he did not bother to compile them into a book. The Quran that we know today was assembled during the reign of the third caliph, Othman (r. 644–656). Likewise, although Allah repeatedly tells Muslims to follow the Prophet, Muhammad neglected to write down (or have it written down by others) his biography, detailing his actions and deeds, for Muslims to follow until the end of the world. Obviously, the Islamic God had also forgotten to remind Muhammad to assemble His verses into a book (i.e., the Quran) or to write down his autobiography (i.e., the *Sunnah*)—the two foundational components of the Islamic creed that Muslims must follow strictly at all time.

After Prophet Muhammad's death, some intelligent Muslims made up for these shortcomings of Allah and His Prophet. They realized that systematic organization of the divine verses and the *Sunnah* would be essential for the survival of the Islamic creed in the uncorrupted, pristine form. Hence, in order to avoid the same kind of corruptions that occurred in Allah's earlier scriptures—the Gospel and the Torah, they first assembled the Quran about two decades after Muhammad's death.

Next, two streams of brilliant Islamic scholars embarked on two separate Herculean projects in order to put Islam on the right track. The first project was to assemble the *Sunnah*, starting with the compilation of the first biography of the Prophet in about 750 CE by the pious Muslim scholar, Ibn Ishaq. Thereafter, many illustrious Muslim scholars and researchers stepped into the field to perform arduous and meticulous research on the life of Prophet Muhammad. They scoured the lands across Arabia—from the Hejaz to Syria, to Persia, to Egypt—for interviewing numerous people and assembled thousands of sayings, deeds and actions of the Prophet. There were six brilliant *hadith* compilers, whose compilations have been recognized as authentic:

1. Al-Bukhari (810–870) collected 7275 authentic *hadiths*, called the *Sahih Bukhari*

2. Muslim b. al-Hajjaj (821–875), a disciple of Bukhari, collected 9200 authentic *hadiths*, called the *Sahih Muslim*

3. Abu Daud (817–888) collected 4800 authentic *hadiths*, called the *Sunan Abu Daud*

4. Al-Tirmidi (d. 892)

5. Ibn Majah (d. 886)

6. Imam Nasai (b. 215 AH)

---

9. *Sahih Muslim by Imam Muslim*, Translated by Siddiqi AH, Kitab Bhavan, New Delhi, 2004 edition, Vol. I, p. 210–11, note 508.

During the phase of compilation of the *Sunnah*, another stream of brilliant Islamic scholars appeared in the field. They focused on the correct interpretations of the Quranic verses and prophetic traditions in order to formulate well-defined laws for the Islamic society. This field, known as the Islamic jurisprudence (*fiqh*), have four major Schools initiated by four outstanding Muslim scholars. They are:

1. The *Hanafi School*, founded by Imam Abu Hanifa (699–767), is largely practised by Muslims in South Asia, Central Asia, Turkey, the Balkans, China and Egypt.

2. The *Maliki School*, founded by Imam Malik bin Anas (715–795), is largely practised by Muslims in North and West Africa and several Arab states.

3. The *Shafii School*, founded by Imam al-Shafii (767–820), is largely practised by Muslims in Southeast Asia, Egypt, Somalia, Eritrea and Yemen among others.

4. The *Hanbali School*, founded by Imam Ahmad ibn Hanbal (780–855), is largely practised in Saudi Arabia and other Arab states.

The *fiqh*, according to famous Muslim historian Ibn Khaldun, is the *'knowledge of the rules of God which concern the actions of persons who are themselves bound to obey the law respecting what is required (wajib), forbidden (haraam), recommended (mandūb), disapproved (makruh) or merely permitted (mubah)'* in Islam.[10] The founders and pupils of the four major Schools of Islamic jurisprudence carried out outstanding research over three centuries to create a compendium of Islamic laws and precepts, collectively known as the Islamic holy laws or the Sharia. With few exceptions, these Schools of Islamic laws differ only in minor details but very little in essence.

Allah, the Islamic God, had presented Islam to all humankind as the perfected final code of life [Quran 5:3]. In other words, Islam is a detailed manual for humankind to lead life as wished by Allah. Therefore, Islam has a solution or guideline for every possible event, situation and action of human life. The Sharia contains divine laws, protocols and precepts for human beings to follow in every situation in life—be it eating, defecating, bathing, having sex, saying prayers, fighting wars or any other circumstances, they may find themselves in.

Sharia laws cover all spheres of Muslim life: spiritual, social, financial and political. There is no separation between the spiritual (religious) and the mundane in Islam. Islam is an all-in-one solution to the worldly problems for humankind. Therefore Islam, affirms Turkish scholar Dr Sedat Laçiner, is *'not only a religion but also the name of a political, economic and cultural system.'*[11] Prof. M Umaruddin (Aligarh Muslim University, India) sees the relationship between Islam and politics as inseparable. He asserts that *'Islam is not a religion in the usual sense of the word. The view that religion has to do only with the inner conscience of man, with no logical relations with social conduct, is completely foreign, rather abhorrent to Islam.'* Emphasizing that the theological precepts of Islam cover all aspects of human life, he adds: *'It is an all-embracing system, a complete code of life, bearing on and including every phase of human activity and every aspect of human conducts.'*[12]

In sum, the Quran and the *Sunnah* are the primary constitutions of Islam. The Sharia laws are derived from these two primary sources. The Quran, the *Sunnah* and the Sharia together constitute the complete foundation of the Islamic creed. They are the indispensable complete guide to the Muslim life and society for all times and places.

---

10. Levy R (1957) *The Social Structure of Islam*, Cambridge University Press, U.K., p. 150

11. Laçiner S, *The Civilisational Differences As a Condition for Turkish Full-Membership to the EU*; Turkish Weekly, 9 Feb. 2005

12. Umaruddin M (2003) *The Ethical Philosophy of Al-Ghazzali*, Adam Publishers & Distributors, New Delhi, p. 307

Chapter III

Life of Prophet Muhammad and the Birth of Jihad

"I have been made victorious with terror." -- Prophet Muhammad, *Bukhari 4:52:220*

"Muhammad is an exalted standard of (human) character." -- Allah, *Quran 68:4, 33:21]*

Prophet Muhammad, believe many Muslims, was created by Allah prior to creating the universe for his eventual appearance on earth in the seventh century for preaching His final creed to humankind. According to a widely circulated tradition, when asked about '*the first thing Allah created before all things,*' Prophet Muhammad answered, '*the first thing Allah created was the light of your Prophet from His light...*'[13] The life of Prophet Muhammad, the highest possible perfection of human life (*insan-i-kamil*) for all time, was full of virtues and devoid of any vices. He had all the good characteristics of a human being—be it in sexual morality or kindness—in the highest possible degrees, while the bad characteristics, he had none or in the least possible degrees. He was infallible and sinless as Allah himself had consecrated him: '*Have We (Allah) not expanded for you (Muhammad) your breast, and taken off from you your burden (sin)*' [Quran 94:1–2]. He was the kindest, fairest, most just, most merciful, most generous and most honest, while he possessed no cruelty or barbarity at all. Allah Himself affirms this saying, '*And We (Allah) have not sent you (Muhammad) but as a mercy to the worlds*' [Quran 21:107].

Prophet Muhammad himself had boasted of possessing the perfect moral character in saying, ''*I have been sent to perfect morals.*'' Imam al-Ghazzali (d. 1111), the great Islamic scholar and revivalist, considered the second-greatest Muslim after Muhammad, '*considered the Prophet as the ideal, the perfect man par excellence, in all aspects of life.*' About the greatness of the Prophet's personal character, al-Ghazzali wrote:

> The apostle always prayed in all humility to Allah for bestowing on him the highest moral qualities and a generous character. He was of exceeding humility and the greatest, the bravest, the justest and the most pious of men... The high standard which the Prophet set in moral

---

13. Haddad GF, *The First Thing That Allah Created Was My Nur*, Living Islam website; http://www.livingislam.org/fiqhi/fiqha_e30.html

behavior as a citizen free or persecuted, as a husband, as a chief, and as a conqueror was never reached by any individual before or since.[14]

Prophet Muhammad, therefore, was the greatest embodiment of good, justice and mercy to humankind. Whatever he did in his life was the best thing to do; howsoever way he dealt with people, Muslim or non-Muslim, was the fairest and most merciful. This chapter will briefly deal with the life of Prophet Muhammad, particularly his dealing with non-Muslims: the Idolaters, Jews and Christians of Arabia, whom he had encountered in his life. It is needless to reiterate that Muslims indisputably believe that Muhammad's dealing with these people (recounted below) was absolutely fair, just and merciful in every respect.

In this chapter, the doctrines of Jihad in Islam, as revealed by Allah in the course of Muhammad's founding the Islamic creed, will be discussed in detail. Having gone through this chapter, readers will be able to grasp the *true meaning of Jihad* as revealed by Allah and the *ideal model of Jihad* in practice, which Prophet Muhammad had established in complete compliance with the commands of Allah.

THE BIRTH AND EARLY LIFE (c. 570–610)

The Prophet of Islam was born in about 570 CE (c. 567–72) in the Arabian Desert city of Mecca in a family of the Quraysh, the chief tribe of the city. Mecca was situated at a strategic location in the desert valley through which passed two major trade-routes: one linked Himyar with Palestine and Syria; the other linked Yemen, the Persian Gulf and Iraq. Because of this strategic location, Mecca acted as the major transit-point for trade-caravans between the Indian Ocean (including East Africa) and the Mediterranean. Through Mecca were transported large quantities of merchandise to and from the Egyptian, Syrian, Roman, Byzantine, Persian and Indian centres of trade. It was thus a bustling centre of trade and commerce and a routine halting place for trade-caravans to stock up supplies of water and other necessities. As a result, the two powers of the region, namely the Persian and Byzantium Empires, sought to control Mecca through alliance with its leaders.[15]

The first Quraysh to assume a position of importance in Mecca was a man by the name of Qusayy bin Kilab. In about 450 CE, he, in alliance with tribes supported by the Byzantine emperor, deposed the reigning Khuza'a tribe and established the Quraysh leadership in Mecca. He instituted ordnances for the governance of Mecca and for the administration of the sacred temple of *Ka'ba*. He is said to have rebuilt the *Ka'ba*—the sacred *House of God*, long neglected by earlier administrators—on a grander scale and instituted in it the goddesses of the Nabataeans, known as al-Lat, al-Uzza and al-Manat. These goddesses were known to be the daughters of God (Hubal or Allah) in Pagan Arab tradition.

Muhammad's parents used to face hardship in their day-to-day life. The death of his father Abdullah, when his mother Amina was six-month's pregnant with him, must have had aggravated the hardships. It was a tradition among the elites in Mecca (i.e., the Quraysh) to give away their children to paid foster-mothers for nursing.[16] About one-week-old Muhammad was given to a Bedouin woman, named Halima, for which his mother could not pay the foster-mother.[17] Halima took Muhammad away to raise him alongside her own son of the same age. Halima brought four-year-old Muhammad back to Mecca to meet his mother. Because Muhammad had allegedly brought good luck to his foster-parents, they wanted to keep him with them until he became a big boy. Accordingly, they took him back with them. But surprisingly, Halima returned him to his mother Amina in Mecca when he was five. While returning him, Halima allegedly told Amina a supernatural story that happened to Muhammad, whereby "*two men in white raiment came to Muhammad and threw him*

---

14. Umaruddin M (2003) *The Ethical Philosophy of Al-Ghazzali*, Adam Publishers & Distributors, New Delhi, p. 66–67
15. Walker B (2002) *Foundations of Islam*, Rupa & Co, New Delhi, p. 37
16. Muir W (1894) *The Life of Mahomet*, London, p. 129–30
17. Ibn Ishaq, *The Life of Muhammad*, trs. A Guillaume, Oxford University Press, Karachi, 2004 imprint, p. 71

down and opened up his belly and searched (something) therein.'' [18] This event was later described by Allah as the consecration of Muhammad by wiping out his sins [Quran 94:1–2]. To corroborate this claim, Muhammad allegedly returned with a new mark between his shoulder-blades; this mark was later explained as his *seal of prophethood* [Sahih Bukhari 4:741, Tirmidhi 1524].

Amina raised Muhammad with good care. Shortly afterwards, she brought Muhammad to Medina, 210 miles north of Mecca, about ten to twelve days' journey. The Khazraj tribe in Medina was related to Muhammad through his great-grandmother belonging to that tribe. Unfortunately, his mother died on the way back to Mecca when Muhammad was only six years old. The orphan Muhammad was then raised first by his loving grandfather Abd al-Mutallib, after whose death by his uncle Abu Talib. However, he faced hard times: he took up the career of a shepherd at a tender age and used to spend lonely time grazing cattle.

Muhammad's marriage at the age of twenty-five with a forty year-old wealthy businesswoman of Mecca, named Khadijah, dramatically changed his fortune and greatly increased his social standing. Muhammad was at first employed by her to run her businesses. Soon, he is said to have impressed his employer by running the business profitably. Impressed by the young, intelligent and able man, fifteen years younger than her; Khadijah proposed to marry him. [19]

Khadijah had an aging cousin, named Waraqa bin Naufal, a man of flexible faith, who—impressed by monotheism—had changed his faith first to Judaism and then to Christianity. [20] Naufal *'was a Christian convert and used to read the Gospels in Arabic,'* says a hadith [Bukhari 4:605]. Khadijah, through her close interaction with Waraqa, had also become influenced by monotheism, Christianity in particular. Muhammad, on his part, used to follow all the idolatrous rituals of the polytheistic religion of his Quraysh tribesmen. But after his marriage, which brought him in close contact with Waraqa and Khadijah, Muhammad abruptly stopped practicing Paganism and became interested in the monotheistic Jewish and Christian theology.

Soon after his marriage, Muhammad is said to have started spending certain period of the year in a cave in the Mount Hira near Mecca for meditation. This is the same cave in which his loving grandfather used to retire for meditation in the holy month of Ramadan. Such retirements to caves for meditation was a common practice amongst the *Hanifs*—a monotheistic sect of Mecca (see below). Islamic tradition says that Muhammad used to spend time in this cave meditating in the pursuit of God. After fifteen years of meditation, Muhammad allegedly received revelation from God for preaching a new religion, Islam.

This idea is similar to the Jewish tradition of Moses' meditation in a cave of Mount Sinai, where he had allegedly conversed with God (Jehovah/Yahweh). Muhammad was likely inspired by that story. There are also references in Islamic literatures informing us that Muhammad used to spend his time in the cave, not alone, but his wife Khadijah and Waraqa also sometimes joined him. Islamic literatures also inform that Muhammad, through Waraqa's connection, often met with Jewish rabbis and Christian priests during the late period of his meditation and the early days of his prophetic mission. It is believed that Muhammad familiarized himself in the scriptures of the monotheistic Jewish and Christian theology during those years, often in the cave of Mount Hira, away from the public sight. The likely purpose of this was to prepare him for the mission of preaching the oneness of God of the Abrahamic faiths among the polytheistic Idolaters of Mecca.

---

18. Ibid, p. 71–72

19. It should be noted here that widowed Khadijah was looking for an able agent to run her businesses. Her nephew, named Khuzaima, once met Muhammad when he was on a business trip overseas with his uncle, Abu Taleb. Khuzaima spotted Muhammad's business talent, which he had mastered while accompanying his uncle's trade-caravans to various destinations since the age of twelve. Khuzaima later introduced him to Khadijah for employing him to run her businesses.

20. Ibn Ishaq, p. 83

PROPHETIC MISSION IN MECCA (610–622)

With this background and after fifteen years of meditation in the cave of Mount Hira, Muhammad one day (aged 40, 610 CE) claimed that he had heard voices from the unseen instructing him in some messages.[21] The first persons to believe him were his wife Khadijah and Waraqa, who persuaded an apparently confused Muhammad saying that God had talked to him through angel Gabriel to preach a new religion. According to a prophetic tradition, Waraqa said to Muhammad: '*That is the same angel whom Allah sent to Prophet Moses. Should I live till you receive the Divine Message, I will support you strongly*' [Bukhari 4:605]. However, Waraqa never embraced Islam and died as a Christian.

Muhammad named his monotheistic God Allah—the name of the chief Pagan deity of Arabia,[22] which was also in general use in the region to denote God. For the first three years, Muhammad preached his alleged divine messages secretly to his close associates, friends and family members before going public about his divine mission. His messages demanded that the *Ka'ba*, considered the *House of God* in the local Pagan tradition, was an exclusive sanctuary of his own God. He claimed that the *Ka'ba* was founded by the Jewish patriarch Abraham and his son Ishmael, both considered highly respected prophets in Islam. He called his new creed the *Religion of Abraham* and urged the Meccan Polytheists to abandon their idolatry and follow his creed. Here is how Muhammad demanded that the Pagans of Mecca follow his creed and claimed that the *Ka'ba* belonged to his own God:

> And whoever shall invent a falsehood after that concerning Allah, such will be wrong-doers. Say: Allah speaketh truth. *So follow the religion of Abraham, the upright. He was not of the idolaters*. Lo! the first Sanctuary (*Ka'ba*) appointed for mankind was that at Becca (Mecca) a blessed place, a guidance to the peoples; Wherein are plain memorials (of Allah's guidance); *the place where Abraham stood up to pray*; and whosoever entereth it is safe. And pilgrimage to the House is a duty unto Allah for mankind, for him who can find a way thither. As for him who disbelieveth, (let him know that) lo! Allah is Independent of (all) creatures. [Quran 3:94–97]

This naturally had caused unhappiness among the pious Quraysh of Mecca. The majority of them adamantly rejected Muhammad's religion. Neither did they hand over the custodianship of the *Ka'ba* to him. After about thirteen years of preaching in Mecca, Muhammad could only obtain a handful of converts, 100 to 150 in all, before he was *allegedly* driven out by the Quraysh and he took refuge in Medina in June 622. After securing himself in Medina, he undertook a ruthless mission to destroy the livelihood and religion of the Quraysh over the next eight years. In 630, he conquered Mecca, took possession of the *Ka'ba*, despoiled the idols therein, and eventually, forced the Idolaters of Mecca to accept Islam on the pain of death.

Before proceeding further, let us first examine a few popular stories prevalent in Muslim societies about Muhammad's departure from Mecca and about the cruelty and intolerance of the Quraysh.

Was Muhammad driven out of Mecca?

Muslims indisputably believe that the Quraysh drove Muhammad and his followers out of Mecca, forcing them to relocate to Medina in 622—a journey, famously known as the *Hijra* or *Hijrat*. According to this story, the Quraysh had sent assassins to kill the beloved Prophet. Being informed of it by angel Gabriel, Muhammad fled Mecca in the company of his trusted disciple and friend, Abu Bakr. As the assassins pursued them, they took refuge inside a cave in Mount Thor about an hour's journey from Mecca. By the time the pursuers came to the cave, pigeons had made nests and laid eggs, whilst spiders had spun webs instantaneously covering the entrance to it. Thinking that no one could have entered the cave a short while earlier, the pursuers left.

---

21. Ibid, p. 111
22. Muhammad's father's name was Abdullah, meaning *slave of Allah*.

Thereafter, Muhammad and Abu Bakr left from there in the darkness of night and reached Medina after a twelve days' journey. This story is presented in Islamic folk-stories and literatures as a miraculous act of God that saved Muhammad.

Although the Quraysh's attempt to assassinate Muhammad remains a popular story in Islamic literatures and an incontestable belief amongst Muslims, there is little credible evidence to substantiate this claim for a number of reasons. Firstly, relocation overseas or attempt to do so was rather common in Muhammad's community during his prophetic mission in Mecca. By 615, the opposition to Muhammad's mission grew strong as a result of his increasing insult of the existing religion, customs and culture. This made his preaching activity somewhat difficult. Muhammad's disciples were now being enticed by their families to return to their ancestral faith. According to al-Tabari, the greatest Islamic historian, the Quraysh were able to seduce some Muslim converts back to Paganism, '*a trial which shook the people of Islam...*' Fearing '*that they will be seduced from their religion,*' Muhammad '*commanded them to emigrate to Abyssinia,*' records al-Tabari.[23] With this instruction, about a dozen of his disciples, who were more vulnerable to family pressures, secretly departed with their families in small groups to Abyssinia (Ethiopia). In 616, a second wave of emigration took place. According to different estimates, 82–111 disciples of Muhammad had migrated there. These self-exiled disciples returned to Mecca and later to Medina after six months to thirteen years. A few of them had converted to Christianity and died in Abyssinia as Christians. It is thought that Muhammad had sent them there not only to protect them from being seduced back to their ancestral religion but also to create a sanctuary there in case he had to relocate elsewhere, because of the failure of his mission in Mecca or because staying in Mecca became truly dangerous.

Faced with Muhammad's increasing defiance and insult of their religion and customs, the Quraysh slapped a social excommunication and economic blockade against his community in 617. It was withdrawn two years later. Although the blockade withdrawn, Muhammad's prophetic mission came to almost a standstill as open preaching became nearly impossible. Under these circumstances, he went to Taif in 619 in search of a new sanctuary. Both Muhammad and the Quran had already insulted al-Lat, the chief deity of the Taifites. But they did not resist his entry into their community.

At Taif, he asked the people to leave their ancestral religion and join his creed. More importantly, he sought to incite a rivalry among the Taifites against the Quraysh with whom they had good trade relations. Muhammad stayed there for ten days and met the leading men to convince them of his religious mission and anti-Quraysh ploy. Ibn Ishaq describes his mission to Taif as thus: '*The apostle sat with them and invited them to accept Islam and asked them to help him against his opponents at home (Mecca).*' But he failed to achieve anything from his two-pronged—prophetic and anti-Quraysh—mission to Taif. Despaired and fearful of increased hostility from the Quraysh upon his return to Mecca, he requested the Taifites before leaving: '*Seeing that you have acted as you have, keep the matter secret.*'[24] The news reached Mecca anyway. Even then, the Quraysh did not show any serious displeasure against him, and he returned to Mecca without facing any hostility.

These precedents of Muhammad's attempt to relocate to Taif in 619 and sending his disciples to Abyssinia twice make it hard to believe that the Quraysh tried to assassinate him, forcing him to relocate to Medina. Muhammad's eagerness to migrate to Medina as early as 620, as narrated below, adds further incredibility to the assassination claim.

His mission stagnant in Mecca, Muhammad caught up with a number of pilgrims from Medina during the pilgrimage season of 620 and preached his creed to them. Six of them converted. Muhammad, describing the difficulty of his mission in Mecca, sought to migrate to Medina and inquired if they will be

---

23. Al-Tabari (1988) *The History of Al-Tabari*, Trs. WM Watt and MV McDonald, State University of New York Press, Vol. VI, p. 45
24. Ibn Ishaq, p. 192–93

able to protect him there.[25] But those converts discouraged him on the account of an ongoing deadly feud between two tribes in Medina and asked him to defer his emigration to a more suitable time.

During the pilgrimage next year, twelve men, including those of the previous year, met Muhammad secretly at a place, called Akaba. They pledged allegiance to his faith, which became known as the *First Oath of Akaba* in Islamic annals.[26] Muhammad sent his Meccan disciple Musab ibn Omayr with them for instructing the neo-converts in their new faith.

Musab's preaching bore fruit in expanding Muhammad's faith in Medina. During the next pilgrimage season (622), seventy-five citizens of Medina (seventy-three men and two women) accompanied Musab to Mecca and held a secret meeting with Muhammad at Akaba again. During the meeting, Muhammad's uncle al-Abbas, who had accompanied him to the secret rendezvous, announced Muhammad's desire to relocate to Medina saying that although the Prophet's kinsmen and disciples would protect him in Mecca, '*But he (Muhammad) preferreth to seek protection from you (Medina converts)... If ye be resolved and able to defend him, then give the pledge. But if you doubt your ability, at once abandon the design.*' To this, the Medina converts replied: '*We have heard what you say. You speak, O apostle, and choose for yourself and for your Lord what you wish.*' Then Muhammad spoke and ended by saying that '*I invite your allegiance on the basis that you protect me as you would your (own) women and children.*' Upon this, Al-Bara (a Medina convert) took his hand and said: '*By Him Who sent you with the truth, we will protect you as we protect our women. We give our allegiance and we are men of war possessing arms which have been passed on from father to son.*' This pledge of the Medina converts, known as helpers or *ansars* in Islam, is called the *Second Oath of Akaba*.[27]

This story makes it clear that Muhammad was obviously not in any impending danger in Mecca at this point in time (622). Even then, he was eager to relocate to Medina on his own accord as early as 620. A couple of months before his relocation to Medina in 622, he secured a pledge for his protection from his Medina converts. The question thus arises: when he was so eager to move to Medina, where the prospect of his religion was already very promising, why would anyone need to drive him out of Mecca? Furthermore, prior to his departure in late May 622, he had already ordered his disciples to move to Medina in early April and they migrated there in small groups over the next two months. Muhammad and his trusted comrade Abu Bakr and their families were the last ones to leave Mecca. Under this background, the following questions warrant a thorough consideration:

1. What was the purpose of Muhammad's eager interest to migrate to Medina and obtaining a guarantee of his protection once relocated?

2. Why did he send his disciples away to Medina over the months prior his own departure?

3. What was he going to do in Mecca alone, where his prophetic mission had come to a standstill?

These circumstances and evidence, which come from the most authentic and authoritative Islamic sources, clearly suggest that Muhammad had firmly and eagerly decided to relocate to Medina. Therefore, no one needed to drive him out or try to kill him, when he was going away on his own accord, saving the Quraysh of his insult, annoyance, and social and family discords, which they had put up with for thirteen years. Furthermore, after Muhammad left for Medina, his disciple Ali (later his son-in-law) along with Abu Bakr's wife and daughter Aisha (she was engaged to Muhammad) remained in Mecca for a few more days. And they did not face any major harm or harassment from the Quraysh.

---

25. Muir, p. 114

26. Ibn Ishaq, p. 198–99

27. Ibid, p. 204; Muir, p. 129–130

Islamic historian Ibn Ishaq informs us that the Quraysh reckoned: '*Muhammad had gained adherents outside the tribe (in Medina), (and) they were no longer safe against a sudden attack.*' Then they wondered upon putting him in irons behind bars, to drive him away, or to assassinate him and the last course of action was adopted.[28] But it does not conform to any logic or reason that, if the cruel Quraysh (as Islamic literatures depict them) were hell-bent on killing Muhammad, they would not persecute Ali and the female-members of Muhammad's and Abu Bakr's families, left behind after Muhammad's miraculous escape. They were not taken captive, tortured and imprisoned in order to force Abu Bakr and Muhammad to surrender. Instead, after Muhammad's successful flight, Talha, who had already gone to Medina, returned to Mecca and took away the family members of Abu Bakr and Muhammad as if nothing had happened.[29]

These factors make it almost impossible to believe that the Quraysh had attempted to assassinate Muhammad or drove him out. Even Allah had seen a prospect of success of Muhammad's mission in Medina and ordered him to relocate there as said Muhammad: '*I was ordered to migrate to a town which will swallow (conquer) other towns and is called Yathrib and that is Medina (Medinat-ul Nabi, abode of the Prophet)*' [Bukhari 3:95]. Allah also gives a concise account of the Quraysh's treatment of Muhammad and his community in a verse [Quran 2:217] revealed later: '*...graver is it in the sight of Allah to prevent access to the path of Allah, to deny Him, to prevent access to the Sacred Mosque, and drive out its members.*' Allah clearly suggests that the people of Mecca simply did not accept Muhammad's creed, prevented others (often the family members) from accepting Islam, and denied Muhammad's community access to the *Ka'ba*. Allah makes no mention that the Quraysh tried to assassinate Muhammad or any other Muslim. By "drive out its members," Allah likely meant that, since the Quraysh did not accept Islam, Muhammad had to relocate to Medina for a better prospect of success. Muhammad himself affirmed such an analysis at the battlefield of Badr. After the Quraysh were defeated, Muslims were unceremoniously throwing their dead-bodies into a mass-grave. Like a psychopath, Muhammad yelled over those dead-bodies: '*O people of the pit [hellfire], you were an evil kinsfolk to your Prophet. You called me a liar when others (Medina people) believed me; you cast me out when others took me in; you fought against me when others fought on my side.*'[30] Here again, Muhammad makes no mention of an attempt to assassinate him. The fighting mentioned here meant the fighting, which he himself initiated after relocating to Medina (described below). Prior to that, there was no fighting between Muslims and the Quraysh, neither could the Medina people fight on Muhammad's side in such battles.

The story of the Quraysh's attempt to assassinate Muhammad was most likely invented by him, hoping that, the people of Medina would more likely show him sympathy when he arrived there or that he had intended to set the people of Medina, particularly his converts, on a hostile term against the Quraysh. The fact that Muhammad, soon after his relocation to Medina, launched an aggressive and violent Jihad against the Quraysh gives credence to such a possibility. Let us also recall here Muhammad's failed attempt to incite enmity amongst the Taifites against the Quraysh in similar fashion three years earlier.

Were the Meccans a cruel people?

Islamic discourse gives the impression that the Quraysh tribesmen of Mecca were probably the most barbaric people, who had inflicted immense cruelty on the Prophet. One Muslim wrote to me that '*many Muslims perished, died under torture, in many horrific ways for 13 years.*'[31] They use such allegations to justify Muhammad's campaign of terror against the Quraysh and his capture of Mecca and destruction of their

---

28. Ibn Ishaq, p. 121–122

29. Muir, p. 165

30. Ibn Ishaq, p. 306

31. Islamic literatures record no incidence of death; no Muslim died in anti-Islam violence during Muhammad's stay in Mecca.

religion. The Quraysh have been repeatedly depicted as uncivilized and cruel oppressors and enemies of Allah in the Quran and the *Sunnah*. Even while in Mecca, Muhammad called them wicked and sinners, who were bent upon "wickedness supreme" [Quran 56:46] and "wretched", who will be thrown into the "midst of a Fierce Blast of Fire and in Boiling Water" [Quran 56:41–42]. Muhammad even denounced and threatened the Pagans of Mecca with temporal consequence in saying, '*thus shall We deal with the guilty. Woe on that day unto the rejecters (of Truth)*' [Quran 77:18–19]. He called himself and his followers the *righteous* and those, who rejected it, were *liars*, *wrong-doers* and *inventors of falsehood*. He consigned the Meccan idolaters to the eternal fire of hell. Some of the initial verses read as follows:

1. 'Then will he be of those who believe, and enjoin patience, (constancy, and self-restraint), and enjoin deeds of kindness and compassion. Such are the Companions of the Right Hand (of God). But those who reject Our Sign… On them will be Fire vaulted over (all round)' [Quran 90: 17–20].

2. 'Those who believe not in the Signs of Allah, Allah will not guide them and theirs will be a grievous Penalty. It is those, who believe not in the Signs of Allah that forge falsehood: it is they who lie!' [Quran 16:104–05].

However, the claim that the Quraysh had inflicted inhuman cruelty on Muhammad and his community, which is widely prevalent in Islamic societies, is very hard to substantiate. Faced with the helpless arid desert environment and hardship of those days, the citizens of Mecca used to be a deeply religious people. They had assembled 360 idols in the sanctuary of their God, the *Ka'ba*, for worshipping in order to earn God's favour. They had also turned the *Ka'ba* into the most venerated object of piety and centre of pilgrimage for the Pagans of Arabia and beyond. They used to hold the *Ka'ba* in similar esteem as do Muslims of today. Muhammad not only groundlessly laid a claim on the *Ka'ba* to be a sanctuary of his own God, his verses also termed the religion of the Pagans to be false.

Despite these insulting remarks and audacious claims and demands, the Quraysh allowed Muhammad and his community to live in Mecca for thirteen years. Muhammad exercised a good degree of freedom to preach his creed for the first seven years until his messages became overtly hostile and insulting to the Quraysh. Although there was opposition to Muhammad's claim on the *Ka'ba,* and later, there arose opposition to his mission engendered by his increasing insults, there is no report of any assault or injury caused to him or to his disciples by the Quraysh. There are some isolated references of torture of some slaves of the Quraysh, who had joined Muhammad's insulting creed. But, those were never serious or life-threatening. In other instances, some Quraysh had prevented their family members (sometimes by locking them at home) from joining Muhammad's community.

A few testimonies left by Muslim chroniclers prove that the Quraysh instead showed remarkable tolerance against Muhammad's overtly hostile attitude and offensive invectives. Al-Zuhri records:

'The unbelievers of the Quraysh did not oppose what he (Muhammad) said. If he passed the place where they sat together, they pointed to him and said: '*This young man of the tribe of Abd al-Muttalib proclaims a message from heaven!*' This they continued to do until Allah began to attack their gods…, and until He proclaimed that their fathers who died in unbelief were lost (to hellfire). Then they began to hate the Prophet and show their enmity to him.'[32]

Although Muhammad's message was hostile and insulting to the religion, gods and customs of the Quraysh, his invitation to them for embracing Islam was turned down rather politely. In one instance, Muhammad's uncle Abu Talib, while passing by a place, found his young son Ali praying with Muhammad. He inquired Ali what he was doing. To this the Prophet replied, '*he (Ali) was following the teaching revealed to him by God*' and invited Abu Talib to follow suit. To this invitation, the old man replied that he could not give up the faith

32. Sharma SS (2004) *Caliphs and Sultans: Religious Ideology and Political Praxis*, Rupa & Co, New Delhi, p. 63; Muir, p. 63

of his fathers, nor could he join in devotions which required '*placing his backside above his head (i.e., prostration while praying).*'[33]

The reaction of the Quraysh to Muhammad's slanderous invectives at their gods and ancestors is recorded by Baihaki in his book *Proof of Prophecy* as a testimony of Amru ibn al Aas, a disciple of Muhammad:

> 'I was once present when the chief among the idolaters assembled at the *Ka'ba*. They were discussing Allah's apostle, and said, '*Never have we had to tolerate from anyone what we have had to tolerate from this man. He slanders our fathers, criticizes our religions and divides our people, and blasphemes our gods. Such grievous things have we tolerated from this man...*' The Prophet who was nearby and hearing this conversation, he responded, 'Men of Quraysh! I will surely repay you for this with interest.'[34]

Despite the fact that the Quraysh adamantly stuck to their ancestral religion and were opposed to Muhammad's mission, they allowed Muhammad to enter the *Ka'ba* as late as in the sixth year of his mission. It becomes clear from the drama of the *satanic verses* [Quran 53:19–20], the plot of Salman Rushdie's novel. According to *The History of Al-Tabari*, the two *satanic verses* in which Muhammad accepted the Pagan deities—al-Lat, al-Uzza and al-Manat—as worthy of worship, were allegedly thrown into Muhammad's mouth by Satan, which Allah later repudiated [Quran 53:21–22].[35] This occurred when Muhammad was holding a reconciliation meeting with Quraysh elders inside the *Ka'ba* in 616.[36] After the Hudaybiya treaty in 628, the Quraysh again allowed Muhammad and his entourage to enter the *Ka'ba* for three days every year to perform the pilgrimage (see below). Now, let us consider a similar hypothetical situation in present-day context:

> Suppose a man from any community of Mecca, or elsewhere in Saudi Arabia, or from anywhere in the world, goes to Mecca and declares in front of an assembly of Muslims that he has received revelations from the true God; that he is the true messenger; that Islam is false; that the *Ka'ba* is the sanctuary of his own God; and that Muslims should abandon their false creed and embrace his new religion.

One should have no difficulty in figuring out what would happen to this alleged new prophet. Obviously, that person might suffer instantaneous death. Indeed, if a person openly makes such a claim in any major mosque in any Muslim country, he will most likely embrace the same fate at the hands of zealous followers of Islam even today despite having the guarantee of free speech and human rights under the U.N. charter. It is easy to draw a comparison of the fervent tendency toward violence amongst today's Muslims with that of those allegedly wretched and wicked Pagans of Mecca of that so-called barbarian age. They never made any physical assault on Muhammad for almost thirteen years despite his continued insult of their religion and culture, and his claim on their most sacred shrine.

Of the impact of Muhammad's prophetic mission on the life and religion of the Quraysh, notes Sir William Muir: '*Their shrine, the glory of Mecca and the centre of pilgrimage from all of Arabia was in danger of being set at nought.*'[37] Even then the Quraysh permitted Muhammad to enter the *Ka'ba* while non-Muslims are barred even today from entering any mosque (forget about *Ka'ba*) in Muslim countries even for a visit. Ever since the founding of Islam to this day, non-Muslims have been barred from entering the city of Mecca and Medina, the two holiest cities of Islam. A number of French citizens were murdered in February

---

33. Glubb JB (Glubb Pasha, 1979) *The Life and Times of Mohammad*, Hodder & Stoughton, London, p. 98
34. Sharma, p. 63–64
35. Al-Tabari, Vol. VI, p. 107
36. Ibid, p. 165-67; Muir, p. 80
37. Muir, p. 62

2007 who happened to be in the prohibited zone near Medina.[38] The intolerant teachings of Islam have transformed such an amazingly tolerant and civilized people of the seventh-century Arabia into such a fanatic and murderous lot. Not only the Arabs, but Muslims anywhere in the world today carry forward the legacy of Islam with similar intolerance and bigotry. And Muhammad used to call those highly tolerant and civilized people of the seventh-century Mecca cruel, wicked and wretched as do Muslims of our time.

Even today, Muslims in many Islamic countries kill those who openly leave Islam, despite the fact that all Muslim countries have signed the *Universal Declaration of Human Right*s of the U.N. charter, which guarantees one's right to change one's belief as one chooses. But the Pagans of the seventh-century Mecca never caused any harm either to Muhammad or to those dozens of free citizens of Mecca, who had converted to his creed. Evidently, Muslims of today are much more intolerant, cruel and uncivilized as compared to those Quraysh Pagans of Mecca.

Exemplary tolerance of Meccans

The society of Mecca at the time of Muhammad was definitely backward and unsophisticated than the more advanced and civilized societies of Persia, Syria, Egypt, and India. The people of Mecca were also a deeply religious community. However, it is tolerance, harmony and accommodation—not intolerance, hatred and violence—toward people of different faiths that characterized those allegedly barbarian people. For example, although the *Ka'ba* was their venerated *House of God* and the heart of their religious devotion, they never considered it solely of their own. Instead, they had allowed all the religious sects of the region and neighboring countries—Southern Arabia, Mesopotamia, Palestine, Syria and other places afar—to place their religious symbols and idols in the sanctuary of the sacred shrine.[39] Since Mecca was an important center of trades and frequent stopover for merchants from far off lands, the Meccans were accommodative of the spiritual needs of those foreign merchants. They housed the idols and religious symbols of the foreigners in the *Ka'ba,* enabling them to perform their religious devotions while in Mecca. These ancient idols from various lands and faiths had formed circles of 360 monolithic figures in the sanctuary of the *Ka'ba.* Even effigies of Abraham and Ishmael and of Mary with the infant Jesus were housed in the *Ka'ba*, representing the Jewish and Christian faiths. When Muhammad conquered Mecca, he ordered the destruction of the idols housed in the sanctuary. According to Turkish Muslim historian Emel Esin, Muhammad allowed the despoiling of the effigy of Abraham and Ishmael but protected that of Mary and Jesus by covering it with his hands.[40] The Quraysh hosted the Jewish and Christian symbols in the *Ka'ba* despite the fact that Christians and Jews perennially rebuked the Pagans for their idolatrous practices. The Syrian merchants were propagating Christianity in Mecca at the time of Muhammad without facing any hostility from the Quraysh.[41] Indeed, a number of Quraysh had converted to Christianity—the prominent amongst them were Waraqa ibn Naufal and Othman ibn Huwayrith—who enjoyed respected and privileged position in Mecca (see below).

Despite Muhammad's intense hatred and insult of the Quraysh's religion, Muslims were permitted to enter the *Ka'ba* for performing pilgrimage therein as already cited. Even the Hindus of India, who worshipped a different set of idols, had access into the sacred *Ka'ba.* Indian merchants brought the idol monolith of goddess al-Manat from the *Ka'ba*, which had disappeared from the shrine, to Somnath (India), where it became a popular deity. The pious Muslim conqueror Sultan Mahmud of Ghazni—determined to wipe out the remaining vestige of idolatry of the *Ka'ba*—attacked Somnath in 1024 for destroying that idol. In trying to protect their revered idol, some 50,000 Hindus perished.[42]

---

38. Globe and Mail (Canada), *Gunmen slay 3 Frenchmen in Saudi Arabia*, 26 Feb 2007
39. Walker, p. 44
40. Esin E (1963) *Mecca the Blessed, Medina the Radiant*, Elek, London, p. 109
41. Tagher J (1998) *Christians in Muslim Egypt: A Historical Study of the Relations Between Copts and Muslims from 640 to 1922*, Trs. Makar RN, Oros Verlag, Altenberge, p. 16
42. Sharma SS (2004) *Caliphs and Sultans: Religious Ideology and Political Praxis*, Rupa & Co, New Delhi, p. 144–45

Given these facts, those Pagans of Mecca were obviously a more tolerant, accommodative and civilized people than Muslims of today. Despite so much irreverence shown and insults hurled by Muhammad toward the religion, gods and customs of the Quraysh, they put up with him for thirteen years. The only cruelty they had shown to him was the two-year social and economic blockade to Muhammad's community (617–619), considered very much a civilized measure for dealing with such cases even today. In terms of compassion, tolerance, accommodation and nonviolence, the idolaters of the seventh-century Mecca were evidently quite a civilized people even by today's standard, despite the unsophisticated and backward nature of their society even at that time. In sum, the Pagans of Mecca, badly vilified by Muslims for the last fourteen centuries, were a very tolerant and civilized people.

MUHAMMAD'S CAMPAIGN OF TERROR AGAINST MECCANS (623–630)

Prophet Muhammad's relocation to Medina turned out to be a blessing for the success of his prophetic mission. This was a very likely outcome given that Musab ibn Omayr's prior mission, even in Muhammad's absence, was successful in drawing a large number of converts to Islam. The Prophet arrived at Medina to a hero's welcome from his eagerly waiting disciples. Medina was populated by a number of Pagan and Jewish tribes, the latter being richer and more influential. Soon more and more citizens of Medina, mostly from the Pagan tribes, started joining his mission.

The Seeding of Jihad

According to Ibn Ishaq, within the first year of his relocation to Medina, Muhammad had signed a treaty with the tribes of the city, which famously became known as the *Constitution of Medina*. This treaty contained clauses underpinning Muhammad's violent intent, particularly against the Quraysh.[43] Two such clauses were:

1. No believer shall be put to death for the blood of an infidel neither shall any infidel be supported against Muslims.

2. The Polytheists (of Medina) shall not take the property or person of the Quraysh under his protection, nor shall intervene against Muslims.

These clauses of the treaty clearly suggest that Muhammad had arrived in Medina with the intent of launching a violent campaign against the Quraysh of his ancestral city, which soon ensued. Muhammad spent about six months to build a communal abode for his community. Once settled himself in, he turned attention to seek revenge against the Quraysh. It appears that Muhammad's disciples were opposed to engaging in violence. Allah came to Muhammad's assistance, revealing a flurry of violence-inciting verses, urging Muslims to engage in Jihad or holy war, initially against the Quraysh and later against all non-Muslims. To convince Muhammad's unwilling disciples, Allah sent down a tailor-made verse, sanctioning fighting as a religious duty: '*Fight in the cause of Allah those who fight you, but do not transgress limits; for Allah loveth not transgressors*' [Quran 2:190]. Until this point, there was no fighting between Muslims and the Quraysh. The Quraysh, however, had adamantly opposed Muhammad's mission, which could be equated to "fighting". Therefore, fighting the Quraysh became divinely sanctioned to Muslims.

For those, who still had concerns about the legitimacy of engaging in unprovoked violence, Allah made it easy for them too as He revealed: '*And slay them wherever ye catch them, and turn them out from where they have turned you out; for tumult and oppression are worse than slaughter...*' [Quran 2:191]. Since the Quraysh had fought Muhammad and drove him out committing a crime tantamount to *worse than*

---

43. Ibn Ishaq, p. 231–33; Watt WM, *Muhammad in Medina*, Oxford University Press, Karachi, 2004 imprint, p. 221–25

slaughter—fighting them, therefore, had become more than legitimate for the sake of justice. Hence, the believers should have no ethical scruples about fighting the Quraysh, because they, fighting the Quraysh, were only rendering justice in the cause of Allah. Allah exhorts them to fight resolutely, which will continue until justice and faith in Allah (i.e., Islam) dominates: '*And fight them on until there is no more Tumult or oppression, and there prevail justice and faith in Allah*' [Quran 2:193]. Before moving further, let us investigate what *Tumult or oppression* in these verses stands for.

Tumult and oppression

The phrase *Tumult or oppression* in verse 2:193 (also *tyranny* in other verses), which stands for *fitnah* in Arabic, has traditionally been understood as idolatry, more accurately, the persistence of the Quraysh in the practice of idolatry, rejecting the call to Islam. But modern scholars of Islam, concerned of non-Muslim and Western audience, have introduced these vague terms for *fitnah* in English translations of the Quran. Influenced by these vague translations, many scholars of Islam are quick to assert that violent Jihad or killing is allowed in Islam only under strict conditions, such as to fight *tumult, oppression* or *tyranny*. It sounds very reasonable. Who doesn't appreciate the noble cause of fighting oppression or tyranny?

But these terminologies require a thorough analysis in order to grasp what tumult, oppression or tyranny truly stands for in the language of the Quran. In Arabic, *fitnah* (also *al-fasad*) means dissension or discord among a group, violation of law and order, or disobedience, a revolution or war against the establishment, or similar things. Given that, the Quraysh were in the helm of the administration of Mecca and Muhammad's community were the dissidents, it is only Muhammad, not the Quraysh, who could commit *fitnah* in Mecca.

How could then the Prophet and the Islamic God, for that matter, accuse the Quraysh of committing *fitnah*? It is probably because, according to verse 2:193 (also 8:39), the Quran was revealed by Allah, the supreme Creator, as the supreme book of law and justice, which must prevail over all religions. Hence, a rejection or opposition to it—which exactly was the Quraysh's reaction to Muhammad's creed—could constitute *fitnah* in the judgement of Muhammad and Allah. And this is exactly how Allah defines *fitnah* in verse 2:217: "…*graver is it in the sight of Allah to prevent access to the path of Allah, to deny Him, to prevent access to the Sacred Mosque, and drive out its members.' Tumult and oppression are worse than slaughter.*' Thus, a simple rejection of the Islamic religion constituted *tumult, oppression and tyranny*, which in turn was deemed *worse than slaughter* in the eyes of Allah and His Apostle.

Readers must bear in mind that this offence of the idolatrous Quraysh was the sole reason for everything Muhammad inflicted upon them as described below. Furthermore, Muhammad's ideal protocol of dealing with the Quraysh and other idolaters of Arabia will, by extension, apply to any idolaters of the world at all time.

Allah entreated Muslims again to extirpate all non-Muslim faiths: '*And fight them on until there is no more tumult or oppression, and there prevail justice and faith in Allah altogether and everywhere; but if they cease, verily Allah doth see all that they do*' [Quran 8:39]. It seems that these verses were not enough to motivate at least some of Muhammad's disciples. They refused to engage in fighting the Quraysh or anyone else because of their dislikes for violence. Allah thereafter came with new verses making fighting a binding duty for all Muslims, they like it or not: '*Fighting is prescribed for you, and ye dislike it. But it is possible that ye dislike a thing which is good for you, and that ye love a thing which is bad for you. But Allah knoweth, and ye know not*' [Quran 2:216].

It also appears that the disciples of Muhammad had initially resisted against engaging in fighting, arguing that Allah had not sanctioned it. But when the desired sanction came down from the heaven, some of the nonviolent, faint-hearted disciples were still undecided about engaging in violence, fearing bloodbath and likely death. Allah admonished such timorous ones amongst Muhammad's followers revealing: '*And those who believe say: Why has not a chapter been revealed (on fighting)? But when a decisive chapter is revealed and fighting is mentioned therein, you see those in whose hearts is a disease look to you with the look of one fainting because of death. Woe to them then!*' [Quran 47:20].

Most of Muhammad's early disciples were the rowdiest, belonging to the lower strata, of the society. Still, on account of their belonging to quite a non-violent and peaceful society, they expressed moral scruples when their Jihad started claiming innocent lives. Allah removed this guilty feeling of Muhammad's followers by taking the responsibility of the cruel acts on Himself: '*So you did not slay them, but it was Allah Who slew them, and you did not smite when you smote (the enemy), but it was Allah Who smote, and that He might confer upon the believers a good gift from Himself; surely Allah is Hearing, Knowing*' [Quran 8:17].

It further appears that some of Muhammad's Meccan disciples were particularly reluctant to engage in fighting or show hostility against the Quraysh, who were after all their own family members, relatives and tribesmen. In order to convince them, Allah revealed verses encouraging them to sever their relationship with their kinfolk. For example, Allah revealed: '*O you who believe! Surely from among your wives and your children there is an enemy to you; therefore beware of them...*' [Quran 64:14].

Allah encourages Muslims to invest all their power and resources in the cause of Jihad, promising them of paying back in full: '*Make ready for them all thou canst of (armed) force and of horses tethered, that thereby ye may dismay the enemy of Allah and your enemy, and others beside them whom ye know not. Allah knoweth them. Whatsoever ye spend in the way of Allah it will be repaid to you in full and ye will not be wronged*' [Quran 8:60]. It appears that some of Muhammad's followers were not willing to invest their wealth and resources in waging Jihad for a simple return in full. Allah, therefore, promised to increase the return manifolds amongst other rewards: '*And what cause have ye why ye should not spend in the cause of Allah? ...Who is he that will Loan to Allah a beautiful loan? For (Allah) will increase it manifold to his credit, and he will have (besides) a liberal Reward*' [Quran 57:10–11]. Still, there were some amongst Muhammad's followers, who were not willing to risk their resources by investing in Allah's Jihadi wars and Allah admonished them thus: '*Behold, ye are those invited to spend in the Way of Allah: But among you are some that are niggardly. But any who are niggardly are so at the expense of their own souls...*' [Quran 47:38].

These verses are the early exhortation and sanction of Allah for convincing Muslims to engage in violent attacks—i.e., Jihad or holy war, particularly against the Quraysh of Mecca. With this divine license for violence, Muhammad ordered the first Jihad raid (*gazwa*) in February 623, only about eight months after his arrival in Medina, against a trade-caravan of the Quraysh passing through a nearby route for the twin purpose of plundering it and harassing the Quraysh. But it failed. Over the next few months, two more raids were ordered, which too were unsuccessful. About twelve months after his relocation to Medina, Muhammad himself started commanding the raids. Over the next few months, he personally commanded three raids, but all went in vain.[44]

The raid of Nakhla

In January 624, the Prophet sent forth a band of eight raiders under the command of Abdullah ibn Jahash for attacking a Meccan caravan at a place, called Nakhla, which was nine days' journey from Medina and only two days' from Mecca. While sending them, the Prophet gave a letter in Abdulla's hand, instructing him to open it after a two-day journey. Abdullah opened the letter at due time, which read: '*When you have read this*

44. Muir, p. 225–228

letter of mine, proceed until you reach Nakhla between Mecca and Al-Ta'if. Lie in wait there for the Quraysh (caravan)...'[45] Abdullah and his party complied and reached Nakhla.

It was the time of *Orma* (i.e., the lesser pilgrimage to the *Ka'ba*). Not to alarm the approaching caravan, one of the Muslim raiders shaved his head to give an impression that they were returning from the pilgrimage, and therefore, could not be hostile. Once the caravan came with their reach, they fell upon it: one attendant of the caravan was killed; two were captured while another escaped. They returned to Medina with the rich caravan and the two prisoners.

It was the sacred month of *Rajab*; one of the four months of the year, when fighting and bloodbath was prohibited in the Arabian tradition. This breach of the age-old sacred custom created great dissatisfaction and outcry among the citizens of Medina, including some disciples of Muhammad. This landed the Prophet in an awkward situation. He initially tried to distance himself from the incidence putting the blame on the perpetrators' shoulders. But seeing that Abdullah and his co-raiders had become heart-broken (which could potentially discourage future raids), Allah quickly came to the rescue by revealing the following verse to justify the bloodshed, even though it took place during the sacred month:

> They ask thee concerning fighting in the Prohibited Month. Say: '*Fighting therein is a grave (offence); but graver is it in the sight of Allah to prevent access to the path of Allah, to deny Him, to prevent access to the Sacred Mosque, and drive out its members.*' Tumult and oppression are worse than slaughter. Nor will they cease fighting you until they turn you back from your faith if they can... [Quran 2:217].

The verse concluded by warning those amongst Muslims, who had shown displeasure over the incident and could potentially leave Muhammad's creed, that '*...And if any of you turn back from their faith and die in unbelief, their works will bear no fruit in this life and in the Hereafter; they will be companions of the Fire and will abide therein*' [Quran 2:217]. With this command, the fighting and killing the Quraysh or any perceived enemy—any time, any where, for any reason—became divinely justified. The Prophet also honored Abdullah with the title of *Amir-ul-Muminin* (Commander of the Faithful).

It needs to be taken into consideration that, prior to this successful plundering raid, Muhammad's community had been suffering from extreme hardships. Therefore, this blood-laden but successful raid had a special significance for Muhammad's community and creed in that it brought them rich booty (spoil of war) to assuage their hardships. Allah made plundering booty lawful to Muslims, revealing: '*Now enjoy what ye have won, as lawful and good, and keep your duty to Allah*' [Quran 8:69]. Allah also revealed a verse, Quran 8:41, on the distribution of booty captured in wars; and accordingly, the Prophet kept a fifth of the plunder as his share and the remainder was distributed amongst the raiders. The two prisoners were exchanged for ransoms bringing more revenues.[46] For Muhammad and his community, this also marked the beginning of embracing plundering and looting of non-Muslim caravans and communities as the major source of livelihood.

The great Battle of Badr

The next, indeed the most famous and significant, raid for Muhammad's prophetic mission came two month later in March 624. He planned to attack and plunder a rich caravan of the Quraysh, which was returning from Syria under the care of Abu Sufyan, the leader of Mecca. On the initiation of this raid, notes Ibn Ishaq, '*when the apostle heard about Abu Sufyan returning from Syria, he summoned the Muslims and said, 'This is the Quraysh caravan containing their property. Go out to attack it, perhaps God will give it as a prey.' The*

---

45. Ibn Ishaq, p. 287; Muir p. 208–209

46. Ibn Ishaq, p. 286–88

people answered his summons, some eagerly, others reluctantly[47] because they had not thought that the apostle would go to war.'[48] The intelligence of Muhammad's intended attack reached Abu Sufyan, who sent forth a messenger to Mecca for sending a rescue-force. In the meantime, he took a different route along the Red Sea Coast evading Muhammad's army and hastened the caravan to reach Mecca safely.

But a rescue mission had already left Mecca to save the caravan as well as to teach Muhammad's plundering brigands a lesson. Muhammad had planned to ambush the caravan near a water-filled oasis, called Badr. Taking position there, he despoiled the water-wells by filling them with sands keeping only one usable next to his camp for the supply of water to his own army. He was unaware that Abu Sufyan had escaped with the caravan. As he heard of the approach of the Meccan army, he thought it was the caravan itself.

When the Meccan army arrived at Badr on the seventeenth day of Ramadan after days of arduous journey through the hot sandy desert, they were tired and badly thirsty. But all the water-wells had been despoiled by Muhammad, preventing them from quenching their thirst. On the Meccan side, there were about 700 (some say 1,000) fighters, while Muhammad had only about 350 raiders. In the bloody confrontation that ensued the next morning, the thirsty Meccan army quickly succumbed and retreated with heavy losses despite their numerical advantage. They lost about fifty men and a similar number were taken prisoners, while Muhammad's party lost only fifteen fighters. Some of the captives were cruelly slaughtered at the battlefield by Muhammad's order.[49]

Emboldened by the stunning victory at Badr, the Prophet soon attacked the Jewish tribe of Banu Qaynuqa of Medina and exiled them (described below).

The disastrous Battle of Ohud

The unbelievable victory at Badr boosted the confidence of Muhammad and his community that God was on their side helping them win against stronger oppositions in battles. Allah also sent down a tailor-made verse to affirm that He was, indeed, assisting Muslims in battles by sending angels so that twenty steadfast Muslim fighters would be able to vanquish 200 opponents [Quran 8:66]. Muhammad soon conducted three more raids on Meccan caravans plundering rich spoils. Exasperated and their life-sustaining commerce made impossible, the Quraysh finally decided to take offensive counteractions. On 23 March 625, some 3,000 Meccan fighters, under the command of Abu Sufyan, engaged about 700 Muslim fighters, commanded by Muhammad, at a place, called Ohud, near Medina. The numerically weak Muslim force quickly caved in and suffered heavy casualties with Muhammad himself got struck by a stone losing a tooth and falling unconscious. In this battle, Muslims lost seventy-four fighters against only nineteen casualties on the Meccan side.

As Muhammad had promised that twenty Muslim fighters, aided by angels, will vanquish 200 opponents before this disastrous battle, this severe loss of life created a great deal of suspicion, including amongst his disciples, about the veracity of his prophetic claim and even a sense of hostility against him. His opponents, particularly the Jews and the hypocrite, Abdullah ibn Obayi (see below for he was a hypocrite), also used the incidence to disparage Muhammad and spread doubts about his prophethood. Allah as usual came to Muhammad's rescue and countered this hostility and suspicion about his prophethood by revealing a long series of verses [Quran 3:120–200].

Regarding the complaint about His earlier assurance of angels' help to Muslims in vanquishing the opponents, Allah put the blame on Muhammad's disciples for their lacking in firmness and patience, revealing: *'Remember thou said to the Faithful: 'Is it not enough for you that Allah should help you with three thousand angels (Specially) sent down?' Yea, if ye remain firm, and act aright, even if the enemy should rush*

---

47. It becomes obvious that even at this time, more than a year after *Jihad* or *holy war* was sanctioned by Allah, many followers of Muhammad were still reluctant to engage in violence.

48. Ibn Ishaq, p. 289

49. Ibid, p. 289–314; Walker, p. 119–20

here on you in hot haste, your Lord would help you with five thousand angels Making a terrific onslaught' [Quran 3:224–25].

Allah insisted that He truly had helped Muslims in the earlier battle at Badr when they had feared defeat; and for that, they should express gratitude to Him: '*Remember two of your parties (amongst Muslims) meditated cowardice (in Badr); but Allah was their protector, and in Allah should the faithful (Ever) put their trust. Allah had helped you at Bad'r, when ye were a contemptible little force; then fear Allah; thus May ye show your gratitude'* [Quran 3:122–23].

Allah also blamed the Muslim fighters for not paying heed to Muhammad's command, which, He held, was responsible for their latest defeat at Ohud: '*When ye climbed (the hill) and paid no heed to anyone, while the messenger, in your rear, was calling you (to fight). Therefore He rewarded you grief for (his) grief, that (He might teach) you not to sorrow either for that which ye missed or for that which befell you'* [Quran 3:153].

Further, Allah cited examples of His earlier prophets and their disciples before Muhammad, who had steadfastly fought in His cause without ever loosing heart and urged Muhammad's followers to do likewise: '*How many of the prophets fought (in Allah's way), and with them (fought) large bands of godly men? But they never lost heart if they met with disaster in Allah's way, nor did they weaken (in will) nor give in. And Allah loves those who are firm and steadfast'* [Quran 3:146].

About those who were slain at Ohud, Allah revealed verses to console their kinsfolk and comrades that they were, in reality, not dead but in a trance; and that they had landed in Paradise where they were rejoicing: '*Think not of those who are slain in Allah's way as dead. Nay, they live, finding their sustenance in the presence of their Lord; they rejoice in the bounty provided by Allah: And with regard to those left behind, who have not yet joined them (in their bliss), the (Martyrs) glory in the fact that on them is no fear, nor have they (cause to) grieve'* [Quran 3:169–70].

Meanwhile in August 625, some five months after the battle of Ohud, Muhammad attacked the Jewish tribe of Banu Nadir of Medina and again exiled them (described below). But having learned a lesson in the disastrous battle of Ohud against the powerful Quraysh, Muhammad stopped his raids on Meccan caravans for some time. The Quraysh did not follow up after their victorious campaign of Ohud any further. Since Muhammad had stopped raiding their caravans, they possibly thought that he had learnt a lesson and posed no further threats. In the meantime, Muhammad took time to consolidate his power by increasing his converts and material support (captured from exiled Banu Qaynuqa and Nadir tribes, see below). After a respite of about one year, he resumed his raids on Meccan caravans in April 626. Increasingly successful raids on rich caravans started making Muslims very rich in spoils, camels and slaves. At this point, seeking to strengthen his plundering brigands, Muhammad had invited nearby non-Muslim tribes to join his raids. Some non-Muslim tribes joined his plundering forays, likely for twin reasons: the greed for the booty and for their own protection from Muhammad's raids. By this time, Muhammad had attacked and exiled two powerful Jewish tribes of Medina, which clearly suggests that those non-Muslim tribes faced a real danger of being attacked by Muhammad if they refused his call.

The Battle of the Ditch (Trench)

The resumption of raids on Meccan caravans sent a clear message that Muhammad's threat to the Quraysh was far from over. Abu Sufyan, therefore, made preparation in April 627 to launch another counterattack for putting an end to Muhammad's threats. He appealed to neighbouring tribes to join hands and many of them, including Banu Ghatafan, Banu Suleim and Banu Asad—who had already suffered from Muhammad's attacks—responded to his call. A huge confederate force of 10,000 men (some say 7,000) assembled behind Abu Sufyan. Muhammad had a capacity to assemble, at best, 3,000 men on his side at this time and the situation looked grave for his community.

Fortunately for Muhammad, he had obtained a Persian convert, the famous Salman the Persian, who gave Muhammad the idea of digging a trench around his abode in Medina. This was a common strategy for fending off enemy attacks in Persia but unknown amongst Arabs. Muhammad instantly grabbed the idea and ordered digging a deep trench around the perimeter of his community. The outer walls of houses were fortified by stones, entrenching Muslims inside. The Quraysh laid a siege on the city. But unfamiliar with the tactic, they failed to overcome the trench. After a long siege, extending beyond twenty days (some say nearly one month), the Meccan army withdrew. There was not much fighting during the siege. Muhammad's side lost only five men, while the Meccan side lost three. Salman, a Christian converted from Zoroastrianism before converting to Islam, whose advice saved the day, was duly appreciated by Muhammad expressing gratitude to him and his community for their depth of knowledge.[50]

As soon as the Quraysh withdrew from the siege, Muhammad accused Banu Qurayza—the last Jewish tribe in Medina—of assisting the Quraysh and attacked them. When the Jews surrendered, he slaughtered the men and enslaved the women and children (described below).

The Conquest of Mecca and capture of the Ka'ba

By 628, Muhammad had either evicted or annihilated all the powerful Jewish tribes of Medina and brought many small tribes of surrounding regions to submission through threats or attacks. He had now become powerful enough to vie for the capture of his ancestral city of Mecca and the *Ka'ba* therein—on which, he had laid a claim very early in his prophetic mission. Furthermore, it was the *Ka'ba* toward which his community in Medina had been turning for years whilst saying prayers. The *Ka'ba* had thus become the most sacred symbol of his religious mission and the biggest prize to be captured. The *Ka'ba* also had a big economic significance (as it is to the Saudis today), because, as the centre of pilgrimage—namely the *Omra* and *Hajj*—for the people of Arabia, it was a coveted revenue-generating venture. Moreover, Allah had dedicated so much effort and space in the Quran for fighting and defeating the Quraysh. Bringing Mecca to submission had therefore become the central mission of Muhammad's prophetic career.

The Treaty of Hudaybiya: In March 628, about one year after the battle of the Ditch and six years after his relocation from Mecca, Muhammad dared marching toward his ancestral city. He invited the surrounding tribes to join his campaign, but his invitation to this dangerous venture was declined. Muhammad marched toward Mecca at the head of some 1,300 to 1,525 armed Muslims during the lesser pilgrimage (*Omra*). The Quraysh learned of Muhammad's approach and swore not to allow him enter their city another time, because of the terrible bloodbath, humiliation and hardships he had caused to them. When Muhammad was apprized of the determination of the Quraysh, he stopped and set up tents at a place called Hudaybiya. He sent forth a message to Mecca that he had come only to perform pilgrimage peacefully and then would return to Medina.

Muhammad was determined to perform the pilgrimage to which the Quraysh were adamantly opposed. Given consideration to Muhammad's military power and capacity to engage in cruelty and bloodbath, the Quraysh decided to negotiate with him in order to avoid a bloody confrontation. At one point in the course of the intense bargaining that followed, Othman—Muhammad's son-in-law and the third caliph of Islam—went to the Meccan camp for negotiation. It was taking time for Othman to return and a rumour spread in the Muslim camp that he had been killed. Muhammad quickly assembled his armed comrades under an acacia tree and bounded them one by one by a pledge to stand by "Othman to the death". This oath became known as the famous *Pledge of the Tree* in Islamic annals. Muhammad had excited his followers' religious fervor in the camp to such a degree that all of them were in a suicidal mood to rush upon the enemy at once. Just about this time, Othman returned to the camp avoiding a sheer bloodbath. Othman returned with the final terms of the treaty and a truce was signed—the famous *Treaty of Hudaybiya*. It demanded cessation of

---

50. Ibid, p. 121–22; Ibn Ishaq, p. 456–61; Muir, p. 306–14

hostility from both sides for a ten-year period. It also stipulated that Muhammad's party would return to Medina this time without visiting the *Ka'ba*, but they would be allowed to perform annual pilgrimage to the *Ka'ba* for three days from the following year.[51]

Here, seeing the determined opposition of the Quraysh, Muhammad pretended that he had come for the pilgrimage, not war. But his original intention was to occupy Mecca as Ibn Ishaq writes: '*The apostle's companions had gone out without any doubt of occupying Mecca because of the vision which the apostle had seen, and when they saw the negotiations for peace and a withdrawal going on and what the apostle had taken on himself, they felt depressed almost to the point of death.*'[52] The signing of the treaty meekly, instead of taking on the Quraysh in a violent confrontation, caused anger amongst some Muslims, including bloodthirsty Omar. However, Muhammad assured them that he was under the instruction of Allah to conclude this treaty and it would bring eventual benefit to his party. Allah took the pain of revealing an entire Sura— Chapter 48 of the Quran (*surah al-Fath* or *Victory*)—to convince Muhammad's party that this treaty was actually more appropriate under the situation and tantamount to a *Victory*, and that the decisive victory would come soon.

Muhammad's breach of the treaty: It took very little time for Muhammad's party to breach the treaty. Abu Bashir, a convert from Mecca, soon killed a Quraysh violating the treaty. He went on to form a raiding brigand consisting of some seventy Muslim marauders and they, with connivance of Muhammad, engaged in attacking Meccan caravans, sparing none of the attendants alive. Ibn Ishaq records of Abu Bahir's actions: '*Then Abu Basir went off until he halted at al-'Is in the region of Dhu'l-Marwa by the sea-shore on the road which Quraysh were accustomed to take to Syria... About seventy men attached themselves to him, and they so harried Quraysh, killing everyone they could get hold of and cutting to pieces every caravan that passed them.*'

The helpless Quraysh gave up on the treaty. Instead, they begged Muhammad "by the ties of kinship" to stop his men from attacking the caravans. After the request, Muhammad brought his raiders back to Medina. A few women converts, who were held up by their families, escaped from Mecca to join Muhammad's community in Medina. They were supposed to be returned according to the treaty. In total disregard of the treaty, Muhammad refused to return them when the Quraysh came to take them back to Mecca.[53]

Muhammad throws away the treaty and attacks Mecca: In two years after the signing of the *Hudaybiya Treaty*, Muhammad's army had become strong enough to overrun the Quraysh. Therefore, he altogether threw away the ten-year treaty and ordered preparations for attacking Mecca. He wanted to take the Quraysh by surprise. As preparations went on, he kept praying to Allah: "*O Allah, take eyes and ears from the Quraysh so that we may take them by surprise in their land.*"[54] In January 630, he marched toward Mecca at the head of a 10,000-strong army.

The invincible Muslim army approached near Mecca at night and camped at place, called Marr al-Zahran. In the darkness of the night, each fighter lighted a fire to show to the Quraysh a glimpse of the huge Muslim army that had assembled. Catching sight of Muhammad's force, his uncle Al-Abbas, who had joined the Muslim camp a while earlier, said, "*Alas, Quraysh, if the apostle enters Mecca by force before they come and ask for protection, that will be the end of the Quraysh forever.*"[55] Before proceeding further, let us investigate the controversy as to who truly breached the treaty.

---

51. Muir, p. 353–59; Ibn Ishaq, p. 500–05

52. Ibn Ishaq, p. 505

53. Ibn Ishaq, p. 507–09; Muir, p. 364–65

54. Ibn Ishaq, p. 544

55. Ibid, p. 547

Who truly breached the Hudaybiya Treaty?

Daniel Pipes, who is hated by Muslims for his objective views on Islam, claims that Muhammad did not breach the treaty, but technically the Quraysh did. He writes, '*Muhammad was technically within his rights to abrogate the treaty, for the Quraysh, or at least their allies, had broken the terms.*'[56] His views fit well with the standard Islamic position that it was the Meccans who broke the treaty.[57] This alleged breach of the treaty by the Quraysh relates to an ongoing feud between two third-party tribes: Banu Bakr and Banu Khuza'a. Banu Bakr was an ally of the Quraysh, while Banu Khuza'a was of Muhammad.

According to Al-Tabari, prior to Muhammad's coming to the scene, a merchant named Malik bin Abbad of Banu Bakr on his trade-journey was attacked by some people of Banu Khuza'a, who killed him and took his property. In retaliation, Banu Bakr killed a man from Banu Khuza'a. In their second turn of attack, Banu Khuza'a killed three brothers—Salma, Kulthum and Dhu'ayb—the leading men of Banu Bakr. In the counter retaliation, Banu Bakr killed a Banu Khuza'a man, named Munabbih, in which a few Quraysh had allegedly assisted Banu Bakr in the darkness of night.[58]

This time, Banu Khuza'a had become Muhammad's *Mawla* (confederate). Hence, the Quraysh, according to scholars like Pipes, breached the *Hudaybiya Treaty* and Muhammad was legally justified in attacking Mecca.

The first thing ignored here is that the Khuza'a tribe was the instigator of the feud with Banu Bakr. Khuza'a had attacked Banu Bakr twice and killed four men. Prior to the latest attack, Banu Bakr had attacked Banu Khuza'a only once, killing one man. Even after the latest attack, Khuza'a had killed four Banu Bakr men, while the latter had killed only two of their opponents. Muhammad's confederates had a surplus of killing two extra men.

The next thing ignored here is that, in the first place, Muhammad had no right to make an attempt to capture Mecca or seek access into the idol-shrine of *Ka'ba*, which led to the signing of the *Hudaybiya Treaty*. And Pipes is totally oblivious to the fact that Muhammad had broken the terms of the treaty at the earliest opportunity and repeatedly—amongst other breaches, by killing a number of the Quraysh and plundering their trade-caravans. It also makes little sense that Muhammad would attack the Quraysh, instead of attacking Banu Bakr, who were directly involved in killing the men of Banu Khuza'a. Muhammad, at best, could come to the assistance to Banu Khuza'a's attack on Mecca, not for his own capture of the city under any logic or reason.

Let us return to Muhammad's attack on Mecca. The Quraysh leader Abu Sufyan, one of the Prophet's fathers-in-law, learning of Muslims' approach, quickly set off in the darkness of night to meet Muhammad for persuading him not to attack the city. On the way, Abu Sufyan met his brother Al-Abbas, who assured him protection and led him to Muhammad. Omar al-Khattab (later the second caliph) came upon them and seeing Abu Sufyan, he cried out: "*Abu Sufyan, the enemy of God! Thanks be to God who has delivered you up without agreement or word.*" He then rushed for his sword, adding: "*Let me take off his head.*"[59]

---

56. Pipes D (2002) *Militant Islam Comes to America*, WW Norton & Company, New York, p. 185

57. *The Taking of Makkah*, Ministry of Hajj (Saudi Arabia), http://www.hajinformation.com/main/b2109.htm

58. Al-Tabair, Vol. VI, p. 160–62

59. Ibn Ishaq, p. 547

Al-Abbas persuaded Omar against taking drastic actions on the ground of his promise to protect Abu Sufyan and brought him to Muhammad. Muhammad asked al-Abbas to bring him back the next morning. When Abu Sufyan was brought back the next morning, the Prophet said, "*Isn't it time that you should recognize there is no God but Allah?*" Abu Sufyan never believed that Mohammed was a prophet and when he hesitated, an angry Muhammad exclaimed, "*Woe to you, Abu Sufyan! Isn't it time that you recognized that I am the apostle of God?*" To this, Abu Sufyan answered, "*As to that I still have some doubt.*" Seeing Abu Sufian's life in immediate danger, al-Abbas quickly intervened, forcefully telling him, "*Submit and testify that there is no God but Allah and Muhammad is the apostle of God before you lose your head.*" Abu Sufyan had no option but to comply. Al-Abbas then requested Muhammad to do something for Abu Sufyan's people. To this, Muhammad said, "*He who enters Abu Sufyan's house is safe, and he who locks his door is safe and he, who enters the mosque (Ka'ba), is safe.*"[60]

On returning to Mecca, Abu Sufyan explained to his people about the futility of opposing Muhammad's advance into their city and asked them not to fight a losing battle. Instead, he famously said, '*Aslim Taslam*', which meant *become Muslims if you want to be safe*. He advised those, who sought to persist in their Pagan religion, to stay indoors or take refuge in his own house. The next morning, Muhammad's army marched into Mecca. One recalcitrant group of Meccans, who had fallen on the way of Khalid ibn Walid's army, showed a meek resistance. Khalid slaughtered those, who fell within his reach, and pursued others, who ran to save their lives up the hill.

Upon capturing Mecca, Muhammad ordered the destruction of all idols of the *Ka'ba*, shouting out, '*Truth has (now) arrived, and Falsehood perished: for Falsehood is (by its nature) bound to perish,*'[61] which Allah later copied as a revealed verse and included in the Quran [Quran 17:81]. Muhammad stood in the middle of the *Ka'ba*, and as he pointed to the idols, passionately worshipped by the devout Meccans for centuries, with a stick one by one, they were smashed into pieces. Muhammad himself destroyed a wooden dove, a deity of the Quraysh.

After the capture of Mecca and pillage of the *Ka'ba*, Muhammad sent Khalid bin Walid to destroy the idol-temple of al-Uzzha at Nakhla, two days' journey from Mecca.[62] A disciple, named Amr, broke the idol-image, called Suwa, adored by the Hudeil tribe; the temple of the famous goddess, al-Manat, worshipped at Kodeid was destroyed by a band of Medina Muslims—former devotees to the goddess.[63] Many of the Pagans accepted Islam on the day Muhammad captured Mecca.

Before proceeding further, let us examine a few popular claims about Muhammad's exemplary dealing with the Quraysh on the occasion of capturing Mecca.

Muhammad's exemplary forgiveness of Meccans

Muslims typically make a number of claims regarding Prophet Muhammad's conquest of Mecca:

1. Firstly, the Muslim army entered the city peacefully and unopposed, welcomed by the Quraysh.

2. Secondly, the Quraysh willingly converted to Islam in large number under no duress.

3. Thirdly, Muhammad showed exemplary forgiveness to the Quraysh by not putting them to death.

---

60. Ibid, p. 547–48

61. Ibid, p. 552

62. Ibid, p. 565

63. Muir, p. 412

Muhammad's peaceful entry into Mecca: Despite Muhammad's attacking Mecca by throwing away the 10-year-long *Hudaybiya Treaty* after just two years, the conquest was still a peaceful act to Muslims. Of course, Muhammad and his disciples had persistently violated the treaty even during those two years. As to the claim of Muhammad's unopposed entry into Mecca, it should not be difficult to realize what would have happened on that day had the Meccans tried to defend their city. What was Muhammad's demand to Abu Sufyan before attacking the city? It was: *Accept Islam or your heads will roll, wasn't it*? And when some wayward Meccan citizens in their stupidity tried to oppose Khalid ibn Walid's army, they became food for the sword of his army. Muslims were allowed unopposed entry, not because they were a peaceful and lovable people, but because, they were deadly and strong enough to overrun the weaker Meccans. The fate of the unfortunate Jewish clans of Medina—especially the horror suffered by the men of Banu Qurayza, who were put to the sword in barbaric manners by Muhammad (described below)—was very much alive in Meccans' minds.

Meccan's willing acceptance of Islam: If the Quraysh had accepted Islam in large numbers on the day of Muhammad's capture of Mecca under no duress, but because of Islam's peaceful message, a question naturally arises: *Why they did not embrace Islam two years earlier when Muhammad had led an expedition to Mecca*? Why did they seek to prevent Muhammad's entry into Mecca with the last drop of their blood, which led to the signing of the *Hudaybiya Treaty*? Moreover, during those two intervening years following the conclusion of the treaty, Muhammad did not do any peaceful and loving things, which might have impressed the Quraysh to embrace Islam in large numbers on the day of his capture of Mecca. Instead, Muhammad breached the treaty at the earliest opportunity and his disciples caused terrible sufferings to the Quraysh by persistently attacking their caravans and killing the attendants. He also threw away the treaty altogether eight years before its expiry. Muhammad had also ordered a number of unprovoked violent raids against other non-Muslim tribes, namely the Jewish stronghold of Khaybar, Banu Soleim, Banu Leith, Banu Murra, Dhat Atlah, Muta, and Banu Nedj amongst others during those two intervening years.[64] Finally, Abu Sufyan's message to his fellow citizen was *Aslim Taslam*—become Muslim if you want to be safe. For their safety, there were only two options before them: first, convert to Islam; and second, take refuge in the mosque (*Ka'ba*) or Abu Sufyan's house. These instances make it clear that it was not the peaceful nature of Islam or Muhammad's peaceful and loving gestures and acts that had convinced the Quraysh to embrace Islam in large numbers on that day.

Muhammad's forgiveness: Prophet Muhammad's sparing the lives of the surrendered Quraysh is portrayed by Muslims as a demonstration of outstanding generosity and forgiveness on his part. Muslims typically cite this as a proof of Muhammad's exemplary kindness toward his enemies. Muslims give an impression that, never in history, a leader showed such out-of-the-world forgiveness and tolerance to his vanquished enemies. *But how could Muhammad, or any other nominally sensible person, slaughter a people, who had already agreed not to resist his capture of their city and their leader (Abu Sufyan) had already accepted Muhammad's religion and prophethood*? Muhammad had also promised to Abu Sufyan not to harm them, if they did not oppose his advance.

It has been clearly demonstrated that the Quraysh never showed any cruelty toward Muhammad when he initially preached his religion in Mecca. They remained within civilized limits in their dealing with him despite his insult of their religion and customs for thirteen years. It was Muhammad, who, nonetheless, had aggressively launched many plundering raids on Meccan caravans that led to a number of bloodletting battles between them. Muhammad's persistent raiding and plundering of Meccan caravans and disruption of their trades had caused immense economic loss and hardship to the Quraysh. More importantly, the Quraysh were the fathers, mothers, brothers, sisters and kinfolk of those Muslims, including Muhammad, who had emigrated from Mecca. Would the cruellest of human being in the world think of putting such close kinfolk, who had already undeservedly suffered so much, to the sword? In the thought of Muslims even of our time,

---

64. Ibid, p. 392–93

Muhammad had not yet committed enough brutality against the Quraysh. To all Muslims, the evidently civilized and tolerant behavior of the Quraysh toward Muhammad was such an unpardonable crime that he should have slaughtered all of them upon his capture of Mecca.

Muhammad's capture of Mecca, nonetheless, was not bloodless either. Khalid ibn Walid had brutally slaughtered those who sought to put up a meek resistance. Muhammad had also ordered execution of ten or twelve Meccan citizens who had earlier abandoned Islam, or had criticized or ridiculed him and his creed. Some of the proscribed persons belonging to influential families, lobbied by their family members, were spared. Eventually, four persons were executed. Amongst them were two singing girls, who had composed songs ridiculing Muhammad.[65] Given the kind of rather humane treatment Muhammad had received from the Meccans against the sort of torment, insults, troubles, bloodshed and hardships he had caused them, no Meccan citizens deserved capital punishment in any sort of sensible justice—especially when, they had unconditionally surrendered their homeland to Muhammad's rule.

Further cruelty of barbaric nature was yet to follow upon Muhammad's conquest of Mecca. After destroying the *Ka'ba*, Muhammad sent Khalid ibn Walid to bring the neighboring tribes into submission. Khalid reached the Jazima (Jadhima) tribe and ordered them to lay down their arms. Ibn Ishaq records: '*As soon as they had laid down their arms, Khalid ordered their hands to be tied behind their backs and put them to the sword, killing a number of them.*'[66] The tribe had already offered submission to Muhammad. On this ground, a few Medina citizens and refugees in Khalid's party intervened, saving the lives of the rest. Moreover, the Jazima tribesmen had never caused any trouble to Muhammad or his community. This cruelty on them, therefore, was nothing less than barbaric. Upon Muhammad's conquest of Mecca, the way he mercilessly destroyed the idol-gods of the Quraysh, put his critics to death, Khalid slaughtered those Meccan citizens who had shown a meek resistance and the heartless way Khalid slaughtered the Jazima tribesmen and so on, it represents an occasion of cruel atrocity on his part, not of forgiveness, kindness and generosity of any kind.

The Prophet had conquered or brought into submission all other Pagan tribes of Arabia using violent or intimidating tactics, which will not be included in this book to keep the discussion short. However, his confrontation with the Quraysh, which was rather sympathetic, gives a prototypic outline of his dealing with the idolatrous people, which will apply to all idolaters of the world at all time.

MUHAMMAD'S DEALING WITH THE JEWS

Jewish influence on Muhammad's mission

It has already been explained that Prophet Muhammad was highly influenced by the monotheistic beliefs of the Jews and Christians. This had, likely, inspired him to launch his own prophetic mission for preaching a monotheistic creed amongst the Polytheists of Mecca for proclaiming the oneness of God. Muhammad obtained the first idea of the Jewish people and their creed and customs when he was on a business-trip to Syria with his uncle Abu Talib at the young age of twelve.[67] In Mecca too, he was friendly with one learned Jewish rabbi, named Abdais ben Salom, who is said to have had recited the Jewish scriptures and explained Jewish traditions to Muhammad. Ibn Ishaq's biography of Muhammad reveals that he used to visit the Beth ha-Midrash, a house for the study of biblical commentaries in Mecca. Muslim commentator Al-Baydawi relates that certain Jews used to repeat ancient history, as recounted in the Torah, to Muhammad. Muhammad

65. Ibid, p. 410-11; Walker, p. 319
66. Ibn Ishaq, p. 561
67. Ibn Ishaq, p. 79–81; Muir, p. 21

is even reported to have had attended Synagogues. This rabbi—who, allegedly, became a Muslim later on and took the name, Abdullah ibn Salam—is believed to be the witness mentioned in Quran 46:10, which affirms an agreement between the Quran and the Jewish scriptures. This verse was intended for exhorting the Jews to accept Muhammad's new religion.[68]

When Muhammad relocated to Medina in 622, a number of Jewish and Polytheistic tribes lived there. The Jews were a thriving, rich and influential community as compared to the less well-off Polytheists. In affirmation of this, renowned Islamic scholar Abul Ala Maududi (d. 1979) writes, '*Economically they (Jews) were much stronger than the Arabs. Since they bad emigrated from more civilized and culturally advanced countries of Palestine and Syria, they knew many such arts as were unknown to the Arabs; they also enjoyed trade relations with the outside world.*'[69] The Jews might have let Muhammad settle in their city without raising any opposition for two reasons. First, Muhammad was preaching a monotheistic creed among the hopeless Polytheists to extirpate idolatry, which the Jews desired as much. Second, Muhammad's religion at this point was friendly and well-disposed toward the Jewish faith, giving the Jews and their scriptures a very respectable rendering in the Quran. At the beginning in Medina, Muhammad continued pouring praise upon the Jews and their faith. He maintained good relations with them and adopted many Jewish customs, namely fasting, circumcision, turning toward Jerusalem while praying and so on (see below).

Muhammad's Exhortation to draw the Jews to Islam

As Prophet Muhammad started preaching his religion actively in Medina, the Polytheists joined his creed in large numbers. But, he made poor impact upon the wealthy Jewish community. To draw the unimpressed Jews to Islam, Allah started revealing verses specially designed to exhort them. For example, there came down a series of verses from Allah relating to the Jewish story of *Genesis* [Quran 2:30–38] and to the Judaic stories of Moses and the children of Israel [Quran 2:240–61]. Then Allah exhorted the Jews and Christians (also monotheistic *Sabians*) to believing in the Quran alongside following their own scriptures to gain His mercy: '*Those who believe (in the Qur'an), and those who follow the Jewish (scriptures), and the Christians and the Sabians, any who believe in Allah and the Last Day, and work righteousness, shall have their reward with their Lord; on them shall be no fear, nor shall they grieve*' [Quran 2:62, also see 22:17].

Allah made many direct exhortations addressing the Jews (and Christians) to accept Muhammad as their prophet too: '*O followers of the Book (Jews and Christians)! indeed Our Messenger (Muhammad) has come to you explaining to you after a cessation of the (mission of the) messengers, lest you say: There came not to us a giver of good news or a warner, so indeed there has come to you a giver of good news and a warner; and Allah has power over all things*' [Quran 5:19]. But all efforts of the Islamic deity to impress and draw the Jews to Muhammad's faith failed utterly.

Jewish doctrines in good light in Islam

The influence of Judaism on Muhammad is further reflected in the fact that he placed higher esteem on the Jewish faith than on idolatry of the Quraysh in the Quran. Jewish patriarch Abraham and his son Ishmael, Prophet Moses and King David (Dawood) and Solomon (Sulaiman) *et al.* of the Jewish tradition have found highly respected position among the prophets of Islam. Indeed, Muhammad even gave a higher status to Moses than to himself [Bukhari 4:610,620].

During the early phase of Muhammad's prophetic mission, the Islamic revelations as well as Muhammad's personal gestures were well-disposed toward the Jewish faith. He is reported to have said, '*He who wrongs a Jew or a Christian will have me as his accuser on the day of judgment.*' His initial gestures

---

68. Walker, p.180–81

69. Maududi AA (1993) *Historical Background to Surah Al-Hashr*, In *Towards Understanding the Quran*, (Trs. Ansari ZI), Markazi Maktaba Islamic Publishers, New Delhi

toward these faiths suggest that he sought to preach a monotheistic faith among the idolatrous Arabs, which would form part of a common faith with Judaism and Christianity. The early verses of the Quran recognize the Jews as a well-regarded people: '*And certainly We gave the Book and the wisdom and the prophecy to the children of Israel (Jews), and We gave them of the goodly things, and We made them excel the nations*' [Quran 45:16]. The Quran says of the Jewish scriptures that it contained God's "guidance and light" [Quran 5:44] and that it was God's blessing and guidance for the righteous [Quran 6:153–54]. The Quran recognizes Palestine (Jerusalem) as a "blessed land" in multiple places. At the beginning, Muhammad looked upon Jerusalem as the centre of his new faith. It is from Jerusalem that he, allegedly, ascended the heaven. He adopted it as the direction of Muslim prayers after migrating to Medina.

Muhammad had also copied the Jewish custom of making contribution to charity, gave it an Aramaic name, *zakat*, and made it one of the five pillars of Islam. Following the Jewish tradition, he also prohibited the eating of pig meat, introduced ceremonial ablutions and purifications, and established the "Sabbath observance" on Saturdays (later changed to Friday). Also following the Jewish customs and practices, he established the fasting of *ashura*—later changed to Ramadan—another of the five pillars of Islam. He, following Jewish traditions, instituted circumcision for Muslim [Abu Dawud 41:5251][70] and claimed to have himself been born circumcised. At the beginning, he used to call himself *Navi*, the Jewish term for *Prophet*.

Muhammad's bitterness with the Jews

The Jews ignored the exhortations of Allah and Prophet Muhammad to embrace Islam. There were many inaccuracies and distortions of Jewish scriptures and traditions in the Quran. For example, Quran 7:157 claimed that Muhammad, allegedly a descendent of Abraham's son Ishmael, was the messiah whose coming was foretold in the Torah. This claim contradicted earlier revealed verses of the Quran, which clearly said that prophethood is bestowed upon the children of Israel only [Quran 45:16] and more specifically upon the family of Isaac and Jacob [Quran 29:27]. Muhammad was an Arab, not an Israelite and his family-line leading up to Ishmael was different from those of Isaac and Jacob. The Jewish rabbis easily refuted his claim of prophethood by pointing to this clear contradiction in the Quran.

Moreover, Ishmael was an illegitimate son of Abraham, born of his relation with an Egyptian concubine, Hagar, of non-Semitic race. He was, therefore, outside God's covenants with Abraham. The Bible also described him as "uncouth and violent" [Gen 16:12]. Hence, God could not bestow prophethood upon Ishmael's posterity. Jews also rejected Muhammad's claim that the Quran was a divine revelation, because it was not revealed in a sacred language, Hebrew or Syriac, but in Arabic, a language of poets and drunkards. The Jews also pointed to multiple errors in Muhammad's versions of the events of the Torah and called him ignorant of Jewish scriptures, which his revelation claimed to affirm. For example, he wrongly accused the Jews of saying that Ezra (Ozayr) was the son of God [Quran 9:30], which they easily refuted. In sum, the Jews rejected Muhammad's claim of prophethood by terming his alleged revelations as garbled, fallacious and, at times, unintelligible.

These bitter arguments and antagonism with the Jews came to a head in about October 623, barely one year after Muhammad's arrival in Medina and shortly before the battle of Badr. Having failed to entice the Jews (also Christians) to Islam, an exasperated and angry Allah now sought to break away from further persuasion of them and revealed: '*And the Jews will not be pleased with you, nor the Christians until you follow their religion. Say: Surely Allah's guidance that is the (true) guidance. And if you follow their desires after the knowledge that has come to you, you shall have no guardian from Allah, nor any helper*' [Quran 2:120].

---

70. References of *hadiths* (or *Sunnah*) from the authentic sources, namely Sahih Bukhari, Sahih Muslim and Sunan Abu Dawud, have been included in the parentheses within the text.

Thereafter, Allah's tone and Muhammad's gesture toward the Jews started changing. Jewish patriarch Abraham now became a "Muslim" and a precursor of Muhammad's own mission: *'Abraham was not a Jew nor yet a Christian; but he was true in Faith, and bowed his will to Allah's (i.e., to Islam)'* [Quran 3:67]. To counter the contradiction regarding the genealogy of prophethood and to give validity to Muhammad's claim to it, Allah now revealed a series of verses to create an entirely new genealogy along the Abraham-Ishmael line of progenies. In order to take away the covenant of His faith from the children of Israel and to place it upon Muhammad, an Arab, Allah now invented a new covenant of His with Abraham and Ishmael, who allegedly had founded Allah's sacred House, the *Ka'ba*, in Mecca. In order to suit Muhammad's prophetic mission centered in Arabia, not in Israel, Allah now claimed that he had given His blessing for a center of His faith surrounding the *Ka'ba* [Quran 2:126–30]. Through a new set of verses [3:67, 2:126–30], Allah created a completely new paradigm of the Abrahamic faith, which should be centered in Mecca, not in Israel and its covenant should follow the Abraham-Ishmael line of genealogy, not the Isaac or Jacob line. In other words, Islam was the original religion that Allah had planned to establish through Abraham (and Ishmael) and Muhammad, the Arab Prophet, came to restore the originally intended religion of Allah to its pure form.

The Jewish Torah, which Allah had initially recognized as divine book containing His "guidance and light" [Quran 5:44] and a blessing and guidance for the righteous [Quran 6:153–54], now became perverted by the Jews [Quran 2:79]. The Jews, earlier recognized by Allah as *'privileged above all people'* [Quran 45:15], now turned to *'those who show the greatest hostility to the believer [Muslims]...'* [Quran 5:82]. Muhammad now started calling himself a *Rasool* (messenger), instead of *Navi*. Having invented a new center of His religion, Allah now sent revelations for changing the direction for prayers from Jerusalem to Mecca [Quran 2:144]. Muhammad also changed the day of Sabbath from Saturday to Friday (*Juma*) and the fasting of *ashura* in accordance with the Jewish tradition to the month-long fasting of Ramadan in accordance with the tradition of the *Hanifs* of Mecca. Muhammad either changed or modified multiple other Jewish customs and practices, which he had adopted after arriving in Medina. The Jews now accused him of being fickle-minded. They also ridiculed him for turning, while praying, toward a piece of Black Stone, a Pagan fetish, housed in the idolatrous temple of *Ka'ba*.

Muhammad's violence against the Jews

In Medina, the Jews, with their razor-sharp criticism of Muhammad's revelations, became an increasing irritant to his religious mission. He had few answers to those criticisms. Emboldened by his stunning victory against the Quraysh at Badr in early 624 and reinforced by his increasing power and resources obtained through a series of plundering raids on trade-caravans, Muhammad now turned his swords against the obstinate, troublesome Jews. With the Badr victory behind him, he assembled the Banu Qaynuqa Jews at their market-place and ominously warned: *"O Jews, beware lest God bring upon you the vengeance that He brought upon Quraysh (at Badr) and become Muslims. You know that I am a Prophet who has been sent (by God)..."*[71] The Jews soon paid a heavy price for ignoring Muhammad's ominous threat.

Attack on Banu Qaynuqa: After this warning, one day in April 624, a youngster of Banu Qaynuqa, allegedly, teased a Muslim woman at the market-place. A Muslim present there killed the Jewish prankster. This man was in turn killed by the Jews in revenge.[72] On the pretext of this brawl, Muhammad besieged the entire community of Banu Qaynuqa, the wealthiest in Medina. After a fifteen-day siege, the Jews surrendered. Muhammad ordered the surrendered men to be tied for their summary execution. At this point, Abdullah ibn Obayi, the chief of the Khazraj clan, who had converted to Islam but had a dubious allegiance to Muhammad's mission, firmly intervened. He urged Muhammad, *"By God, would you cut down these 700 men in one morning?"* Abdullah pleaded, *"Oh Muhammad, deal kindly with my clients."* It should be noted that Banu Qaynuqa was an ally of Abdullah's tribe. When the Prophet tried to ignore his pleas, Abdullah

---

71. Ibn Ishaq, p. 363
72. Muir, p. 241

caught him by the collar of his robe and insisted, "*By God, I will not let you go until you deal kindly with my clients.*" He further cautioned, "*I am a man, circumstances may change!*"[73]

Abdullah was an influential leader and Muhammad prudently relented from slaughtering the prisoners. Instead, he exiled them to Syria. They were given three days to leave and were forbidden to take any implements of their trade. Once the Jews left, Muhammad quickly took possession of their homes and properties, which he distributed amongst his disciples as sacred booty obtained through Jihad in the cause of Allah.

About this time, he ordered assassinations of those who criticized his creed and actions. The victims included a 120-year-old poet, named Abu Afaq, who had composed verses condemning Muhammad's violent acts. Another victim was poetess Asma bte Marwan, a mother of five, who had composed verses condemning Muhammad for killing Abu Afak and his other violent activities. A third victim was the Jewish poet Kaab ibn Ashraf, who composed verses condemning Muhammad's brutality at Badr and inspiring the Quraysh to avenge the defeat.[74]

According to Ibn Ishaq, Muhammad gave general approval of slaying the Jews at this time, saying, "*Kill the Jew that falls into your power.*" Thereafter, Muhayyisa, a Jewish convert to Islam, happened to come across a Jewish merchant, named Sunayna. Muhayyisa fell upon the unfortunate merchant and killed him. Muhayyisa's family had social and business relations with Sunayna and benefited from him. His elder brother Huwayyisa confronted him for murdering the valuable man, saying, "*You enemy of God, did you kill him when much of the fat on your belly comes from his wealth.*" The younger brother ominously responded, "*Had the one who ordered me to kill him ordered me to kill you, I would have cut your head off.*" Impressed by the barbaric attitude and commitment that Muhammad's creed had instilled in the younger brother, Huwayyisa exclaimed, "*By God, a religion which can bring you to this is marvellous!*' and he became a Muslim,'* records Ibn Ishaq.[75]

Attack on Banu Nadir: Muhammad's next atrocity against the Jews of Medina came in August 625. A few months after the disastrous battle of Ohud, Muhammad, along with companions Abu Bakr, Omar and Ali *et al.*, went to the house of Banu Nadir leader for the mediation of a dispute in which a disciple of Muhammad had killed a man from a tribe allied to Banu Nadir. In the midst of the meeting, Muhammad suddenly '*got up (saying to his companions, 'Don't go away until I come to you') and he went back to Medina.*'[76] His companions waited for a long while and when Muhammad did not return, they also left. According to Ibn Ishaq, Muhammad later accused Banu Nadir of conspiring to kill him by throwing stones from the roof of the house (interestingly, none of his companions who waited there for so long saw anyone on the roof). He then charged the Jewish tribe with treason and ordered them to evacuate their settlements on the pain of death. Some commentators also cite Banu Nadir's commercial dealings with Abu Sufyan of Mecca prior to the disastrous battle of Ohud as a reason for Muhammad's hostility against them. However, the Quran explains the reason as follows: '*Allah had decreed banishment for them... because, they resisted Allah and His Messenger: and if any one resists Allah, verily Allah is severe in Punishment*' [Quran 59:3–4]. In other words, Banu Nadir's rejection of Islam was the reason for Muhammad's attack on them.

Abdullah ibn Obayi—repeatedly condemned as a hypocrite in the Quran—again denounced Muhammad's charge of treason against Banu Nadir as baseless and even threatened to fight on their side. Allah cites this in the Quran: '*the Hypocrites say (to Banu Nadir)... 'If ye are expelled, we too will go out with you, and we will never hearken to any one in your affair; and if ye are attacked (in fight) we will help you'. But Allah is witness that they are indeed liars*' [Quran 59:11]. When the Jews, emboldened by

---

73. Ibn Ishaq, p. 545–46; Walker, p. 184
74. Ibn Ishaq, p. 675–76,367
75. Ibn Ishaq, p. 369
76. Ibid, p. 437

Abdullah's pledge of support, did not leave, Muhammad attacked and seized them in their forts. In order to hasten their surrender, notes Ibn Ishaq, '*the apostle ordered that the palm-trees should be cut down and burnt, and they (Banu Nadir) called out to him, 'Muhammad, you have prohibited wanton destruction and blamed those guilty of it. Why then are you cutting down and burning our palm-trees?*''[77] They surrendered at length on the condition of letting them go to exile. Muhammad took possession of their swords, cuirasses, and helmets along with their assets, homes and firms, which he distributed amongst his followers.

The slaughter of Banu Qurayza: Muhammad's most horrendous act of cruelty against the Jews came in April 627, immediately after the *Battle of the Ditch* in which the Meccans had seized the Muslims at Medina. Islamic literatures record that during that siege, the Quraysh had approached Banu Qurayza for assistance to which they, allegedly, had agreed. But in reality, they remained neutral throughout that protracted confrontation. In fact, Banu Qurayza had lent their spades and other tools to Muhammad for digging the trench that saved his community. After the Quraysh withdrew, Muhammad accused Banu Qurayza of spying and breaking treaty, which probably never existed.[78] Allah affirms this accusation in the Quran as follows: '*And He [Allah] brought those of the People of the Scripture (i.e., Banu Qurayza Jews) who supported them (i.e., the Quraysh) down from their strongholds, and cast panic into their hearts...*' [Quran 33:26]. It is difficult to grasp how Banu Qurayza, sitting in their *strongholds*, as claimed Allah, could help the Quraysh fighters. However, this was good enough reason for Allah and Muhammad to attack and besiege them for nearly a month in their forts before they surrendered.

Abdullah ibn Obayi again condemned Muhammad's attack on Banu Qurayza. But he was not far from death and his power had weakened as most of his followers had joined Muhammad. Now, Muhammad could easily ignore him. The surrendered Jews offered to go to exile like the Banu Nadir tribesmen exiled two years earlier. Muhammad rejected the proposal; instead, he decided to slaughter all their adult males, some 800 to 900 of them. Their adulthood was determined by the growth of pubic hair.[79] The women and children were captured as slaves and their homes and properties were as usual confiscated and distributed amongst Muslims. The Islamic God gave an emphatic sanction to these barbaric atrocities by revealing: '*...Some ye slew and ye made captive some. And He (Allah) caused you to inherit their land and their houses and their wealth, and land ye have not trodden. Allah is ever able to do all things*' [Quran 33:26–27].

Following this, a trench was dug at the market-place; and in Muhammad's presence, those 800–900 captives were brought to the brink of the trench with their hands tied behind and were beheaded with swords before pushing the dismembered bodies into it. Muhammad himself chopped off the heads of two Jewish leaders. The spectacle went on from morning through the day and continued by torchlight into the night. This ghastly massacre created revulsion even in Karen Armstrong, who is immensely popular amongst Muslims for her relentless campaign to correct Western misconceptions about Islam. She was so disgusted that she compared it to the Nazi atrocities on the Jews.[80] This cruel massacre can obviously be called the *First Holocaust* of the Jews.

---

77. Ibid

78. Watt WM (1961) *Islam and the Integration of Society*, Routledge & Kegan Paul; London, p. 19. Indeed, there existed no treaty at all. *The Constitution of Medina*, which is peddled as the treaty in question by Muslims was never signed by any Jewish tribes. According to Montgomery Watt, whose books on Islam are widely published in Pakistan, there were nine contracting parties in this document and they were the Muslims and Arab Pagan tribes, who had become essentially Muslim by converting to Islam in large numbers after Muhammad's arrival in Medina.

79. Abu-Dawud 38:4390: Narrated Atiyyah al-Qurazi: "I was among the captives of Banu Qurayzah. They (the Companions) examined us, and those who had begun to grow hair (pubic) were killed, and those who had not were not killed..."

80. Armstrong K (1991) *Muhammad: A Western Attempt to Understand Islam*, Gollanz, London, p. 207.

A Jewish woman, whose husband was beheaded, demanded the same fate for herself too than becoming a slave to her husband's murderers. Her wish was granted and she accepted death with a smiling face. Muhammad's young wife Aisha, who witnessed the massacre, later used to say that this heroine's smile as she embraced death was to haunt her ever after. According to Ibn Ishaq, '*Aisha used to say, 'I shall never forget my wonder at her good spirits and her loud laughter when all the time she knew that she would be killed.*''[81]

Another old Jewish man, named al-Zabir, who had earlier saved lives of some Muslims, was offered pardon. But he declined it saying that he had no desire to live anymore, since all of his dear ones were gone. Ibn Ishaq records of him saying: ''*What does an old man without family and without children want with life.*'' Muhammad shouted: ''*Yes, you too will join them—in the fire of Hell*'' and order his execution.[82]

Of the properties of Banu Qurayza captured as the sacred booty, Muhammad kept one-fifth as his own share and the rest were distributed amongst his followers. The captive women and children were also distributed likewise. The young and pretty ones amongst the female captives became sex-slaves; Muhammad himself took a beautiful woman, named Rayhana, as his own concubine. He took her to bed on the same night after slaughtering the men. Some of the women were sold overseas for acquiring weapons and horses for using in future battles of which records Ibn Ishaq: '*Then the apostle sent Sa'd b. Zayd al-Ansari... with some of the captive women of B. Qurayza to Najd and he sold them for horses and weapons.*'[83]

Attack on the Jews of Khaybar: With the extermination of Banu Qurayza, Medina was cleansed of the Jews. Muhammad's attention now turned to the Jewish community away in Khaybar, another powerful Jewish stronghold in the Arabian Peninsula, located about seventy miles north of Medina on the way to Syria. He was particularly resentful of the exiled Banu Nadir Jews, who had resettled there after their expulsion from Medina. Its leader Abu Rafi was among the confederate army that laid siege on Medina in the battle of the Ditch. Therefore, revenge against Abu Rafi and his community was due.

Soon afterwards (627), Muhammad sent an expedition to Khaybar under the command of Ali, which yielded no result except the capture of camels and flocks. Muhammad then sent a band of assassins to murder Abu Rafi. The assassins on a friendly pretension got access into the house of Abu Rafi and dispatched him. When the successful assassins returned to Medina, the Prophet exclaimed: ''*Success attend you!*'' ''*And thee, O Prophet!*'' they replied.'[84] Another such assassination mission was sent forth to murder Osier (Yuseir), the leader of Khaybar. But the Jews were very alert this time round and the mission failed.

Then in January 628, Muhammad openly sent a delegation of thirty Muslims to Khaybar for negotiations with its leader. After their arrival, they assured Oseir that '*Muhammad would make him ruler over Khaybar and treat him with distinction and gave him a solemn guarantee of safety.*' Upon this assurance, a delegation of thirty Khaybar men, led by Oseir, headed for Medina. Each Jewish man sat behind a Muslim on the camel and when some distance away from Khaybar, Muslims fell upon the Jews and killed them with only one escaping. When this brutal murder of the Jews was recounted to Muhammad, he thanked God, saying, ''*Verily, the Lord hath delivered you from an unrighteous people.*''[85]

Next in May 628, the Prophet set upon an expedition against Khaybar with himself at the command of 1,600-strong army. They approached Khaybar secretly by night. According to Ibn Ishaq, when the workers of Khaybar came out in the morning with their spades and baskets, they saw the apostle and the army. So, '*they cried, 'Muhammad with his force' and turned tail and fled. The apostle said, 'Allah akbar! Khaybar is destroyed.*''[86] When the sanguinary battle ensued, Muslims at length achieved victory with ninety-three

---

81. Ibn Ishaq, p. 465; also Walker, p. 185–86
82. Ibn Ishaq, p. 466
83. Ibid, p. 465
84. Muir, p. 348
85. Ibid, p. 349
86. Ibn Ishaq, p. 511; also see Bukhari 2:68

Jewish defenders and nineteen Jihadis slain. Following the assassination of Abu Rafi, his young grandson Kinana had become the leader of the Banu Nadir Jews. He was protecting his treasures hiding in a secret location, which Muhammad was informed of by a renegade Jew. For extracting information about the whereabouts of the treasure, Muhammad tortured Kinana at length placing fire on his chest. However, the treasure was found and Kinana was put to death.

After the victory in Khaybar, '*their warriors (fighting-age men) were killed; the children and women were taken was captives*' [Bukhari 2:14:68]. '*The women of Khaybar were distributed among the Muslims,*' records Ibn Ishaq.[87] Among the captives were three prized women: Safiya, Kinana's seventeen-year-old beautiful wife, and two of her virgin cousins. Prophetic traditions inform us that Safiya had initially fallen to the share of Muhammad's Jihadi comrade Dihyah b. Khalifa al-Kalbi. When someone informed him of her exquisite beauty, worthy of the Prophet only, Muhammad wanted her for himself, as says Muslim 8:3329 (also Bukhari 5:512): '*Anas, (Allah be pleased with him) reported: Safiya (Allah be pleased with her) fell to the lot of Dihyah in the spoils of war, and they praised her in the presence of Allah's Messenger (may peace be upon him) and said: We have not seen the like of her among the captives of war.*' Hearing this, Muhammad ordered that Dihyah and Safiya be brought to his presence. When the Prophet looked at her, he said to Dihyah, ''*Take another slave-girl from the captives.' The Prophet set her free and married her*' [Abu Dawud 19:2992]. According to Ibn Ishaq, '*He gave orders that Safiya was to be put behind him and threw his mantle over her, so that the Muslims knew that he had chosen her for himself.*'[88] Dihyah was consoled with the two young cousins of Safiya.

Muhammad distributed the huge spoil confiscated in the expedition amongst his holy warriors. He wanted to expel the surrendered Jews [Bukhari 3:531]. But Muslims did not have enough manpower to cultivate the confiscated lands as records a hadith [Abu Dawud 19:3008]: '*...they (Muslims) did not have sufficient laborers to work on it.*' Muhammad, therefore, allowed the Jews to stay in the possession of the lands on two conditions: first, ''We *will let you stay on this condition as long as we wish*'' [Bukhari 3:531] and second, half of the produce (fruits and vegetation) must be surrendered to Muslims as tax [Bukhari 3:521–24].

After the Khaybar incidence, the terrified Jewish tribe of Fadak quickly offered submission to Muhammad on the condition of surrendering half of the produce of their lands. Subsequently, other Jewish strongholds of Arabia—Kamus, Watih, Solalim, and Wadi al-Kora etc.—were also forced to submit or exiled. Before his death, Muhammad ordered his companions to exterminate the Jews and Christians from the Arab lands. According to Ibn Ishaq, the Prophet, while in his death-bed, instructed '*that two religions should not be allowed to remain in the peninsula of the Arabs.*'[89] Consequently, the second Caliph Omar expelled the Jews of Khaybar in 638; and by the end of his reign (d. 644), no Jews and Christians remained in the Arabian Peninsula [Bukhari 3:531, Abu Dawud 19:3001].[90]

MUHAMMAD'S DEALING WITH THE CHRISTIANS

Prof. Edward Said laments that Islam was believed to '*be demonic religion of apostasy, blasphemy and obscurity*' in Christian Europe during most of the Middle Ages and the early part of Renaissance.[91]

---

87. Ibid, p. 515

88. Ibid

89. Ibid, p. 525

90. Muir, p. 381

91. Said EW (1997) *Islam and the West* In *Covering Islam: How the Media and Experts Determine How We See the Rest of the World*, Vintage, London, p. 5–6

'Christians long viewed Islam as a heretical movement stemming from their own faith,' notes Pipes.[92] Ignaz Goldziher claims that *'Muhammad did not proclaim new ideas… (His) message was an eclective composite of religious ideas and regulations'* from Jewish, Christian and other sources.[93] While the Quran itself agrees to Jewish and Christian influence on Islam; the Pagan, Zoroastrian, Sabian and other pre-Islamic beliefs and rituals were also incorporated into the Islamic creed. Samuel Zwemer concludes that Islam "is not an invention but a concoction" of old ideas.[94] Amidst these claims that Islam was founded by mixing existing religious ideas, particularly from Christianity and Judaism, the issue of Prophet Muhammad's dealing with the Christians will be addressed here in a comprehensive way in order for the readers to grasp all these claims about Islam's foundation and its relationship with Christianity. It will help the reader understand how Christianity in particular had dominantly influenced Muhammad's mission and the conception of his theology and how his attitude and tone of his creed toward Christians and their faith gradually changed as Islam became increasingly firm-footed.

Christian Influence on Muhammad's mission and creed

According to the eighth-century Christian theologian John of Damascus (d. 749), Muhammad's religion was an errant form of Christianity. Muhammad, he wrote, *'having happened upon the Old and the New Testaments, in all likelihood through an Arian monk, organized his new sect.'* German Philosopher Nicholas of Cusa (d. 1464) found in the Quran a strand of Nestorianism, a sect of Christianity, widely diffused in the Middle East during early the Christian centuries.[95]

Islamic literatures affirm that Muhammad had his first contact with Christianity through a learned Nestorian monk, named Bahira, whom he had met at the age of twelve (some say nine) while on a trade-trip to Syria with his uncle Abu Talib. On this journey, Muhammad had received the first dose of familiarity with the Christian religion, customs and rituals while passing through the predominantly Christian regions of Syria. It is said that Bahira was highly impressed by Muhammad's interest in religious discussions and had allegedly seen in him a coming prophet as go Muslim legends.[96] Bahira is said to have had communicated certain Christian doctrines and laws, and had recited inspired Biblical passages, to him. On Muhammad's gaining Biblical knowledge from Bahira, notes Ibn Ishaq: *'There he gained knowledge from a book… handed on from generation to generation.'*[97] Muhammad was to embody those knowledge and teachings later in the Quran so that the Arabs get acquainted with the concept of one true god.

As already discussed, Muhammad was very likely trained in the scriptures of the Jewish and Christian faiths prior to receiving his revelation from God. There are a good deal of references in Islamic literatures, which suggest that Muhammad, prior to embarking on his own prophetic mission, had familiarized himself with the Christian and Jewish scriptures and was inspired by the central concept of the "oneness of god" of these creeds. His first intimate contact with Christianity came from his marriage of twenty-four years with Khadijah, who had strong connection with Christian theology through her Christian cousin Waraqa ibn Naufal. Waraqa had even translated a portion of the gospels into Arabic. *'Waraqa attached himself to Christianity and studied its scriptures until he had thoroughly mastered them,'* records Ibn Ishaq.[98] He was, as noted, the first person to affirm Muhammad's divine communication with Gabriel and was instrumental in persuading Muhammad to launch his prophetic mission. Zayd ibn Haritha, a slave of Khadijah, whom Muhammad had adopted as his son, was also a Christian.

---

92. Pipes D (1983) *In the Path of God*, Basic Books, New York, p. 77

93. Goldziher I (1981) *Introduction to Islamic Theology and Law*, Trs. Andras & Ruth Hamori, Princeton, p. 4–5

94. Zwemer S (1908) *Islam: A Challenge to Faith*, New York, p. 24

95. Walker, p. 188

96. Al-Tabari, Vol. 6, p. 45

97. Ibn Ishaq, p. 79–81

98. Ibid, p. 99

When Muhammad went on a business-trip to Syria in charge of Khadijah's caravan at the mature age of about twenty-five years, he met one Nestorian monk, Nastur or Nestor, who had allegedly embraced Muhammad as a prophet.[99] Moreover, Muslim commentator Husayn said that the Prophet used to go to a certain Christian every evening for listening to the Torah and *Injil* (gospels).[100] Islamic literatures also inform us that Waraqa and Khadijah introduced Muhammad to Christian monks, who lived in Mecca. One such person was Addas, a Christian monk from Nineveh, who had settled in Mecca. Khadijah brought Muhammad to Addas who, in a long conversation, had explained the significance of angel Gabriel as the transmitter of divine messages to prophets.

Benjamin Walker summarizes other contacts of Muhammad with Christianity.[101] One Tamim al-Dari, a Christian, is said to have had influenced Muhammad's eschatological ideas. One Kayis of the Abdul Kayis tribe was a Christian whose house Muhammad used to frequent. Jabra, a young Greek Christian and a sword-cutter by profession, had settled in Mecca. He was well-versed in the Torah and the teachings of Jesus. Muhammad used to frequent his house. Muhammad also frequented the house of Abu Takhiba, a Greek Christian. Abu Rokaya of the Christian Tamim tribe was known for the purity of his life. His devotion to religion and selflessness had earned him the title of "monk of the people". Muhammad had associated with him, who, later on, became a Muslim. Some Rahman of Yamama was believed by Muhammad's contemporaries to have given him some Christian ideas. Ibn Ishaq confirms that Muhammad had contacts with certain Rahman of Yamama. Other commentators recognize Rahman to be Musaylima, a famous preacher in prophetic garb from Yamama. Musaylima had become a formidable opponent of Islam after Muhammad's death. A series of sanguinary battles between Muslims and Musaylima's followers ensued and he was killed (discussed later).

Mecca also had substantial contact with overseas Christians. Some Christian tribes of the region maintained commercial depots in Mecca and had their representatives there. '*Such were the Christian tribes of Ijl, affiliated by a pact with the Koraysh (Quraysh) clan of Sahm, and the Ghassan, affiliated to the Koraysh clan of Zuhra and having a privileged establishment in the vicinity of the Kabaa itself,*' notes Walker. Furthermore, '*Mecca had a small but influential Christian population—both Arab and foreign, slave and free, from Abyssinia, Syria, Iraq and Palestine*'—who '*worked as artisans, masons, traders, physicians and scribes,*' adds Walker. Some Muslim chronicler also wrote about the presence of a Christian cemetery in Mecca.[102]

Manichean influence: Manichaeism, a heretic sect founded by Mani (d. 276) of Ectaba by mixing Christian, Zoroastrian and Buddhist ideas, had flourished in Hira (Mesopotamia) at the time of Prophet Muhammad. Since Mecca had a flourishing trade and commerce with Hira, the ideas of Manichaeism had undoubtedly reached Mecca. Mani had claimed that he was the Paraclete, who, Jesus had promised, would come; that he was the last and the final prophet in the prophetic succession; that he received his revelation from the divine creator; and that Jesus was not crucified but a different person was put in his place. All these fundamental beliefs of Manichaeism seemed to have influenced Muhammad and found prominent place in Islam.

Nestorian influence: Nestorianism, another Christian sect founded by Nestorius (d. 451), the bishop of Constantinople, was also flourishing in Persia and reached Mecca during Muhammad's time. Muhammad's meeting with Nestorian monks have been mentioned already. Nestorians were puritanical and opposed to showing images of Jesus and the Cross. These ideas have found firm place in Islamic doctrines. This was reflected in the widespread protests and violence by Muslims, leading to many deaths in February 2006, over

---

99. Muir, p. 21

100. Walker, p. 190

101. Ibid, p. 190–91

102. Ibid, p. 180

the publication of Muhammad's images in a Danish paper. In Islam, the depiction of living beings, particularly of Prophet Muhammad, in images and pictures are banned.

Influence of hermitic Christian monks: The ascetic Christian monks of the time also had profoundly influenced Muhammad's theological ideas. According to both Islamic and Pagan chronicles, Christian monks had set up monastic communities along the roads of Egypt, Asia Minor (modern Turkey), Syria, Palestine, Mesopotamia and Arabia. They dedicated themselves to good works, acts of charity, and care for the poor, the sick and the orphaned—the abandoned girls in particular. At night, exhausted travelers and trade-caravans used to break their journey at these monastic communities, where the hermits would offer these wayfarers welcome, shelter and hospitality. Muhammad, having traveled extensively throughout the region for business-trips, must have been very familiar with these monasteries; he had enjoyed their hospitality himself. Monk Bahira treated him with a copious meal on his first business-trip to Syria.[103] These monks had made a positive impression on Muhammad's mind and he gave their lifestyle an honourable homage in the Quran:

1. 'Spend your money for good: to help your parents, your family, orphans, wayfarers, and the needy.' [Quran 2:215]

2. 'Be kind to parents, relatives, orphans, the needy, neighbors, and travelers.' [Quran 4:36]

Another major feature of Islam, picked by Muhammad from Christian monks, is the prayer rituals. The monks, dedicated to the practice complete chastity, had devoted themselves to prayers multiple times a day. Their prayer rituals comprised of reverential postures: standing with palms together, bowing down, kneeling, and sitting on the heels. Muhammad had undoubtedly copied this mode of prayer rituals into Islam. According to CJ Archer's *Mystic Elements in Muhammed* (1924), the monks also used to engage in prayer rituals late into the night believing that *"Prayer is better than sleep."*[104] The early-morning Muslim call to prayer (*adhan*) has incorporated this line. So impressed was Muhammad by some aspects of these monks' lifestyle, namely devotion to god, generosity and acts of charity, that he honorably referred to them in the Quran: '...*of the followers of the Book (Christians), there is an upright party; they recite Allah's communications in the nighttimes and they adore (God)... they enjoin what is right and forbid the wrong and they strive with one another in hastening to good deeds, and those are among the good*' [Quran 3:113–14].

But already married and engaged in a material life long before starting his prophetic mission, Muhammad condemned monasticism, which, he claimed, was *not ordained by God*, but invented by Christians [Quran 57:27].

Othman ibn Huwayrith's effort to introduce Christianity in Mecca: Another person warrants mention here is Othman ibn Huwayrith, who was an influential leader in Mecca and a cousin of Muhammad's first wife, Khadijah. According to Ibn Ishaq, Othman had broken with Polytheism. Appalled by idolatry in the *Ka'ba*, he '*went to the Byzantine emperor and became a Christian. He was given high office there.*'[105] In 605, about five years before the start of Muhammad's divine mission, Othman returned to Mecca. On the strength of a Byzantine imperial grant, he laid claim on the Government of Mecca intending to reform existing Polytheism of the city. Opposed by the ruling Meccans, he fled to Syria where he was assassinated.[106]

The sermon of Qiss ibn Sayda in the Okaz fair: Muhammad is also known to have attended sermons in the annual fair of Okaz near Mecca. His encounter with Qiss ibn Sayda ('Qiss' means 'priest') in the Okaz fair needs a mention here. Islamic tradition relates that some time before Muhammad's mission commenced, Qiss ibn Sayda—the bishop of Najran, belonging to the Iyad tribe—preached in the fair. He

---

103. Al-Tabari, Vol. VI, p. 44–45; Ibn Ishaq, p. 80
104. Walker, p. 62
105. Ibn Ishaq, p. 99
106. Walker, p. 66

spoke "as though in ecstasy", chanting the rhymed prose (*sai*) in the then Arab poetic style, reminiscent of early Quranic *suras*. One sermon read:

> 'O Ye, people draw near / And hear, and fear / Signs are read / Not to be gainsaid / Stars that set and rise / Sea that never dries.

> And roofed above, the skies / On earth below that lies / Rain is shed / Plants are fed / Male and female wed.

> Time flying and time fled / O mortals say / Where are the tribes today / That once did disobey / The rules of goodness / Where are they?

> Verily doth Allah give / Light to those who seek to live!'

The bishop then went on to preach about human frailties, the grace of God and the coming *Judgment Day*. Muhammad listened to the sermon "as though spellbound" and was deeply moved. This sermon had stirred his mind and soul as renowned Muslim scholar al-Jahiz (d. 869) records a prophetic tradition that Muhammad himself recalled '*how vividly he remembered the scene, the man, the eloquent words and the persuasive message.*' In later years, when a deputation from the Iyad tribe visited Mecca, Muhammad enquired with them about Qiss and was informed that he had died (c. 613). Saddened by the news, Muhammad spoke kindly of him as one, who had preached the "true universal faith".[107]

In the Okaz fair, Jewish preachers also delivered sermons. Preachers of both religions used to rail at the Arab tribes, spurning them for practicing idolatry and warning them of the coming punishment in hell. Muhammad used to go to the fair and listen to the sermons of Jewish and Christian preachers. Despite the mutual hostility between the Jews and Christians, the similarity of these two religions—both having a unitary God, a revealed divine book and a prophet of their own; both fervently denouncing idolatry; and of course, the fear of coming punishment in hell in those sermons—had likely stirred young Muhammad's mind profoundly.

Influence of other beliefs and legends on Muhammad's creed

In order to understand better the foundation of Muhammad's prophetic mission, it is necessary to digress here briefly to include the influence of other beliefs, customs and legends that had inspired and played critical roles in the formulation of his creed.

Influence of the Hanifs: The influence of one Zayd ibn Amr of the *Hanif* sect demands a mention here. *Hanif*, a Syrian Christian loanword, meant one who had moved away from idolatry. During Muhammad's time in Arabia, it loosely referred to monotheists: Jews, Christians, Zoroastrians and *Sabians*. In Mecca, the term *Hanif* more specifically referred to those, who, under the Jewish and Christian influence, had moved away from Paganism and were trying to reform idolatry into monotheism. Ibn Ishaq notes on the beliefs of *Hanifs* at Mecca:[108]

> …they were of the opinion that their people had corrupted the religion of their father Abraham, and that the stone (i.e., black stone in *Ka'ba*) they went around was of no account; it could neither hear, nor see, nor help. '*Find for yourself a religion,*' they said; '*for by God, you have none.*' So they went their several ways in the lands, seeking the *Hanifiya*, the religion of Abraham.

Apart from Zayd ibn Amr, Othman ibn Huwayrith and Waraqa ibn Naufal were also *hanifs*.

Zayd was an uncle of Omar, Muhammad's close companion and the second caliph of Islam. He called himself a follower of Abraham's religion and used to write poetry disparaging heathenish practices of

---

107. Ibid, p. 90
108. Ibn Ishaq, p99

his tribe. He had condemned female infanticide and idolatry. Every year during the month of Ramadan, he used to spend time in retirement in a cave of Mount Hira.

In about 595, Muhammad (age 24–25) met Zayd on the way and conversed with him and offered him some flesh of an animal sacrificed to idols. Zayd refused the meat, scolded Muhammad for practicing idolatry and rebuked him for eating flesh offered to Pagan Gods. Muhammad later had said, "*After that I never knowingly stroked one of the idols, nor did I sacrifice an animal to them.*" Zayd used to sit in the courtyard of the *Ka'ba* and pray: "*O God, I do not know how you desire to be worshipped. If I knew, I will surely worship you.*" Mocked by the people, he went to Syria and then to Iraq to question the rabbis and monks. On his way back in 608, he was killed by bandits.[109]

Muhammad appears to have been influenced by Zayd's doctrines and practices so deeply that all of them were later incorporated into Islam. Indeed, Muhammad at the beginning used to call his disciples *Hanif.* The Quran affirms that Muhammad was only preaching the original and pure religion (monotheism) of Abraham [Quran 21:51], who "was not of the polytheists" [Quran 16:123]. In other words, Abraham was a *Hanif.*[110] In a later verse, Quran 3:67, he introduced the term "Muslim" and Abraham was now a Muslim and a *Hanif* (i.e., not a Polytheist).

In his teachings, Muhammad had consigned all non-Muslims, including his doting uncle Abu Talib and his mother Amina, to the fire of hell. But he made an exception by invoking the mercy of God on Zayd. Ibn Ishaq writes, when Muhammad was asked: "*Ought we to ask God's pardon for Zayd b. Amr?*' He replied, '*Yes, for he will be raised from the dead as the sole representative of a whole people.*'"[111] The Prophet added, "*He is one of those destined for paradise. I have seen him there.*"[112] This clearly points to a towering influence that Zayd (and *Hanifs* in general) had on Muhammad and in the formulation of his doctrines.

Other Monotheistic influences: The Jews and Christians obviously had the strongest influence in the formulation of Muhammad's creed. Contacts with the Jews had increased dramatically after his migration to Medina. Other monotheistic creeds existing in the region, such as the fire-worshipping Zoroastrianism (i.e., *Persi*) of Persia and the star-worshipping *Sabianism,* also influenced Muhammad. He incorporated various thoughts and codes of these beliefs into Islam. Alongside the Jews and Christians, the Quran also mentions the *Sabians* as the people of the Book [Quran 5:69] and depicts the Zoroastrians (*Madjus/Magians*) favorably [Quran 22:17]. He incorporated the Zoroastrian concept of heaven and hell in Islam. His swearing *by the Star* in the Quran [71:15] clearly shows a *Sabian* influence.

Polytheistic Influence: Growing up in the vicinity of the *Ka'ba,* a center of vibrant religious activities, Muhammad was deeply influenced by religious piety. The Polytheistic creed and tradition that he grew up with also left their marks on Muhammad's new faith. For example, *Hajj* and *Omra,* which were Polytheistic rituals of pilgrimage to the sacred temple of *Ka'ba,* were incorporated into Islam with minor changes. Concerning *Hajj,* the only change Muhammad made is that the sacrifice of animals was now done to an invisible Allah, instead of to idol-gods previously.

A careful analysis of the events surrounding Muhammad's life clearly suggests that he was particularly influenced by the prevailing monotheistic communities worshipping a singular God. His contacts and discussions with Jewish and Christian believers and preachers appear to have greatly inspired his mind with the concept of a unitary God. The concept of God's rigorous judgment and the horrifying punishments in hell in these religions—unknown to Pagan traditions of the Quraysh—must have filled his mind with the fear of God's vengeance after death. Ibn Huwayrith's fateful mission to reform Meccan Paganism to Christianity,

---

109. Ibid, p. 99–103; Walker, p. 89

110. Those not Polytheists in Mecca were called *Hanifs.*

111. Ibn Ishaq, p. 100

112. Walker, p. 90

only five years before Muhammad's own mission, must have had impacted his inspiration and resolve for establishing a monotheistic creed among the misguided idolaters of Mecca.

Christian thoughts in Islam

The suggestion that Muhammad was strongly influenced by Christian theology, and that he was possibly trained in it prior to his prophetic mission, is reflected in the fact that many concepts of Christianity were later copied in the Quran as the divine verses from Allah. The Prophet had evidently copied the existing style of prayer rituals of the Christian monks. When Muhammad sent away a number of his followers to settle in Abyssinia in 615, they were honorably received and protected by the Christian king there. According to Al-Tabari, the emigrants later said, "*We came to Abyssinia and were hospitably lodged by the best of hosts. We had security to practice our religion*" without being persecuted or hearing unpleasant words.[113] This event had evidently created a favorable impression of Christianity in Muhammad's mind as judged from the fact that verses revealed by Allah from this time onwards started giving a very good appraisal of Christianity (also Judaism). This trend continued until the first year after Muhammad's relocation to Medina.

In the Quran, Allah addresses Jesus: '*I will make those who follow thee superior to those who reject faith, to the Day of Resurrection*' [Quran 3:55]. The Quran also records that Christians are free from pride and most inclined to entertain feelings of friendship toward Muslims [Quran 5:82], which clearly referred to the Abyssinia king's hospitality to Muslim exiles. Following his triumphant entry into Mecca in January 630, Muhammad ordered the destruction of the idols and erasure of the paintings from the walls and pillars. The effigies of Abraham and Ishmael, as already noted, were also destroyed. But Muhammad protected the image of Mary and infant Jesus by placing his hand over it.

Parallel Biblical passages in the Quran: Muhammad did not only absorb Christian rituals and ideas, but he also copied many passages from the Bible almost as such or with minor modifications. A few such instances are listed here:[114]

1. 'The righteous shall inherit the earth' [Quran 21:105] was taken directly from the Bible [Ps 37:29]

2. A verse from Mark's Gospel reads: '*For the earth bringeth forth fruit of herself; first the blade, then the ear and after that the full corn of the ear*' [Mark 4:28]. The Quran renders it thus: '*They are the seeds that putteth forth its stalk, then straighten it and its growth in the ear and riseth upon its stem*' [Quran 48:29].

3. Jesus said: '*it is easier for a camel to pass through the eye of a needle than for a rich man to enter the kingdom of heaven*' [Matt. 19:24]. According to the Quran, '*Heaven's gates shall not open to those who charge us with falsehood, nor shall they enter paradise until a camel passeth through the eye of a needle*' [Quran 7:40].

4. On the Day of Judgment, says the Bible, '*the heavens shall roll together into a scroll*' [Isa. 34:4]. The Quran says, '*On that day will we roll up the heavens as one rolleth up written scrolls*' [Quran 21:104].

5. '*Where two or three person meet together in my name, there am I in the midst of them,*' says the Bible [Matt. 18:20]. The Quran puts it: '*Three persons cannot meet together secretly but God is the fourth*' [Quran 58:7].

---

113. Al-Tabari, Vol. VI, p. 99.

114. Ibid, p. 93

6. The Bible says, '*There are many other things which Jesus did, which if written down, I suppose that even the world could not contain the book that should be written*' [John 21:25]. The Quran puts it: '*If the seas were ink, it would be insufficient for the words of the Lord*' [Quran 18:109].

Christian terminology in Islam: The major terminology of Islam was also borrowed from those in Christian religious usage. "Islam" (also "Muslim"), meaning "submission to God", has its root in the Semitic term '*SLM* and was in Christian usage to mean "devotion to God". The term "Quran" originates from the Christian Aramaic term *Kerana*, then in usage to mean readings of the sacred texts in church services. The word *sura* originates from the Aramaic Christian term *sutra*, meaning portion of the scripture, and the word *aya*, meaning verse or sign, were also taken from Christian usage. There are other Islamic terms that were then in Christian use.

Jesus and Bible in good light in the Quran: The Quran accords an honorable status to Jesus and the Bible. It states that God sent Jesus as a sign of mercy for mankind [Quran 19:21]. It affirms that the Gospel (*Injil* from 'Evangel') is a divine book, which was given to Jesus and that God has planted mercy in the hearts of those who follow him [Quran 57:27]. The Quran confirms Christian Gospels as the guide to mankind [Quran 3:3], which contains the truth [Quran 9:111] and gives guidance and light [Quran 5:46]. The Quran also regards Virgin Mary (Maryam) as a highly esteemed woman. Having been chosen above all women of the world, the Quran says, she was purified by God [Quran 3:37] and maintained in purity [66:12]. She '*was a saintly woman*' [Quran 5:75]. God breathed His spirit into her womb; and hence, the birth of Jesus was a creative act of God vested upon an immaculate virgin, who kept her maidenhood [Quran 19:21, 21:91]. Those who follow the Gospel will enjoy bounties from both above and below, asserts the Quran [5:69].

No novelty in Islam: It is evident that all types of religious thoughts and practices—namely Christian, Jewish, Zoroastrian, *Hanifite*, Pagan, and popular legends, and myths—which were current in Arabia during Muhammad's time, have found place in the Quran, either as such or in modified forms. Indeed, Allah did reveal, or Muhammad did innovate, almost nothing new in the formulation of Islam. There is rarely, if at all, a doctrine, ritual or practice in Islam that was not current in the existing religious beliefs, social customs and popular myths and legends. Allah and Muhammad only assimilated the existing ideas, thoughts and practices into Islam. Scholars, such as Ignaz Goldziher and Samuel Zwemer, are, therefore, correct in insisting that Muhammad created no new ideas but only mixed the existing ideas and practices into a new concoction. In agreement, Ibn Warraq writes:

> Muhammad was not an original thinker; he did not formulate any new ethical principles, but merely borrowed from the prevailing cultural milieu. The eclectic nature of Islam has been recognized for a long time. Even Muhammad knew Islam was not a new religion and the revelation contained in the Quran merely confirmed the already existing scriptures. The prophet always claimed affiliations with the great religions of the Jews, Christians and others.[115]

Christianity obviously had the most inspiring impact on Muhammad's mission, initially intended for reforming the Paganism in Mecca. Christian doctrines and practices were most widely assimilated into Islam. Therefore, the historical Christian belief that Islam was a heretic sect of their own religion is largely justified.

Condemnation of Christianity in the Quran

During the first five years of Muhammad's prophetic mission, when nearly twenty out of 114 chapters of the Quran were revealed, his verses mentioned very little about the Bible or Christianity. Only after Muhammad

---

115. Ibn Warraq (1995) *Why I am not a Muslim*, Prometheus Books, New York, p. 34

had sent away some of his disciples to Christian Abyssinia in 615, the new verses started affirming Biblical stories. This trend continued until some early period of Muhammad's mission in Medina.

It is likely that, after seeing no prospect in getting the Meccan Polytheists flock to his faith, Muhammad directed his attention to the Christians and Jews who might join his mission, if he affirmed their faiths in his new creed. It also became a tactical necessity to keep the Christians of Abyssinia—who had accorded great hospitality to the Muslim refugees—on a friendly term. The Quraysh, who had trade-relations with Abyssinia, had sent a deputation to the Christian king to have the Muslim settlers expelled or deported to Mecca. They complained to the king that Muslims were setting up a heretical sect. The king wanted a proof of their heresy before taking any action. When the king summoned the Muslim settlers to his court and questioned about their allegedly heretical doctrines, Jafar, their spokesman, cleverly read out from *sura Maryam* that talks about Virgin Mary, John the Baptist and the miraculous birth of Jesus, affirming the Christian faith. This pleased the king; he refused to expel the Muslim refugees.[116]

Despite affirming the Christian faith in the Quran for years and exhorting them to join Muhammad's creed, Christians (Jews too) did not flock to his faith in significant numbers. The exhortation to Christians and Jews continued for over a year after his relocation to Medina, but all efforts went in vain. Instead, they started harassing Muhammad on the basis of many inaccuracies about their faiths in his verses. They turned to be his major critics and irritants. His attitude toward them started hardening. Despite borrowing so heavily from Christian (also Jewish) doctrines to formulate his creed, he now would not hesitate to condemn the Christians (and Jews) for their reluctance to embrace Islam. He accused the Christians of misunderstanding or forgetting their scriptures [Quran 5:14]. Out of his own misconception of the Trinity, whereby he thought Christian believed in three Gods, he attacked them: '*They surely are infidels who say that God is the third of the three*' [Quran 5:73] and urged them to '*believe therefore in Allah and His messengers, and say not, Three (Gods)*' [Quran 4:171].

In line with the Jewish thoughts, Muhammad now denied the divinity of Jesus and his incarnation. Jesus was not a son of God, for '*God begetteth not*' [Quran 112:3]. '*It is not befitting to (the majesty of) Allah that He should beget a son,*' says the Quran [19:36]. Allah revealed that it would be far from the glory of God to have a son [Quran 4:171]. Ibn Ishaq relates a story of Muhammad rebuking two Christian divines about their belief that God has a son. Then they asked back: "*Who was his father, Muhammad?*" An affirmer of the virgin birth of Jesus himself, he had no ready answer and kept silent.[117] He needed time to find an answer and later received a verse, which says, '*God can create what He will. When He decrees a thing, Allah createth what He willeth: When He hath decreed a plan, He but saith to it, 'Be' and it is!*' [Quran 3:47].

The Quran now invoked Allah's curse on Christians who said Christ was the son of God [Quran 9:30]. Muhammad also denied that Jesus died on the Cross as the Quran says, '*they slew him not nor crucified him;*' instead, '*Allah raised him up unto Himself*' during his apparent crucifixion [Quran 4:157–58]. This idea was copied from Manichaeism as already mentioned. It should be understood that if the death of Jesus on the Cross for the sin of mankind is denied, the Christian faith loses much of its claimed greatness.

Muhammad's hostility toward Christians

Exasperated with the Christians, critical of his faith, Muhammad no longer remained content with only condemning many doctrines of Christianity. The Christian priests, who were preventing their faithful from joining Muhammad's mission, were now condemned by Muhammad as greedy and devourer of people's wealth, which they do not spend in Allah's mission, as the Quran says: '*...the (Christian) monks devour the wealth of mankind wantonly and debar (men) from the way of Allah. They who hoard up gold and silver and spend it not in the way of Allah, unto them give tidings (O Muhammad) of a painful doom...*' [Quran 9:34].

---

116. Walker, p. 109
117. Ibid, p. 199

Allah now started condemning Christians for perverting His true creed and promised His vengeance against them [Quran 9:30]. Allah's attitude now became hostile toward Christians and started inciting hatred against them by revealing: '*O Ye who believe! Choose not for guardians such of those who received the Scripture before you (Christians, Jews)... keep your duty to Allah if ye are true believers*' [Quran 5:57]. He now condemned Christians, the transgressors of truth, to hell, where they will abide forever [Quran 5:77, 98:6].

The scholars of Islam often mention only the favourable references of Christianity in the Quran to show that the Islamic creed is very friendly toward Christians. Evidently, those verses were tailor-made for exhorting the Christians to join Islam and accept Muhammad as their prophet, abandoning Christianity. But when Allah's desperate effort failed to impress them, numerous hostile and violence-inciting verses came down from the heaven, which those scholars will never mention. Some of those hostile verses are listed below:

1. Jews and Christians believe in idols and false deities. [Quran 4:51]

2. 'Those (Christians and Jews) are they whom Allah hath cursed.' [Quran 4:52]

3. Allah has stirred up enmity and hatred amongst Christians. [Quran 5:14]

4. Jews and Christians are losers. [Quran 5:53]

5. Christians will be burned in the fire of hell. [Quran 5:72]

6. Christians are wrong about the Trinity. For that, they will have a painful doom. [Quran 5:73]

7. Do not choose the Jews, Christians, or disbelievers as guardians. [Quran 5:57]

8. Do not take Jews or Christians for friends. If you do, Allah will consider you to be one of them. [Quran 5:51]

9. Christians and Jews are perverts. Allah himself fights against them. [Quran 9:30]

10. There will be a painful doom to the rich and greedy Christian monks… [Quran 9:34]

11. Jews and Christians are evil transgressors. [Quran 5:59]

12. Evil is the handiwork of the Jewish rabbis and Christian priests. [Quran 5:63]

13. Christians and Jews must believe what Allah has revealed to Muhammad; if not, Allah will turn them into apes, as He did to the Sabbath-breakers. [Quran 4:47]

14. Fight against the Christians and Jews '*until they pay the tribute (jizyah) readily, being brought low in humiliation.*' [Quran 9:29]

Muhammad's anti-Christian hostility in his death-bed

Prophet Muhammad's hostility toward Christians continued well into his death-bed. The Prophet fell terminally ill and he was in severe pain and moaning aloud all night. His wife Aisha, hoping to console him, said which Muhammad himself used to say when others were in pain: "*O Prophet, if any of us had moaned like this, you would surely have reprimanded her.*" He replied, "*Yes, but I burn with the fever-heat twice as strong.*"[118] The next morning the pain worsened and he almost became unconscious. Another wife Umm Salama suggested of giving him a concoction of Abyssinian recipe, which she had learned while in exile

---

118. Ibid, p. 141

there. Having revived from its effect, Muhammad became suspicious of what he had been made to drink and ordered all the women in the chamber to take the same medicine. In his presence, the medicine was poured into each woman's mouth.

The conversation on the Abyssinian remedy moved to Abyssinia itself. Two of his wives, Umm Salama and Umm Habiba, both having been exiles in that country, spoke of the beautiful cathedral of Maria there and the wonderful pictures on its walls. Overhearing this, an exasperated Muhammad cried out: *"The Lord, destroy the Jews and Christians. Let the Lord's anger be kindled against them. Let there remain throughout Arabia no faith except Islam."*[119] This dying wish of the Prophet was carried out to conclusion by his immediate successors by expelling the Jews and Christians from Arabia.

Muhammad's threatening missives to Christian rulers

In 628, when Muhammad was not strong enough even to capture Mecca, he sent emissaries proclaiming his prophethood to the distant Arab kings of Yamama, Oman and Bahrain, summoning them to embrace Islam. Responses from Oman and Bahrain were non-committal. Hauda ibn Ali, the Christian head of Yamama, the most powerful man in Arabia, sought a share in Muhammad's prophethood. On receiving the reply, Muhammad cursed him and Hauda died after a year. Missives, demanding conversion to Islam, were also sent to powerful foreign Christian rulers: Emperor Heraclius of Rome (Constantinople), Ghassanid Prince Harith VII and the Christian governor of Egypt. His missives at Rome and Ghassan were received with scorn and as an "emissary of a madman". The Roman governor of Egypt did not embrace Islam but returned a friendly reply along with two beautiful slave-girls (sisters) as a gift to Muhammad. The Prophet added the younger, beautiful Maria the Copt to his harem as a sex-slave.

Muhammad's expeditions against Christians

Later on, when Muslims achieved power, Muhammad launched military campaigns against all those kings who had rejected his missives. But satisfied with the prized gift, Maria the Copt, he never launched an attack against Egypt, although his successors did after his death.

In September 629, Muhammad sent a strong force of 3,000 Jihadis to Muta, a Christian border-district in Syria. Muhammad instructed his commanders to summon the Christians to embrace Islam, and if they refused, to draw the sword against them in the name of Allah. The Christians had assembled a large force to confront the Muslim aggressors. In the battle, Muslims suffered severe losses: two leading Muslim generals, Zayd and Jafar, were slain. Only Khalid ibn Walid's brilliant maneuvres saved the life of the rest.[120]

In February 630, Muhammad sent a force under Amr ibn al-As to the Christian tribes of Oman, summoning the ruler to embrace Islam and pay taxes. Some of the tribes accepted Islam, whilst the Mazuna tribe were forced to surrender half of their land and property in order to keep their Christian faith. In the same month, a missive was sent to the Christian prince of Himyar, demanding submission to Islam and payment of required tithes, taxes and tributes. They were also ordered to speak the Arabic, instead of Himyar. If refused, they were to be regarded as the enemies of Allah. In order to save lives, the prince replied back accepting Islam.[121]

In October 630, Muhammad assembled 30,000 horses and foots to launch an expedition against the Byzantine frontier in Syria. Two years earlier, Emperor Heraclius and the Ghassanid prince of Syria had rejected Muhammad's missives summoning them to embrace Islam. After arriving at Tabuk near the Syrian border, Muhammad stopped and set up tents. He sent out missives to various principalities, demanding that they embrace Islam or pay *jizyah* tax. Yohana (John) ibn Ruba, the Christian prince of the Ayla tribe, made a

---

119. Ibid, p. 142; also Ibn Ishaq, p. 523
120. Ibn Ishaq, p. 532–40; Muir, p. 393–95
121. Walker, p. 204–05

treaty with Muhammad agreeing to pay *jizyah* as protection against attack on his people. Muhammad halted at Tabuk for twenty days and brought a few small communities into subjection. Muhammad now wished to march ahead to make encroachment into the Syrian territory, the main objective of the campaign. While he was making the preparation, intelligence arrived that a large Greek force had assembled at the border to confront the Muslim army. The report disheartened his troops, forcing him to retreat without realizing his ardent desire.

While in Tabuk, Muhammad had sent Khalid ibn Walid to the Oasis of Duma, ruled by Arab Christian prince Okaydir ibn Abdul Malik of the Kalb tribe. Okaydir was out on hunting with his brother when Khalid ambushed them, killed his brother and brought Okaydir to Medina as a prisoner. Okaydir was forced to convert to Islam and sign an agreement to pay customary taxes. After Muhammad's death, Okaydir revolted. To avenge his disobedience and apostasy, Khalid returned to Duma, killed the prince and sacked his community.

Muhammad's dealing with Christian delegations

Muhammad's manner of dealing with Christians can be gauged from the way he had handled a few Christian delegations in 631. After Muhammad's capture of Mecca in 630, delegations from terrified tribes across Arabia poured into Medina to seek protection from his attacks. In February, an embassy from the influential Christian tribe of Banu Hanifa came to visit Muhammad in Medina. Although unclear what transpired in the discussion, before they returned, the Prophet handed them a vessel of water left from his ablution and ordered them that, on their return, they tear down their churches, sprinkle the site with the water and build a mosque at its stead. A month later, an embassy of sixteen men, made up of partly Christians from the Taghlib tribe, wearing gold crosses, paid a visit to Muhammad. He signed an agreement with them whereupon they could keep their faith but could not baptize their children into the Christian faith.[122] That means, the children became the property of Muslims.

On another notable occasion, a Christian delegation of fourteen men from Nejran visited Muhammad in the same year. They were led by Abdul Masih of the Kinda tribe, Bishop Abu Haritha of the Bakr tribe and a representative of the noble Dayan family. Muhammad recited passages from the Quran to them, and out of politeness, they agreed that he had a message for his people. But when he pressed them to embrace Islam, they declined. Much argument between the two parties on religious matters followed without reaching an agreement. Finally, Muhammad suggested of holding a fighting match between the two parties on cursing each other, so that the curse of God will fall on the families of those who were lying. The Christian delegation refused to participate in such mean acts.[123] Allah has related this story in the Quran as follows: '*But whoever disputes with you in this matter after what has come to you of knowledge, then say: Come let us call our sons and your sons and our women and your women and our near people and your near people, then let us be earnest in prayer, and pray for the curse of Allah on the liars*' [Quran 3:61].

Before taking a leave, Muhammad assured the delegation that their practice of religion will not be molested and their lands and properties will not be confiscated. But later in the same year, Muhammad sent Khalid to force the people of Nejran to embrace Islam. Knowing Khalid's reputation as a brutal mass-murderer, some of them quickly submitted to Islam. However, more pressing battles on other fronts diverted Khalid's attention elsewhere and most of the people of Nejran remained Christian until Muhammad's death. Later on, Caliph Omar launched a new campaign to exterminate the remaining Christians from Arabia. Under a fresh threat of attack and decimation, most of the Nejran tribesmen embraced Islam. In 635, Omar sent a large number of their prominent citizens, scholars and religious leaders to exile.[124]

---

122. Muir, p. 458
123. Ibid, p. 458–60
124. Walker, p. 207

In 632, the Prophet was preparing for an expedition when he suddenly fell terminally ill. His dying wish to cleanse entire Arabia of other religions was taken up by the successive caliphs. Muslim armies first set upon a campaign to convert the whole of Arabia by force. Soon, they turned attention to the Christian tribes of Central Asia. Musaylima of Yamama, allegedly under a revelation that pre-dated the start of Muhammad's mission, was preaching a mainly Christian version of religion. He had sent a letter to Muhammad recognizing him also as a prophet and appealed for preaching their religions within their regions without hostility. Rejecting Musaylima's offer, Muhammad replied, "*From Muhammad the apostle of God to Musaylima the liar... The earth is God's. He lets whom He will of His creatures inherit it and the result is to the pious.*"[125]

Musaylima was known to be very popular and his following was no less strong than Muhammad's. Abu Bakr sent an expedition against Musaylima whose expanding popularity was threatening the nascent faith of Islam. In the first battle of Yamama, Muslims were defeated by Musaylima's followers. In the second battle in 634, Muslims suffered so worse a defeat that there was hardly a house in Medina where the sound of wailing was not heard. Most importantly, thirty-nine of Muhammad's chief companions, including the best Quran rememberers, died in this battle. A few months later in 634, Abu Bakr turned to dreaded Khalid, sending him with a large force to exterminate Musaylima. A fierce battle ensued at Akraba, which famously became known as the "garden of death". Musaylima was slain; ten thousand of his followers were massacred; the rest of the population were forcibly converted to Islam.[126] No significant Christian presence remained in Arabia thereafter.

This is the life of Prophet Muhammad, who, Muslims believe, was indisputably the greatest, kindest and most merciful human being ever to walk on the earth.

STATUS OF NON-MUSLIMS IN ISLAM AS ACCORDED BY MUHAMMAD

Based on Prophet Muhammad's treatment of non-Muslims, let us evaluate the status he had given to different kinds of infidels: Pagans, Jews and Christians of the Arabian Peninsula.

Idolaters in Islam

Prophet Muhammad tried to preach Islam among the idolaters of Mecca for thirteen years, but failed to make much progress. Although the majority of the Meccans rejected his message, he faced no violent hostility from them despite the fact that his messages were hateful and insulting to their religion, customs and ancestors, and that he claimed the *Ka'ba* belonged to his God. The only hostility the Quraysh had shown was the two-year social and economic blockade on Muhammad, a rather civilized measure. The Pagans of Mecca had, undoubtedly, shown remarkable tolerance in the face of hostile, irreverent attitude and actions of Muhammad. Seeing no hope of success of his mission in Mecca, and that his mission was doing very well in Medina in his absentia, Muhammad relocated there (622).

Allah later termed the Meccans' rejection of Islam "tumult and oppression", which was "worse than slaughter". To avenge the rejection, Allah sanctioned attacking and killing the Meccan citizens [Quran 2:190–93]. He found the Meccans' rejection of His new religion so offensive and unpardonable that He made killing and fighting those rejecters a binding duty upon Muslims, even if they disliked it [Quran 2:216]. Allah made fighting and killing the Meccan idolaters legal even during the prohibited months (for fighting), such as their killing in the first successful Jihad attack in Nakhla [Quran 2:217].

After the controversial, but successful, blood-letting Jihad raid at Nakhla, a number of major confrontations—the battles of Badr (624), Ohud (625) and the Ditch (627)—took place between Muslims of Medina and the idolaters of Mecca. These confrontations culminated in Muhammad's conquest of Mecca in 630. He took possession of the Meccans' sacred idol-shrine of *Ka'ba*, destroyed the idol-gods therein and transformed it into the sacred house of the Islamic God.

---

125. Ibn Ishaq, p. 649
126. Ibid, p. 209

Although many idolaters of Mecca submitted to Islam on that day, the recalcitrant ones were allowed to stay in the practice of idolatry, based on an agreement Muhammad had reached with Meccan leader Abu Sufyan. This concession lasted only for one year. During the next *Hajj* pilgrimage (631), Allah suddenly revealed a number of verses (9:1–5)—particularly verse 9:5—which commanded the annihilation of idol-worship by giving the idolaters a choice between conversion to Islam and death: '*Then, when the sacred months have passed, slay the idolaters wherever ye find them, and take them (captive), and besiege them, and prepare for them each ambush. But if they repent and establish worship and pay the poor due, then leave their way free...*'

With this command, the practice of idol-worship was completely banished from Arabia during Muhammad's life-time. A choice between death and acceptance of Islam, therefore, became the standard sanction in Islam for the Pagans, idolaters, animists, heathens and atheists.

Jews in Islam

Prophet Muhammad initially exhorted the Jews to embrace Islam and accept him as their prophet. When they adamantly rejected this offer, he decided to deal with them harshly. First, he attacked the Jewish tribe of Banu Qaynuqa of Medina soon after his stunning victory against the Quraysh at Badr. After defeating the Jewish tribe, he wanted to slaughter the surrendered Jews as records Al-Tabari: '*They were fettered and he (Muhammad) wanted to kill them.*'[127] But a strong intervention by Abdullah ibn Obayi—the famed hypocrite of Islamic annals—prevented Muhammad from slaughtering the Jews *en masse*. Instead, he exiled the whole community from their ancestral homes.

When Muhammad next attacked Banu Nadir, the second major Jewish tribe of Medina, the following year on a flimsy excuse and Abdullah ibn Obayi, still a powerful leader, threatened to fight on the Jewish side. The Prophet again settled for exiling them. When the last Jewish tribe of Banu Qurayza was attacked two years later, Muhammad ignored weakened Abdullah's condemnation and went back to his original plan, which was intended for dealing with the Banu Qaynuqa Jews three years earlier. He slaughtered all the grown-up men and enslaved the women and children. The captured wealth of Banu Qurayza and captive women and children were distributed amongst his followers. The young and prettier ones among the female captives were reduced to sex-slaves. The Prophet also sold some of women overseas to acquire horses and weapons.

In sum, when the Jews rejected Islam, Muhammad attacked them one by one in which the adult males were to be executed and the women and children enslaved. This remained the final writ for the Jews in the book of Prophet Muhammad.

Christians in Islam

There was no major Christian presence around Mecca and Medina. Therefore, Muhammad did not have the kind of bitter and sustained confrontations with the Christians as he had wih the Pagans and Jews. However, his intent of dealing with the Christians can be traced in a few letters he sent to overseas Christian kings or governors: of Bahrain, Oman, Egypt, Syria, and Byzantium. Here, two letters will be dealt with: one sent to the Christian kings of Oman (628) and the other to the Christian prince of the Ayla tribe during his expedition to Tabuk (630). The Oman government Website keeps a copy of Prophet Muhammad's letter to the Oman kings:[128]

---

127. Al-Tabari, Vol. VII, p. 86

128. This document has now been removed from the Oman Government Website (http://www.mofa.gov.om/oman/discoveroman/omanhistory/OmanduringIslam). Wikipedia preserves a copy of it at http://www.wikiislam.com/wiki/Quotations_on_Islam#Official_Oman_Site

After God empowered Muslims to enter Mecca, Islam became the prevailing power and was spread by use of fear... The prophet then saw it preferable to contact neighbouring kings and rulers, including the two kings of Oman, Jaiffar and Abd, sons of Al Julanda, through peaceful means. History books tell us that the prophet had sent messages to the people of Oman, including a letter carried by military escort from Amr Ibn Al Aas to Jaiffar and Abd, sons of Al Julanda, in which, he wrote: '*In the name of God the Merciful and the Compassionate, from Muhammad bin Abdullah to Jaiffar and Abd, sons of Al Julanda, peace be on those who choose the right path. Embrace Islam, and you shall be safe. I am God's messenger to all humanity, here to alert all those alive that nonbelievers are condemned. If you submit to Islam, you will remain kings, but if you abstain, your rule will be removed and my horses will enter your arena to prove my prophecy.*'

At this point in 628 CE, suggests the letter, the choice given to Christians was to embrace Islam to buy safety. If not, they were to face the wrath of Islam, which meant war, death and destruction plus the likely enslavement of the women and children. This was the same treatment Muhammad had meted out to the Banu Qurayza Jews. In his letter, sent to the prince of the Ayla tribe (October 630), the Prophet wrote: '*...Believe or else pay tribute [Jizyah]... Ye know the tribute. If ye desire security by sea and by land, obey Allah and his apostle... But if ye oppose and displease them, I will accept nothing from you **until I have fought against you and taken captive your little ones and slain the elder**; for I am the apostle of Allah in truth...*'[129]

In two years, suggests this letter, the provision for dealing with the Christians had changed to some extent. On top of the choice of embracing Islam or death (plus enslavement of their women and children), they now have a third choice of paying poll-tax (*jizyah*) by accepting Muhammad as the master of their territory. A similar option was also extended to the Jews of Khaybar in August-September 628, about one-and-a-half years after slaughtering the Banu Qurayza Jews. After defeating the Jews of Khaybar, the women and children were carried away as slaves. The surviving Jewish men were spared and allowed to tend their lands as long as Muslims needed them on the condition of surrendering fifty percent of the produce as tribute. Allah subsequently codified this new paradigm as the final protocol for dealing with the Jews and Christians in verse 9:29 (revealed in 631): '*Fight those who believe not in Allah, nor the Last Day, nor hold that forbidden which hath been forbidden by Allah and His Messenger, nor acknowledge the religion of Truth [Islam], (even if they are) of the People of the Book [Jews & Christians], until they pay the Jizya with willing submission, and feel themselves subdued.*'

The Jews and Christians are recognized as the privileged *People of the Book* in Islam. Even then, if they fail to accept Islam, Muslims must fight them until they are defeated and agree to pay *jizyah* tax as a symbol of their humiliated and subjugated status to supreme Islam. By this divine decree [9:29], Allah commands Muslims to attack the Jewish and Christian communities and nations. After defeating them, Muslims can enslave their women and children in the way the Prophet dealt with the Jews of Banu Qurayza and Khaybar. If the vanquished Christians and Jews willingly accept the supremacy and sovereignty of Islam and agree to pay the humiliating *jizyah*, land-tax and other tributes, they should be allowed to live on with a host of disabilities as enshrined in the *Pact of Omar* (see in next chapter).

Before Prophet Muhammad died about a year later, he seemed to have changed his mind again, whereby he wanted to give no quarters to the Jews and Christians in Islamic territories, similar to the way the idolaters had already been exterminated from Arabia. This was spelled in one of his three final wishes in his death-bed that '*two religions should not be allowed to remain in the peninsula of the Arabs.*' A hadith also affirms this: '*It has been narrated by 'Omar b. al-Khattab that he heard the Messenger of Allah say: 'I will expel the Jews and Christians from the Arabian Peninsula and will not leave any but Muslim*'' [Muslim

---

129. Muir, p. 402

19:4366]. Accordingly, Caliph Omar cleansed the Arabian Peninsula of the Jews and Christians [Bukhari 3:39:53].

Islam, therefore, accords a choice between conversion to Islam and death to Polytheists (Pagans, idolaters, heathens, animists and atheists etc.), while the Christians and Jews are to be reduced into a humiliated and heavily exploited subhuman entity. It should be noted that a greater majority of the world population during Muhammad's time were Polytheists living in India, China, South and North America, and Africa. Many of these peoples, notably in India and China, had created valuable and creative civilization since the ancient times. With one stroke of the theology of Islam, they were rendered to be either brutally converted to Islam or violently dispatched to the fire of hell by a rather uncultured and backward people, who had no achievements of note until that time.

MUHAMMAD'S JIHAD AND ITS OUTCOME

Prophet Muhammad's Jihad, his *struggle or fight in the cause of Allah*, obviously consisted of all his actions and deeds—peaceful, persuasive or military—in the propagation of Islam among the people of Arabia and in extending the geographical domain of Islam. During the course of his prophetic mission, particularly after his relocation to Medina whereupon the doctrine of Jihad entered the body-politic of Islam; Prophet Muhammad had turned his small community of followers into an overpowering military force in the Arabian Peninsula. The most prized outcome of his struggle in the cause of Allah was his founding of a powerful Islamic state, the nascent Islamic caliphate of Medina. During this epoch-making phase of his prophetic career, Muhammad had evidently created three major paradigms of Jihadi actions as follows:

1. Forced conversion of the infidels, particularly the Polytheists.

2. Imperialism: the conquest of the lands of the Polytheists, Jews and Christians for establishing Islamic rule.

3. Slavery and slave-trade: for example, the enslavement of the women and children of Banu Qurayza and selling some of them by Prophet Muhammad.

Prophet Muhammad established these prototypical models of Jihad in strict observance of the divine commands of Allah. Using the Prophet's Medina caliphate as the launching-pad, the Islamic holy warriors, the Jihadis, burst out of Arabia after his death for spreading Islam and expanding its political domain to far corners of the world. In carrying forward the God-ordained campaigns of Jihad, the Muslim holy warriors meticulously replicated the three major prophetic models of Jihad paradigms throughout the ages of Islamic domination.

Prophet Muhammad had instilled in his followers such dedication and bravery for fighting in the interest of Islam that, within a decade of his death, Muslim Jihadis had overrun the great empire of Persia, while making significant and irreversible encroachment into the world's most powerful empire, the Byzantium. Within a century of his death, Islam had created the world's largest kingdom (caliphate) spreading from Arabia at a whirlwind speed to Transoxiana and Sindh (India) in the East, conquering all of Egypt and North Africa and had reached the heart of France in Europe. How the three prime prototypical models of Jihadi actions, set forth by Prophet Muhammad, impacted the later history of Islam will be discussed in the following chapters.

Chapter IV

Propagation of Islam:
By Force or Peacefully?

'So when the sacred months have passed away, then slay the idolaters wherever you find them, and take them captives and besiege them and lie in wait for them in every ambush, then if they repent and keep up prayer and pay the poor-rate (i.e., they become Muslim), leave their way free to them; surely Allah is Forgiving, Merciful.'

-- Allah, *Quran 9:5*

'The basis of the obligation of jihad is the universality of the Muslim revelation. God's words and God's message is for all mankind; it is the duty of those who have accepted them to strive (jihada) unceasingly to convert or at least subjugate those who have not. This obligation is without limit of time or space. It must continue until the whole world has either accepted the Islamic faith or submitted to the power of the Islamic state.'

-- Bernard Lewis, *The Political Language of Islam*, p. 73

'The spread of Islam was military. There is a tendency to apologize for this and we should not. It is one of the injunctions of the Quran that you must fight for spreading of Islam.'

-- Dr Ali Issa Othman, Islamic scholar, Palestinian sociologist and advisor to the United Nations Relief and Works Agency on education, *The Muslim Mind*, p. 94

THE EARLY WARS FOR SPREADING ISLAM

Whether Islam was propagated through violence or peaceful missionary activity (*da'wa*) has been the subject of intense debates for a long time, more so in recent decades. A search of the Internet on this topic reveals numerous articles and commentaries and dozens of books by pro-Islam authors staunchly denying the use of violence in the spread of Islam. However, the founding of Islam by Prophet Muhammad (discussed already) and its subsequent history (to be discussed in this book) are littered with countless battles and wars, which claimed hundreds of millions of human lives. Before going into this discussion, let us first take a brief look at the sanguinary history of Islam in its founding years and decades.

53

Prophet Muhammad's biographies by pious Islamic historians list 70–100 failed or successful raids, plundering expeditions and wars, undertaken by him, during the last ten years of his residence in Medina. He had personally led seventeen to twenty-nine of them. Below is a list of the major expeditions and battles, which the Prophet had directed or commanded in person:

623 CE — Battle of Waddan

623 CE — Battle of Safwan

623 CE — Battle of Dul-Ashir

624 CE — Battle of Nakhla

624 CE — Battle of Badr

624 CE — Battle of Banu Salim

624 CE — Battle of Eid-ul-Fitr and Zakat-ul-Fitr

624 CE — Battle of Banu Qaynuqa

624 CE — Battle of Sawiq

624 CE — Battle of Ghatfan

624 CE — Battle of Bahran

625 CE — Battle of Ohud

625 CE — Battle of Humra-ul-Asad

625 CE — Battle of Banu Nadir

625 CE — Battle of Dhatur-Riqa

626 CE — Battle of Badru-Ukhra

626 CE — Battle of Dumatul-Jandal

626 CE — Battle of Banu Mustalaq Nikah

627 CE — Battle of the Trench

627 CE — Battle of Ahzab

627 CE — Battle of Banu Qurayza

627 CE — Battle of Banu Lahyan

627 CE — Battle of Ghaiba

627 CE — Battle of Khaybar

628 CE — Campaign to Hudaybiya

630 CE — Conquest of Mecca

630 CE — Battle of Hunsin

630 CE — Battle of Tabuk

Prophet Muhammad died in 632 and Abu Bakr, his father-in-law, became the first caliph of the Islamic state. The aggressive wars for the purpose of expanding the domain of Islam and spreading the Islamic faith continued:

>   633 CE — Battles at Oman, Hadramaut, Kazima, Walaja, Ulleis, and Anbar
>
>   634 CE — Battles of Basra, Damascus and Ajnadin

Caliph Abu Bakr was allegedly assassinated in 634. Omar al-Khattab, another father-in-law and companion of the Prophet, became the second caliph. The mission to expand the Islamic territory continued under his direction:

>   634 CE — Battles of Namaraq and Saqatia
>
>   635 CE — Battles of Bridge, Buwaib, Damascus and Fahl
>
>   636 CE — Battles of Yermuk, Qadisiyia and Madain
>
>   637 CE — Battle of Jalula
>
>   638 CE — Battle of Yarmuk, conquest of Jerusalem and Jazirah
>
>   639 CE — Conquest of Khuizistan and movement into Egypt
>
>   641 CE — Battle of Nihawand
>
>   642 CE — Battle of Ray in Persia
>
>   643 CE — Conquest of Azerbaijan
>
>   644 CE — Conquest of Fars and Kharan

Caliph Omar, who played the pivotal role in the expansion of the Islamic state, was murdered in 644. Othman, a son-in-law and companion of the Prophet, became the next caliph and the conquests continued:

>   647 CE — Conquest of the island of Cypress
>
>   648 CE — Campaign against the Byzantines
>
>   651 CE — Naval battle against the Byzantines
>
>   654 CE — Islam spreads into North Africa

Caliph Othman was also murdered in 656. Ali, the husband of the Prophet's daughter Fatimah, became the new caliph. During this time, just over two decades after Muhammad's death, internal dissension and conflicts badly afflicted the Islamic community. This led to intra-Islam battles, such as the *Battle of the Camel* between Ali and the Prophet's wife Aisha and the *Battle of Siffin* between Ali and Mu'awiyah. As a result, wars against the infidels died down. Under Caliph Ali, only two notable wars were waged against the infidels:

>   658 CE — Battle of Nahrawan
>
>   659 CE — Conquest of Egypt

Ali was murdered with a poisoned dagger in 661, ending the era of the Rightly Guided Caliphs or *Khilafat Rashidun*. The Umayyad dynasty, headed by Mu'awiyah, came to power. Wars of conquest for expanding the Islamic kingdom once again resumed in full force.

>   662 CE — Egypt falls to Islamic rule
>
>   666 CE — Sicily attacked by Muslims
>
>   677 CE — Siege of Constantinople

687 CE — Battle of Kufa

691 CE — Battle of Deir ul Jaliq

700 CE — Military campaigns in North Africa

702 CE — Battle of Deir ul Jamira

711 CE — Invasion of Gibraltar and conquest of Spain

712 CE — Conquest of Sindh

713 CE — Conquest of Multan

716 CE — Invasion of Constantinople

732 CE — Battle of Tours in France

740 CE — Battle of the Nobles.

741 CE — Battle of Bagdoura in North Africa

744 CE — Battle of Ain al Jurr

746 CE — Battle of Rupar Thutha

748 CE — Battle of Rayy

749 CE — Battle of Isfahan and Nihawand

750 CE — Battle of Zab

772 CE — Battle of Janbi in North Africa

777 CE — Battle of Saragossa in Spain

Many smaller and unsuccessful campaigns, undertaken during the same period, have been excluded from this list. For example, attacks on India frontiers had started in 636 during the reign of second Caliph Omar. After many attempts over a period of eight decades to establish a permanent foothold for Islam in India, success finally came in 712 when Muhammad bin Qasim conquered Sindh. To this long list, we must add another long list of wars on numerous fronts in the later centuries, like those in India, started by Sultan Mahmud of Ghazni in 1000 and continued as long as Muslims held the power in India. The Umayyad Caliph Mu'awiyah (661–80) tried to capture Constantinople for five years (674–78) during which he launched a number of unsuccessful and often disastrous attacks. Later on, the campaign to capture Constantinople was revived in 716, which also failed suffering severe reverses. More attempts were made to capture it over the next centuries before Muslims ultimately wrestled the prized center of Christianity in 1453.

Despite this long list of aggressive and bloody wars against non-Muslims, waged by Prophet Muhammad, the succeeding caliphs and other Muslim rulers, Muslims have their way of explaining away those blood-letting atrocities and are still able to argue that Prophet Muhammad was a peaceful man and that non-Muslims all over the world accepted Islam because of the essence of peace and justice inherent in the Islamic creed. In this chapter, these arguments will be discussed in detail mainly in the context of the Muslim population growth in medieval India under the Muslim rule. It must be noted beforehand that the version of Islam, enforced in India, was based on the *Hanafi* School—the mildest amongst the four major Schools of Islamic laws. This is the only School that gives legal right to life to idolaters by provisionally elevating them to the status of *dhimmi* (tolerated people), clearly violating the canonical Quranic dictum, which demands their conversion on the pain of death [Quran 9:5].

PROPAGATION OF ISLAM: QURANIC COMMANDS & PROPHETIC MODEL

The Meccan period of Prophet Muhammad's religious mission involved no use of arms except that his messages were insulting, derogatory and offensive to the religion, customs and ancestors of the people. Nonetheless, Muhammad showed his intent for future violence in some of his statements during this early period even though his community was very weak. He clearly expressed his intent for future violence in his statement (noted already): '*Men of Quraysh! I will surely repay you for this with interest.*' A number of verses revealed during the first five years of his prophetic mission threatened the Quraysh with earthly punishments, such as threats of destroying them [Quran 77:16–17]. For example, the Quran [77:18] threatened the Quraysh: '*...thus shall We deal with the guilty.*' But these earthly punishments at this stage were to come from Allah. The Prophet also demonstrated his intent of hostility against the Quraysh when he went to Taif in 619 to find a sanctuary, where he tried to incite enmity amongst Taifites against the Meccans.

Muhammad expressed his clearest and decisive intent for violence in the *Second Pledge of Akaba*, just before his relocation to Medina. In this pledge, he obtained a promise for his protection from his Medina converts with their blood. What was the need of this promise? In Arab towns, such as in Mecca and Medina, people from foreign lands used to come freely and set up businesses and even engage in peaceful missionary activities. If Muhammad was going to Medina to settle down peacefully, nobody was going to harm him. When he sent his disciple Musab to Medina a year earlier, he actively preached Islam and obtained large number of converts; he faced no hostility from the citizens of Medina. Therefore, Muhammad needed the pledge for his protection, because he had already decided to unleash violence: first, against the Quraysh, then against all humanity for establishing Islam—the final, perfected religion of Allah—on the global scale (see next Chapter).

The rule of the game indeed changed completely after his relocation to Medina. The war against the infidel world, declared by the Prophet through the *Second Pledge of Akaba*, was soon unleashed. The verses of Jihad, entreating Muhammad and his disciples to take up arms against the Quraysh, soon started pouring down from Allah. The punishment of the Quraysh will now be meted out by the hands of Muhammad and his disciples, not by Allah. And those who die while fighting the infidels will receive Allah's succor in the next life: '*Thus (are ye commanded): but if it had been Allah's Will, He could certainly have exacted retribution from them (Himself); but (He lets you fight) in order to test you, some with others. But those who are slain in the Way of Allah, He will never let their deeds be lost*' [Quran 47:4].

Prophet Muhammad himself was candid about it, as Narrated by Ibn 'Omar: *Allah's Apostle said*: '*I have been ordered (by Allah) to fight against the people until they testify that none has the right to be worshipped but Allah and that Muhammad is Allah's Apostle, and offer the prayers perfectly and give the obligatory charity, so if they perform that, then they save their lives and property from me except for Islamic laws and then their reckoning (accounts) will be done by Allah*' [Bukhari 1:24].

Within seven months of his relocation to Medina, the Prophet started sending military expeditions for raiding and plundering trade-caravans of the Quraysh and the first success came at Nakhla after about eighteen months. The rest of his mission in Medina, as recounted in the previous chapter, was obviously a monotonous tale of continuous raid, plunder, war, mass eviction, slaughter and enslavement of non-Muslims until he died in 632.

By the time Muhammad died, the city of Mecca and Medina was completely denuded of the infidels. The Prophet had already extirpated idolatry from the newly founded Islamic state in Arabia by giving them the choice between Islam and death in accordance with Quran 9:5. Some residual Jewish and Christian communities still existed in some remote parts of the Arab Peninsula; they were expelled by his immediate successors in accordance with his dying wishes. They were, however, tolerated as humiliated and exploited *dhimmi* subjects in the conquered Muslim lands outside Arabia.

Guided by the Quran, the prophetic model for the propagation of Islam, therefore, consisted of converting the idolaters at the pain of death. The Jews were to be attacked and expelled from their lands as happened to Banu Qaynuqa and Banu Nadir. In other instances—Muhammad's dealing with the Jews of Banu Quraiza, for example—they were attacked, their males were slaughtered *en masse*, and their women and children were made Muslim through enslavement. In Khaybar, after defeating the Jews, their women and children were driven away as slaves. The surviving men were allowed to tend the land on the condition of paying half of the produce as tribute until Muslims had sufficient manpower to cultivate the captured land.

Regarding Christians, when the Prophet sent emissaries to Christian kings and princes, he demanded that they convert to Islam or face the wrath of his army. In other instances, he ordered the Christians not to baptize their children, thereby incorporating the latter into Islam. Jews and Christians were finally placed into the same category of *dhimmi* subjects in verse 9:29. Thereafter, they could generally be attacked, their males slaughtered in the battle, their women and children enslaved, and the rest could be tolerated as *dhimmi* subjects, if they accepted the degrading terms of *dhimmitude* (see *Pact of Omar* below).

The thirteen-year prophetic mission of Muhammad in Mecca, during which he obtained about 150 converts, was somewhat peaceful, while the last ten years in Medina was overwhelmingly violent, involving plundering raids of non-Muslim caravans and wars against their communities. In the process, the infidels were slaughtered, evicted and enslaved *en masse* or converted to Islam on the pain of death.

The Meccan period of Muhammad's prophetic mission was obviously a complete failure. Therefore, the violent phase of Muhammad's prophetic mission in Medina, which enabled him to put Islam on a firm footing, was the dominant mode of his propagation of Islam. To be noted here that Muhammad had shown indications of future violence even during his preaching mission in Mecca when he was militarily very weak. Had his community in Mecca been powerful enough, violence would very likely have started in Mecca itself. Dr Muhammad Muhsin Khan of the Islamic University at Medina, translator of the Quran and al-Bukhari hadiths, agrees to such a possibly as he says, '*at first 'the fighting' was forbidden, then it was permitted, and after that it was made obligatory.*'[130] Contemporary scholar Dr Sobhy as-Saleh quotes brilliant medieval Egyptian theologian Imam Jalaluddin Al-Suyuti (d. 1505), famously known as *Ibn al-Kutb* (the Son of Books), on why the permission of Jihad from heaven came gradually: "*The command to fight the infidels was delayed until the Muslims become strong, but when they were weak they were commanded to endure and be patient.*"[131] Dr as-Saleh adds the opinion of another famous medieval Egyptian theologian Abi Bakr az-Zarkashi (d. 1411) that "*Allah, the most high and wise, revealed to Mohammad in his weak condition what suited the situation, because of his mercy to him and his followers. For if He gave them the command to fight while they were weak it would have been embarrassing and most difficult, but when the most high made Islam victorious He commanded him with what suited the situation, that is asking the people of the Book to become Muslims or to pay the levied tax, and the infidels (Polytheists) to become Muslims or face death.*"[132]

It is, therefore, undeniable that violence, prompted by carefully unraveled divine verses, was the lifeline of Prophet Muhammad's propagation of Islam and his founding of the nascent Islamic state in Medina. Violent Jihad is the heart of Islam; without it, Islam would, most likely, have died a natural death in the seventh century itself. This ideal model of the propagation of Islam was meticulously embraced by the Prophet's immediate successors and later Muslim rulers. During the late period of Islamic domination, Ottomans was wreaking havoc in the Balkan and Eastern Europe, while reaching the Gates of Vienna, the heart of Europe and the Holy Roman Empire, for the second time in 1683. Meanwhile, Mughal Emperor Aurangzeb (r. 1658–1707) was wreaking havoc on the infidels of India, destroying thousands of Hindu

---

130. Khan MM (1987) *Introduction*, in *The Translation of the Meanings of Sahih Al-Bukhari*, Kitab Bhavan, New Delhi, Vol. I, p. XXVI

131. Sobhy as-Saleh (1983) *Mabaheth Fi 'Ulum al- Qur'an*, Dar al-'Ilm Lel-Malayeen, Beirut, p. 269

132. Ibid, p. 270

temples and converting the Hindus and other non-Muslims by the sword and other measures of compulsion (discussed below).

MUSLIM SCHOLARS ON THE WARS FOR SPREADING ISLAM

The long list of wars involving immense bloodbath cannot be disregarded by Muslims when critics accuse that Islam was spread by the sword. Many of these battles took place thousands of miles away from the Islamic heartland of Arabia. One has to be credulous in the extreme to believe, as claim Muslims, that these multitudes of battles were defensive in nature. The Muslim homeland in the Arabian Peninsula was never under invasion by the Persians, Spaniards or Indians. When Pope Benedict highlighted this violent nature of Islam in a lecture in Germany in September 2006 by pointing to a 1391 conversation between a Byzantine emperor and a Muslim scholar,[133] the Muslim world raised an international outcry. They unleashed acts of violence and vandalism, which led to burning and torching of churches and death of a number of people. Clerics from Britain (and also Somalia) ordered the assassination of the Pope for insulting the Prophet.[134] Muslims' indulging in unbridled vandalism, violence and acts of terrorism in reaction to such allegations only proves those allegations true.

While the majority of Muslims take recourse of violent protests against these allegations, Islamic scholars pick up the pen to rebut them. Today's most influential Muslim scholar, Dr Sheikh Yusuf al-Qaradawi—whom the London Mayor Ken Livingstone embraced as a voice of "moderation and peace" in the Islamic world—condemned the Pope's comment as follows:

> The Pope spoke about Islam without reading first its scriptures, the Noble Quran, and Prophet Muhammad's hadiths, but sufficed to cite a conversation between a Byzantine emperor and a Persian Muslim intellectual... To say that Prophet Muhammad brought evil and inhuman things, like spreading faith by the sword, is either a calumny or pure ignorance, in effect.[135]

Dr Zakir Naik, the president of the Islamic Research Foundation (Mumbai, India), is another brilliant Islamic scholar, highly respected across the Muslim world for his voice of reason and scientific investigation of Islam. Both al-Qaradawi and Naik have explained the allegation of Islam's propagation through violence as what Muslims universally call the *widespread misconception* about Islam. The arguments of these two famous scholars of Islam will be discussed here. Al-Qaradawi lists four main reasons behind the wars that were undertaken by Prophet Muhammad and the later caliphs of Islam:[136]

1. For protecting sovereignty of the Islamic state

2. For overcoming tyranny of foreign rulers

---

133. Pope quoted Emperor Manuel II Palaeologus (1391): *"Show me just what Muhammad brought that was new, and there you will find things only evil and inhuman, such as his command to spread by the sword the faith he preached."*

134. Doughty S and Mcdermott N (2006) *The Pope must die, says Muslim*, Daily Mail (UK), 18 September

135. Islam Online, *Muslims Insist on Pope's Apology*, 15 Sept, 2006; http://www.islamonline.net/English/News/2006-09/15/01.shtml

136. Yusuf Al-Qaradawi (2007) *The Truth about the Spread of Islam*, Islam Online website, 06 Aug; http://www.islamonline.net/servlet/Satellite?pagename=IslamOnline-English-Ask_Scholar/FatwaE/FatwaE&cid=1135167134062

3. For freeing weak countries from the oppression of tyrannical rulers

4. For removing tyranny and oppression

Protecting sovereignty of the Islamic state

In defending the wars undertaken by Muslim rulers against foreign kingdoms in the early phase of Islam, the learned al-Qaradawi writes:

> ...the emerging Muslim state in Madinah not only had to prove its sovereignty, but it also had a message of mercy and justice to deliver to all mankind and an ideology to practice. Any state seeking change of this kind at that time would usually be confronted with hostility and aggression from the great powers (Byzantine and Persian empires). These powers saw the emerging Muslim state and its principles as a threat to their interests. They believed that this would lead to an inevitable confrontation between the two parties. Hence, Muslims at that time were in a situation to undertake what is referred to nowadays as a defensive war, so that they could defend their territories against the prospective threats of the neighboring countries that differed with the Muslim state's ideology and interests.

Al-Qaradawi did not specify the sovereignty of which Islamic state, he was talking about. From where did the Islamic state in Medina come in the first place? Was not the Prophet a refugee there? What claim, as a refugee settler, could the Prophet possibly have on the land of Medina? Did the Jews of Banu Qaynuqa launch an attack on Muslims (or Islamic state), which gave Muhammad no option but to undertake a defensive attack on the Jewish community in 624? This attack took place just over one-and-a-half years after Muhammad was graciously allowed to settle down in Medina by the Pagan and Jewish tribes of the city.

As described already, Muhammad attacked the Banu Qaynuqa Jews because a Jewish prankster teased a Muslim woman in the market-place. He is said to have pulled the cloth of the woman causing her embarrassment. For this, a Muslim killed the prankster; the Jews, in turn, killed the Muslim man. On this excuse, Muhammad attacked the whole community of Banu Qaynuqa and was about to slaughter them *en masse*, if not for intervention by Abdullah the hypocrite. Although this incidence is said to be the reason for Muhammad's attack on Banu Qaynuqa, more authoritative sources—namely Ibn Ishaq's and al-Tabari's biographies of Muhammad—give a simpler reason (non-reason) for the attack. Al-Tabari, citing the account of al-Zuhri, talks of a verse being brought by Gabriel to Muhammad, which said, '*And if thou fearest treachery from any folk, then throw back to them their treaty fairly*' [Quran 8:58]. Whereupon, Muhammad said, "*I fear Banu Qaynuqa*" and '*the Messenger of God advanced upon them.*'[137]

Evidently, if the latter account is true, there was at all no ground for Muhammad to attack the Jewish tribe. And it was solely the courageous intervention of Abdullah ibn Obayi that prevented Muhammad from slaughtering the surrendered Jews *en masse*—his original plan. Instead, he had to be content with exiling them. Even if the account of the teasing incidence is true, the prankster did not deserve to be killed over such a minor incidence. Muhammad's decision to attack the entire tribe over this negligible incidence, the working of an individual prankster, fails the least civilized standard of justice. His plan to slaughter the Jewish tribe *en masse* and their ultimate expulsion was nothing less than barbaric.

Prophet Muhammad similarly attacked the Jewish tribes of Banu Nadir in 625 and Banu Qurayza in 627. Again the question arises: Did the Banu Nadir Jews attack Muslims or their state, forcing Muhammad to undertake a defensive counterattack? The reason for Muhammad's attack of Banu Nadir was his unsubstantiated accusation of their plotting to kill him about which no one else, including his disciples, had any clue. Inventing this baseless allegation, he attacked the Jewish tribe and exiled them. The Banu Qurayza Jews had done nothing to Muslims, but the Prophet accused them of breaking a treaty, which never seems to have existed (discussed already). The ghastly massacre of the Banu Qurayza tribesmen was Muhammad's

---

137. Al-Tabari, Vol. VII, p. 86

original plan for dealing with Banu Qaynuqa in 624, which he could not act upon because of Abdullah's intervention. Muhammad opted for exiling Banu Nadir in 625, when Abdullah, still powerful, threatened to fight on their side. In the attack on Banu Qurayza in 627, Muhammad, ignoring weakened Abdullah's condemnation, put his original plan for dealing with the Jews into action after years of frustration. Abdullah, a compassionate and just person, has been repeatedly vilified as the greatest "hypocrite" in the Quran, *Sunnah* and other Islamic literatures.

The bottom-line is that, in the first place, the Muhammad had no right to found a state of his own in a land he was graciously welcomed to settle down in his time of distress. And he founded the embryonic Islamic state in Medina through extreme cruelty on the innocent people of the city, the Jews in particular, by exiling, slaughtering and enslaving them *en masse*.

Al-Qaradawi's reference of hostility against the Islamic state of Medina from the two powerful empires, Persia and Byzantium, is a baseless fabrication. Neither the Byzantine nor the Persian rulers ever showed hostility toward the Muslim state. Instead, it was Muhammad who aggressively sent letters to the world's most powerful rulers, those of Persia and Byzantium, in 628, calling on them to embrace Islam or face dire consequence. At this time, Muhammad's community was a weak force, not even capable of overrunning the small city of Mecca. Appropriately, the two most powerful rulers of the world simply ignored Muhammad's threatening letters without taking any action against him.

Not taking Muhammad's threats seriously proved too costly for both empires. Two years later, Muhammad himself dared launching an aggressive expedition with 30,000-strong army against the Byzantine border and reached Tabuk near Syria. Over the next two decades, the Islamic army, pursuing Muhammad's unrealized dream, overran the Persian Empire and made significant encroachment into Byzantium—all aggressively under no provocation, threat or hostility of any kind. Muhammad himself had incited hostility by demanding that the Byzantine and Persian rulers submit to Muhammad's rule. But the world most powerful emperors ignored petty Muhammad's hostile aggrandizement to their own peril.

Overcoming tyranny of foreign rulers

Muslims waged wars against foreign nations, adds al-Qaradawi, in the just cause of

> overcoming the tyranny of the rulers of other countries who prevented their subjects from listening to the call of Islam. The Muslims had (by Almighty Allah's order) to make Islam known to the people of other countries, but the tyrant rulers would not allow their subjects to listen to the word of Islam and the call of the Qur'an... The tyranny of the rulers at that time hindered the spread of the universal call of Islam. So when the Prophet (peace and blessings be upon him) sent letters to rulers of the nearby countries inviting them to Islam, he (peace and blessings be upon him) told them that if they rejected the call, they would be responsible for misguiding their subjects. For example, he (peace and blessings be upon him) said in his letter to the emperor of the Byzantine Empire, '*If you reject this call, you will be responsible for misguiding your Arisiayin [peasants].*' He (peace and blessings be upon him) also wrote to the Persian Emperor, '*If you refuse the call of Islam, you will be responsible for misguiding the Magians (Zoroastrians),*' and to Al-Muqawqis (governor of Egypt) he wrote, '*If you refuse the call of Islam, you will be responsible for misguiding the Copts.*' ...Hence, the wars in which the Muslims engaged against the rulers of other countries led to the removal of the barriers between the common people of these countries and Islam. With this, they could choose for themselves, without fear of punishment, either to believe or disbelieve in Almighty Allah, bearing the full responsibility for their own choices.

Before discussing these arguments, first take note of how al-Qaradawi contradicts himself. In the earlier passage, he claimed that the Byzantine and Persian hostility had forced Muslims to undertake defensive wars—a claim, which in itself is completely baseless or born out of ignorance. In his next point, he himself exposes the baselessness or ignorance of his claim by asserting that Muslims had to launch the aggressive war, because the rulers of Persia, Rome and Egypt had hindered the spread of the universal message of Islam; not because, they were under any threat from those two powerful empires. Then he cites a line, not the whole letter, which Prophet Muhammad had sent to the rulers of those nations. Here is what Ibn Ishaq records about the letter sent to Byzantine Emperor Heraclius: *'The apostle's letter with Dihya b. Khalifa al-Kalbi came to Heraclius saying, 'If you accept Islam you will be safe; if you accept Islam, Allah will give you double reward; if you turn back, the sin of the husbandmen will be upon you.'*[138] Similarly, Muhammad's letter to the kings of Oman (noted already) demanded: *"Embrace Islam, and you shall be safe… If you submit to Islam, you will remain kings, but if you abstain, your rule will be removed and my horses will enter your arena to prove my prophecy."*

Contrary to what al-Qaradawi tells us, these letters sent by Muhammad to foreign kings and emperors were not meant for exhorting them to accept Islam through peaceful means. The central message was: *Embrace Islam and you will be safe*; if not, the wrath of Muhammad's horsemen would befall them. These letters obviously threatened violence if those rulers refused to embrace Islam. This was unlike the peaceful preaching of today's Christian missionaries or the propagation of Buddhism since ancient times to this day.

Now let us agree with al-Qaradawi that the Prophet's letter said, *'if they rejected the call, they would be responsible for misguiding their subjects.'* But how could the rejection of Muhammad's letter of submission to Islam by those rulers amount to misguiding their people? And what justifies attacking those foreign lands by Prophet Muhammad and later caliphs just because his letter of invitation was rejected? If Muhammad's protocol of spreading Islam was peaceful, instead of threatening them at the first instance and then attacking them, he should have sent his missionary teams to those lands to invite the people to Islam peacefully. There is no mention in Islamic literature of any initiative undertaken by Muhammad and later caliphs of sending preachers to Persia, Egypt and Byzantium for the peaceful propagation of Islam. Here is what second Caliph Omar al-Khattab wrote to the Iranian Sovereign, Yazdgerd III, demanding his submission or face destruction:

> To the Shah of the Fars, I do not foresee a good future for you and your nation save your acceptance of my terms and your submission to me. There was a time when your country ruled half the world, but see how now your sun has set. On all fronts your armies have been defeated and your nation is condemned to extinction. I point out to you the path whereby you might escape this fate. Namely, that you begin worshipping the one god, the unique deity, the only god who created all that is. I bring you his message. Order your nation to cease the false worship of fire and to join us, that they may join the truth.

> Worship Allah the creator of the world. Worship Allah and accept Islam as the path of salvation. End now your polytheistic ways and become Muslims that you may accept Allah-u-Akbar as your savior. This is the only way of securing your own survival and the peace of your Persians. You will do this if you know what is good for you and for your Persians. Submission is your only option.[139]

Al-Qaradawi wants to tell us that if the American President rejects a letter calling for his submission to the universal message of Islam—say, from the Saudi King or Iranian President, America will then become a legitimate target for conquest by Muslims. Indeed, the messianic Iranian President Mahmoud Ahmadinejad called on President Bush and the American people to convert to Islam twice in 2006. Similarly, the leaders of

---

138. Ibn Ishaq, p. 655

139. *Letter of Omar, Khalifat of Arabs to Shahanshah of Persia*; http://www.youtube.com/watch?v=fwnKblyx96s; accessed 10 Sept, 2008

al-Qaeda have been making repeated calls to the infidel world, particularly the United States, to submit to Islam. Therefore, America is already a valid target for violent attack and conquest by Muslims for President Bush's obstruction of the propagation of the universal message of Islam amongst Americans. Of course, al-Qaeda has already attacked the United States and continues its effort to attack her at every possible opportunity to bring her down to the feet of Islam. If he has the power to defeat America, President Ahmadinejad will most likely attack the *great Satan* in the same way Muslim Arabs attacked his infidel ancestors of Persia in the seventh century. Al-Qaradawi plainly supports such a notion in his arguments.

Freeing weak countries from oppressive rulers

On his third point, al-Qaradawi says:

> Since Islam strives to free humans from being enslaved by other humans, it had a mission to deliver the weak people from suffering oppression at the hands of their powerful occupiers... Hence, Muslims, by Allah's instructions, took it upon themselves to deliver the weak people from the oppressive foreign rule... The Byzantines in Egypt used to exploit the prosperity of Egypt and oppress its people to such a degree that the Egyptians warmly welcomed the Muslims' opening (fath) of Egypt. In fact, the Muslims succeeded in entering Egypt and freeing it from the Byzantine occupation with only 8,000 soldiers.

It is most ridiculous on al-Qaradawi's part to assert that '*Islam strives to free humans from being enslaved by other humans,*' when the Quran most overtly sanctions slavery and that Muslims have remained the masters of enslaving free men, women and children from the days of Prophet Muhammad to the present day (see Chapter VII). And once again, he negates his earlier claim that Muslims' war against Persia and Byzantium was a defensive one to protect the sovereignty of the nascent Muslim state. Here, he clearly agrees that Muslims waged an **offensive** war, but for an allegedly noble cause: for freeing the people, oppressed by the cruel Persian and Byzantine regimes.

Did Prophet Muhammad and later Muslim rulers embark upon the conquest of foreign lands for freeing the people from their oppressive rulers and overlords? There is no evidence at all to suggest so. Islamic literatures make no mention of a request to Prophet Muhammad or later Muslim rulers from the governor or the people of Egypt to save their country from the tyranny and oppression of their Byzantine overlords. Neither is there any record of a plea from the people of Persia and Byzantium, entreating the Prophet or later Muslim rulers, to liberate them from their oppressive and tyrannical rulers. Instead, when the Prophet wrote his letter to the Egyptian governor in 628, his letter flatly threatened the governor that "embrace Islam and you will be safe". Muhammad made no mention of a noble desire to free Egypt and its people from Byzantine oppression.

What one gathers from al-Qaradawi's rebuttal of the allegations about Islam's propagation through violence is that the Muslim invaders launched numerous wars against foreign lands for spreading the universal message of Islam amongst those peoples. In other words, he himself admits that Muslims raised swords against foreign nations absolutely for spreading Islam—*the universal message of Islam* in his words. In his own arguments, the learned Sheikh himself establish the fact that Islam was indeed spread by the sword—the allegation, he had intended to refute at the outset.

Removing tyranny and oppression

Al-Qaradawi further claims that those wars undertaken by Muslim rulers were intended for abolishing the tyranny and oppression of Persian and Byzantine rulers upon their people. Let us examine briefly what kind of justice and peace Muslim invaders brought to the conquered people, allegedly tyrannized and oppressed by their former rulers.

When the Jews of Medina obstructed the propagation of the universal message of Islam, the Prophet attacked them, exiled the Banu Qaynuqa and Nadir tribes and slaughtered the men of Banu Qurayza and enslaved their women and children. When Caliph Omar conquered Jerusalem in 638, the devastation and pillage was so extensive that, the next year, *'thousands died as a result of famine and plague consequent to the destruction and pillage.'* During the Muslim campaigns of 634, *'the entire region between Gaza and Caesarea was devastated; four thousand peasants—Christians, Jews and Samaritans who were simply defending their lands—were massacred. During the campaign of Mesopotamia between 635 and 642 CE, monasteries were sacked, monks killed and Monophysite Arabs executed or forced to convert. In Elam, the population was put to the sword...'*[140]

In Muhammad bin Qasim's first successful foray into India, as recorded by al-Biladuri and Muhammad al-Kufi (in *Chachnama*): at Debal, *'the temples were demolished, a general massacre endured for three days; prisoners were taken captive;'* at Nairun, *'the idols were broken, and mosques founded despite its voluntary surrender;'* at Rawar and Askalanda, *'all the men in arms were put to the sword, and the women and children carried away captive;'* at Multan, *'all men capable of bearing arms were massacred; six thousand ministers of the temple were made captive, besides all the women and children.'*[141]

The three-day period of general massacre, which became an oft-repeated paradigm in many Islamic conquests, was set as an example by Caliph Omar. Having taken the city of Alexandria in 641, ordered by Caliph Omar, the population suffered three days of horrendous carnage, pillage and plunder. After the fall of Constantinople in 1453, Sultan Mehemet allowed his soldiers *'three days of unrestricted pillage to which they were entitled. They poured into the city... They slew everyone they met in the streets, men, women and children without discrimination. The blood ran in rivers down the steep streets...'*[142] Amir Timur or Tamerlane, on his campaign to India—undertaken for fulfilling his obligation of waging holy war against the infidels—slaughtered 100,000 captives in a single day in Delhi in December 1399.[143]

Al-Qaradawi tells us that the conquest of Egypt was so welcomed by the oppressed inhabitants that only 8,000 soldiers were required to capture it. Here is a sample of the gifts the inhabitants in Egypt received from the Islamic harbingers of peace. The horror unleashed by Caliph Omar's forces after taking Alexandria is noted above. According to Ibn Warraq, when Amr advanced into Egypt and captured the city of Behnesa near Fayum, he exterminated the inhabitants. Nobody was spared, irrespective of surrendered or captured, old or young or woman. The same happened to the citizens of Fayum and Aboit. On the early Islamic conquests adds Ibn Warraq:[144]

> At Nikiu, the entire population was put to the sword. The Arabs took the inhabitants to captivity. In Armenia, the entire population of Euchaita was wiped out. Seventh century Armenian chronicles recount how the Arabs decimated the population of Assyria and forced a number of inhabitants to accept Islam and then wrought havoc in the districts of Daron, southwest of Lake Van. In 642, it was the turn of the town of Dvin to suffer. In 643, the Arabs came back with "extermination, ruin and slavery".

Such was the kind of peace and justice that Muslim warriors brought to the conquered people by destroying, what they call, the existing "tyranny, oppression and injustice" of incumbent rulers. Apart from the barbaric

---

140. Ibn Warraq, p. 219

141. Eliot HM and Dawson J, *The History of India As Told by the Historians*, Low Price Publications, New Delhi, Vol. I, p. 469

142. Runciman S (1990) *The Fall of Constantinople, 1453*, Cambridge, p. 145; Bostom AG (2005) *The Legacy of Jihad*, Prometheus Books, New York, p. 616–18

143. Lal KS (1999) *Theory and Practice of Muslim State in India*, Aditya Prakashan, New Delhi, p. 18

144. Ibn Warraq, p. 220

cruelty perpetrated by Muslim invaders in the course of conquests, the establishment of Muslim rule did not alleviate the oppression and exploitation of the vanquished subjects either. For example, as early as in the reign of Caliph Omar, the taxes imposed on the conquered people were quite burdensome. According to Muslim historian Prof. Fazl Ahmed, a Persian slave named Abu Lulu Firoz, burdened by excessive tax, went to the caliph one day and said: *"My master squeezes too heavy a tax out of me. Please get it reduced."*[145] Omar refused the plea. Angered by it, Abu Lulu stabbed the caliph to death the next day.

Naik also concurs with al-Qaradawi on the motive of aggressive wars under taken by Muslim rulers as he wrote: *'The fight against oppression may, at times, require the use of force. In Islam, force can only be used to promote peace and justice.'*[146] We will see how the Islamic rule of justice and peace in India had reduced the non-Muslims of an otherwise prosperous country into beggars at the doors of Muslims within a short time. They had to sell their wives and children in the slave-markets to pay for the grinding taxes imposed on them. The most helpless and destitute amongst them took refuge in jungles to live amongst animals; they survived by highway robbery and on what was available in the wilderness (discussed later).

Furthermore, al-Qaradawi's claim that the Muslim invaders were jubilantly welcomed by the conquered people—seeking liberation from their tyrannical and oppressive rulers—does not hold any water either. As cited above, even the general peasants used to take up arms against Muslim invaders. Some 4,000 of such peasants, who had taken up arms against invading Muslims, were massacred in the region between Gaza and Caesarea in 634. At Debal, Muhammad bin Qasim slaughtered the inhabitants for three days. Was this massacre perpetrated because the Hindus had welcomed Qasim's army with opened hands? In Constantinople in 1453, Muslim soldiers engaged in massacring the inhabitants for three days flooding the streets with blood. Some 30,000 peasants in Chittor had taken up arms alongside their Rajput rulers even against liberal and magnanimous Akbar the Great in 1568. When they surrendered, Akbar ordered their massacre.[147] Such was the jubilant welcome the Muslim invaders received from the allegedly oppressed people of the invaded lands.

Islamic invaders, according to the records of mostly Muslim historians, faced stiff resistance from the invaded people. If they welcomed the invading Muslim conquerors, Qasim needed not slaughter the inhabitants for three days at Debal. Al-Kufi records in *Chachnama* that *'The infidels (of Debal) made a rush upon the Arabs from all sides and fought so bravely and steadily that the army of Islam became irresolute and their lines were broken up...'*[148] In the Muslim conquest of India, rarely people embraced Islam voluntarily because of its appealing message. In general, the adults fell to the sword of Islamic warriors while the helpless women and children were enslaved. In some instances, the Muslim invaders overran territories without much resistance—not because the people warmly welcomed the Muslim invaders, but because they sought to avoid extermination by fighting losing battles.

On Sultan Mahmud's attack of Somnath in 1024, records Ibn Asir, *'Band after band of defenders (Hindus) entered the temple of Somnath, and with their hands clasped round their necks, wept and passionately entreated him (not to attack). Then again, they issued forth to fight until they were slain but few were left alive... The number of the slain exceeded fifty thousand.'*[149] These were just the ordinary people who sought to defend the dignity of their sacred temple. This temple was reconstructed three times by the devout Hindus, as Muslim invaders repeatedly destroyed it. These are definitely not instances of what one understands to be jubilant welcome of the occupation army, but of stiff resistance against them, by the conquered people.

---

145. Ahmad F, *Hazrat Omar bin Khattab—The Second Caliph of Islam;* http://path-to-peace.com/omer.html

146. Naik Z (1999), *Was Islam Spread by the Sword?*, Islamic Voice, Vol. 13-08, No.152

147. Smith VA (1958) *The Oxford History of India*, Oxford University Press, London, p. 342

148. Sharma, p. 95–96

149. Elliot & Dawson, Vol. II, p. 470–71

The words of famous Islamic scholar and historian, Alberuni, on the exploits of Sultan Mahmud's repeated invasions of India, will suffice to summarize what the Muslim conquerors had brought upon the conquered peoples. Alberuni (973–1050), an outstanding Persian scholar, was captured by Sultan Mahmud during his conquest of the Central Asian state of Khwarizm in 1017. Mahmud brought him to his capital Ghazni and appointed as an official in his court. Mahmud brought Alberuni to India in the course of his invasions. He traveled across India for twenty years and studied Indian philosophy, mathematics, geography and religion from Hindu pundits. He wrote of the Muslim conquest of India: '*Mahmud utterly ruined the prosperity of the country and performed there wonderful exploits, by which the Hindus became like atoms of dust scattered in all direction, and like a tale of old in the mouth of the people. Their scattered remains cherish, of course, the most inveterate aversion toward all Muslims.*'[150]

Welcome in Spain

In isolated instances, however, some elements among the conquered people had probably welcomed Muslim invasions; welcome by the Jews in Spain is an oft-repeated example. This claim, however, is not supported by historical documents, as notes Stephen O'Shia, '*Many have conjectured that Muslims were welcomed as liberators by the Jews of Iberia, but no documentary evidence backs up this assertion.*'[151] However, the consequence of the alleged welcome of the Muslim invaders by the Spanish Jews was not pleasant for them either.

Spain was then under the Visigothic rule. Visigoths were a Germanic people from North Europe, commonly called the Barbarians, who had captured Spain in the early fifth century. Unlike the Muslim invaders, who usually forced Islam upon the vanquished people at the pain of death and through enslavement, the Visigoths later adopted the Christian faith of the conquered land. At the beginning, the Visigothic rulers were tolerant to all the citizens irrespective of Jews, Christians or Pagans. But their subsequent Catholicization worsened their tolerance of Jews. In 633, the Catholic bishops, who held the power of confirming the election of kings, declared that all Jews must be baptised. Thereafter, treatment of the Jews worsened.

The Visigothic kings, also foreign invaders like Muslim invaders, had badly exploited the peasants. The native Iberian people in Spain were mainly serfs working as underpaid farm-laborers for the ruling Visigothic families. As a result, when Musa ibn Nusair, the caliph's governor to North Africa, attacked Spain, '*The peasants, who would provide the bulk of the Visigoth armies, armed with sticks and spears and hating their rulers, would not fight (Muslim invaders).*'[152] Although the Jews and peasants of Spain were initially not necessarily unhappy with the Muslim invasion, what soon followed was quite an unpleasant experience for them. The Muslim invaders unleashed looting, pillage, slaughter, forced conversion, and enslavement of women and children—amongst whom were 30,000 white virgins from the Visigothic nobility alone.[153] According to AS Triton, '*On one of his expeditions, Musa destroyed every church and broke every bell. When surrendered, the Muslims took the property of those killed in the ambush, of those who fled to Galicia, of the churches, and the church jewels.*'[154]

After Islamic conquest began in 711, Spain sustained serious turmoil and brutality for more than four decades. A semblance of stability returned, only after Umayyad prince Abd al-Rahaman, fleeing the pursuant Abbasid assassins, arrived in Spain to found the Umayyad dynasty (756–1071). While applying the

150. Sachau EC (2002) *Alberuni's India*, Rupa & Co., New Delhi, p. 5–6 (first print 1888)

151. O'Shea S (2006) *Sea of Faith: Islam and Christianity in the Medieval Mediterranean World*, Walker & Company, New York, p. 69

152. Fregosi P (1998) *Jihad in the West*, Prometheus Books, New York, p. 91

153. Lal (1999), p. 103

154. Triton AS (1970) *The Caliphs and Their Non-Muslim Subjects*, Frank Cass & Co Ltd, London, p. 45

discriminatory Islamic laws against the *dhimmi* Jewish and Christian subjects, the Umayyad rulers—historically dubbed as "Godless" by orthodox Muslims and the *ulema* (for reasons, see Chapter V, Section: *How Muslim world excelled intellectually and materially?*)—ruled with some measure of tolerance. They were generally disrespectful of Muhammad's religion and did not overtly pressurize non-Muslims anywhere to convert as long as they filled the treasury.

Those Jews, who allegedly saw the Muslim inavders as liberators, soon found the reality to be otherwise as they were subjected to various indignities and exploitations. The Muslim rulers soon imposed the discriminatory *jizyah* (poll-tax), *kharaj* (tribute, land-tax) and other kinds of taxes, applicable to *dhimmi* subjects under Islamic rule. Building of churches and synagogues became banned. Instead, the Jews and Christians, enslaved *en masse*, had to serve as laborers on demolishing churches for building mosques in their steads from the columns and materials extracted from them. They were banned from carrying weapons, ride horses, wear shoes, ring church bells, wear anything green, or resist Muslim assaults in accordance with the *Pact of Omar* (see below). Proclaiming the divinity of Jesus and attempting conversion from Islam were capital offence all along.

Hundreds of Jews were killed near Cordoba and other parts of Spain between 1010 and 1013. Protests by Muslims against the employment of non-Muslims in government services resulted in riots in 1066; the entire community of 4,000 Jews of Grenada were massacred. The real nightmare was to descend upon the non-Muslims of Spain—Jews, Christians and Mozarabs (arabized Christian slaves), with the arrival of the orthodox Almoravid (1085–1147) and Almohad (1133–1270) invaders from North Africa, ousting the Umayyads. These pious orthodox rulers spread terror against the infidels wherever they went. In 1143, Almohad Caliph al-Mumin ordered the deportation of the Jews and Christians, who refused to convert to Islam.[155] The Jews were converted to Islam at the pain of death or deported by Almohad caliphs—namely al-Mumin (r. 1133–63), Abu Yakub (r. 1163–84) and al-Mansur (r. 1184–99). The Christians of Grenada were deported to Morocco by Almoravid rulers in 1126.[156]

The Jews, including the family of famous Jewish theologian, philosopher and physician Moses Maimonides (1135–1204)—facing the choice of conversion to Islam, death or exile after the Almohad conquest of Cordoba in 1148—chose exile. Since similar persecution of Jews existed in much of the Muslim lands, the Maimonides family failed to settle first in Morocco, then in Palestine. Scouring the Islamic land in the Muslim guise for nearly two decades, they finally settled in Fustat (Egypt). Maimonides left glimpses of the persecution, the Jews suffered, in Muslim lands in his writings, particularly in *The Epistle to the Jews of Yemen* (1172).[157] He wrote of the Muslim persecution and forced conversion of Jews to Islam in Yemen, North Africa and Spain that '*the continuous persecutions will cause many to drift away from our faith, to have misgivings, or to go astray, because they witnessed our feebleness, and noted the triumph of our adversaries and their dominion over us.*' He added,

> 'God has hurled us in the midst of this people, the Arabs, who have persecuted us severely, and passed baneful and discriminatory legislation against us, as Scripture has forewarned us, 'Our enemies themselves shall judge us' (Deuteronomy 32:31). *Never did a nation molest, degrade, debase and hate us as much as they....*'

Emphasizing that '*we were dishonored by them beyond human endurance*', Maimonides continued,

> We have acquiesced, both old and young, to inure ourselves to humiliation, as Isaiah instructed us: '*I gave my back to the smiters, and my cheeks to them that plucked off the hair*' (50:6). All this notwithstanding, we do not escape this continued maltreatment which well nigh crushes us.

---

155. Walker, p. 247

156. Ibn Warraq, p. 226,236

157. Maimonides M (1952) *Moses Maimonides' Epistle to Yemen: The Arabic Original and the Three Hebrew Versions*, ed. AS Halkin, trans. B Cohen, American Academy for Jewish Research, New York.

No matter how much we suffer and elect to remain at peace with them, they stir up strife and sedition, as David predicted, '*I am all peace, but when I speak, they are for war*' (Psalms 120:7). If, therefore, we start trouble and claim power from them absurdly and preposterously we certainly give ourselves up to destruction.

HOW SO MANY HINDUS SURVIVED IN INDIA?

Naik applies a different ploy to refute the allegation that Islam was propagated through violence. He counters it by arguing that if Islam was spread by the sword, there could not have survived so many non-Muslims in India and the Middle East. He writes:

> Overall, the Muslims ruled Arabia for 1400 years. Yet today, there are 14 million Arabs who are Coptic Christians, i.e. Christians since generations. If the Muslims had used the sword there would not have been a single Arab who would have remained a Christian.

> The Muslims ruled India for about a thousand years. If they wanted, they had the power of converting each and every non-Muslim of India to Islam. Today more than 80% of the people of India are non-Muslims. All these non-Muslim Indians are bearing witness today that Islam was not spread by the sword.

Al-Qaradawi counters Naik in claiming that sword was applied to create the atmosphere for spreading the universal message of Islam:

> ...the sword may conquer lands and occupy states, it will never be able to open hearts and inculcate faith in people. The spread of Islam only occurred after a while, after the barriers between the common people of these countries and Islam were removed. At this point, they were able to consider Islam within a peaceful atmosphere, away from the disturbance of war and the battlefields. Thus, non-Muslims were able to witness the excellent morals of the Muslims...

Dr Fazlur Rahman, a renowned Islamic scholar, who had to flee Pakistan and take refuge in the United States for his allegedly moderate views on Islam, also agrees with al-Qaradawi. Rahman asserts that '*Jihad (by the sword) becomes an absolute necessity*' for instituting the religio-social world-order underlined in the Quran. He asks: '*How can such an ideological world order be brought into existence without such means?*' Quite puzzlingly, he then blasts what he calls *Christian propaganda* for popularizing the slogan that '*Islam was spread by the sword*' or '*Islam is a religion of the sword.*' He, however, candidly agrees that the sword came first in creating a conducive environment before Islam could be propagated. He writes, '*...what was spread by the sword was not the religion of Islam, but the political domain of Islam so that Islam could work to produce the order on the earth that the Quran seeks... But one can never say that Islam was spread by the sword.*'[158]

On the question of Jihad, Abdel Khalek Hassouna, the Secretary General of the Arab League (1952-71), similarly said in interview (1968) that '*Islam was not imposed by the sword as its enemies claim. People were converted to Islam by their own choice because the life it promised them was better than their previous life. **Muslims invaded other countries to ensure that the Call (to Islam) would reach the masses everywhere.***'[159]

These renowned Muslim scholars had set out to refute the allegation that Islam was spread by the sword. In the process, they have inadvertently agreed that the sword had indeed played the pivotal role in the propagation of Islam. If analyzed carefully, their statements clearly affirm that the sword was the *primary*

---

158. Sharma, p. 125
159. Waddy C (1976) *The Muslim Mind*, Longman Group Ltd., London, p. 187

weapon in the propagation of Islam: the sword was applied first; the propagation of Islam came next—the latter, they claim, came through peaceful means. A couple of questions need to be asked in this regard:

1. How peaceful was the propagation phase of Islam?

2. Didn't the initial sword-phase played any role in the spread of Islam?

The answer to these questions will be found as one goes through this book. It will be demonstrated, based on the records of Muslim historians, that the conversion of the vanquished to Islam started rights on the battle-field on a grand scale. Let us now address the following two issues concerning the claims of these Muslim scholars:

1. First, did non-Muslims rush to the umbrella of Islam upon realizing that the message of Islam was one of peace and justice?

2. Second, if Islam was spread by the sword, why are there still fourteen million non-Muslims in the Middle East and 80 percent of the people are Hindus in India after about fourteen and ten centuries of Islamic rule, respectively?

A brief account of what had descended upon the people of the Middle East and India in the initial Muslim assaults has already been described. Sultan Mahmud made seventeen devastating assaults in Northern India between 1000 and 1027 CE. Three decades after Sultan Mahmud's first assault, Alberuni recorded in his book, *Alberuni's India* (*Indica*, 1030 CE), that the Hindus had become "atoms of dust" in the lands conquered by Muslims; and those, who survived, cherished '*the most inveterate aversion towards all Muslims.*' Alberuni further wrote that the Hindus '*frighten their children with us (Muslims), our dress and our ways and customs*' and decry us as "devil's breed" and that they regard '*everything we do as opposite of all that is good and proper.*'[160] The reason for the Hindu repugnance toward Arab Muslims were the complete banishment of Buddhists from countries like Khurasan, Persia, Iraq, Mosul and Syria, first by the Zoroastrians and then by Muslims. And then Muhammad bin Qasim forayed into India, conquered the cities of Brahmanabad and Multan, and went as far as Kanauj. And '*all these events planted a deeply rooted hatred in their hearts,*' adds Alberuni. Ibn Battutah witnessed many Hindu rebels and warriors, who, instead of submitting to Muslim rules or converting to Islam, had taken refuge in inaccessible mountains near Multan and Aligarh, while Mughal Emperor Babur, late in the Muslim rule in India, noted the same in Agra (see below). In the reign of rather kind-hearted Jahangir (d. 1627), hundreds of thousands, probably millions, of Hindus had taken refuge in jungles across India and taken to rebellion; Jahangir hunted down 200,000 of them in 1619–20 and sold them in Iran.[161]

Alberuni proves that, some three decades after Sultan Mahmud's first invasion, India's Hindus failed to see the message of peace and justice in Islam. If they did, they would have rushed to embrace Islam, instead of showing "inveterate aversion" and "deeply rooted hatred" against Muslims. Other Muslim scholars, travelers and merchants, who visited India during the early centuries of Islam, also expressed similar frustrations. Islamic rule came to the India proper in 712 and it appears that the Hindus did not grasp Islam's appealing message of peace and justice for centuries, as Prof. Habibullah writes, '*direct conversions at the beginning must have been rare; an early report, quoted by a tenth-century Arab geographer, complains that Islam had not made a single convert in India.*'[162] Merchant Sulaiman (851), who traveled to India and China, stated: '*In his time, he knew neither Indian nor Chinese who had accepted Islam or spoke Arabic.*'[163] Ibn

160. Sachau EC (1993) *Alberuni's India*, Low Price Publications, New Delhi, p. 20–21

161. Elliot & Downson, Vol. VI, p. 516; Levi (2002) *Hindus Beyond the Hindu Kush: Indian in the Central Asian Slave Trades*, Journal of the Royal Asiatic Society, 12(3), p. 283–84

162. Habibullah ABM (1976) *The Foundations of Muslim Rule in India*, Central Book Depot, Allahabad, p. 1

163. Sharma, p. 110

Battutah and Emperor Babur witnessed amongst Hindus strongly hostile feelings toward Islam more than six and eight centuries after Islam was implanted in India, so did Emperor Jahangir after nine centuries.

What can be gleaned from this analysis is that the Hindus obviously failed to grasp the beauty of Islam well into the dying days of Muslim rule in India; instead, they were hostile toward it. We will see (Chapter VI) that, within a century of founding the Muslim sultanate in Delhi in 1206, the Hindus—pauperized by extreme exploitation, namely the imposition of *jizyah*, *kharaj* and other kinds of onerous taxes—started begging at the doors of Muslims. They could escape from this desperate situation simply by accepting Islam, but they were not doing so. We will see the testimonies of Muslim chroniclers and European travelers that, as late as in the seventeenth century, the Hindus were taking their wives and children to slave-markets for selling them to pay up the grinding taxes. Muslim officers were also forcibly carrying away the children of destitute Hindus for selling them for exacting taxes (see Chapter VII). Still, they were not converting to Islam.

The vast expanse of thick jungles, which existed all over India, had also provided a valuable defence for the survival of Hindus as suggested by many Muslim historians and rulers. Ibn Battutah, traveling to India in the reign of Sultan Muhammad Shah Tughlaq (r. 1325–51) found near Multan, Hindu *'rebels and warriors, who maintain themselves in the fastness of (inaccessible) mountains...'* On his journey with a convoy of the Delhi Sultan to China, Ibn Battutah found near Kol (Aligarh) that Hindu rebels who had taken refuge in "an inaccessible hill", from where they made frequent attacks on the Muslim-ruled territories. His convoy engaged in repelling one such rebel attack on a Muslim town, routing and killing them to the last man.[164] The great Sufi scholar Amir Khasrau describes similar incidents in his *Suh Nipher*. In his memoir *Mulfuzat-i-Timuri*, barbarous invader Amir Timur (Tamerlane) records that he was warned by his nobles about the defence of Indians, which *'consists of woods and forests, and trees, which, interweaving stem with stem and branch with branch, render it very difficult to penetrate into that country... the soldiery, and landholders, and princes, and Rajas of that country inhabit in the fastness of those forests, and live there like wild beast.'*[165]

When Babur, the first Mughal ruler, invaded India in the 1520s, he noted of the survival strategy of the inhabitants that *'in many parts of the plains thorny jungles grow,'* which provides good defence, behind which the people *'become stubbornly rebellious.'* The defiant and successful strategy of hiding in jungles was noticed by Babur upon his arrival in Agra of which he wrote, *'neither grain for ourselves nor corn for our horses was to be had. The villagers, out of hostility and hatred to us, had taken to thieving and highway robbery; there was no moving on the roads... All the inhabitants had run away (to jungles) in terror.'*[166]

These testimonies give us a good deal of idea about the continuous, determined resistance of Hindus against resented Muslim invaders and rulers of India. This will also help one comprehend how so many Hindus might have managed to survive the Muslim assaults in India spanning so many centuries. Indeed, Islamic chronicles on India is littered with examples of Indian rulers and their soldiers, rebels and commoners, under attack by Muslim invaders and rulers, frequently taking refuge in the inaccessible jungles and mountains to save their lives.

Evidently, there was, amongst Hindus, strong resistance against and repugnance toward Islam; they took refuge in inaccessible jungle and mountain hideouts to save lives, and to avoid capture and enslavement for their conversion to Islam. Large numbers of peasants, refusing to pay exorbitant taxes to Muslim rulers, were leaving their farms to take refuge in jungles. Still, others were bearing the burden of crushing *dhimmi* taxes, rather than embracing Islam to get rid of the burden. After Aurangzeb reintroduced the humiliating *jizyah* in 1679 (earlier abolished by enlightened Akbar, r. 1556–1605), a great multitude of Hindus from all walks of life thronged to Delhi and laid a sit-in protest outside the royal palace. In order to disperse the

164. Gibb HAR (2004) *Ibn Battutah: Travels in Asia and Africa*, D K Publishers, New Delhi, p. 190,215
165. Elliot & Dawson, Vol. III, p. 395
166. Lal (1999), p. 62–63

stubborn protesters, Aurangzeb set his elephants and horses upon them. *'Many fell trodden to death under the feet of the elephants and horses'* and at length, *'they submitted to pay the jizyah,'* wrote Khafi Khan.[167]

This clearly proves that even one millennium after the Muslim invaders came to India, the Hindus—still unable to find anything appealing or worthwhile in Islam—were ignoring so much privilege and inducements to convert to Islam. Instead, they were undertaking such dangerous protests and still, ending up paying the humiliating *jizyah*, onerous *kharaj* and other kinds of crushing taxes by doggedly adhering to their ancestral faith.

Moreover, many of those—who had converted to Islam under various circumstances, including at the point of the sword—were willing to revert to their ancestral religion at the earliest opportunity. Sultan Muhammad Shah Tughlaq had enslaved and converted two brothers, Harihara and Bukka, from the Deccan in 1326. Ten years later, the sultan sent them back with an army to the Deccan to control the chaotic situation there. Far away from the capital Delhi, they not only returned to the Hindu fold but also threw away the Islamic yoke from South India by founding the Vijaynagar Kingdom.[168] Vijaynagar became a powerful Hindu kingdom and flourishing centre of Indian civilization and the greatest impediment against Islamization of South India for over 200 years.

When deviant Akbar allowed a free choice in religion, many of the Hindus, earlier converted to Islam by force, reverted to their ancestral faith. Muslim women started marrying Hindu men and embrace Hinduism. In one instance, when Emperor Shahjahan was returning from an expedition to Kashmir, he discovered that Hindu men in Bhadauri and Bhimbar were marrying Muslim women as a part of social custom. And some of the women had adopted the faith of their Hindu husbands. Shahjahan declared such promiscuous marriages illegal and ordered his officers to separate the Muslim women from their Hindu husbands.[169] It is no wonder then that Maulana Abul Kalam Azad, the first Education Minister of Independent India, condemned Akbar terming his *'tolerant rule as the near-suicide of Indian Islam'* and praised the fanatic Sufi master, Shaykh Ahmad Sirhindi, who had revolted against Akbar and urged for the restoration of Hindu persecution (discussed later).[170]

In Kashmir, records *Baharistan-i-Shahi*, Hinduism *'had been stamped out in the reign of Sultan Sikandar the Iconoclast,'* through their mass-conversion by the sword and wholesale destruction of Hindu temples.[171] Sultan Sikandar (r. 1389–1413) *'was constantly busy in annihilating the infidels and destroyed most of the temples...,'* records Haidar Malik Chadurah.[172] When Sikandar's successor Sultan Zainul Abedin (aka Shahi Khan, r. 1417–67), another deviant Muslim ruler, permitted the converted Hindus to revert, records Sydney Owen, *'many Hindus (i.e., Hindus converted to Islam by force) were re-admitted into the Hindu fold.'*[173] *Baharistan-i-Shahi*, an anonymous Persian chronicle (1614), regretfully records of the ascendancy of Hinduism and decline of Islam under Sultan Zainul Abedin that,

> '...the infidels and their corrupt and immoral practices attained such popularity that even the *ulema*, the learned (Sufis), the Sayyids (nobles) and the Qadis (judges) of this land began to observe them without exhibiting even the slightest repugnance for them. There was none to

167. Lal (1999), p. 118

168. Smith, p. 303–04

169. Sharma, p. 211

170. Elst K (1993) *Negationism in India*, Voice of India, New Delhi, p. 41

171. Pundit KN (1991) *A Chronicle of Medieval Kashmir*, (Translation), Firma KLM Pvt Ltd, Calcutta, p. 74 (This authoritative seventeenth-century Persian chronicle, entitled *Baharistan-i-Shahi*, was written anonymously. It has been translated by Prof. KN Pundit under the title, *A Chronicle of Medieval Kashmir*.)

172. Chadurah HM (1991) *Tarikh-i-Kashmir*, ed. & trans. Razia Bano, New Delhi, p. 55

173. Owen S (1987) *From Mahmud Ghazni to the Disintegration of Mughal Empire*, Kanishka Publishing House, New Delhi, p. 127

forbid them to do so. It resulted in a gradual weakening of Islam and a decay in its cannons and postulates; idol-worship and corrupt and immoral practices thrived.'[174]

Under the later administration of Malik Raina, the Hindus were again converted *en masse* to Islam by force. During the subsequent laxity, they reverted back to Hinduism again. Under the instigation of Amir Shamsud-Din Muhammad Iraqi, the greatest Sufi saint of Kashmir, General Kaji Chak carried out "wholesale massacre" of these apostates on the holy festival day of *Ashura* (Muharram, 1518 CE), slaughtering 700–800 of the leading men (see Chapter IV, Section: *Brutal Conversion in Kashmir*). Pundit Jawaharlal Nehru, the socialist historian and first prime minister of independent India—who is eager to whitewash Islamic atrocities in India—also records of similar willingness of the forcibly converted Kashmiri Muslims to revert to their former faith, albeit four centuries later. He wrote in *The Discovery of India* that,

> In Kashmir, a long-continued process of conversion to Islam had resulted in 95 per cent of the population becoming Moslems, though they retained many of their old Hindu customs. In the middle of nineteenth century, the Hindu ruler of the state found that very large numbers of these people were anxious to return *en bloc* to Hinduism.[175]

WHY SO MANY PEOPLE IN INDIA ARE STILL HINDUS?

The historical records cited above make it obvious that the Hindus of India were never impressed by Islam. Instead, the trend was exactly the opposite: that is, an eagerness to leave the fold of Islam to rejoin Hinduism. On rare occasions, when a liberal Muslim ruler came to power and gave the citizens free choice in matters of religion, Islam declined and Hinduism and other local religions flourished, as admitted by Muslim historians and scholars.

This discussion gives enough evidence as to why some 80 percent of the people in subcontinental India remained non-Muslim after so many centuries of Muslim rule. It will be noted below that the Hindus resolutely endured extreme social, cultural and religious degradation, humiliation and deprivation as well as crushing burden of discriminatory taxes and still stuck to their ancestral religion even after a millennium of brutal Islamic rule.

Another factor warrants consideration here is that, although Muslims theoretically ruled India for over eleven centuries, they hardly ever managed to secure a complete hold over the entire country. During the first three centuries after Qasim's foray into Sindh in 712, Muslim rule remained confined to a tiny Northwest area of vast India. The fact that a huge majority of the population in those parts are now Muslims proves that Muslim rulers could impose Islam more effectively in areas, where they had strong political power over a longer period of time.

Only under the great commandership of Akbar the Great (r. 1556–1605), most parts of India came under the sway of Muslim rule. But then, Akbar was a great apostate of Islam and did not help the cause of spreading Islam. During his five-decade reign, the Muslim population probably dwindled, instead of expanding. Following Akbar, the policy of Islamization did not get a strong hold as a policy of the state during the next fifty years, ruled by his son Jahangir and grandson Shahjahan.

When Akbar's great grandson fanatic Aurangzeb (r. 1658–1707) captured power, Islamization and forced conversion became the focus of the state. But during his reign, revolts were taking place in all corners of the kingdom. According to Bernier, during Aurangzeb's brutal reign, the powerful and defiant Rajput and

---

174. Pundit, p. 74

175. Nehru J (1946) *The Discovery of India*, The John Day Company, New York, p. 264

72

Maratha princes used to enter the courtyard of his palace always mounted on their horses, well-armed and well-attended by their men.[176] When Aurangzeb banned non-Muslims from carrying weapons in conformity with the *Pact of Omar* and Sharia laws, the defiant and dangerous Rajputs had to be exempted. Despite Aurangzeb's dreaded policies and atrocities against his infidel opponents, defiant Hindu rebels like Shivaji and Rana Raj Singh wrote letters, protesting the re-imposition of *jizyah*. When his officers (*amin*) went to collect *jizyah*, one of them was killed and another was humiliated by Hindus pulling by his beard and hair before sending back empty-handed.[177]

Even during the period of most firmly established Mughal rule of Akbar and Jahangir, their influence across the country remained rather fragile. Jahangir wrote in his memoir, *Tarikh-i-Salim Shahi*, that "*the number of turbulent and disaffected never seems to diminish; for what with the examples made during the reign of my father, and subsequently of my own, ...there is scarcely a province in the empire in which, in one quarter or the other, some accursed miscreant will not spring up to unfurl the standard of rebellion; so that in Hindustan never has there existed a period of complete repose.*" Summarizing the Hindu defiance, notes Dirk H. Kolf, '*millions of armed men, cultivators or otherwise, were its (government's) rivals rather than subjects.*' According to Badaoni of Akbar's court, Hindus often warded off attacks of Muslim army from their jungle hideouts. Those, who took to the forest, stayed there eating wild fruits, tree-roots and coarse grain if and when available.[178] These examples would give one sufficient idea about how some 80 percent of the population of the subcontinental India remained non-Muslims after so many centuries of Islamic rule.

HOW CONVERSION TOOK PLACE IN INDIA?

In light of the evidence presented above, the question should not be about how some 80 percent of the Indians remained non-Muslims after so many centuries of Muslim rule. Instead, it should be asked, why and how as many as 20 percent of the Indians became Muslim despite their defiant resistance against Islam. How could the Muslim population swell when Hindus found Islam so repugnant, as attested by the records of many Muslim chroniclers and rulers?

Conversion by the sword

Conversion by the sword was initiated by Prophet Muhammad by giving the Polytheists a choice between death and conversion to Islam in compliance to Allah's command in Quran 9:5. The Hindus, therefore, were supposed to be given a choice between death and Islam.

When Muhammad bin Qasim began the conquest of Sindh, he exercised the policy of converting the people of a territory, which gave a fight, at the pain of death. He gave quarters to the people, if they submitted to his invading army without giving a fight. He did not force them to convert. When the report of his latter lenient policy reached his patron Hajjaj in Baghdad, disapproving the leniency, he wrote to Qasim:

> '...I learnt that the ways and rules you follow are conformable to the (Islamic) Law. Except that you give protection to all, great and small alike, and make no difference between enemy and friend. God says, '*Give no quarter to Infidels, but cut their throats.*' Then know that this is the command of the great god. You should not be too ready to grant protection... After this, give no

---

176. Bernier F (1934) *Travels in the Mogul Empire (1656–1668)*, Revised Smith VA, Oxford, p. 40,210

177. Lal (1999), p. 118–119

178. Lal (1994), p. 64

protection to any enemy except to those who are of rank (i.e., accept Islam). This is a worthy resolve, and want of dignity will not be imputed to you.'[179]

Having received this command from Hajjaj, Qasim followed it through in his next conquest of Brahmanabad, sparing none who did not embrace Islam. According to al-Biladuri, '*eight, or some say twenty-six thousand, men were put to the sword.*'[180] However, putting the great multitude of Hindus, who often refused to embrace Islam, to death was difficult. Instead, giving them quarters for raising taxes was a more lucrative alternative. Qasim later wrote to Hajjaj in this regard. In response, Hajjaj wrote back:

> 'The letter of my dear nephew Muhammad Kasim has been received and the fact understood. It appears that the chief inhabitants of Brahmanabad had petitioned to be allowed to repair the temple of Budh and pursue their religion. As they have made submission, and agreed to pay taxes to the Khalifa, nothing can be properly required from them. They have been taken under our protection (*dhimmi*), and we cannot in any way stretch out our hands upon their lives or property.'[181]

Hindus were, thus, accepted as *dhimmi* subjects, which spared them from conversion by the sword. The Godless Umayyad rulers were more interested in filling the treasury by extracting higher taxes from non-Muslim subjects than converting them to Islam. For example, al-Hajjaj harshly treated those, who converted to Islam.[182] When a group of non-Muslims came to him to inform their acceptance of Islam, al-Hajjaj refused to recognize their conversion and ordered his troops to return them to their villages.[183] The first Umayyad Caliph Mu'awiyah desperately wanted the Egyptian Copts not to convert to Islam, '*claiming that if they all convert to the true religion (Islam), they will cause the treasury a great loss in income from the jizyah.*'[184]

The leniency, accorded to Hindus by the Godless Umayyads, was obviously a violation of the canonical Islamic laws of the Quran and *Sunnah*. This irreverent concession was later included in the Hanafi laws; all other Schools of Islamic laws demand death or conversion of Polytheists. Therefore, as far as forced conversion is concerned, the infidels of India suffered the mildest of persecution.

Following the extermination of the Godless Umayyad dynasty in 750, the more orthodox rulers often converted Hindus at the pain of death. Saffaride ruler Yakub Lais captured Kabul in 870 and took the prince of Kabul prisoner. He put the king of Ar-Rukhaj to death, destroyed and plundered the temples and *the inhabitants were forced to embrace Islam*. He returned to his capital loaded with booty, which included heads of three kings and many statues of Indian divinities.[185]

In Sultan Mahmud's conquest of Kanauj, '*the inhabitants either accepted Islam or took up arms against him to become the food of Islamic swords,*' records his secretary Abu Nasr al-Utbi.[186] In the captured of Baran, records al-Utbi, '*since God's sword was drawn from the scabbard, and the whip of punishment was uplifted... ten thousand men proclaimed their anxiety for conversion and their rejection of idols.*'[187]

After conquering a city, Sultan Mahmud—an educated cultured man and a master of Islamic jurisprudence (*fiqh*)—would normally slaughter the men of fighting age, enslave their women and children

179. Elliot & Dawson, Vol. I, p. 173–74
180. Ibid, Vol. I, p. 122
181. Sharma, p. 109
182. Bulliet RW (1979) *Conversion to Islam and the Emergence of a Muslim Society in Iran*, N. Levtzion ed., *Conversion to Islam*, Holmes and Meier Publishers Inc., New York, p. 33
183. Pipes (1983), p. 52
184. Tagher, p. 19
185. Elliot & Dawson, Vol. II, p. 419
186. Ibid, p. 26
187. Ibid, p. 42–43

and force the remaining inhabitants to embrace Islam. He used to place on the throne a converted prince, who must run the affairs of the state according to Islamic laws and oversee the propagation of Islam and the suppression of idol-worship. One such converted prince was Nawasa Shah. After Sultan Mahmud retired from India, records al-Utbi, '*Satan had got the better of Nawasa Shah, for he was again apostatizing towards the pit of plural worship... So the Sultan went swifter than the wind in that direction, and made the sword reek with the blood of his enemies.*'[188] This means that Sultan Mahmud did not simply convert the Hindus by the sword in his campaigns in India, but he also made it sure that the converts did not revert to their ancestral faith after his return to Ghazni. We will see in Chapter VI (Section: *1947 Riots and Massacres: Who is responsible?*) that, in the course of India's Partition in 1947, a few million Hindus and Sikhs were converted to Islam at the pain of death in East and West Pakistan.

Conversion through enslavement

In the first successful encroachment into India, Muhammad bin Qasim put large numbers of men to death in Debal, Brahmanabad and Multan. It appears that the adult men of weapon-bearing age, who fell within the reach of the Muslim army in the course of the assaults, were ruthlessly slaughtered. Undoubtedly, many of the grown-up men fled in all directions to escape the sword, leaving the vulnerable women and children behind, who were carried away as slaves. *Chachnama* records that Qasim's assault on Rawar yielded 60,000 slaves. In the final stages of his conquest of Sindh, says *Chachnama*, about 100,000 women and children were enslaved.[189]

The number of women and children enslaved by Muslim invaders has not been recorded systematically for all the campaigns. It can be surmised that each of Qasim's major assaults in Sehwan, Dhalila, Brahmanabad and Multan yielded similar numbers of captives. His brief exploit of three years in the Sindh frontier of India (712–15) had likely yielded a few hundred thousand slaves. He always forwarded one-fifth of the captives and other spoils—the share of the state, according to the Quran [8:41], prophetic traditions and Sharia—to the caliph in Damascus and distributed the rest amongst his soldiers. These slave women and children became the property of Muslims and entered the house of Islam by default. When those children grew up to be adult Muslims in a few years, the males were drafted into the Muslim army for waging new holy wars against the Hindus, who had been their kinfolk and coreligionists a few years earlier. In other words, in the short time-span of a decade, these captured children had become the weapon for the Muslim state to wage new Jihad expeditions for extending the domain of Islam, for converting the vanquished infidels, for enslaving their women and children, and for plundering their wealth. Even during the upheaval of the Partition of India (1946–47), some 100,000 Hindu and Sikh women were enslaved, carried away and married off to Muslims (Chapter VI).

Enslaved women as reproduction tools

The female captives, in compliance with Quranic sanctions and prophetic traditions, were used as sex-slaves by their Muslim masters (see Chapter VII on Slavery). Therefore, they did not only add to the growing Muslim population, but also became valuable tools for expanding the Muslim populace through procreation. When those women, especially the ones of childbearing age, were taken away, the Hindu men, who had fled, came back to find that their women and children gone. As a result, they did not have sufficient partners for the procreation. That means, wherever Muslims made a successful assault, procreation in the Hindu community dropped sharply. On the other hand, the few thousand Muslim soldiers who came to India with Muhammad bin Qasim had plenty of sex-partners for reproduction to the maximum capacity. Even Emperor Akbar had amassed 5,000 beautiful women in his harem. Sultan Moulay Ismail of Morocco (r. 1672–1727) had sired

---

188. Ibid, p. 33
189. Lal (1994), p. 18–19

about 1,200 children through his 2,000–4,000 thousand wives and sex-slaves.[190] The extensive enslavement of the vanquished Hindus, particularly the women—who were engaged in the breeding of Muslim children—helped the rapid growth of the Muslim populace.

Therefore, wherever Muslims made successful inroads, they reduced the Hindu population directly by slaughtering the men in large numbers and taking away the women and children as captives. It indirectly reduced the Hindu populace by rendering the remnant Hindu men unprocreative by depriving them of childbearing female partners. Since those women became the vehicle for breeding Muslim offspring instead, the final result was a reduction of the Hindu populace and a sharp rise in the number of Muslims. The growing Muslim population was to be maintained by the toiling of the vanquished Hindus, subjected to grinding taxes. This is roughly the same protocol, which Prophet Muhammad had applied to the Jews of Banu Qurayza and Khaybar.

Qasim's three-year-long exploits in India, therefore, not only added a few hundred thousand Hindus to the fold of Islam instantly through enslavement, but the enslaved women also acted as the vehicle of reproduction, swelling the Muslim populace in lips and bounds. Initiated by the Prophet, this protocol was applied by Muslim invaders and rulers everywhere; in India, Emperor Akbar banned the practice in 1564 although rather unsuccessfully. In his expeditions to India, Sultan Mahmud slaughtered the men in large numbers and carried away a great multitude of mainly women and children as slaves. Al-Utbi records that Sultan Mahmud had taken 500,000 people captives in his campaign of 1001–02. In his assault in Ninduna (Punjab), he captured so many slaves that '*they became very cheap…*,' wrote an elated al-Utbi. In Thanesar (Haryana), Mahmud enslaved 200,000 and returned with 53,000 slaves in 1019.[191]

Based on the records of Muslim historians, Sultan Mahmud's repeated invasions of Northern India had reduced the Hindu population by about two million as estimated by Prof. KS Lal.[192] Many of them were slaughtered in the course of the assaults; the rest—a larger number—were carried away as slaves at the point of the sword and instantly became Muslim.

Later on, Sultan Muhammad Ghauri (Muizzuddin, d. 1206) of Khurasan and his General Kutbuddin Aibak joined hands to consolidate Muslim power in India, which led to the establishment of direct Muslim rule in India, the Sultanate of Delhi, in 1206. According to the testimony of Muhammad Ferishtah, three to four hundred thousand *Khokhars* (Hindus) were converted to Islam by Muizzuddin. *Fakhr-i-Mudabbir* sums up the exploits of Muizzuddin and Aibak as thus: '*even poor (Muslim) householder became owner of numerous slaves.*'[193]

The capture of slaves remained a general policy in Muslim-ruled India until the reign of apostate Akbar (r. 1556–1605), who prohibited mass enslavement in battle-fields. Despite the ban, the age-old tradition continued with vigor even in his reign. His frustrated advisor, freethinker Abul Fazl, says in *Akbar Nama* that '*many evil-hearted and vicious officers used to proceed to the villages and mahals to sack them.*' In these sackings, normally the women and children were driven away. In Akbar's reign, affirms Moreland, '*It became a fashion to raid a village or a group of villages without any obvious justification, and carry off the inhabitants as slaves.*'[194] It is no wonder then that Abdulla Khan Uzbeg, a general of Akbar, had boastfully declared:

---

190. Milton G (2004) *White Gold*, Hodder & Stoughton, London, p. 120

191. Lal (1994), p. 20

192. Lal KS (1973) *Growth of Muslim Population in Medieval India*, Aditya Prakashan, New Delhi, p. 211–17

193. Lal (1994), p. 43–44

194. Moreland WH (1995) *India at the Death of Akbar*, Low Price Publications, New Delhi, p. 92

'I made prisoners of five *lacs* (500,000) of men and women and sold them. They all became Muhammadans. From their progeny, there will be crores (one crore = ten million) by the Day of Judgment.'[195]

After Akbar's death, Islamization was gradually revived during the subsequent reigns of Jahangir and Shahjahan. On Emperor Jahangir, seen as a liberal and kind-hearted ruler, records *Shash Fath-I Kangra* that '*he devoted all his exertions to the promulgation of the Muhammadan religion...*' and that his '*whole efforts were always directed to the extinguishing of the fire of Paganism...*'[196] According to *Intikhab-I Jahangir Shahi*, when Jains in Gujarat built splendid temples, attracting many devotees, '*Emperor Jahangir ordered them to be banished from the country and their temples to be demolished. Their idols were thrown down on the uppermost step of the mosque, so that it might be trodden upon*' by Muslim worshippers.[197] Emperor Shahjahan was more orthodox than his father Jahangir.

It is Aurangzeb (r. 1658–1707), who brought back the full-scale profession of slavery and forced conversion into the state policy. Even after the British capture of Bengal in 1757, slave-taking by Muslim rulers was still going on with vigor around India. According to *Siyar-ul-Mutakhirin*, after Ahmad Shah Abdali's victory in the *Third Battle of Panipat* in 1761, the prisoners, famished due to deprivation of food and drink, were paraded in long lines before being beheaded and the '*women and children who survived were driven off as slaves—twenty-two thousand, many of them of the highest rank in the land.*'[198] About two decades earlier, Nadir Shah of Iran invaded India (1738). After committing harrowing atrocities and plunder in which some 200,000 people were slaughtered, he returned with thousands of slaves and a great sum of treasure.

It should not be difficult now to grasp that slave-taking helped swell the Muslim population in India, probably, like no other sources. General Abdulla Khan Uzbeg has described it most accurately in his boastful statement cited above. The contribution of the enslaved women in the growth of Muslim population has been succinctly described by Arnold: '*Women slaves turned concubines could increase the Muslim population by leaps and bounds when captured in large numbers.*'[199] In agreement, Muhammad Ashraf opines that '*the slaves added to the growing Muslim population of India.*'[200] However, he is somewhat incorrect in that the slaves did not simply add to the growing Muslim population; instead, it is slaves who formed the mass of the Muslim population in the initial years and decades. Whilst slaves continued to be added, it was the offspring of slaves, who mainly swelled the Muslim populace in the subsequent period.

Opposed to the views of modern Islamic scholars—Sheikh al-Qaradawi, Dr Zakir Naik and Dr Fazlur Rahman *et al.*—the conversion and growth of the Muslim population clearly started right at the time of conquests: through forced conversion of the vanquished by invaders like Sultan Mahmud and Yakub Lais, and through universal enslavement of the women and children on grand scales at the point of the sword, since the enslaved by default became Muslims. The women, especially the young ones, were the major target of enslavement by Muslims right from the time of Prophet Muhammad. Subsequently, those enslaved women became the major tool for the breeding and growth of the Muslim populace.

Humiliation & economic burdens contributing to conversion

Islam recognized the monotheistic Jews and Christians as *dhimmi* subjects. Although Allah gave Polytheists—namely Hindus, Buddhists, and Animists etc.—a choice between death and conversion, the

---

195. Lal (1994), p. 73

196. Elliot & Dawson, Vol. VI, p. 528–29

197. Ibid, p. 451

198. Lal (1994), p. 155

199. Arnold TW (1896) *The Preaching of Islam*, Westminster, p. 365

200. Ashraf KM (1935) *Life and Conditions of the People of Hindustan*, Calcutta, p. 151

Godless Umayyads, upon the conquest of Sindh in India, came across too great a number of recalcitrant Polytheists to put to the sword. Generally lax in enforcing Muhammad's religion and more interest in inflating the treasury from taxes, they, instead, spared the great multitude of India's Polytheists to use them as the source of revenue. Therefore, they elevated them into the category of *dhimmi* subjects in violation of the Quran [9:5]. The *dhimmis* were generally subjected to extreme degradation and humiliation socially, and exploitation economically, which acted as a huge coercive inducement for them to embrace Islam. The *Pact of Omar*, promulgated by the second caliph of Islam (some authors attribute it to Caliph Omar II, r. 717–20), outlines the general treatment meted out to *dhimmi* subjects under Islamic rule.

The Pact of Omar: This pact is quoted in *Kitab ul-Umm* (Mother of Books) of Imam Shafi'i, the founder of the Shafi'i School of Islamic laws. After the Arabs overran Syria, this agreement was signed between Caliph Omar and the Christian chief of Syria, under the Caliph's dictation. It demands a complete and humiliating subjugation of *dhimmis* to Muslim rule, that they pay discriminatory taxes as a symbol of their lowly status, and suffer many other degrading and dehumanizing socio-political disabilities. Caliph Omar sent a letter to the patriarch of Syria setting the terms of their subjection to Islam, the salient points of which were as follows:[201]

'I, and all Muslims, promise you and your fellow Christians security as long as you keep the conditions upon you, which are:

1. You shall be under Muslim laws and no other, and shall not refuge to do anything we demand of you.

2. If any of you say anything about the Prophet, his religion and the Quran what is unfitting, he is debarred from the protection of Allah, the commander of the Faithful and all Muslims. The condition on which security was given will be annulled and your life will be outside the pale of law.

3. If one of you commits fornication with or marries a Muslim woman, or robs a Muslim on the high way, or turns a Muslim from his religion, or helps their enemies or shelters a spy, he has broken the agreement, and his life and property is without the law.

4. He who commits lesser harm than this to the goods and honor of a Muslim shall be punished.

5. We shall watch your dealing with the Muslims, and if you have done anything unlawful for a Muslim, we shall undo it and punish you.

6. If you or other unbelievers ask for judgment, we shall give it according to the Muslim law.

7. *You shall not display in any Muslim town the crosses, nor parade your idolatry, nor build a church or place of assembly for your prayer, nor beat the Nakus (church bell), nor use your idolatrous language about Jesus, the son of Mary (i.e., Jesus is the son of God), to any Muslim.*

8. You shall wear the *zunnar* (cloth belt) above all your clothes (as a distinguishing mark), which must not be hidden.

9. You shall use peculiar saddles and manners of riding and make your *kalansuwas* (cap) different from those of the Muslims by a mark you put on them.

10. You shall not take the crest of the road, nor the chief seat in the assemblies when Muslims are present.

---

201. Triton, p. 12–24

11. Every free adult male of sound mind shall pay poll-tax (*jizyah*), one *dinar* of full weight, at new year. He shall not leave his town till he has paid.

12. A poor man is liable for his own *jizyah* till it is paid; poverty does not cancel your obligation to pay the *jizyah*, nor abrogate the protection given to you. If you have anything, we shall take it. *Jizyah* is the only burden as long as you live and travel in the Muslim land, except as merchants.

13. You may not enter Mecca under any conditions. If you travel with merchandise, you must pay one-tenth to the Muslims. You may go wherever you like except Mecca. You can stay in Muslim land except the Hedjaz (Hejaz), where you may stay only three days till you depart.'

These were the standard terms that must be imposed upon Jews and Christians (also on Polytheists in countries under *Hanafi* laws) in an ideal Islamic state. The terms in the *Pact of Omar* for dealing with *dhimmis* is clearly in agreement with the sanction of Allah [Quran 9:29] and prophetic tradition. Therefore, the *Pact of Omar*, wrote Abu Yusuf, the great eighth-century *Hanafi* jurist, '*stands till the day of resurrection.*'[202] The Jews and Christians (also Hindus in India), who were rightfully the free-spirited and honorable people in their own homeland, now had to bear this crushingly humiliating and exploiting subjection to Muslim invaders. It is not hard to imagine the psychological pressure such treatments would create on them to convert to Islam.

Jizyah and humiliation: The practice of imposing *jizyah* on *dhimmi* subjects will give one a clear idea of the social degradation they faced in Muslim states. The payment of *jizyah* was not like writing away a check or sending money to the collector's office. Instead, the *dhimmi*, demands Allah, must '*pay the jizyah with willing submission, and feel themselves subdued (humiliated)*' in the process [Quran 9:29]. Paying *jizyah* in "willing submission" and "humiliation" meant that it had to be paid according to a demeaning protocol that would engender such an impact on the *dhimmi*. The great Islamic commentator al-Zamakhshari (d. 1144) interprets the Quranic verse 9:29 on *jizyah* payment as thus:[203]

'The *jizyah* shall be taken from them with belittlement and humiliation. (The *dhimmi*) shall come in person, walking not riding. When he pays, he shall stand, while the tax-collector sits. The collector shall seize him by the scruff of the neck, shake him and say: '*Pay the jizyah!*' and when he pays it, he shall be slapped on the nape of his neck.'

The famous sixteenth-century Egyptian Sufi scholar ash-Sharani describes the ritual of *jizyah* payment in his *Kitab al-Mizan* as thus:[204]

'The *dhimmi*, Christian or Jew, goes on a fixed day in person to the emir appointed to receive the poll-tax (*jizyah*). He sits on a high throne. The *dhimmi* appears before him, offering the toll-tax on his open palm. The emir takes it so that his hand is on top and the *dhimmi's* below. Then the emir gives him a blow on the neck, and who stands, before the emir drives him roughly away... The public is admitted to see this show.'

Let us have a look at how these standard theories were applied in India. Emperor Aurangzeb, having reimposed *jizyah* (earlier abolished by apostate Akbar in 1564) on the Hindus in 1679, promulgated the following protocol for the payment of *jizyah*:

---

202. Ibid, p. 37
203. Ibn Warraq, p. 228–29
204. Triton, p. 227

'The *jizyah* lapses on the death and acceptance of Islam... The non-Muslim should bring himself the *jizyah*; if he sends it through his deputy it should not be accepted. At the time of payment, non-Muslim must keep standing, while the chief should keep sitting. The hand of the non-Muslim should be below and that of the chief above it and he should say '*Make payment of jizyah, O! non-Muslim...*''[205]

When Sultan Alauddin Khilji sought advice from learned scholar Qazi Mughisuddin regarding the collection of *kharaj* (land-tax), the Qazi prescribed a similar protocol, adding that "*should the collector choose to spit into his mouth, he opens it. The purpose of this extreme humility on his part and the collector's spitting into his mouth, is to show the extreme subservience incumbent on this class, the glory of Islam and the orthodox faith, and the degradation of the false religion (Hinduism).*"[206] Similarly, Persian scholar Mulla Ahmad wrote to remind liberal and tolerant Sultan Zainul Abedin of Kashmir (1417–67) that "*the main object of levying the jizyah on them is their humiliation... God established jizyah for their dishonor. The object is their humiliation and (the establishment of) the prestige and dignity of the Muslims.*"[207]

Popular Sufi master Shaykh Ahmad Sirhindi (1564–1624), frustrated by Emperor Akbar's tolerant and liberal policies toward non-Muslims, which violated Islamic laws, wrote to the emperor's court: "*The honor of Islam lies in insulting the kufr (unbelief) and kafir (unbelievers). One who respects the kafirs dishonors the Muslims... The real purpose of levying the jizyah on them is to humiliate them to such an extent that they may not be able to dress well and to live in grandeur. They remain terrified and trembling.*" Similar were the views of Sufi saint Shah Walliullah (d. 1762) and of many other leading Islamic scholars and Sufi masters throughout the period of Muslim rule in India.[208]

These measures, meant for the extreme humiliation of *dhimmis*, were to remind them of their utterly degraded socio-political status in Muslim states. It should not be difficult to conceive the kind of psychological pressure such subjection of the Hindus to utmost humiliation and degradation had created on them to convert to Islam. To humiliation was added the lure of avoiding the economic burden of paying discriminatory extra taxes: *jizyah*, *kharaj* and others. The humiliation aside, *jizyah* was relatively light on the scale of economic burden. The worst burden was the crushing *kharaj*. During the reign of Sultan Alauddin Khilji (1296–1316), the peasants had literally become bonded slaves of the government, since up to 50–75 percent of the produce was taken away in taxes, mainly as *kharaj*. Even during the reign of Akbar, *kharaj* was fixed at '*one-third, but in reality it came to two-thirds*' of the agricultural produce in Kashmir. In Gujarat, the peasants had to hand over three quarters of the produce in around 1629 in the reign of Emperor Shahjahan.[209]

As already noted, the Hindus were reduced to such a desperate situation by the crushing economic exploitation that they were taking refuge in jungles to evade the torture of tax-collectors. Just by reciting the Islamic profession of faith—the *Shahada: [I testify that] there is no god but Allah, and Muhammad is the messenger of Allah*, the Hindus could relieve themselves from all these economic burdens, sufferings and humiliation. This coercive incentive for conversion seemed to have worked brilliantly as testified by Sultan Firoz Shah Tughlaq (r. 1351–88) in his memoir *Fatuhat-i-Firoz Shahi*:

I encouraged my infidel subjects to embrace the religion of the prophet, and I proclaimed that every one who repeated the creed and became a Musalman should be exempted from the *jizyah*, or poll-tax. Information of this came to the ears of the people at large, and great numbers of Hindus presented themselves and were admitted to the honor of Islam. Thus they came forward

---

205. Lal (1999), p. 116

206. Ibid, p. 130

207. Ibid, p. 113

208. Ibid, p. 113–14

209. Ibid, p. 132, 134

day by day from every quarter, and, adopting the faith, were exonerated from the *jizyah*, and were favored with presents and honor.[210]

Therefore, regarding conversion to Islam and the growth of the Muslim population in lands conquered by Muslim invaders, the first wave of converts came through enslavement at the point of the sword. Thereafter, their offspring continued swelling the rank of Muslims. Invaders like Sultan Mahmud, after conquering a city, converted the population to Islam at the pain of death, which contributed substantially to the Muslim populace. In some cases, the inhabitants, under attacks by the brutal and invincible Muslim army, submitted without giving a fight fearing sheer death and destruction and involuntarily converted to Islam, adding themselves to the Muslim population. The next prominent, likely the largest, contribution came from the coercive compulsion of the infidel subjects to convert for relieving themselves from the humiliating *jizyah*, crushing *kharaj* and other discriminatory taxes.

Conversion under brutal Aurangzeb

Muslim rulers added many other kinds of illegitimate inducement and compulsion to convert the infidels to Islam. Ibn Askari writes in his *Al-Tarikh* that Emperor Aurangzeb offered privileges such as administrative posts in the empire, freedom of the criminals from prison, settlements of disputes in favor, and honor of imperial parade among other inducements for conversion.[211] As a result, many notorious criminals must have joined the Islamic creed. This trend is quite active even today; hardened criminals are converting to Islam in prisons, especially in Western countries.

The present demography of the Muslim population of Northern India was shaped largely during the reign of brutal Aurangzeb because of the large-scale conversion by force and other coercive compulsions. The *Gazette of North West Provinces* (NWP), which included modern-day state of Uttar Pradesh and Delhi territories, states: *"Most Muslim cultivators assign the date of their conversion to the reign of Aurangzeb and represent it as the result of sometimes persecution and sometimes as made to enable them to retain their rights when unable to pay revenue."* (This trend must have had extended across the provinces during Aurangzeb). European courtier Niccolao Manucci, who lived in India during the reign of Aurangzeb, also affirms this in saying, *"Many Hindus unable to pay (taxes) turned Muhammadan to obtain relief from the insults of the collectors"*; and Aurangzeb used to take delight in it. Thomas Roll, the president of the English factory in Surat wrote that *jizyah* was exacted by Aurangzeb for the duel purpose of enriching the treasury and for *"forcing the poorer sections of the population to become Muslims."*[212]

On 15 December 1666, Aurangzeb decreed an order for expelling the Hindus from duties in the Royal court and provinces, and to replace them by Muslims.[213] This further pressurized the Hindus to convert to Islam in order to save their livelihood. He pressurized Hindu *zamindars* (landlords) to become Muslim or lose their job or even face death. Devi Chand, the *zamindar* of Manoharpur, was dispossessed from his position and thrown into prison. Aurangzeb sent his *Kotwal* (executioner) instructing him that if Devi Chand becomes Musalman, spare him; if he refused, kill him. Devi Chand agreed to embrace Islam, if he would be restored to *zamindari*. He became a Muslim, his life was spared and the *zamindari* restored.[214] Ratan Singh,

210. Elliot & Dawson, Vol. III, p. 386

211. Roy Choudhury ML (1951) *The State and Religion in Mughal India*, Indian Publicity Society, Calcutta, p. 227

212. Sharma, p. 219

213. Exhibit No. 34, Bikaner Museum Archives, Rajasthan, India;   Available at: http://according-to-mughal-records.blogspot.com/

214. Exhibit No. 41, Bikaner Museum Archives.

who was dispossessed from gaining his father's *zamindari* state of Rampura in Malwa, received the state back by becoming Muslim.[215]

In other instances, Muslims used to invent false charges against Hindus of insulting Islam and they were forced to embrace Islam as punishment. The Council of Surat recorded similar strategy for conversion in 1668. When Muslims owed money to Hindu money-lenders (*bania*) but did not want to pay back, "*the Muhammadan would lodge a complaint to the Kazi (judge) that he had called the Prophet names or spoken contumaciously of their religion, produce a false witness or two and the poor man was forced to circumcision and made to embrace Islam.*"[216]

Aurangzeb also promulgated an order in 1685 to his officers of the provinces to encourage the Hindus to convert to Islam by offering that '*each Hindu male, who becomes a Musalman, is to be given Rupees four and each Hindu woman Rupees two*' from the treasury.[217] Four Rupees was equivalent to a month's earning of a male. Given that conversions also brought relief from *jizyah*, *kharaj* and host of other crushing taxes along with relief from the humiliation and degradation, this incentive had a much larger inducement for conversion than its monetary value. One Mughal document records the conversion of 150 Hindus by Shaikh Abdul Momin, the Faujdar of Bithur, by offering them *saropas* (robes of honour) and cash.[218]

Aurangzeb converted the pundits of Kashmir *en masse* by force. The aggrieved pundits came to Sikh Guru Tegh Bahadur Singh of Punjab for help. When the Guru went to the court of Aurangzeb to enquire about the unlawful conversion of Kashmiris, he was imprisoned and tortured at length for weeks demanding his own conversion. He (also two of his disciples) was ultimately beheaded. It appears that until the time of Aurangzeb, Hindus were still a substantial, if not dominant, part of the population in Kashmir. The spade-work of Aurangzeb has transformed the beautiful Himalayan Queen state of India into an overwhelmingly Muslim-dominated one, and the most fanatic one, too. During Aurangzeb's reign, similar policies must have been in force elsewhere in India having effective Muslim control.

Brutal Conversion in Kashmir

Violent and coercive conversion of the Hindus did not remain confined to the central Muslim power based in Delhi. It also spread to the provinces where Muslim rulers remained often independent and enforced the writ of Islam on the subjects as their pious duty. Kashmir will suffice as an example.

In the reign of Sikandar Butshikun (1389–1413), he and his prime minister, a Brahmin convert to Islam, teamed up to unleash harrowing persecution of Kashmiri Hindus. Sikandar, records Ferishtah, issued an order

> '*proscribing the residence of any other than Mahomedans in Kashmeer; and he required that no man should wear the mark on his forehead (as worn by Hindus)... Lastly, he insisted on all golden and silver images (idols) being broken and melted down, and the metal coined into money. Many of the bramins (Brahmins), rather than abandon their religion or their country, poisoned themselves; some emigrated from their native homes, while a few escaped the evil of banishment by becoming Mahomedans. After the emigration of the bramins, Sikundur (Sikandar)*

---

215. Sharma, p. 220

216. Ibid, p. 219–20

217. Bikaner Museum Archives, Exhibit No. 43

218. Ibid, Exhibit No. 40

*ordered all the temples in Kashmeer to be thrown down... Having broken all the images in Kashmeer, he acquired the title of the Iconoclast, **Destroyer of Idols**.*[219]

According to learned Ferishtah (d. 1614), this was the greatest deed of Sultan Sikandar.

Succeeding the Iconoclast, his son Ameer Khan (or Ally Shah)—guided by his father's fanatic prime minister—continued the butchery of remaining Hindus. They *'persecuted the few bramins who still remained firm in their religion; and by putting all to death, who refused to embrace Mahomedism. He drove those who still lingered in Kashmeer entirely out of that kingdom,'* adds Ferishtah.[220] Later on, in the reigns of Malik Raina and Kaji Chak, the Hindus were converted to Islam by the sword, often accompanied by their mass slaughter (described below). These historical records should leave one in no doubt about the measures that were instrumental in converting the masses of Indian infidels to Islam.

DECEPTIVE PROPAGANDA ABOUT CONVERSION

Voluntary conversion

Modern Islamic scholars and historians (also many non-Muslim ones) have created a thick smokescreen of myths surrounding the means by which Muslim population grew in medieval India and elsewhere. This myth is that the conquered infidels embraced Islam on their own accord, after they discovered Islam's message of peace and justice. The records of medieval Islamic historians, travelers, invaders and rulers prove such assertions thoroughly groundless. Chronicles of European travelers and courtiers on India, especially of the Mughal period, also concur with the records of Muslim historians. All those records suggest that the Hindus had nothing but disdain and resentment toward Muslims. The evidence for the conversion of non-Muslims to Islam, impressed by its message, is nonexistent. The most peaceful means of conversion of the Hindus recorded in medieval documents was the lure of ridding themselves of the crippling misery and wretched humiliation caused by the draconian *kharaj, jizyah* and other onerous taxes. Such coercive methods of conversion, solely to avoid an abominable alternative, can not be termed peaceful or voluntary. Voluntary conversion might have taken place, but only in rare instances—much overwhelmed by the violent, coercive ones.

Conversion of lower caste Hindus

Muslims in India make lofty claims that it is mostly the socially discriminated and oppressed lower caste Hindus who had converted to Islam because of its message of equality for all. However, the medieval Islamic chroniclers, who sometimes kept quite detailed records of the conversion, have left no references to the fact that the lower caste Hindus flocked to Islam in order to run away from oppression and tyranny of the upper caste Hindus. There might have been a higher proportion of conversion amongst lower caste Hindus, but for an entirely different reason. They were the poorest in the society and the crushing *kharaj, jizyah* and other taxes had naturally hit them the hardest. A closer look at the Muslim population in the subcontinent reveals that conversions had taken place across all levels of the society. The fact that some 70 percent of the Hindus in India still belong to lower castes negates the claim that they, impressed by Islam's superior message, had flocked to its banner in overwhelming numbers.

According to a recent study, commissioned by the Andhra Pradesh government, the forefathers of some 85 percent of Muslims today belonged to lower castes.[221] That means, if fertility remained the same amongst Muslims and Hindus, twice as many lower caste Hindus likely converted to Islam compared to the

---

219. Ferishtah MQHS (1829) *History of the Rise of the Mahomedan Power in India*, translated by John Briggs, D.K. Publishers Distributors (P) Ltd, New Delhi, Vol. IV (1997 imprint), p. 268
220. Ibid, p. 269
221. *85% of Muslims in India were SC, backward Hindus: Report*, Indian Express, 10 August 2008.

upper caste ones. It should be considered, however, that the lower caste Hindus, through persuasive preaching, converted to Buddhism and, to a good extent, to Christianity at high frequencies. If the same happened in conversion to Islam as well, the proportion of the lower caste people were obviously much higher in the past—probably as high as 80 percent of the Hindus in medieval India—when Islamic conversions took place. That means that the frequency of conversion to Islam was not that higher amongst lower caste Hindus than those of the upper caste. The somewhat higher frequency can be accounted for by the fact that Islamic imposition of grinding taxes affected the poorer lower caste Hindus more severely. In truth, when the Islamic invaders and rulers engaged in ceaseless campaigns over the centuries, in which they enslaved in tens to hundreds of thousands at the point of the sword and converted them to Islam, they had little time or concern to discriminate who belong to the lower caste and who didn't.

Historically, Muslims took little interest in finding out which section of the people were converting to Islam. It is some Europeans, who, based on some isolated incidents, first created the hype that the lower caste Hindus converted to Islam to escape oppression of the Hindu society. Thereafter, Muslim scholars, stung by the charges of forced conversion, have jumped on the opportunity to emphasize the peaceful voluntary conversion of low caste Hindus to Islam in large numbers in India. Khondkar Fazl-i Rabbi, diwan to the Nawab of Murshidabad, claimed in the 1890s that lower class Hindus such as weavers and washermen had accepted Islam in Bengal. He, however, emphasized that such converts formed a small minority of the Muslim populace.[222]

It is important to note that, throughout the entire period of Muslim rule, the lower caste Hindus and Sikhs joined the resistance and rebellion against Muslim rulers in large numbers; in many cases, it was the lower caste Hindus, who led the revolts. A few examples will be given here. Khusrau Khan, an enslaved and castrated Hindu convert to Islam, got his patron Sultan Kutbuddin Mubarak Khilji killed in 1320 and wiped out the sultan's leading Muslim officers. Khusrau Khan had allied with 20,000 Bewari Hindus (also called *Parwari* by some authors) from Gujarat.[223] Their aim was to wipe out Islam from the Delhi seat of power. According to Ziauddin Barani, '*In the course of four or five days, preparations were made for idol worship in the palace*' and '*Copies of the Holy book (Quran) were used as seats, and idols were set up in the pulpits of the mosques.*'[224] Medieval chroniclers Ziauddin Barani, Amir Khusrau and Ibn Battutah recognize the Bewaris as low caste Hindus having '*bravery and readiness to lay down their lives for their masters.*'[225]

The lower caste Hindus took up arms in large numbers even against liberal and more equitable Akbar the Great. It is noted already that, in Akbar's attack of Chittor in 1568, some 40,000 peasants—the lower caste Hindus—fought on the side of 8,000 Rajputs. They had put up such an obstinate resistance that enraged Akbar, abandoning his general measure of dealing with captives, ordered the massacre of the 30,000 surrendered peasants. Similarly, Shivaji (d. 1680), who had founded the Maratha Kingdom, defying Aurangzeb, was a low caste Hindu (see Chapter VI, Section: *Tolerance & chivalry of Hindu rulers during Muslim period*). The Marathas, who were low caste Hindu peasants, kept the resistance up until 1761; Ahmad Shah Abdali came from Afghanistan to decimate them in the *Third Battle of Panipat*. The low caste Hindus of all kinds all over India—Bewaris, Marathas, Jats, Khokhars, Gonds, Bhils, Satnamis, Reddis and others—kept fighting the Muslim invaders from the beginning to the last days of Islamic domination. The Khokhar peasants (or Gukkurs)—who, according to Ferishtah, '*were a race of wild barbarians, without either religion or morality*'[226]—offered the strongest of resistance to Sultan Muhammad Ghauri, such as in Multan. Multan was conquered by Qasim in 715. Five centuries after Islam was brought to Multan, the Khokhar peasants, not impressed by its message, took up arms against Sultan Ghauri. The sultan returned to crush the Khokhars, in

222. Rabbi KF (1895) *The Origins of the Musalmans of Bengal*, Calcutta, p. 113
223. Farishtah, Vol. I, p. 224
224. Elliot & Dawson, Vol. III, p. 224
225. Lal KS (1995) *Growth of Scheduled Tribes and Castes in Medieval India*, Aditya Prakashan, New Delhi, p. 73
226. Ferishtah, Vol. I, p. 104

which, records Ibn Asir, '*he defeated the rebels, and made their blood flow in streams.*'[227] However, Khokhars eventually secured the assassination of Sultan Ghauri in 1206 in a war camp. Twenty Khokhars, who had lost their relations to Ghauri's attack, entered the sultan's tent in a daring sally and dispatched him with daggers.[228] More than two centuries later, in Yahya bin Ahmad's *Tarikh-I Mubarak-Shahi*, we come across one Jasrath Shaika Khokhar, who turned to be the most inveterate infidel enemy of the Muslim rulers (1420–30s).

Indeed, it is often the higher caste Hindus fought on the Muslim side against the rebellious lower caste Hindus. For example, after Aurangzeb moved his capital to the South, Jat peasants in the North rose in rebellion. They started attacking the caravans carrying merchandise, revenues and provision headed to the Royal Court in the South. Aurangzeb sent a royal army, consisting of upper caste Rajput and Muslim soldiers, to attack and put an end to the Jat rebels. After a long siege, the fort of the Jats at Sinsani (in Rajasthan) was stormed in January 1690, but with heavy casualties on both sides. Some 1,500 Jats lost their lives, while 200 Mughals and 700 Rajputs were slain or wounded on the imperial side.[229] It is, therefore, thoroughly groundless to claim that the lower caste Hindus happily embraced Islam to free themselves from the upper caste Hindu oppression.

The most extensive conversion to Islam has taken place amongst Buddhists. At the time of Islam's invasion of India, Buddhism was dominant in Northwest (today's Pakistan, Afghanistan etc.) and Eastern (e.g., Bengal) India. Buddhism has been wiped out almost completely in both regions. In Bengal, as high as 60 percent of the people had converted to Islam during the Muslim rule. An overwhelming majority of those, who retained their pre-Islamic faiths, were not Buddhist but Hindu, mostly belonging to low castes. There is no caste system or caste tyranny in Buddhism; it is, undoubtedly, more egalitarian and peaceful than Islam. What then had prompted their conversion to Islam? And why Islam failed to convert the great multitude of the low-caste Hindus of Bengal, the ones oppressed by the upper-caste Hindu tyranny!

Peaceful conversion by Sufis

Another lofty claim of mythic proportion being perpetuated about conversion to Islam is that a heterodox variety of Muslims, namely the Sufis, had propagated Islam through peaceful missionary activity. British historian Thomas Arnold (1864–1930)—desperate to alter the centuries-old European discourse of Islam as a violent faith—initiated this propaganda in the 1890s, which has been embraced by numerous Muslim and non-Muslim historians and scholars. As summarized by Peter Hardy, the following instances led Arnold to his conclusion:

> …in 1878, a settlement report for the Montgomery district in the Panjab quoted Lieutenant Elphistone as follows: '*It [the town of Pakpattan] contains the tomb of the celebrated saint and martyr Baba Farid, who converted a great part of the Southern Punjab to Muhammadanism, and whose miracles entitle him to a most distinguished place among the pirs (Sufi saints) of that religion.*' The settlement report for the Jhang district makes similar claims for Shaykh Farid al-Din. In the Punjab Census report of 1881, Ibbeston adds the name of Bana al-Huq of Multan to that of Baba Fraid as the two saints to whom '*the people of western plains very generally attribute their conversion.*' The Bombay Gazetteer for the Cutch, published in 1880, ascribes the conversion of the Cutchi Memons to witnessing the miracles of one Sayyid Yusu al-Din a descendent of Sayyid Abd al-Qadir Jilani. Elsewhere in the Bombay Presidency, Sayyid Muhammad Gesu Daraz is said to have converted Hindu weavers to Islam. In the North-Western Provinces, data in an Azamgarh settlement report, collected in 1868, included a tradition among Muslim *zaminders* of the district that "the teaching of some Moslem saint" had been responsible

---

227. Elliot & Dawson, Vol. II, p. 297–98
228. Ibid, p. 233–36; Ferishtah, Vol. I, p. 105
229. Lal (1995), p. 90

for their ancestor's conversion to Islam. In Bada'un, Shaykh Jalal al-Din Tabrizi, who later went to Bengal, is said with one look to have converted a Hindu milkman. It was from this and much other material that Arnold reached his conclusion that vast number of Indian Muslims are descendent of converts in whose conversion force played no part and in which only the teaching and persuasion of peaceful missionaries were at work.[230]

The major reference, on which Arnold based his conclusion that peaceful conversion by Sufis played major role in conversion to Islam, was a generic reference in the 1884 *Bombay Gazetteer* that Sufi saint Ma'bari Khandayat (*Pir* Ma'bari) came to the Deccan in about 1305 as a missionary and converted a large number of Jains to Islam.[231] This document gives no specifics on the means *Pir* Ma'bari employed in his conversion; the same applies to other claims (these claims are often unsubstantiated and legendary in nature) cited above. However, older documentation on *Pir* Ma'bari by Muslim chroniclers, as studied by historian Richard Eaton, reveals the measures *Pir* Ma'bari had applied in converting the infidels. According to Muhammad Ibrahim Zubairi's *Rauzat al-Auliya* (1825–26), *Pir* Ma'bari Khandayat came to the Deccan as a holy warrior:

> 'During the period of Ala al-Din Khalaji (Alauddin Khilji, d. 1316), the Shah of Delhi, he (*Pir* Ma'bari) accompanied the camp of the army of Islam in the year A.H. 710 (A.D. 1310–11) when buried treasures of gold and silver came to the hands of Muslims and the victory of Islam was effected.'[232]

A hagiographic record adds:

> '(*Pir* Ma'bari) came here and waged Jihad against the rajas and rebels (of Bijapur). And with his iron bar, he broke the heads and necks of many rajas and drove them to the dust of defeat. Many idolaters, who by the will of God had guidance and blessings, repented from their unbelief and error, and by the hands of (*Pir* Ma'bari) came to Islam.'[233]

Another tradition says that *Pir* Ma'bari had expelled a group of Brahmins from their village in Bijapur. Muslim literatures portray *Pir* Ma'bari as a fierce wager of Jihad against the infidels wielding an *iron bar*. This gave him his last name, *Khandayat*—literally meaning *blunted bar*.

Eaton has particularly become an influential propagator of the paradigm that Islam was spread peacefully by the Sufis. He says that Islam came to areas, where Muslim powers could not reach, *'with the appearance of anonymous, itinerant holy men whom the local population might associate with miraculous power.'* Eaton then goes on to describe a popular Muslim folk-story in Bengal that a Muslim *pir* with occult power appeared in a village, built a mosque, healed sick people with his miraculous power and his fame spread far and wide. Thereupon, hundreds of people came to visit him with *'presents of rice, fruits and other delicious food, goat, chickens and fowls,'* which he never touched but distributed among the poor. *'This humane quality of the Sufis,'* asserts Eaton, made the mosque a centre of Islam from where it reached far and wide.[234]

One intriguing thing about Eaton is that his own research of the medieval literatures on Indian Sufis for his Ph.D. thesis, published in *Sufis of Bijapur 1300–1700*, failed to find any trace of peace in the views and actions of Sufis and in their method of conversion. He found that all the revered Sufis, particularly the earlier ones to arrive at Bijapur, were fierce Jihadis and persecutor of Hindus; an example, that of *Pir* Ma'bari, is cited above. His research outcome was so damning to his tendentious, love-stricken views about the Sufis that

---

230. Hardy P (1979) *Modern European and Muslim Explanations of Conversion to Islam in South Asia: A Preliminary Survey*, In N. Levtzion ed., p. 85

231. Arnold, p. 271

232. Eaton RM (1978) *Sufis of Bijapur 1300-1700*, Princeton University Press, p. 28

233. Ibid, p. 30

234. Eaton RM (2000) *Essays on Islam and Indian History*, Oxford University Press, New Delhi, p. 32

Muslims in India protested against his book leading to its ban in India. But Eaton would not stop spreading his fallacious and unfounded views about Sufis.

For a rational person, the stories of spiritual and occult power of Sufis are nothing but fantastical myths. Such legends, upon thorough research, have indeed been found, according to Prof. Muhammad Habib, to be "latter day fabrication" (see below). Concerning conversion, historical records and circumstantial evidence lend little support to the paradigm that Sufis made great contribution in converting the infidels to Islam peacefully. In India, no historical documents mention that the Sufis converted the Hindus and other infidels to Islam in large numbers through *peaceful* means. The great liberal Sufi scholar Amir Khasrau (fourteenth century) mentions in his chronicles many incidents of enslavement of the infidels by Muslim rulers in large numbers for their conversion, but makes no mention of any incidence of peaceful preaching by a Sufi saint that drew the Hindus to Islam in significant numbers. The ideology of Indian Sufis and their involvement in the conversion of the infidels will be dealt here in some detail.

Origin of Sufism: Allah made Jihad a binding duty for Muslims whereby they must keep fighting until Islam—the perfect, universal guidance to human life—becomes the sole religion in the world [Quran 2:193]. Allah has purchased the life of believers, who must devote to His command and engage in Jihad—and slay and be slain in the process—in order to gain Paradise [Quran 9:111]. Allah blesses those who get slain in Jihad, the martyrs, with straight landing in Paradise: '*And say not of those who are slain in the way of Allah: They are dead. Nay, they are living, though ye perceive (it) not*' [Quran 2:154]. Allah encouraged Muslims to renounce their kindred relationships with '*fathers, and your sons, and your brethren, and your wives, and your tribe*', plus the allure of earthly indulgence and pleasures for single-mindedly "striving in Allah's way" [Quran 9:24].

Prophet Muhammad acted upon these commands of Allah in the course of founding his new creed: his followers dedicated themselves to the cause of Allah—to prayers and fasting etc. and more prominently, to Jihad—for making Islam the only religion on the earth. After relocating to Medina, where the doctrine of Jihad was revealed by Allah, Prophet Muhammad and his militant community engaged prominently in aggressive and violent Jihad, comprising plundering raids and wars against the infidels, for founding the nascent Islamic state and lived almost solely on the spoils they captured. Martyrdom gained while fighting Jihad, decreed Allah [Quran 2:154], was the surest means of gaining access to Paradise: the central aim of Muslims' every action in this life. Therefore, those who died in those holy wars had the best of fortune: that is, they became martyrs earning a direct ticket to Islamic Paradise.

During early years and decades of Islam, the inspiration to embrace martyrdom drew large numbers of recruits to the profession of Jihad. For securing a place in Islam's sensual Paradise—filled with black-eyed and full-breasted celestial virgins for serving sex to the blessed [Quran 44:51–54, 78:31–33]—through martyrdom, these Jihadis renounced kindred and social bonds and earthly indulgence to devote themselves solely to Allah's cause. Their lifestyle became somewhat "ascetic"—devoid of social intercourse and dedicated to prayers, and prominently, to opportunities for engaging in Jihad for gaining martyrdom. This was roughly the mode of the early Islamic vision of life, which Prophet Muhammad had instilled, with the sanctions of Allah, amongst his pious followers.

During early Islam, particularly in the days of Prophet Muhammad, all male Muslims of fighting-age and in good physical condition were supposed to participate in Jihad campaigns. As the Islamic state quickly expanded and became more organized, the state began recruiting the Jihadis as regular soldiers putting them on the state-payroll. Still others, inspired solely by the spirit of Jihad for achieving martyrdom and Paradise, dedicated themselves as volunteers for fighting in Allah's cause. These volunteer Jihadis, variously described as *enthusiasts* or *adventurers*, used to engage in Jihad when opportunities for war against the infidels arose. They were paid, not from state treasury, but from the *zakat* fund—meant solely for the religious cause. The share of the sacred booty also became a part of their livelihood.

After Muhammad bin Qasim opened up a new frontier for Jihadi conquests in Northwest India with his 6,000 Arab soldiers, "adventurers, eager for plunder and proselytism", streamed into Sindh from Muslim lands swelling Qasim's army.[235] The desire for martyrdom was so strong amongst devout Muslims that they were willing to travel hundreds of miles to foreign lands to engage in Jihadi wars. '*It was for this reason,*' writes Daniel Pipes, '*that about 20,000 volunteers traveled 1,000 miles in 965, from Iran to Syria, for the opportunity to fight Byzantium.*' The Ottoman conquerors drew Muslim warriors from far-off Muslim lands flocking to engage in Jihad against Christians in the Balkan.[236]

After the initial surge, the Jihad expeditions became relatively infrequent. The surviving volunteers, called *Ghazis*—dedicated to Allah and an ascetic life—took abodes in forts or fortified lines at the frontiers, called *ribat* (pickets), hoping that opportunities for martyrdom operations against infidel territories across the frontier would arise. New volunteers, seeking martyrdom, continued to be attracted to this relatively idle band of *Ghazis*. They continued to exist along with the *ribat* in Andalusia (Spain) until the fourteenth century.[237]

The *Ghazis*—also known as *Murabits,* roughly meaning "mounted frontiersmen"—waited in those militant recluses, ready to respond to the call of Jihad, sometimes for a very long time. With fewer engagements in Jihad and away from their families and society, they increasingly got accustomed to an isolated, somewhat monastic, life. The life of some of them became increasingly idle, sedentary and nonviolent. Devoted to Allah and renounced worldly indulgence, their mode of life slowly transformed into a more nonviolent and sex-starved one, similar to that in Christian and Buddhist monasteries. In time, these Jihadi frontier recluses became transformed into ascetic *ashrams*, as notes Sir Hamilton Gibb, '*it (ribat) was associated with the rise of the ascetic and mystical movement within Islam (i.e., Sufism)... Later on, Jihad was interpreted to apply to the inward and spiritual struggle against the temptations of the world.*'[238]

Certain elements from within *ribats* started professing a quietist and nonviolent vision of life, which, they had become increasingly accustomed to. They started preaching withdrawal from the society, and avoidance of luxury and ostentation of which, writes Umaruddin, '*Their object was the avoidance of every indulgence which entangled the soul and prevented its development.*'[239] In time, the followers of this quietist doctrine became known as Sufis, who withdrew from warfare; the *ribat* was now ascetic hermitage, convent or hospice for the devotees to congregate for living the religious life.[240] According to Benjamin Walker,

> Many Sufi orders were established on monastic principles and eminent Sufis wrote in praise of poverty, and extolled the ideal of the beggars (fakirs) and the religious mendicants (dervishes). A small number voluntarily embraced such a way of life, giving up the delights of the world—wealth, fame, feasts, women and companionship—and seeking instead penury, anonymity, hunger, celibacy and solitude—even welcoming abuse and disgrace as a means of strengthening the spirit by remaining indifferent to censure and ridicule.[241]

The precursor of Sufism was therefore rooted in militant Islamic orthodoxy. It arose, notes Umaruddin, also as a reaction '*against intellectualism of the rationalist and the philosopher, the ungodly ways of the ruling classes.*'[242] The Abbasid rulers had pushed the Arab (Islamic) cultures into the background and adopted the

---

235. Elliot & Dawson, Vol. I, p. 435
236. Pipes (1983), p. 69
237. Gibb, p. 33
238. Ibid
239. Umaruddin, p. 61
240. Gibb, p. 33–34
241. Walker, p. 305
242. Umaruddin, p. 58–59

jahiliyah ways and manners of the pre-Islamic Persian civilization (superseded by Islam), *'which encouraged laxity in morality.'* The philosophers, on the contrary, *'believed in the infallibility of Plato and Aristotle'*—not of the prophets. To counter these tendencies, adds Umaruddin, arose the *'doctrines of Sufism and its rules of conduct were based on the Quran and the lives of the Prophet and his companions.'*

According to Umaruddin, in the early *'stage of development, Sufism was not very different from Islam (i.e., orthodox Islam). In their doctrine, they emphasized some truths of Islam (more),'*[243] whilst paying less attention to others. Later on, some stream of Sufis became dramatically transformed and opposed to the rigid formality of orthodox Islam, which had become a set of outward rituals and ceremonies, hardly fulfilling the spiritual need of the soul. They deviated from the original orthodox path and considered the outward ritualism of Sharia regulations *'as the lowest scales of a person's spiritual evolution. The life and disciplines of a Sufi are designed to lead one on a mystical journey through progressive stages from law to liberation, from orthodoxy to illumination, from knowledge of self to the extinction (fana) of selfhood in the Godhead.'*[244] Slowly there opened floodgate of numerous innovation and compromise in Sufi doctrines, some of which amounted to heresy, irreverence, and the breach of Islam. In time, some deviant Sufis reached the un-Islamic doctrine of pantheism, which unifies the Creator with man and all creations into a single entity. In classical Islamic sense, pantheism is a sacrilegious doctrine—professing self-absorption, self-effacement, self-annihilation—which allegedly leads to confluence of the individual with God. At this stage of development, they do not require a guide (i.e., a prophet) or law-book (i.e., the Quran). They give up almost all rituals required in orthodox Islam and the Sharia: fasting, prayers, Hajj pilgrimage and so on. In Islamic society, they became identified as *bisharia*—i.e. outside the Sharia or Islam.

Imam Ghazzali (d. 1111), who made the Sufism into acceptable in the mainstream Islamic society, wrote of the aim of a Sufi that,

> 'The Sufis endeavored to emulate each and every aspect of the Prophet's life. The retirement of the Prophet to the cave of Hira for meditation for a certain period of time every year, set an example to the Sufis to retire from society. The practice of ecstasy and self-annihilation was founded on the Prophet's habit of absorption into prayers. The ascetic aspects of Sufism are based on the simplicity of the life followed by the Prophet... He washed his clothes, repaired his shoes, milked his goats, and never on any occasion did he take his fill.'[245]

Indian Sufis: Although some Sufis deviated completely from Islam, majority of them remained largely orthodox. Ghazzali enabled Sufism triumph in Muslim societies in the twelfth century. He basically weaved the Islamic orthodoxy into the body of Sufism, expunging deviant ideas and rituals, which made Sufism more acceptable amongst Muslims. Therefore, it is the orthodox strain of Sufism that got acceptance in the Muslim society, thanks to Imam Ghazzali. The deviant *beshariyah* Sufis often suffered brutal persecution and even death. For example, Sultan Firoz Shah Tughlaq (d. 1388), an austere orthodox believer, records in his memoir that he had put Sufi Shaykh Ruknuddin of Delhi, who called himself a *Mahdi* (messiah) and *'led people astray into mystic practices and perverted ideas by maintaining that he was Ruknuddin, the prophet of God.'* People killed Ruknuddin and some of his followers; they *'tore him into pieces and broke his bones into fragments,'* records the Sultan.[246]

When the central Asian Turks established direct Muslim rule in India (1206), Sufism, the Ghazzalian orthodox Sufism to be accurate, had gained wide acceptance in Muslim societies. Following the trail of Muslim invaders, Sufis poured into India in large number. The great Sufi saints of India—namely

---

243. Ibid, p. 62

244. Walker, p. 304

245. Umaruddin, p. 59–60

246. Elliot & Dawson, Vol. III, p. 378–79

Nizamuddin Auliya, Amir Khasrau, Nasiruddin Chiragh, Khwaja Moinuddin Chisti and Jalaluddin *et al.*—held rather orthodox and intolerant views. They held the *Ulema*, the orthodox scholars of Islam, in great esteem and advised their disciples to follow their rulings in religious laws and social behavior. Influenced by the unorthodox, controversial doctrines and practices of famous Arab-Spanish Sufi ideologue Ibn Arabi (d. 1240), Moinuddin Chisti and Nizamuddin Auliya were the most unorthodox and liberal amongst India's Sufis. Annoying the orthodox, they had adopted musical sessions (*sama*) and dancing (*raqs*) in their rituals. However, when it came to the real question of Islam, they never took a stand against classical orthodoxy; they always put the *Ulema* ahead of them in religious matters. To the question of whether dancing and playing of musical instruments, as had been adopted by Sufi dervishes, were permissible, Auliya said, *"What is forbidden by Law (Sharia) is not acceptable."* On the question of whether the controversial Sufi devotional practices were permissible or not, he said, *"Concerning this controversy at present, whatever the judge (orthodox Ulema) decrees will be upheld."*[247]

The Sufis of India had no contradiction with the *Ulema*; both had a common goal—the interest of Islam, but to be achieved through different methods. Auliya used to say, '*What the Ulema seek to achieve through speech, we achieve by our behavior.*' Jamal Qiwamu'd-din, a long-time associate of Auliya, never saw him miss a single *Sunnah* of the Prophet.[248] Other prominent Sufis held even more orthodox views. The great Sufi saint Nasiruddin Chiragh, for example, purged and purified deviant aspects of the Sufi practices. According to Prof. KA Nizami, he prohibited all deviant (from Sharia) rituals and practices that had entered the Sufi community, saying, *"Whatever Allah and His Prophet have ordered, do it and whatever Allah and His Prophet have forbidden you against, you should not do."* Nizami adds: '*He brought Sufi institution in harmony with Sunnah. Wherever there was a slightest clash, he proclaimed the supremacy of the Sharia Laws.*'[249]

Views of Sufis: In this section, the views of prominent Sufis, particularly of India, on infidels and the violent Islamic doctrines, such as Jihad, will be summarized in order to understand their mind and ideology. Ghazzali, the greatest Sufi ideologue, held rather orthodox and violent views on Jihad. He advised fellow Muslims that,

> '...one must go on Jihad at least once a year... One may use a catapult against them when they are in a fortress, even if among them are women and children. One may set fire on them and/or drown them... One may cut down their trees... One must destroy their useful book (Bible, Torah etc.). Jihadists may take as booty whatever they decide...'[250]

About the protocol of the payment of *jizyah* in humiliation by a *dhimmi*, he wrote:

> '...the Jews, Christians and the Majians must pay the *jizyah*... On offering up the *jizyah*, the *dhimmi* must hang his head while the official takes hold of his beard and hits on the protuberant bone beneath his ear.'

He follows it up with prescribing a number of standard disabilities for *dhimmis* as enshrined in the Sharia and the *Pact of Omar*. He wrote:

> 'They are not permitted to ostensibly display their wine or church bell... their houses may not be higher than the Muslim's, no matter how low that is. The *dhimmi* may not ride an elegant horse

247. Sharma, p. 226
248. Nizami KA (1991a) *The Life and Times of Shaikh Nizamuddin Auliya*, New Delhi, p. 138
249. Nizami KA (1991b) *The Life and Times of Shaikh Nasiruddin Chiragh-I Delhi*, New Delhi, p. 100,103
250. Bostom, p. 199

or mule; he may ride a donkey only if the saddle is of wood. He may not walk on the good part of the road. They have to wear patches... and even in the public bath, they must hold their tongues...'[251]

The prominent Indian Sufis did not leave behind a comprehensive commentary about their ideas of non-Muslims or on issues, like Jihad. However, their isolated comments on such issues, whenever opportunities arose, give a good deal of idea about their views on these subjects. In general, their views on the infidels and Jihad were of the mould of Ghazzali, the greatest Sufi master.

Nizamuddin Auliya (1238–1325), toeing the orthodox line, condemned the Hindus to the fire of hell, saying: '*The unbelievers at the time of death will experience punishment. At that moment, they will profess belief (Islam) but it will not be reckoned to them as belief because it will not be faith in the Unseen... the faith of (an) unbeliever at death remains unacceptable.*' He asserted that '*On the day of Resurrection when unbelievers will face punishment and affliction, they will embrace faith but faith will not benefit them... They will also go to Hell, despite the fact that they will go there as believers.*'[252] In his *khutba* (sermon), Nizamuddin Auliya condemned the infidels as wicked, saying, '*He (Allah) has created Paradise and Hell for believers and the infidels (respectively) in order to repay the wicked for what they have done.*'[253]

Auliya's thought on Jihad against non-Muslims can be gleaned from his statement that *Surah Fatihah*, first chapter of the Quran, did not contain two of the ten cardinal articles of Islam, which were "***warring with the unbelievers*** *and observing the divine statutes...*" He did not only believe in warring with the unbelievers or Jihad, he came to India with his followers to engage in it. He participated in a holy war commanded by Nasiruddin Qibacha in Multan. When Qibacha's army was in distress facing defeat, Auliya rushed to him and gave him a magical arrow instructing: "*Shoot this arrow at the direction of the infidel army.*' ...*Qibacha did as he was told, and when daybreak came not one of the infidels was to be seen; they all had fled!*'[254] When Qazi Mughisuddin inquired about the prospect of victory in the Jihad launched in South India under the command of Malik Kafur, the Auliya uttered in effusive confidence: '*What is this victory? I am waiting for further victories.*'[255] The Auliya used to accept large gifts sent by Sultan Alauddin from the spoils plundered in Jihad expeditions and proudly displayed those at his *khanqah* (lodge).[256]

Khwaja Moinuddin Chisti (1141–1230), probably the second-greatest Sufi saint of India after Nizamuddin Auliya, demonstrated a deep-seated hatred toward Hindu religion and its practices. On his arrival near the Anasagar Lake at Ajmer, he saw many idol-temples and promised to raze them to the ground with the help of Allah and His Prophet. After settling down there, Khwaja's followers used to bring every day a cow (sacred to Hindus) near a famous temple, where the king and Hindus prayed, slaughter it and cook kebab from its meat—clearly to show his contempt toward Hinduism. '*In order to prove the majesty of Islam, he is said to have dried the two holy lakes of Anasagar and Pansela (holy to Hindus) by the heat of his spiritual power.*'[257] Chisti also came to India with his disciples to fight Jihad against the infidels and participated in the treacherous holy war of Sultan Muhammad Ghauri in which the kind and chivalrous Hindu King Prithviraj

---

251. Ibid

252. Sharma, p. 228–29

253. Nizami (1991a), p. 185

254. Ibid, p. 232

255. Ibid

256. Sharma, p. 200

257. Ibid, p. 230

Chauhan was defeated in Ajmer. In his Jihadi zeal, Chisti ascribed the credit for the victory to himself, saying: '*We have seized Pithaura (Prithviraj) alive and handed him over to the army of Islam.*''[258]

Amir Khasrau (1253–1325), Shaykh Nizamuddin Auliya's exalted disciple, is lauded as the greatest liberal Sufi poet of medieval India. His coming to India, deem many modern historians, as a blessing for the subcontinent. He had the good fortune of working at the royal court of three successive sultans. Regarded as one of India's greatest poets, he is also credited with being a great contributor to Indian classical music and the creator of *Qawwali* (Sufi devotional music). The invention of the *Tabla* (an Indian drum) is usually attributed to him.

There is little doubt about Amir Khasrau's achievements in music and poetry. But when it came to the fallen infidels and their religion, his bigoted Islamic zeal was very much evident. In describing Muslim victories against the Hindu kings, he mocks their religious traditions, such as "tree" and "stone-idol" worship. Mocking the stone-idols, destroyed by Muslim warriors, he wrote: '*Praise be to God for his exaltation of the religion of Muhammad. It is not to be doubted that stones are worshipped by the Gabrs (derogatory slang for idolaters), but as stones did no service to them, they only bore to heaven the futility of that worship.*'[259]

Amir Khasrau showed delight in describing the barbaric slaughter of Hindu captives by Muslim warriors. Describing Khizr Khan's order to massacre 30,000 Hindus in the conquest of Chittor in 1303, he gloated: '*Praise be to God! That he so ordered the massacre of all chiefs of Hind out of the pale of Islam, by his infidel-smiting swords... in the name of this Khalifa of God, that heterodoxy has no rights (in India).*'[260] He took poetic delight in describing Malik Kafur's destruction of a famous Hindu temple in South India and the grisly slaughter of the Hindus and their priests therein.[261] In describing the slaughter, he wrote, '*...the heads of brahmans and idolaters danced from their necks and fell to the ground at their feet, and **blood flowed in torrents**.*' In his bigoted delight at the miserable subjugation of Hindus and the barbarous triumph of Islam in India, he wrote:

> The whole country, by means of the sword of our holy warriors, has become like a forest denuded of its thorns by fire? Islam is triumphant, idolatry is subdued. Had not the Law granted exemption from death by the payment of poll-tax, the very name of Hind, root and branch, would have been extinguished.[262]

Amir Khasrau described many instances of barbaric cruelty, often of catastrophic proportions, inflicted by Muslim conquerors upon the Hindus. But nowhere did he show any sign of grief or remorse, but only gloating delight. While describing those acts of barbarism, he invariably expressed gratitude to Allah, and glory to Muhammad, for enabling the Muslim warriors achieve those glorious feats.

Other Sufis: Another great Sufi saint to come to India was Shaykh Makhdum Jalal ad-Din bin Mohammed, popularly known as Hazrat Shah Jalal, who had settled in Sylhet, Bengal (discussed later). Apart from these highly revered Sufi saints, there were other great Sufi personalities, namely Shaykh Bahauddin Zakaria, Shaykh Nuruddin Mubarak Ghaznavi, Shaykh Ahmad Sirhindi and Shaykh Shah Walliullah *et al.*, who have often been condemned by some modern historians for their relatively orthodox views. For example, Shaykh Mubarak Ghaznavi—a great Islamic scholar and Sufi saint of the Suhrawardi order—had utter disrespect and violent hatred of non-Muslims (*kafirs*) and their religion, as he reminded the sultans that ''*Kings will not be able to discharge their duty of protecting the Faith unless they overthrow and uproot kufr and kafiri (infidelity), shirk (associating partners to God, polytheism) and the worship of idols, all for the*

---

258. Ibid

259. Elliot & Dawson, Vol. III, p. 81–83

260. Ibid, p. 77

261. Ibid, p. 91

262. Ibid, p. 545–46

sake of Allah and inspired by a sense of honor for protecting the din of the Prophet of God.''[263] However, in case of an impossible situation, he advised, ''*...if total extirpation of idolatry is not possible owing to the firm roots of kufr and the large number of kafirs and mushriks, the kings should at least strive to disgrace, dishonor and defame the mushriks and idol-worshipping Hindus, who are the worst enemies of God and His Prophet.*''[264]

Although condemned by modern historians, these Sufi saints were highly popular in their days, respected by the *Ulema* and especially in ruling circles, thereby wielding critical influence on the formulation of state-policies. Sufi masters Bahauddin Zakaria and Nuruddin Mubarak held the highest Islamic epithet— the *Shaykh al-Islam*, normally bestowed upon the most learned scholars of Islam. Without going into further detail of the views of those popular but more orthodox Sufis, let us now examine the role, Sufis played, in the propagation of Islam.

Sufis in the propagation of Islam: Sufis have been credited with converting large masses of infidels to Islam through peaceful missionary activity. But this claim comes with little supporting evidence. Two points must be taken into consideration beforehand in this discussion. First, Sufis became an organized and accepted community in the thirteenth and early fourteenth century. By this time, the peoples of the Middle East, Persia, Egypt and North Africa had become largely Muslim. The Sufis could not have played significant roles in their conversion. In agreement, says Francis Robinson, Sufis played a leading part in '*the remarkable spread of Islam from the thirteenth century onwards.*'[265] Second, the Sufis almost invariably needed the power and terror of the sword to create the dominance of Islam first before their alleged peaceful mission of propagating Islam could proceed.

The attitude and mindset of the greatest Sufi saints of medieval India, discussed above, were hardly different from those of the orthodox, who advocated for the use of unconditional force in accordance with the Quran, the *Sunnah* and the *Sharia* for converting the infidels. The famous Sufis of India invariably supported violent Jihad for making Islam victorious. India's greatest Sufi saints—Nizamuddin Auliya and Moinuddin Chisti—themselves came to India to participate in holy war against the infidels, which they both did. Auliya had also sent forth Shaykh Shah Jalal, the greatest Sufi saint of Bengal, with 360 disciples to take part in a holy war against King Gaur Govinda of Sylhet (see below). The renowned Sufis of Bijapur also came there as holy warriors for slaughtering the infidels and establishing Islamic rule (noted already).

Conversion by Sufis in Bengal: The claim that Sufis *peacefully* converted the non-Muslims to Islam in large numbers is not supported by historical records. Furthermore, most Sufis were intolerant, of violent Jihadi mindset, and even, were themselves Jihadis. While discussing these issues in a friendly conversation with two learned secular Bangladeshi scholars, they informed me that, at least in Bangladesh, Sufis had propagated Islam through *peaceful* means. This agrees with Nehemia Levtzion's assertion that '*Sufis were particularly important in achieving the almost total conversion in eastern Bengal.*'[266]

An investigation of two greatest Sufi saints of Bengal outlined below will give us an inkling of the roles Sufis played in the proselytization and how peaceful it was. Two Jalaluddins, Shaykh Jalaluddin Tabrizi (d. 1226 or 1244) and Shaykh Shah Jalal (d. 1347), were the greatest Sufi saints of Bengal. Shaykh Jalaluddin Tabrizi came to Bengal after Bakhtiyar Khilji conquered Bengal defeating the Hindu King Lakshman Sena in 1205. He settled in Devtala near Pandua (Maldah, West Bengal). He is said to have "converted large number of *Kafirs*" to Islam but the method of his conversions is unknown. According to Syed Athar Abbas Rizvi, '*a kafir (Hindu or Buddhist) had erected a large temple and a well (at Devtala). The Shaikh demolished the*

263. Ibid, p. 179
264. bid, p. 183
265. Robinson F (2000) *Islam and Muslim History in South Asia*, Oxford University Press, New Delhi, p. 31–32
266. Levtzion N (1979) *Toward a Comparative Study of Islamization*, in *Conversion to Islam*, p. 18

temple and constructed a takiya (khanqah)...'[267] This will give one a good deal of idea about the kind of means this great Sufi saint had employed in converting the *kafirs* to Islam.[268]

Shaykh Shah Jalal, the other great Sufi saint of Bengal, had settled in Sylhet. He is regarded as a national hero by Bangladeshi Muslims. Shah Jalal and his disciples are credited with converting a large majority of Bengalis to Islam through *truly* peaceful means.

When Shah Jalal came to settle in Sylhet in East Bengal (now Bangladesh), it was ruled by a Hindu king, named Gaur Govinda. Before his arrival in Bengal, Sultan Shamsuddin Firuz Shah of Gaur had twice attacked Gaur Govinda; these campaigns were led by his nephew, Sikandar Khan Ghazi. On both occasions, the Muslim invaders were defeated.[269] The third assault against Gaur Govinda was commanded by the sultan's Chief General Nasiruddin. Shaykh Nizamuddin Auliya sent forth his illustrious disciple Shah Jalal with 360 followers to participate in this Jihad campaign. Shah Jalal reached Bengal with his followers and joined the Muslim army. In the fierce battle that ensued, King Gaur Govinda was defeated.[270] According to traditional stories, the credit for the Muslim victory goes to Shah Jalal and his disciples.

As a general rule, every victory in Muslim campaigns brought a great many slaves, often tens to hundreds of thousand, who involuntarily became Muslim. Undoubtedly, on the very first day of Shah Jalal's arrival in Sylhet, he helped conversion of a large number of *kafirs* by means of their enslavement at the point of the sword—a very *peaceful means* of propagating Islam indeed! Ibn Battutah, who paid a visit to Shah Jalal in Sylhet, records that his effort was instrumental in converting the infidels who embraced Islam there.[271] But he gives no detail of the measures the Sufi saint employed in the conversion. One must take into consideration that Shah Jalal '*came to India with 700 companions to take part in Jihad (holy war)*'[272] and that he fought a bloody Jihad against King Gaur Govinda. These instances give a clear idea of the tools he had applied in converting the Hindus of Sylhet.

In another instance, Sufi saint Nur Qutb-i-Alam played a central role in making a high profile convert in Bengal. In 1414, Ganesha, a Hindu prince, revolted against Muslim rule and captured power in Bengal. The ascension of a Hindu to power created strong revulsion amongst both the Sufis and the *Ulema*. They repudiated his rule and enlisted help from Muslim rulers outside of Bengal. Responding to their call, Ibrahim Shah Sharqi invaded Bengal and defeated Ganesha. Nur Qutb-i-Alam, the leading Sufi master of Bengal, now stepped in to broker a truce. He forced Ganesha to abdicate and Ganesha's twelve-year-old son Jadu was converted to Islam and placed on the throne under the name of Sultan Jalaluddin Muhammad.[273] This conversion by a Sufi saint, call it peacefully or at the point of the sword, proved a boon for Islam. The Sufis (also the *Ulema*) trained the converted young sultan in Islam so well that he became a bloody converter of the infidels to Islam through extreme violence. There took place, says the *Cambridge History of India*, a wave of conversions in the reign of Jalaluddin Muhammad (1414–31).[274] About Jalaluddin's distinguished role in converting the Hindus of Bengal to Islam, Dr James Wise wrote in the *Journal of the Asiatic Society of*

---

267. Rizvi SAA (1978) *A History of Sufism in India*, Munshiram Manoharlal Publishers, New Delhi, Vol. I, p. 201

268. In Kashmir, great Sufi saint Sayyid Ali Hamdani also destroyed a temple to set up his *Khanqah*. There is a likely parallel between the methods these two Sufis applied in converting the Hindus (see below).

269. There is a tradition that king Gaur Govinda was attacked because of his punishing one Shaykh Burhanuddin and his son for slaughtering a cow. A piece of the cow-meat was stolen and dropped on the king's temple, which infuriated the king. Such stories should be considered in the light of the facts that Muslims attacked every corner of India, often repeatedly and it is unlikely that they had or needed a valid reason like this in each case.

270. *Hazrat Shah Jalal*, Wikipedia, http://en.wikipedia.org/wiki/Hazrat_Shah_Jalal

271. Gibb, p. 269

272. *Shah Jalal (R)*, Banglapedia; http://banglapedia.search.com.bd/HT/S_0238.htm

273. Sharma, p. 243-44

274. Smith, p. 272

Bengal (1894) that '*the only condition he offered was the Koran or death... many Hindus fled to Kamrup and the jungles of Assam, but it is nevertheless possible that more Mohammedans were added to Islam during these seventeen years (1414–31) than in the next three hundred years.*'[275]

Prof. Ishtiaq Hussain Qureishi makes an interesting observation that the Sufis in Bengal played significant missionary role in converting the Hindus and Buddhists but on an "orthodox" line.[276] This means that the Sufis of Bengal were doctrinally strict; therefore, doctrinal compromise and peaceful persuasion were unlikely part of their methods as orthodoxy demands the use of unconditional force in converting the infidels. Ishtiaq lends credence to the orthodoxy of Bengal Sufis in saying that '*They established their khanaqahs and shrines at places (i.e., temples) which already had a reputation for sanctity before Islam.*' Ishtiaq wants to tell us that the establishment of their *khanqahs* at the place of former Hindu or Buddhist temples (after destroying them), a recurring phenomenon amongst Sufis everywhere, facilitated the conversion of the native infidels as Levtzion agreeingly put it, '*(the Sufis) established their khanaqahs on the sites of Buddhist shrines, and (it) fitted well into the religious situation in Bengal.*'[277]

It is incredulous in the highest degree to suggest that the Hindus and Buddhists of Bengal loved it more that the Sufis destroyed their temples and build *khanqahs* thereon, to which the natives could easily connect.[278] Indeed, India's history is replete with instances that the Hindus and other non-Muslims always welcomed Muslims when settled among them peacefully, but revolted against them when attacked their religion. The unceasing rebellion and strife that Muslim invaders instigated amongst native Indians were as much political as it was for the invaders' attacks on their religious institutions and culture—a fact, repeatedly affirmed by Jawaharlal Nehru in his writings. The reigns of liberal Akbar and Zainul Abedin (in Kashmir), who disbanded religious persecutions and allowed religious freedom, were most peaceful and prosperous. This proves that Indians never liked it when Muslims, be it the rulers or the Sufis, defiled their religious symbols. Moreover, the Buddhists, the dominant converts to Islam in Bengal, had earlier embraced Buddhism voluntarily leaving their former Hindu faith, because of the peaceful and non-violent nature of Buddhism. Muslims' attack on their temples and shrines, and converting those to mosques and *khanqahs* had undoubtedly created amongst them a greater revulsion, not a favorable impression, toward Islam.

Conversion by horrifying Sufis in Kashmir: Persian chronicles, *Baharistan-i-Shahi* and *Tarikh-i-Kashmir* (1620), give somewhat detailed accounts of the involvement of Sufi saints in the conversion of Hindus of Kashmir to Islam. The greatest Sufi to arrive in Kashmir was Amir Shamsud-Din Muhammad Iraqi. He formed a strong alliance with Malik Musa Raina, who became the administrator of Kashmir in 1501. Earlier Sultan Zainul Abedin (1423–74), the only tolerant and liberal Muslim ruler of Kashmir, had allowed religious freedom enabling the flourishing Hinduism, '*which had been stamped out in the (earlier) reign of Sikandar the Iconoclast.*'[279] With the patronage and authority of Malik Raina, records *Baharistan-i-Shahi*, '*Amir Shamsud-Din Muhammad undertook wholesale destruction of all those idol-houses as well as total ruination of the very foundation of infidelity and disbelief. On the site of every idol-house he destroyed, he ordered the construction of a mosque for offering prayers after the Islamic manner.*'[280] *Tarikh-i-Kashmir*, a historical account of Kashmir written by Haidar Malik Chadurah, who served in Sultan Yusuf Shah's Court (1579–86), records: '*Sheikh Shams-ud-Din reached Kashmir. He began destroying the places of worship and the temples of the Hindus and made an effort to achieve the objectives.*'[281] A medieval chronicle, entitled

275. Lal KS (1990) *Indian Muslims: Who are They*, Voice of India, New Delhi, p. 57

276. Qureishi IH (1962) *The Muslim Community of the Indo-Pakistan Subcontinent* (610–1947), 'S-Gravenhage, p. 74

277. Levtzion N (1979) in *Conversion to Islam*, p. 18

278. For the Sufis, building of their *khanqahs* at the site of destroyed temples was meant for showing their utter contempt and disrespect for the religion of infidels.

279. Pundit, p. 74; also discussed above

280. Ibid, p. 93–94

281. Chadurah HM (1991) *Tarikh-Kashmir*, ed. & trans. Razia Bano, Delhi, p. 102–03

Tohfat-ul-Ahbab, records that '*on the instance of Shamsud-Din Iraqi, Musa Raina had issued orders that everyday 1,500 to 2,000 infidels be brought to the doorstep of Mir Shamsud-Din by his followers. They would remove their sacred thread (zunnar), administer Kelima (Muslim profession of faith) to them, circumcise them and make them eat beef.*' There they became Muslim. *Tarikh-i-Hasan Khuiihami* notes of the conversion of Hindus to Islam by Shamsud-Din Iraqi that '*twenty-four thousand Hindu families were converted to Iraqi's faith by force and compulsion (qahran wa jabran).*'[282]

Later on in 1519, Malik Kaji Chak rose to the rank of military commander under Sultan Muhammad Shah. And '*one of the major commands of Amir Shamsud-Din Muhammad Iraqi carried out by him (Kaji Chak) was the massacre of the infidels and polytheists of this land,*' says *Baharistan-i-Shahi*.[283] Many of those, converted to Islam by force during the reign of Malik Raina, later reverted to polytheism (Hinduism). A rumor was spread that these apostates '*had placed a copy of the holy Quran under their haunches to make a seat to sit upon.*' Upon hearing this, the enraged Sufi saint protested to Malik Kaji Chak that,

> '*This community of idolaters has, after embracing and submitting to the Islamic faith, now gone back to defiance and apostasy. If you find yourself unable to inflict punishment upon them in accordance with the provisions of Sharia (which is death for apostasy) and take disciplinary action against them, it will become necessary and incumbent upon me to proceed on a self-imposed exile.*'[284]

It must be noted that Shaykh Iraqi's complaint does not mention the alleged disrespect of the Quran but simply emphasize the Hindus' abandonment of Islam after accepting it. In order to appease the great Sufi saint, Kaji Chak '*decided upon carrying out wholesale massacre of the infidels,*' notes *Baharistan-i-Shahi*. Their massacre was scheduled to be carried out on the holy festival day of *Ashura* (Muharram, 1518 CE) and '*about seven to eight hundred infidels were put to death. Those killed were the leading personalities of the community of infidels at that time.*' Thereupon, '*the entire community of infidels and polytheists in Kashmir was coerced into conversion to Islam at the point of the sword. This is one of the major achievements of Malik Kaji Chak,*' records *Baharistan-i-Shahi*.[285] This horrifying action, of course, was order by the great Sufi saint.

Sayyid Ali Hamdani was another famous Sufi saint, who had arrived in Kashmir earlier in 1371 or 1381. The first thing he did was to build his *khanqah* on the site of '*a small temple which was demolished...*'[286] Before his coming to Kashmir, the reigning Sultan Qutbud-Din paid little attention to enforcing religious laws. Muslims at all levels of the society, including the *Qazis* and theologians of those days, paid scant attention to things permitted or prohibited in Islam. The Muslim rulers, theologians and commoners had tolerantly and comfortably submerged themselves in Hindu tradition.[287] Horrified by the un-Islamic practices of Kashmiri Muslims, Sayyid Hamdani forbade this laxity and tried to revive orthodoxy. Sultan Qutbud-Din tried to adopt the orthodox way of Islam in his personal life but '*failed to propagate Islam in accordance with the wishes and aspirations of Amir Sayyid Ali Hamdani.*' Reluctant to live in a land dominated by the infidel culture, customs and religion, the Sufi saint left Kashmir in protest. Later on, his son Amir Sayyid Muhammad, another great Sufi saint of Kashmir, came during the reign of Sikandar the idol-breaker. The partnership of holy Sayyid Muhammad and Sikandar the Iconoclast succeeded in wiping out idolatry from Kashmir as discussed above. And '*the credit of wiping out the vestiges of infidelity and heresy*'

---

282. Pundit, p. 105–106

283. Ibid, p. 116

284. Ibid, p. 117

285. Ibid

286. Ibid, p. 36

287. Ibid, p. 35

from the mirror of the conscience of the dwellers of these lands,' goes to the holy Sufi saint Sayyid Muhammad, notes *Baharistan-i-Shahi.*[288]

Conversion by Sufis in Gujarat: Sultan Firoz Shah Tughlaq (r. 1351–88) had appointed Furhut-ul-Mulk as the governor of Gujarat. Undertaking tolerant policies toward Hindus, notes Ferishtah, Furhut-ul-Mulk *'encouraged the Hindu religion, and thus rather promoted than suppressed the worship of idols.'*[289] As usual, this caused revulsion among *'the learned (Sufis) and orthodox (Ulema) Mahomedans of Guzerat, fearing lest this conduct should be the means of eventually superseding the true faith (Islam) in those parts.'* They addressed the Delhi Sultan explaining the liberal Muslim governor's political views and *'the danger (it posed) to the true faith, if he were permitted to retain his government.'* After receiving the complaint, Sultan Firoz Shah *'convened a meeting of the holy men (Sufi saints) at Dehly and in conjunction with them appointed Zuffur (Moozuffur Khan)'* as the viceroy of Gujarat.[290]

This Moozuffur Khan—requested as well as chosen by the Sufi saints—soon ousted tolerant Furhut-ul-Mulk from Gujarat and unleashed brutal terror against Hindus, including their forced conversion and general destruction of their temples. In 1395, *'He proceeded to Somnath, where having destroyed all the Hindoo temples which he found standing; he built mosques in their stead and left the learned men (Sufis) for the propagation of the faith and his officers to govern the country.'*[291]

This example once again proves that the Sufis were generally intolerant of any tolerance certain kind-hearted and liberal Muslim rulers accorded to non-Muslims. The question further arises: how did the Sufis, left behind by Moozuffur Khan in Somnath, propagate Islam among the terror-stricken Hindus after all their temples had been destroyed?

The Sufis of Gujarat and Delhi wanted the ouster of tolerant governor Furhut-ul-Mulk from Gujarat for not suppressing idol-worship (i.e., Hindu religion). It should, therefore, leave one with no doubt that the Sufis, left behind by Moozuffur Khan, meticulously worked in conjunction with the Muslim officers on enforcing the writ of Islamic laws and suppressing the Hindu religion. That means, the Sufis made it sure that the destroyed temples were not rebuilt and that the Hindu religion was not practised to ensure the suppression of idol-worship. Of course, they might have acted like Sufi saint Shamsud-Din Iraqi of Kashmir—whose followers, aided by Muslim soldiers—brought 1,500–2,000 infidels to his *khanqah* everyday and forcibly converted them to Islam.

The Real Sufi contribution in conversion: If Sufis were to play a major role in the propagation of Islam as popular notion goes, it must have happened in India; because, the Islamic conquest of India started in real earnest right at the time, when Sufism had become properly organized and widely accepted in Muslim societies for the first time. It has been noted that Khwaja Moinuddin Chisti came to Ajmer with Sultan Muhammad Ghauri's army just when Muslim conquest was making a hold in Northern India. As accounted above, none of the greatest Indian Sufis had a mentality needed for the peaceful propagation of Islam. Khwaja Moinuddin Chisti, Nizamuddin Auliya and Shaykh Shah Jalal came to engage in holy war in India and, indeed, participated in Jihadi wars involving slaughter and enslavement of the Hindus. Nizamuddin Auliya encouraged Sultan Alauddin's barbaric holy wars, and expressed obvious delight at victories in his blood-letting Jihad campaigns, and delightfully accepted large gifts from his plundered booty.

These are only the stories of the most revered and tolerant Sufi saints of medieval India. All indications suggest that, instead of taking on a missionary profession for propagating Islam through *peaceful*

---

288. Ibid, p. 37

289. Ferishtah, Vol. IV, p. 1

290. Ibid

291. Ibid, p3

means, the Sufis were invariably the spiritual and moral supporter of bloody holy wars that were waged by Muslim rulers. They were even prominent participants in them. In Kashmir, it is the Sufis, who inspired bloody Jihad that involved whole-sale destruction of Hindu temples and idols, slaughter of Hindus and their forced conversion to Islam. The mentality, attitude and actions of these illustrious Sufis saints of medieval India—whether in Ajmer, Bengal, Bijapur, Delhi or Kashmir—differed very little. Hence, the role Sufis played in conversion all over India may not have been very different from the one, they played in Kashmir.

It should be noted that the Muslim rulers of India were incessantly undertaking holy wars against the multitude of Hindus. Many of these wars involved mass slaughter of the vanquished and enslavement of tens to hundreds of thousands of women and children for their conversion to Islam. Not a single famous Sufi saint ever objected to this cruel and barbaric practice and means of converting the infidels *en masse* to Islam. No great Sufi saint of India ever made a statement, condemning these barbaric acts. They never asked the rulers to stop their barbaric expeditions and means of conversion on the pain of death. None of them ever said: '*Do not capture the Hindus for conversion to Islam in this cruel manner. Leave the job to us. That's our mission to be achieved thorough peaceful persuasion.*' Instead, they offered unstinted support, indeed encouragement; and even, eager participation, in those barbaric wars.

The instances of Sufis' involvement in converting the Hindus in Kashmir, Gujarat and Bengal gives clear idea about the means they applied in perfect harmony with their deranged ideology and attitude toward non-Muslims and their creeds. In Kashmir, they were the ones to inspire the rulers to unleash brutality against the Hindus and their forced conversion. There is no evidence to support the claim that they converted non-Muslims through *peaceful* means in large numbers. If such conversions ever took place—those, at best, played a peripheral role in the overall conversion in medieval India. Their role elsewhere was, likely, even less prominent.

Few documentations of peaceful conversion by Sufis: Muslim historians have left piles of documentation of the infidels being forced to convert in the battlefields and through enslavement in large numbers in the course of ceaseless Muslim expeditions to all corners of medieval India. Not a single document makes mention of an occasion, in which a Sufi converted the Hindus to Islam in significant numbers through *nonviolent* means.

Sultan Mahmud enslaved 500,000 Hindus in his first expedition to India, who instantly became incorporated into Islam. Shams Shiraj Afif records that Sultan Firoz Tughlaq converted a great number of Hindus to Islam by offering them relief from the oppressive and humiliating *jizyah* and other onerous taxes,[292] which is also claimed by the sultan himself (discussed above). According to Afif, he had collected 180,000 Hindus boys as slaves; '*Some of the slaves spent their time in reading and committing to memory the holy book, others in religious studies, others in copying books.*'[293] Even during the rule of enlightened Akbar, who had prohibited enslavement and forced conversion, his not-so-illustrious General Abdulla Khan Uzbeg, who ruled Malwa for only about two years, had converted 500,000 infidels to Islam through enslavement.[294] The forefathers of today's Muslims of North West Provinces converted to Islam mostly during the reign of fanatic Aurangzeb in order to avoid persecution, attain privileged rights, and to be relieved of the burdensome discriminatory taxes.

In the midst of this dominant coercive mode of conversion, there exists few evidence or record that the Sufis made significant contributions to proselytization. Based on historical investigation of conversion in medieval India, noted Habib, '*The Musalmans have no missionary labor to record... We find no trace of*

---

292. Sharma, p. 185

293. Elliot & Dawson, Vol. III, p. 341

294. Lal (1994), p. 73

missionary movement for converting non-Muslims.' He added that medieval Islam *'failed to develop any missionary activity;'* and that, in India, *'we have to confess frankly that no trace of a missionary movement for the conversion of the non-Muslims has yet been discovered.'* He further added: *'Some cheap mystic books now current attribute conversions to Muslim mystics on the basis of miracles they performed... But all such books will be found on examination to be latter-day fabrication.'*[295] Rizvi's investigation on the Sufi mystics of medieval India also led him to conclude that *'the early mystic records (Malfuzat & Maktubat) contain no mention of conversion of the people to Islam by these Saints.'* Nizamuddin Auliya was India's greatest Sufi saint. But his biographical memoir *Fawaid-ul-Fuad* records the conversion of only two Hindu card-sellers by him.[296]

In instances of large-scale conversion, in which Sufis were involved, their roles were to incite the rulers into unleashing violence and cruelty on non-Muslims leading up to those conversions. The evidence recounted above makes it overwhelmingly clear that the Sufi mystics took little interest or initiative in peaceful missionary activity. Indeed, they were opposed to such engagements. For example, when the zealous proselytizer, Sultan Muhammad Shah Tughlaq, wanted to employ the Sufis for missionary work, notes Mahdi Hussain, it faced strong opposition from the Sufi community.[297] Whenever Sufis were involved in the conversion, their method was obviously not peaceful.

Moreover, most of the Indian Sufis, who came from Persia and the Middle East, did not speak Indian languages to transmit Islam's messages to ordinary people effectively. They never learned the hated *jahiliyah* Indian languages, while masses of Indian natives were illiterate; they rarely learned Arabic or Persian. Finally, the Hindus of our time, particularly those of the lower caste, are much better able to judge the superior message of equality, peace and social justice, allegedly contained in Islam. Today, the message of Islam is reaching to every corner of India in well-expounded and clear language through so many easily accessible and innovative means. If it was the greatness of Islam's message, which impressed tens of millions of Indian infidels to embrace Islam during the Muslim rule, the rate of their conversion to Islam should be greater today than at any previous time.

Conversion by traders in Southeast Asia

The conversion of the infidels to Islam by Muslim traders, particularly in Southeast Asia, is emerging as a new paradigm. In a *The Time of India* article, Atul Sethi terms the claim—that *'Islam was brought to India by Muslim invaders'*—a misconception. Attempting to clear the misconception, he wrote:[298]

> Most historians now agree that India's introduction to Islam was through Arab traders and not Muslim invaders, as is generally believed. The Arabs had been coming to the Malabar Coast in southern India as traders for a long time, well before Islam had been introduced in Arabia... Writes H G Rawlinson, in his book, *Ancient and Medieval History of India*, 'The first Arab Muslims began settling in the towns on the Indian coast in the last part of the 7th century.' They married Indian women and were treated with respect and allowed to propagate their faith. According to B P Sahu, head of the department of history of Delhi University, Arab Muslims began occupying positions of prominence in the areas where they had settled by the 8th and 9th centuries... In fact, the first mosque in the county was built by an Arab trader at Kodungallur, in

295. Lal (1990), p. 93

296. Ibid, p. 93–94

297. Ibid, p. 94

298. Sethi A, *Islam was brought to India by Muslim invaders*, The Time of India, 24 June, 2007; also Qasmi MB, *Origin of Muslims in India*, Asian Tribune, 22 April 2008

what is now Kerala, in 629 AD. Interestingly, Prophet Mohammed was alive at that time and this mosque in India would probably have been one of the first few mosques in the world, thus highlighting the presence of Islam in India long before the Muslim invaders arrived.

In 916–17, renowned Muslim traveler and chronicler Al-Masudi *'described a settlement in Chaul (twenty-five miles south of modern Bombay) of tens of thousands of Muslims whose ancestors had come from Arabia and Iraq to engage in the pepper and spice trade. This settlement, granted a degree of political autonomy by the local raja, was composed mainly of Arabs who had been born in Chaul and had intermarried considerably with the local population.'*[299]

Obviously, Muslim traders arrived in India long before the Muslim invaders started digging their feet in Sindh in 712. Based on such examples, it is claimed that these traders—not the Muslim invaders and warriors—spread Islam in India and many other places. Malaysia, Indonesia, Southern Philippines and Southern Thailand in Southeast Asia have emerged as the ideal example of the propagation of Islam through this mode. To negate the use of force in the conversion of non-Muslims to Islam, Zakir Naik asks, *'Indonesia is a country that has the maximum number of Muslims in the world. The majority of people in Malaysia are Muslims. May one ask, 'Which Muslim army went to Indonesia and Malaysia?''* And the reply comes: *'The ruler's back then volunteered in submitting to present-day religion (i.e., Islam) from traders of the silk route and maritime route'* (personal communication). *Daniel Pipes answers Naik's question as thus: 'Dar al-Islam also expanded peacefully when kings converted; for example, Parameswara, the ruler of Malacca in 1410 and thereafter his city was the major center of Islam in Southeast Asia.'*[300] Similarly, Arab League Secretary General Abdel Khalek Hassouna asserted (1968): *'Islam spread to China, Malaysia, Indonesia and the Philippines without fighting.'*[301]

Indonesian historian Raden Abdulkadir Widjojoatmodjo notes on the conversion of non-Muslims to Islam in Indonesia that,

> 'In the whole history of the conversion of Indonesia, there was no trace of any outward force. For the Holy War is not the only way to spread the true religion. According to the theory, it is only allowed to resort to the use of force, when exhortation and preaching have proved to be in vain.'[302]

Widjojoatmodjo is honest in agreeing that the use of force in the form of "Holy War" for conversion is sanctioned in Islam, but sees no evidence of its use in Indonesia. He is, however, candid that it would have been applied had the infidels of Indonesian Archipelago resisted the persuasive means of conversion.

During the thirteenth to fifteenth century, prior to the spread of Islam in Southeast Asia, there were three powerful kingdoms in the region: Srivijaya (Malaysia), Majapahit (Indonesian archipelago) and Siam (Thailand). The people followed a syncretic religion: a mix of Hinduism, Buddhism and Animism. Islam appeared to have established contact with Indonesia as early as at the time of third Caliph Othman (d. 656) through Muslim traders on their way, via sea-route, to China. Later on, Muslim traders became more involved in trades in the Sumatran trading ports in Srivijaya between 904 and the mid-twelfth century. After Islam established itself in India, Muslim traders came in increasing numbers from Indian costal ports of Gujarat, Bengal and South India and also some from China. These Muslim traders, who always carried religious mission with them, settled in the coastal port-cities, namely Malacca and Samudra or Pasai (in Aceh, Java) in Northern Sumatra. They intermarried with the local infidel women creating Muslim communities. Muslim traders, likely settled in the region in the early tenth century, had established notable presence in Northern

---

299. Eaton (1978), p. 13

300. Pipes (1983), p. 73

301. Waddy, p. 187

302. Widjojoatmodjo RA (1942) *Islam in the Netherlands East Indies*, in *The Far Eastern Quarterly*, 2 (1), p. 51

Sumatra toward the end of the thirteenth century. By this time, they had established two small city kingdoms: one at Samudra (Pasai) and another at Perlak in the Indonesian archipelago. Ibn Battutah visited the Muslim city-kingdom of Samudra in 1345–46.

Until this point in time, the local infidels, it seems, did not converted to Islam in significant numbers. Muslims, exploiting the liberal and tolerant local culture, engaged in intermarriages with the local women, and with the offspring, slowly built up their communities. In three to four centuries, they were numerous enough to found small Muslim city-kingdoms, namely in Samudra and Perlak. And soon, they were waging brutal Jihad against the surrounding infidels. After visiting the Sultanate of Samudra, Ibn Battutah noted that the reigning Sultan al-Malik az-Zahir was a "most illustrious and opened-handed ruler". It is because,

> He was constantly engaged in warring for the Faith (Jihad against the infidels) and in raiding expeditions... His subjects also take a pleasure in warring for the Faith and voluntarily accompany him on his expeditions. They have the upper hand over all the infidels in their vicinity, who pay them poll-tax to secure peace.[303]

Still until the end of the fourteenth century, Islam had achieved very little success in converting the infidels and had its presence only in small isolated pockets. That was going to change dramatically with the conversion of King Parameswara of Srivijaya through a deceptive ploy. Parameswara ruled from Palembang. The Srivijaya kingdom was in decline at the time and Majapahit had become its overlord. Because of a dispute with the Majapahit ruler, he was forced to shift his capital from Palembang to safer Temasek Island (Singapore). In a skirmish with the forces of Majapahit, Parameswara killed prince Temagi of Siam, ally of Majapahit. The angered Siamese king, allied with Majapahit, waged a string of battles against Srivijaya in an attempt to capture and kill Parameswara. Parameswara retreated and fled from Temasek Island: first to Muar, then to Malacca, making the latter his new capital in 1402.

By this time, Muslims, settled centuries ago, had a significant presence in the port city of Malacca. Mainly merchants in profession, they were crucial for Malacca's flourishing trade with India. Muslims, therefore, received welcome in Parameswara's court and slowly increased their presence in his court and influence on his political fortune. Muslims were drafted into his army and he was becoming increasingly dependent on them to stave off attacks from Siam and Majapahit. About this time, the Muslim advisors of Parameswara offered to send in more Muslim soldiers to fight on his side, if he would convert to Islam. Parameswara rejected the offer. As his struggle with his sworn enemies continued over the succeeding years, his position became increasingly precarious.

At this juncture, the Arab merchants presented him with a damsel from Pasai of mix breed, born of a marriage between her Arab father and Indonesian mother. She was a maiden of great beauty. Parameswara fell in love with the beautiful slave-girl and she became pregnant in his harem. Childless Parameswara had been longing for an heir to his kingdom. When he proposed to marry the damsel to make the child a legitimate heir, she insisted that he must convert to Islam prior to marrying her. With his increasingly weakened and precarious position needing the support of Muslim soldiers, compounded by his desperate desire for an heir, Parameswara eventually agreed. He converted to Islam and brought her to the palace as a legitimate queen.

Malacca Sultanate and the intensification of Jihad: After embracing Islam in 1410, Parameswara transformed the Hindu kingdom of Srivijaya into a Muslim Sultanate—the Sultanate of Malacca, and assumed the title of Sultan Iskandar Shah. After his conversion, his half-Muslim Queen and Muslim soldiers and courtiers transformed him into a strict Muslim. Ma Huan, a Chinese Muslim, visited Sultan Iskandar Shah in 1414 as a Secretary Dragoman of an envoy of Chinese Emperor Yung Lo. He found the Sultan was already a "very strict believer in the faith".[304]

---

303. Gibb, p. 274
304. Widjojoatmodjo, p. 49

Small-scale violent Jihad against the infidels in Southeast Asia had started as soon as Muslims attained some power in Samudra in the early fourteenth century as recorded by Ibn Battutah. After the founding of the Malacca Sultanate, Jihad intensified for achieving the greater glory. The Sultanate became the center for waging large-scale Jihad expeditions against neighboring kingdoms for expanding the domain of Islam. His Muslim army—now inspired by the Islamic zeal of fighting in the cause of Allah for gaining martyrdom or becoming *Ghazi*—dramatically changed the fortune of the precariously weakened Malacca Sultan. From a point of near doom, Parameswara, now Sultan Iskandar Shah, and his descendants, soon gained ascendancy in political power over the neighboring kingdoms. The Sultanate expanded; at its height, it encompassed much of today's Malaysian Peninsula, Singapore and the greater regions of Eastern Sumatra and Borneo. Later on, Borneo seceded from Malacca to become an independent Sultanate. For long, Malacca remained the center of Southeast Asian Islam, comprising Malaysia, Aceh, Riau, Palembang and Sulawesi.

In the course of the fifteenth century, the Sultanate of Malacca waged Jihad against neighboring states and destroyed the powerful Majapahit Kingdom and also weakened Siam. When Muslim warriors overran Java in 1526, the Majapahit Kingdom ceased to exist. The Sultanate continued its rivalry with the surviving Thai Kingdom, capturing territory from the south. In the course of late fifteenth and early sixteenth centuries, Muslim invaders were poised to storm into the Thai capital of Ayuthaya. For some time, it seemed that the Muslim holy warriors would overrun Siam.

But the coincidental arrival of the mercantile Portuguese fleets along the naval route to the Malacca Strait at this critical juncture, which led to an internecine conflict between the Portuguese and the Malacca Sultan, served as a welcome relief for beleaguered Siam. In 1509, the Portuguese fleet, led by Admiral Lopez de Sequira, reached the Malacca Strait. The reigning Sultan Mahmud Shah, prompted by a Muslim-Portuguese conflict in India, attacked the Portuguese fleet and forced them to flee. In 1511, another Portuguese fleet from Cochin (India), commanded by Viceroy Alfonso d'Albuquerque, came to Malacca and conflict ensued again. After forty days of fighting, Malacca fell to the Portuguese on August 24. Sultan Mahmud Shah fled Malacca. Over the next years and decades, internecine conflicts continued between the Portuguese and Muslim forces.

This distraction and eventual dismantling of the Malacca Sultanate by the Portuguese saved Siam from collapsing to Muslim rule. In the seventeenth century, Siamese rulers made alliance with the seafaring Portuguese and Dutch powers, which succeeded in countering the threat of Muslim attack. In the eighteenth century, Siam counterattacked in order to recover the lost territory. It overran and annexed the declining Muslim Sultanate of Pattani.

The spread of Islam in the Philippines: The Muslim region of the Philippines, comprising the Mindanao and Sulu Islands, is another example where Islam, claim Muslims and many scholars, was spread peacefully by traders. Which Muslim army went to the Philippines to spread Islam by the sword, ask Muslims? It was Muslim traders and Sufis coming from India and the Malay Peninsula spread Islam there, they claim, through peaceful missionary activity.

Islam was allegedly brought to the Sulu Archipelago of the Southern Philippines by Arab trader Makhdum Karim in 1380. He settled there and constructed a mosque—the oldest mosque in the region. But conversion of the largely Animist Filipinos to Islam on a large scale did not occur until the Malacca Sultanate gained political ascendancy in the Malay Peninsula and Indonesian Archipelago. In the 1450s, Shari'ful Hashem Syed Abu Bakr, a Malaysia's Johore-born Arab warrior, sailed with a force northward from Borneo to the Sulu Islands and founded the Sultanate of Sulu in 1457. With the force of Islamic political power, the conversion of the Animist population to Islam began in real earnest. By the end of the fifteenth century, forward Jihad from Sulu, patronized by the Borneo Sultanate, had brought most of Visayas (Central Philippines), half of Luzon (Northern Philippines) and the islands of Mindanao in the south under Muslim control. Continued incursions by Muslim Jihadis intensified the spread of Islam among the terrified Animist populace. Following the trail of Muslim holy warriors, Islam spread from Sulu to Mindanao and reached the Manila area by 1565.

The local Filipinos organized into small Barangays—groups based on village or tribal community—offered sporadic and feeble resistance against well-organized Muslim incursions. The arrival of the Spanish colonists in the Cebu Islands in 1521, from where they slowly expanded their control over the Philippines, eventually halted the further spread of Islam. By this time, a major section of the Animist population of Southern Philippines had been converted to Islam. When the Spaniards spread their political control over Filipino islands, the Animist population, threatened and brutalized by the Muslim warriors, did not offer much resistance to the new imperialists. But the Muslim-held islands offered fierce, protracted resistance.[305] The native forces allied with the Spaniards tried to take control of Muslim-held islands but failed. The Spanish occupiers, however, rolled back the rival Muslim invaders from some areas and sealed off the further territorial expansion and spread of Islam. Mindanao and the Sulu Archipelago, which had been thoroughly Islamized, remained under Muslim control and remain Islamic till today.

Method of conversion in Southeast Asia: Indisputably, Muslims first came to Southeast Asia as traders and settled down in the port-cities among the native people. Taking opportunities of the liberal and tolerant local culture, they freely intermarried with the infidel women, who bore Muslim children. In intermarriages, even the powerful King Parameswara could not retain his own religion and convert his concubine damsel: half Muslim and half Indonesian. Since Muslims started settling down in Southeast Asia in the early tenth century, procreation through intermarriages, it appears, was the main tool for the growth of the Muslim population. There might have been conversion of some servants and employees engaged by Muslim merchants, which, given the repulsive attitude Muslims entertained against non-Muslims, facilitated a more harmonious relationship between the two parties. Furthermore, the Islamic sanction that Muslim men can have up to four wives, engage in temporary marriages (*mut'ah*)[306] and keep unlimited concubines (sex-slaves) might have helped the Muslim population grow faster.

In this early period of the Muslim settlement in Southeast Asia, not many people converted to Islam because of its superior message. In the 1290s—nearly four centuries after the Muslim settlement began—only two small Muslim city-kingdoms were established in Northern Sumatra. After King Parameswara converted and founded an Islamic Sultanate in Malacca, Islam spread quickly as conquest of the Malay Peninsula, Indonesian Archipelago, Philippines and Southern Thailand proceeded apace. The Malacca Sultanate remained in Muslim control for less than a century before the Portuguese ousted them. And within that short time, a large section of the population had been converted.

What enabled the conversion of the otherwise resistant infidels of Southeast Asia to Islam so quickly after Muslims gained political power?

To historians like Richard Eaton and Anthony Johns among many others, it was now the turn of the Sufis, who came mainly from India, to spread Islam quickly among the until-now-resistant infidels through peaceful persuasion. But even in Eaton's testimony, there is absolutely no clear record or evidence to suggest that the Sufis converted the infidels to Islam. Nor is there any indication of the method they might have used in the conversion. According to Eaton, there are only some fragmentary writings about "enormously influential Javanese Sufis (*kiyayi*)" of the nature of "fantastic legends".[307] Based on these unsubstantiated evidence, these scholars are quick to assert that the conversion was of peaceful nature and the credit goes to Sufis. In a wilful assertion, Syed Naguib al-Attas notes: '*I am inclined to believe that it was the Sufis who actually propagated*

---

305. Pipes (1983), p. 266

306. It is said that the Pasai damsel, presented to Parameswara, was born of a *mut'ah* marriage.

307. Eaton (2000), p. 39

and finally made it possible for Islam to become well established among the people. With regard to Malaya, I feel almost certain that Islam was propagated by the Sufis.' His assertion is, however, based on no evidence at all as he himself quickly adds: *'There may not be direct evidence to support this theory.'*[308]

Such Sufi legends, most likely of concocted nature, are much more common in India. It has been noted already how unsuccessful the Sufis were in peaceful conversion of the infidels in India and how horrifying they were, when successful as in Kashmir. According to Widjojoatmodjo, Ibn Battutah found the Muslim ruler of the Samudra Sultanate performing *'his religious duties with utmost zeal. He belonged to the madhab (School) of Imam Shafi'i.'*[309] The Shafi'i law was adopted by Muslims in Southeast Asia. It prescribes the choice of death or conversion to Islam to idolaters, such as Hindus, Buddhists and Animists, to which the pre-Islamic people of Southeast Asia belonged. Ibn Battutah's description shows that as soon as Muslims gained political power as in Samudra, they started brutal Jihad against the surrounding infidels.

Just four years after Parameswara's conversion to Islam, Ma Huan—the Chinese Muslim Dragoman—found him a "very strict believer in the faith". It means that he was strictly applying the Shafi'i laws in his Sultanate. It gives one a good deal of idea about the policies Sultan Iskandar and his descendants applied to their non-Muslim subjects. Given the tiny Sultanate of Samudra could unleash such brutality against the surrounding infidels, it could have served as a model for the Sultanate of Malacca to follow, if not a more lethal coercive force was applied by the much more powerful Malacca Sultans.

Some insight into how Islam was being propagated in the Muslim-ruled Malay Peninsula and Indonesian Archipelago beginning in the early fifteenth century can come from the parallel conversions in Gujarat, with which the Southeast Asian Muslim Sultanates had a close contact. Gujarat was a major source of Muslim traders and Sufis who came to the Malay and Indonesian Archipelagos at the time. The role played by the Sufis in India, particularly in Gujarat, probably acted as model for the Sufis of Southeast Asian Muslim Sultanates to follow. The Sufis of South Indian coasts had an equally close, if not closer, relationship with the Southeast Asian port-cities through trades. The fact that South India also follows the same Shafi'i law as in Southeast Asia, the method of the South Indian Sufis was most likely a model for the conversion of infidels in the Malay and Indonesian Archipelagos. And we have noted of how *Pir* Ma'bari Khandayat from the South Indian coastal town of Ma'bar (Coromandel) came to Bijapur for waging Jihad against the Hindus and exiling the Brahmins from their homelands in the course of Islamizing the area.

The intolerance of the Muslim rulers, Sufis and *Ulema* of Southeast Asia regarding the infidels was, in all likelihood, more heightened than those of India (probably except South India). It is because the Shafi'i laws, which they followed, accord mandatory death or conversion to the polytheists; while the Hanafi laws, practised in India, accord them a more tolerant *dhimmi* status. Indeed, Shafi'i laws are the strictest against giving quarters to infidels in a territory conquered by Muslims. In accordance with Quran 9:2—which says: *'Go ye, then, for four months, backwards and forwards, (as ye will), throughout the land, but know ye that ye cannot frustrate Allah (by your falsehood) but that Allah will cover with shame those who reject Him'*— Shafi'i (also Hanbali) laws give exactly four months for the infidels to convert, while other Schools give up to one year.[310] The conversion of the otherwise resistant Southeast Asian infidels to Islam was much more complete than those of India within a much shorter time. The Malacca Sultanate was in existence for only a century before the Portuguese dismantled it in 1511. This suggests that a greater coercion was most likely applied in the conversion of the Hindu-Buddhist-Animist infidels of Malaysia, Indonesia and the Philippines to Islam.

---

308. Al-Attas SN (1963) *Some Aspects of Sufism as Understood and Practice Among the Malays*, S Gordon ed., Malaysian Sociological Research Institute Ltd., Singapore, p. 21

309. Widjojoatmodjo, p. 49

310. Rudolph P (1979) *Islam and Colonialism: The Doctrine of Jihad in Modern History*, Mouton Publishers, The Hague, p. 31

About the Sufis of Southeast Asia, writes Eaton: '*enormously influential Sufis... who seem occasionally to have assisted the sultans to power and occasionally to have used their considerable influence with rural masses to undermine the sultan's power.*'[311] Such references are good enough examples for Dr. Eaton to conclude that those popular and revolutionary heroic Sufis initiated a mystical, spiritual and intellectual movement for the synthesis of an Islam '*tinged with Hindu-Buddhist and native Javanese conceptions,*' transforming '*Hindu Java with Muslim Java*' through a humane, peaceful process, of course.

What Eaton ignores, or is unaware of, is the fact that the Sufis engaged in similar political movements everywhere, not in Java alone. Sometimes, they allied with rulers to persecute the infidels. At other times, they allied with the Muslim masses against the wayward Muslim rulers, who were tolerant toward non-Muslims. According to Bernard Lewis, Muslim rulers often had '*fears of the dangerous pent-up energies that the dervish leaders (Sufi saints) could control and release at will. Under the Seljuk and Ottoman Sultans, there were even dervish rebellions, which at times offered a serious threat to the established order.*'[312]

Sufism itself developed, as noted already, as a reaction against the deviant Abbasid rulers; because, they patronized the un-Islamic Persian culture and promoted moral laxity in violation of Islam. In Kashmir and Gujarat, Sufis allied with the rulers to persecute the Hindus. Sufi saint Sayyid Ali Hamdani, failing to incite the Kashmiri Sultan to persecuting the Hindus as per Islamic principles, left the country in protest. Shaykh Ahmad Sirhindi, the leading Sufi saint of his time, joined hands with the Muslim masses and the *Ulema* to wage revolt against Emperor Akbar's liberal and tolerant policies toward non-Muslims.

On rare occasions, the Sufis allied against pious Muslim rulers. In one such instance, some 700 followers of *Pir* Budhu Shah, a Sufi saint, had joined the revolt of Guru Gobind Singh against the tyranny of Emperor Aurangzeb. But this alliance did not impress the Hindus and Sikhs of Gobind Singh's force to convert to Islam. The Sufis generally allied with the rulers to enforce the writ of Islam, particularly on the non-Muslim subjects. They allied with the Muslim masses against rulers, who failed to enforce the writ of Islam, particularly the persecution of non-Muslims. The involvement of the Sufis of Java in political movements against or in favor of the rulers was unlikely for a reason different from it was elsewhere. Even if they ever joined forces with the persecuted infidels, there is no reason to believe that such alliance led to their voluntary conversion to Islam in large numbers.

It has been noted already that the ruthlessness that Islamic holy warriors exhibited in their campaigns often terrified the infidels into submission and acceptance of Islam. The Jihad incursions by Muslim rulers in Southeast Asia were no less brutal and terrifying. Prof. Anthony Reid, who thinks that '*Islam was more egalitarian*' in Southeast Asia, notes: '*Malaya lost much of its population as a result of the campaigns (by Muslim ruler) of Aceh in the period of 1618–24.*'[313] Similarly, when Sultan Agung of Mataram, hailed as a great Muslim monarch of Southeast Asia, besieged Surabaya and its nearby towns with 80,000 troops for five years (1620–25), his troops devastated all the rice crops and even poisoned water and stopped its flow to the city by damming up the river. Consequent to these campaigns, all but 500 of the 50,000–60,000 inhabitants remained there; the rest had died or left the city from the resulting misery and famine.[314]

Moreover, wars waged by Muslim rulers in Southeast Asia appeared to have targeted mass-conversion of the people by force. For example, in the sixteenth century, the Makassarese of Sulawesi were prominent amongst those resisting Islam. The Muslim ruler of Makassar, says the local chronicle of Bulo-bulo (Sindjai region), invited the recalcitrant Makassarese to accept Islam and threatened war if refused. A

---

311. Eaton (2000), p. 28

312. Lewis B (2000) *The Middle East*, Phoenix, London, p. 241

313. Reid A (1988) *Southeast Asia in the Age of Commerce 1450–1680*, Yale University Press, New Haven, Vol. I., p. 35,18

314. Ibid, p. 17

prominent Makassarese leader '*defiantly declared that he would not bow to Islam even if the rivers flowed with blood, as long as there were pigs to eat in the forests of Bulo-bulo. Miraculously, the story goes, all the pigs disappeared that very night, so the chief and all his men were obliged to convert.*'[315] One would be credulous in the extreme to believe that the pigs disappeared just like that miraculously. What, in actuality, might have led to mass conversion of the Makassarese is the threat of violence or a real war.

According *Hikayat Banjar*, the chronicle of Banjarmasin (Indonesia) dating mid-seventeenth century, '*the Islamization of Banjarmasin was effectively determined when opposing claimants to the throne decided on single combat to avoid a civil war.*'[316] This again proves that Muslim rulers of Southeast Asia waged wars for the express purpose of converting the subdued people; when they won, conversion of the masses was a compulsion, not a choice. Based on such examples, argues MC Ricklefs, '*Conversion by arms may have occurred (in Java) when a Muslim dignitary defeated a non-Muslim, whereupon the vanquished and his people would presumably embraced Islam.*'[317]

The numerous Jihadi expeditions the Malacca and other Sultanates in Southeast Asia embarked upon for their territorial expansion undoubtedly yielded great multitudes of slaves, who generally had to embrace Islam. Enslavement became most extensive in the region after the Muslim capture of power. When the Portuguese came to Islamic Southeast Asia, they found it hard to hire men for work on wage, because almost all the people were slaves to one master or another. Persian chronicler Muhammad ibn Ibrahim wrote in 1688 that "*It is their custom to rent slaves. They pay the slave a sum of money, which he gives to his master, and then they use the slave for that day for whatever work they wish.*" Similarly, Portuguese author Joao de Barros wrote in 1563: "*You will not find a native Malay, howsoever poor he be, who will lift on his own back his own things or those of another, however, much he be paid for it. All their work is done by slaves.*"[318] Hwang Chung, a Chinese traveler reported in 1537 that the people of Melaka "*say that it is better to have slaves than to have land, because largely slaves are a protection to their masters.*"[319] According to Reid, '*many members of the slave-owning merchant class had strong roots in the Islamic world, which had a clear body of law on slaves as property.*'[320] This suggests that it is Muslim merchants who had promoted slavery in Muslim Southeast Asia so extensively.

When Ibn Battutah visited the Samudra Sultanate, the sultan presented to him two slave girls and two men servants.[321] Battutah also mentions of slaves owned by the infidel ruler of Mul-Jawa, who entertained Battutah for three days; one of his slaves sacrificed himself with his own hands, says Battutah, '*for the love of him (the ruler).*'[322] This means that slavery obviously existed in pre-Islamic Southeast Asia. The citizens of the Thai Kingdom had to work for the king for half of their time, notes Reid.[323] This was a kind of slavery, too. In pre-Islamic Southeast Asia, slaves were probably owned by the rulers and high officials, not by common merchants; the latter became widespread under the Muslim rule. Most importantly, slaves owned by Muslims generally had to convert to Islam, which was not the case previously.

Raiding non-Muslim territories became a constant phenomenon after Muslim powers were established in Southeast Asia. It was '*a period of Javanese history characterized by almost incessant warfare,*' says Ricklefs.[324] A substantial part of the population, the so-called savages, lived in the hills. Over five centuries after Muslims came to power in the early fifteenth century, those animist hill peoples

---

315. Ibid, p. 35

316. Ibid, p. 124

317. Ricklefs MC (1979) *Six Centuries of Islamization in Java*, in N. Levtzion ed., p. 106–07
318. Reid (1988), p. 131
319. Ibid, p. 129
320. Ibid, p. 134
321. Gibb, p. 275
322. Ibid, p. 277–78
323. Reid (1988), p. 132
324. Ricklefs in N. Levtzion ed., p. 106

completely disappeared as a result of their incorporation, through enslavement, into the Muslim populace of Malaya, Sumatra and Borneo '*by a mixture of raiding, tribute and purchase, especially of children.*'[325] '*Certain small sultanates, notably Sulu, Buton and Tidore, began to make profitable business of raiding for slaves in eastern Indonesia or the Philippines and marketing the human victims to the wealthy cities—or to the expanding seventeenth-century pepper estates of southern Borneo,*' adds Reid.[326] In Muslim wars in Southeast Asia, the enslavement was often complete: the entire population were enslaved and carried away. For example, Thomas Ivye reported in 1634 that an English Party went about looking in vain for two days for the once-flourishing Sumatran town of Inderagiri to buy pepper. No trace of the town was found. They later learned that its whole population were carried away in an Acehnese Muslim invasion six years earlier to a location three days' journey up the river.[327] These enslaved people—belonging to the polytheistic Hindu, Buddhist and Animist creeds—were unlikely allowed to keep their faiths by their Muslim captors of Shafi'i persuasion.

Although the Spaniards occupied the Philippines and kept pressure on the Muslim-controlled regions in the south, the Moro Muslim raiders kept their Jihad alive by making continued incursions into Spanish-occupied territories for capturing slaves. They enslaved, claimed Archbishop of Manila in 1637, on an average 10,000 Catholic Filipinos annually over the previous thirty years. It is estimated that the Moro holy warriors had enslaved some two million non-Muslims during the first two centuries of the Spanish rule in the Philippines beginning in 1665.[328] Thereafter, the Spanish and Portuguese naval patrols became increasingly effective in stopping the Moro Jihad raids. Still, the Southern Filipino Muslims, according to a conservative estimate, brought 200,000–300,000 people to the Sulu Sultanate through enslavement between 1770 and 1870.[329] In the late nineteenth century, enslavement was extensive in the Malay Peninsula and Indonesian Archipelago: some 6 percent of the population in the Perak Sultanate were slaves in 1879, about one-third in the eastern regions of West Sumatra in the 1860s, 30 percent in the Muslim-ruled region of North Sulawesi and as high as two-thirds or more in parts of North Borneo in the 1880s.[330] Here, one must take the fact into consideration that Europe banned slavery in 1815, pressured Muslim rulers to follow suit and intervened in slave-trade by force whenever possible.

These examples of large-scale slavery would give readers a clear idea of how the conversion had taken place in Southeast Asia. Muslim rulers also waged wars for the express purpose of converting the vanquished populace under compulsion. Moreover, continuous Muslim incursions, sufferance of horrible social degradation accorded to infidel subjects by Muslim rulers as per Islamic laws and the burden of onerous discriminatory taxes—*kharaj, jizyah* and others—had also undoubtedly imparted a *coercive compulsion* upon them to convert to Islam. An understanding of the terror Islamic rulers of Southeast Asia had stricken among the infidel populace can be surmised from a testimony of Dutch general Cohen (1615). People told him that "*the Pangeran of Banten fears no Portuguese, Spanish, Hollanders or Englishmen, but only the (Muslim King of) Mataram. From the latter, he says, no one can flee, but for the others the whole mountains are sufficient for us, they cannot follow us there with their ships.*"[331] In the midst of this desperate situation, Muslim preachers, Sufis and the *Ulema* might have made some contribution in converting those persecuted, humiliated, pauperized and terrified infidels. But such conversions likely had a very nominal

325. Reid (1988), p. 133

326. Ibid

327. Ibid, p. 122–23

328. Reid A (1983) *Introduction: Slavery and Bondage in Southeast Asian History*, in *Slavery Bondage and Dependency in Southeast Asia*, Anthony Reid ed., University of Queensland Press, St. Lucia, p. 32

329. Warren JF (1981) *The Sulu Jone, 1768-1898: The Dynamics of the External Slave Trade, Slavery and Ethnicity in the Transformation of a Southeast Asian Maritime State*, Singapore University Press, Singapore, p. 208.

330. Clarence-Smith WG (2006) *Islam and the Abolition of Slavery*, Oxford University Press, New York, p. 15–16

331. Reid (1988), p. 122

impact, because '*from the fourteenth century to the end of the nineteenth century, the (Indonesian) archipelago saw almost no organised Muslim missionary activity.*'[332] Historians, like Eaton, should take note of this fact before drawing their conclusions based on vague, unsubstantiated historical legends. This means that there was no organized missionary activity (the same is the case in India), conducted by either the Sufis or the *Ulema*; therefore, very few conversions occurred through such persuasive means. Conversion must have come predominantly through the exertion of the state: by the sword, large-scale enslavement and other means of coercive compulsion, as happened in India.

When Muslims came and settled in Southeast Asia, they obviously could convert the local people freely, such as through intermarriage or business contact. Unlike Muslims, who never allow their coreligionists to leave Islam, the converted infidels or their Muslim converters never faced persecution from the generally tolerant local people. Under such a conducive environment, if Islam's message had such a great appeal, the persuasive preaching by Sufis, traders or whosoever should have been almost as successful prior to Muslim conquest, as it became after. The fact that conversion through preaching was negligible prior to the conquest, the triumph of the sword undoubtedly became the primary weapon in converting Southeast Asia's infidels to Islam.

The same paradigm applies to India. Al-Masudi's record clearly suggests that, prior to the arrival of the Muslim invaders, expansion of the Muslim population were mainly through procreation aided by intermarriages in the tolerant culture of India. Al-Masudi suggests that conversion, other than through intermarriage, was rare. But after Muslim invaders brought the sword of Islam to India in three waves: first in early eighth century by Muhammad bin Qasim, then in the early eleventh century by Sultan Mahmud and finally in the late twelfth century by Sultan Ghauri, the Muslim population grew in leaps and bounds through large-scale conversion of native Indians in the face of brutal Muslim assaults, through their enslavement *en masse* and other forms of coercion.

CONCLUSION

Historian De Lacy O'Leary writes on the subject of conversion of non-Muslims to Islam that,

> 'History makes it clear however that the legend of fanatical Muslims sweeping through the world and forcing Islam at the point of the sword upon conquered races is one of the most fantastically absurd myths that historians have ever repeated.'[333]

If history is about studying factual evidence left to posterity in the records of scholars and chroniclers of the time, then O'Leary could not possibly consider this notion about the spread of Islam to be "the most fantastically absurd myth". Of course, he would be correct, if myths and facts were synonymous. Like O'Leary, there are far too many modern Muslim historians and their fellow travelers of non-Muslim variety— particularly of the leftist-Marxist leaning—who think that investigating history is not about enumerating and unearthing facts, but about hiding them while writing sophistry. This becomes the trend particularly when it comes to writing the history of Islam. But those, who wish to find unvarnished truth about Islamic history, say in India, they should go back to the writings of Al-Kufi (*Chachnama*), Al-Biladuri, Alberuni, Ibn Asir, al-Utbi, Hasan Nizami, Amir Khasrau, Ziauddin Barrani, Sultan Firoz Tughlaq, Emperor Babur and Jahangir, Badaoni, Abul Fazl, Muhammad Ferishtah and many more such medieval historians.

Dr Ali Issa Othman, a reputed Palestinian sociologist and advisor to the United Nations Relief and Works Agency (UNRAWA) on Education, said on the propagation of Islam that, "*The spread of Islam was*

---

332. Van Nieuwenhuijze CAO (1958) *Aspects of Islam in Post-Colonial Indonesia*, W. van Hoeve Ltd, The Hague, p. 35

333. O'Leary DL (1923) *Islam at the Cross Roads*, E. P. Dutton and Co, New York, p. 8

military. There is a tendency (amongst Muslims) to apologize for this and we should not. It is one of the injunctions of the Quran that you must fight for spreading of Islam."[334] The records and first-hand witness accounts of the medieval chroniclers, historians and rulers heartily agree with candid Othman's paradigm.

Finally, it should not be forgotten that the protocol used for converting the infidels to Islam in India was the mildest in the world. Let's conclude by recalling that even Prophet Muhammad, the most charismatic preacher of Islam, failed to convert the infidels of Arabia, including his own kinfolk, in substantial numbers except by the sword.

---

334. Waddy, p. 94

Chapter V

The Arab-Islamic Imperialism

'(Allah) hath made you (Muslims) His agents, inheritors of the earth' and *'promised to... make them rulers in the earth.'*

-- Allah, *Quran 24:55, 6:165*

'And fight them on until... there prevail justice and faith in Allah altogether and everywhere.'

-- Allah, *Quran 8:39*

'...the Arabs were the most successful imperialists of all time, since to be conquered by them (and then to belike them) is still, in the minds of the faithful, to be saved.'

-- V.S. Naipaul, *Among the Believers*, p. 142

———

Citizens of former colonies generally harbor animosity toward present-day European countries because of latter's past colonial rule. This ill-feeling continues to feature prominently in their collective national psyche and in intellectual, literary and political discourse. European nations had colonized countries in Asia, Africa, South America and Australasia without racial or religious discrimination. But their colonial past continues to incite the strongest anger and hatred amongst Muslims.

The predominantly non-Muslim former colonies, such as India, Singapore, Hong Kong, Philippines, Vietnam, South Africa, and Brazil among others—leaving aside their resentment for the past colonial injustices—have moved on in a mature fashion to forge valuable economic, political, educational and cultural ties with their former colonial masters. This prudent approach has enabled them to make significant developmental gains and progress since achieving independence. South South Korea, for example, has managed to overcome the resentment against her former brutal colonial master Japan (1910–45) and has forged a strong alliance with the latter, instead. On the other hand, the Muslim world has busied itself in the futile exercise of constantly harking back to the past colonial wrongs. Instead of looking inward to identify the cause of their hopeless current plight, they find it convenient to hold the past colonial masters responsible for all their present shortcomings and failures.

Anti-colonial resentment remains so intense amongst Muslims that it plays a critical role in fuelling the ongoing anti-West hatred and violence amongst Islamic radicals. According to playwright and performer Adam Broinowski, suicide bombing by Muslim extremists is associated with '*the legacy of colonialism and the resentments*' against it and '*probably involves a protest against (past) imperialism.*'[335] The legacy of European colonialism across the continents '*has helped produce large, monolithic and increasingly restive Islamic populations with a multi-generational sense of grievance,*' which fuels homegrown terrorism in the U.S. and Europe, thinks Jon Perr.[336]

However, it is surprising that Muslims refuse to acknowledge that their own past was not only imperialist but also no less brutal and devastating to the people whom they fell upon. 'Islam offers a faith untainted by colonialism and racism,' claims Rocky Davis, aka, Shaheed Malik, an Australian Aboriginal convert to Islam. According to him, 'the difference between the Muslim and Christian faiths: one is for the oppressed and one's for the oppressor, one's for the colonizer and one for the colonized.'[337] He told the ABC Radio that,

> Christianity is a culture of invasion, and if anyone can tell me that it's not, I need people to openly debate whether it be on live TV or in front of an audience, that Christianity was used as a weapon to invade all the world's indigenous peoples, Canadian Indians will tell you, Maoris will tell you, Cook Islands will tell you, Africans will tell you, the English used Christianity to invade and conquer and enslave... And I was never invaded by a Muslim country. Everywhere the Christians went, they plundered and they robbed and they murdered and they enslaved, and they raped.[338]

The Muslim Arabs, who were mostly uncultured lawless desert Bedouins, launched a massive campaign of ruthless conquest of the world from the Arabian Peninsula in the 630s. Within a century, they had established a huge kingdom spanning vast tracts of Asia, the entire Middle East, North Africa, and Spain. In the process, they exterminated a great multitude of people through mass slaughter, destroyed great civilizations of the time, and obliterated the cultural heritage of many peoples forever. This violent and destructive aspect of Islamic expansionism, which was followed by the centuries of devastating colonial rule, will be discussed in this chapter.

ISLAMIC IMPERIALISM: QURANIC COMMANDS & PROPHETIC MODEL

Colonialism can be described as a system of governance in which powerful states establish sovereignty over weaker states or peoples for exploiting the wealth—resources, labor and market—of the ruled. It also often degrades latter's socio-political norms and cultural values. Imperialism, although used interchangeably with colonialism, refers more specifically to the political power and control exercised by powerful states over weaker ones either by indirect influence or by direct military power. Colonialism, therefore, is of wider scope in which imperialism is imbedded.

The Quran entails an ideology for establishing a religio-political imperial state on the global scale through Jihad or holy war. Islam is a religious, social and political creed—all imbedded in one—a complete way of life. Allah commands Muslims to wage ceaseless Jihad, comprising violent raids and wars, against the infidels for establishing the all-encompassing religious-social-political system of Islam over the whole earth. For example, the Quran commands:

---

335. The Age, *Deadly disease without cure*, 19 June 2007

336. Perr J, *Homegrown Terrorism in the U.S. and Europe*, Perrspectives.com, 13 August 2006.

337. *A new faith for Kooris*, The Sydney Morning Herald, 4 May 2007

338. ABC Radio, *Aboriginal Da'wah - 'Call to Islam'*, 22 March 2006;
http://www.abc.net.au/rn/talks/8.30/relrpt/stories/s1597410.htm

1. 'And fight them (the infidels) on until there is no more Tumult or oppression [non-Islamic faiths], and there prevail justice and faith in Allah' [Quran 2.193].

2. 'And fight them on until there is no more tumult or oppression, and there prevail justice and faith in Allah altogether and everywhere' [Quran 8.39].

To Allah belongs the heaven and earth and everything in it, says the Quran [24:42, 34:1]. Allah holds the supreme and absolute authority over the heaven and earth [Quran 57:5, 67:1] and has made Muslims the inheritor of the latter for establishing a global Islamic rule. The Quran says: '*(Allah) hath made you (His) agents, inheritors of the earth*' [Quran 6:165] and that '*has promised to... make them rulers in the earth*' [Quran 24:55]. As Muslims wage Jihad against the infidels, Allah will come to their assistance to help them acquire their lands gradually and will eventually bring the whole earth under their control; Allah's global caliphate will, thus, be realized:

1. 'Do they not see that We are bringing destruction upon the land by curtailing it of its sides?'

2. 'See they not that We gradually reduce the land (in their control) from its outlying borders?'

Allah would help Muslims, if need be, by destroying the communities of the unyielding infidels to appropriate their land, of course, to hand it over to Muslims:

> And how many a community have We destroyed that was thankless for its means of livelihood! And yonder are their dwellings, which have not been inhabited after them save a little. And We, even We, were the inheritors. [Quran 28.58]

Allah made good of these lofty promises, too. It was Allah, Who helped Muslims wrestle the lands of Jewish tribes of Medina. Allah claims that He helped Muslims acquire the lands and properties of Banu Qaynuqa and Banu Nadir by expelling them from their lands: '*(Allah) it is Who hath caused those of the People of the Scripture (Banu Nadir Jews etc.) who disbelieved to go forth from their homes unto the first exile*' by casting terror in their hearts and bestowed whatever Allah had grabbed from them as spoil (the land and properties) unto His messenger [Quran 59:2–6]. As concerns the Jewish tribe of Banu Qurayza, '*Allah did take them down from their strongholds and cast terror into their hearts*' enabling Muslims slay some of them and make the rest prisoners [Quran 33:26] and '*made you (Muslims) heirs of their lands, their houses, and their goods, and of a land which ye had not frequented (before)*' [Quran 33:27].

Indeed, over the centuries since the birth of Islam, Muslims clearly believed Allah was helping them achieve victory and acquire the lands of the infidels in their Jihadi conquests. Al-Biladuri, the eminent Muslim historian of the Abbasid court (mid-ninth century), asserts that it was Allah who had conquered the lands of Medina Jews for Muslims.[339] Al-Utbi notes of Sultan Mahmud's victory of over King Jaipal at Peshawar (1001–02) that '*God bestowed upon his friends such amount of booty as was beyond all bounds and all calculation, including five hundred thousand slaves, men and women. The sultan returned with his followers to his camp, having plundered immensely, by God's aid, having obtained victory, and thankful to God, the lord of the universe.*'[340] In the late sixteenth century, the Ottoman archives noted of their defeat at the battle of Lepanto (1571) that "*The fleet of the divinely guided Empire encountered the fleet of the wretched infidels, and the will of Allah turned the other way.*"[341] Such references that it was God, who was giving the Muslim holy warriors victory in their Jihad against the infidels, are universal in Islamic chronicles.

In order to complete the inheritance of the earth, which Allah has bestowed upon Muslims, they must kill the Polytheists wherever found and enslave their women and children (for converting to Islam) [Quran 9:5]. This way, Muslim will capture their lands and clear the way for establishing Islamic rule. For acquiring the lands under the control of the Monotheists—the Jews and Christians, for example—Muslims must fight

---

339. Hitti PK (2002) *History of the Arabs*, Palgrave Macmillan, London, p. 21,33

340. Elliot & Dawson, Vol. II, p. 26

341. Lewis B (2002) *What Went Wrong: Western Impact and Middle Eastern Response*, Phoenix, London, p. 12

them until they are subdued and subjugated to Muslim rule [Quran 9:29]. This way Muslims must complete the establishment of an imperial Islamic state of global expanse.

The global imperial Islamic state also has a colonial dimension of economic exploitation and gains. Allah commands Muslims to plunder the wealth of the infidels in Jihadi wars as sacred booty: '(*Allah) inherited you their land, their homes, their money, and lands you had never stepped on. God is able to do all things*' [Quran 33:27]. Allah not only commands Muslims to plunder booty, He also takes a share of it: '*And know that out of all the booty that ye may acquire (in war), a fifth share is assigned to Allah and his Messenger...*' [Quran 8:41]. Furthermore, Allah commands Muslims to impose taxes upon the defeated and subjugated *dhimmi* subjects, the Jews and Christians etc. [Quran 9:29], for enriching the coffer of the Islamic state.

Therefore, the Quran evidently outlines a module for the establishment of a colonial state of global expanse, albeit of divine nature. Prophet Muhammad had meticulously acted upon every command of Allah and established, with Allah's unfurling assistance, a prototypical model of Islamic rule, which was ideally colonial and imperial in nature. He came to Medina with his followers from a foreign land as refugees. He soon established a foreign rule and an Islamic state in Medina by exterminating the non-submissive Jewish tribes one after another, while the Pagans—through coercion or the lure of booty—became assimilated into his militant religious community. Once the foreign Islamic rule was established in Medina, it became the launching-pad for further conquest and imperial expansion beyond its borders.

The ideal example of establishing a colonial rule by Prophet Muhammad was the conquest of Khaybar. Under no provocation, he led a large Muslim army against Khaybar in May 628. After defeating the Jews, he put the men of fighting-age to death, captured their wealth and treasures, and carried away their women and children as slaves. The surviving Jewish men (the old ones) were spared and allowed to tend their lands. The Prophet imposed upon them a heavy tax, 50 percent of the produce, to be remitted into the overseas treasury of the Islamic state, based in Medina. But this arrangement was to continue until Muslims were capable of taking possession of the Khaybar lands by themselves. The second Caliph Omar (d. 644) later expelled the Jews altogether in accordance with the Prophet's last wishes.

Similarly, Allah granted the "women, children, and flocks" of the Hawazin and Thaqif tribes '*as booty to His Messenger, who divided the spoils among those Quraysh who had recently embraced Islam,*' records al-Tabari.[342] By the time Muhammad died, he had established a nascent Islamic empire in the Arabian Peninsula by expanding colonial Islamic domination over the Christian, Jewish and Pagan strongholds. Whenever, he conquered a foreign land by the force of arms or by threats—the people, particularly the idolaters, were converted to Islam on the pain of death, their religious institutions were destroyed, and restrictions were imposed on their religious and cultural practices. Most of all, he plundered the wealth and treasures, including enslaving the women and children of the vanquished, and imposed taxes, namely *jizyah* and *kharaj*, upon them. This was a perfect template of colonial rule, involving both economic exploitations and socio-cultural degradations to the extreme.

Muhammad's conquest of Khaybar was evidently a perfect example of conquering a foreign land for establishing a colonial rule. The difference between the prophetic and later European models of colonial rule is that the Europeans, in most instances, did not enslave the women and children of the conquered lands and send them to the imperial capitals of Europe. Secondly, the Europeans probably never evicted the entire population from the lands they conquered and colonized.

This ideal model of imperial expansion and colonial exploitation established by Prophet Muhammad was, after his death, embraced by his immediate successor caliphs and later Muslim rulers throughout the entire period of medieval Islamic domination. Within two decades of Muhammad's death, the powerful Persian Empire was under the feet of Islam, while Byzantium, the most powerful empire of the time, had lost

---

342. al-Tabari, Vol. IX, p. 3

a big chunk of its crown territory to the ever-expanding Islamic empire. Toward the late medieval period, when the Ottoman sultans were at the forefront of imperial Islamic expansion, the Islamic army, under the banner of Jihad, reached the gates of Vienna twice in their effort to incorporate Europe into the Islamic empire.

Islam, therefore, was founded at its birth as an imperial, colonial power by Prophet Muhammad in accordance with the divine instructions of Allah. In time, Islam went on to establish the greatest colonial empire of the medieval world and sustained the longest period in the history of imperial colonialism. Later on, the rival European colonists started dismantling it in the mid-eighteenth century. But how many people in the world have heard the term "Islamic imperialism" or "Islamic colonialism", although European colonialism is first thing one learns about world history.

THE PERCEPTION OF ISLAMIC RULE

Muslims, growing up in the subcontinent, are taught to be proud of Islam's heroic and glorious past in India. Special adulation is reserved for the three great Islamic heroes, Muhammad bin Qasim, Sultan Mahmud of Ghazni and Mughal Emperor Aurangzeb, for their decisive roles in firmly establishing the Muslim faith in Hindustan. Qasim was the first to bring the light of Islam to the India proper through his conquest of Sindh in 712. Then Sultan Mahmud came along in 1000 CE and made seventeenth brilliant expeditions to India, bringing with him an unrelenting determination to further the spread of Islamic glory amongst benighted infidels of the subcontinent. From a Muslim perspective, he became a model of perseverance for spreading the light of Islam. Drawing on Sultan Mahmud's undying determination as an example, Muslim children are told to increase their determination and perseverance to achieve their goals in life.

Emperor Aurangzeb (r. 1658–1707) is another great Islamic hero amongst Muslim rulers of India; he played a critical role in saving Islam in India by reversing enlightened Akbar's deviant and liberal policies, harmful to Islam. Akbar had attempted to synthesize a new composite religion, called *Din-i-Ilahi*—religion of God, which could extinguish the light of Islam in India forever. His great grandson Dara Sikoh followed in his footsteps to reinvigorate the synthesis of Islam, Hinduism and Buddhism. Aurangzeb, a fanatical Sunni Muslim, waged Jihad against his heretical brother Dara Sikoh, the heir-apparent to the throne, and put him to death on the accusation of apostasy. Aurangzeb also patronized the composition of the *Fatwa-i-Alamgiri*, a great compendium of *Hanafi* laws, which, neglected for a long time, helped bring the wayward Islam to the right path in India. In sum, Aurangzeb rescued and revived a decaying Islam and saved it from its decadence and likely extinction in India. He also prospered it by patronizing the conversion of non-Muslims to Islam by force and other forms of compulsion and inducements. During his fifty-year rule, he brought the full force of Islam to bear on the state policy—so much so that, the majority of the Muslims in Northern India trace their Islamic roots to their ancestors' conversion in Aurangzeb's reign. These three great Islamic conquerors and rulers brought and propagated the light of the glorious *religion of truth* in the dark, decadent and idolatrous land of India. Islam's arrival marked the beginning of a great civilization in India, replacing its worthless *jahiliyah* (ignorance) past. So goes the Islamic discourse!

This remains the general impression of Islamic rule in India not only amongst Muslims; it is also the dominant opinion amongst modern historians of non-Muslim backgrounds. The history books in Pakistan teach: 'Before Mohammed (Qasim) there is blackness: slavery, exploitation. After Mohammed, there is light: slavery and exploitation vanish.'[343] In India, the general theme of this School of history writing has been succinctly described by Shashi Sharma:

---

343. Naipaul VS (1981) *Among the Believers: An Islamic Journey*, Alfred A Knopf, New York, p. 143

The pre-Muslim past of India was just a caboodle of decay, superstition, inequality, and oppression. Nothing credible or worthy ever took place within her boundaries. It was Islam that brought all that Indians could boast of with pride as the positives of their civilization: the Sufis, kebab, *ghazals*,[344] religious devotion, human brotherhood, and of course Amir Khasrau. Did Arabia not wallow in the darkness of incompetent ignorance till the light of Islam brought her to the threshold of culture?[345]

When the same historians write about the British rule in India, they find it to be the darkest period in India's history—a period of tyranny, oppression and extreme exploitation—with the sole aim of plunder and economic extraction for swelling the British coffer.

This *Islam the benefactor* view of history writing is widespread globally, as notes Ibn Warraq: '*Open any modern introductory book on Islam and the chances are you will find that it begins by singing the praise of a people who conquered, in an incredibly short period, half the civilized world—of a people who established an empire that stretched from the banks of the Indus in the East to the shores of the Atlantic in the West. The volume will recount in positively glowing terms a time when Muslims ruled over a vast population of diverse peoples and cultures.*'[346] Pundit Jawaharlal Nehru, for example, writes on the spread of Islam: '*The Arabs... in a fine frenzy of enthusiasm and with a dynamic energy, had spread out and conquered from Spain to the borders of Mongolia, carrying with them a **brilliant culture**...*'[347] No historian can get away with such effusive eulogy of the vast empires of Cyrus and Alexander the Great of the ancient world, much less so of the European empires of the more recent past.

When modern historians cover the history of European colonial empires, the British and the French ones for example, they are invariably described in extremely negative, indeed derogatory, terms. Those are narrated as a period of terrible exploitation, injustice, and misery brought upon the colonized people by their foreign masters. European rules overseas are invariably labeled as colonialist or imperialist, which carries a shameful, degrading and negative connotation. If a British historian were to paint the picture of the British colonial rule in a positive light with beneficial consequences, he/she would be pilloried, ridiculed and castigated to the extreme.

Intriguingly, the great majority of people of the world, including those on whom the Islamic rule was brutally imposed by foreign Muslim invaders, have rarely heard of anything called Islamic imperialism or colonialism. Muslims, and even a large majority of the non-Muslims of the subcontinent, will neither believe nor agree that the long period of Islamic hegemony over a vast area of the world, including their own country, can be rightly called imperialism or colonialism. The Arab, Persian, Turk and Berber Muslim invaders conquered many nations and imposed Islamic rule permanently in most instances. Muslims never consider these Muslim rules in foreign lands to be imperial or colonial in nature. The PBS documentary on Islamic history, widely used as teaching materials in American schools, calls the vast empire that Islam had founded to be an *empire of faith*, not a colonial empire.

As discussed in the previous chapter, Muslims believe that Islamic conquests were meant for humane and charitable reasons. Islamic conquerors came, they hold, never to exploit but with the purpose of liberating the masses from the tyranny and oppression of incumbent rulers; they came for integrating with the natives and for enriching and nourishing the conquered nations in the fields of economics, culture, arts, education and science. In India, the Muslim rulers imported the one *true* faith—a religion of "social equality and justice" as its core value and things that apparently had never existed. The founding father of Pakistan, Muhammad Ali Jinnah, demanded this in a speech addressed to the American people in February 1948: "*It (Islam) has taught*

---

344. *ghazals* are a kind of song

345. Sharma, p. 111

346. Ibn Warraq, p. 198

347. Nehru (1946), p. 222

equality of men, justice and fair-play to everybody. We are inheritors of these glorious traditions."[348] That is probably true because the double-mouthed Jinnah—agreeing with the Quran that '*O ye who believe! Truly the Pagans are unclean*' [Quran 9:28]—thought that the Hindus were a filthy people; and to keep away from them, he led the campaign for creating a separate homeland for Muslims, carefully choosing its name, *Pakistan* or *Land of the "Pure"* (i.e. pure Muslims). So much for the Islamic "equality of men, justice and fair-play to everybody" and Jinnah's belief in the same!

WHY ISLAMIC RULE IS *NOT* COLONIALISM?

The early Muslims of the Arabian Peninsula and, later on, their Persian, Turkish, Berber and Mongol Muslim protégés crossed great distances to attack and conquer foreign territories in order to establish Islamic rule and spread Islam. They ruled those lands for a few centuries in some places and have been ruling to the present day in others (albeit briefly interrupted by European colonists). They have made the majority of those nations Islamic forever. In places like India, the Balkans and Eastern Europe, Muslim rulers failed to convert the people in substantial numbers, either because of their tenacious adherence to indigenous culture and religion, defying the Muslim persecution and enforcement, or because that the relatively short period of Muslim rule deprived them of sufficient time to convert the masses.

In Europe, Islamic imperial rule started with the conquest of Spain in 711 and lasted until 1492. From Spain, they penetrated deep into Europe, reaching the heart of France, where they were defeated at Tours in 732 by Charles Martel. This defeat restricted the Muslim expansion in Europe from the Iberian front at the French border ever after; Muslims ruled Spain for nearly eight centuries before they were completely ousted from power in 1492. This was a temporary but crucial blow to the raging expansion of Islam in Europe. In summarizing the general sentiment regarding this battle, notes Nehru: "*On the plains of Tours*,' a historian has said, '*the Arabs lost the empire of the world when almost in their grasp. There can be no doubt that if the Arabs had won at Tours, European history would have been tremendously changed. There was no one else to stop them... Instead of Christianity, Islam would have then become the religion of Europe, and all manners of other changes might have taken place.*'[349] If not for this victory of Martel, wrote Edward Gibbon, "*perhaps the interpretation of the Quran would now be taught in the schools of Oxford and her pulpit might demonstrate to a circumcised people the sanctity and truth of the revelation of Mahomet.*"[350]

However, the Jihadi zeal of Muslims to conquer the globe for establishing a global Islamic suzerainty, as commanded by Allah, could hardly be extinguished. In attempts to consolidate their conquest of Europe, they intensified their attacks on the Mediterranean coastal cities and islands off Italy in the early ninth century. In 813, they devastated and occupied Centumcellae, Ischia and Lampedusa. In the same year, they attacked the Sardinia and Corsica Islands. Centumcellae was devastated again in 829.

In 840, the Arabs made an incursion deep into Italy and devastated the monastery of Subiaco. In 840, they conquered the coastal towns off Benevento; Carolingian Emperor Ludovico II succeeded in ousting them in 871. In 845, they penetrated deep inland capturing Capo Miseno (Naples) and Ponza near Rome, making it their base for attacking Rome. In 846, they ransacked Brindisi and conquered Taranto near the Southwest tip of Italy; Byzantine Emperor Basil I succeeded in freeing Taranto in 880.

On 28 August 846, a Muslim fleet arrived at the mouth of river Tiber and sailed to attack Rome. Meanwhile, a Muslim army from Civitavecchia and another from Portus and Ostia marched on-land to join the attack. They failed to penetrate the enclosing walls, solidly defended by the Romans. The Arabs vandalized and plundered the churches of St. Peter and St. Paul. The Saxons, Longobards, Frisians and Franks

---

348. Jamal K, *Founding fathers' descendants condemn emergency*, The News International, 20 November, 2007
349. Nehru J (1989) *Glimpses of World History*, Oxford University Press, New Delhi, p. 146
350. Pipes (1983), p. 86

staunchly defended St. Peter, perishing to the last man. Muslims destroyed all the churches of the district of Suburb. Pope Leo IV briefly fled Rome and appealed for help from neighboring kingdoms. Responding to his plea, Marquis Guy of Spoleto counterattacked and defeated the Arabs. While fleeing partly toward Civitavecchia and partly toward Fondi, Muslims indulged in ruin and devastation of the country. At Gaeta, the Longobard army clashed with them again. Guy of Spoleto found himself in serious difficulty, but the Byzantine troops of Cesarius from Naples arrived in time to rescue him. This attack prompted Pope Leo IV to undertake the construction of the Civitas Leonina in 848 to protect the Vatican Hill.

In 848, they sacked Ancona. The next year, a huge Muslim naval fleet set off to attack Rome and met an Italian naval fleet at the mouth of the river Tiber near Ostia. In the battle, the Arabs were routed. In 856, they attacked and destroyed the Cathedral of Canosa in Puglia. In 861, they assaulted Ascoli and, after slaughtering the children, carried away the inhabitants as slaves. In 872, they attacked and besieged Salerno for six months. In 876, they attacked Latium and Umbria slaughtering the inhabitants, enslaving them and sacking the villages before marching toward Rome; they turned the Roman country into an unhealthy desert. Pope John VIII (872–82) defeated the Arabs at Circeo and freed 600 enslaved Christians from eighteen Muslim vessels. He attempted to expel the Arabs after the depredations, but with little help from European kings forthcoming, he failed and was forced to pay tribute.

Muslims continued their devastation of Latium both on the coast and inland, consolidating their conquest of the Roman country: they went on to capture Tivoli (Saracinesco), Sabina (Ciciliano), Narni, Nepi, Orte, Tiburtino countries, Sacco valley, Tuscia and Argentario Mountain. Their depredations continued through the 880s and 890s. In the early tenth century, Muslims were planning to establish an Emirate in Southern Italy. In 916, Marquis Adalbertus of Tusca, Marquis Albericus of Spoleto, Prince Landulf of Capua and Benevento, Prince Gaimar of Salerno, the dukes of Gaeta and Naples and Byzantine Emperor Constantine entered into an anti-Arab alliance, with Pope John X personally heading the land troops. The Arabs were totally defeated and mainland Italy was freed from the Muslim invaders.

The Mediterranean island of Sicily, where Muslims had founded a long-lasting Emirate, suffered the first Jihad raid, involving pillage and plunder, in 652; it was repeated in 669, 703, 728, 729, 730, 731, 733, 734, 740 and 752. The early Muslim incursions (652–752) in Sicily failed to gain a foothold for Islam. The conquest of Sicily began in real earnest when an Aghlabid Arab army from Tunis landed in Mazara del Vallo in 827. This started a long series of battles: Palermo fell in 831, Pantelleria in 835 and Messina in 843. Cefalù and Enna resisted the Muslim conquest for years before being conquered and burned down in 858 and 859, respectively. Syracuse offered strong resistance for long; the Arabs overran it in 878, massacring the entire population. Sicily was lost. Palermo, renamed al-Madinah, became the new Islamic capital; Arabic language replaced Greek. A native counterattack against the Muslim occupation of Sicily had started in 827. But a Norman conquest, begun in 1061, eventually expelled Muslims in 1091.

On another front, Muslims eventually overran entire Eastern Christendom, centered in Constantinople. In the famous conquest of Constantinople in 1453, the Ottoman holy warriors slaughtered the inhabitants for three days and the rest were enslaved. The Ottoman Jihadis, bypassing Constantinople, had already crossed over to Europe in the 1350s. After a couple of decades of see-saw battles, the Ottomans gained extensive victories capturing Bulgaria and the Balkans in the 1380s and went on to attack Venice in 1423. The capture of Constantinople in 1453 further facilitated the Ottoman conquest of Europe. They captured the entire Balkan Peninsula, moved toward Russia capturing Crimea, and laid unsuccessful siege twice on Vienna, the heart of Western Europe and the Holy Roman Empire, in 1529 and 1683. Muslims at some point ruled the whole of Spain, Portugal, Hungary, Yugoslavia, Albania, Greece, Bulgaria and Romania. They ruled parts of France, Germany, Switzerland, Italy, Austria, Poland, Czechoslovakia and the Soviet Union. By the sixteenth century, extensive Ottoman conquest had reduced Europe into a truncated, cornered Christian landmass, desperately resisting an inescapable takeover by the Ottoman Islamic army. Busbecq, the ambassador of the Holy Roman Empire to Istanbul (1554–62), resonated this desperate sentiment as he went on to say, it was only the threat from Safavid Persia to the Turkish Empire that saved the imminent Ottoman conquest of Europe.[351]

The second defeat of the Ottoman invaders in Vienna (1683) decisively proved the supremacy of European powers over their age-old tormentors; the fortune of the perennial Islam-Europe conflict dramatically changed in Europe's favor. This not only marked the end of Islamic expansion, but also the beginning of its decline. The Ottomans were progressively expelled, eventually from all parts of Western Europe. They continued ruling some Balkan regions until the early twentieth century. Muslims were not only expelled from Europe, starting in mid-eighteenth century, Britain, Holland, France, Italy and Spain eventually captured most of the Islamic lands. Russia took large parts of Central Asian and Eastern European regions, while China, Burma and Thailand also recaptured lands, previously conquered by Muslims.

The European counter-adventure into the Muslim world led to the transfer of political control of most Muslim-ruled territories into European hands by the early twentieth century. Only the regions inaccessible or having little economic incentives—namely Afghanistan and Saudi Arabia as well as Iran and the Ottoman Turkey—remained outside the European control. This period of European imperialism became known as the colonial era. When European colonial powers eventually withdrew from their colonies, countries, dominated by Muslims in population, came under Islamic governance. Elsewhere, where Muslims were in the minority, such as in India, Muslims lost political power to indigenous majorities—the rightful inheritor of the land. In some countries, such as in Nigeria, Muslims, despite being the minority, retained political domination.

The critical point to be considered here is that the Muslim invaders captured those foreign territories by means of brutal invasions and ruled them in an authoritarian fashion for many centuries, turning some of those lands Islamic forever. The European colonists also came from afar to occupy and establish their rule, but the method they employed was, in many instances, certainly less brutal than that of Muslims. Compared to the Muslim invasion, the British occupation of India came at much less bloodshed, and injury and disruption of civilian life.

The question, therefore, arises: How can one of the two foreign rules in India be considered abhorrent colonialism or imperialism, the other not? The popular counter to this enquiry is given by Dr Taj Hashmi, a Professor of Comparative Religion at York University (Canada): '...*unlike the British invaders, Muslim rulers considered India home, as they did not have any metropolis like London to siphon off Indian wealth and resources.*'[352]

There are two fundamental assertions in this claim, which warrant an in-depth analysis. First, the Islamic rule in foreign countries was not motivated by exploitation. Second, the Muslim invaders considered the foreign lands as their own home; and that, they worked for its development and enrichment. The European rule was, on the contrary, driven by the exactly opposite motivation: solely to exploit the alien people and their resources. It is, however, not true that the European colonists never called the conquered lands their home. In certain African countries—South and North America, and Australasia, they have settled in large numbers. Had the British rule continued in India, say for nearly a millennium like the Muslim rule, many more Britons would have eventually called India their home.

ECONOMIC EXPLOITATION IN ISLAMIC EXPANSION

Who could argue that the European colonial rule was not primarily meant for the exploitation of the resources, cheap labor, and markets of foreign lands, aimed at enriching the treasuries of European capitals? After all,

---

351. Lewis (2002), p. 10

352. Hashmi T, News from Bangladesh website; 2 June 2005

the cities like London, Paris, Amsterdam, Madrid and Lisbon owed their prosperity and affluence in those days to the wealth generated from economic exploitations overseas. Many prominent European families to this day owe their comfortable and affluent status to the entrepreneurial and rags-to-riches success of a colonist ancestor, who made his fortune in tea, spices, rubber, sugar or shipping.

But, what was the true motive of Islamic invasion and rule around the world? Was it not motivated by economic exploitations as well? Let us go back to the foundations of Islam to see how Prophet Muhammad's exploits in terms of economic extractions had influenced the later Islamic expansion.

The model of plunder and economic exploitation, which the Prophet had established in his conquests—of Khaybar, for example—became the *modus operandi* in subsequent Muslim invasions during the early centuries of Islam. After all, anything the Prophet did was, for Muslims, not only a stamp of approval to do likewise, but, theologically, was also the most ideal example Muslims must strive to emulate in their actions and deeds. The *Pact of Omar* also gives a similar outline for extracting taxes from the conquered *dhimmi* subjects. When early Muslim invaders conquered Syria, Jerusalem and Egypt etc., the Christian and Jews were made to pay *jizyah* to the treasury of the Medina caliphate and suffer other forms of humiliating impositions applicable to *dhimmi* subjects in a Muslim state. Furthermore, Caliph Omar devised a system of land-tax, called *kharaj*, imposed on *dhimmis* in conquered Muslim territories.

Making his successful inroads into Sindh in 712, Muhammad bin Qasim looted and plundered vast sums of treasures and wealth, and captured a great multitude of women and children as slaves after killing the men in large numbers. Qasim always sent the state's share of one-fifth of the loot and captured slaves, the divinely sanctioned "spoil of war" (*anfal*) as per the Islamic creed, to the caliph in Damascus. After every successful campaign, the state's one-fifth share of the booty was meticulously put aside for forwarding to the caliph. Al-Kufi records in *Chachnama* that 20,000 captives of both sexes along with the looted wealth were forwarded to the caliph in one occasion.[353] The caliph would add some of the prettiest of the young women to his harem; others would be given as gifts to his nobles and generals; and the remainder sold for generating revenues for the treasury.

Prophet Muhammad used to take possession of the most prized female captives, such as Safiya, the beautiful young wife of Khaybar leader Kinana, for keeping as his own concubine. Qasim, likewise, sent the female captives of special value or significance—of exquisite beauty or royal and noble blood—as a special gift and mark of respect to the caliph. When two daughters of King Dahir were taken captive by Qasim, he duly forwarded them to Caliph al-Walid, who made them part of his harem.

The cost of Qasim's initial assaults in Sindh stood at 60 million *dirhams*, financed by the treasury of the caliph. Months before Qasim was recalled from his three-year mission to Sindh, the one-fifth share of the booty, sent to governor al-Hajjaj in Iraq, was counted to be 120 million *dirhams*.[354] Hajjaj quickly settled debt to the caliphal treasury and wrote a letter to Qasim, saying: '*My nephew, I had agreed and pledged myself, at the time you marched with the army, to repay the whole expense incurred by the public treasury in fitting out the expedition to the Khalifa Walid bin Abdul Malik bin Marwan, and it is incumbent on me to do so.*'[355]

Qasim imposed *jizyah* and *kharaj* taxes on the Hindu subjects according to the laws formulated by Caliph Omar, based on the principles set down in the Quran and *Sunnah*. *Chachnama* records: '*Muhammad Qasim fixed the poll-tax upon all the subjects according to the laws of the Prophet. Those who embraced the Muhammadan faith were exempted from slavery, the tribute (kharaj) and the poll-tax (jizyah); and from those who did not change their creed, a tax was exacted.*'[356] With the capture of Sindh, the Hindus simply became serfs in their ancestral land of centuries, which became property of the Muslim state. They had to pay the

---

353. Lal (1994), p. 19
354. Elliot & Dawson, Vol. I, p. 470–71
355. Ibid, p. 206
356. Ibid, p. 182

land-tax (*kharaj*) fixed as followed: '*The land tax was usually rated at two-fifths of the produce of wheat and barley, if the field were watered by the public canals; three-tenths, if irrigated by wheels or other artificial means; and one-fourth, if altogether unirrigated...*' This was in accordance with the original institution of Omar, when he '*assessed the cultivated land (Sawad) of Iraq.*'[357] To be noted here that Hindu laws stipulate the tax as one-sixth to one-twelfth of the produce.

Of the revenues generated from these taxes, state's one-fifth share was routinely forwarded to the caliphal treasury. The province of Sindh possibly combined with Multan yielded annual revenue of 11.5 million *dirhams* (~ £270,000 in 1860s) and 150 pounds of aloe-wood for the caliphal treasury. This included the poll-tax, the land-tax and other customs duties. The annual yield of public revenue, remitted to the caliphal treasury from other provinces of the Muslim caliphate, has been estimated by Elliot and Dawson as follows:[358]

1. Markhan: 400,000 *dirhams*

2. Sijistan: 460,000 *dirhams*, 300 variegated robes, and 20,000 pounds of sweetmeats

3. Kirman: 4,200,000 *dirhams*, 500 precious garments, 20,000 pounds of dates, and 1,000 pounds of caraway seeds

4. Tukharistan: 106,000 *dirhams*

5. Kabul: 1,500,000 *dirhams* and 1000 heads of cattle (~700,000 *dirhams*)

6. Fars: 27,000,000 *dirhams*, 30,000 bottles of rose-water and 20,000 bottles of black currants

7. Khultan: 1,733,000 *dirhams*

8. Bust: 90,000 *dirhams*

These facts clearly demonstrate that the rule imposed in Sindh by Muhammad bin Qasim was nothing less than a foreign rule imposed from the distant caliphal heartland in Arabia. The same applies to other foreign lands Muslim had conquered. It becomes clear that the Muslim invaders came to Sindh not only to rule but also to exploit and skim off the wealth and resources for remitting to the caliphal head-quarter in Damascus (later in Baghdad). This protocol is very similar to the one, which the Europeans applied in their colonies. It is noted already that the taxes imposed by Muslim rulers on the Hindus of India were so crushing that they even had to sell their wives and children in order to meet the tax demand. This, according to the chronicles of contemporary Muslim historians and European travelers, was common during the reign of Emperor Shahjahan and Aurangzeb (c. 1620–1707). Large numbers of Indian peasants also took refuge in jungles for failing to pay the crushing taxes.

When the second wave of Islamic invasion was unleashed on India by Sultan Mahmud (1000), the authority of the Baghdad caliph had become relatively weak. Defying the weak Abbasid caliphs of Baghdad, the Fatimids established independent rule in Egypt in 909; Umayyads were ruling Spain independently since 756. The Abbasid caliphs of Baghdad still retained a significant sway over Sultan Mahmud, the brutal invader of India. When Mahmud defeated Abdul Malik of Khurasan, Caliph Al-Qadir Billah—pleased with the rising, powerful general—recognized him as the *amir* (leader) and bestowed upon him the titles of *Yamin-ud-Daulah* (Right Hand of the State) and *Amin-ul-Millah* (Trustee of the Community). With this caliphal blessing, Sultan Mahmud started his attacks in Northwest India in about 1000 CE. In return for the caliphal recognition and blessing, Mahmud used to send large amount of money and presents to the caliph from his plunder and tribute obtained in India, consisting of "all kinds of wealth". According to *Tarikh-i-Alfi*, Sultan Mahmud kept aside

---

357. Ibid, p. 474
358. Ibid, p. 471–472

one-fifth of his booty, which included 150,000 slaves, for sending to Baghdad.[359] This means his kingdom was a full province of the Baghdad caliphate. His son and successor, Sultan Masud, also received the endowment and recognition of the caliph, after promising '*to send him (caliph) every year a sum of 200,000 dinars, 10,000 pieces of cloths, besides other presents.*'[360]

Sultan Mahmud's brutal assaults on India brought Punjab in Northest India under the Ghaznivid rule. Some 150 years later, the Afghan Ghaurivid sultans, Muhammad Ghauri (d. 1206) and his brother Ghiyasuddin, began their assaults on Northern India, which led to the founding of the Muslim Sultanate in Delhi in 1206. Both Sultan Muhammad Ghauri and later Tajuddin Yildoz (d. 1216), the rulers of Ghazni, had received caliphal recognition and blessings from Baghdad. Sultan Iltutmish (d. 1236) of Delhi, having defeated Yildoz, received the caliphal investiture. Although the details are not recorded in every case, the caliph bestowed the prized investiture only in return of substantial wealth and presents. The blessings of the caliph of Baghdad, and later of Cairo (after Mongols drove them out of Baghdad) continued to be bestowed upon the sultans of Delhi in return for large amounts of wealth sent to the central seat of Islamic power. Sultan Firoz Tughlaq (d. 1388) received investiture from the caliph, as he records: '*A diploma was sent to me fully confirming my authority as deputy of the khilafat, and the leader of the faithful (caliph) was graciously pleased to honour me with the title of Saiyidu-s Salatin.*'[361]

The contemporaneous historian, Ziauddin Barani, writes of Muhammad Tughlaq's (d. 1351) generosity toward the caliph, now based in Egypt, that '*So great was the faith of the Sultan in the Khalifas (caliphs) that he would have sent all his treasures in Delhi to Egypt, had it not been for the fear of robbers.*'[362] Ghiyasuddin—a descendent of the defunct Baghdad caliphal family, now of little significance—came to Delhi during Muhammad Tughlaq's reign. The Sultan's generosity toward his Egyptian overlords can be gauged from his endowment on this unrelated and rather insignificant visitor, as summarized in the *Cambridge History of India*:

> …the vessels in his (Ghiyasuddin's) palace were of gold and silver, the bath being of gold and on the first occasion of his using it, a gift of 40,000 *tangas* was sent to him; he was supplied with male and female servants and slaves. He was allowed a daily sum of 300 *tangas*, though much of the food consumed by him came from the royal kitchen; he received in fee the whole of Sultan Alauddin's city of Siri, one of the four cities which composed the capital, with all its gardens and lands and a hundred villages; he was appointed governor of the eastern district of the province of Delhi; he received 30 mules with trappings of gold and whenever he visited the court, he was entitled to receive the carpet on which the king sat.[363]

When an insignificant and unrelated guest, like Ghiyasuddin, could receive such bounteous wealth and endowment from the sultan, it is not difficult to guess how much wealth he used to send to the caliph in Cairo. The independent sultans of Bengal (1337–1576), Jaunpur, and Malwa also received separate caliphal investitures in exchange of large sums of money and gifts. For example, Caliph al-Mustanjid Billah sent to Sultan Mahmud Khilji (1436–69) of Malwa robes of honor and recognition, which he accepted in return for large amount of gold and silver. Even some rebels of the Delhi Sultanate received the investiture of the caliph in return of money, gold and slaves.[364]

Undoubtedly, the Delhi Sultanate was in effect a province of the central Islamic caliphate. This formal relationship was disrupted after Amir Timur (Tamerlane), the brutal Jihadi invader, destroyed the Tughlaq dynasty (1399). The name of the Arab caliph was dropped from the Delhi coins. This was

---

359. Lal, p. 19–20

360. Lal (1999), p. 208

361. Elliot & Dawson, Vol. III, p. 387

362. Lal (1999), p. 210

363. Haig W (1958) *Cambridge History of India*, Cambridge University Press, Delhi, Vol. III, p. 159

364. Ahmed A (1964) *Studies in Islamic Culture in the Indian Environment*, Clarendon Press, Oxford, p. 10

necessitated by the fact that Timur left Delhi after his barbarous invasion declaring himself the emperor of India and placing the Sayyids at the throne. Realizing the threat of brutal Timur and the importance of his approval, the Sayyid sultans recognized Timur and his successors as the caliph and sent tribute to the Timurid capital of Samarkhand. According to Ferishtah, the first Sayyid Sultan Khizr Khan, '*held the government for Teimoor (Timur), in whose name he caused the coins to be struck, and the Khootba (prayer sermon) to be read. After the death of Teimoor, Khootba was read in the name of his successor, Shahrokh Mirza; to whom he sometimes even sent tribute...*'[365] The Islamic overlordship of the Delhi Sultanate moved to Samarkhand, not abolished. Akbar the Great (r. 1556–1605)—as powerful as any other Muslim ruler: Ottoman or Persian— later declared his independence from foreign overlordship. Therefore, from 712 to early sixteenth century, the Muslim-ruled part of India was basically a province of the wider Islamic world.

Besides sending revenue and gifts to the caliphal headquarters of Damascus, Baghdad, Cairo or Samarkand from India, Islam's holy cities of Mecca and Medina amongst others also received generous donations in money, gifts and presents even in the Mughal period, when the Indian rulers had declared their independence from foreign overlords. Emperor Babur (r. 1525–30) in his autobiography records the gifts and presents he had sent "in the cause of God" to the holy men of Samarkhand, Khurasan, Mecca and Medina. In one place, he wrote, ''*We gave one Shahrukhi (coin) for every soul in the country of Kabul and the vale-side of Varsak, man and woman, bonded and free, of age or non-age.*'' Even apostate Akbar showed generosity toward the city of Mecca and Medina as records *Humayun Nama*: ''*Though debarred from leaving Hindustan himself, he helped many others to fulfil this primary duty of their faith (Hajj), and opened wide his purse for their expenses. Each year, he named a leader of the caravan and provided him with gifts and ample funds for the two cities. When Gulbadan Begum, his paternal aunt, went to Hajj, sultan Khawja took among other presents 12,000 dresses of honor.*'' Mughal Emperor Akbar (r. 1556–1605), Jahangir (r. 1605–27) and Shahjahan (r. 1628–58) used to send subsistence to the religious men of Persia, Rum (Constantinople) and Azerbaijan as allowance "from God'" for "His servants", be they in Hindustan or any other Muslim countries. Emperor Shahjahan also used to send expensive gifts to Mecca.[366]

This is how the money and resources, extracted from the sweat and toil of non-Muslim subjects of India, used to be siphoned to the treasuries of the Islamic caliphate in Damascus, Baghdad, Cairo or Tashkent, to the Islamic holy cities of Mecca and Medina, and to the pockets of the Muslim holy men throughout the Islamic world. At the same time, the infidels of India were being reduced to awful misery.

It is a well-documented, but deliberately ignored, paradigm that Muslim conquests, from the time of Prophet Muhammad, were intended for plundering and looting the wealth and resources of the conquered people. The second purpose was to capture slaves, predominantly the women and children, who were converted to Islam and sold to Muslim owners and employed in all manner of menial servitude in the households of their Muslim masters (see Chapter VII on Slavery). The young and beautiful female captives became sex-slaves in the harem and households of rulers, generals, nobles and common Muslims. They served triple purposes: firstly, they provided labor for the comfort of their Muslim master; secondly, they served the master sexual pleasures; and thirdly, they acted as breeding tools for swelling the Muslim populace. The third purpose of the Muslim conquest of foreign lands was to impose the grinding *jizyah*, *kharaj* and other sundry taxes upon the vanquished people and a part of the revenue went to the central treasury.

Prophet Muhammad set a paradigm of conquest and the expansion of Islamic rule, whereby he used to conquer foreign lands by aggressive threats or violent attacks. Once a foreign land or community has been defeated, their wealth and treasures were invariably looted and one-fifth of the plunder went to state treasury, belonging to Allah and his Prophet, handled by the latter. When a community offered resistance, such as Banu Quraiza or Khaybar, after defeating them, he slaughtered their grown up men *en masse* and enslaved the women and children. The Prophet imposed taxes, namely *kharaj* (land-tax, tribute) and *jizyah* (poll-tax), on the conquered people. The revenue was remitted to the treasury overseen by him. After Muhammad's death,

---

365. Ferishtah, Vol. I, p. 295; Lal (1999), p. 210
366. Lal (1999), p. 212

the one-fifth share of the booty and slaves went to the treasury of the caliphate. In the post-prophetic era, the Muslim army became a formidable and rarely defeated force; during this time, the examples set by the Prophet were meticulously applied albeit on a grander scale. The examples documented by contemporaneous Muslim historians and European travelers recounted above confirm that the prophetic model of imperial conquest and colonial exploitation was consistently, although often with less severity, applied throughout the history of Islamic conquests.

Like in European colonial rule, the economic exploitation of the vanquished *dhimmi* subjects and the siphoning of their wealth and resources to Muslim capitals in foreign lands were a common motive of Islamic conquests and subsequent rules over vast parts of the world. The economic exploitation was the main aim of the European colonial powers: the British, Dutch and French. For Islamic colonial expansion, it was the secondary aim. The primary aim of Islamic imperial expansion, initiated by the Prophet in the name of fighting in the cause of Allah, was to spread the Islamic faith over all peoples at all corners of the globe. They slaughtered a great multitude of infidels and ruthlessly destroyed their religion, culture and civilization. In this respect, the Islamic colonists, like the Portuguese and Spanish, had largely identical aims: religious expansion as well as economic exploitations.

THE CULTURAL IMPERIALISM OF ISLAM

Allah says in the Quran that He has perfected Islam as a religion and chosen it for all mankind as His favour and proclaimed it to dominate over all other religions:

1. This day have I perfected your religion for you, completed My favour upon you, and have chosen for you Islam as your religion. [Quran 5:3]

2. It is He Who has sent His Messenger with Guidance and the Religion of Truth, to proclaim it over all religion: and enough is Allah for a Witness. [Quran 48:28]

Islam, as noted already, is a complete package for humankind, encompassing the religious, social, cultural and political, indeed, every aspect of life and society. Muslims universally believe that Islam is a "complete code of life". Islam, therefore, is a complete civilizational religion of divine nature. The society of believers—founded by Prophet Muhammad and his early successors, the *Rightly Guided Caliphs*—in Medina (622–661) was the ideal civilization that must transcend all corners of the world. Allah's proclamation of Islam over all religions and peoples must be achieved, as noted already, by the muscles of the believers through Jihad.

At the birth of Islam under Muhammad, pre-Islamic civilizations—cultures, customs and religions—became recognized as belong to the age of ignorance (*jahiliyah*). Those were superseded by the divinely guided civilization established by Muhammad and his community of believers. Prophet Muhammad acted single-mindedly to erase the previous Pagan civilization—namely the religious practices, culture and customs of Arabia, even of his own kinfolk—by giving them the choice of death or Islam in accordance with Allah's command in Quran 9:5. As Muslim holy warriors sprang out of Arabia for fighting in the cause of Allah and conquered vast territories, including the world's greatest civilizations of Persia, Byzantium and India etc., the vanquished peoples suffered extensive destruction of their cultures, customs and religious practices. Therefore, apart from the crushing economic exploitations and terrorizing political exertions, Muslim invaders and rulers caused unprecedented and incalculable cultural and civilizational devastations to humanity.

The great pre-Islamic conquerors—namely Alexander the Great, Cyrus the Great, the Germanic peoples (Vandals, Visigoths, Ostrogoths etc.) in Europe, and the Sakas and Huns in India—either got themselves assimilated in the culture, religion and society of the conquered lands or facilitated a syncretic synthesis of the conquering and conquered cultures. In the Islamic era, the Mongol invaders also eventually assimilated themselves in the civilizations of the conquered peoples: '*In China and Mongolia, most of them*

124

became Buddhists; in Central Asia they became Muslims; perhaps some in Russia and Hungary became Christians.'[367] But the Islamic conquerors acted on destroying the culture of the conquered infidels because of the fundamental Muslim belief that the vestiges of the pre-Islamic *jahiliyah* age must be replaced by the perfect religious, political and cultural civilization of Islam. From India to Spain, the destruction of countless numbers of Pagan temples, Buddhist monasteries, Christian churches, Jewish synagogues, and so on bears testimony of the widespread destruction of non-Islamic cultures by Muslim invaders. The Islamic conquests, therefore, came at "extraordinary cultural costs",[368] which remains thoroughly unacknowledged. Instead, the Muslim invaders, surprisingly, have been widely credited with enriching the civilizations of the conquered. In comparing and contrasting the impact of European and Arab (Islamic) rules on the cultural and civilizational aspects of the ruled, Ibn Warraq laments:

> Although Europeans are constantly being castigated for having imposed their insidious and decadent values, cultures and language on the Third World, no one cares to point out that Islam colonized lands that were the home of advanced and ancient civilizations, and that in doing so, Islamic colonialism trampled under foot and permanently destroyed many cultures.[369]

Therefore, apart from the purpose of economic exploitation and political domination, the Islamic invaders also came with an over-riding mission of cultural imperialism. Islam comes with the *mantra* that Prophet Muhammad was the greatest and the perfect example of human life; Muslims must try to emulate his life, actions and deeds in every detail possible. Muhammad, being an Arab and fountainhead of the Islamic creed—a non-Arab person, by embracing Islam, ideally seeks to mimic the life of Muhammad, an Arabo-Islamic overlord. It becomes his life-long mission to become an Arab in lifestyle and Islamic in religious belief, forgoing his own cultural and civilizational values, precepts, and practices. Sir VS Naipaul met one Mr. Jaffrey—a British educated Journalist, living in Tehran. Born and educated in Lukhnow (India), Mr. Jaffrey, a Shiite Muslim, had grown up with the dream of "*jame towhidi*, the society of the believers", a dream of re-creating the culture and society of the earliest days of Islam, founded by Prophet Muhammad in Medina. In his dream of living such a life, he quit Hindu-dominated India in 1948 for Pakistan. Not satisfied with the Sunni Muslim society and its treatment of Shiites, he moved to Shiite Iran, where he worked in the English-language daily, *Tehran Times*. He was disappointed again, because '*Iran under the Shah was a tyranny, and the great wealth when it came led to corruption and sodomy and general wickedness.*'[370] Then there came the Islamic revolution, something Mr. Jaffrey could be delighted about. Iran under the Ayatollahs, ruling as the spiritual and political sovereign in the fashion of the Prophet, was closest to the *jame towhidi* Mr. Jaffrey had been dreaming for. Such a dream is rather universal amongst pious Muslims, the so-called fundamentalists, everywhere, the West included.

Behind Mr. Jaffrey's story lies a very fundamental Muslim urge: that is, how far a Muslim, highly trained in Western secular education, is willing to go in order to live an Arabo-Islamic religious, social, cultural and political life, forgoing his ancestral culture and tradition. Of the Arab cultural hegemony imposed by Islam on the conquered and converted peoples, Anwar Shaikh writes:[371]

> …it becomes the duty of all converts to Islam that they must accept the Arab cultural hegemony, that is, subordinate all their national institutions to those of Arabia, adopt Islamic law, learn

367. Nehru J (1989) *Glimpses of World History*, Oxford University Press, Delhi, p. 222

368. Crone P & Cook M (1977) *Hagarism: The Making of the Islamic World*, Cambridge University Press, Cambridge, p. VIII

369. Ibn Warraq, p. 198

370. Naipaul VS (1998) *Beyond Belief: The Islamic Incursions among the Converted Peoples*, Random House, New York, p. 144–45

371. Shaikh A (1998) *Islam: The Arab Imperialism*, The Principality Publishers, Cardiff, Chapter 7

Arabic and Arab manners, love Mecca and Arabs to acknowledge Muhammad as the Model of Behaviour because being an Arab he loved and enforced everything that was Arabian. Still worse, they must hate their own culture and motherland to such an extent that it becomes *Dar-ul-Harb*, i.e. a living battlefield.

When one takes a closer look at Islamic countries across the continents, the pernicious impact of Islam on the cultural heritage of a vast number of peoples of wide religious, cultural, racial and geographical diversity becomes easily discernable. It is remarkable to wonder at how the culture and tradition of Muslims of Bangladesh, Pakistan, Afghanistan, Malaysia and Indonesia in Asia, of Iran, Syria and Palestine in the Middle East, of Egypt, Sudan, Algeria and Somalia in Africa, and of Turkey and Chechnya in Europe—having Hindu, Buddhist, Zoroastrian, Animist, Christian, Jewish and Pagan roots before the Muslim invasions—have essentially been transformed into a quite similar Arabo-Islamic one with some variations here and there. More remarkable is the way their culture and outlook on life differ from the people belonging to their pre-Islamic roots living around them. This has all happened despite nearly two centuries of disruption by European colonial rule in many of these countries, during which period a determined effort was made to secularize as well as to preserve and rediscover the lost or diminished pre-Islamic socio-cultural heritage of those lands.

The desire for seeing the entire globe turned Islamic in all aspects of life and society is universal amongst faithful Muslims. I have known many Muslims with high academic qualifications from Bangladesh, Pakistan, India and elsewhere living in the West. Although they would never ever think of quitting their host societies for living the Islamic life of their own country or elsewhere in the Muslim world, they never hide their agony of living in a horribly decadent society and culture of the West. There is a burning desire amongst them to see the Western society and culture—the economic, and to some degree, the political aspects (democracy etc.) aside—being replaced by the morally perfect Islamic ways. The increasingly popular Sharia-compliant finance amongst Muslim immigrants is likely to restructure the economic aspect of the Western society, too.

It should be understood that, at the time of Islam's birth, Zoroastrian Persia, Hindu-Buddhist India, Pagan-Coptic Egypt, Pagan-Buddhist China and Christian Byzantium were the world's finest of civilizations, all having long cultural histories and achievements in arts, architecture, education, literature and science. Islam, on the contrary, was founded in the essentially lawless Bedouin Arab Peninsula, when these civilizations had achieved much greater advancement than the unsophisticated Arabs. It is remarkable that Islam has completely effaced the pre-Islamic civilizations from the great lands of Iran, Iraq, Syria, Egypt and Palestine amongst others. Egypt is heir to the earliest and finest civilization of the ancient world, lasting 3,000 years. But the Egyptian Muslims, a non-Arab people, are all now Arabs. Lamenting this degenerating transformation of the Egyptian society, notes Anwar Shaikh, '*look at Egypt... This wonderful land of science, art, culture and godly manners, came down with a thud to touch its nadir when Islam took over its destiny. There are no Egyptians anymore. They all have become Arabs!*'[372]

What is astonishing is the way today's pious Muslims, the descendants of those great civilizations, despise the remnants of their original heritage. The Algerian Islamist movements, for example, took up arms in the 1990s and have killed up to 200,000 of their fellow countrymen in trying to arabize their country completely, to dissociate itself from its Berber African past. It should be noted here that their pre-Islamic Berber ancestors, repulsed by the Islamic invaders and their creed, had put up the staunchest resistance against the Arabs in Africa. According to Ibn Khaldun, the Berbers had apostatized for twelve times before the Arab invaders could decisively impose Islam on them. The fierce Berber resistance forced the Arabs to withdraw several times from the Maghrib.[373]

---

372. Ibid

373. Levtzion N (1979), Toward a Comparative Study of Islamization, In N. Levtzion ed., p. 6

Muslims, by converting to Islam, profess to live by the Quran and prophetic examples in all aspects of life; they become Arabo-Islamic cultural slaves. It becomes incumbent upon them not only to ape the Arabo-Islamic way of life, but also to destroy their pre-Islamic culture, tradition and achievements, repudiated by the Arabo-Islamic civilization. For them, their motherland remains a *Dar al-Harb*—a land of war, until it has been purified religiously, politically and culturally: '*These non-Arab Muslims develop a special sense of contempt for their own cultures and motherlands under the pretence of believing in the Muslim nationhood.*'[374]

Pious Muslims in the subcontinent, therefore, entertain a strong desire to see their countries completely cleansed of the idolatrous Hindu religion, tradition and culture. Muslims created Pakistan at the cost of millions of lives for founding a pure land for them. A similar movement has continued in Muslim-dominated Kashmir since 1947. Similarly, the devout Muslims in Iran want to see all vestiges of pre-Islamic religious and cultural traditions expunged from their country as soon as possible. Following the Iranian revolution, the Ayatollahs, who aimed to re-create the social, political and religious society founded by the Prophet, banned teaching of ancient Iranian history in schools and universities and the teachers in these disciplines had to resign. The pious Egyptian Muslims, likewise, have an eager desire to see the remnants of the pre-Islamic Coptic Christians and their culture and tradition, blotted out forever from Egypt.

In travelling to Pakistan, Indonesia, Malaysia and Iran in the late 1970s and early 1990s, Naipaul noticed a pervasive desire amongst well-educated Muslims for obliterating the so-called un-Islamic ways and traits of their societies and to destroy the remnant of their pre-Islamic cultural heritage. Observing an uncompromising Arab imperialistic affliction imparted by Islam amongst pious Indonesian Muslims, Naipaul wrote: '*The cruelty of Islamic fundamentalism is that it allows only to one people—the Arabs, the original people of the Prophet—a past, and sacred places, pilgrimages, and earth reverences. These sacred Arab places have to be the sacred places of all the converted peoples. Converted peoples have to strip themselves of their past; of the converted peoples nothing is required but the purest faith (if such as thing can be arrived at), Islam, submission. It is the most uncompromising kind of imperialism.*'[375]

Based on his observation of Islam's pernicious impact on the conquered and converted non-Arab peoples and their culture and civilization, notes Naipaul, '*To the convert his land is of no religious or historical importance; its relics were of no account; only the sands of Arabia are sacred.*'[376] Observing the pervasive Arab cultural hegemony amongst Muslims in Sindh—obsession for the Arab faith, Arab language, Arab dress, Arab names etc.—twelve centuries after its conquest, wrote Naipaul:[377]

> …there probably has been no imperialism like that of Islam and the Arabs. The Gauls, after five hundreds years of Roman rule, could recover their old gods and reverences; those beliefs hadn't died; they lay just below the Roman surface. But Islam seeks as an article of faith to erase the past; the believers in the end honour Arabia alone; they have nothing to return to.

This urge for obliterating their pre-Islamic past is not just an idle desire amongst Muslims. In their respective homelands, they have been actively and violently working on destroying the vestiges of non-Islamic religious, cultural and traditional traits—the residues of their pre-Islamic *jahiliyah* heritage. For example, the Taliban Islamists demolished eighteen centuries-old Bamiyan Buddha statues in Afghanistan in 2001; Islamists bombed a first-century rock carving of Buddha in the Swat valley in northwest Pakistan in September 2007; they bombed the wondrous ninth-century Borobudur Buddhist temple in Central Java (Indonesia) in January 1985; Islamists in Egypt attacked world's oldest monastery at Deir Abu Fana in June 2008. In April 2006, Ali

---

374. Shaikh, Chapter 7

375. Naipaul (1998), p. 64

376. Ibid, p. 256

377. Ibid, p. 331

Gomaa, Egypt's top Islamic jurist and Grand Mufti, issued a religious edict based on Islamic text, declaring the exhibition of statues as un-Islamic. It was feared that Islamist may use this edict to unfurl their rage against the rich pre-Islamic heritage of Egypt as the editor of the *Akhbar Al Adab* magazine noted, '*We don't rule out that someone will enter the Karnak temple in Luxor or any other Pharaonic temple and blow it up on the basis of the fatwa.*'[378] The Ayatollahs of Iran have been systematically destroying the pre-Islamic monuments and mausoleums under one excuse or another over the last three decades.

A determined effort to obliterate all that is not Islamic is also witnessed in the continued Muslim ethnic-cleansing of Hindus in Bangladesh and Pakistan. Following the Partition of India in 1947, Hindus constituted about 25–30 percent of the population in East Pakistan (now Bangladesh), while about 10 percent in Pakistan. Today, their numbers have dwindled to about 10 percent in Bangladesh and 1 percent in Pakistan. The major cause of this massive loss of Hindu population in Muslim-majority Bangladesh and Pakistan is the result of a steady exodus of Hindus to India because of the miserable treatment, they experience. Conversion, mostly under various compulsions, also contributes, to a lesser extent, to their falling numbers. Kidnapping of Hindu (also other non-Muslim) girls and forcing them to marry thuggish Muslim men, widespread rapes of their women, seizure of their property and lands, their mass eviction at times of turmoil and creation of other kinds of social pressures compel the Hindus—not willing to convert—to leave their ancestral homes and resettle in India. A recent study in Bangladesh found that nearly ten million Hindus were forced to leave the country between 1964 and 2001 because of communal conflicts and deprivations. Some 2.6 million acres of Hindu land was grabbed by Muslims from 1965 to 2006.[379] Naeem Mohaiemen, a film-maker and commentator, has this to say on the treatment of non-Muslim citizens in Bangladesh:

> We are not only a class elite, but also a Muslim elite that ravages this country and renders all others as shadow citizens. From the Vested Property Act onwards, there are laws, understandings, social norms, politics and quiet discrimination that have rendered our Hindu, Christian, Buddhist, *Adivasi* (Aboriginal), and *Pahari* (Hill) citizens as sub-human—frozen out of schools, jobs, politics, culture, and lived life.[380]

In Egypt, the indigenous Coptic Christian population continues to dwindle resulting from persecution by Muslims. In order to apply pressure on Christians, Muslims build a mosque in every street where there happens to be a church. On a regular basis, Muslims indulge in riots against Christians and vandalize their properties, churches and businesses (frequently reported in the media) and create other social problems, which force the Copts either to convert to Islam or migrate, mostly, to the West. In one latest incidence, a 20,000-strong Muslim mob with stones and butane gas cylinders besieged some 1,000 Christians inside the Coptic Orthodox Church of the Virgin Mary in West Ain Shams (Cairo) on its opening day. Overnight Muslims turned the first floor of a newly-built building facing the Church into a Mosque and started praying there. As security forces tried to disperse them, '*the Muslim mob attacked the church...*, broke its doors and demolished its entire first floor. The mob were chanting Jihad verses as well as slogans saying "we will demolish the church" and "we sacrifice our blood and souls, we sacrifice ourselves for you, Islam."[381] Recently, a number of Hindu girls in London were reported to have been terrorized by Muslim youths for converting them to Islam to such an extent that they were given police protection.[382] When such a thing happens in Britain, what happens to non-Muslims in Muslim-majority countries is easy to guess.

---

378. *Fatwa against statues triggers uproar in Egypt*, Middle East Times, 3 April 2006

379. *Hindus lost 26 lakh acres of land from 1965 to 2006*, The Daily Star, Dhaka, 15 May 2008

380. Mohaiemen N, *Tattered blood-green flag: Secularism in crisis*, Daily Star, Bangladesh, 26 Feb, 2007

381. *20,000 Muslims Attack a Church in Cairo*, Assyrian International News Agency, 26 November, 2008

382. Daily Mail, *Police protect girls forced to convert to Islam*, 22 Feb, 2007

Likewise, the Arab Christian population is decreasing rapidly in the Middle East countries; they have been fleeing mainly to the West to escape discrimination and persecution. The city of Bethlehem in the West Bank in Palestine, once dominated by Christians, is now a predominantly Muslim city. Christians constituted 60 percent of the population in 1990, which dwindled to 40 percent in 2000 and currently stand at only about 15 percent. According to Justus Reid Weiner, an international human rights lawyer and lecturer at the Hebrew University, with connivance and even abetment of the Fatah-led Palestinian Authority, Christian Arabs suffer frequent human rights abuses at the hands of Muslims, which include, '*intimidation, beatings, land theft, firebombing of churches and other Christian institutions, denial of employment, economic boycotts, torture, kidnapping, forced marriage, sexual harassment, and extortion.*'[383] These problems force them to migrate elsewhere. On the other hand, the city of Nazareth, the birthplace of Jesus in Israel—dominated by Christians since 1848—continues to be a dominantly Christian city. According to an estimate based on recent trends, the Christian community may disappear altogether from the Muslim-controlled Palestinian territories of West Bank and Gaza within the next fifteen years as a result of their increasing persecution and maltreatment.[384]

On the other hand, the Muslim population continues to swell in Hindu-majority India. Muslims in Nigeria constituted about 40 percent of the population at the time of gaining independence from Britain in 1960, but are now probably in the majority. In Bosnia-Herzegovina, there were 43.5 percent Muslims prior to the mid-1990 civil war; their number increased to over 50 percent in 2008. In Israel, despite large influx of Jewish immigrants from all over the world, Muslims continue to maintain their proportion of the population. In whichever country Muslims are minorities, they are either growing faster than the rest or maintaining their share of the population. But non-Muslim minorities in Islamic countries have been dwindling fast without exceptions.

Shahada, the fundamental creed of Islam, says, "There is no God but Allah" [Quran 6:102,106; 2:163]. Islam—the religious, social, cultural and political order sanctioned by Allah, the supreme only true sovereign of the universe—must replace all else and dominate over all peoples. For establishing an all-embracing Islamic cultural imperialism—that is, Islam, as the only and the complete way of life for all peoples as demanded by Allah—Muslims must wage Jihad in whatsoever way they can [Quran 2:193, 8:39]. The ongoing pogrom of non-Muslims in Islamic countries, which goes on with little opposition from the wider Muslim populace, is, consciously or subconsciously, the enforcement of the Islamic cultural imperialism—a fundamental writ of Islam.

Therefore, the vast treasure of cultural and civilizational heritage, which humankind has lost due to Islamic onslaughts, is not a cause of regret for the overwhelming majority of Muslims. To devout Muslims, it is instead a cause for jubilation; because, their destruction is a meritorious and divinely binding duty for them. Naipaul rightly noted: '*It (Islam) has had a calamitous effect on converted peoples. To be converted you have to destroy your past, destroy your history. You have to stamp on it, you have to say 'my ancestral culture does not exist, it doesn't matter.*''[385] A campaign to finish off the vestiges of *jahiliyah* religion, tradition, culture and heritage that comes within the power of Muslims is ongoing in full measure across the continents. Muslims must transform the entire world into a uniform Arabo-Islamic society by founding an imperial Islamic state globally—in which, Islam will be the only ideology and the complete guide to all aspects of life for all. In today's postcolonial Muslim world, such a socio-cultural transformation has been taking place at an ever accelerating rate, particularly where Muslims dominate the population. The process of Arabo-islamization of the global culture has now started even in the West by Muslim immigrants.

---

383. Weiner JR (2008) *Palestinian Crimes against Christian Arabs and Their Manipulation against Israel*, in *Institute for Global Jewish Affairs Bulletin*, No. 72, 1 September 2008

384. Lefkovits E, *'Christian groups in PA to disappear'*, Jerusalem Post, 04 December 2007

385. Ezard J, *Nobel dream comes true for VS Naipaul*, The Guardian, 12 October, 2001

CONTRIBUTION OF ISLAM TO CONQUERED LANDS

We have already analyzed whether the Muslim invaders went to India (and everywhere else) for the purpose of colonial-style economic exploitations. Muslims deny that this ever happened. Islamic invaders repeatedly attacked the territories of innocent Hindus; in the process, they plundered immense wealth, slaughtered a great many of them, and enslaved their women and children in large numbers. One-fifth of the plunder and captives went to the caliphal treasury. Once the Islamic rule was established, crushingly discriminatory taxes of all sorts were imposed on the unconverted infidel subjects reducing them to such misery that the Hindus of otherwise prosperous India were begging at the doors of Muslims and selling their women and children to settle burdensome taxes as early as in the reign of Sultan Alauddin Khilji (r. 1296–1316), within a century of founding the sultanate in Delhi. Still, others were taking refuge in the jungle to avoid the torture of tax-collectors. To Muslims, these were not acts of colonialism-style exploitation of the native people. Instead, these, to them, were acts of great social justice and egalitarianism brought to India by the Muslims invaders. Hashmi, succinctly present this paradigm of Muslim thinking:[386]

> 'Muslims brought high culture to India. Fruits like water melon, apple, grape, apricot, varieties of nuts, saffron, perfume, gun powder, mosaic, porcelain, pointed and horse shoe arches, domes and minarets in architecture, sitar and *tabla* and refined musical notes, horses, turban, leather shoes, stitched or tailored garments replacing dhotis and saris and sarongs (*lungi*), ice, rose water and social egalitarianism were brought by Muslim rulers, merchants and Sufis to India...'

Discussion about all these good or beneficial things Muslims brought to India is outside the scope of this book. It is, however, pertinent to mention here that these beneficial things had no basis in Islamic teachings; many of these had no roots in the Arab learning and heritage either (In fact, music, poetry, art, and architecture etc. are explicitly disapproved in Islam). Instead, those had been appropriated from the existing pre-Islamic culture and tradition of the advanced civilizations of Persia, Egypt, Syria and Byzantium, which Muslims had conquered or made contact with.

Muhammad Asghar, an author and critic of Islam, wrote in response to Hashmi's hyperbolic claim that,

> It is a good point that justifies occupation of a country by a foreign force for introducing certain things the invaded nation did not or could not have. Can we apply the same logic to justify certain things that are now happening in our world? The Iraqis did not have hamburgers and sandwiches nor were they wont to eating steak and other things the Americans usually eat. Nor were they able to build skyscrapers, dams and other modern things. They were also living under a repressive and perpetual dictatorship for over thirty years. So Americans invaded Iraq to introduce its own high culture among the Iraqis. Their presence in Iraq now enables the Iraqis to eat hamburgers, sandwiches and they are also being taught how to build tall buildings. They are giving them lessons on democracy. In a short time, Americans would turn the Iraq into a civilized nation; it being a replication of what the Muslims had done to the medieval Indian people.

Despite the fundamental difference between the two cases, Asghar gives a perfect reply to Tashmi's bizarre justification of the senseless brutality the Muslim invaders wrought upon innocent Indians. It is also important to analyze the veracity of Hashmi's claim about the high culture, social egalitarianism, art, architecture, musical instruments, and of course, those great Sufi saints that Islam had brought to India. A few questions need addressing in this regard:

---

386. Hashmi, op cit

1. Did Arabs and their culture, within which Islam had its foundation, had anything to do with these contributions?

2. Were those Arab innovations?

3. Was the Arab society at Prophet Muhammad's time so rich in all these spheres of socio-cultural, intellectual and material development?

The underdeveloped society of the Arabs

Historical records of the Arab society and culture belonging to the prophetic era suggest that such was not the case. Both pre-Islamic and early Islamic literatures show that the Arabian Peninsula at Prophet Muhammad's time was inhabited by an unsophisticated people, having a nominal or rudimentary culture and civilization to speak of. Their social, political and civilizational developments were embryonic as compared to well-developed contemporaneous civilizations of India, Persia, Egypt, and Syria (the Levant). The city of Mecca, situated in the midst of barren deserts, had little agriculture as attested even by Allah: '*I have settled some of my posterity in an uncultivable valley near unto Thy holy House (Ka'ba)...*' [Quran 14:37]. As a result, the people of Mecca had very little daily work. They used to survive on occasional trade and revenues obtained from pilgrims to the *Ka'ba* and taxing the caravans traveling along the important trade-routes passing through Mecca. The more belligerent and adventurous ones amongst them engaged in raids and plunder for making a living. The nomadic Arab tribes, a substantial part of the population, were wont to scouring the desert to eke out a living; this tradition continued well into the twentieth century prior to the discovery of oil.

The people of Prophet Muhammad's ancestral city, Mecca, lived a relatively idle life. For a living, they seized whatever they could as occasional opportunities presented. With a plenty of time at hand, engaging in sexual activities seemed to have been one of their favorite pastime. Maxime Rodinson, a prominent Islamic historian, quotes Rabbi Wathan about the then Arab society:

> 'Nowhere in the world was there such a propensity toward fornication as among the Arabs, just as nowhere was there any power like that of Persia, or wealth like that of Rome, or magic like that of Egypt. If all the sexual licenses in the world were divided into ten parts, nine of these would be distributed among the Arabs and the tenth would be enough for all the other races.'[387]

Similarly, Ronald Bodley notes of the cultural traits of the Arabs of Mecca that,

> There was Amr Ibn al-As, the son of a beautiful Meccan prostitute. All the better Meccans were her friends, so that anyone, from Abu Sufian down, might have been Amr's father. As far as anyone could be sure, he might have called himself Amr Ibn Abu Lahab, or Ibn al-Abbas or "Ibn anyone else" among the Koreishite upper ten. According to Meccan standards of that time, it did not matter who had sired him.[388]

Some readers might think that this was probably the universal norm of the time, but such was not the case. In fact, many of the victims of Islam—the Persians, for example—despite having to accept Islam under whatsoever circumstances, continued to despise the rather indolent and uncultured Arabs. The Persians (Iranians), even to this day, celebrate with great fanfare the death of despised second Caliph Omar, who brought the great Persian civilization down to the feet of Bedouin Arabs. Despite being forced into Islam, the social elites of the many advanced civilizations that were conquered by Islamic invaders had low regards for their Arab masters. They used to ridicule many Islamic rituals and decry their insignificant achievements. They used to glorify their own national achievements and contributions. They took great pride in their own

---

387. Rodinson M (1976) *Muhammad*, trs. Anne Carter, Penguin, Harmondsworth, p. 54
388. Bodley RVC (1970) *The Messenger: The Life of Muhammad*, Greenwood Press Reprint, p. 73

rich cultural heritage and even sought to restore their pre-Islamic civilization to replace the brutally imposed Islamic customs and precepts.

Shu'ubiya was one such anti-Arab movement among the Persians, Egyptians and Palestinians, which rose to prominence during the second-third Islamic centuries. One exponent of this movement was the great Persian General Khayder bin Kawus (aka Afshin), who served under the liberal, freethinking Abbasid Caliph al-Mutasim (d. 842). Despite achieving great military success for the Islamic empire, Afshin had only disdain for the Arab culture and Islamic religion. Ignaz Goldziher notes of him that '*He was so little a Muslim that he cruelly maltreated two propagandists of Islam who wished to transform a pagan temple into a mosque; he ridiculed Islamic laws.*' Defying Islamic taboos of *haraam-halal*, '*He ate meat of strangled animal, and also induced others to do so by saying that such meat was fresher than that of animals killed according to the Islamic rites,*' adds Goldziher. He ridiculed various Islamic customs, such as circumcision and '*dreamt of the restoration of the Persian Empire and the 'white religion' and mocked the Arabs, Maghribines, and Muslim Turks.*'[389] General Afshin, accused of apostasy and conversion to his ancestral religion of Zoroastrianism, was thrown into prison where he died in 841.[390]

While taking great pride in their own national and historical achievements, the *Shu'ubiya* proponents never failed to point fingers at the underdeveloped Bedouin culture of the Arabs by calling them wild, uncouth, and uncivilized. They claimed that it was the Persians from whom they learned manners. They portrayed the Arabs as tent-dwellers, sheep-herders, camel-drivers, desert-squatters and lizard eaters. According to Ismail al-Thaalibi, they denounced the prevalent culture of sodomy among the Quraysh (This affirms the unbridled and decadent sexual and moral standing of the Arabs noted above).[391] Similar movements, dedicated to proving the superiority of indigenous culture over the imposed Arab culture, also took roots among the Egyptian Copts, the Nabatean Arabs, and most likely, amongst every other people, whom the Arabs had conquered. Firuzan (or Abu Lulu), who assassinated Caliph Omar in 644 to avenge the atrocities committed by the Arab invaders in Persia, is revered as a hero in Iran even today.[392]

These instances speak volumes about the stunted cultural, social and political development of the Arabs—amongst whom, Islam originated and flourished and upon whose cultural norms, the Islamic creed was based. The kind of unbridled cruelty and culture of sexual slavery, sodomy and huge harems (see Chapter on Slavery), which the Muslim invaders brought along and implanted in far-flung parts of the Muslim world, is a reflection of the lacking in moral and cultural development in the primitive Bedouin Arab society at the time.

The question, then, naturally arises: In what way, and to what extent, was it possible for such an uncultured, underdeveloped people to offer things valuable to the world's greatest civilizations: India, Persia, Egypt, the Levant and Byzantium?

The Arabs in the seventh century seem to have excelled over their conquered peoples only in sexual indulgence and poetry. Large harems and widespread sex-slavery introduced by Muslim invaders all over the conquered lands clearly prove the amoral nature of their sex culture. In poetry, the pre-Islamic Arabs had excelled over their immediate neighbors. However, Islam categorically condemns poets and poetry [Quran 26:224; Bukhari 8:175–176; Muslim 28:5609]. Still, the Greek poetry excelled the Arab ones. While Muslims

---

389. Goldziher I (1967) *Muslim Studies*, trs. CR Barber and SM Stern, London, Vol. I, p. 139

390. Endress G (1988) *An Introduction to Islam*, trs. C Hillenbrand, Columbia University Press, New York, p. 172

391. Al-Thaalibi I (1968) *Lata'if Al-Ma'arif. The Book of Curious and Entertaining Information*, ed. CE Bosworth, Edinburgh University Press, p. 25

392. Mohammad-Ali E, *Tomb of Firuzan (Abu-lolo) in Kashan to be Destroyed*, The Circle of Ancient Iranian Studies website, 28 June 2007; http://www.cais-soas.com/News/2007/June2007/28-06.htm (As noted elsewhere, Muslim sources allege that Abu Lulu assassinated Omar over a dispute over tributes)

boast of enriching India with poetry, *ghazals*, arts, architectures and science; except in poetry, the Arabs had no excellence in any of these talents and had absolutely nothing of their own devising to offer to India.

We have noted of Nehru saying in effusive eulogy of how the Arabs carried a "brilliant culture" from one corner of the world to another. Contradicting himself, two pages later, he writes: *'(The Arabs) soon left their simple ways of living and developed a more sophisticated culture... Byzantine influences came to them... when they moved to Baghdad, the traditions of old Iran affected them.'*[393] Nehru may draw whichever conclusions he may wish, but a people of "simple ways of living" could offer nothing valuable to highly developed civilizations that they had devoured. The Arabs could only learn and usurp, which they did in the very words of Nehru—from Byzantium, Persia.

Prohibition of intellectual pursuits in Islam

Many of the intellectual pursuits in which the medieval Muslim world had excelled—namely in art and architecture, music and poetry, science and learning etc.—are categorically prohibited in Islam. For example, Allah prohibits Muslims from indulging in ostentation and luxury in this world: *'We (Allah) would certainly have assigned to those who disbelieve in the Beneficent Allah (to make) of silver the roofs of their houses and the stairs by which they ascend. And the doors of their houses and the couches on which they recline, And (other) embellishments of gold; and all this is naught but provision of this world's life, and the hereafter is with your Lord only for those who guard (against evil)'* [Quran 43:33–35]. This means that ostentation and luxury in this world is for the bedevilled disbelievers only; Muslims must scrupulously abstain from it. Muslims must not engage in play and amusement, as says Allah: *'What is the life of this world but play and amusement? But best is the home in the hereafter, for those who are righteous. Will ye not then understand?'* [Quran 6:32].

Allah clearly prohibits ostentation in architecture and building and indulgence in amusement and play (music, poetry etc.). Prophet Muhammad, therefore, said of those Muslims, who would think musical instrument lawful, that they will be destroyed and transformed to apes and pigs [Bukhari 7:494B]. According to another tradition, the Prophet had instructed Ali: *'I send you, as God sent me, to break lutes and flutes.'*[394] About creating buildings on a grand scale, Muhammad, agreeing with Allah, said: *'Truly the most unprofitable thing that eats the wealth of a believer is building'* and that *'Every expense of the believer will be rewarded except the expense of the building.'*[395] Neither did the Prophet himself engage in creating ostentatious buildings despite founding a powerful Islamic state in Medina. The two early mosques, he built— one in Koba and the Prophet's mosque in Medina—were simple structures until his death. Rain used to leak through the roof of his ramshackle mosque in Medina. When his companions asked if it should be repaired, he answered: *'No, a mosque should be simple and modest, a booth, like the booth of Moses.'*[396]

Neither is Allah in favor of creative pursuits, such as in science, philosophy and intellectual learning. Prophet Muhammad was illiterate and Allah proudly glorifies this quality of the Prophet: *'Those who follow the messenger, the Prophet who can neither read nor write, whom they will find described in the Torah and the Gospel...'* [Quran 7:157]. Allah also warns Muslims against being inquisitive and asking creative question about the world: *'O ye who believe! Ask not questions about things, which, if made plain to you, may cause you trouble... Some people before you did ask such questions, and on that account lost their faith'* [Quran 5:101–02]. Prophet Muhammad also advised his followers against asking creative questions and to follow pliantly whatever Allah had revealed: *'Allah's Apostle said, 'Satan comes to one of you and says, 'Who created so-and-so? 'till he says, 'Who has created your Lord?' So, when he inspires such a question, one*

---

393. Nehru (1946), p. 224
394. Walker, p. 283
395. Hughes, p. 178
396. Walker, p. 271

should seek refuge with Allah and give up such thoughts' [Buhkari 4:496; Muslim 1:242–43]. Prophet Muhammad himself did not undertake any initiative to promote sciences, arts, architecture or other creative learning during his rule in Medina.

The Islamic revelation, vouchsafed in the Quran, was believed by the pious to be the complete encyclopedia of universal knowledge directly revealed by the omniscient Creator. Quran 3:164 says, *'Allah did confer a great favor on the believers when He sent among them an apostle from among themselves rehearsing unto them the signs (knowledge) of Allah, sanctifying them in scripture and wisdom while, before that, they had been in manifest error.'* In other words, through the Quran, Allah has opened all his true knowledge, wisdom and guidance to humankind; all that which humanity has known prior to the coming of Islam are manifestly erroneous. Allah claims, from the Quran, the encyclopedia of His knowledge, no knowledge of the natural world has been left out: *'There is not an animal (that lives) on the earth, nor a being that flies on its wings; but (forms part of) communities like you. Nothing have we omitted from the Book...'* [Quran 6:38]. Allah insists that the Quran is not a forged book but His true guidance and wisdom, containing all knowledge what existed before and what was to come, sent down from the heaven with everything clearly explained: *'In their histories, there is certainly a lesson for men of understanding. It is not a narrative which could be forged, but a verification of what is before it and a distinct explanation of all things and a guide and a mercy to a people who believe'* [Quran 12:111].

Therefore, the knowledge and guidance contained in the Quran, hold pious Muslims, are all, which one needs to live a perfect life in this world. A Muslim can secure an auspicious life in Paradise—the sole aim of Muslim life in this world—only by assiduously adhering to the prescriptions and proscriptions of the Quran. In affirmation of this fundamental belief in Islam, Prof. Umaruddin writes: *'The Muslims came very early to believe that, with the advent of Islam, all previous system of thoughts were abrogated. The Quran was considered to be the only true guide to humanity that promised success in this world and the next.'*[397] Dr Ali Issa Othman, likewise, affirms that the Quran is "a motivator of thought and an end of knowledge" for Muslims.[398] Therefore, patronized by Abbasid rulers, when the translation of ancient manuscripts from Greece, India and Egypt etc. made them accessible to Muslims, they were stunned that such vast treasure of knowledge and wisdom was known to humankind before Islam. In order to conform to Islam's repudiation of the knowledge and wisdom of pre-Islamic times as erroneous and misleading, *'Certain caliphs, it is said, ordered the originals of the Greek and Latin manuscripts'* to be cast into flames after their translation into Arabic. This was intended for destroying the evidence of their pre-Islamic origin, so that they could be passed on as product of the Islamic age. Consequently, *'scores of Greek and Latin texts mentioned in the ancient writings now survive only in their Arabic versions.'*[399]

The early Muslims, therefore, had no interest in, but only disdain for, such social, cultural, intellectual, political and material achievements. This naturally led to neglect and decline of such endeavors in the lands Muslims conquered. Islam's contempt for art, poetry, music, science and architecture etc. had a debilitating impact on them, as says Guillaume, the legacy of Islam *'has proved least valuable where the religion has exercised the strongest influence.'*[400] Alberuni in his eyewitness account of Islam's deleterious impact on sciences and learning in India wrote that *'Hindu sciences have retired far away from those parts of the country conquered by us, and have fled to places which our hands cannot yet reach, to Kashmir, Benaras, and other places.'*[401] On the contributions of Muslim invaders to India, Rizwan Salim writes:

397. Umaruddin, p. 42

398. Waddy, p. 15

399. Walker, p. 289

400. Arnold T and Guillaume A eds. (1965) *The Legacies of Islam*, Oxford University Press, p. V

401. Lal (1999), p. 20

Savages at a very low level of civilization and no culture worth the name, from Arabia and West Asia, began entering India from the early century onwards. Islamic invaders demolished countless Hindu temples, shattered uncountable sculpture and idols, plundered innumerable palaces and forts of Hindu kings, killed vast numbers of Hindu men and carried off Hindu women. This story, the educated—and a lot of even the illiterate Indians—know very well. History books tell it in remarkable detail. But many Indians do not seem to recognize that the alien Muslim marauders destroyed the historical evolution of the earth's most mentally advanced civilization, the most richly imaginative culture, and the most vigorously creative society.[402]

Islam egalitarian or racist?

Concerning social egalitarianism and equity, much credit has been attributed to Islam without making a thorough study or understanding of the creed. The assertion of Hashmi and Reid regarding Islam's egalitarianism is noted already. Nehru says that Islam brought a *'flavour of democracy and equality,'* which appealed to the masses of Arabia and neighbouring nations.[403] Regarding Islam's egalitarian nature, Bernard Lewis, a respected Islamic historian, argues:[404]

> There is much truth in this assertion... the Islamic dispensation does indeed bring a message of equality. Not only does Islam not endorse such systems of social differentiation (racism, caste system etc.), it explicitly and resolutely rejects them. The actions and utterances of the Prophet, the honoured precedents of the early rulers of Islam as preserved by tradition, are overwhelmingly against privilege by decent, by birth, by status, by wealth, or even by piety and merit in Islam.

Lewis adds that any deviation from these basic principles was non-Islamic, indeed, anti-Islamic innovation. He is, however, quick to assert the degraded status of slaves, unbelievers and women in Islam, sanctioned by its holy writ, remained unquestioned throughout the history of Islam.[405]

It is, however, uneducated to assert that Islam brought equality amongst all peoples, irrespective of race, color or nationality: Arabs or non-Arabs, Blacks or Whites. Islam in its divine writ of the Quran is a racist and Arab supremacist religion. Allah glorifies Arabs as the best of peoples, His chosen race, whom He will help in establishing their supremacy and domination over all peoples of the earth. This is somewhat like the Israelites, who are G-d's chosen people, but the expanse of their domination is to remain confined to Israel alone. The Arabs of Hejaz, asserts the Islamic God, are the best of nations (peoples, races) in the world: *'Ye are the best of peoples, evolved for mankind, enjoining what is right, forbidding what is wrong, and believing in Allah...'* [Quran 3:110]. According to Muhammad's early biographer Ibn Sa'd, the Prophet also claimed the same in saying:

> 'God divided the earth in two halves and placed (me) in the better of the two, then He divided the half in three parts, and I was in the best of them, then He chose the Arabs from among the people, then He chose the Quraysh from among the Arabs, then He chose the children of 'Abd al–Muttalib from among the Banu Hashim, then he chose me from among the children of 'Abd al–Muttalib.'[406]

In fact, Allah had wished Islam to be a religion solely for the Arabs, to whom no revelation had been sent before: *'Or do they say, 'He (Muhammad) has forged it?' Nay, it is the Truth from thy Lord, that thou mayest admonish a people (Arabs) to whom no warner has come before thee: in order that they may receive guidance'* [Quran 32:3]. Allah chose Muhammad's Quraysh tribe as the best race to lead the world under the

---

402. Salim R, *What the invaders really did*, Hindustan Times; 28 December1997

403. Nehru (1989), p. 145

404. Lewis (2002), p. 91

405. Ibid, p. 91–92

406. Ibn Sa'd AAM (1972) *Kitab al-Tabaqat*, Trans. S. Moinul Haq, Kitab Bhavan, New Delhi, Vol. I., p. 2

banner of Islam says a prophetic tradition: '*Allah's Apostle said, 'Authority of ruling will remain with Quraysh, and whoever bears hostility to them, Allah will destroy him as long as they abide by the laws of the religion*' [Bukhari 4:56:704].

Therefore, the Islamic deity clearly revealed Islam to be an Arab-supremacist religion—opposed to what many great scholars have to say about the egalitarian nature of Islam. Not only that, the Islamic deity is also a white supremacist—that is, an anti-Black racist—who will turn the doomed unbelievers *black* on the day of Judgement:

1. 'On the Day of Judgment wilt thou see those who told lies against Allah; their faces will be turned black...' [Quran 39:60]

2. 'On the Day when some faces will be white, and some faces will be black: To those whose faces will be black (will be said): '*Did ye reject Faith after accepting it? Taste then the penalty for rejecting Faith.*' But those, whose faces will be white, they will be in Allah's mercy...' [Quran 3:106–07]

3. 'For those who do good is good (reward) and more (than this); and blackness or ignominy shall not cover their faces... And those who have earned evil... they shall have none to protect them from Allah—as if their faces had been covered with slices of the dense darkness of night...' [Quran 10:26–27]

The Arab supremacism and anti-Black racism were not simply the divine writ in Islam to sit idle; they were a living reality since the early time of Islam to the present day. Today, the Middle East Arabs treat their Muslim coreligionists from countries like Bangladesh or Africa with contempt and belittlement. Famous Islamic scholar Ignaz Goldziher, out of his ignorance of the Quranic scruples, also thought that Islam taught unequivocal equality of all Muslims before God. Goldziher is, therefore, unnecessarily at pain for the Arabs' historical disregard for Islam's alleged equality for all, as he says, '*the Muslim teachings of the equality of all men in Islam remained a dead letter for a long time, never realized in the consciousness of Arabs, and roundly denied in their day to day behaviour.*'[407]

After the Arab Muslims burst out of Arabia, and conquered vast territories and established rule over them, they never conceded equality to the non-Arab converts; they were the ruling lords and the Muslims of other races were second-class subjects. Of course, that's how it was to be in the writ of Allah. The Arabs treated the non-Arab converts with belittlement, subjecting them '*to a whole series of fiscal, social, political, military and other disabilities.*'[408] The Arabs exercised a policy of apartheid against their non-Arab Muslim brethren. According to *Cambridge History of Islam*,

> They lead them into battles on foot. They deprived them of booty.[409] *They would not walk on the same side of the street with them, nor sit at the same repast.* In nearly every place, separate encampments and mosques were constructed for their use. Marriage between them and the Arabs was considered a social crime.[410]

Islam was born, undoubtedly, to be a global imperialism ruled by the Arabs, and preferably, by the Quraysh—the tribe of Prophet Muhammad. Therefore, throughout history, it became a fashion, indeed a necessity for legitimacy, for Muslim monarchs to link their genealogy to the Arabs, more specifically, to the clan of Quraysh. Well into mid-twentieth century, the dark-skinned Nawab of Bahawalpur (Sindh), who had an

---

407. Goldziher, p. 98

408. Lewis B (1966) *The Arabs in History*, Oxford University Press, New York, p. 38

409. Examples of these treatments will be found in the chapter on Slavery.

410. Ibn Warraq, p. 202

obsession for white women for producing brighter children, fanatically claimed his ancestry to the Abbasid family of the Quraysh clan. The latest *Encyclopedia of Islam* has categorically dismissed this claim.[411] In Southeast Asia, the Mongol-looking rulers of the Sulu Sultanate claimed their descent from the Prophet to reinforce their Islamic credentials for legitimizing their hold on power. Historically, the Muslim monarchs in North Africa normally claimed their ancestry to the Arabs. Sultan Moulay Ismail (d. 1727) had claimed his descent from the family of the Prophet. Shah Ismail (r. 1502–24), the founder of the Safavid dynasty in Persia, despite being a Turk and embracing Persian culture, claimed his descent from Muhammad. Such claims amongst Muslim monarchs throughout history are almost universal. It is still the Arabs, who rule in North Africa in many cases, namely in Sudan and Morocco.

Allah obviously takes the least of liking for the Black people amongst the races. Accordingly, the Blacks suffered the worst treatment and cruelty in the hands of Arab invaders. The Arabs had turned Africa into a slave-hunting and breeding ground over the centuries (see Chapter VII)—a fate that haunts them till today in one form or another, such as in Sudan (Chapter VII; Section: *Revival of slavery in Sudan*). Since early Islam, many famous poets of the Arabs were Blacks, who frequently expressed their sufferance of racism and belittlement from the Arabs in such lamenting terms as '*I am black but my soul is white*' or '*Women would love me if I were white.*' Noting that racism in the modern sense of it was absent in pre-Islamic Arabia, Lewis adds,

> The Islamic dispensation, far from encouraging it, condemns even the universal tendency to ethnic and social arrogance and proclaims the equality of all Muslims before God. Yet, from the literature, it is clear that a new and sometimes vicious pattern of social hostility and discrimination had emerged within the Islamic world.[412]

Lewis is obviously unaware of the Arab supremacist and anti-Black racist dispensation imbedded in the holy scripture of Islam; and what has transpired and continues to this day (Arabs are the most racist people in the world today) is what the Islamic God unequivocally intended.

Undoubtedly, there existed social differentiation of one kind or another in all societies at the time of Islam's birth. But Islam, founded by assimilating the ideas, precepts and values current in the under-evolved Arab society, could offer very little, if at all, in such things as high culture and social egalitarianism to advanced civilizations like India, as Hashmi would have us believe. The unbridled slavery (including sex-slavery), huge harems, horrible social degradation and humiliation plus extreme economic exploitation of non-Muslim subjects—the hallmarks of Islamic rule in India—do not bare any semblance of what one understands by high culture and social egalitarianism. They, instead, symbolize quite the opposite. Muslim rulers, unlike the British, did not take any initiative to undermine or abolish the social ills, namely the widow burning (*sati*) and caste system, which afflicted pre-Muslim India. In fact, some of these social ills aggravated under the Muslim rule (see next chapter).

On the oft-repeated and well-received, but baseless, claim that Islam brought high culture, human brotherhood and social egalitarianism, Anwar Shaikh wrote:[413]

> Islam has caused more damage to the national dignity and honour of non-Arab Moslems than any other calamity that may have affected them, yet they believe that this faith is the ambassador of: 1) Equality, and 2) Human love... This is a fiction which has been presented as a fact with an unparalleled skill. In fact, the Prophet Muhammad divided humanity into two sections—the Arabs and the non-Arabs. According to this categorisation, the Arabs are the rulers and the non-Arabs are to be ruled through the yoke of the Arab Cultural Imperialism... The Islamic love of

---

411. Naipaul (1998), p. 329-31

412. Lewis (1966), p. 36

413. Shaikh A (1995) *Islam: The Arab National Movement*, The Principality Publishers, Cardiff, Preface

mankind is a myth of even greater proportions. Hatred of non-Moslems is the pivot of the Islamic existence. It not only declares all dissidents as the denizens of hell but also seeks to ignite a permanent fire of tension between the Moslems and non-Moslems...

Islam's extirpation of egalitarian Buddhism

At the time of Islamic expansion, Buddhism—the most peaceful, nonviolent and egalitarian ancient faith system—was a flourishing faith in Central and Southeast Asia, while having strong presence in parts of India (Bengal, Sindh etc). Islam inflicted the most complete extirpation of Buddhism wherever it went; this has been pointed out by Alberuni as cited already. In describing Bakhtiyar Khilji's barbarous extermination of the Buddhists of Bihar in 1203, notes Ibn Asir,[414] *'taking the enemy unawares,'* *'Muhammad Bakhtiyar, with great vigor and audacity, rushed to the gate of the fort and gained possession of the place. Great plunder fell into the hands of the victors. Most of the inhabitants of the place were Brahmans with shaven heads (actually Buddhist monks). They were put to death.'* When he reached the famous University of Nalanda, adds Ibn Asir, *'a large number of books were found there.'* So extensive was the slaughter that when the Muhammadan army inquired about the content of the books, no one could tell them because *'all the men had been killed,'* records Ibn Asir.[415] Nalanda University, in fact, had a huge nine-storey library. When it was confirmed that there was no copy of the Quran inside, Bakhtiyar Khilji burned it into ashes.

Dr BR Ambedhkar, a Buddhist convert from Hinduism and the chief architect of the Indian Constitution, had taken side with Muslims in their fight for creating Pakistan in the 1940s, calling it their *legitimate right*. On the impact of Islamic invasions on Buddhism in India, wrote Ambekar, *'no doubt that the fall of Buddhism in India was due to the invasions of the Musalmans.'* Describing Islam's idol-destroying mission in India and elsewhere, he wrote:

> 'Islam came out as the enemy of the *'But'*. The word *'But'* as everybody knows, is the Arabic word and means an idol. Thus the origin of the word indicates that in the Moslem mind idol worship had come to be identified with the Religion of the Buddha. To the Muslims, they were one and the same thing. The mission to break the idols thus became the mission to destroy Buddhism. Islam destroyed Buddhism not only in India but whatever it went. Before Islam came into being Buddhism was the religion of Bactria, Parthia, Afghanistan, Gandhar, and Chinese Turkestan, as it was of the whole of Asia...'

Ambedkar informs us that Islam did not only strike blows at the Buddhist religion, but also destroyed its centers of learning, as he wrote: *'The Mussalman invaders sacked the Buddhist universities of Nalanda, Vikramshila, Jagaddala, Odantapuri to name only a few. How the Buddhist priesthood perished by the sword of the Muslim invaders has been recorded by the Muslim historians themselves.'* To describe Islam's fatal blow to Buddhism in India, Ambedkar wrote: *'Such was the slaughter of the Buddhist priesthood perpetrated by the Islamic invaders. The axe was struck at the very root. For by killing the Buddhist priesthood, Islam killed Buddhism. This was the greatest disaster that befell the religion of the Buddha in India.'*[416]

Furthermore, the Muslim rulers were as caste-minded as the upper caste Hindus in dealing with the lower caste peoples. They never tried to empower low-caste Hindus in their employment. When Muslim rulers started employing some Hindus in the army and other services, particularly in the Mughal reign, they always looked up to upper-caste Rajputs and Brahmins, while the oppressed low-caste Hindus and Sikhs

---

414. In the attack of Bihar, Bakhtiyar had two brave brothers, Nizamuddin and Shamsuddin, in his army. Author Ibn Asir had met Shamsuddin at Lakhnauti in 1243.

415. Elliot & Dawson, Vol. II, p. 306

416. Ambedkar BR (1990) *Writings and Speeches: Pakistan or The Partition of India*, Government of Maharashtra, Vol. III, p. 229–38

raised revolts. It has been noted already that Aurangzeb sent an army, predominantly consisting of Rajputs, to crush the low-caste Jat rebels at Sinsani in 1690, in which 1,500 Jats were killed.

About Hashmi's assertion that Islam brought the Sufis—Amir Khasru, Nizamuddin Auliya and Moinuddin Chisti being prominent amongst them—to India, it could bear some credit if Muslim rulers had brought an epoc-making thinker like Aristotle, Isaac Newton or Albert Einsten. However, it is already noted how Amir Khasrau, the allegedly great liberal Sufi poet, took sadistic delight in the destruction of Hindu temples and massacre of Hindus by Islamic marauders. Other greatest Indian Sufi saints, Auliya, Moinuddin Chisti and Shah Jalal *et al.*, came to India for fighting Jihad and slaughtering the Hindus. Auliya expressed delight at the successful expeditions of massive looting, slaughter and slave-taking in India and happily accepted gifts from the plunder. Other great Sufis, those in Kashmir and Gujarat, inspired and brought terror and destruction upon Indians.

The Arabs, affirms this discussion, had nothing to offer to India and other great civilizations and nations they had conquered within a short time after Muhammad's death. The immediate effect of Islamic onslaughts was a decline in existing arts, culture, literature, architecture, science and learning in those civilizations; their destructions of many centers of learning, from India to Egypt, bears a clear testimony to that. These intellectual and material endeavours flourished again amongst Persians, Egyptians, and Syrians etc. out of the resilience of their pre-Islamic cultural and civilizational heritage. Even Nehru, who generally paints a rosy picture of the Muslim rule in India, failed to identify any positives that Islam could offer to India. He wrote:

> The Moslems who came to India from outside brought no new technique or political or economic structure. In spite of a religious belief in the brotherhood of Islam, they were *class bound* and feudal in outlook. In technique and in the methods of production and industrial organization, they were inferior to what prevailed in India. Thus their influence on the economic life of India and the social structure was very little.[417]

How the Muslim world excelled intellectually and materially?

After the initial surge of the brutal, iconoclastic assaults of Islamic invaders, these unsophisticated Bedouin Arabs faced the impossible task of managing the world's advanced civilizations. Having little knowledge, expertise and discipline needed for the administration of advanced organized states, they were forced to make many theological compromises and absorbed many of the advanced pre-Islamic human endeavors they came across in the conquered lands. They had to fall back upon the advanced *jahiliyah* system and expertise of the indigenous people in social, political, financial, trading and educational administration. The Arabs let the often-unconverted people to run those affairs, while engaging themselves in conquests.

As a general rule, Muslim rulers found the Jews proficient in finance, the Greeks skilled in engineering, architecture, and arts, and the Christians in law, medicine, education and administration. They found it convenient and prudent to employ some of these infidels to continue in their respective professions. As a result, much of the contributions in early centuries of Islam, which Muslims consider as Islamic, came from the mind, toil and sweat of the much despised non-Arab infidels. The level of Muslim rulers' dependence on non-Muslims can be gauged from the fact that nearly two-and-a-half century after Islam's birth, when Caliph Mutawakkil expanded his library in 856, he could not find an educated Muslim scholar to lead the venture. Consequently, he had to entrust the job to a Christian scholar, Honayn Ibn Ishaq, despite his hatred and persecution of Jews and Christians.

After absorbing the initial blow, music, art, literature, architecture and science flourished in the Islamdom, to which the Arabs of the desert had very little, if at all, to contribute. They all evolved out of the indigenous and vibrant pre-Islamic heritage of the advanced non-Arab nations and civilizations Muslims had

---

417. Nehru (1946), p. 265

conquered. This also came at the compromise of Islamic teachings, since these achievements were the manifestations of pre-Islamic *jahiliyah* heritage, canceled by Islam. Many of these endeavors are also overtly condemned by Allah and Prophet Muhammad as discussed already. Islam was born not to nurture but to destroy them. Prophet Muhammad and the later Muslim invaders set out to accomplish this goal by launching aggressive attacks on the existing non-Islamic civilizations one after another. Despite making significant inroads into obliterating those *jahiliyah* achievements in the early phase of Islamic conquests, they eventually failed to realize their goal completely due to the resilience of those deeply-rooted cultures and civilizations—some thousands of years old. The ascension of the Godless Umayyads to power quite early in Islam (661) dramatically changed the political and ideological circumstances in many respects from the course that was set forth by the Prophet.

Although not within the scope of this book, it is worth discussing briefly that the majority of the Umayyad rulers had deep-seated disdain for Prophet Muhammad because of the sustained and bloody rivalry between Muhammad and Meccan leader Abu Sufyan, father of Mu'awiyah, the first Umayyad Caliph. Mu'awiyah himself was staunchly opposed to Islam. When Muhammad conquered Mecca in 630, Abu Sufyan had to embrace Islam. A large number of Meccans accepted Islam on that day, but Mu'awiyah didn't. The next year, when Allah revealed verse 9:1–5 to force the idolaters to convert to Islam at the pain of death, all Meccans had to embrace Islam but Mu'awiyah didn't; he fled to Yemen. Only after Yemen and entire Arabia was taken by Muslims, Mu'awiyah reluctantly embraced Islam.

Therefore, Mu'awiyah and most Umayyad rulers had little respect for Islam and the Quran. In the battle of Siffin in 657 against fourth Caliph Ali, Mu'awiyah, knowing the kind of reverence Muslims show to the holy Quran, instructed his troops to stick its pages at the tip of their spears.[418] Seeing this, Ali's troops refused to fight and technically lost the battle. Following their ascension to caliphal power, the Umayyads were responsible for the death of many members of Ali's family. In the reign of Mu'awiyah's son Yazid I, Husayn, son of Ali and grandson of Muhammad, was killed in a cruel manner in the battle of Karbala (680). Husayn had revolted against Yazid's authority and in the confrontation at Karbala, Husayn's troops were cut off from the source of drinking water to avenge the incidence of Badr—in which Muhammad had similarly cut off Abu Sufyan's troops from water. The dismembered heads of the slain men, women and children were brought to the governor of Basra, while the head of Husayn was sent to Caliph Yazid in Damascus for displaying publicly. Sahih Bikhari [5:91] records of the treatment of the decapitated head of Husayn that '*The head of Al-Husain was brought to 'Ubaidullah bin Ziyad and was put in a tray, and then Ibn Ziyad started playing with a stick at the nose and mouth of Al-Husain's head and saying something about his handsome features.*'

Mocking Allah's promise in the Quran [14:9] to destroy the rebellious like the way '*the people of Noah, and Ad, and Thamud*' were destroyed previously, Caliph al-Walid II (d. 743) tore out that page of the Quran, stuck on a lance and shot it into pieces by an arrow and challenged: '*Do you rebuke every opponent? Behold, I am that obstinate opponent! When you appear before your Lord on the day of resurrection; say that Walid has torn you in this manner.*'[419] The irreverent Walid II was an '*intensely cultivated man, surrounded with poets, dancing girls, and musicians and lived a merry life of the libertine, with no interest in religion.*'[420]

During most of the ninety-year Umayyad rule (660–750), except a short period of relative orthodoxy (715–21), the Umayyad rulers did all kinds of sacrilegious acts to undermine Islam. The only thing the Umayyads had whole-heartedly embraced from the Islamic creed is the doctrine of its war for their conquest. Mu'awiyah—under whom the Islamic world achieved its greatest expansion yet—was a master Arab

---

418. Some sources claim a copy of the Quran was raised as a sign of calling to resolve the dispute through mediation.

419. Walker, p. 237; also Ibn Warraq, p. 243

420. Ibn Warraq, p. 243

imperialist. Although, the Umayyads exploited the doctrine of Jihad for their conquest, they never took serious interest in propagating the religion of Muhammad; instead, they opposed the conversion of the vanquished as discussed already.

Abu Sufyan, unlike Muhammad, was an elite and the leader of Mecca; his family was one of the most educated in the city. It is during the Umayyad dynasty, the descendants of Abu Sufyan, that interest in the battered creative pursuits—in art and architecture, music and poetry, science and learning—were slowly revived. Later on, the persianized Abbasids further propped up and expanded these initiatives, ushering in the *golden age* of the medieval Muslim world.

The Muslim world had, indisputably, excelled over the rest between the ninth and the twelfth century. This is because Muslims had overrun the world's greatest civilizations—Egypt, Persia, India and the Levant—incorporating their wealth, brains and accumulated intellectual treasure. The Hellenic civilization, following the trail of Alexander's conquest, had moved eastwards from Greece to Alexandria and the Levant. Thus, the intellectual treasure of classical Greece also became incorporated into the Islamic world. Europe, battered by the so-called Barbarians from the North—the Vandals, Goths, Vikings etc.—and under obscurantist Christian influence, had sunk into darkness. Under these circumstances, which else could be the leading civilization of the world? After the initial battering by zealous Muslims, the vigorous pre-Islamic civilizations, which Islam had devoured, revived themselves in the vast Islamic world. It was not Arabs, but the Persians, Indians, Greeks and Levantines—many of them non-Muslims—who rejuvenated and nurtured intellectual and material endeavors in the Muslim world. The translation of foreign manuscripts, which was central for the medieval Islamic world's excellence, was already occurring in pre-Islamic Persia. And in the Muslim period, the translations—patronized by the Godless Umayyads and wayward persianized Abbasids— were done entirely by non-Muslim scholars, mostly Christians; none of the translators were Muslims. Given the prohibition of the Islamic theology to many of these endeavors, little credit should go to Islam for the medieval Muslim world's excellence; it must go to the pre-Islamic civilizations that Islam had violently appropriated and internalized.

CALLING THE COLONIES HOME

It is true that, everywhere Muslims went as invaders, they sought to make the place their home, which has not always been the case with the European colonists. But, it was only expected of Muslims because Allah commands them to conquer the world and make it Islamic in all respect. Allah made Muslims the inheritor of the earth. It was, therefore, incumbent upon Muslims to wrestle the ownership the world from non-Muslims. Unlike the European colonists, Muslims became the owner of the foreign lands they conquered (all Schools of Islamic laws also affirm this); they could not return those lands to previous owners. The Muslim invaders' love for the conquered lands was so great that they have completely destroyed the indigenous culture, tradition and people forever in many cases. Muslims see this as an object of pride, as Hashmi boastfully says, '*unlike the British invaders, Muslim rulers considered India home.*' In praise of this trait of the Muslim invaders, Nehru similarly writes: '*Their dynasties became Indian dynasties, and there was a great deal of racial fusion by intermarriage... They looked to India as their home country and had no other affiliations.*' On the other hand, says Nehru, '*The British remained outsiders, aliens and misfits in India...*'[421]

Like Muslims, many European settlers in Africa, the Americas and Australasia have made the former colonies their home, too. Muslims see their settlement in the conquered lands as an object of pride, and receive praise for it from many quarters. But the European settlers often receive opposite reactions; instead of praise, they receive suspicion, contempt and even violence. This may appear rather perplexing, but there is more to add. In many conquered lands where Muslims have become the majority population, they generally

---

421. Nehru (1946), p. 233-34

remain desperately poor with very little contribution to modern civilization. They excel mostly in areas, such as fanaticism, violence, terrorism, human right violation and so on. Where Muslims form a minority population, such as in India, Thailand, Singapore, China, Eastern Europe, Russia and elsewhere, they remain relatively backward and poorer than their unconverted fellow citizens. In many cases, they have become an ongoing burden for these predominantly non-Muslim nations. The Muslim rulers in India, for example, perpetrated terrible cruelty against indigenous non-Muslims and horrible social degradation and grinding economic exploitation of them for more than a millennium to few centuries in different parts of the country. But after the majority Hindus retook control of their country following the British withdrawal in 1947, Muslims have continued to fall behind in the new knowledge-based and technology-driven economy. The Indian government has been instituting special economic incentives to Muslims at the tax-payers' expense. In the State of Kerala, a certain percentage of jobs have been reserved for Muslims, because of their failure to compete openly. The State of Andhra Pradesh and Tamil Nadu are in the process of introducing similar measures—a process, which will likely spread all over India eventually.

These tax-payers, predominantly Hindus, were terribly exploited, oppressed, terrorized, and degraded during the centuries of Muslims rule. Some commentators have quite correctly termed these special economic incentives to Muslims as the restoration of the same old discriminatory *jizyah*, which Muslim rulers had imposed upon non-Muslims; the British abolished it. However, there is a notable difference between the pre-colonial practice and this post-colonial restoration of *jizyah*. It was Muslims who extracted *jizyah* from the Hindus and other non-Muslims during the pre-colonial Islamic rule. In the new policy, it is now the ruling Hindus (the dominant tax-payers), who voluntarily pay, instead of extracting it. In either case, it is the Hindus, classed as *dhimmi* in the Islamic law in India, who end up paying the *jizyah*, whilst Muslims enjoy the benefit. This agrees with the canonical Islamic law.

On the other hand, the European settlers have been very productive and contributory citizens in their adopted homelands. In Zimbabwe for example, the European settlers, despite their meager numbers, formed the backbone of the nation's economy before they were evicted from their farms in recent past. Despite being such valuable citizens, they have received contempt and hatred of the indigenous people, and persecution by the government. The White settlers in Zimbabwe are accused of being the evil remnants of the British colonialism, continuing the exploitation of the colonial age. In order to finish off this remnant of the colonial exploitation, the Zimbabwe government, after gaining independence in 1980, launched a land reform program to confiscate the White-owned lands for transferring to Black farmers. In 2000, Robert Mugabe's government gave a free-hand to Blacks to capture the white-owned farmlands by force, if necessary. This led to mob-violence against the White farmers causing a number of deaths.[422] A huge 110,000 square-kilometers of the White-owned farmland was seized in this violent land-grabbing campaign.[423]

As a result of this anti-White campaign, the white farmers left Zimbabwe in large numbers. However, much of the confiscated land, now occupied by the Blacks, who lack in the knowledge and expertise of modern agriculture, lies uncultivated. The lack of capital investment and an insouciant attitude toward hard work among the Blacks also contribute to this. The previously rich farmland is now left unproductive causing serious economic hardships, plunging Zimbabwe into its worst famine in living memory. Two thirds of the 11.6 million people of Zimbabwe were facing severe food shortage (2007).

When the British colonists left Zimbabwe in 1980, it was the most prosperous nation in the continent, famously known as the *bread basket* of Southern Africa. Now Zimbabwe struggles to feed its people; a staggering 45 percent of whom are considered malnourished; the prospect of famine looms large, continuously. The vaingloriously gratifying act of unceremonious and violent expulsion of the White farmers presented an occasion to Robert Mugabe's supporters for joyous dancing in the streets. But this imprudent act

---

422. *White farmers held in Zimbabwe*, BBC News, 7 August 2001

423. Wikipedia, *Land reform in Zimbabwe*, http://en.wikipedia.org/wiki/Land_reform_in_Zimbabwe

has caused devastating and irreparable damage to the economic life of Zimbabwe. The inflation in Zimbabwe runs at 100,000 percent a year.[424]

This decolonizing sentiment continues to reverberate in many former colonies where Europeans have settled in large numbers. The black supporters of South African President Thabo Mbeki, who consider Robert Mugabe as an ally and a "hero of the (anti-colonial) resistance movement", also want to see the Zimbabwean scenario being replicated in their own country. Max Hastings writes of Mbeki that *'many of his own voters applaud Zimbabwe's land confiscations and, indeed, the ruthless treatment of its white rump.'*[425] This happens despite the fact that these white settlers constitute the mainstay of the national economy; without whom, those nations will face serious economic consequence.

On the other hand, the Muslim settlers as well as the local converts have become a serious economic handicap in the lands previously conquered by Muslim. If one looks at India, it becomes evident that the conversion of the indigenous Hindus to Islam has, on the whole, imparted a severe handicap on them. Although not genetically different from the Hindus, Muslims in India continue to fall behind in almost every positive achievement: education, science, prosperity and so on. Still, they take great pride in their imagined superiority of being Muslim. They receive praise even from many non-Muslims for calling the conquered lands their home. Last but not the least, Muslims continue to despise the Hindus and their *jahiliyah* culture, which they strive to destroy completely; the campaign for this is being invigorated with increasing radicalization of India's Muslims in recent decades. If they become successful in completely Islamizing India, it will, in all probability, turn her with the vast population into big handicap for the world.

---

424. Angus Shaw, *Zimbabwe inflation passes 100,000%, officials say*, Guardian, 22 February 2008
425. Hastings M, *I'll never lament the passing of white rule in Zimbabwe*, Guardian, 27 Feb 2007

Chapter VI

Islamic Imperialism in India

'Swords flashed like lightning amid the blackness of clouds, and fountains of blood flowed like the fall of setting star. The friends of God defeated their opponents... the Musalmans wreaked their vengeance on the infidel enemies of God, killing 15,000 of them... making them food of the beasts and birds of prey... God also bestowed upon his friends such an amount of booty as was beyond all bounds and calculations, including five hundred thousand slaves, beautiful men and women.'

-- Sultan Mahmud's minister al-Utbi on his campaign to India

'(Sultan) Mahmud utterly ruined the prosperity of the country and performed there wonderful exploits, by which the Hindus became like atoms of dust scattered in all direction... This is the reason, too, why Hindu sciences have retired far away from those parts of the country conquered by us, and have fled to places which our hands cannot yet reach, to Kashmir, Benaras, and other places.'

-- Alberuni, Great Muslim scholar and scientist, d. 1050

'The Hindu women and children went out begging at the doors of the Musalmans.'

-- Egyptian Sufi saint Shamsuddin Turk on Sultan Alauddin's crushing exploitation of Hindus

---

The history of the Indian subcontinent since early eighth to the mid-twentieth century was characterized by two consecutive foreign rules: Islamic and British. The Islamic invasion and rule started with Muhammad bin Qasim's capture of Sindh in 712 and officially ended after the Sepoy Mutiny in 1857. The British colonial occupation, in effect, started in 1757 and ended in 1947.[426]

Directed by governor of Baghdad Hajjaj bin Yusuf and blessed by Caliph al-Walid of Damascus, Qasim inaugurated the Islamic conquest and rule of India in 712. Muslim rulers finally achieved near-total control of India in the 1590s under Mughal Emperor Akbar. The Muslim control of India expanded a bit further under Aurangzeb (1658–1707). The defeat of Nawab Siraj-ud-Daulah of Bengal by British mercenaries of the East India Company in the *Battle of Plassey* in 1757 signaled the beginning of the end of the Islamic rule. When Tipu Sultan of Mysore—the last independent Muslim ruler—was defeated in 1799, Muslim rule in India effectively ended. Most parts of India came under *de facto* British control with the

---

426. Some coastal parts of India, such as Goa, also came under Portuguese control in the sixteenth century.

incorporation of Punjab in 1850. The British mercenaries retained Muslim rulers as the "puppet head of state" until the Sepoy Mutiny uprisings of 1857. The direct British imperial rule was introduced in 1858.

Following a long campaign for independence by Indian nationalists, the British rulers finally relinquished their sovereignty over India on 26 January 1947 and India became independent on August 14–15 of the same year. After many centuries of foreign domination, an independent subcontinent—albeit partitioned into two states: India and Pakistan—eventually emerged for the first time, free to determine her own future.

Curiously, of the two foreign rules in India, only one—the British rule—is termed colonial and singled out for condemnation by historians, scholars and citizens of the subcontinent and elsewhere. A conscious and deliberate effort has been made to whitewash the no-less dark and disastrous and much longer period of Islamic rule. Quite oddly, the Islamic rule is mostly shown in a positive light by most of the leading modern historians and writers. This remains the dominant theme in modern history writing, not only in Islamic Pakistan and Bangladesh, but also in Hindu India. The people of the subcontinent, both Muslim and non-Muslim, are constantly told stories of the 190-year British rule and how cruel and economically exploitative it was. But the manifestly greater brutalities, exploitation and iniquities of the Islamic invasions and much longer period of Muslim rule are rarely, if ever, mentioned. When the Muslim rule in India is discussed, it is usually described as something positive, beneficial, and even as *glorious*. For example, Nehru, who was at the forefront of whitewashing Islamic atrocities in India, says, '*Islam brought an element of progress to India.*'[427]

The future stability of India is increasingly threatened by rising radicalism, intolerance and militancy amongst its sizable Muslim population. The British imperialism in India, which no longer affects India's future, is frequently cast as the demonic villain in Indian discourse. But factual investigation and discussion about the deleterious impact of the Islamic rule have hitherto remained largely shrouded in a policy of silence or denial, or a *de-facto* taboo subject in India. The elite historians, intellectuals and writers adamantly refuse to acknowledge the real consequence of the Islamic conquest, while vigorously delving into every negative detail of the British rule—details, which are inconsequential to India's future. While they are highly vocal in condemning, what they perceive as, the lasting negative impact of the British rule; they take refuge in a peculiar silence or negation about the same concerning the Islamic rule. Most surprisingly, even many historians from the Hindu background with Marxist leanings have allied with their Muslim counterparts to paint a gloriously rosy picture of the Islamic rule and its legacy. This viewpoint, however, shows a wilful disregard for an overwhelming body of recorded evidence left behind by Muslim historians and chroniclers of those times.

The past European colonial rules across the continents have been roundly condemned and demonized by historians and intellectuals everywhere to the extent that most Europeans, suffering from the past colonial guilt, feel ashamed and candidly acknowledge the misdeeds of their forefathers. About how this altogether negative view of British rule evolved in India, notes Ibn Warraq:

> After the first heady days of independence in 1947, Indian historians poured out "nationalist" histories that found no redeeming features in the British Empire. Later, every ill, every failure, every shortcoming of the new country in the 1960s and 1970s was ultimately traced back to the period of the British presence, to past British exploitation.[428]

But Islam's blood-drenched expansionist invasion and rule—from the Middle East to India, to Europe, to Africa—is '*held up as something which Muslims can be proud of, something to be lauded and admired,*'

---

427. Nehru (1989), p. 213
428. Ibn Warraq, p. 198

laments Ibn Warraq. For example, the Organization of Islamic Conference (OIC) Secretary-General Ekmeleddin İhsanoğlu of Turkey demands Turkey's accession into the European Union based on Islam's contribution to Europe in its colonial past. He recently said: '*We argue that Islam is among the founding elements of Europe. The Ottomans ruled for five centuries in the Balkans, and Muslim rule in Andalusia lasted eight centuries... Islam cannot be regarded as an extrinsic element in Europe. It is one of the founding elements of the European civilization.*'[429] Despite the fact that today's India is impossible without the British contributions: from education to administration, from governance to healthcare, a similar statement on Britain's contributions to India by a British statesman will undoubtedly raise an international outcry.

An objective study of the Islamic invasion and subsequent Muslim rule in India is very important at this juncture, when the future security and stability of India is seriously challenged by Islamic terrorists: both homegrown and foreign. Indeed, the stability and security of Muslim Bangladesh and Pakistan are much more vulnerable to Islamic terrorist threats. This study will attempt to evaluate the largely untouched impact of the Islamic rule in subcontinental India and its continued legacy. It is needless to emphasize again that the Islamic rule in India was as much imperial and colonial as was the British rule.

THE ISLAMIC CONQUEST AND RULE

One central theme in modern history writing in India is that there was great harmony, peace and brotherhood between Muslims and Hindus (and other non-Muslims) prior to the British occupation. Having captured power in India, the British rulers created disharmony between Muslims and Hindus, which continues to blight India to this day.

If one looks at historical records left by leading Muslim historians and rulers, the claim that Hindu-Muslim disharmony never existed before the British engendered it appears furthest from the truth. Regrettably, the unavoidable truth is that religious tolerance and harmony between Hindus and Muslims hardly existed ever since the Islamic invaders set foot in India. Let us examine the trail of the Hindu-Muslim relationship in India throughout the centuries of Muslim invasion and rule.

Muhammad bin Qasim's invasion: Inspired by the edicts of the Quran and *Sunnah* (as noted already), Hajjaj sent Qasim with a 6,000-strong army toward India, instructing him to kill all able-bodied men and to enslave the women and children in the course of his conquests. After capturing Debal in Sindh, Qasim's army massacred the residents for three days. In Brahmanabad, between 6,000 and 16,000 men of weapon-bearing age were slaughtered; in Multan, all men of weapon-bearing age were ordered to be killed. *Chachnama* records that Qasim's successful assault in Rawar yielded 60,000 slaves.[430] Qasim slaughtered tens of thousands of Indian defenders and enslaved their women and children on a grand scale, a few hundred thousand in all, during his three-year stint in Sindh. In addition, temples were demolished, sculptures and idols shattered, and mosques built in their stead. Plundering of Hindu establishments, temples and palaces yielded great quantities of booty.

Sultan Mahmud's campaigns: Sultan Mahmud, in his seventeen plundering expeditions into Northern India (1000–27), revived Qasim's momentous exploits of slaughter and destruction with greater ferocity and magnitude. In his forays one after another, Sultan Mahmud used to slaughter the adults mercilessly; capture the women and children as slaves in the tens to hundreds of thousands; and loot and confiscate whatever

429. Kamil Subasi, *Ihsanoğlu: Islam not just a guest in Europe*, Today's Zaman, 9 October, 2008

430. Lal (1994), p. 18

booty (*khams*) his army could lay their hands upon. In his foray into Northwest India in 1001–02, wrote al-Utbi:

> Swords flashed like lightning amid the blackness of clouds, and fountains of blood flowed like the fall of setting star. The friends of God defeated their opponents... the Musalmans wreaked their vengeance on the infidel enemies of God, killing 15,000 of them... making them food of the beasts and birds of prey... God also bestowed upon his friends such an amount of booty as was beyond all bounds and calculations, including *five hundred thousand slaves*, beautiful men and women.[431]

In the capture of Nagarkot (Kangra) in 1008, the booty amounted to 70,000,000 dirhams in coins and 700,400 mounds of gold and silver, besides plenty of precious stones and embroidered cloths. Sultan Mahmud, marched to attack Thanesar in 1011 '*for the purpose of planting the standard of Islam and extirpating idolatry,*' writes al-Utbi. In the ensuing battle, '*blood of the infidels flowed so copiously that the stream was discolored, notwithstanding its purity, and people were unable to drink it... The Sultan returned with plunder which is impossible to count. Praise be to Allah for the honor he bestows upon Islam and Musalmans!*'[432]

In the conquest of Kanauj, '*the inhabitants either accepted Islam or took up arms against him to become the food of the Islamic sword. He collected so much booty, prisoners (i.e., slaves) and wealth that the fingers of those who counted them would have been tired.*' Al-Utbi continues: '*Many of the inhabitants of the place fled and were scattered abroad like so many wretched widows and orphans... Many of them thus effected their escape and those who did not fly were put to death. The Sultan took all seven forts in one day, and gave his soldiers leave to plunder them and take prisoners.*'[433]

As noted already, Alberuni of Mahmud's court depicted his invasions of Hindustan as having '*utterly ruined the prosperity of the country*' and his brutality of the inhabitants was such that '*the Hindus became like atoms of dust scattered in all directions*' and cherished '*the most inveterate aversion toward all Moslems.*'[434] In his forays to India, notes Nehru, '*he became a terror all over the north. ...Most Muslims adore him; most Hindus hate him.*'[435] '*After Mahmud's raids and massacres, Islam was associated in northern India with barbarous cruelty and destruction,*' adds Nehru.[436]

Ghaurivid invasions: The third wave of Islamic conquest and expansion in India by the Ghaurivid invaders in the late twelfth century finalized the founding of Muslim rule in India in 1206. The Persian historian Hasan Nizami, in his *Taj-ul-Ma'sir*, records of Muhammad Ghauri's conquest of Ajmer that '*one hundred thousand groveling Hindus swiftly departed to the fire of hell*' and the invaders '*obtained so much booty and wealth that you might have said that the secret depositories of the seas and hills had been revealed.*' Sultan Ghauri marched forward to attack Delhi and '*torrents of blood flowed on the field of battle...*'[437]

In the 1193 campaign of Muhammad Ghauri's general Qutbuddin Aibak in Aligarh, '*by the edge of the sword, they (Hindus) were dispatched to the fire of hell,*' notes Nizami. The slaughter was so extensive that '*Three bastions were raised as high as heaven with their heads, and their carcasses became food for

---

431. Elliot & Dawson, Vol. II, p. 26

432. Ibid, p. 40-41

433. Ibid, p. 45-46

434. Lal (1999), p. 20

435. Nehru (1989), p. 155

436. Ibid, p. 209

437. Elliot & Dawson, Vol. II, p. 215–16

beasts of prey. The tract was freed from idols and idol worship and the foundations of infidelity were destroyed.[438]

In Aibak's expedition to Benares, *'which was the centre of the country of Hind... here they destroyed nearly one thousand temples, and raised mosques on their foundations; and the knowledge of the law (Sharia) became promulgated, and the foundations of religion were established,'* adds Nizami.[439] In January 1197, Qutbuddin Aibak advanced against Nahrwala, the capital of Gujarat and *'fifty thousand infidels were dispatched to hell by the sword and from the heaps of the slain, the hills and the plains became of one level'* and *'more than twenty thousand slaves, and cattle beyond all calculation fell into the hands of the victors.'*[440] On Aibak's brilliant achievement in the expedition to Kalinjar in 1202, records Nizami: *'The temples were converted into mosques... and the voices of summoners to prayer ascended to the highest heaven and the very name of idolatry was annihilated.'* *'Fifty thousand came under the collar of slavery and the plain became black as pitch with Hindus,'* continues Nizami.[441] On the Ghaurivid invasions, notes Nehru: *'These Muslims were fierce and cruel to begin with... The first effect of Muslim invasion was an exodus of people to the south... when the new invasions came and could not be checked, crowds of skilled craftsmen and learned men went to southern India.'*[442]

These examples of mass slaughter of the hapless Hindus, their enslavement and forced conversion to Islam in large numbers, the destruction of countless Hindu temples and their replacement with mosques and the wholesale looting and plundering of their wealth were not isolated examples. Instead, they were the standard practice in the numerous conquests and wars, which became a familiar feature in India throughout the Islamic rule. Sultan Alauddin Khilji (r. 1296–1316) and Muhammad Shah Tughlaq (1325–1351) were great persecutors and exploiters of the infidels of India. Sultan Firoz Tughlaq (1351–88) was the kindest amongst Delhi Sultans. He was very careful when his wars put lives of Muslims, whether of his side or his opponent's, in danger. Still, in his campaign to Bengal, records Shiraj Afif, *'The heads (of the slain Bengalis) were counted and amounted to rather more than 180,000.'*[443]

All earlier Muslim rulers had exempted the Brahmans from *jizyah* payment. But a zealously pious Muslim that Sultan Firoz was, thinking that this was a religious error and that *'the Brahmans were the very keys of the chamber of idolatry,'* he imposed *jizyah* on them as well.[444] He staunchly suppressed idol-worship and destroyed many Hindu temples. He appointed spies to inform him about idol-worship and building of temples in his kingdom. He records many instances of his destroying Hindu temples and murdering the priests. In one instance, he writes in his memoir, *Futuhat-I Firoz Shahi*: *'(Hindus) now erected idol temples in the city and in the environs in opposition the Law of the Prophet which declares that such temples are not to be tolerated. Under Divine guidance, I destroyed these edifices and killed those leaders of infidelity who seduced others into error, and lower orders I subjected to stripes and chastisement, until this abuse was entirely abolished.'*[445] In another instance, he received information that the Hindus had erected a new idol-temple in the village of Kohana; they assembled in it and performed their religious rites. He records: *'I ordered that the perverse conduct of the leaders of this wickedness should be publicly proclaimed and that they should be put to the death before the gate of the palace. I also ordered that the infidel books, the idols, and the vessels used in their worship... should all be publicly burned. The others were restrained by threats*

---

438. Ibid, p. 224

439. Ibid, p. 223

440. Ibid, p. 230

441. Ibid, p. 231

442. Nehru (1989), p. 208–9

443. Elliot & Dawson, Vol. III, p. 297

444. Ibid, p. 366

445. Ibid, p. 380

and punishments, as a warning to all men, that no zimmi (dhimmi) could follow such wicked practices in a Musulman country.'[446]

The independent Bahmani sultans of Gulbarga and Bidar in Central India '*considered it meritorious to kill a hundred thousand Hindu men, women and children every year,*' noted *Abdul Kadir Badaoni.*[447] It was a rule of the Bahmani sultans of the Deccan Sultanate '*to slay a hundred thousand Hindoos in revenge of the death of single Mussulman,*' records Ferishtah. As a result, when King Dev Raya II captured two Muslim soldiers in a war, Sultan Alauddin Ahmad Shah Bahmani II (1436–58) swore that '*should Dew Ray (Dev Raya II) take away the lives of the two captive officers, he would revenge the death of each by the slaughter of a hundred thousand Hindoos.*' Terrified Dev Raya not only released the Muslim prisoners, he also promised to pay tribute to the Sultan.[448]

Amir Timur noted in his memoir, *Malfuzat-I Timuri*, that he invaded India to fulfil his Islamic duty of waging holy war against the infidels '*to become a ghazi (infidel slayer)... or a martyr.*' On his order to slaughter a large number of captives in his possession on the eve of his assault on Delhi (December 1398), he wrote: '*When this order became known to the ghazis of Islam, they drew their sword and put their prisoners to death. 100,000 infidels, impious idolaters, were slain*' on that single day.[449]

Under Aurangzeb: During the late period of Islamic rule under Emperor Aurangzeb (r. 1658–1707), India witnessed large-scale destruction of Hindu temples and schools, and slaughter of the infidels (Hindus, Sikhs etc.). According to his official chronicle, *Ma-Asir-I Alamgiri*, the Emperor learnt in 1669 that '*foolish Brahmans were in the habit of expounding frivolous books in their schools and the students and learners— Musalmans as well as Hindus—came there, even from long distances, led by desire to become acquainted with the wicked sciences they taught.*' An infuriated Aurangzeb, therefore, '*ordered all the provincial governors to destroy, with a willing hand, the schools and temples of the infidels; and they were strictly enjoined to put an entire stop to the teaching and practicing of idolatrous forms of worship.*'[450] '*Hindus were not allowed to wear any marks of honor, to ride elephants etc... The heaviest burden of all was the poll-tax on non-Moslems, or jizyah, introduced in 1679...*'[451] Aurangzeb was a champion defiler of Hindu temples; he destroyed thousands of them. Of the mind-blowing record of despoiling of temples in the year 1679 alone, records *Ma-Asir-I Alamgiri*:

1. '*Khan Jahan Bahadur arrived from Jodhpur, bringing with him several cartloads of idols, taken from the Hindu temples that had been razed.*' Some of these idols were '*placed beneath the steps of the grand mosque, there to be trampled under foot.*'

2. When Prince Muhammad Azam and Khan Jahan Bahadur proceeded to Udaipur "to effect the destruction of temples of the idolaters," some twenty Rajput princes revolted to protect the temples and "those fanatics" were sent to hell and "the temple was now clear, and the pioneers destroyed the images."

3. Aurangzeb ordered the destruction of three temples constructed by the Rana of Udisagar. Returning from the campaign, Hasan Ali Khan stated '*the temples situated near the palace and one hundred and twenty-two more in the neighboring districts, had been destroyed.*'

446. Ibid, p. 381

447. Lal (1999), p. 62

448. Farishtah, p. 267–68

449. Elliot & Dawson, Vol. III, p. 394,436

450. Ibid, Vol. VII, p. 183–184; also Bikaner Museum Archives, Exhibit No. 9

451. Antonova K, Bongard-Levin G and Kotovsky G (1979), *A History of India*, trs. Judelson K, Progress Publishers, p. 255

4. Aurangzeb proceeded to Chittor, where *'Temples to the number of sixty-three were demolished.'*

5. Upon executing the order *'to effect the destruction of the idol-temples of Amber,'* Abu Turab reported *'that threescore and six of these edifices had been leveled with the ground.'*[452]

More than 200 Hindu temples were destroyed in 1679 alone by Aurangzeb's order. It is not difficult to guess how many thousand temples were destroyed during his fifty-year reign, which some estimates put at up to 5,000. The defenders of the temples were also often wiped out. He did not spare even his own brother Dara Sikoh, whom he declared an apostate for taking interest in Hinduism and had him executed. As mentioned already, Aurangzeb killed Sikh Guru Tegh Bahadur Singh, along with two of his associates, for objecting to his forced conversion of the Kashmiri Hindus.

The Persian ruler Nadir Shah, in his invasion of India in 1738, killed some 200,000 people and returned with a huge quantity of booty and a large number of slaves, including a few thousand beautiful girls. Alain Danielou (d. 1994), French scholar of Indian philosophy, religion, history and arts, described Nadir Shah's assault of Delhi as follows: *'...for a week his soldiers massacred everybody, ransacked everything, and razed the entire countryside, so that the survivors would have nothing to eat. He went back to Iran taking with him precious furniture, works of art, horses, the Kohinoor diamond, the famous Peacock throne, and 150 million rupees in gold.'*[453] The plunder was so huge *'that Nader Shah stopped taxation in Iran for a period of three years, following his triumphant return.'*[454]

The scale of the destruction of Hindu, Buddhist, Jain and Sikh religious institutions by Muslims in India have few parallels in the history of conquests. In most instances, after a temple was destroyed, the idols and treasures therein were carried away, while the remains of the destroyed temple were often used as materials for the construction of a mosque at its place. The *Kwat-ul-Islam* (Might of Islam) mosque in Delhi was constructed from the materials of seventeen destroyed temples of the area.[455] The priests of the temples and monasteries were normally slaughtered, as joyfully narrated by Amir Khasrau and Sultan Firoz Tughlaq amongst others (mentioned already).

These vivid descriptions of savagery of Muslim invaders and rulers are drawn exclusively from the records of leading Muslim historians of the time; they generally recorded these catastrophic brutality and destruction with delightful religious pride. In summarizing the zeal for the destruction of temples by Muslim invaders and rulers, Francis Watson writes:

> Their minds filled with venom against the idol-worshippers of Hindustan, the Muslims destroyed a large number of ancient Hindu temples. This is a historical fact, mentioned by Muslim chroniclers and others of the time. A number of temples were merely damaged and remained standing. But a large number—not hundreds but many thousands—of the ancient temples were broken into shreds of cracked stone. In the ancient cities of Varanasi and Mathura, Ujjain and Maheshwar, Jwalamukhi and Dwarka, not one temple survives whole and intact from the ancient times.[456]

Even the most magnanimous amongst Muslim rulers, the reputedly *enlightened* Akbar, had ordered the massacre of about 30,000 surrendered Hindu peasants at Chittor (1568) for supporting the Rajput princes.

---

452. Elliot & Dawson, Vol. VII, p. 187–88

453. Danielou A (2003) *A Brief History of India*, trs. Kenneth F. Hurry, Inner Traditions, Rochester, p. 290

454. Nader Shah, Wikipedia, http://en.wikipedia.org/wiki/Nadir_Shah

455. Watson F and Hiro D (1979) *India: A Concise History*, Thames & Hudson, India, p. 96

456. Ibid, p. 96

When 8,000 Rajput soldiers were slain in the siege, their women—some say 8,000 in number, who were ordered to be enslaved—embraced death by jumping into fire to avoid dishonor and sexual slavery.[457] As noted already, Emperor Jahangir wrote that 500,000 to 600,000 people were slaughtered during the combined rule of his father (enlightened kind-hearted Akbar) and his own (1556–1627).

The Islamic brutality and savagery in India, begun with the invasion of Sindh, continued into the reign of the last independent Muslim ruler Tipu Sultan (1750–99), seen as a nationalist "hero" of India for his brave resistance against the British. According to the *History of Mysore* by Hayavadana Rao, Tipu Sultan had put 700 men, women and children of the Iyengar community of Mysore to death on the day of Dipavali celebration in the 1790s; for, the latter had allegedly made a pact with General Harris, the British Governor of Madras and Tirumaliyengar. According to Mohibbul Hasan, a Mughal General known by his initial M.M.K.F.G. recorded in his account of Tipu Sultan's life (corrected by Tipu's son) that the Sultan had killed 10,000 Hindus and Christians and enslaved 7,000 of them in his wars against Travancore. The enslaved were carried away to Seringapatam, where they were circumcised, made to eat beef and forced to convert to Islam.[458] Muslim chronicler Kirmani in his *Nishan-e Haidari* records that 70,000 Coorgis were forcefully converted to Islam by Tipu Sultan. Some modern historians dispute this as an exaggeration by the author to represent the Sultan as a *champion of Islam*.[459] Whether the number is correct or not, these modern historians happily affirm that converting the infidels by the sword was obviously considered glorious even at these dying days of Muslim rule in India.

Alain Danielou, in describing the Muslim invasion of India, writes: '*From the time Muslims started arriving, around 632 AD, the history of India becomes a long, monotonous series of murders, massacres, spoliations, and destructions. It is, as usual, in the name of "a holy war" of their faith, of their sole God, that the barbarians have destroyed civilizations, wiped out entire races.*' Mahmud Ghazni, continues Danielou, '*was an early example of Muslim ruthlessness, burning in 1018 the temples of Mathura, razing Kanauj to the ground and destroying the famous temple of Somnath, sacred to all Hindus. His successors were as ruthless as Ghazni: 103 temples in the holy city of Benaras were razed to the ground, its marvelous temples destroyed, its magnificent palaces wrecked.*' Indeed, the policy of the Muslim invaders in India '*seems to have been a conscious systematic destruction of everything that was beautiful, holy, refined (to Indians),*' concludes Danielou.[460]

American historian Will Durant, who thinks that the Muslim conquest of India was probably the bloodiest in history, wrote: '*The Islamic historians and scholars have recorded with utmost glee and pride of the slaughters of Hindus, forced conversions, abduction of Hindu women and children to slave-markets, and the destruction of temples carried out by the warriors of Islam during 800 AD to 1700 AD. Millions of Hindus were converted to Islam by the sword during this period.*'[461] Indeed, this sadistic glorification of the Islamic brutality of Indian infidels was a common theme in Muslim history writing until the last days of Islamic domination. The works of Muhammad al-Kufi, al-Biladuri, al-Utbi, Hasan Nizami, Amir Khasrau and Ziauddin Barani amongst many others bear the testimony of that.

The massacre and enslavement of the conquered infidels and destruction of their religious institutions by Muslim invaders in India have few parallels in history. The Hindu Kush Mountain was named so because of the huge number of Hindu slaves from India, caught up in inclement weather, died there while being transported to Islamic Central Asia. According to Ibn Battutah (described in 1333), Hindu Kush 'means *"Slayer of Indians" (i.e. Hindus), because the slave boys and girls who were brought from India die there in*

457. Lal KS (1992) *The Legacy of Muslim Rule in India*, Aditya Prakashan, Delhi, p. 266–67

458. Hasan M (1971) *The History of Tipu Sultan*, Aakar Books, New Delhi, p. 362–63

459. Tippu Sultan, Wikipedia, http://en.wikipedia.org/wiki/Tipu_Sultan

460. Danielou, p. 222

461. Durant W (1999) *The Story of Civilization: Our Oriental Heritage*, MJF Books, New York, p. 459

large numbers as a result of the extreme cold and the quantity of the snow.'[462] The number of those frozen to death in Hindu Kush is uncertain. According to Moreland, 'their number was so large that the price of the survivors remained low in foreign markets.'[463]

INDIA BEFORE THE COMING OF ISLAM

An advanced civilization

Prior to Muslim conquest, India was one of the world's top civilizations with significant achievements—in science, mathematics, literature, philosophy, medicine, astronomy, architecture and so on—to its credit. Indian mathematicians conceived the mathematical concept of *zero* and founded the basics of algebra. The persianized Abbasid caliphs, inspired by the pre-Islamic Persian pursuit of knowledge,[464] sent scholars and merchants to India for collecting documents and texts on science, mathematics, medicine and philosophy. According to Nehru, '*In subjects, like medicine and mathematics, they learned much from India. Indian scholars and mathematicians came in large numbers to Baghdad. Many Arab students went to Takshashila in North India, which was still a great university, specializing in medicine.*'[465]

An Indian scholar brought two seminal mathematical works to Baghdad in 770. One was the *Brahmasiddhanta* (known to Arabs as Sindhind) of the great seventh-century Indian mathematician, Brahmagupta. It contained early ideas of algebra. In the ninth century, famous Muslim mathematician and astronomer Muhammad ibn Musa al-Khwarizmi combined the Indian work with Greek geometry to found the mathematical system of algebra. Khwarizmi became known as the *father of algebra*. The term algorithm (or algorism), the technique of performing arithmetic calculations developed by al-Khwarizmi using Indian numerals, is the latinized version of his name. The second manuscript contained the revolutionary system of denoting number, including the concept of *zero*, unknown elsewhere. Muslim scholars used to call this Indian numbering system, "Indian (Hindi) numerals"; the Europeans later gave it the name, "Arabic numerals".[466] Although Muslims made significant contributions in these achievements, they often, in an act of self-gratification, claim all the credit for these plagiarized developments. Pre-Islamic India had a great tradition in creating magnificent and sensual sculptures, and building wondrous architectures. After the coming of Muslim invaders, Indian builders and craftsmen mixed Islamic ideas to their own, creating a new Indo-Islamic mosaic in the new building and architecture, which became integrated into the "heritage" of the self-declared Islamic civilization.

Alberuni (d. 1050) has recorded many of these ancient Indian achievements in his famous work, *Indica*, published in 1030. Arabic scholar Edward Sachau translated this book in 1880 and published under the title of *Alberuni's India* (1910). Sachau writes: '*To Alberuni, the Hindus were excellent philosophers, good mathematicians and astronomers.*'[467] Alberuni summarizes Indian achievement in mathematics as follows:

---

462. Gibb, p. 178

463. Moreland WH (1923) *From Akbar to Aurangzeb*, Macmillan, London, p. 63

464. Patronized by the pre-Islamic Sassanian kings of Persia, the great Nestorian learning centre of Jundhishpur had become a flourishing centre for translating the ancient works of Greek, Indian and other origin. Under king Khosro I (531–579), it had become a melting pot of Syrian, Persian and Indian scholars. Khosro I sent his own physician to India in search of medical books. These were then turned from Sanskrit into Pahlavi (Middle Persian), and many other scientific works were translated from Greek into Persian or Syriac.

465. Nehru (1989), p. 151

466. Eaton (2000), p. 29

467. Sachau, Preface, p. XXX

They do not use the letter of their alphabet for numerical notation, as we use the Arabic letters in the order of Hebrew alphabet... The numerical signs which *we* use are derived from the finest forms of the Hindu signs...The Arabs, too, stop with the thousand, which is certainly the most correct and the most natural thing to do... Those, however, who go beyond the thousand in their numeral system, are the Hindus, at least in their arithmetical technical terms, which have been either freely invented or derived according to certain etymologies, whilst in others both methods are blended together. They extend the names of the orders of numbers until the eighteenth order for religious reasons, the mathematicians being assisted by the grammarians with all kinds of etymologies.[468]

According to Alberuni, Indian learning, such as the fables of *Kalila* and *Dimna* and books on medicine, including the famous *Charaka*, came to the Arab world, through either direct translation from Sanskrit into Arabic or through first translation into Persian, and then, from Persian into Arabic. Sachau also thinks that the influx of knowledge from India to Baghdad took place in two different phases of which, he writes:

> As Sindh was under the actual rule of Khalif Mansur (753–74), there came embassies from that part of India to Baghdad, and among them scholars, who brought along with them two books, the *Brahmasiddhanta* of Brahmagupta, and his *Khandakhadyaka* (Arkanda). With the help of these pundits, Alfazari, perhaps also Yakub ibn Tarik, translated them. Both works have been largely used, and have exercised a great influence. It was on this occasion that the Arabs first became acquainted with a scientific system of astronomy. They learned from Brahmagupta earlier than from Ptolemy.[469]

Sachau adds that there was another influx of Hindu learning into the Arab world during the reign of Caliph Harun al-Rashid (r. 786–808). The famous ministerial family of Barmak from Balkh, who had outwardly converted to Islam but never abandoned their ancestral crypto-Buddhist tradition after generations,

> ...sent scholars to India, there to study medicine and pharmacology. Besides, they engaged Hindu scholars to come to Baghdad, made them the chief physicians of their hospitals, and ordered them to translate from Sanskrit into Arabic books on medicine, pharmacology, toxicology, philosophy, astrology, and other subjects. Still in later centuries, Muslim scholars sometimes traveled for the same purposes as the emissaries of the Barmak, e.g. Almuwaffuk, not long before Alberuni's time...[470]

Moreover, the Arabs also translated Indian works on many other subjects, including on snakes, poison, veterinary art, logic and philosophy, ethics, politics, and science of war. '*Many Arab authors took up the subjects communicated to them by the Hindus and worked them out in original compositions, commentaries and extracts. A favorite subject of theirs was Indian mathematics, the knowledge of which became far spread by the publications of Alkindi and many others,*' adds Sachau.[471]

The eleventh-century Spanish Muslim scholar Said al-Andalusi—in his book, *The Categories of Nations*, on world science—acknowledges India very positively and describes it as a major center for science, mathematics and culture. The treatise recognizes India as the first nation to have cultivated science and praises Indians for their wisdom, ability in all the branches of knowledge and for making useful and rare inventions. It adds:

---

468. Ibid, p. 160–61
469. Ibid, p. XXXIII
470. Ibid, p. XXXIII-XXXIV
471. Ibid, p. XXXVI

To their credit, the Indians have made great strides in the study of numbers and of geometry. They have acquired immense information and reached the zenith in their knowledge of the movements of the stars (astronomy) and the secrets of the skies (astrology) as well as other mathematical studies. After all that, *they have surpassed all the other peoples in their knowledge of medical science* and the strengths of various drugs, the characteristics of compounds and the peculiarities of substances (chemistry).[472]

Many early Islamic scholars (seventh–eighth century) left records of a vibrant and wealthy India, having many populous and prosperous cities (discussed below). Of the pre-Islamic civilization of India, notes Francis Watson:[473]

It is clear that India, at the time when Muslim invaders turned toward it (8th to 11th centuries), was the earth's richest region for its wealth in precious and semi-precious stones, gold and silver, religion and culture, and its fine arts and letters. Tenth century Hindustan was also far more advanced than its contemporaries in the East and the West for its achievements in the realms of speculative philosophy and scientific theorizing, mathematics and knowledge of nature's workings. Hindus of the early medieval period were unquestionably superior in more things than the Chinese, the Persians (including the Sassanians), the Romans and the Byzantines of the immediate proceeding centuries. The followers of Siva and Vishnu on this subcontinent had created for themselves a society more mentally evolved—joyous and prosperous too—than had been realized by the Jews, Christians, and Muslim monotheists of the time. Medieval India, until the Islamic invaders destroyed it, was history's most richly imaginative culture and one of the five most advanced civilizations of all times.

Look at the Hindu art that Muslim iconoclasts severely damaged or destroyed. Ancient Hindu sculpture is vigorous and sensual in the highest degree—more fascinating than human figurative art created anywhere else on earth. (Only statues created by classical Greek artists are in the same class as Hindu temple sculpture). Ancient Hindu temple architecture is the most awe-inspiring, ornate and spell-binding architectural style found anywhere in the world. (The Gothic art of the cathedrals in France is the only other religious architecture that is comparable with the intricate architecture of Hindu temples). No artist of any historical civilization has ever revealed the same genius as ancient Hindustan's artists and artisans.

The ancient Greeks undoubtedly had made greater contributions in science, medicine and philosophy than other ancient civilizations, but India was definitely a leading civilization in all spheres of intellectual achievements.

A tolerant and humane society

Apart from India's intellectual and scientific achievements, Said al-Andalusi noted: '*The Indians, as known to all nations for many centuries, are the metal (essence) of wisdom, the source of fairness and objectivity. They are peoples of sublime pensiveness, universal apologue...*' Indeed, India was not only a distinguished civilization in its achievements in science, literature, philosophy, arts, and architecture but also had distinguished itself from the invading Muslims in terms of its humanity, chivalry and ethical behavior. Prior to Islamic invasions, Hindu kings and princes of India used to engage in wars, like in any major civilization of the time, but such wars were relatively infrequent. Affirming this, Muslim traveler Merchant Sulaiman writes in his *Salsilatut Tawarikh* (851): '*The Indians sometimes go to war for conquest, but the occasions are rare.*' Ibn Battutah, while traveling with Sultan Muhammad Tughlaq's diplomatic convoy to the Chinese emperor,

---

472. al-Andalusi S (1991) *Science in the Medieval World: Book of the Categories of Nations,* Translated by Salem SI and Kumar A, University of Texas Press, Chapter 5.

473. Watson & Hiro, p. 96

was surprised to observe that the Hindu rulers of Malabar showed great respect for each other's territory and exercised restraint against warfare. In Malabar, he wrote, '*there are twelve infidel sultans, some of them strong with armies numbering fifty thousand men, and others weak with armies of three thousand. Yet there is no discord whatever between them and the strong does not desire to seize the possessions of the weak.*'[474] Muslim invaders had unfurled continuous warfare in India (and everywhere else) not only against the Hindus but amongst themselves; there were ceaseless revolts by Muslim generals, chiefs and princes all over India during their entire period of Islamic rule. Battutah's astonishment is then quite understandable. Sulaiman adds that the Indian kings even did not maintain troops in regular pays. They used to be paid only when they were called in for fighting. Once the war is over, '*They then come out (to civilian life), and maintain themselves without receiving anything from the king.*'[475]

Indians used to observe high ethical conventions and behavior in times of both peace and war. Wars and battles were normally limited to the martial class, the *kshatriyyas*, of opposing parties, who used to clash mostly in open battle-fields. They used to follow a code of honor and sacrificing it for the sake of victory or material gain was deemed a shame worse than death. Even famous Muslim historian Al-Idrisi wrote that Hindus never departed from justice (discussed below). The religious teachers and priests and the non-combatants, particularly the women and children, were normally left unmolested in wars. Religious symbols and establishments—namely temples, churches and monasteries—and civilian habitations were generally not attacked, pillaged and plundered. War booty, a major divinely-sanctioned object of the Islamic holy war, was not a part of war and conquest in pre-Islamic India. The women of the defeated side were normally not captured or their chastity not violated, contrary to the practice in other contemporaneous civilizations—China and Greece, for example.

Merchant Sulaiman affirms some of these ethical conducts of Indian wars. He says: '*When a king subdues a neighboring state, he places over it a man belonging to the family of the fallen prince, who carried on the government in the name of the conqueror. The inhabitants would not suffer it to be otherwise.*'[476] The tenth-century Muslim chronicler, Abu Zaidu-l Hasan, wrote about the conquest of the kingdom of Kumar (Khmer) by the Maharaja of Zabaj (Srivijaya or Java).[477] The young, haughty prince of Kumar had expressed his desire to conquer Zabaj and hearing this, the king of Zabaj attacked the Kumar kingdom. After the Maharaja seized the palace of Kumar and killed the prince, '*He then made a proclamation assuring safety to everyone, and seated himself on the throne.*' He then addressed the *wazir* (chief minister) of Kumar that,

> 'I know that you have borne yourself like a true minister; receive now the recompense of your conduct. I know that you have given good advice to your master if he would but have headed it. Seek out a man fit to occupy the throne, and seat him thereon instead of this foolish fellow.' The Maharaja then returned immediately to his country, and *neither he nor any of his men touched anything belonging to the king of Kumar*.[478]

The ancient Greek traveler and historian Megasthenes (c. 350–290 BCE) recorded his observation of the peculiar traits of Indian warfare during his visit to India. Alain Danielou has summarized his observations as follows:

---

474. Gibb, p. 232

475. Elliot & Dawson, Vol. I, p. 7

476. Ibid

477. The Southeast Asian kingdoms of Srivijaya, Java and Khmer were then an extension of the Indian civilization with a firmly rooted Hindu-Buddhist religious influence. The famous Muslim historian al-Masudi had met Zaidu-l Hasan in Basra in 916, reproduced this story in his *Meadows of Gold*.

478. Elliot & Dawson, Vol. I, p. 8–9

Whereas among other nations it is usual, in the contests of war, to ravage the soil and thus to reduce it to an uncultivated waste; among the Indians, on the contrary, by whom husbandmen are regarded as a class that is sacred and inviolable, the tillers of the soil, even when battle is raging in their neighborhood, are undisturbed by any sense of danger, for the combatants on either side in waging the conflict make carnage of each other, but allow those engaged in husbandry to remain quite unmolested. Besides, they never ravage an enemy's land with fire, nor cut down its trees.[479]

Prof. Arthur Basham (d. 1986), the leading authority on ancient Indian culture and Oriental civilizations, writes about ancient Indian codes of war that '*In all her history of warfare, Hindu India has few tales to tell of cities put to the sword or of the massacre of non-combatants. The ghastly sadism of the kings of Assyria, who flayed their captives alive, is completely without parallel in ancient India. To us the most striking feature of ancient Indian civilization is its humanity.*'[480] Hiuen Tsang, a seventh-century Buddhist pilgrim from China to Nalanda University, recorded that the country was little injured despite enough rivalries between the ruling princes of India. Faxian, a fourth-century Chinese pilgrim to India, marveled at the peace, prosperity, and high culture of Indians. Having grown up in war-torn China, says Linda Johnson, he was deeply impressed by a land whose leaders were more concerned with promoting commerce and religion than with slaughtering substantial portion of the population.[481]

Muslim code of war

It is evident from the discussion so far that the Islamic invaders of India brought a totally different code of war, based on the Quran and the *Sunnah*. Contemporary Muslim historians inform us that, as a general rule, they used to slay all enemy soldiers on the battlefield. After the victory, they often fell upon the civilian villages and towns often slaughtering the men of fighting age. They sacked and plundered the households for booty, and sometimes burned down the villages and towns. Of the civilian population, the Buddhist monks and priestly Brahmins, in whom the common people reposed their trust, became special targets for extermination. The centers of infidel religion and learning—namely Hindu and Jain temples, Buddhist monasteries, Sikh *Gurdwaras* and indigenous educational institutions—were their prime targets for desecration, destruction and plunder. The women and children were captured as slaves in large numbers. They kept the young and beautiful women captives as sex-slaves, others were engaged in household chores, and the rest were sold. The magnitude of the booty, the captives included, was a measure of the glory and success of military missions; this is reflected in their glorifying narratives by leading medieval Muslim historians. When large numbers of infidels were slain, Sultan Muhammad Ghauri, Qutbuddin Aibak and Emperor Babur *et al.* used to raise "victory-towers" with their heads to celebrate the achievement. Sultan Ahmad Shah Bahmani (1422–36) of the Deccan Sultanate attacked the Vijaynagar kingdom, in which records Ferishta, '*wherever he went he put to death men, women and children without mercy, contrary to the compact (not to molest civilians) made between his uncle and predecessor Mahomed Shah and the Rays of Beejanuggar. Whenever the number of slain amounted to twenty thousand, he halted three days and made a festival in celebration of the bloody event. He broke down also the idolatrous temples and destroyed the colleges of the Brahmins.*'[482] The Muslim invaders and rulers committed all these barbaric acts for the sake of Islamic holy war in the cause of Allah as commanded in the Quran and prophetic examples. The Prophet's attack of the Jewish tribe of Banu Qurayza of Medina (627) or the Jews of Khaybar (628) and his manner of dealing with them served as an ideal example for emulation by later holy warriors of Islam.

The contrast between the Hindu and Islamic codes of war was clearly exhibited in Sultan Muhammad Ghauri's attack on King Prithviraj Chauhan of Delhi and Ajmer (1191). Muhammad Ghauri was

---

479. Danielou, p. 106

480. Basham AL (2000) *The Wonder That Was India*, South Asia Books, Columbia, p. 8–9

481. Johnson L (2001) *Complete Idiot's Guide to Hinduism*, Alpha Books, New York, p. 38

482. Ferishtah, Vol. II, p. 248

defeated and captured in his first attack. Despite his many brutal attacks on the northern borders of India, involving mass murder, enslavement, plunder and pillage, Prithviraj Chauhan forgave and honorably released the aggressor without inflicting any punishment or humiliation. Within a few months, Ghauri regrouped and attacked Prithviraj again defeating the chivalrous Hindu King.[483] Muhammad Ghauri repaid Prithviraj's earlier generosity by pulling out his eyes before killing him.[484]

Further evidence of the contrast between the Hindu and Muslim codes of war comes from Ferishtah's narration of Deccan Sultan Muhammad Shah's attack against King Krishna Ray of Vijaynagar kingdom in 1366. Muhammad Shah had vowed to slaughter 100,000 infidels in the attack and *'the massacre of the unbelievers was renewed in so relentless a manner that pregnant women and children at the breast even did not escape the sword,'* records Ferishtah.[485] The Muslim army in a treacherous surprise-attack put Krishna Ray on the flight and 10,000 of his soldiers were slain. Muhammad Shah's *'thirst for vengeance being still unsatisfied, he commanded the inhabitants of every place around Vijaynagar to be massacred,'* records Ferishtah.

Krishna Ray dispatched ambassadors to make peace, which Muhammad Shah refused. Thereupon, one of the Sultan's favorite advisor reminded him that *'he had only sworn to slaughter one hundred thousand Hindus, and not to destroy their race altogether.'* The sultan replied that *'twice the number required by this vow might have been slain,'* yet he was neither willing to make peace nor spare the subjects.[486] This means that nearly 200,000 people were slaughtered in this campaign. The ambassadors were, at length, able to conclude peace by paying a large sum of money on the spot and pleaded with the Sultan to let them speak. According to Ferishtah, *'Being permitted to speak, they observed that no religion required the innocent to be punished for the crimes of the guilty (kings), more especially helpless women and children: if Krishn Ray had been in fault, the poor and feeble inhabitants had not been accessory to his errors. Mahomed Shah replied that decrees of Providence (i.e., from Allah such as in Quran 9:5 to slaughter the idolaters) had been ordered what had been done, and that he had no power to alter them.'* At length, the ambassadors were able to rouse a humane sense in Muhammad Shah, as adds Ferishtah, *'(he) took an oath that he would not, hereafter, put to death a single enemy after a victory, and would bind his successors to observe the same line of conduct.'*[487] On the contrast between the Hindu and Islamic codes of war, John Jones observes: *'It is a curious fact that the hideous and bloody monster of religious intolerance was hardly known in India until, first the followers of Mohammed and secondly, the disciples of the meek and lowly Jesus (i.e. Portuguese), began to invade the land.'*[488] Arthur Schopenhauer (d. 1860), one of the greatest nineteenth-century philosophers, narrates the sordid tale of the Islamic invasion of India as follows: *'...the endless persecutions, the religious wars, that sanguinary frenzy of which the ancients (of India) had no conception! The destruction or disfigurement of the ancient temples and idols, a lamentable, mischievous and barbarous act still bears witness to the monotheistic fury... carried on from Mahmud, the Ghaznevid of cursed memory, down to Aurangzeb... We hear nothing of this kind in the case of the Hindoo.'*[489] English novelist Aldous Huxley (1894–1963), in likening the atrocious history of Islam with that of later Christianity, wrote in *Ends and Means*:

483. Dutt, KG, *The Modern Face of Ang Kshetra*, Tribune India, 17October 1998

484. Prithviraj III, Wikipedia, http://en.wikipedia.org/wiki/Prithviraj_Chauhan

485. Ferishtah, Vol. II, p. 195

486. Ibid, p. 196–97

487. Ibid, p. 197

488. Jones JP (1915) *India - Its Life and Thought*, The Macmillan Company, New York, p. 166

489. Saunders TB (1997) *The Essays of Arthur Schopenhauer: Book I : Wisdom of Life*, De Young Press, p. 42–43

It is an extremely significant fact that, before the coming of the Mohammedans, there was virtually no persecution in India. The Chinese pilgrim Hiuen Tsang, who visited India in the first half of the seventh century and has left a circumstantial account of his 14 years in the country, makes it clear that Hindus and Buddhist lived side by side without any show of violence. Neither Hinduism nor Buddhism is disgraced by anything corresponding to the Inquisition; neither was ever guilty of such iniquities as the Albigensian crusade or such criminal lunacies as the religious wars of the 16th and 17th centuries.[490]

Indisputably, Buddhism, Jainism and Sikhism arose in India as a revolt against Hinduism. Although Hinduism had its shortcomings, these new religious off-shoots grew from the midst of the Hindu society without facing any persecution of the type Islam brought to India or meted out to its revolting heretics throughout Islam's history. The Christian persecution and brutality caused death of millions of Pagans, Jews, heretics, apostates and witches in Europe, South America and India's Goa. In Islam, Prophet Muhammad himself had ordered execution of critics and apostates of Islam, while the killing and torture of apostates and heretics have continued ever since to this day. It should be noted that Buddhism was a flourishing religion in Central and Southeast Asia and was quite vigorous in parts of India at the time of Islam's birth. Islam has nearly extinguished this most humane and peaceful ancient religious creed from India. It extinguished Paganism from Arabia by the sword in the life-time of Muhammad. Zoroastrianism in Persia and Christianity in the Levant, Egypt, and Anatolia etc. have suffered near extinction caused by the violent exertions of Islam. It should be noted that, to escape the brutal persecution of Islam, tens of thousands of Zoroastrians (Persis) fled to India, where—welcomed by the Hindu society—they live as a peaceful and well-off community till today. However, they suffered Islamic persecution in India too, after the Muslim invaders later occupied India. Sultan Ibrahim, a Ghaznivid descendent of Sultan Mahmud, marched to India; and according to historian Nizamuddin Ahmad, the author of *Tabakat-I Akbari*, '*he conquered many towns and forts, and amongst them were a city exceedingly populous, inhabited by a tribe of Khurasani descent (Persis), whom Afrasiyah had expelled from their native country. It was completely reduced... he took away no less than 100,000 captives.*'[491]

Indian tolerance in the eyes of Muslim chroniclers

The humanity, tolerance and chivalry of Indians also caught the attention of Muslim historians. The Arab geographer Abu Zaid wrote of the rulers and people of Sarandib (Sri Lanka), an extension of Indian civilization, that in late ninth century, '*There are numerous colonies of Jews in Sarandib, and people of other religions, especially Manicheans. The King allows each sect to follow its own religion.*'[492] Al-Masudi, a famous Muslim historian and traveler, writing in the early tenth century, describes the disposition of the most powerful Indian king, Balhara, toward Muslim settlers of his kingdom. He placed Balhara (Rashtrakuta dynasty, South India) in the same league of the world's three greatest monarchs: the caliph of Baghdad, the emperors of China and Constantinople.[493] On Balhara's treatment of Muslims, noted al-Masudi: '*Of all the kings of Sindh and India, there is no one who pays greater respect to the Musalmans than Balhara. In his Kingdom, Islam is honored and protected.*'[494] Al-Masudi's description (916–17) of a large Muslim community near Bombay, created by Arabian and Iraqi pepper and spice traders who had settled there, is already noted. This Muslim community was '*granted a degree of political autonomy by the local raja*' and

---

490. Swarup R (2000) *On Hinduism Reviews and Reflections*, Voice of India, p. 150–51

491. Elliot & Dawson, Vol. V, p. 559

492. Ibid, Vol. I, p. 10

493. Nehru (1989), p. 210

494. Ibid, p. 24

they *'intermarried considerably with the local population.'*[495] About the status of Muslims in Balhara's kingdom, al-Istahkri wrote (c. 951): *'It is a land of infidels, but there are Musalmans in its cities and none but the Musalmans rule them on the part of Balhara.'*[496]

Ibn Haukal—renowned tenth-century Arab traveler and geographer and the author of famous treatise, *Surat al-Ardh* or *The face of the Earth* (977)—observed while traveling in the region between Cambay and Saimur that *'The inhabitants were idolaters, but the Musalmans were treated with great consideration by the native princes. They were governed by the men of their own faith... They had erected their mosques in these infidel cities and were allowed to summon their congregations by the usual mode of proclaiming the time of prayer.'*[497] Al-Idrisi also gives a similar account of the treatment of Muslims in the territory of Balhara: *'The town is frequented by large number of Musalman traders who go on business. They are honorably received by the king and his ministers and find protection and safety.'* Al-Idrisi continues: *'The Indians are naturally inclined to justice, and never depart from it in their actions. Their good faith, honesty, and fidelity to their engagements are well known, and they are so famous for these qualities that people flock to their country from every side.'* He was further impressed by Indian's "love of truth and horror of vice".[498] Even modern Muslim historian Habibullah states that *'Muslims were treated by the Hindus with generosity and respect and allowed them freedom, even to govern themselves.'*[499]

These ethical principles of Indians were rooted in its civilizational value system. King Ashoka seemed to have deviated from these principles in his ambition to become a great conqueror. However, he was left devastated by the casualties that occurred in the conquest of Kalinga, in which about 100,000 soldiers and commoners died. Subsequently, he became a great humanist and used to feel frightened by wars; he became an avowed anti-war activist. Killing the infidels in large numbers by Muslim conquerors was a common occurrence, generally glorified by Muslims at all levels—including by most of their greatest intellectuals.

Evidently, the Indian rulers showed generosity, humanity and chivalry toward Muslims, despite suffering terrible cruelty at the hands of ruthless Muslim invaders. This generosity and chivalry was demonstrated very early, when the Hindus revolted and ousted the Muslim rulers from Sindhan during the reign of Caliph Al-Mutasim (833–42). Despite suffering so much slaughter, destruction, pillage, enslavement and defilement of their temples over two centuries, the Hindus *'respected the mosque, which the Musalmans of the town visited every Friday, for the purpose of the reading of usual offices and praying for the Khalif.'*[500]

Tolerance & chivalry of Hindu rulers during the Muslim period

Indian rulers exercised the principle of Hindu tolerance, generosity and chivalry toward Muslims well into the last days of Islamic domination; by this time, Muslim invaders had inflicted terrible cruelty upon the Hindus and destruction of their religion for nearly a millennium in some parts. During the period of the Muslim rule in India, courageous Indian princes and commoners, revolting against the Muslim invaders, occasionally curved out Hindu kingdoms. Vijaynagar was one such Hindu kingdom (1336–1565) in South India (Andhra Pradesh, Tamil Nadu and Kerala). Constantly under attack by Muslim rulers, sometimes it exercised independence, and paid tribute to Muslim overlords at other times. Still, Vijaynagar rose to be one of the greatest empires in the world of the time. Abdur-Razzak of Herat, who came to Vijaynagar in 1443 as an envoy of the Mongol Khan of Central Asia, wrote, *"The city is such that eyes has not seen nor ear heard of any place resembling it upon the whole earth."*[501] Paes, a Portuguese traveler, visiting Vijaynagar in 1522,

---

495. Eaton (1978), p. 13

496. Ibid, p. 27

497. Elliot & Dawson, Vol. I, p. 457

498. Ibid, p. 88

499. Sharma, p. 89

500. Elliot & Dawson, Vol. I, p. 450

501. Ibid, Vol. IV, p. 106

found it "*large as Rome and very beautiful to the sight*"; it was "*the best-provided city in the world... for the state of the city is not like other cities, which often fails of supplies and provisions, for in this everything abounds.*"[502] As goes the legend, it was '*a kingdom so rich that pearls and rubies were sold in the market-place like grain,*' notes Naipaul.[503] Razzak's eyewitness account somewhat affirms this legend, saying: '*The jewellers sell their rubies and pearls and diamonds and emeralds openly in the bazar.*'[504] In late 1564, four neighboring Muslim sultanates joined hands to destroy the great Hindu civilization of Vijaynagar that had lasted over 200 years. In a five-month seize, it was burnt to ashes in January 1565. English historian Robert Sewell noted of the destruction that "*so splendid a city; teaming with a wealthy and industrious population in the full plentitude of prosperity... seized, pillaged and reduced to ruins, amid scenes of savage massacre and horrors begging description.*"[505] On the massacre and pillage of the fleeing Hindus, notes Ferishtah, '*the river was dyed red with their blood. It is computed by the best of authorities that above one hundred thousand infidels were slain during the action and in the pursuit. The plunder was so huge that every private man in the allied army became rich in gold, jewels, tents, arms, horses, and slaves...*'[506]

Let us return to the tolerance of the Vijaynagar kings. In order to fortify his army to stave off Muslim attacks, King Dev Raya II (1419–49), records Ferishtah, '*gave orders to enlist Mussulmans (of his kingdom) in his service, allotting them estates, and erecting a mosque for their use in the city of Beejanuggar (Vijaynagar). He also commanded that no one should molest them in the exercise of their religion and moreover, **he ordered a Koran to be placed before his throne on a rich desk, so that the faithful (Muslims) can perform their ceremony of obeisance in his presence without sinning against their laws.**'[507] However, this tolerance and promotion of treacherous Muslims in the army eventually proved costly for Vijaynagar, the only standing Hindu civilization in India. By the mid-sixteenth century, Muslims had become a significant force in the army. When the confederate force of the surrounding sultanates attacked Vijaynagar in 1564–65, two large Muslim battalions, each having 70,000–80,000 soldiers, deserted King Ramraja. Because of these two Muslim commanders' treachery, Ramraja fell into Muslim hands. Sultan Hussein Nizam Shah ordered his beheading immediately. This led to the collapse of Vijaynagar, noted Caesar Frederick, who visited the place two years later in 1567.[508]

It should, however, be acknowledged that some degree of intolerance had been sinking in Ramraja's army. He had become very powerful and started capturing domains from the neighboring Muslim sultanates, threatening latter's existence. In the course of incursions into Muslim domains, his forces started paying in the same coin as Muslims had been doing ever since they started attacking India in the 630s, and more importantly, against Vijaynagar over the previous 200 years. His forces started disrespecting mosques, offering Hindu prayers in them and even destroyed some; they even violated Muslim women in the 1558 attack of Ahmednagar, ruled by Hussein Nizam Shah, records Ferishtah.[509] However, these sacrilegious acts, it appears, were not approved by the Hindu monarch. On one occasion, his Muslim soldiers sacrificed a cow—sacred to Hindus—in the Turukvada area in Vijaynagar offending the Hindus. Ramraja's offended officers and nobles, including his own brother Tirumala, petitioned to him about the sacrilege. To be noted that even today a similar offence against Islam in a Muslim-majority country, say in Bangladesh or Pakistan, will incite Muslim mobs to violence, even probably bloodbath. Ramraja, however, refused to prohibit the

---

502. Nehru (1989), p. 258

503. Naipaul VS (1977) *India: A Wounded Civilization*, Alfred A Knopf Inc., New York, p. 5

504. Elliot & Dawson, Vol. IV, p. 107

505. Nehru (1989), p. 259

506. Ferishtah, Vol. III, p. 79

507. Ibid, p. 266

508. Majumdar RC ed. (1973) *The Mughal Empire*, in *The History and Culture of the Indian People*, Bombay, Vol. VII, p. 425

509. Ferishtah, Vol. III, p. 72,74

sacrifice of cows by his Muslim soldiers, saying that, it will not be right to interfere in their religious practices and that he was only the master of the bodies of his soldiers, not of their souls.[510]

During the reign of fanatic Aurangzeb (d. 1707) toward the end of the Islamic domination in India, his Maratha opponent Shivaji was consolidating power and expanding his kingdom. When Shivaji started incursions into Mughal territories in the South, Aurangzeb, still a prince, wrote to his general Nasiri Khan and other officers to enter Shivaji's territory from all sides for '*wasting the villages, slaying the people without pity and plundering them to the extreme,*' records Qabil Khan in *Adab-i-Alamgiri*. They were further instructed to show no mercy in slaying and enslaving,[511] an age-old Muslim practice. But Shivaji, a deeply religious man, never indulged in extreme cruelty and violence in kind. Even his inveterate critic Khafi Khan, in his *Muntakhab-ul-Lubab*, could not but admire Shivaji's lofty ideals in saying: '*But he (Shivaji) made it a rule that whenever his followers were plundering, they should not do harm to the mosques, the Book of God (Quran), or the women of anyone.*'[512]

Shivaji put his words in actions too. Despite the fact that Muslim rulers used to enslave the Hindu women in tens of thousands and reduce them to sex-slavery, he abstained from such abhorrent practices even defying the temptation of very beautiful captive women. One of his officers had captured a beautiful Muslim girl in 1657 and presented her to Shivaji. Shivaji praised her as prettier than his own mother Jija Bai, honorably gave her dresses and ornaments, and sent her back to her people, escorted by 500 horsemen.[513] Obviously, such acts of chivalry made Khafi Khan appreciate his hated enemy.

Shivaji also made good of his promise to respect the religious institutions and symbols of all, including Muslim's. Despite the fact that, his opponent Aurangzeb destroyed thousands of Hindu temples— more than 200 in 1979 alone, Shivaji scrupulously refrained from defiling Muslim mosques, *madrasas* or shrines. Instead, he was very respectful of them. He particularly venerated the Sufis, and even provided them subsistence and build *khanqah* for them at this own cost. Notably, Baba Yakut of Keloshi was one such Sufi saint who had received Shivaji's succor.[514]

Shivaji refrained from excessive bloodbath as well. While Muslim invaders and rulers quite commonly slaughtered the Hindus in tens of thousands—even tolerant and humane Akbar massacred 30,000 surrendered peasants in Chittor (1568), Shivaji never engaged in such cold-blooded mass-murder of his opponents captured in wars. When he attacked Surat in 1664, its Mughal governor Inayat Khan fled and the 500-strong Muslim army was taken prisoner. From his hiding place, Inayat Khan sent an envoy to negotiate peace, in the guise of which the envoy unsuccessfully fell upon Shivaji with a concealed dagger. Seeing the treachery and thinking that Shivaji was slain, his soldiers raised a cry to kill the Muslim prisoners. Shivaji stood up from the ground quickly and forbade any massacre. The enraged Shivaji, however, quenched his anger by putting four prisoners to death, amputated hands of twenty-four and spared the rest.[515] Such vengeance was, however, rare for him; it was obviously highly restrained, even more restrained than that of the later British mercenaries.

In his administration, notes Jadunath Sarkar, he '*brought peace and order to his country, assured the protection of women's honor and the religion of all sects without distinction, extended the royal patronage to the truly pious men of all creeds (Muslims included), and presented equal opportunities to all his subjects by opening the public service to talent, irrespective of caste or creed.*'[516] An illiterate and deeply religious

---

510. *Journal of the Bombay Brach of the Royal Asiatic Society*, Vol. XXII, p. 28

511. Sarkar J (1992) *Shibaji and His Times*, Orient Longham, Mumbai, p. 39

512. Ghosh SC (2000) *The History of Education in Medieval India 1192-1757*, Originals, New Delhi, p. 122

513. Sarkar, p. 43

514. Sarkar, p. 288; Ghosh, p. 122

515. Sarkar, p. 76

516. Ibid, p. 302

orthodox Hindu—Shivaji's even-handed, tolerant and just policy toward his heterogeneous mix of citizens, that included Muslims, was unthinkable in his days of Muslim-ruled India.

However, Shivaji engaged in raiding and plundering of the territory of his sworn Muslim enemies. Based in a part of India, in which *'rice cultivation was impossible and wheat and barley grow in very small quantities,'* Shivaji had little choice. He told the Surat governor of Aurangzeb in this regard that *'Your Emperor has forced me to keep an army for the defence of my people and country. That army must be paid for by his subjects.'*[517] This justification will probably not stand for all of his raids. He was ambitious of establishing a native Hindu kingdom opposed to the persecuting, discriminatory foreign Muslim rulers; his raids were definitely aimed at achieving this goal, too. Nonetheless, whatever defects he had in his actions, he was no match for the plundering activities of his Muslim counterparts and the persecution, discrimination and humiliation the latter meted out to their non-Muslim subjects.

These examples, which come mainly from the writings of Muslim historians, clearly testify to the humane, chivalrous, tolerant and free nature of the Indian society, conspicuously different from what the Muslim invaders and rulers had brought in their trail. Many Muslim historians and non-Muslim observers in the late period of Muslim rule also affirmed this. In praise of Indians, Abul Fazl, the minister of Emperor Akbar, wrote: *"The inhabitants of this land are religious, affectionate, hospitable, genial, and frank. They are fond of scientific pursuits, inclined to austerity of life, seekers after justice, contended, industrious, capable in affairs, loyal, truthful and constant..."* In the Vijaynagar kingdom, noted Duarte Barbosa, *"every man may come and go, and live according to his creed without suffering any annoyance, and without enquiring whether he is a Christian, Jew, Moor (Muslim) or Heathen. Great equity and justice is observed by all."* Mulla Badaoni, a relatively bigoted chronicler of Akbar's court, failed to deny the freedom and tolerance that existed in Indian society as he wrote: *"Hindustan is a nice place where everything is allowed, and no one cares for another (i.e., not interferes in others' affairs) and people may go as they may."*[518]

Coming to such a land of humanity, freedom and tolerance, the Muslim invaders committed utmost slaughter and cruelty; they killed tens of millions and enslaved a greater number. They destroyed temples in the thousands and looted and plundered India's wealth in measures beyond imagination as recorded by contemporary Muslim historians with gloating joy. Kanhadde Prabandha, an Indian chronicler, leaves an eyewitness account of the activities of Islamic invaders (1456) as thus: *"The conquering army burnt villages, devastated the land, plundered people's wealth, took Brahmins and children and women of all classes captive, flogged with thongs of raw hide, carried a moving prison (of captives) with it, and converted the prisoners into obsequious Turks."*[519] Such barbarism Muslim invaders committed with the purpose of carrying out their religious duty. The orthodox *Ulema* as well as the Sufi divines often condemned the Muslim rulers for their failure to put a complete end to the filth of idolatry and unbelief in India. For example, Qazi Mughisuddin reminded Sultan Alauddin that *'Hindus were deadliest foes of the true Prophet,'* who must be annihilated or subjected to worst degradation.[520]

The ruthless and relentless savagery and massacre of Hindus, Buddhists, Sikhs and Jains, committed by Muslim invaders and rulers in India, will surpass the massacre of South American heathens by the Spanish and Portuguese invaders. Of the estimated ninety million natives in the continental Latin America in 1492, only twelve million survived after a century.[521] The overwhelming majority of these deaths resulted from European and African diseases—namely the "childhood diseases" like measles, diphtheria and whooping cough as well as smallpox, *falciparum* malaria and yellow fever—involuntarily brought by the colonists. The native people lacked acquired immunity to these foreign diseases, which caused huge numbers of death.

---

517. Ibid, p. 2,290

518. Lal (1994), p. 29

519. Goel SR (1996) *Story of Islamic Imperialism in India*, South Asia Books, Columbia (MO), p. 41–42

520. Lal (1999), p. 113

521. Elst, p. 8

Within a century, most of the people of the lowland tropical regions were literally wiped out, while as high as 80 percent of the highland population of Andes and Middle America also died from these diseases.[522] Nonetheless, the colonists also killed the Pagan natives, probably in the millions, often on religious grounds. The Europeans, too, did not have acquired immunity to *falciparum* malaria and yellow fever of African origin; they also died in large numbers from these diseases contracted from African slaves brought to the Americas.

Based on historical documentation and circumstantial evidence, Prof. KS Lal estimates that the population of India stood at about 200 million in 1000 and it dwindled to only 170 millions in 1500, in spite of the passage of five centuries.[523] Between sixty and eighty million people died at the hands of Muslim invaders and rulers between 1000 and 1525, estimates Lal. The possibility of annihilation of such a large number of Indians by Muslim invaders and rulers may appear a suspect. However, in the war of independence of Bangladesh in 1971, the Pakistani army killed 1.5 to 3.0 million people in just nine months. It occurred in our modern age of flourishing journalism, but the world hardly took a notice of it. Moreover, a large number of the victims in this case were their co-religionists, the Muslims of East Pakistan. Hence, it is entirely possible that Muslim invaders and rulers, who came with the mission of extirpating idolatry from India, could easily have slaughtered as many as eighty million Indian infidels over a period of ten centuries in such a vast land.

HINDU-MUSLIM DIVIDE: A BRITISH INVENTION?

One aspect of the British imperialism in India, which critics of the subcontinent have obsessively used for demonizing the British, was their "Divide and Rule" policy. These critics claim that the British rulers created animosity between Hindus and Muslims as a premeditated stratagem to weaken the unity and neutralize the collective resistance of Indians for facilitating their continued occupation and exploitation. They argue that this clever ploy kept the Hindus and Muslims of India divided; they fought each other over their religious differences, allowing the British rule to continue unimpeded.

An overwhelming majority of the people in Bangladesh, India and Pakistan also think that this British-created religious divide is the root cause of the internecine communal troubles that have continued to plague India to this day. They entertain a deeply-entrenched belief that religious animosity between Hindus and Muslims was totally unknown in India before the British rulers came and devised this cunning and malevolent scheme to keep the Hindus and Muslims at each other's throat.

This hyperbolic criticism of the British "Divide and Rule" policy has been consumed voraciously and regurgitated frequently by all and sundry: Hindus and Muslims, progressives and obscurantists, liberals and zealots. There existed, believe critics, a wonderful relationship of amity, tolerance, brotherhood and co-operation between the Hindus and Muslims before the devious and manipulative British spoiled it all. Even Nehru painted a picture that the British deliberately created a division between the Hindus and Muslims. India's Congress Party viewed this conspiracy theory as a major underlying cause of the continued Hindu-Muslim conflicts in post-independence India; and all blame was conveniently heaped, in absentia, on the former colonists.

The British rulers undoubtedly exploited the religious division amongst Indians to their advantage. But the question that must be asked is: Was there a unity and brotherhood between Hindus and Muslims during the centuries of Muslim rule in pre-British India?

522. Curtin PD (1993) *The Tropical Atlantic of the Slave Trade*, In M Adas ed., *Islam & European Expansion*, Temple University Press, Philadelphia, p. 172.

523. Lal (1973), p. 25–32

The claim that a utopian harmony existed in pre-British India is not at all supported by available historical evidence; it, instead, point to the contrary. During the centuries of Muslim rule in India, every major Hindu temple was destroyed and many of them were replaced by mosques, often with towering minarets, as a twin symbol of Islam's triumph as well as the subjugation and humiliation of the Hindus. Even after the British mercenaries first landed in India as traders in early 1600s, Aurangzeb (r. 1658–1707) was destroying thousands of temples and forcing the Hindus all over India to convert to Islam. Islamic persecution and brutality virtually extinguished the light of Buddhism in India, a vibrant religion in parts of India when the Muslim invaders came. The Sikhs and Jains also suffered their share of terrible atrocity during the Muslim rule.

Could such blatant persecution of India's natives—the Hindus, Buddhists, Jains and Sikhs—by Muslim invaders and rulers possibly foster a brotherly and harmonious relationship between Muslims and non-Muslims?

If the answer is "yes", then the much smaller hostility shown by the Hindus against Muslims in recent years, such as in their largely justifiable campaign to restore the destroyed Ram temple at the site of the Babri mosque in Ayodhya, must also be fostering tolerance, amity and unity between them. Undeniably, there could not but exist a huge divide between Muslims and the non-Muslims in pre-British India resulting from the extreme persecution of non-Muslims by Muslim rulers.

The myth that a serene harmony and peace existed between Muslims and non-Muslims in pre-British India—propagated by Secular-Marxist and Muslim historians—is nothing but an absurd falsification of history. It contradicts all existing historical evidence, comprising loads of documents left by contemporary Muslim chroniclers and rulers. This alleged harmony and peace is also contradicts the core principles of Islam, which view the idolatrous natives of India as the inveterate enemy and demands their outright extermination.

British exploitation of Hindu-Muslim divide: Obviously, there existed a huge chasm between Muslims and non-Muslims of India. The British mercenaries, after arriving in India, witnessed it themselves for a long time before they started capturing power in 1757. In front of their own eyes, Emperor Aurangzeb destroyed thousands of Hindu temples; they witnessed his bloody, bitter, ceaseless struggles with Marathas, Sikhs and others. The British later exploited this pre-existing discord and animosity to their advantage. For example, in the wake of the Sepoy Mutiny, the Chief Commissioner Sir Henry Lawrence addressed an assembly of Hindu and Muslim sepoys in Lucknow that,[524]

> Soldiers! Some persons are abroad spreading reports that the Government desires to interfere with the religion of their soldiers; you all know this to be a transparent falsehood. ...Alamgeer (Aurangzeb) in former times, and Hyder Ali in later days, forcibly converted thousands of Hindoos, desecrated their fanes [religious places], demolished their temples, and carried ruthless devastation amongst their household gods. Come to our times. Many here present will know that Runjeet Singh never permitted his Mohammedan subjects to call the pious to prayer—never allowed the muezzin to sound from the lofty minarets which adorn Lahore, and remain to this day a monument of their magnificent founders. The year before last a Hindoo could not have dared to build a temple in Lucknow. All this is changed. Now, who is there who would dare to interfere with our Mohammedan or Hindoo subjects...?

This example not only points to a British exploitation of the division between Muslims and non-Muslims, but also affirms the historical truth that this divide had existed since long before the British capture of power. Whether because of this divisive British ploy or not, it is a fact that the Hindus and other non-Muslims of

---

524. Brown RC (1870) *The Punjab and Delhi in 1857*, Atlantic, Delhi, p. 33

India did not support the Sepoy Mutiny as enthusiastically as did Muslims. The Sikhs and Ghurkhas supported the British. The Sikhs obviously did not forget the extreme brutality they had suffered under Aurangzeb (see p. 183–84). They helped the British to recapture Delhi. The Scindia in the North and many other states were on the British side, too.

Why should the Sikhs and Hindus participate in the mutiny anyway? Although the British held the executive power, Muhammad Shah Jaffar was still the official head of India at the time. Shah Jaffar is much eulogized by today's Indians—both Muslim and non-Muslim—as a great revolutionary patriot for instigating the Sepoy Mutiny. But he was essentially fighting to drive the British mercenaries out of India for reestablishing the lost Muslim sovereignty of the yesteryear, not for restoring political power to the people of India. Upon Shah Jaffar's appeal, Muslims across India considered the Sepoy Mutiny to be a Jihad against the British for reinstating the lost Islamic domination. In the course of the Sepoy Mutiny, Shah Jaffar declared himself the Emperor of India and issued coins in his name, the standard way of asserting Islamic imperial status. His name was added to the *khutbah* (sermon) in Muslim prayers, which symbolized the acceptance by Muslims that he was the *Amir* (leader) of India.

The Ottoman stand on the Sepoy Mutiny did not help Muslim's Jihad against the British Raj either. Following the ouster of Muslim rulers by the British, India's Muslims—generally hateful of living under non-Muslim rule—pledged their allegiance to the powerful Ottoman sultan, accepting him as their caliph. But the British assistance to the Ottomans in the Crimean war against Russia helped the Raj obtain an Ottoman order *'advising the Indian Muslim not to fight against them (the British),'* which was read out in mosque sermons around India. The Ottoman sultan, instead of showing support, *'condemned and abhorred the atrocities committed by the Mutineers...'*[525] Obviously under the Ottoman influence, the prominent Muslim scholars and *ulema* of India met in Calcutta in 1857 and issued a *fatwa*, in view of the British government's cordial relationship with the Ottoman sultan, the caliph of Islam, that *"jehad against the British nation is unlawful."*[526] According to Salar Jang, the Muslim prime minister of Hyderabad, *"the whole influence of the (Ottoman) Caliphate was used most unremittingly from Constantinople to check the spread of Mutiny"* and to rally the Indian Muslims around the British Raj in order to pay the debt, he owed, to Great Britain for the British support in the Crimean war.[527] Because of this discouraging position of the Ottoman sultan, the *de facto* political and spiritual head of Indian Muslims, their enthusiasm for the anti-British Jihad lost steam. *"At the bidding of their caliph,"* adds Salar Jang, *"the most warlike of the native races (Indian Muslims)... gave their unstinted support to the British connection at the supreme moment (of the revolt)."*

Following the suppression of the Mutiny, the British Raj understood that their prospect of long-term rule in India lies in exploiting the long-existing bitter religious discord between Muslim and non-Muslim Indians. Thereafter, they applied a divisive ploy, particularly in the army, by putting the Hindu, Muslim and Sikh soldiers in separate quarters—never to serve in the same unit again.[528]

In their Jihad to oust the British rulers, the defunct Mughal leaders (*Nawabs*) tried to win the support of Hindus by offering them various incentives. For example, they agreed to hand-over the hotly contentious Ram temple/Babri Mosque site in Ayodhya to Hindus in order to assuage their anti-Muslim discontent, thereby coaxing them to join the Mutiny. Many Hindu soldiers in the British force jointly revolted with their Muslim colleagues. Hindus in the United Provinces, Delhi, parts of Central India and Bihar joined the revolt in large numbers. But, on the whole, the participation of Hindus and other non-Muslims in the mutiny was less enthusiastic; elsewhere, they sided with the British.

---

525. Ozcan A (1977) *Pan Islamism, Indian Muslims, the Ottomans & Britain (1877-1924)*, Brill, Leiden, p. 16

526. Ibid, p. 20

527. Ibid, p. 17

528. Braudel F (1995) *A History of Civilizations*, Translated by Mayne R, Penguin Books, New York, p. 242

The Sepoy Mutiny, in all likelihood, meant for reestablishing the days of *jizyah* and slavery for non-Muslims, which the British had abolished. The Sepoy Mutiny, according to Nehru, was an effort to reestablish the old feudalism, which he abhorred. '*The Revolt of 1857–58 was the last flicker of feudal India,*' he asserts.[529] Would it have been wise for India's non-Muslims to throw their lot in with the Muslims, drive out the British and return to the Mughal rule once again? The British exploitation was possibly as bad as the Muslim one. Otherwise, they were definitely freer, less molested, more respectable, and even somewhat privileged under the British Raj than what they had enjoyed under the previous Muslim rule. '*The British period—two hundred years in some places, less than a hundred years in others—was a time of Hindu regeneration,*' notes Naipaul.[530] For them, returning to *dhimmitude* under the Islamic yoke once again was clearly a less attractive choice.

HINDU-MUSLIM DISCORD, PARTITION OF INDIA & BRITISH COMPLICITY

The British rulers have also been roundly blamed, particularly by Hindus, for the Partition of India in 1947. As the movement for India's independence started building up following the founding of the Indian National Congress Party in 1885, a Hindu-Muslim tension also started building up over the political control of independent India. The founding of the All India Muslim League Party later in 1906 further boosted the tension. It took a violent turn in the 1920s and more dangerously, in the 1940s—leading to the eventual Partition of the subcontinent in 1947 into two states: India and Pakistan. The Partition-related riots caused as many as two million deaths. The British Raj has been summarily condemned for this devastating violence. However, the British complicity in the Partition and the violence connected to it demands a thorough examination.

A fomenting nationalist movement was sweeping across India in the early twentieth century. It gained manifold momentum after Mahatma Gandhi arrived from South Africa in 1914. His nonviolence movement, clothed in Hindu religious principles (*ahimsa* etc.), greatly aroused the Indian masses. The overwhelming response to Gandhi's call for the boycott of the 1919 Constitution on 20 September 1920 and for civil disobedience in December 1921 made it clear that the days of the British imperialism in India had been numbered.

During this time, there arose two separate movements amongst India's Muslims. The pious started the "*Khilafat* (Caliphate) Movement" (1919–23). Earlier, as British mercenaries started ousting Muslim rulers one after another, Muslims of India increasingly looked to the Ottoman sultan as their political head and savior. This trend was inspired by the teachings of the widely popular Sufi master Shah Walliullah (d. 1762), who, seeing that Muslim power in India was crumbling, recognized the Ottoman sultan as *Amir al-Muminin*, the *leader of the believers*. After the ouster of Tipu Sultan in 1799, Muslim allegiance overwhelmingly lied with the Ottomans, which can be gathered from their pliant response to the Ottoman opposition to Sepoy Mutiny.

The Anglo-French forces occupied much of the Ottoman Empire during the First World War and partitioned it into small independent states. This infuriated Muslims worldwide. The indignant pious Muslims in India, in their rage against the British interference in Ottoman affairs, waged a campaign for ousting the British from India. They were in favor of establishing a pan-Islamic caliphate spanning all Muslim lands of the world headed by the Ottoman caliph. They wanted India to be a part of it after the eviction of the British. The Congress Party led by Mahatma Gandhi and Jawaharlal Nehru—desperate to oust the common enemy, the British—joined this Islamist movement. It lost favor among the Congress Party leaders following the

529. Nehru (1989), p. 415

530. Naipaul (1998), p. 247

barbaric Muslim violence against innocent Hindus in Malabar (Kerala, 1921), known as the "Mopla Rebellion" (see below). It was abandoned altogether when Kemal Ataturk dismantled the Ottoman caliphate in 1923.

The nationalist minded Muslims started a second campaign for creating a separate Muslim state. The idea was floated with the founding of the Muslim League Party in 1906, but gained momentum after the death of the *Khilafat* Movement. This separatist movement was initiated, because Muslims feared that they might have to live in an independent democratic India politically dominated by the majority Hindus. This fear was clearly reflected in Allama Muhammad Iqbal's criticism of democracy as a system of governance, in which, "heads are counted, not weighed". Muhammad Iqbal (his family had converted to Islam from Hinduism not long ago), pathologically blinded by the supremacist Islamic ideology, thought that '*All land belongs to the Muslims, because it belongs to their God.*'[531] Therefore, although all the great thinkers and Nobel laureates of India were Hindu, the Muslim heads weighed higher than the Hindu ones to bigoted Iqbal. It may be noted here that, in the course of unleashing mindless violence for seceding Pakistan in 1947, the Muslim League Party, led by Muhammad Ali Jinnah, circulated secret pamphlets amongst Muslims, saying: "*One Muslim should get the right of five Hindus, i.e., each Muslim is equal to five Hindus.*"[532] Having realized the impossibility of gaining the old Muslim political ascendancy in united India, Iqbal presented a firm and clear blueprint of Pakistan as a separate homeland for Muslims in his Presidential Address in the *All-India Muslim League Meet* in Allahabad on 29 December 1930.[533] In pointing to the incompatibility of Islam with a secular-democratic polity, Iqbal noted:

> 'Is religion a private affair? Would you like to see Islam as a moral and political ideal, meeting the same fate in the world of Islam as Christianity has already met in Europe? Is it possible to retain Islam as an ethical ideal and to reject it as a polity, in favor of national polities in which (the) religious attitude is not permitted to play any part? This question becomes of special importance in India, where the Muslims happen to be a minority. The proposition that religion is a private individual experience is not surprising on the lips of a European. In Europe the conception of Christianity as a monastic order, renouncing the world of matter and fixing its gaze entirely on the world of spirit, led, by a logical process of thought, to the view embodied in this proposition. The nature of the Prophet's religious experience, as disclosed in the Quran, however, is wholly different.'

Therefore, Muslims needed a state, in which the religious scruples will be thoroughly integrated into the polity, as added Iqbal:

> 'The religious ideal of Islam, therefore, is organically related to the social order which it has created. The rejection of the one will eventually involve the rejection of the other. Therefore the construction of a polity on national lines, if it means a displacement of the Islamic principle of solidarity, is simply unthinkable to a Muslim. This is a matter which at the present moment directly concerns the Muslims of India.'

Muslims, therefore, needed a separate state, as Iqbal goes on to articulate the "Two Nation" theory:

> 'I would like to see the Punjab, North-West Frontier Province, Sindh and Baluchistan amalgamated into a single state. Self-government within the British Empire, or without the

---

531. Elst, p. 41

532. Khosla GD (1989) *Stern Reckoning: A Survey of Events Leading Up To and Following the Partition of India*, Oxford University Press, Delhi, p. 313

533. Sherwani LA ed. (1977) *Speeches, Writings, and Statements of Iqbal*, Iqbal Academy (2nd Edition), Lahore, p. 3–26.

British Empire, the formation of a consolidated Northwest Indian *Muslim state* appears to me to be the final destiny of the Muslims, at least of Northwest India.'

In a 1937 letter to Jinnah, Iqbal candidly agrees that his proposed separate Muslim state was meant for saving '*Muslims from the domination of Non-Muslims*' and also proposed to include the Muslim-dominated far-off Bengal in such a state, saying: '*Why should not the Muslims of North-West India and Bengal be considered as nations entitled to self-determination just as other nations in India and outside India are.*'[534] Just before his death in 1938, Iqbal urged Muslims to rally around Jinnah, saying,

> 'There is only one way out. Muslims should strengthen Jinnah's hands. They should join the Muslim League. Indian question, as is now being solved, can be countered by our united front against both the Hindus and the English. Without it our demands are not going to be accepted. People say our demands smack of communalism. This is sheer propaganda. These demands relate to the defence of our national existence.'[535]

The campaign for creating Pakistan gathered momentum under Jinnah's stewardship. Muslim League passed the "Lahore Resolution" in 1940 demanding the creation of a separate independent Muslim state, Pakistan. The resolution said, '*...the areas in which Muslims are numerically in a majority, as in the north-western and eastern zones of India, are grouped to constitute "independent states" in which the constituent units will be autonomous and sovereign.*'[536]

Having exercised their brutally mighty lordship over the non-Muslims for so long, Muslims' historical pride could not bear to let them become a minority but equal citizens in an independent secular-democratic India. They unleashed mindless violence in their secessionist campaign for founding a Muslim homeland (see below), which convinced the British that the Hindus and Muslims could not live together. These circumstances led to the eventual division of subcontinental India in 1947. Islam, fundamentally, thinks Anwar Skaikh, is an ideology of "Divide and Rule". He thinks this Islamic Divide and Rule, not the divisive British policy, was responsible for the Partition of India:[537]

> ...but the wound inflicted by their (Islamic invaders') ideology i.e. Islam, which brought them to India, cannot be effaced from memory because instead of healing, this hurt has turned into an incurable abscess. Though 95 percent of all Muslims descend from the original population and the remaining 5 percent also qualify as Indians owing to their permanent residence over the centuries, they all want to be considered as a separate Muslim nation, dedicated to the belief that their motherland is a *Dar-ul- Harb*. It is this iniquitous philosophy, which caused the partition of India. What the Arabs (Arab invaders) failed to do themselves, the Arabian doctrine of Divide and Rule has done for them.

As Muslim zealotry for creating a separate Islamic state gathered strength, there arose a nationalistic Hindu movement, which opposed the division of their motherland. This neo-Hindutva movement is often viewed as an equally culpable partner in the Partition-related riots and bloodbath. But, indisputably, Muslims' unwillingness to accept a united and democratic India with a non-Muslim majority population was the primary reason for the violence and massacres that took place during the Partition.

The Hindutva nationalists have also received severe condemnation for the continued communal tension and violence in independent India. In the first place, the birth of Hindutva movement was a natural reaction to Muslims' unreasonable, bigoted campaign to include India into a pan-Islamic Caliphate as

---

534. Allama Iqbal Biography; http://www.allamaiqbal.com/person/biography/biotxtread.html

535. Iqbal and Pakistan Movement; http://www.allamaiqbal.com/person/movement/move_main.htm

536. Menon VP (1957) *The Transfer of Power*, Orient Longman, New Delhi, p. 83

537. Shaikh (1998), Chapter 7

intended by the *Khilafat* Movement (aided by Gandhi and Nehru *et al.*), to their separatist demand for creating an independent state dividing India, and to their indulgence in mindless violence against the Hindus (e.g., Mopla Rebellion) to achieve their goal.

Muslims came to India as brutal invaders and ruled for centuries. They inflicted utmost cruelty, including mass slaughter and enslavement of native Indians, engaged in massive plundering and looting of their wealth and perpetrated large-scale destruction of their religious symbols and institutions. The economic exploitations aside, the British rule came somewhat as a relief to India's non-Muslims after their sufferance of enduring Islamic brutality and humiliation. As the British rulers were about to leave, returning India's sovereignty to the people after so many centuries of foreign rule, Muslims became hell-bent on dividing the land. Although a great multitude of Indians had become Muslim during Islamic conquests and rule resulting from forced conversion, enslavement and other forms of persecution and economic compulsions, they had no right to divine India based on a foreign ideology so brutally imposed on the people. Muslims' demand for an independent homeland and unleashing of mindless violence to achieve it, therefore, created the perfect ground for the rise of nationalist sentiments and religious zealotry amongst Hindus. Consequently, for the first time, some Hindus as a religious entity rose up as a militant religio-nationalistic force to confront the instigatory Muslims from dividing their country. Particularly after the Mopla violence (1921), Hindu cultural, religious, political and nationalistic ideas were floated. In 1925, a Hindutva organization, *Rashtriya Swayamsevak Sangh* (RSS), was founded on Hindu and Hindustani nationalism. It was a natural reaction to the long period of historical injustice and to the ongoing Muslim bigotry, intolerance and violence.

THE 1947 RIOTS & MASSACRES: WHO IS RESPONSIBLE?

The blame for the Partition of British India and the related violence has been primarily placed on the British, particularly by the Hindus. India's Congress Party believed, notes Koenraad Elst, that an evil factor (the British) was *'forcing a partition on an unwilling brotherhood of Hindus and Muslims.'*[538] Major literary works on the Partition—such as Khushwant Singh's novel *Train to Pakistan*, Bhishm Sahni's novel *Tamas* (made into film) and Urabhavi Butalia's collection of Partition-related Testimonies in *The Other Side of Silence*—have been projected in a way to put more blame on the Hindus by highlighting the cases of Hindu violence. However, the most common impression among the people of the subcontinent is that the Hindus and Muslims were equally guilty of the violence and cruelty that occurred during the Partition. Most research works on the issue are also done in a directed way to even out the blame on the Hindus and Muslims. An objective analysis of the 1947 violence will be presented here. This will help readers to judge how much blame should be shared by each of the three parties involved: a) the British Raj, b) Muslims and Islamist movements, and c) Hindus and Hindutva movement.

The Mopla Rebellion

In order to understand the violence in the course of independence of India and her eventual Partition in 1947, let us first go to Malabar in South India in 1921 to witness the kind of mindless brutality Muslims could perpetrate on their innocent Hindu neighbors. It is noted that Muslim traders had allegedly settled amongst tolerant Hindus in the Malabar Coast in 629 and intermarried with the Hindu women to form their communities, while some low-caste Hindus had also allegedly converted voluntarily. By the early nineteenth century, they had become substantial in number (currently about one-fourth). Often ignited by Sufi masters, they were now powerful enough to go on a Jihadi path, against the Portuguese occupiers and Hindus. According to Robinson, they developed *'a tradition of holy war and martyrdom... it has been manifest in*

---

538. Kamra AJ (2000) *The Prolonged Partition and Its Progroms*, Voice of India, New Delhi, p. VII

outbreaks of religious violence—there were thirty-two, for instance between 1836 and 1919.[539] The victims of their Jihadi outbursts were always the innocent Hindus.

In 1921, Muslims in Malabar (called *Mopla*) unleashed a heinous wave of violence against innocent Hindus, which became known as the "Mopla Rebellion". This rebellion was instigated by two Muslim organizations: *Khuddam-i-Kaba* and *Central Khilafat Committee*. These movements were in favor of founding a pan-Islamic Caliphate. According to Ambedkar, they preached the doctrine that *'India under the British government was Dar-ul-Harb and therefore, the Muslims must fight against it, and if they could not, they must carry out the alternative principle of Hijrat (departure to a Muslim land).'*[540] Although the rebellion was against the British, in their absence, Muslims unleashed terror on their innocent Hindu neighbors. Ambedkar recounts the horrific barbarity committed by the Moplas as thus:

> The Hindus were visited by a dire fate at the hands of the *Moplas*. Massacres, forcible conversions, desecration of temples, foul outrages upon women, such as ripping of pregnant women, pillage, arson and wholesale destruction—in short, all the accompaniments of brutal and unrestrained barbarism, were perpetrated freely by the *Moplas* upon the Hindus... The number of Hindus who were killed, wounded or converted is not known. But the number must have been enormous.

JJ Banninga, who lived in India between 1901 and 1943, published an account of this horrific brutality.[541] Banninga records the verdict of a three-judge panel that tried some of the leading culprits:

> 'For the last hundred years at least, the Moplah community has been disgraced from time to time by murderous outrages. In the past, these have been due to fanaticism... their tutored mind is particularly susceptible to the inflammatory teachings that *Paradise was to be gained by killing Kafirs*. They would go out on the warpath, killing Hindus no matter whom... no grievance seems to have been necessary to start them on the wild career.'

On the atrocities, adds Banninga:

> ...wells were filled with mutilated bodies; pregnant women cut into pieces; children torn from their mother's arms and killed; husbands and fathers tortured, flayed, burned alive before the eyes of their wives and daughters; women forcibly carried off and outraged; homes destroyed... not less than 100 temples were destroyed or desecrated; cattle slaughtered in temples and their entails placed around the necks of the idols in place of garlands of flowers; wholesale looting.

According to Moplas, notes Robinson, "10,000 lives were lost".[542]

Mahatma Gandhi, a supporter of the *Khilafat* Movement—embracing the brutal *Moplas* as "among the bravest in the land" and "God-fearing", and to downplay the quantum of the brutality—wrote in his magazine *Young India*: *'Whilst I was in Calcutta, I had what seemed definite information that there were only three cases of forced conversions... But I don't think that it seriously interferes with Hindu-Muslim unity.'*[543] But in reality, a large number of Hindus were converted.

---

539. Robinson, p. 247

540. Ambedkar, Vol. 8, p. 163

541. Banninga JJ (1923) *The Moplah Rebellion of 1921*, in *Moslem World 13*, p. 379–87

542. Robinson, p. 247

543. Gandhi K (1921) *Young India*, September 8 edition

Direct Action riots in Calcutta

The Caliphate Movement died down after the Mopla Rebellion. Let us now move on to the Partition-related violence, which started a year before the independence on August 14–15, 1947. In mid-1946, the idea of a separate Muslim state was still being resisted and efforts were being made to form an interim government, giving equal representation to Hindus and Muslims. Muslims, being only about 20 percent of the population to 75 percent Hindus, the Congress Party objected to this arrangement. Instead, they agreed to an arrangement, having six Hindu and five Muslim representatives with another from the remaining religious groups. Jinnah was opposed to this new arrangement; and washing his hands off further negotiations, he called a meeting of the *Muslim League Council* in Bombay on 29 July 1946. The crux of the resolution, reached at the meeting, read:[544]

> 'It has become abundantly clear that the Muslims of India would not rest with anything less than the immediate establishment of an independent and full sovereign State of Pakistan... the *Council of the All-India Muslim League* is convinced that now the time has come for Muslim nation to resort to *Direct Action* to achieve Pakistan and get rid of the present slavery under the British and contemplated future caste Hindu domination.'

What would that "Direct Action" be? When Jinnah was pressed on whether the Direct Action would be violent or nonviolent, he replied, ''*I am not going to discuss ethics.*'' Nawabzada Liaquat Ali Khan, later the first Prime Minister Pakistan, told the *Associated Press* (U.S.A.): ''*We cannot eliminate any method. Direct Action means any action against the law.*'' Sardar Abdur Rab Nishtar, who became the Minister for Communication and Governor of Punjab in independent Pakistan, made it ominously clear: '*Pakistan could only be achieved by shedding blood and, if opportunity arose, the blood of non-Muslims must be shed, for 'Muslims are no believers in ahimsa (non-violence).*''[545] It is abundantly clear what this Direct Action was going to be all about. On Jinnah's attitude and violent instigation, wrote *News Chronicle* (U.K.): ''...*there can be no excuse for the wild language and abandonment of negotiations... Mr. Jinnah is totally wedded to complete intransigence, if, as now seems the case, he is really thirsting for a holy war.*''[546]

Calcutta, the capital of the Muslim-majority (54.3 percent) province of Bengal, which had a Muslim League government, was chosen for unleashing Jinnah's Direct Action on 16 August 1946. To grasp the purpose of this Direct Action rally, let us review the highly inflammatory propaganda, which had been circulated amongst Muslims preceding the event:

> Pamphlets issued both in Urdu and Bengali by Muslim League painted highly romanticized wordy pictures of would-be violent scenes of the Direct Action. In one such pamphlet, one finds imagery of the thousands of Muslims armed with swords killing Hindus to make rivers of blood flow through the streets of the city. In another, a Bengali poem warns the Hindus whose heads were about to roll as armed bands of Muslims were approaching.[547]

To such blood-curdling provocative propaganda, a Hindu response was published in the *Dainik Basumati* newspaper on 11 August 1946, which defiantly stated: ''*The Muslim League-wallahs (members) should know*

---

544. Khosla, p. 38

545. Ibid, p. 43

546. Ibid, p. 44

547. Sugata Nandi (2006) *Locating the Origins of a Criminal Riot*,
http://mail.sarai.net/pipermail/urbanstudygroup/2006-April/000824.html

that mere threats will not work. They (Hindus) are known to face bullets and bayonets with a smile... they do not accept defeat even for a moment... The League is free to test our resolve but only at its own peril.'' Three days later the main news story of the paper was titled, *Large Scale Clash of the Hindus and Muslims Feared Ahead.*[548]

The allusions to these violence-inciting pamphlets were put into action by militant Muslims on August 16, the day of Direct Action. The Mayor of Calcutta SM Usman urged a million Muslims to congregate at the rally. To inaugurate the Direct Action, Jinnah chose the date, eighteenth of Ramadan, the day of Prophet Muhammad's stunning victory in the *Battle of Badr* against a three times stronger opposition. The Muslim League pamphlet, urging Muslims to attend the rally in large numbers, read:[549]

> 'Muslims must remember that it was in Ramzam that the Quran was revealed. It was in Ramzan that the permission for *Jehad* was granted. It was in Ramzam that the battle of Badr, the first open conflict between Islam and Heathenism (i.e., idolatry, which equates Hinduism) was fought and won by 313 Muslims; and again it was in Ramzan that 10,000 under the Holy Prophet conquered Mecca and established the kingdom of Heaven and the commonwealth of Islam in Arabia. Muslim League is fortunate that it is starting its action in this holy month.'

While another leaflet, entitled *Munajat for the Jehad*, was to be read out in mosque prayers. It included the above passage and added:[550]

> 'By the grace of God, we are ten cores (100 millions) in India but through our bad luck we have become slaves of the Hindus and the British. We are starting a *Jehad* in Your Name in this very month of Ramzan. Pray make us strong in body and mind—give Your helping hand in all out actions—make us victorious over the *Kafers*—enable us to establish the Kingdom of Islam in India and make proper sacrifices for this *Jehad*—by the grace of God may we build up in India the greatest Islamic kingdom in the world.'

Another Bengali pamphlet, *Mogur* (Club), wrote of the auspicious holy month event: *''The day for an open fight which is the greatest desire of the Muslim nation has arrived... The Shining gates of heaven have been opened for you. Let us enter in thousands. Let us all cry out victory to Pakistan, victory to the Muslim nation and victory to the army which has declared a Jehad.''* The Mayor of Calcutta issue a leaflet, showing Jinnah with a sword, which read:[551]

> 'We Muslims have had the Crown (of India) and ruled... Be ready and take your sword. Think you, Muslims, why we are under the *kafirs* today. The result of loving *kafirs* is not good. O *kafir*! Do not be proud. Your doom is not far and the general massacre will come. Show our glory with swords in hands and will have a special victory.'

Still another leaflet, urging Muslims to come to the rally with their swords, added: *''We shall see who will play with us, for rivers of blood will flow. We shall have the swords in our hands and the noise of takbir (Allahu Akbar, Allah is Great). Tomorrow will be dooms day.''*

Huseyn Shaheed Suhrawardy—the Chief Minister (CM) of Bengal, also holding the portfolio of Law and Order—took it upon himself to execute the Direct Action for what it was going to be. In order to remove police interference in the coming violence, Suhrawardy, as the Minister of Law and Order, ordered the

---

548. Ibid
549. Khosla, p. 51
550. Ibid, p. 51–52
551. Ibid, p. 52–53

transfer of Hindu police officers from key posts in Calcutta, putting twenty-two out of twenty-four police stations in Muslim hands; two were controlled by Anglo-Indians. The Muslim League activists mobilized the hooligans and unruly elements amongst Muslims and armed them with all kinds of weapons. Congress leader Kiron Shankar Ray drew the attention of the police to these ominous developments; it was ignored. On the morning of the day of Direct Action, Muslim hooligans paraded the streets of Calcutta armed with *lathis*, spears, daggers, hatchets and even guns. The European Superintendent of Police at the Howrah Bridge stopped a crowd heading for the rally; from them, '*lathis, spears, daggers, knives, unburnt torches, empty soda water bottles, tins containing kerosene oil, rags soaked in oil, ready for being used in setting fire to houses, were collected.*'[552]

On CM Suhrawardy's Direct Action speech, writes Yasmin Khan, '*if he did not explicitly incite violence, certainly gave the crowds the impression that they could act with impunity, that neither the police nor the military would be called out and that the ministry would turn a blind eye to any action that they unleashed in the city.*'[553] At the close of the rally, these armed militants poured into the thickly-populated Hindu neighborhoods of Calcutta and started a gory rampage: looting, burning and massacre. The police, instructed as they were, remained indifferent, watching the burning and looting of Hindu and Sikh homes and businesses with utter nonchalance. Suhrawardy, arrived at the Police Headquarter, took charge of the Control Room and directed the police, preventing them from taking any action against Muslim rioters, looters and murderers, but he directed the police to take quick action against any complaint of Hindu retaliations. Inspector Wade had arrested eight Muslims, who were looting at Mallick Bazaar Market wearing Red Cross bands; Suhrawardy ordered their immediate release.[554] Muslim shops were marked "Mussalman shop - Pakistan" to save them from looting and burning. The homes of the Congress Party leaders were attacked and set on fire; newspaper publishing houses were attacked and attempted to set on fire. The Fire Brigade was prevented by unruly Muslim mobs from putting out fires in non-Muslim homes and properties. Hindu temples were vandalized and set on fire; Medical colleges, schools and students hostels came under Muslim attacks, vandalism and intimidation.

Justice Khosla of Lahore High Court recounts of the carnage: '*The streets were strewn with dead bodies and the corpses... There were stories of children having been hurled down from the roofs of houses. Young children were reported to have been boiled in oil. Others were burnt alive. Women were raped and mutilated and then murdered.*' The Muslim rioters had their sway in the carnage and plunder for one-and-a-half days, before the Hindus and Sikhs recovered from their shock, plucked courage and began hitting back. Suhrawardy had delayed calling the army; he called in the army as soon as the Hindu and Sikh retaliation began. However, things had gone out of hands; the Hindus and Sikhs, two-thirds of the city's population, unleashed violence in like manners wreaking havoc on Muslims. Three organizations that collected the dead bodies for the burial had gathered 3,173 corpses in all. These excluded those buried by the family members, thrown into the rivers and washed away, and those burnt to ashes. The total deaths were to the tune of 5,000. Of the dead, brought to hospitals or died there, 138 were Muslims against 151 Hindus plus sixty-two others—that is, some 43 percent were Muslim deaths in this count. Of the homes and properties set on fires, 65 percent belonged to Hindus, 20 percent to Muslims and 15 percent to government and others.[555]

Although the properties lost by Muslims were negligible as compared to non-Muslim losses, the count of the dead was not as good a reading—definitely unlike the spectacular success of the Prophet's Jihad at Badr—which the Muslim League had hoped to achieve. Disappointed by Allah's lack of favour and the unpleasant outcome, the Muslim League leaders blamed the *kafirs*, vehemently asserting '*that the rioting was*

---

552. Ibid, p. 54

553. Khan Y (2007) *The Great Partition: The Making of India and Pakistan*, Yale University Press, p. 64

554. Khosla, p. 59

555. Ibid, p. 63-66

started by the supporters of the Congress and some of them even went so far to say that the Hindus had prepared a deeply laid plan to commit wholesale murder of Muslims to discredit the Muslim League.'[556]

Nehru's reaction to the Direct Action riots was, noted *Time*, ''*Either direct action knocks the Government over, or the Government knocks direct action over.*''[557] PC Lahiry, a freedom fighter against the British and a member of the Provincial Legislative Assembly of post-independence East Pakistan, writes of this tragedy:

> The well-thought plan of the Muslim League to frighten and terrorize the Congress and the Hindus to submit to the demand of the League for a separate sovereign state of Pakistan was frustrated in Calcutta, because the Hindus (and Sikhs) did not lag behind the Muslims in aggressiveness and killing. A large number of Muslims also died.[558]

Following the Calcutta riots, Muslims in Bombay started rioting on September 2, on the day the Interim Congress Government took office. The violence lasted several days leaving over 200 people dead.

Anti-Hindu riots move to East Bengal

Disappointed with the outcome of the Direct Action and to avenge the death of their Muslim brethren in Calcutta, Muslims in East Bengal, where they were in the majority, took it upon themselves to continue the savagery on the Hindus in their midst. A series of sustained riots took place; the riots of *Noakhali-Tippera* of 1946–47, known as the *Noakhali* riots, rate a special mention. Since the late nineteenth century, rising Islamic fundamentalism—fueled by the puritanical Saudi *Wahabbism* and *Anjuman Society*—had been sweeping across Bengal, particularly Noakhali, where the population was predominantly Muslim (80–85 percent).[559] This radicalization was seen as a primer for the riots in Noakhali and other districts (Feni, Comilla) across East Bengal, affecting some 350 villages.[560] According to Lahiri, '*Having thus failed in Calcutta, the Muslim League selected another venue in the district of Noakhali, where the Hindus were only 18 percent of the total population, for the nefarious deed of arson, loot, abduction and rape of the Hindu women, mass-conversion of faith and killings.*'[561] The first news of the Noakhali violence reached Bengal Congress Office in Calcutta on 15 October 1946 from the Party members in Noakhali in the form of a telegram, which read:[562]

> 'Houses burned on mass scale / Hundreds burnt to death / Hundreds killed / Otherwise large number Hindu girls forcibly married to Moslems and abducted / All Hindu temples and images desecrated / Helpless refugees coming to Tippera District / Golam Sarwar leader inciting Moslems to exterminate Hindus from Noakhali…'

The Noakhali riots were ignited by this *Pir* (Sufi master), Maulvi Gholam Sarwar, by grossly exaggerating the stories of Calcutta riots and putting all blames on the Hindus. Muslim clerics in public Islamic gatherings (*waaz mahfil*) preached hatred against the Hindus regarding the Calcutta riots. In order to instigate Muslims into orgasmic violence, rumors were spread amongst them that the Hindus had brought armed Sikh and Hindu hooligans from Calcutta to Noakhali to massacre them. By mid-October, records Khosla: '*Hundreds of murders had been committed, thousands of women had been dishonored and carried away or compelled to*

---

556. Ibid, p. 66

557. *Direct Action*, Time, 26 Aug, 1946; http://www.time.com/time/magazine/article/0,9171,933559,00.html

558. Lahiri PC (1964) *India Partitioned and Minorities in Pakistan*, Writers' Forum, Calcutta, p. 6

559. Batabyal R (2005) *Communalism in Bengal: From Famine to Noakhali, 1943-47*, SAGE Publications, p. 295–96.

560. Ibid, p. 270–71

561. Lahiri, p. 7

562. Khan, p. 68

*marry Muslims. Whole villages had been burnt down and razed to the ground. **All the entire Hindu population of the district had been robbed of all they possessed and then forcibly converted to Islam.**'*[563]

Hindu temples were defiled and the idols smashed. There were about 400,000 Hindus living in Noakhali; at least *95 percent of them were converted to Islam* on the pain of death. *'The converted persons were made to read kalma,*[564] *slaughter cows and eat their flesh,'* records Khosla. Up to 5,000 people were murdered, estimated 99 percent of the non-Muslim houses looted and 70–90 percent of them burned down. A similar spectacle transpired in the neighboring Tippera District. Gandhi, at the frail age of seventy-seven, came to Noakhali on November 6 to assuage the harrowing riots. He walked door to door of Muslim homes preaching *ahimsa* and urging them to accept Hindus as their friendly neighbors, while encouraging the Hindus, who had taken shelters in refugee camps, to have courage and return home.[565]

Hindu counterattack in Bihar

In the days from the Direct Action to the Noakhali riots, an atmosphere of hostility was brewing up in Bihar. In Calcutta, there were thousands of businesses and workshops, belonging to people from Bihar. With businesses destroyed, and fear and insecurity prevailing, they headed back to Bihar abandoning Calcutta, their adopted home. They brought with them *'the harrowing tales of massacre, rape, arson and plunder which they related stirred the emotion of the Bihari Hindus,'* notes Khosla.[566] Fuel was added into this mix by systematic instigations of explosive nature by Bihari Muslims. On the day of the Direct Action in Calcutta, the Bihar Muslim League held a meeting locally, in which speakers emphasized the strength of the sword, which had enabled their past successes and achievements. Referring to the assertions of leading Muslim League leaders, said speaker Syed Muhammad Abdul Jalil: *"Their (Hindu's) attack and their conduct is based on nonviolence but... our representatives, Qaid-e-Azam (Jinnah), Nazimuddin and Suhrawardy, have made it clear that, to us, nonviolence means nothing. When we want to fight, we shall make use of whatever weapons we have."*

Shaheedul Haq of the Muslim Students Federation announced the basic creed of Jihad in the most provocative terms, saying, *"for a Muslim the way to haven lay both in killing and being killed by a Hindu."*[567] To this explosive rhetoric and boiling resentment amongst Bihari Hindus over what had happened to the Hindus in Calcutta—including those from Bihar, the final dose of provocation was added by the Muslim League President of Biharshariff, who was the Secretary of the Cloth Distribution Committee. He stamped every cloth ration card with the words *"Allah-ho-Akbar, Leyke rahenge Pakistan* (Allah is great, we will not rest until creating Pakistan)."[568]

Then in mid-October, the horrors of the Noakhali riots started arriving. *Statesman* broke the story of murder, loot and arson in Noakhali on 16 October 1946, followed by similar stories over the subsequent days. Amidst this situation, leaflets containing direct incitement to violence, produced by the Secretary of the local Muslim League in South Bihar, were recovered in various parts of Bihar. Calling Hindus the "enemies of Islam", the author said of himself to be *"one whose head is to be found besmeared with the blood and dust of the battle-field."* Another leaflet, addressed to Jinnah, read: *"So far we have given sufficient time to Indian infidels. It is time to remove the darkness of infidelity (i.e., Hinduism) and illuminate the whole of universe by resplendent Islam. To accomplish this sublime cause we must slaughter the infidels, as was done in the early*

---

563. Khosla, p. 68

564. *Kalma* is the Muslim profession of faith.

565. Khosla, p. 69–76

566. Ibid, p. 77

567. Quran 9:111, *Allah hath purchased of the believers their persons and their goods in return of Paradise: they fight in His cause, and slay and are slain – a promise binding on Him in truth, through the Law, the Gospel, and the Qur'an.*

568. Khosla, p. 79

days (of Islam in Arabia).'' Still another leaflet, originated from Calcutta, purportedly contained Jinnah's instruction '*for the destruction of Hindu religion and culture, conversion and murder of Hindus, murder of nationalist Muslims (they opposed Partition), Congress leaders and bestial attacks on Hindu women.*'[569]

It was sinking amongst the Bihari Hindus that the whole thing—mayhem, massacre, forced conversion, enslavement, rapes and plunder—was a well-orchestrated stratagem of the Muslim League to terrify the Hindus and Congress into conceding the demand for Pakistan. Sensing a prospect of troubles, the political leaders urged for calm, while the provincial government issued stern warning against trouble-making, which went in vain. On October 25, there started serious outbreak of violence and atrocity, which peaked on November 3–4 and then rapidly died down. '*During those twelve days, the Hindus of Bihar let their passions loose upon their Muslim brethren and drank deep the cup of revenge,*' notes Khosla. Police tried its best to handle the situation even-handedly, but was unsuccessful in containing the surge of violence. Gandhi, hearing of the violence, started fasting unto death in protest; this news cooled down the violence quickly. The Bihari public (Hindus) also played their part in stemming the violence. Nehru, who visited Bihar during the violence, told the Legislative Assembly on 14 November 1946 that '*a much more powerful factor in the restoration of order was the fact that a large number of persons, chiefly Biharis, spread out all over the villages and faced the masses. News of the Mahatma's proposed fast also had a powerful effect.*'[570] According to an estimate of Khosla, the casualties included 5,334 Muslim and 224 Hindu deaths. But the Muslim League leaders exaggerated the number out of all proportions, claiming 20,000 to 30,000 Muslim deaths.[571]

Riots move to Pakistan

From Bengal and Bihar, the flash-point of riots later moved to the provinces of present-day Pakistan. The Hindu retaliation in Bihar became the focal propaganda tool for the Muslim League to launch the next phase of violence. The Muslim League Party from North-West Frontier Province (NWFP) and other parts of Pakistan sent activists to Bihar to find out what happened there. Joined by students from the Aligarh Muslim University (near Bihar), they brought stories of what had transpired there: a number of skulls of the victims, images, bricks from damaged mosques, and mutilated pages of the Quran—allegedly of the Bihar riots. They showed these to Muslims in the Muslim-dominated areas of Northwest India, particularly in NWFP. With these exaggerated propaganda stories, mixed with all sorts of anti-Hindu rhetoric and blood-curdling slogans—''*We will avenge Bihar in the Frontier (NWFP)*'' and ''*Blood will be avenged by blood*''—they incited Muslim mobs to anti-Hindu communal frenzy. Violence against Hindus as well as Sikhs soon started in the Hazara District of NWFP in December 1946, which quickly spread to most areas of today's Pakistan.[572] It is not possible to give all the details in the short space here, but only brief account of a subset of events will be included.

In NWFP, non-Muslims constituted only 8 percent of the population. In the attack, the miniscule Hindu and Sikh population were easily overwhelmed; their shops and businesses were looted and set on fire; Hindu temples and Sikh *gurdwaras* were plundered and defiled. Although the mobs concentrated mainly on plundering and burning the businesses and religious places, they also killed a number of Hindus and Sikhs and their women were often carried away and forcibly married off to Muslims. The violence remained confined mainly in Hazara and, to some extent, in Dera Ismail Khan Districts until January (1947), but the launching of a Civil Disobedience Movement by the Muslim League in February intensified the violence, spreading to all districts of the provinces. Mobs, led Muslim League activists, now started mass conversion of the Hindus and Sikhs, accompanied with plundering and arson.

---

569. Ibid, p. 80–81

570. Ibid, p. 81–83

571. Kamra, p. 14

572. Khosla, p. 264–65

In April 1947, large-scale violence, looting and arson started in the town of Dera Ismail Khan and surrounding villages, forcing non-Muslims to withdraw to distant quarters from their homes and businesses, which, after looting, were set on flames. Assaults continued for three days, destroying and gutting 1,200 Hindu and Sikh shops; the city turned into smouldering ruins. In some villages, the entire Hindu and Sikh population were murdered or converted to Islam on the pain of death. Hindus and Sikhs, trying to flee, were waylaid by Muslim mobs and murdered; their women were abducted. Violence continued in NWFP unabated through the period of Partition in August 1947 until January 1948. On 22 January 1948, a Muslim mob— armed with guns, spears and hatchets, and assisted by 500–600 Muslim League militias—attacked a refugee camp in Parachinar, sheltering some 1,500 Hindus and Sikhs. In the attack, 138 were killed, 150 injured and 223 women carried away.[573]

In the Muslim-dominated West Punjab, violence began somewhat late. On 4 March 1947, Hindu and Sikh students brought out a rally in Lahore to protest Muslims' demand for creating Pakistan. Police opened fire on it killing a number of them. A separate procession in another part of the city was also attacked by Muslim National Guards. These incidents set Muslims on a violent fury; they attacked and stabbed the Hindus and Sikhs, plundered their shops and businesses before setting them on fire. By the evening, thirty-seven Hindus and Sikhs were dead. From Lahore, rioting soon spread to all the Muslim-dominated districts of Punjab: Amritsar, Rawalpindi, Multan, Jhelum and Attock.[574] On the spread of the violence, Akbar Hussain, the Chief Secretary to Government (Punjab), said: "*With the news of grave events radiating from Lahore, there has been bloodbath and burning in many districts and rural areas have paid the price levied by insensate fury, as well as towns.*"[575]

On March 5, violence spread to all parts of Lahore, Hindu homes and properties were vandalized, looted and set on fire. The Hindus and Sikhs were killed. Violence died down on March 11. Muslims in Amritsar, where they had strong but not dominant presence, initiated violence on March 6, by attacking a train at Sharifpura killing the Hindu and Sikh passengers. The train reached the Amritsar Station with Hindu and Sikh dead-bodies, including three in the women's compartment. The Muslim orgy of violence, massacre and arson had begun in Amritsar: hospital were littered with dead-bodies and the injured with '*heads almost severed from bodies, bellies ripped open with intestine protruding from the wound, arms and legs chopped off and all kind of horrible injuries,*' records Khosla. On March 7, there was a 'veritable inferno' with fires raging over parts of the city. Hindu and Sikh shops and businesses were vandalized and set on fire. By March 8, there were 140 deaths and numerous wounded, although many more bodies were consumed in the inferno and buried under falling buildings. The violence in Amritsar continued for one whole week: the Hindus and Sikhs suffered heavily in life and properties; all the non-Muslim owned factories but one, the Jawala Flour Mill, were destroyed.

Also on March 5, Muslim mobs in Multan (West Punjab)—armed with clubs, spears and daggers and shouting: "*Leke rahenge Pakistan, Pakistan zindabad* (We will wrestle Pakistan, Long live Pakistan)"— attacked a procession of Hindu and Sikh students, wounding several of them; it ignited barbarous violence amongst Muslims. For three days, Muslim hooligans marched about attacking the Sikhs and Hindus with swords, daggers and hatchets killing them and looting their businesses and homes before burning them down. The barbarous hooligans even attacked the Sri Krishan Bhagwan Tuberculosis Hospital, butchered the patients and doctors and set it on fire. The temples and *gurdwaras* were plundered and defiled, idols smashed, and many set on fire. The devotees on many temple premises, namely the Jog Maya, Ram Tirath, Devpura and Devta Khu temples, were massacred. Young Hindu and Sikh girls were enslaved and carried away.

---

573. Ibid, p. 267–73
574. Ibid, p. 101–02
575. Ibid, p. 105–06

In the towns and villages of Rawalpindi District, Hindus and Sikhs suffered the worst of pre-Partition violence: slaughter, rape, enslavement, mass conversion, plunder and arson. Only a few examples of these will be included in the short space here. On March 6, Muslim mobs in Rawalpindi started attacking Hindu and Sikh houses, setting them on fire, butchering the inmates, forcibly converting them to Islam and cutting off the hair and beard of many Sikhs. In some areas, Sikhs and Hindus were in equal strength and they counterattacked causing substantial loss on the Muslim side. Muslims called in reinforcements from neighboring villages, outnumbering the Hindus and Sikhs. The killing and pillage continued for three days. On March 7 or 8, Muslim League invited eleven Hindu and Sikh representative for forming a Peace Committee for establishing peace and harmony. Muslim mobs seized them, killing seven on the spot; two were able to escape.

In the villages of Rawalpindi, armed Muslims—shouting blood-curdling slogans and beating drums—approached a non-Muslim village, surrounded it, looted the properties and killed a few residents, terrorizing the rest to embrace Islam. They looted homes and enslaved and carried away the young and beautiful girls and women; the young women were often molested and raped in the open, while mobs went about burning the houses and shops. In desperation, records Khosla,[576]

> Some women would commit suicide or suffer death at the hands of their relations with stoic indifference; others would jump into wells or be burnt alive uttering hysterical cries. The men would come out and meet death in a desperate sally against the marauders... Some villages were completely wiped out. Houses and shops were looted and then burnt down and demolished. Conversions saved the lives of many but not their property. Refusal to accept Islam brought complete annihilation. The men were shot or put to the sword. In some cases, small children were thrown in cauldrons of boiling oil. In one village men and women who refused to embrace Islam were collected together and after a ring of brambles and firewood had been placed around them they were burnt alive. A woman threw her four-month old baby to save it from burning. The infant was impaled upon a spear and thrown into the fire.

On March 10, a Muslim mob from neighboring communities swarmed Doberan, a village of 1,700 residents, the majority of whom were Sikhs. The Hindus and Sikhs took shelter in a local *gurdwara*, as Muslims plundered the deserted houses and set them on fire. When Muslims attacked the *gurdwara*, besieged Sikhs counterattacked with a few firearms they had, but suffered heavy casualties and soon ran out of ammunition. The Muslim raiders offered them safety, if handed over the arms. Some three hundred of them came out, surrendering the weapons. They were placed in one Barkat Singh's house, but at night, kerosene was poured into it and set on fire, burning the surrendered inmates alive. The next morning, Muslim attackers broke the doors of the *gurdwara*; the remaining Sikh inmates came out wielding swords and perished to the last man.

There were numerous such horrid incidents. And these were only the pre-Partition violence. Terror, massacre, plunder, enslavement, mass conversion, rapes and burning of Hindu and Sikh lives and properties of many folds greater ferocity and quantum came in late July onwards as the Partition of Pakistan was eventually agreed upon. The details of these too-numerous later incidents cannot be included here. Suffice it to say that, through the days of the Partition well until early next year, Muslims unleashed violence and bloodshed on the Hindus and Sikhs in every part of present-day Pakistan, where Muslims constituted 60–92 percent of the population. Gurbachan Singh Talib in his book, *Muslim League Attack on Sikhs and Hindus in the Punjab 1947*, has listed 592 instances of major attacks in Punjab and other districts of greater Pakistan—all initiated by Muslims under no provocations of similar kinds.[577]

---

576. Ibid, p. 107–08

577. Talib SGS (1991) *Muslim League Attack on Sikhs and Hindus in the Punjab 1947* (compilation), Voice of India, Appendix, Atrocities, chapters 9-11

Sikh and Hindu Retaliation

In the pre-Partition phase of violence and terror from August 1946 till late July 1947, namely in Calcutta, East Bengal, NWFP and Punjab (including Amritsar), Muslims had a near monopoly. The Hindu retaliation in Bihar was a result of Muslims' instigation in Calcutta (included many Bihari victims) and Noakhali, which was further fueled by incitements by local Muslims. But the Muslim violence on the Pakistan side went on almost unabated in one part or another. Meanwhile, the Sikhs, who had suffered horribly in NWFP and West Punjab, moved to different parts of East Punjab, including Amritsar. Amritsar had already suffered a horrid wave of Muslim violence and destruction. They brought their harrowing tales of sufferance and Muslim barbarity, naturally igniting outrage and even a sense of retaliation amongst Sikhs, particularly in Amritsar—already wounded by unprovoked Muslim brutality. Their innocent coreligionists had been slaughtered in large numbers and converted *en masse*; their women were raped, enslaved and carried away; their homes, businesses and properties were looted and burned down; *gurdwaras* were plundered and defiled.

A flame of retaliation was ignited, particularly amongst those, who had come from the other side empty-handed with their family members killed, wives and daughters raped and carried away as well as those who had already suffered horrid violence in Amritsar earlier in March. In late July 1947, Lahore was in flames again; this ignited the Sikhs and Hindus in Amritsar, already fuming with anger, into unleashing violence on their Muslim neighbors. Further Fuel was added to the Sikh anger by their loss of Sheikhpura, which became part of Pakistan. It is the most sacred place for them, the birthplace of Guru Nanak Dev, founder of Sikhism. In August, violence flared up in equal measure on both sides of the Partition line in Punjab. From Amritsar, violence spread quickly to other districts of East Punjab: Gurdaspur, Jalandhar, Hoshiarpur, Ludhiana and Ferozepore, and later in Haryana.

The Sikh violence mainly focused on killing Muslims and looting their properties. There were some incidents of kidnapping of Muslim women and some of them married off to Sikh men. However, authorities, who tried their best to protect Muslims, recovered most of the kidnapped Muslim women and returned to their families. On the background of centuries of Muslim brutalities and those in the course of the Partition beginning with the Direct Action, the Sikhs of East Punjab had become convinced that peaceful coexistence with Muslims would not be feasible; therefore, driving Muslims out from their midst was a major motive of their retaliations (discussed below).

On the India side, Delhi, where Muslims had strong presence in some areas, also witnessed large-scale violence, all instigated by Muslims. The Muslim League had tried to ignite violence in Delhi in November 1946 by arming the Muslim hooligans. In the course of the Partition in August 1947, Muslims were armed again with '*automatic weapons, country-made cannons, rifles, bombs, mortars and missiles.*'[578] Muslim blacksmiths and motor mechanics became producers of weapons; Muslim rioters were provided with wireless transmitters and receiving sets for exchanging messages, thirteen of which amongst other deadly weapons were recovered.

On 21 August 1947, a bomb exploded in the house of a Muslim student in Shahadara, probably accidentally while assembling it. On the night of September 3, another bomb, allegedly thrown by Muslims, exploded in the Qarol Bagh Hindu neighborhood. Following this, a communal frenzy erupted amongst Muslims in the area; armed mobs paraded the streets, and shot Dr Joshi, a non-Muslim resident, when he went out to reason with them. Following this event, Muslim mob violence spread to other parts of Delhi. On September 6, they began widespread looting and stabbing in the capital. A Muslim mob attacked the District Jail and killed a Hindu warden; they battled with the police, which was 60 percent Muslim.

On the morning of September 8, records a police report, a police patrol found Muslims firing on Hindus in the Subzimandi area. In the confrontation, many policemen were also injured; Assistant Sub-Inspector had to be sent to Hospital. The battle between the Muslim mob and the police lasted the whole day;

---

578. Khosla, p. 282–83

the Police Station was also shot at. Muslims also started attacking the Hindu villages in the outskirt of Delhi, burning them down. These unremitting provocations—in the context of what had transpired since the Direct Action and what was happening to the helpless Hindus (and Sikhs) on the Pakistan side—ended restraint of the Hindus of Delhi. They started attacking and murdering Muslims, who, although found armed, were outnumbered; their houses were sometimes burned down. Police had recovered from Muslim houses a number of unlicensed guns, daggers and knives, 154 bombs, forty-five mortars, 1,950 rounds of rifle ammunition, thirteen wireless transmitters, a number of hand-grenades, Sten-gun cartridges and chemicals. According to police records, 507 Muslims perished in the violence with seventy-six Hindu deaths; probably equal numbers went unreported.[579]

Premeditated ethnic cleansing of Hindus and Sikhs

The violence during the Partition forced nearly twenty million people to cross the border: Hindus and Sikhs from Pakistan to India and Muslims from India to Pakistan. The Muslim League, it appears, not only wanted a separate homeland, they also wanted it purely for Muslims, cleansed of the infidels: Hindus and Sikhs. The violence they perpetrated during the course of the Partition, it appears, was a premeditated stratagem, carefully orchestrated by the Muslim League, to ethnically cleanse the non-Muslims from Pakistan. On Muslim League's incitement of the ethnic-cleansing of non-Muslims, the *Times of London* wrote, '*League's reckless propaganda causes Punjab tragedy.*'[580] The incitement and demagoguery of Jinnah and other top Muslim League leaders, argue Collins and Lapierre, convinced Muslims that '*in Pakistan, the **Land of the Pure**, Hindu moneylenders, shopkeepers and zamindars (Sikh landlords) would disappear... if Pakistan is ours, so too are shops, farms, houses and factories of the Hindus and Sikhs.*'[581] Collins and Lapierre add: '*The central Post Office in Lahore was flooded with thousands of postcards addressed to the Hindus and Sikhs. They depicted men and women being raped and slaughtered. On the back was the message: 'This is what is happening to our Sikh and Hindu brothers and sisters at the hands of Muslims when they take over.' These postcards were part of a campaign of psychological warfare, conducted by the Muslim League, to create panic among Sikhs and Hindus.*'[582] An officer sent a letter, dated 5 September 1947, from the Lahore Government House to Governor-General Jinnah, read: "*I am telling everyone that I don't care how the Sikhs cross the border, the great thing is to get rid of them as soon as possible. There is still little sign of the 300,000 Sikhs in Lyallpur moving, but in the end they too will have to go.*"[583]

Whether in Calcutta, Noakhali or the Muslim-dominated Districts of present-day Pakistan, the police—dominated by or exclusively made up of Muslims—maintained indifference and even participated in the vandalism, plunder, arson and killing. It is already noted of how Suhrawardy directed the police in the Calcutta riots. Regarding the abetment of the Bengal Muslim League government and the police in the Direct Action violence, the words of *Sher-e-Bangla* (Tiger of Bengal) AK Fazlul Huq,[584] the CM of undivided Bengal (1937–43) and later briefly of East Pakistan (1954), are worth taking note here. In describing his eyewitness account of the savagery in an address to the Bengal Legislative Assembly on 19 September 1946, he said: "*It seemed ...that some modern Nadir Shah had come upon Calcutta and had given up the city to rapine, plunder and pillage. Sir, each time I tried to get in touch with police officers, I was told that I was to contact the Control Room.*" His desperate effort to contact the police and government officials was unsuccessful. Of the government and police inaction, he added:[585]

---

579. Ibid, p. 242–85

580. *Times of London*, 19 March 1947

581. Collins L & Lapierre D (1975) *Freedom at Midnight*, Avon, New York, p. 330

582. Ibid, p. 249

583. Khosla, p. 314

584. Fazlul Huq was kicked out of the Muslim League in 1940 for advocating for an undivided India.

585. Ibid, p. 307

'Police officer would not listen, the Control Office would not control, the Government Houses would not listen, Sir, in these circumstances the Great Killing went on and it is undisputed that this would never have happened if the police and the military had taken strong measures on Friday, the 16th, when the trouble began. It would have been nipped in the bud that very day, and, therefore, the conclusion is inevitable that although the police may not be responsible for the origin of disturbances, they are directly responsible for the great loss of human life, and if an impartial enquiry is held and these officers can be spotted, my opinion is that they deserve to be hanged, drawn and quartered publicly, on charges of murder and abetment of murder...'

In violence during the Partition in the districts of today's Pakistan, notes Gurbachan Singh Talib:

'... police and military—which, by now, were entirely composed of Muslims on the Pakistan side, due to the partition of personnel and assets between India and Pakistan—gave not only active assistance and encouragement to the rampaging Muslim mobs, but often-times led them, directed their operations, and finished off the job of murder where the mobs could not succeed single-handed. By August, the non-Muslim populations of Lahore had been reduced to only a fraction of their former numbers. But still more than 100,000 Hindus and Sikhs remained in Lahore.'[586]

According to a Civil and Military Gazette report, the Sikhs, in particular, had refused to leave Lahore saying that Lahore was their home. This refusal proved calamitous for them as '*the destruction, devastation, and massacre soon rained on the Hindus and Sikhs and nine thousand of their corpses were left to rot on the streets of Lahore causing a terrible stench.*'[587] According to Talib, on 10 August 1947, almost all Hindu and Sikh localities were set alight. Fires were raging in Chune Mandi, Bazaz Hatta, Sua Bazar, Lohari Gate, Mohalla Sathan and Mozang. Everywhere, police led the attacks in non-Muslim areas. Describing the terrible massacre in Lahore in early August 1947, the special correspondent of *The Hindustan Times* reported: "*Seventy per cent of the casualties of the last three weeks in West Punjab were inflicted by the communally maddened troops and policemen. The victims of their bullets numbered thousands. The massacre at Sheikhupura, which was their handiwork, puts into shade the slaughter at Jalianwala Bagh.*"[588]

In fact, from the very beginning, police abetted and even participated in the violence and vandalism against Hindus and Sikhs on the Pakistan side. On 5 March 1947, a Muslim mob, assisted by National Guards, started looting non-Muslim shops at Rang Mahal in Lahore. When the Hindus and Sikhs offered resistance, the Muslim Sub-Inspector arrived with a police-force and opened fire on the defenders. When a young Hindu man argued with the Sub-Inspector, the latter shot him dead.[589] When Muslims unleashed violence in Amritsar on 6 March 1946, the Hindu policemen were replaced by Muslim ones in the violence-stricken area; on their complicity to the violence records Khosla, '*Muslim Magistrates assisted by Muslim police officials... lent their support and connivance to the miscreants.*' Similarly, in the violence in Rawalpindi, the Magistrate and the police offered indifference and abetment. When a senior Sikh Advocate asked the Magistrate for police assistance, records Justice Khosla, '*the Additional District Magistrate accused him of spreading rumors and added that he was endangering his own life.*'[590] Such was the response of the authority and law enforcement agencies in the pre-Partition violence in Muslim-dominated areas. In the course of the Partition in August 1947, the participation of the police and government authority in the

---

586. Talib, op cit

587. Ibid

588. The Jalianwala Bagh massacre in Punjab was the worst violence committed by the British in the course of Independence movement of India. It caused 379 deaths according to British records, while up to 1,000 in Indian claims.

589. Khosla, p. 101–02

590. Ibid, p. 103,106

renewed, intensified violence became much more prominent, an example of which has been cited already. In massacre of the Hindus and Sikhs of Lahore in August 1947, the Baluch Regiment took a very prominent part, while the District Magistrate of Jhang, Pir Mubarak Ali Shah, was seen firing from a rifle and leading the mob.[591]

On the Indian side of the Partition, authorities mostly tried to curtail the violence. On the disparity in responses of authorities on the two sides of the border, notes Khosla, '*while the Government of India and the East Punjab Government mobilized all their resources to quell the disturbances, the West Punjab Government gave encouragement to the rowdy elements by many official and unofficial acts.*'[592] Nonetheless, some police officers, particularly in East Punjab (Ambala area for example)—undoubtedly instigated by what their Muslim counterparts were committing on the Hindus and Sikhs on the other side of the border—showed indifference and connivance to the Sikh retaliation; some of them even participated in the murder and looting. Such incidents were, however, rather infrequent and a number of such culprit police officers were arrested. No such actions were taken against the culprit police and government officials in Pakistan.

Ethnic cleansing of Muslims

As noted already, on the India side of the Partition, ethic cleansing occurred mainly in East Punjab. The very late Sikh retaliation against Muslims under utmost ongoing provocations cannot be judged properly without taking the historical context into account. Guru Nanak, the founder of Sikhism, a contemporary of Mughal invader Babur, witnessed latter's mass slaughter of Hindus and destruction of their temples. Nanak, giving a vivid account of Babur's vandalism in Aimanabad in his *Babur Vani*, denounced the invader's barbarism in no uncertain terms. He also described Muslim cruelties against the Hindus in the form of a complaint to God, as enshrined in the *Granth Sahib*, the Sikh Scripture:

> 'Having lifted Islam to the head, You have engulfed Hindustan in dread... Such cruelties have they inflicted, and yet Your mercy remains unmoved... Should the strong attack the strong, the heart does not burn. But when the strong crush the helpless, surely the One who was to protect them has to be called to account... O' Lord, these dogs have destroyed this diamond-like Hindustan, (so great is their terror that) no one asks after those who have been killed and yet You do not pay heed....' (Mahla 1:36).

Islamic cruelties were later to fall upon the followers of Guru Nanak, too. Emperor Jahangir condemned Sikh Guru Arjun Dev to torture-until-death on the accusation of supporting a revolt, led by Prince Khusrau, son of Jahangir. Later on, ordered by Aurangzeb, Guru Tegh Bahadur Singh was tortured in the cruelest manner before being beheaded as he prayed, for complaining against forced conversion of the Kashmiri Hindus. In 1705, Aurangzeb attacked Guru Gobind Singh (son of Guru Tegh Bahadur) and his followers, and besieged them in their fortress. Having given the promise of safe passage, Aurangzeb's army treacherous fell upon Gobind Singh's followers when they came out, decimating them and their family, including Gobind Singh's. Although the Guru survived on this occasion and was on the run, his death was eventually secured in 1707 by Wazir Khan, Aurangzeb's governor of Sirhind (in Punjab).

In the context of these cruelties, in which the Sikh prophets were put to death by Muslim rulers one after another, the Sikh resentment against Muslims can hardly be underestimated. We must recall here the Sikh assistance to the British during the Muslim-instigated Sepoy Mutiny. Then there were the Mopla Rebellion and Muslims' insistence on dividing India (to which Sikhs were opposed), followed by Muslim brutalities starting in Calcutta affecting their Sikh coreligionists there, which spilled over the Sikhs in today's Pakistan and even in Amritsar in East Punjab. The Sikhs in East Punjab, it appears, had realized that it was

---

591. Ibid, p. 122,179

592. Ibid, p. 119

impossible to live in peace with the Muslims in their midst. This becomes abundantly clear from a statement released by Sikh leaders against the illegitimate Sikh violence in East Punjab, which read:[593]

'We do not desire friendship of the Muslims and we never may befriend them. We may have to fight again but we shall fight a clean fight—man killing man. This killing of women and children and those who seek asylum must cease at once… There should be no attacks on refugee trains, convoys and caravans. We ask you to do so in the interest of your own communities, reputations, character and tradition than to save the Muslims.'

In this oddly-worded appeal for calm, there was also a call to fight only if the Muslim men take it up, without harming the women and children, and those seeking refuge. Evidently, there was, in this appeal, an underlying angst against Muslims, in which the historical persecution of the Sikhs by Muslim invaders and rulers and the ongoing Muslim brutality of Sikhs had played their part.

Muslims also suffered heavy casualties and ethnic cleansing in the princely states of Alwar and Bharatpur, which were outside of British control. The ethnic Muslims, called Meos, lived in these fiefdoms in large numbers. The Hindu violence, according to an estimation of Ian Copland, killed 30,000 Meos and drove about 100,000 of them out. However, this violence in Rajasthan took place at a later stage. The Hindu violence was provoked, they claimed, for '*The killings of Hindus at Noakhali and Punjab had to be avenged,*' notes Copland. Who instigated the violence is not known as Copland writes: '*Separating "aggressors" from "victims" in this context is difficult, perhaps even pointless. Both sides were culpable.*'[594] The aggressive violence unleashed by Meos on Hindu villages in the outskirts of Delhi had likely instigated the violence in neighboring Alwar. According to Khosla, '*In some villages (of Delhi), trouble was started by the Meo residents. Hindu villages were attacked and burnt down. The Meos were ultimately driven out and many of them were wiped out in the neighboring State of Alwar.*'[595] There was also a separatist movement among the Meos; they wanted to create an independent Muslim state, called Meostan, in the heart of Rajasthan.

In the course of the Partition, estimated 600,000 to two million people died; about a hundred thousand predominantly Hindu and Sikh women were raped; a similar number were enslaved and carried away. Likely a few million Hindus and Sikhs were converted to Islam on the pain of death, some 95 percent of the 400,000 Hindus in Noakhali alone. Of the casualties, the numbers were roughly evened out between Muslims and non-Muslims. The heavy casualties Muslims suffered were mainly in East Punjab. The Partition also led to displacement of an estimated nineteen million people across the borders. Based on the 1951 Census of displaced persons, some 14.5 million people crossed the border on the Punjab side of the Partition. Of them, 7,226,000 Muslims went to Pakistan from India, while 7,249,000 Hindus and Sikhs moved to India from Pakistan immediately after the Partition. On the Bengal side of the Partition, 3.5 million Hindus moved from East Pakistan to India, while only 700,000 Muslims migrated in the opposite direction.[596] It should be understood that the Muslim migration was generally of more willing nature since they overwhelmingly wanted a separate Muslim homeland, and that migration to a Muslim land from the infidel-dominated *Dar al-Harb* (e.g., Hindu India) was widely promoted by Muslim organizations in their separatist campaign.

In terms of property, the Hindu and Sikh loss much surpassed that of Muslims. The Hindus and Sikhs all over India were wealthy communities particularly in business and industrial establishments. The Hindus in East Bengal prior to the Partition, although a minority, possessed 80 percent of the national wealth. According to Kamra, '*The majority of the buildings and properties in each town of East Bengal, in some*

---

593. Ibid, p. 288

594. Copland I (1998) *The Further Shore of Partition: Ethnic Cleansing in Rajasthan 1947, Past and Present*, Oxford, 160, p. 203–39

595. Khosla, p. 284

596. *Partition of India*, Wikipedia, http://en.wikipedia.org/wiki/Partition_of_India

cases more than 85 percent of the urban properties, belonged to Hindus.'[597] In NWFP, the minorities (Hindus, Sikhs, Christians) constituted only 8.2 percent of the population, but the Hindus alone paid 80 percent of the income-tax of the province; in Lahore, non-Muslim minorities owned 80 percent of the property.[598] The Muslim violence, it seems, was unleashed with a premeditated intent of capturing the huge Hindu and Sikh properties and businesses by driving them out. The Muslim League propaganda that if Pakistan was theirs, so were the properties of non-Muslims has been cited above. Bengal Congress leader Kiron Shankar Roy, in a press statement on 22 July 1947, referred to the expectation of East Bengal Muslims as thus: "*There is a notion among ordinary Muslims in the Eastern Pakistan region that after August 15, the houses and land of the Hindus there will automatically pass into the possession of Muslims, and that the Hindus will be a sort of subject race under the Muslims of that area.*"[599] This attitude applied more emphatically to the rampaging Muslims of Punjab, where '*each one of them thought that he had become a Nawab (provincial governor).*'[600]

Who bears the responsibility?

Clearly, the responsibility for the great human tragedy and suffering, engendered by the Partition, falls mostly on Muslims. They started the secessionist movement in the first place; and they were generally the instigators of the violence and eviction that followed. They started a campaign of gory violence a year ahead of the Partition in order to press their demand for creating Pakistan. They engaged in much more vicious violence as their demand for Pakistan was met and the Partition eventually took place. The Direct Action, according to Muslim League and mosque propaganda, was a Jihad, the re-enactment of Muhammad's Jihadi *Battle of Badr*. The overall motive of the Muslim violence was to cleanse the newly created Islamic "Land of the Pure" from the filthy infidels. This fitted perfectly well with Prophet Muhammad's example of founding the first Islamic state in Arabia by mass eviction and slaughter of the Jews and extermination of the Polytheists.

In the course of the Partition in August, riots took place everywhere inside West Pakistan. In East Pakistan (East Bengal), violence was tactfully prevented in the days of the Partition, but harrowing mob violence against Hindus returned in February 1950. This violence was instigated, over Pakistan's failed attack in Kashmir, by the Pakistani press, radio and Muslim leaders—calling Hindus "saboteurs", "enemy agents", "fifth columnists" and "disloyal elements" amongst all kinds of false propaganda. On February 6 and 7, Radio Pakistan announced: "*Brethren! You have heard about the inhuman atrocities that are now being perpetrated in India and West Bengal. Will you not gather strength?*" Such false stories were also splashed over the pages of newspapers in East Bengal. Pakistan Radio announced that 10,000 Muslims were killed in Calcutta, while *Pashban*, a Bengali daily in Dhaka, raised the figure to 100,000.[601] Such false propaganda instigated Muslims to unleash harrowing mob violence against Hindus all over Eastern Pakistan. Mass murder, rapes, abduction of women, mass conversion, arson and plunder took place, which cannot be accommodated here in detail. For an example, Jawaharlal Nehru gave a figure of Hindu casualty of 600 to 1,000 in Dhaka, which was lower than the true figure; in the villages of Rajapur Police Station, some 150 Hindus were killed and the rest were converted to Islam; some 1.5 million Hindus fled from East Bengal to India, according to a figure given by Nehru.[602]

---

597. Kamra, p. 3

598. Khosla, p. 120,258

599. Hindustan Times, 22 July 1947

600. *Civil and Military Gazette*, Lahore, 30 December 1948

601. Kamra, p. 55,57

602. Ibid, p. 59,66,105

The Hindus and Sikhs did not incite violence proactively; but they merely, and rather belatedly, reacted in kind. Inside India, in the course of the Partition in August 1947, besides violence in East Punjab, Delhi, Alwar and Bharatpur, riots also took place in Aligarh, Bombay and Jammu and Kashmir amongst others. In these places, Muslims had strong presence and these riots were initiated and/or instigated by them. In Kashmir, for example, the Pathan Muslims enslaved the young Hindu women, carried them away and sold in the markets of Jhelum District in Pakistan.[603] The Hindu and Sikh violence, in most cases, was retaliation against the Muslim ones, including in East Punjab, where Muslims suffered worst Sikh retaliations. Muslims' unprovoked harrowing violence—in Calcutta, Noakhali, West Punjab, NWFP, and even, in Amritsar in East Punjab among other places—had, undoubtedly, tested the patience of the Sikhs and Hindus to an utmost degree, and instigated them to engage in violence in like manners. Overall, the Hindus and Sikhs showed great restraint; most places inside India, where Muslims were minority, remained largely calm.

Undoubtedly, the separatist Muslims should bear almost the entire responsibility for the Partition-related violence and bloodbath: firstly, for their demand of a separate state, and secondly, for inciting and initiating unprovoked violence and bloodbath that took place. The British rulers and the Hindus and Sikhs (including Hindutva groups) deserve very little share of the blame.

ISLAM'S IMPACT ON THE
SOCIAL, INTELLECTUAL & CULTURAL LIFE OF INDIA

The worst impacts of Islamic colonialism in India were the widespread violence against non-Muslims, crushing economic exploitation of them and their enslavement on a grand scale (see next chapter) by the Muslim invaders and rulers. Moreover, many existing social and cultural ills of the Indian society—*sati*, child marriage and caste system etc.—worsened under the Muslim rule. Islamic rule also engendered new social ills, such as the *thuggee* cult and *jauhar*, in India. After the British takeover, some of these, namely *jauhar*, and *thuggee* cult, disappeared; the British also made serious efforts to abolish or suppress the rest of India's social afflictions. Islamic rule also had a crippling impact on the health of education and learning in India.

On Education and learning

Education and learning was one of the worst victims of the Islamic colonialism in India. Muslim rulers and invaders destroyed India's indigenous education system. For education, they built mosques and *madrasas*, solely for Muslims. It is noted already that pre-Islamic India had high standards in education, literature, science and medicine, and founded famous centers of learning, namely at Nalanda (427–1197), Taxila, Kanchi, Vikramasheela, Jagaddala and Odanthapura. Situated at the then Buddhist center of learning in today's Bihar, the Nalanda University was one of the world's first residential universities with dormitories for students. In its heyday, it accommodated over 10,000 students and 2,000 teachers. It had a huge nine-storey library, where meticulous copies of texts were produced and preserved. Nalanda was also the most global university of its time, attracting pupils and scholars from Korea, Japan, China, Tibet, Indonesia, Persia and Turkey.[604] In 1197, Bakhtiyar Khilji destroyed the University, slaughtered all of its shaven-head Buddhist teachers, and burned its immensely rich library. Prior to the Muslim conquest of India, many Muslim students from Baghdad came to Taxila University to study Medicine in particular. All these reputed universities were destroyed by Muslim invaders and rulers; they ceased to exist after the Muslim occupation of India. On the impact of Islamic invasions on science and learning in India, said Alberuni (noted already) that Hindu

603. Talib, p. 201

604. Nehru (1989), p. 122; also *Nalanda* in Wikipedia, http://en.wikipedia.org/wiki/Nalanda

sciences and learning had retired far away from the Muslim-occupied areas.[605] During the relatively liberal rule of Akbar, Hindus had rebuilt thousands of temples, which also acted as Hindu schools. Later on Aurangzeb, having noticed that Muslim pupils also attended those temple-schools, filling their minds with sinful *kuffar* (un-Islamic) teachings, ordered their destruction, thereby destroying the revived Hindu education system. Other Muslim rulers, such as Sultan Ahmad Shah Bahmani in the South, broke "idolatrous temples" and "destroyed the colleges of the Brahmins".[606]

The Muslim invaders, instead of building schools for secular education and learning, frequently destroyed the non-Muslim centers of learning they came across. When Caliph Omar conquered Egypt (641), the great Library of Alexandria was destroyed.[607] They burned the royal Zoroastrian library at Ctesiphon after the conquest Persia. Similar spectacle befell the libraries in Damascus (Syria) and Spain. In 1171, Sultan Saladin destroyed the great Library of Cairo, after ousting the heretical Fatimid rulers. Destruction of libraries and universities in India has been mentioned.

Muslim rulers in India built only Islamic schools, namely *muktabs* and *madrasas*, often linked to mosques, solely for training Muslim students in their religion and other crafts for administrative and military duty, useful for the Muslim state. Learning Arabic and Persian language and memorizing the Quran, prophetic tradition and Islamic laws were the major subjects of study. Limited training was also given in agriculture, accountancy, astrology, astronomy, history, geography and mathematics, needed for running the state.[608] The students of a *madrasa*, recorded Islamic historian and poet Allam Shibli (d. 1914), were provided with room, carpet, food, oil, pen and paper, sweets and fruits. Ibn Battutah on his travels across India sometimes stayed in *madrasas*. In one *madrasa* of 300 rooms, he found students being taught the Quran and provided with daily food and yearly allowance of clothes. He found in another *madrasa*, where he lodged for sixteen days, that the students were daily served excellent foods: chicken loaves, *Poloo* and *Korma* (meat dishes) and plate of sweets.[609]

These schools were exclusive preserves for Muslim pupils; non-Muslim students had no access to them. Muslim rulers only engaged Muslims in their administration. Educating the Hindus was, therefore, unnecessary. Most importantly, the filthy non-Muslims were not allowed to enter the perimeter of religious palaces, like *madrasas* and mosques; it remains the practice even today. Later on, when apostate Akbar opened his administration to employment of people of all creeds, he opened the door of *madrasas* to non-Muslim students and incorporated the study of Sanskrit and Hindu religious scriptures, such as Upanishad.[610] Akbar even unbelievably tried to dispense with the study of Arabic, the language of the Prophet and the Quran, in the context that he promulgated his own new religion, *Din-i-Ilahi*.[611] Islamic education was now irrelevant.

---

605. Sachau (2002), p. 6

606. Ferishtah, Vol. II, p. 248

607. Some modern scholars, such as Phillip K Hitti, deny this on the ground that the Library of Alexandria could not exist because it was destroyed during the invasion of Julius Caesar in 48 BC. But, according to Theodore Vrettos (*Alexandria, City of the Western Mind*, The Free Press, New York, 2001, p. 93-94): 'Caesar's soldiers set fire to the Egyptian ships, and the flames, spreading rapidly in the driving wind, consumed most of the dockyard, many structures near the palace, and also several thousand books that were housed in one of the buildings. From this incident, historians mistakingly assumed that the Great Library of Alexandria had been destroyed, but the Library was nowhere near the docks... Some 40,000 book scrolls were destroyed in the fire, which were not at all connected with the Great Library; they were account books and ledgers containing records of Alexandria's export goods bound for Rome and other cities throughout the world.'

608. Ghosh, p. 22

609. Ibid, p. 23

610. Ibid, p. 22

611. Ibid, p. 29

In the 630–650s, Hiuen Tsang, the famous Chinese pilgrim to Nalanda University, found Indian education system quite well-organized: both boys and girls, at the age of seven, started the study of five *Shastras*—Grammar, Science of arts and crafts, Medicine, Logic, and Philosophy. From Hiuen Tsang's account, notes Nehru, '*it appears that primary education was comparatively widespread, as all the monks and priests were teachers, and there is no lack of them. Hiuen Tsang was much struck by the love of learning of the Indian people...*'[612] It is no wonder then that Indian civilization had achieved such great height in her intellectual endeavors, even affirmed by many Muslim historians, including Alberuni and al-Andalusi. The coming of Alexander to the Indus valley brought India in contact with classical Greek civilization; India absorbed latter's achievements, particularly in art. With classical Greece in decay, India exceled the world in science, learning and other human endeavors at the time of Islam's birth. It is noted that many Arab students came to the Taxila University in the early Abbasid period. Large numbers of Indian mathematicians and physicians were engaged by Caliph Harun al-Rashid (d. 813); Indian physicians set up hospitals and medical schools in Baghdad.[613]

Even Nehru, always eager to say good things about Islam, complained that Muslim rulers did not build one good college in eight centuries. They took very little interest in secular education, especially in science. Even enlightened Akbar the Great, who was illiterate, undertook no major interest in promoting science; in philosophy, he solely focused on founding his own religion of no secular or practical value. Except widening the *madrasa* curricula to include Indian language and Hindu scriptures, he built no major schools, universities and research centers for promoting science, philosophy and other creative learning, when great things were happening in Europe. Although Akbar reduced the burden of taxes and offered toleration to all subjects, '*his mind was not directed to raising the general level of education and training,*' writes Nehru.[614] Sitting on one of the world's greatest and wealthiest seat of power, Akbar received clocks from the Portuguese and the British mercenaries; he received printed books from the Portuguese Jesuits of his courts; but his mind was never curious to find out how these technologies worked. Muslim rulers, including Akbar, built only sumptuous monuments, citadels and palaces to commemorate and perpetuate their vain greatness, often much outdoing their counterparts of vigorous Europe in the age of *Renaissance*. It is no wonder then that India, despite being a creative and learned civilization previously, made no notable contribution to science, philosophy and literature during the Muslim rule.

Caste system worsened

The most emphatic claim, Muslims make, about Islam's contribution to India, is that it brought egalitarianism; in Islam, every body is equal: no high or low, no high-caste or outcaste. Seeing this liberty and equality, claim Muslims, large numbers of low-caste Hindus eagerly converted to Islam; this saved them from the oppressed and ignominious life offered by the Hindu society.

The issue of the conversion of low-caste Hindus has already been discussed. However, the conversion did not elevate their social standing in the Muslim community. Fazl-i Rabbi, following European leads, was the first Muslim to try to make a case for the willing conversion of the low-caste Hindus to Islam. He, however, found that conversion to Islam did not change their social position and the family status; they still could associate with Muslims of similar status only.[615] Similarly, Ashraf—who sees Islam as a religion of "equality and fraternity" and that it opened doors to low-caste Hindus for rising higher in society—found, based on mostly Islamic sources, that '*With his conversion to Islam, the average Muslim did not change his*

---

612. Ibid, p. 124

613. Nehru (1989), p. 154,151

614. Ibid, p. 313

615. Rabbi, p. 60–61

188

old environment, which was deeply influenced by caste distinction and general social exclusiveness.'[616] Wise witnessed in Bengal that some Bediya outcastes of the Hindu society had converted some thirty years ago (c. 1850) and become practising Muslims, *'but they cannot enter the public mosque or find a place in the public graveyard. From a social point of view they are still aliens with whom no gentleman will associate or eat. The treatment of the Chandal by the Sudra is in no respect more rigorous or harsh than that of the Bediyas by the upper ranks of Muhammadans.*'[617]

In sum, the converted low-caste Hindus socially remained the same in the Muslim community. Even today, they are outcaste, a socially degraded people. They are no better off than their Hindu counterparts, probably rather worse. Conversion to Islam did not uplift their overall caste-sufferance; instead, it has probably worsened their overall situation because, Muslims in India, including converts from the upper caste, continue falling behind economically and intellectually. They also commit human rights violation within their community, including suppression of women's rights and honor killing.

Islam, in fact, worsened the overall caste situation in India. The caste system, as horrible as it is, was a reality in pre-Islamic India. However, ancient manuscripts, namely *Arthashastra* of Kautilya and *Nitisara*, suggest that it was not so rigid. The social structure in the middle ages, notes Nehru, *'may have been open to merit or capacity, as the Nitisara says... Occasionally men from the lower castes made good. Sudras were even known to become kings... A more frequent method of rising in the social scale was for a whole sub-caste to go a step up.'* Sometimes, there were power-struggles between the upper and lower caste and *'more often they ruled jointly and accommodated each other,'* adds Nehru.[618] The dominant reality was, however, that the Brahmins and *Khasttriyahs*, the two castes at the top, ruled and the rest toiled. But the coming of Islam to India, argues Nehru, *'made its caste system, which till then had an element of flexibility in it, more rigid and fixed.'*[619]

Islam also worsened the standing of the caste system in India by driving larges number of upper caste Hindus down the ladder. There are numerous examples of destitute Hindus taking refuse in jungles all over India either to wage rebellion against Muslim oppressions or to escape torture of the tax-collectors for failing to meet the crushing tax demands. During the reign of Ghiyasuddin Balban (aka Ulugh Khan Balban, r. 1265–85), hundreds of thousands of Hindus, whose wealth and abode had been plundered and ravaged and families decimated, had taken refuge in the jungle settlements and engaged in night-time robbery. The Sultan resolved to decimate these bandits and rebels (*Muwattis*), first in the jungles and hills around Delhi. He directed his chiefs *'to slay the men, to make prisoners of the women and children, to clear away the jungles and to suppress all lawless proceedings,'* records Barani.[620] In the campaigns to suppress these rebels, *'one hundred thousand of the royal army were slain by the Muwattis,'* while *'great number of the Muwattis were put to the sword'*.[621] The Sultan then marched out of Delhi proceeding to the neighborhood of Kampil and Pattiali, where he spent five to six months putting the *Muwattis* to the sword. He then on marched to Katehar to exterminate the turbulent rebels surrounding the districts of Badaun and Amroha, where *'the blood of the rioters ran in streams, heaps of slain were to be seen near every village and jungle, and the stench of the dead reached as far as the Ganges,'* adds Barani.[622]

---

616. Ashraf KM (1935), *Life and Condition of the People of Hindustan (1220–1550 A.D.)*, Journal of Asiatic Society of Bengal, Letters, p. 191.

617. Wise J (1894) *The Muhammadans of Eastern Bengal*, Journal of the Asiatic Society of Bengal, Vol. 63, 3:1, p. 61

618. Nehru (1989), p. 132

619. Ibid, p. 157

620 Elliot and Dawson, Vol. III, p. 105

621 Ibid, p. 104–05

622 Ibid, p. 105–06

Sultan Ghiyasuddin Tughlaq (1320–25) had applied a taxation policy that left the Hindu peasants to bare subsistence. His successor Muhammad Tughlaq (1325–51) increased the tribute by another 5–10 percent. This reduced the farmers to desperate poverty and they *'threw off their allegiance and betook themselves in the jungles,'* causing failure of cultivation and reduced grain production; a situation of general famines and *'thousands upon thousands of people perished of want (of food),'* records Barani.[623] When he sent a force to exterminate the rebels of the mountain of Kara-jal, the rebels cut off the passage of their retreat and the *'whole force was thus destroyed at one stroke, and out of all these chosen body of men, only ten horsemen could return to Delhi.'*[624] The country of Doab near Delhi, when reduced to ruin through "heavy taxation" and brutal campaigns, desperate Hindus formed bands and took refuge in the jungles, leaving the country in ruins. The sultan hunted them down from their jungle hide-outs: *'the whole of that country was plundered and laid waste and the heads of the Hindus were brought in and hung upon the ramparts of the fort of Baran,'* recounts Barani.[625]

According to British indigo merchant William Finch who came to India in 1611, Emperor Jahangir (d. 1628) used to go on hunting with thousands of his favorite soldiers every year, which lasted for months. He order to encircle a large tract of jungle or desert and *'whatever is taken in this enclosure is called the King's sykar or game, whether man! Or beast and whatever let aught escape loses his life, unless pardoned by the king. All the beasts thus taken, if man's meat, are sold, and the money given to the poor.'*[626] Obviously, a large number of these miserable jungle dwellers got killed in Jahangir hunting game. Still, another 200,000 were caught in 1619–20 and he sent them to Iran for selling.[627]

Even in the reign of tolerant and kind-hearted Akbar, large numbers of Hindus had been living in jungles. According to *Akbar Nama*, in the twenty-seventh year of his reign, he ordered his officers that *'if the occupants of the hill forts, trusting in the security of their fastness, should engage in freebooting,'* they should be admonished, chastised and, if necessary, *'their country was to be laid waste.'*[628]

This clearly shows that large numbers of non-Muslims—hundreds of thousands, probably millions—took shelter in jungles away from the normal social life. These jungle dwellers of all classes and creeds lived and waged revolts together and survived on whatever came their way: wild fruits, leaves, grains and animals. Together, they became the new *untouchables*: there was no going back to the society; they won't be accepted either. One major reason for their rejection could have been their eating meats of wild animals in desperate hunger. Once consumed meat, there is no place for them back in the society, particularly in the upper castes. The lower caste, therefore, naturally swelled further under the Muslim rule.

In sum, Muslims probably took away a chunk of Indian outcastes out of Hindu fold, and socially kept them where they previously had been, but in a different community. At the same time, Muslim rule worsened the institution by making it more rigid as well as by pushing a large number of Hindus down the social ladder.

Islam created the practice of Jauhar

Jauhar was a custom amongst Hindu women of committing suicide by jumping into fire in order to avoid capture for enslavement and sexual violation by the Muslim invaders and raiders. This practice was unknown in pre-Islamic India. Since Muslim armies started attacking the borders of India in 634; they, if successful, plundered the wealth and drove away women and children as slaves. The Islamic marauders had launched

---

623 Ibid, p. 238
624. Ibid, p. 241–42
625. Ibid, p. 242
626. Ibid, Vol. VI, p. 516
627. Levi, p. 283–84
628. Elliot & Downson, Vol. VI, p. 64

eight more plundering and enslaving forays on the borders of India before Qasim, by conquering Sindh in 712, brought to the India proper the prophetic tradition of kidnapping and enslaving the womenfolk of the vanquished for keeping as sex-slaves. In his three-year tenure in Sindh, he had enslaved a few hundred thousand women and children. Sultan Mahmud had carried away 500,000 captives from India in 1001–02 and large numbers of them on other occasions. When Qasim conquered Sindh, women in the palace set themselves on fire in order to avoid capture and sexual violation. This trend continued even into the reign of enlightened Akbar. In his conquest of Chittor (1568), when Akbar ordered enslavement of the women of the 8,000 slain Rajput soldiers,[629] some 8,000 of them committed *Jauhar* to avoid dishonor and sexual slavery. Chittor witnessed three major occurrences of *Jauhar* when it was attacked by Alauddin Khilji (1303), Bahadur Shah of Gujarat (1535) and Akbar (1568). In fact, the practice continued into the days of 1947 Partition, when many Hindu and Sikh women saved their honor by setting themselves on fire, jumping into wells and consuming poisons as already noted.

Sati worsened under the Muslim rule

Sati, the Hindu funeral ritual of burning the wives alive with their dead husbands, was a pre-Islamic custom in India. Muslim rulers took no serious initiative to ban or suppress the practice. Only Akbar, the distinguished apostate of Islam until then, was opposed to the practice but made no effort to abolish it. According to *Akbar Nama*, he only tried '*to prevent any woman being forcibly burnt.*'[630]

The institution of *sati* undoubtedly worsened under the Muslim rule. According to Ibn Battutah, it was an optional practice as he writes, '*The burning of the wife after her husband's death is regarded by them as commendable act, but not compulsory... she is not forced to burn herself.*'[631] However, the practice became heightened during the Muslim invasions and rule in India; for, the continuous warfare that Muslims ignited in India, in which they killed Hindus (men) in large numbers as a matter of great pride, the wives of the slain, who survived enslavement, obviously embrace *sati*. Ibn Battutah leaves an eyewitness testimony of this: '*Once in the town of Amjari (Amjhera near Dhar) I saw three women whose husbands had been killed in battle and who had agreed to burn themselves... I rode out with my companions to see the way in which the burning was carried out.*'[632]

There is another reason that might have aggravated the practice of *sati* under the Muslim rule. Because of the prohibition of widow marriage in Hindu tradition, these women, if still young, obviously became the target of rape, kidnapping or enslavement by Muslims. It should be understood that kidnapping of Hindus by Muslims, often for selling, were common. In Malabar, never occupied by Muslims, the Mopla Muslims had a rather small presence. Still they used to kidnap Hindus, particularly the children, in the eighteenth century and sell them to European traders, especially in the Dutch port of Cochin.[633] This factor, undoubtedly, had made the widows embrace *sati* in larger numbers and created greater social pressure to do so.

Islam promoted child-marriage

Muslim's abduction and enslavement of Hindu women for subjecting them to rape and sex-slavery encouraged Hindu parents to marry off their daughters at younger age. This must have had worsened the tradition of child-marriage in India under the Muslim rule. Dhan Gopal Mukerji, author of *Caste and Outcast*,

---

629. Nizami KA (1989) *Akbar and Religion*, Idarah-i-Adabiyat-i-Delhi, New Delhi, p. 107,383–84

630. Elliot & Downson, Vol. VI, p. 68–69

631. Gibb, p. 191-2

632. Ibid, p. 192

633. Clarence-Smith, p. 30

argues that the oppressive Muslim rule in India forced Hindus to abandon some of their well-evolved traditions. According to him, before reaching the age of maturity, girls were betrothed to young Hindu boys, so that they could be protected from Muslim predators. The Muslim rule, therefore, aggravated the institution of child-marriage in India. The British rulers went to great lengths to suppress the institution.

Even today, this is a reality for the Hindu minorities (and other non-Muslims) in Bangladesh and Pakistan, where there are high rates of kidnapping and rape of Hindu women. The incidence of kidnapping and rape of Hindu women in Pakistan and Bangladesh has been discussed already. According to my contacts with secular-minded Muslims and Hindus from Bangladesh, Hindu girls, especially the beautiful ones, are often married off at younger age or sent over to India to save them from being kidnapped or raped by thuggish Muslims. According to the Pakistan Minorities Concern network, nearly 50 Hindu and 20 Christian girls were kidnapped in 2005; the majority of them were forcibly converted to Islam. Similar abduction and forced conversion of non-Muslim girls and their forced marriage to Muslims occur in Palestine and Egypt etc. on a regular basis. If not for the pressure on Muslim governments to protect the human rights of their citizens from international organizations (e.g., the E.U. and U.N.), foreign governments (the U.S. in particular) and human rights bodies, the fates of non-Muslim women in Islamic countries would have been quite different from what they are today. Slavery and sexual exploitation of non-Muslim women are still alive and well in certain Muslim countries in Africa and the Middle East (see next chapter).

Islam created the deadly thuggee cult

Thuggees were a religio-cultural cult of the Hindu goddess *Kali*, which the British crushed in the 1830s. They used to engage in night-time robbery and strangle their victims—often the wayfarers and travelers—to death. They filled the streets of India with lawlessness and terror at nightfall. They had murdered tens, possibly hundreds, of thousands of people. The British eradicated the cult through a process of selective assassination, covert operation, infiltration, solid police work and a clemency for former *thuggees* who cooperated and surrendered.[634]

The name *thag* (*thuggee*) first appears in Ziauddin Barani's *Tahrikh-I Firoz Shahi*. In the reign of Sultan Jalaluddin Feroz Shah Khilji (1290–96), records Barani, the sultan had captured one thousands *thags* by befriending a member of their community. He pardoned them and deported to Lakhnauti.[635] The *thuggee* cult seems to have originated very early after Islamic depredators started their devastating assaults on the population of India. We have noted that hundreds of thousands of Hindus had taken refuge in jungles during the Muslim rule. The rowdy and daring ones amongst them had taken to the profession of night-time robbery of highway caravans and travelers. Almost all medieval Islamic chronicles make mention of rebels—having taken refuge in the jungle hideouts and fastness of mountains—taken into highway robbery. Their homes and properties plundered and burned down and the women and children carried away, they took to the jungle. Others, failing to meet the demand of exorbitant taxes, joined them. For survival, these jungle-dwellers took to robbery; Muslim chroniclers and rulers call them despicable highway robbers. In time, they likely mixed religious inspirations to give their desperate profession a boost. They often assembled under a spiritual head, a Hindu monk.

Ibn Battutah records that their caravan, consisting of '*twenty-two horsemen, partly Arabs and partly Persian and Turks,*' was attacked by a band of Hindu rebels including two horsemen, coming down from the inaccessible mountains of Multan. '*My companions were men of courage and ability and we fought stoutly with them killing one of the horsemen and about twelve of the foot-soldiers. I was hit by an arrow... We*

---

634. *Thugee*, Wikipedia, http://en.wikipedia.org/wiki/Thugee

635. Elliot & Dowson, Vol. III, p. 141

carried the heads of the slain to the castle of Abu Bak'har... and suspended them from wall,' adds Battutah.[636] These were obviously *thuggees*, although Battutah was probably not familiar with their local name. Emperor Jahangir hunted down 200,000 jungle-dwelling rebels just noted above. Many of those rebels were obviously engaged in the profession of *thuggee*. Nicholas Withington who traveled in India during 1612–14, while awed by Jahangir's wealth, witnessed extreme poverty amongst common folks and many had taken into robbery for making a living. His group was caught by one such robber, obviously a *thuggee*, who took away their belongings and weapons. Withington leaves the *'first competent account of the Indian thugs at a time when the Mughal Empire was in the heyday of its power,'* says RC Prasad.[637]

The *thuggee* cult was obviously a Muslim creation, which, with the British effort, quickly disappeared. In 629, at the time of Islam's birth in Arabia, Hiuen Tsang traveled thousands of miles from China to arrive at Nalanda. Of the ordinary people of India, he wrote: *"In money matters, they are without craft, and in administering justice, they are considerate... They are not deceitful or treacherous in their conduct and are faithful in their oaths and promises... With respect to criminals, these are few in numbers, and only occasionally troublesome."*[638] The Muslim invaders had driven these peaceful and highly ethical people in large numbers into jungles; they had no way but to fill the streets of India at night-time to engage in robbery for survival, and thus causing terror to caravans and travelers.

These are but a few instances of Islam's impact on the social, cultural and intellectual life of India. In other instances, for example, Hiuen Tsang witnessed girls in India taking part in education alongside the boys. India's greatest mathematical achievement, the decimal system that we use today, was the work of three great mathematicians: Bhashkaracharya, Lilavati and Brahmagupta; Lilavati was a woman, daughter of Bhashkaracharya.[639] Marco Polo of Venice, visiting South India twice (1288 & 1293), witnessed a very praiseworthy woman, named Rudramani Devi, who was the ruler of the Telugu country. She ruled for forty years.[640] The Muslim invaders—who engaged in widespread enslavement, kidnapping and rape—drove India's womenfolk from the social life into the confines of homes. The coming of Islam to India *'reduced the freedom of its women folks,'* notes Nehru, adding that Hindus put their women behind the *purdah* (veil) by Muslim influence.[641]

At about the time of establishing Muslim rule in India, the vigor of Indian civilization in creativity had been stagnating. It happened with any civilization in those times; the dazzle of ancient Greece did not last long. *'India was too much in a rut. It was becoming unchanging and unprogressive,'* says Nehru.[642] On the positive influence of Islam, which came to India through Sultan Mahmud's brutal invasions, writes Nehru: *'Islam shook up India. It introduced vitality and an impulse for progress in a society which was becoming wholly unprogressive. Hindu art, which had become decadent and morbid, and heavy with repetition and detail, undergoes a change in the North. A new art grows up, which might be called Indo-Muslim, full of energy and vitality. The old Indian master-builders draw inspiration from the new ideas brought by the Muslims.'*[643]

---

636. Gibb, p. 190–91

637. Prasad RC (1980) *Early Travels in India*, Motilal Banarsidass, New Delhi, p. 261–66

638. Nehru (1989), p. 123–24

639. Ibid, p. 132

640. Ibid, p. 210–11

641. Ibid, p. 157,149

642. Ibid, p. 208

643. Ibid, p. 209

Nehru's assertion that Islam brought a civilization-changing vitality to India is quite hyperbolic, if not unfounded. We do not see anything worth noting. Alberuni, an eyewitness of Sultan Mahmud's invasions, has left a totally opposite opinion on the issue as already noted. Nehru himself says that it was the Indian master-builders who used their brains and labor to build what the Muslim invaders wanted reflecting their religious symbols; and many aspects of this, too, were usurped by Muslims from the pre-Islamic Persian, Egyptian and Byzantine civilizations. Nehru himself says that Mahmud took large numbers of Indian architects and builders with him to Ghazni for building a magnificent mosque there.[644] Obviously, Muslim invaders even did not know how to build what they wanted. No doubt, it was the Indian brain, Indian labor (in the form of wretched slaves), and Indian wealth (obtained through reinless plunder and exorbitant taxes) were most liberally poured into these useless follies of no values to India's natives. These institutions, instead, became the strong fortress from where horrible persecution and exploitation of the common masses were unleashed over the centuries.

Nehru is probably correct that Indian civilization was stagnating. This may give one an impression that Indian civilization had become obscurantist, which so easily turned to darkness and gave way to numerous social ills with the coming of Muslim invaders. It did not know how to rejuvenate and progress. There is, however, no ground for such an assumption. On the basis of what Muslim invaders wanted, Indian builders, craftsmen and artisans created magnificent buildings and monuments, the so-called Indo-Muslim architecture. And as soon as the British came with progressive ideas—freedom, secular education, rule of law, democracy and human rights—non-Muslim Indians quickly embraced them with open arms, a hallmark of Indian civilization since ancient times. '*The Hindus, especially in Bengal, welcomed the New Learning of Europe and the institutions the British brought. The Muslims... out of old religious scruples stood aside,*' notes Naipaul.[645] Historically speaking, Muslims took very little interest in secular education and learning. During the British rule, Muslims staunchly resisted modernity and did not avail themselves of the British-instituted modern education and learning. They considered secular learning un-Islamic and assiduously avoided it. Consequently, they were left behind, while the Hindus, availing of the new learning opportunities, progressed and prospered. In East Bengal for example, Hindus were the minority prior to the Partition, but the '*educational institutions of East Bengal were almost entirely built by the Hindus... 90 percent of the teachers were Hindus.*'[646]

The British Raj, having gained control of most of India in about 1850, albeit with the disturbances of Sepoy Mutiny of 1857–58 in some areas, started reorganizing India's education system by founding three universities in 1857: in Calcutta, Bombay and Madras. In the new environment of educational, scientific and cultural intellectualism, India's literary and scientific geniuses, mostly Hindus, bloomed within a short time. In about half a century, Indian poets and scientists were vying for the Nobel Prize. India's greatest minds—for example the Nobel laureates, namely Rabindranath Tagore, the Chandra Shekhars, Hargobind Khorana and Abdus Salam, and other literary and scientific luminaries, namely Jagadish Chandra Bosu, Satyan Bose, Prafulla Chandra Roy, Nazrul Islam, and Allama Iqbal *et al.*—all bloomed in the new intellectual environment, many within a very short time. The great reformers of religion, tradition and culture of Indian society, namely Raja Ram Mohan Roy (d. 1833), Swami Vivekananda (d. 1902) and Ishwar Chandra Bidyasagar (d. 1891) *et al.*, also bloomed very quickly under the British-fostered socio-political atmosphere, creative intellectualism and culture of freedom. These factors clearly suggest that the vigorous and creative civilization of India, brutally suppressed and deprived of opportunities by Muslim invaders and rulers, was eagerly waiting to flourish at the earliest opportunity.

---

644. Ibid, p. 155

645. Naipaul (1998), p. 247

646. Kamra, p. 3

No doubt there was some resistance amongst Hindus to the British-initiated social and cultural reforms in India, but it was meek at best. Overall, the Hindus quickly understood that institutions of *sati*, female infanticide, child marriage, prohibition of widow marriage and caste system, which had lasted hundreds to thousands of years, were unconscionable ills of their society. *Thuggees*, the lawless ruffians, persistently roamed the streets of India throughout the period of Muslim rule, despite their killing and capturing in hundreds of thousands by Muslim rulers. But under the British rule, they quickly understood that the age-old brutality was gone; they quickly returned to civilian life after the new rulers took civilized measures to rein them. The relatively short period of British rule, lasting less than 100 to 190 years in different areas, had created a heightened degree of awareness amongst low-caste Hindus about their degraded social status and affronted dignity, opposed to what they deserved as respectable human beings. This awareness had become so strong that they, under Ambedkar's leadership, even launched a campaign in the 1940s for an independent state for themselves, free from upper-caste Hindus.[647] Some of those ills—female infanticide, child-marriage, caste discrimination—still persist to some extent in Indian society; they are, however, legally banned and there is a universal understanding amongst all Indians that those are ethically wrong. It is only about time, they will disappear.

ISLAM'S IMPACT ON RELIGIOUS DEMOGRAPHICS: PAST & PRESENT

The conversion of the Hindus and other non-Muslims into Islam through terror, enslavement and coercive economic compulsion during the Muslim rule has been addressed already. Undoubtedly, without the British interference, the religious demography of the population in Bangladesh, Pakistan and India would have looked very different from what it is today. The demographics of Muslim versus non-Muslim populations in countries like Afghanistan, Egypt, Iraq, Iran, Saudi Arabia, Yemen, Turkey and Syria, where European colonists exerted no or short-lived political power, would tell it all. One must take into account that even in the course of 1947 Partition, a few million Hindus and Sikhs were forcibly converted to Islam.

On the Muslim rulers' failure to effectively Islamize India, despite their brutal and economically crushing measures, says Fernand Braudel, '*India survived only by virtue of its patience, its superhuman power and its immense size.*'[648] Indeed, the Muslim invaders never really got a complete and effective hold over vast India, preventing its extensive Islamization. It was not anti-Islam resistance of the Hindus, and their love for Indian culture and religion alone that helped the Hindu civilization to survive. The Islamic sultanate was founded in India at a time when the Islamic power-house at Baghdad was in a state of decline; the political authority had been split amongst regimes based in Baghdad, Egypt and Spain. Then, there came the Mongols, reducing Muslim powers in Central Asia and Baghdad to rubbles. The Muslim rulers of India also maintained their relative independence from central Islamic powers, offering only loose allegiance to the caliphs of Baghdad, Egypt and Samarkand. The absence of a strong central Islamic power when Muslim invaders came to India was a handicap in exerting effective Muslim authority over vast India.

Afghanistan was historically an integral province of India, which Sultan Mahmud brought under permanent Muslim sovereignty in 1000 CE. The stamp of Islamic power has kept a firm hold over Afghanistan ever since, and one can see the change in Muslim versus non-Muslim demographics there. The same applies to Pakistan, where Muslim invaders set up the first Islamic colony and Islam has kept a strong hold over it ever since. According to a 1998 census, Pakistan is demographically 96.28 percent Muslim.

---

647. Bandyopadhyay S (1998) *Changing Borders, Shifting Loyalties: Religion, Caste and the Partition of Bengal in 1947*, Asian Studies Institute, Victoria University of Wellington, New Zealand, p. 4-5

648. Braudel, p. 232

A tangible Muslim sovereignty over most parts of India was established only in the reign Emperor Akbar (r. 1556–1605), leaving some southern-most part (Malabar, Goa etc.) aside. But Akbar undertook a policy of secularization; he even tried, albeit unsuccessfully, to supersede Islam with his own syncretic religion. Islam undoubtedly experienced a decline in his reign. Akbar's policy was slowly reversed in the reign of his son Jahangir (1605–27) and grandson Shah Jahan (1627–58) gradually reviving Islamization. Interrupted for a century, Islamization returned to full-force in the reign of Aurangzeb (1658–1707). It is already noted that Aurangzeb's reign was instrumental in converting bulk of the Muslim population of North India. Soon after Aurangzeb's death, the British mercenaries started consolidating power, eventually ending forced conversion and creeping Islamization in India. Even Aurangzeb's reign witnessed ceaseless revolts all over India; the Muslim authority was falling apart at the time of his death. The half-a-century of somewhat effective Islamization over most parts of India under Aurangzeb has contributed substantially to the shaping of current demography of Muslim population, particularly in Northern India. Hence, it will be easy to understand how continued Islamic rule, without the British interruption, would have impacted the Muslim versus non-Muslim demographics in the subcontinent.

The change of religious demographics in the Muslim-dominated Bangladesh and Pakistan since 1947 will give one a clear idea of how an uninterrupted Muslim rule would have changed the overall religious demographics in the subcontinent. In East Pakistan (Bangladesh), Hindus, 25–30 percent of the population after the Partition, are now about 10 percent. In Pakistan, Hindus constituted about 10 percent of the population after the Partition; their number dwindled to 1.6 percent in 1998. A large number of them were either forcibly converted or driven out in the new wave of violence in 1950 (and thereafter) over Pakistan's failure in Kashmir. Today, it is frequently reported that Hindu (also Christian) girls are routinely kidnapped by Muslims in Pakistan, convert them to Islam, and force them to marry Muslims. According to Pakistan Minorities Rights groups, some 600 Hindus, Sikhs and Christians are forcibly converted to Islam every year.[649] This and a host of other social problems and psychological pressure on the Hindus force them either to convert to Islam or relocate to India. This has effected the change in religious demographics in Pakistan over the past six decades as noted above.

Similar circumstances cause the decline of Hindu population in Bangladesh. After the 2001 general election in Bangladesh, the winning pro-Islam *Bangladesh Nationalist Party*, allied with the Islamist *Jamaat-e-Islami Party*, unleashed a wave of persecution—including humiliation, torture, rape and even murder—of Hindus for supporting the defeated somewhat-secular *Awamy League Party*. One investigative report in the leading *Daily Star* newspaper in Dhaka documented nearly 1,000 rapes of Hindu women in the district of Bhola alone. The victims '*included eight-year-old Rita Rani and seventy-year-old Paru Bala.*'[650] This pogrom forced an estimated 500,000 Hindus to flee Bangladesh and take refuge in India in the aftermath of the 2001 election.[651]

MUSLIM RULE AND POVERTY

From historical data, it becomes evident that the predominant contribution of Islam to India was the large-scale massacre of India's non-Muslims, the enslavement of their women and children in great numbers, the wholesale destruction of religious places, the eradication of non-Muslim educational institutions causing serious decline in science and learning, and the reduction of non-Muslims to abject poverty through extreme

---

649. *Pakistani Christians asked to choose between 'conversion' or 'death'*, Christian Today, Australia, 11 Sept 2008; http://au.christiantoday.com/article/pakistani/4282.htm

650. *Harrowing tales of depravity*, Daily Star (Dhaka), 10 November 2001

651. Lundström J (2006) *Rape as Genocide under International Criminal Law, The Case of Bangladesh*, Global Human Rights Defense, Lund University, p. 29-30

economic exploitation. The Hindus of prosperous of India were begging at the doors of Muslims as early as in the reign of Alauddin Khalji (1296–1316), just nine decades after the founding of Islamic rule in Delhi.

The British occupation later brought some kind of relief to the savagery, destruction and plunder wrought by Muslim invaders and rulers upon India's non-Muslims. The British rule, however, did not attenuate the economic misery of Indians to any significant extent. The British rule was based on a policy of economic exploitation, aimed at generating revenue for the British treasury. Javier Cuenca Esteban estimates that the '*net financial transfers from India to Britain reached a peak of £1,014,000 annually in 1784–1792 before declining to £477,000 in 1808–1815.*'[652] The British did not engage in plundering the households, temples etc. as did the Muslim rulers, but they imposed high taxes on India's farmers. Taxes were high, about one-third of the produce. This was the same rate on paper charged by Sultan Alauddin Khilji, who indeed charged 50 percent in order to reduce the peasantry to extreme poverty for preventing disaffection and rebellion amongst Hindus. Taxation became the worst under Muhammad Tughlaq (1325–51) reducing the peasantry to extreme poverty and beggary; in the Mughal reign, taxes could reach as high as three quarters in some areas.

Under the British, the situation was badly worsened by the homegrown *zamindars*, the tax-collectors for the Raj; they charged another one-third for their own keeping. This was mindless, because, the British invested a good part of the revenues in education, healthcare, development of infrastructures and running the state-machinery, but the amount collected by the *zamindars* was entirely for their own keeping. However, the British must take as much responsibility for their failure to regulate those policies of the *zamindars*. The British also forced the peasants to change cultivation from food-crops to cash-crops: indigo, jute, cotton, and tea etc., useful for the booming industries in Britain. As a result, the production of food-crops for local consumption reduced. The British traders also flooded India's market with cheaper industrial products from Britain, causing a decline of the archaic indigenous industries; this caused further economic hardships to a large number of people. All these factors caused hardships to Indians under the British rule. However, one must take into consideration that the archaic industry of India was going to collapse anyway as the world was irreversibly changing to capitalist industrialization.

The British occupation of India undoubtedly came at a much less brutality and bloodbath. They, nonetheless, committed their share of brutality mainly in the course of the Sepoy Mutiny (1857–58). The British atrocity in the Sepoy Mutiny was gory; but atrocities were committed by both sides. The British became more brutal after the cruel betrayal of Nana Sahib at Cawnpore (Kanpur). On 5 July 1857, some 210 British women and children, left in Nana's custody, were butchered, hacked to pieces and thrown down the well.[653] The mutineers also slaughtered innocent children and raped the white women in Lucknow. These incidents of cold-blooded murder of innocent women and children and rapes enraged the British, including the public in Britain. The British soldiers committed shameful, disproportionate atrocities in revenge on the mutineers. However, the unarmed civilian population, particularly the women and children, a prime target for enslavement by Muslim invaders and rulers, rarely suffered British cruelties. In the course of the independence movement, British atrocities were minimal; the Jalianwala Bagh massacre was the major incidence, killing a few hundred people.

Undoubtedly, the Islamic rule in India was much more devastating and debilitating than the British one. But defying all logic and reason, Muslims as well as non-Muslim secular-Marxists of the subcontinent see the advent of Islam in India as a great blessing, while the British rule as the greatest curse. Islam allegedly brought, they say, equality, justice, emancipation, art, culture, architecture, and prosperity, in which India

---

652. Clingingsmith D & Williamson JG (2005) *India's Deindustrialization in the 18th and 19th Centuries*, Harvard University, p. 9

653. Nehru (1989), p. 414; also *Indian Rebellion* of 1857, Wikipedia; http://en.wikipedia.org/wiki/Indian_Rebellion_of_1857

should take great pride. In glorifying Arab imperialism that extended to India, respected Marxist historian MN Roy calls the *Arab Empire* a magnificent monument to the memory of Muhammad.

Contrary to this Marxist assessment, it has been made abundantly clear that the Arabs—the founders of Islam—had nothing to contribute to the more developed outside world, except in poetry, which, too, became prohibited in Islam. Nehru, who keeps contradicting himself, also negates this Marxist view-point in saying, '*The Afghans brought no new element of progress; they represented a backward feudal and tribal order.*'[654] Naipaul, slamming the Marxist assessment, asserts that Hindu civilization was left "terrorized", "wounded" and "destroyed" by Islamic invasions. He says, '*Islamic rule in India was at least as catastrophic as the later Christian (British) rule. The Christians created massive poverty in what was a most prosperous country; the Muslims created a terrorized civilization out of what was the most creative culture that ever existed.*'[655]

Like Naipaul, the Marxist-socialist historians, Nehru included, predominantly focus on the poverty caused by the British in their history writing. Fair enough! That is indeed an indisputable fact. What is conspicuously absent in their writings is the impact of Islam on the poverty in India. What was the effect of Islamic rule on poverty?

Many mentions have been made of how astonished the Muslim invaders and chroniclers were by the riches of India. About the riches in pre-Islamic India, wrote Abdullah Wassaf in his *Tazjiyatul Amsar* (1300 CE), '*the charms of the country and the softness of the air, together with the variety of its wealth, precious metal, stones, and other abundant productions, are beyond description.*' In a poetical note, he adds, '*If it is asserted that Paradise is in India; Be not surprised because Paradise itself is not comparable to it.*'[656] Hajjaj was so awed by the one-fifth share of the booty received from Qasim on one occasion that he '*prostrated himself before God, offered thanksgiving and praises, for, he said, **he had in reality obtained all the wealth and treasures and dominion of the world**.*'[657] In 1311, Malik Kafur returned after sacking South India; his loot, according to Nehru, included '*50,000 maunds (1 maund = 37.3 kg) of gold, a vast quantity of jewels and pearls, and 20,000 horses and 312 elephants.*'[658] According to Barani,[659] Malik Kafur's booty was so immense that the '*old inhabitants of Delhi remarked that so many elephants and so much gold had never before been brought to Delhi. No one could remember anything like it, nor was there anything like it recorded in history.*'[660]

The Islamic invaders came to a country of such riches to unleash terrible plundering, looting and exploitation, causing great misery and sufferings to the people. Alauddin Khilji (d. 1316) sucked the peasantry to such an extent that they were left with enough for bare sustenance; the rest was taken away in all kinds of taxes. Alauddin had reduced Indian peasants to such misery that Maulana Shamsuddin Turk, a Sufi saint from Egypt, wrote in delight, '*the Hindu women and children went out begging at the doors of the Musalmans.*' Such miserable condition forced many peasants to sell their wives and children for paying up the taxes.[661] Later on, Sultan Ghiyasuddin Tughlaq (r. 1320–25) continued the exploitation such that '*there should be left only so much to the Hindus that neither, on the one hand, they should become arrogant on account of their wealth, nor, on the other, desert their land in despair,*' wrote Barani. Next Muhammad bin Tughlaq (r. 1325–51) increased the tax further, forcing the peasants to leave their lands and take refuge in jungles, from where he hunted them down like wild beasts. As noted already, in the glorious days of Mughal

---

654. Nehru (1946), p. 261

655. Outlook India, *V.S. Naipual interview*, 15 November 1999

656. Elliot & Dawson, Vol. III, p. 29

657. Sharma, p. 95

658. Nehru (1989), p. 213; also Ferishtah, Vol. I, p. 204

659. Barani puts the number of elephants at 612, the amount of gold at 96,000 *maunds*.

660. Elliot & Dawson, Vol. III, p. 204

661. Lal (1994), p. 128–131

rule, kind-hearted Jahangir had hunted down 200,000 jungle-dwellers in 1619–20. Twenty-seven years into kind-hearted Akbar's reign, numerous Hindus lived in the fastness of mountains as noted above. This means desperate poverty persisted in India even throughout the glorious Mughal rule.

The policy of extreme exploitation of the non-Muslim peasantry, except probably with some measure of relief under Akbar, continued through the reign of Jahangir and beyond. On Muslim rulers' deliberate policy of causing crushing impoverishment of the peasants, notes Fernand Braudel, '*The levies it (Hindus) had to pay were so crushing that one catastrophic harvest was enough to unleash famines and epidemics capable of killing a million people at a time. Appalling poverty was the constant counterpart of the conquerors' opulence, including the splendor of palaces and feasts in Delhi.*'[662] The situation got worse under the reign of Shahjahan (d. 1658) and Aurangzeb (d. 1707). The Muslim rulers '*founded its luxury on India's general poverty*' and India, under the Muslim rule, experienced '*a series of famine, a fabulous death-rate...,*' adds Braudel.[663]

LEGACY

It is already explained that the erasure of the contemptuous pre-Islamic *jahiliyah* heritage is an essential part of the fundamental Islamic doctrine. It is incumbent upon "true believers" to blot out the vestiges of erroneous, obsolete pre-Islamic religious, cultural and civilizational traits and acquisitions from the lands they live in. Therefore, after Islam took control of the Middle East in the seventh century, notes Lewis, '*The most ancient languages—the Egyptian, Assyrian, Babylonian, Hittite, old Persian, and the rest—were abandoned and remained unknown until they were exhumed, deciphered, interpreted and restored by Orientalist scholars to history... For a long time, the effort was exclusively the work of the non-Middle Easterners, and it remains predominantly so.*'[664] In agreement, writes Ibn Warraq, '*the sciences of Egyptology, Assyriology, and Iranology were the exclusive concerns of the European and American scholars. It was left to the dedicated archeologists to recover and give back to mankind a part of its glorious past.*'[665]

However, in recent years, the fundamentalist Muslims, in Egypt for example, are seeking to destroy those revived past glories by destroying the pyramids and other archeological and architectural treasures of the pre-Islamic era. The Taliban fundamentalists in Afghanistan obliterated the pre-Islamic Bamiyan Buddha statues. The Islamic regime in Iran has been systematically obliterating the great pre-Islamic Persian heritage under one excuse or another over the past three decades. This campaign has been gaining strength and will, in all likelihood, expand and intensify in Islamic countries in the coming decades.

Indisputably, the Portuguese and Spaniards amongst European colonists, wrought havoc upon the colonized peoples, such as in South America and the Portuguese-controlled Goa in India. But, if the records of medieval Muslim historians and rulers are taken into consideration, the Muslim invaders undoubtedly committed no lesser atrocity against the colonized people. They killed an estimated eighty million natives in India, a similar number in the Middle East and Central Asia, a larger number in Africa and more in Europe. The Spanish and Portuguese imperialism was obviously cruel, but the Islamic one was no less cruel as far as atrocities against the colonized are concerned. Other European colonial powers—with notable exception, such as in Australia—behaved reasonably well for that time.

---

662. Braudel, p. 232

663. Ibid, p. 233–34

664. Lewis (2000), p. 245

665. Ibn Warraq, p. 202

What are the continued legacies of European and Islamic colonialism—in the subcontinent, for example? In India, the positive impact of the British-instituted education, legal and healthcare systems, roads, railway and irrigation systems, secular-democracy, rule of law and telecommunication, along with their efforts to abolish a whole host of social ills cannot be discounted in today's India. But what can India boast of about Islam's beneficial legacy? Indian Muslim friends tell me that India had nothing before the Muslim invasion. *'Islam gave India the Taj Mahal, the Red Fort,'* they say. Islam *'inspired the king of what was then the world's wealthiest empire to build a tomb—the Taj Mahal—in honour of his wife,'* argues Irfan Yusuf.[666] India's pre-Islamic standing in science, art and architecture has been discussed already. Also discussed, how these fanciful follies, the so-called great Islamic contributions, were built by sucking the blood of the colonized people, and of course, by their brain and labor, too. Most importantly, without these follies, India will be as great a nation today, but not without the legacy of the British Raj. Naipaul writes on the distinction between the British and Islamic legacies in Pakistan that,

> The Moguls had built forts, places, mosques, and tombs. The British in the second half of the nineteenth century had put up buildings to house institutions. Lahore was rich in the monuments of both periods. Ironically, for a country that talks so much about Islamic identity, and even claimed to be a successor to Mogul power, it was the Mogul monuments that were in decay: the fort, Shah Jehan's mosque, the Shalimar Gardens, the tombs of both Emperor Jehangir and his great consort Noor-Jehan… The British administrative buildings live on. The institutions they were meant to house are still more or less the institutions the country depends on.[667]

Waleed Iqbal, a grandson of Muhammad Iqbal, the man behind the Pakistan idea, told Naipaul that *'going back further to the times of the Mogul, the law was simply dictatorial. The British-given courts, and the British procedural laws of 1898 and 1908, were still all that the country had. They met a need; that was why they had lasted.'*[668]

This does not mean that the British occupation was essential for these ideas and institutions to come to India. Since ancient times, Indian civilization, while being creative itself, was very assimilative of foreign ideas. The developments of the *Renaissance* and Enlightenment Europe would have trickled into India with relative ease. However, Islam's hold on India, if continued, would have been an impediment. The Muslim power was decaying in India and many would believe that the Hindus and Sikhs' were about to displace Muslims from power. That was very much a possibility. However, it must be taken into consideration that, nowhere in the world, the Muslim colonists were dislodged from power without foreign interference. Muslim power had decayed in India a few times previously. Amir Timur had thoroughly devastated the already decaying Islamic power in Delhi; Muslims still came back and asserted their political control. If not with internal power, with foreign reinforcements, Muslim could still keep their hold on power. Did not Ahmad Shah Abadali, upon fervent appeals from India's pious Muslims, like great Sufi master Shah Walliullah, come to India thrice to wreak havoc and decimate the Maratha opposition in his last foray in 1761? Earlier, amidst chaotic political situation in India, Muslims had appealed for outside help; responding to it, Babur came from Central Asia and founded the powerful Mughal Empire.

The overall impact of the Islamic imperialism on India was undoubtedly worse than the British one. A look at the current mess in Islamic Bangladesh and Pakistan clearly shows the continued legacy of Islamic imperialism in the subcontinent. The Hindu India, absorbing progressive European ideas, has steadily marched ahead after gaining independence. Pakistan and Bangladesh, the heirs of the legacy of Islamic imperialism, have harked back to Islam and regressed. If European imperialism deserves condemnation, Islamic imperialism deserves no less.

---

666. Yusuf I, *Violence against women won't stop until men speak out*, New Zealand Herald, 12 Sept. 2008
667. Naipaul (1998), p. 255–56
668. Ibid, p. 256

The negative impact of the European imperialism on the former colonies of Africa, Americas, Asia and elsewhere has now ended with their withdrawal. But the footprints, left behind by the Islamic imperialism, continue to cause misery, even havoc, in the lands Muslims had conquered. Muslim converts' failure to cope up with the rest of the citizens, such as in India, has been discussed already. There is no end in sight for this ongoing pernicious impact of Islam. On the contrary, wherever the European colonists have left their footprints, namely as settlers in Canada, United States, Australasia and South Africa among other places, they have been an asset for those nations.

Critics and historians, who engage in evaluating the impact of the Islamic and British rules in India, should pay heed to what India's latest Prime Minister Manmohan Singh and the first Prime Minister Jawaharlal Nehru said about the British and Islamic impact on India. In a speech at Oxford in 2005, Singh, breaking tradition, said of his assessment of the British impact on India, '*Today, with the balance and perspective offered by the passage of time and the benefit of hindsight, it is possible for an Indian prime minister to assert that India's experience with Britain had its beneficial consequences too.*' He added: '*Our notions of the rule of law, of a constitutional government, of a free press, of a professional civil service, of modern universities and research laboratories have all been fashioned in the crucible where an age-old civilization met the dominant Empire of the day.*'[669]

Nehru, on the other hand, rather reluctantly drew the unavoidable conclusion on Islam's impact on India that '*Islam did not bring any great social revolution in its train which might have put an end to a large extent to the exploitation of masses. But it did lessen this exploitation so far as the Muslims are concerned...*'[670] Nehru's appreciation of Muslim rulers' racist policy of relieving exploitation of the miniscule Muslim population was possible only by sucking the blood, heart and soul of the much larger non-Muslim population.

---

669. Rediff.com, *British Raj was beneficial: PM*, 9 July 2005; http://us.rediff.com/news/2005/jul/09pm1.htm
670. Nehru (1989), p. 145

Chapter VII

Islamic Slavery

'Allah sets forth (another) Parable of two men: one of them dumb, with no power of any sort; a wearisome burden is he to his master; whichever way he directs him, he brings no good: is such a man equal with one who commands Justice, and is on a Straight Way?'

-- Allah, in *Quran* 16:76

'(Allah) brought those of the People of the Scripture... and cast panic into their hearts. Some (adult males) ye slew, and ye made captive some (women and children).'

-- Allah, in *Quran* 33:26–27

It is written in the Quran that all Nations who should not have acknowledged their (Muslims') authority were sinners; that it was their right and duty to make war upon whoever they could find and to make slaves of all they could take as prisoners; and that every Mussulman who should be slain in battle was sure to go to Paradise.

-- Tripoli's London ambassador Abd al-Rahman to Thomas Jefferson & John Adams (1786) on by what right the Barbary States enslaved American seamen.

———————

Slavery is a socio-economic institution, in which some human individuals, called slaves, become property of others, called masters or owners. Devoid of freedom and liberty, slaves are expected to provide loyal and diligent service for the comfort and economic well-being of their masters. Deprived of any human rights, slaves are the unconditional possession of their owners: mere chattels, having no right to leave, refuse work, or receive compensation for their labor. The position of slaves in society in many respects is akin to that of domesticated animals. Just as cows, horses and other beasts of burden are trained and utilized for economic advantage, such as for pulling carts or plowing fields—slaves are exploited for the benefit, comfort and economic well-being of the owner. Slave-trade, integral to slavery, involves buying and selling of human beings as a commodity like any other commercial transaction. Slavery, in essence, is the exploitation of the weak by the strong and has a very long history.

One major criticism of the West by all, and particularly by Muslims, pertains to the trans-Atlantic slave-trade by European powers and their mindless exploitation and degrading treatment of slaves in the Americas and West Indies. Muslims are often quick to point fingers at the European slave-trade; they often claim that the exploitation of slaves enabled countries like the United States to amass the huge wealth they enjoy today. One young Muslim, born in America, wrote: '*Do you know how the American slave-hunters went to Africa, seized the black people and brought them to America as slaves? America's economic power owes a great deal to the labor of those slaves*' (personal communication). Terming the 350-year trans-Atlantic slave-trade '*the worst and most cruel slavery*' in history, the Nation of Islam Minister Louis Farrakhan claims that some white Americans do not know that '*they are in the privileged position... today based on what happened to us (Blacks)*' in the past.[671] An overwhelming majority of Muslims believe that Islamic history is devoid of the abhorrent practice of slavery. Rocky Davis (aka Shahid Malik), an Australian Aboriginal convert to Islam, told the ABC Radio that '*Christianity were the founders of slavery. Not Islam.*'[672] When Muslims in India talk about the practice of slavery in the subcontinent—they talk about the harrowing tales of how the Portuguese transported slaves from coastal areas of Goa, Kerala and Bengal in terrible conditions. It is already noted that history books in Pakistan teach that before Islam, there was exploitation and slavery, which vanished with the coming of Islam. They will never talk about the slavery that Muslim invaders and rulers practiced on a grand scale in India.

This Muslim silence about the widespread practice slavery under Islamic rules, such as in India, likely results from their ignorance of historical facts. In modern history writing in India, there is extensive whitewashing of the atrocities that took place during the Muslim invasions and the subsequent Islamic rule. Such distortions of the true picture of Islamic history compound Muslims' ignorance about Islamic atrocities in medieval India and create an erroneous perception amongst them about the extensive slavery practised by Muslim rulers. As recounted throughout this book, slavery was regrettably a prominent institution throughout the history of Islamic domination everywhere. It also had unique features, namely large-scale concubinage, eunuchs, and *ghilman* (described below).

THE QURANIC SANCTION OF SLAVERY

The institution of slavery in Islam was formalized in the following Quranic verse, in which Allah distinguishes free human beings or masters, who exercise justice and righteousness, from the dumb, useless and burdensome ones, the slaves:

> Allah sets forth (another) Parable of two men: one of them dumb, with no power of any sort; a
> wearisome burden is he to his master; whichever way he directs him, he brings no good: is such
> a man equal with one who commands Justice, and is on a Straight Way? [Quran 16:76]

Allah warns the believers against taking the slaves as equal partner in status and in sharing their wealth, lest they have to fear them as anyone else:

---

671. Farrakhan L, *What does America and Europe Owe?*, Final CalL, 2 June 2008

672. ABC Radio, *Aboriginal Da'wah - "Call to Islam"*, 22 March 2006;
http://www.abc.net.au/rn/talks/8.30/relrpt/stories/s1597410.htm

…do ye have partners among those whom your right hands possess (i.e., slaves, captives) to share as equals in the wealth We have bestowed on you? Do ye fear them as ye fear each other? [Quran 30:28][673]

Allah recognizes some human beings, namely the masters, as more blessed by Himself than the less favored slaves as part of His divine plan. He warns Muslims against sharing His gifts to them equally with their slaves. Those who would take slaves as equal, warns Allah, would deny Him:

Allah has bestowed His gifts of sustenance more freely on some of you than on others: those more favoured are not going to throw back their gifts to those whom their right hands possess, so as to be equal in that respect. Will they then deny the favours of Allah? [Quran 16:71]

Allah does not only sanction the institution of slavery, He also gave divine blessing to masters (Muslim men only can own slaves) to have sex with the female slaves:

And those who guard their private parts, Except in the case of their wives or *those whom their right hands possess*—for these surely are not to be blamed [Quran 70:29–30]

And who guard their private parts, except before their mates or those whom their right hands possess, for they surely are not blameable [Quran 23:5–6]

Therefore, if there are women amongst the captives or slaves, Muslims are divinely sanctioned to have sex with them as they do with their wives. This verdict of Allah founded the institution of sex-slavery or slave-concubinage in Islam, which was widespread in the pre-colonial Muslim world and continued well into the mid-twentieth century. As far as legal marriage is concerned, there is a limitation of four wives for a man at one time [Quran 4:3], but no such limitation on the number of sex-slaves.

Allah also gave a divine sanction to Muslims for acquiring female slaves for sexual engagement by waging wars against the infidels:

O Prophet! surely We have made lawful to you your wives whom you have given their dowries, and those whom your right hand possesses out of those whom Allah has given to you as *prisoners of war*… [Quran 33:50]

Muslims can engage in sex with the captured slave women even if they are married, but not with the married free Muslim women:

Also (prohibited are) women already married, except those whom your right hands possess… [Quran 4:24].

There are other verses in the Quran that talks approvingly of slaves and capturing them in wars. Thus, according to the divine commands of the Islamic God as enshrined in the holy Quran, Muslims are allowed to keep slaves. They can amass slaves by waging wars, have sex with the female slaves, and of course, use them as they wish. For Muslims, having sex with female slaves is as legal as having sex with their married wives. Slavery appears to be one of the most desired divine privileges in Islam, since Allah took the pain of reminding Muslims about this *divine right* time and again in so many verses.

---

673. Famous scholar Abu Ala Maududi in his interpretation of this verse notes: "When you do not make your own slaves partners in your wealth, how do you think and believe that Allah will make His creatures partner in His Godhead?" [Maududi AA, *Towards Understanding the Quran*, Markazi Muktaba Islami Publishers, New Delhi, Vol. VIII]. In other words, associating partners with Allah, which is the most abhorrent thing to do in Islam, is tantamount for a man to take his slaves as equal partner.

THE PROPHETIC MODEL OF SLAVERY

Allah did not rest with repeatedly reminding Muslims to engage in slavery, but also took the initiative to guide Prophet Muhammad on how to enslave the infidels, such as in the following verse:

> And He (Allah) brought those of the People of the Scripture (i.e., Banu Qurayza) who supported them (i.e., the Quraysh) down from their strongholds, and cast panic into their hearts. *Some (adult males) ye slew, and ye made captive some* (women and children)... [Quran 33:26–27]

In this verse, Allah charged the Banu Qurayza Jews with supporting the Quraysh of Mecca "from their strongholds" against Muslims in the battle of the Trench (627). Based on this unsubstantiated accusation, Allah commanded that some of the Jews, the adult males, were to be slain, and the rest, the women and children, enslaved. The Prophet duly complied with this divine command. He distributed the enslaved women and children among his disciples, himself acquiring one-fifth of them. The young and pretty ones amongst the female captives were made sex-slaves; the Prophet himself took beautiful Rayhana, whose husband and family members had been slain in the massacre. He took her to bed on the same night.[674]

After conquering Khaybar the following year, Muhammad carried away their women and children as slaves. In many other attacks, the Prophet and his followers enslaved and carried away the women and children of the vanquished. Therefore, after aggressively attacking and defeating the infidels, enslaving the women and children became a model of Muhammad's wars. Some of the slaves could be sold or ransomed for generating revenues. The young and pretty ones amongst the female captives became sex-slaves.

Since emulating Muhammad in action and deed is central to living a good Muslim life in Islamic thought, Muslims duly embraced his model of slavery (comprising enslavement, slave-trade and slave-concubinage) and perpetuated it during the later centuries of Islamic domination. Muhammad's example of dealing with the Jews of Banu Qurayza or Khaybar became the standard template for capturing slaves. This led to a massive rise in enslavement, sex-slavery and slave-trade in medieval Islamdom. After Muhammad's death, Muslims—armed with sanctions of the Quran and *Sunnah*—embarked on an unbridled mission of waging holy war to conquer the world for the purpose of spreading Islam and expanding Islamic rule. As Islam burst out of Arabia, Muslim invaders became adept at capturing the vanquished infidels, particularly the women and children, in large numbers as slaves.

In Islamic thoughts (as noted already), the civilizations preceding and outside of Islam are *jahiliyah* or erroneous in nature, invalidated with the coming of Islam. Only Muslims were in the sole possession of truth in the form of the true faith of Islam. In their thoughts, the world outside the boundary and religion of Islam, notes Bernard Lewis, '*was inhabited by the infidels and barbarians. Some of these were recognized as possessing some form of religion and a tincture of civilization. The remainder, polytheists and idolaters, were seen primarily as sources of slaves.*'[675] Muslims captured slaves in such great numbers that slave-trade became a booming business enterprise; markets across the Muslim world became teeming with slaves. Accordingly, '*it goes to the credit of Islam to create slave trade on a large scale, and run it for profit like any other business,*' writes Lal.[676]

---

674. Ibn Ishaq, p. 461–70

675. Lewis (1966), p. 42

676. Lal (1994), p6

SLAVERY IN THE ANCIENT WORLD

Slavery was not an Islamic invention, nor did Islam have a monopoly in it. Likely originated in the age of savagery, slavery had been a prominent feature of all major civilizations throughout recorded history. Slavery existed in Babylonia and Mesopotamia, and was prevalent in ancient Egypt, Greece and Rome before the advent of Christianity. Slavery is approved in Christian scriptures and was practiced in the medieval Christendom.

Ancient Egypt. In ancient Egypt, slaves provided the labor-force in the construction of Pyramids. According to famous Greek traveler Herodotus (484–425 BCE), some 100,000 slaves worked for twenty years in the construction of the Great Pyramid at Giza, one of the seven wonders of the ancient world, built by Cheops, a Pharaoh of Egypt's Old Kingdom (r. 2589–2566 BCE).[677] Recorded from legendary accounts, this figure was obviously an exaggeration. It, nonetheless, informs us that slaves were used in large numbers in such ventures in those times. Pharaohs in Egypt used to capture slaves in wars or purchase them from foreign lands. They were the property of the state, not of private citizens, but were often presented as gifts to generals and priests.

Ancient Greece. In the ancient city states of Greece, namely Athens and Sparta, slavery was integrated into the socio-economic and political system. Alongside the free citizens and foreigners, there were the helots: the slave class, working as serfs in agricultural and other menial activities. This, assume many scholars, allowed the elites and free citizens to engage themselves in intellectual pursuits among other activities, likely contributing to the stunning intellectual, political, scientific and literary achievements of classical Greece. The bulk of the Greek peasants did not own lands and had to give away a large proportion of their crop to landlords. As a result, they fell into debt and ultimately offered themselves as slaves, forming the helot class. At one point, Athens is said to have had a staggering 460,000 slaves against only 2,100 free citizens. Slaves were treated mildly in Athens compared to those in Sparta. Later, the constitution of Draco (621 BCE) and the laws of Solon (638–558 BCE) made them property of the state, which improved their condition. The decree of Solon also banned enslavement because of debts. The slaves now possessed some basic rights and could not be put to death except by the state.

Roman Empire. In the ancient Roman Republic and early Roman Empire, about 15–20 percent of the population were slaves.[678] During Emperor Augustus Caesar (r. 63 BCE–14 CE), one master, it is said, left behind 4,000 slaves.[679] Until the second century BCE, masters could legally kill a slave although occurred rarely. The Cornelian Law (82 BCE) forbade masters from killing a slave. The Petronian Law (32 BCE) forbade masters from forcing slaves into warfare. Under Emperor Claudius (r. 41–54 CE), if a master neglected the health of his slaves resulting in death, he was guilty of murder. Dio Chrysostom—a famous orator, writer, philosopher, and historian—had devoted two Discourses (14 and 15) delivered at the Forum condemning slavery during Emperor Trajan (r. 98–117 CE). *De Clementia* (1:18), authored by Seneca the Elder (c. 54 BCE–39 CE), records that masters—cruel to slaves—were publicly insulted. Later on, Emperor Hadrian (r. 117–138 CE) renewed the Cornelian and Petronian laws. Ulpian, a Stoic lawyer under Emperor Caracalla (r. 211–217 CE), made it illegal for parents to sell their children into slavery. Diocletian (r. 284–305 CE), the last notable Pagan Emperor of Rome, made it illegal for a creditor to enslave a debtor and for a man to sell himself into slavery for paying up a debt. Constantine the Great (r. 306–337 CE) prohibited the separation of family members during the distribution of slaves. Evidently, the condition of slaves was slowly improving in the pre-Christian Roman Empire.

---

677. Ibid, p2

678. Slavery, Wikipedia, http://en.wikipedia.org/wiki/Slavery

679. Lal (1994), p. 3

Ancient China. In ancient China, rich families owned slaves for doing menial works in the fields and at home. The Emperor usually owned slaves in hundreds and even in thousands. Most of the slaves were born to slave-mothers. Some became slaves for failing to pay up debts; others were captured in raids and wars.

Ancient India. There are few mentions of slavery in ancient India, another great civilization since early antiquity. Megasthenes (c. 350–290 BCE), the famous Greek traveler, who was familiar with slavery in Greece and other countries he had visited, failed to notice the existence of slavery in India. He wrote, "*All Indians are free. None of them is a slave... They even do not reduce foreigners to slavery. There is thus no question of their reducing their own countrymen to slavery.*"[680] Similarly, Muslim chroniclers, who left abundant records of large-scale Islamic slavery in India, never mention any incidence of slavery in the pre-Islamic Hindu society. However, slavery did exist in ancient India, because references of slaves are found in *Rigveda* (ancient Hindu scripture) and other philosophical and religious literature, including in the teachings of Buddha.

Buddha (c. 563–483 BCE) enjoined his followers to assign only the amount of work to slaves that they could easily do. He also advised masters to attend to slaves when they fell ill. Kautaliya (aka Chanakya), a teacher of the Taxila University whose protégé Chandragupta Maurya founded the great Maurya dynasty (c. 320–100 BCE), had prohibited masters from punishing slaves without reasons; the defaulters were to be punished by the state. Emperor Ashoka (r. 273–232 BCE) of the Maurya dynasty, in his *Rock Edict IX*, advised masters to treat their slaves with sympathy and consideration. Ancient Hindu scripture *Rigveda* mentions of slaves being given as presents and rulers giving female slaves as gifts. Slaves in India served as domestic servants in the palaces of rulers and in the establishments of aristocrats and priests. It is likely that those, who failed to pay up debts, were reduced to slavery in India.[681]

It, however, appears that the practice of slavery in ancient India was much lower and that slaves received more humane treatment compared to those in contemporary Egypt, Greece, China and Rome. In India, slaves were never considered a commodity for trading; there was no slave-market. Slave-trade was never a feature of India's economic system until Muslims brought the practice to India.

Slavery in Christianity. Slavery is clearly recognized, even sanctioned, in the New Testament [Mat 18:25, Mark 14:66]. For example, Jesus advised people in debt to sell themselves along with their family members into slavery to pay up [Mat 18:25]. Similarly, a number of St. Paul's verses, such as Eph 6:5–9, Cor 12:13, Gal 3:28 and Col 3:11 etc., recognize slavery or slaves (the bonded) and the free man.

These New Testament sanctions had likely encouraged Christians to enslave the infidels (non-Christians). Obviously, slavery was gradually declining in the pre-Christian Roman Empire; the condition of slaves was improving. When Christians rose to imperial power after Emperor Constantine's conversion in the fourth century, the trend reversed. For example, pro-Christian Emperor Flavius Gratianus (r. 375–383) enacted an edict that a slave, who accused his master of a crime, should be burned alive. In 694, the Spanish monarchy, under pressure from the church, ordered the Jews to choose baptism or slavery. The church Fathers and Popes justified slavery in the medieval Christendom on religious grounds. They continued supporting the slave-trade even in the face of rising opposition against the institution in Europe. '*The Churches, as everyone knows, opposed the abolition of slavery as long as they dared,*' writes Bertrand Russell.[682]

---

680. Ibid, p. 5

681. Ibid, p. 4

682. Russell B (1957) *Why I Am Not a Christian*, Simon & Schuster, New York, p. 26

ENSLAVEMENT BY MUSLIMS IN INDIA

Muslim invaders and rulers engaged in large-scale enslavement of the infidels wherever they went: Europe, Africa and Asia. In this discussion, slavery by Muslims in medieval India as recorded by contemporaneous Muslim historians will be presented in some detail. Brief accounts of Islamic slavery in Africa, Europe and elsewhere in Asia will also be presented.

By Muhammad bin Qasim: Islam's assault on Indian frontiers started during Caliph Omar with the attack and pillage of Thana in 636, just four years after Prophet Muhammad's death. Eight more such plundering expeditions followed under succeeding caliphs: Othman, Ali and Mu'awiyah. These early assaults by Muslim invaders sometimes yielded booty and slaves besides slaughter and pillage, but failed to gain a foothold for Islam in India. With Caliph al-Walid's blessings, Hajjaj bin Yusuf sent two expeditions to Sindh, led by Ubaidullah and Budail. Both campaigns failed suffering heavy casualties; both commanders were slain. Sorely wounded at heart, Hajjaj next sent his nephew and son-in-law Qasim at the head of 6,000 soldiers. He overran Debal in Sindh in 712, digging a firm and lasting foothold of Islam in Hindustan. Debal, records famous Muslim historian al-Biladuri, '*was taken by assault, and the carnage endured for three days... the priests of the temple were massacred.*'[683] He put the males above seventeen years of age to the sword and enslaved the women and children. The total number of captives taken in Debal is not recorded; but among them were 700 beautiful women, who had taken refuse in temples, records *Chachnama*. Caliph's one-fifth share of the booty and slaves, which included seventy-five damsels, was sent to Hajjaj. The rest were distributed amongst his soldiers.[684]

In the attack of Rawar, records *Chachnama*, '*When the number of prisoners was calculated, it was found to amount to thirty thousand persons, amongst whom were the daughters of the chiefs, and one of them was Rai Dahir's sister's daughter.*' One-fifth of the prisoners and the spoils were sent to Hajjaj.[685] As records *Chachnama*, when Brahmanabad fell to Muslims, in which 8,000 to 26,000 men were slain, '*One-fifth of all the prisoners were chosen and set aside; they were counted as amounting to twenty thousand in number, and the rest were given to the soldiers.*'[686] This means, about 100,000 women and children were enslaved in this assault.

One consignment of caliph's share of the booty included 30,000 women and children and slain Dahir's head. Among the captives were a few girls of Sindh nobility. Hajjaj forwarded the caravan of booty and slaves to Caliph al-Walid in Damascus. '*When the Khalifa of the time read the letter,*' records *Chachnama*, 'he *praised Almighty Allah. He sold some of those daughters of the chiefs, and some he granted as rewards. When he saw the daughters of Rai Dahir's sister, he was so much stuck with her beauty and charms, and began to bite his fingers with astonishment.*'[687]

In the attack of Multan, records al-Biladuri, there were, among the captives, '*ministers of the temple, to the number of six thousand.*'[688] This figure should give us an idea of total number of women and children enslaved in Multan. Qasim undertook similar expeditions in Sehwan and Dhalila among others. His rather small feat in Sindh over a short period of three years (712–15) might have yielded to the tune of three hundred thousand slaves in all.

---

683. Elliot & Dawson, Vol. I, p. 119-20; Sharma, p. 95
684. Lal (1994), p. 17
685. Elliot & Dawson, Vol. I, p. 173
686. Ibid, p. 181
687. Sharma, p. 95–96
688. Elliot & Dawson, Vol. I, p. 122–23,203

During 715 to 1000 CE: After Qasim's recall in 715, Muslim campaigns of slaughter and enslavement became somewhat subdued, but low-intensity campaigns continued nonetheless. During the reign of the only orthodox Umayyad Caliph Omar (717–20), his lieutenant Amru bin Muslim made several Jihad expeditions against Hindu territories and subdued them; these undoubtedly had yielded slaves. During Caliph Hasham bin Abdul Malik (r. 724–43), Sindh military chief Junaid bin Abdur Rahman engaged in a number of victorious campaigns. In his attack of Kiraj, he *'stormed the place, slaying, plundering, and making captives.'* In his incursions against Ujjain and Baharimad, he burnt down the suburbs and plunder great booty.[689] Booty invariably included captives.

After the orthodox Abbasid dynasty was founded in 750, Caliph al-Mansur (r. 755–74) sent Hasham bin Amru for waging holy war against Hindu territories. He *'subdued Kashmir and took many prisoners and slaves...'*[690] He attacked many places between Kandahar and Kashmir, and every victory must have yielded captives, which are not recorded.

Great Muslim historian Ibn Asir (Athir) records in *Kamil-ut Tawarikh* that during Caliph Al-Mahdi's reign, Abdul Malik led a large naval Jihad expedition against India in 775. They disembarked at Barada and in the sustained battle with the people of the neighborhood, the Muslim army prevailed. *'Some of the people were burned, the rest were slain and twenty Musalmans perished in testimony of their faith,'* records Asir.[691] The number of captives is not recorded.

During Caliph al-Mamun's reign (r. 813–33), Commander Afif bin Isa led an expedition against the revolting Hindus. After defeating and slaughtering them, the surviving 27,000 men, women and children were enslaved.[692] The next Caliph al-Mutasim's governor of Sindh, Amran bin Musa, attacked and defeated Multan and Kandabil, and *'carried away its inhabitants'* as captives.[693] In about 870, Yakub Lais attacked Ar-Rukhaj (Aracosia) and the enslaved inhabitants were forced to embrace Islam.[694]

By Ghaznivid invaders: Nearly three centuries after Qasim's exploits, Sultan Mahmud launched seventeen devastating incursions into Northern India (1000–27), involving mass slaughter, plunder, destruction of temples and enslavement in large numbers. In his attack of King Jaipal in 1001–02, records al-Utbi: *'God bestowed upon his friends such amount of booty as was beyond all bounds and all calculation, including five hundred thousand slaves, men and women.'* Among the captives were King Jaipal and his children and grandchildren, and nephews, the chief men of his tribe and his relatives.[695] He drove them away to Ghazni for selling.

In the attack of Ninduna (Punjab) in 1014, writes al-Utbi, *'slaves were so plentiful that they became very cheap; men of respectability in their native land were degraded by becoming slaves of common shop-keepers (in Ghazni).'* From the next year's assault in Thanesar (Haryana), the Muslim army *'brought 200,000 captives so that the capital appeared like an Indian city; every soldier of the army had several slaves and slave girls,'* testifies Ferishtah. From his expedition to India in 1019, he brought 53,000 captives. Of his seventeen expeditions to India, the campaign to Kashmir was the only failure. In each victorious campaign, he plundered booty, which normally included slaves, but their records have not been recorded systematically. Caliph's one-fifth share of the booty was kept aside, which, records *Tarikh-i-Alfi*, included 150,000 slaves.[696] This means that a minimum of 750,000 slaves were captured by Sultan Mahmud.

---

689. Ibid, p. 125–26
690. Ibid, p. 127
691. Ibid, Vol. II, p. 246
692. Ibid, p. 247–48
693. Ibid, Vol. I, p. 128
694. Ibid, Vol. II, p. 419
695. Ibid, p. 25–26
696. Lal (1994), p. 19–20

Mahmud (d. 1030) did the spade-work for founding an Islamic Sultanate in Punjab, where the Ghaznivid dynasty ruled until 1186. In 1033, his not-so-illustrious son, Sultan Masud I, launched '*an attack on the fort of Sursuti in Kashmir. The entire garrison was put to the sword, except the women and children, who were carried away as slaves.*'[697] In 1037, Sultan Masud, having fallen ill, made a vow '*to prosecute holy war against Hansi,*' if he recovered. Having recovered, he attacked and captured Hansi. According to Abul Fazl Baihaki, '*The Brahmans and other higher men were slain, and their women and children were carried away captives.*'[698]

The rather weak Ghaznivid Sultan Ibrahim attacked the districts of Punjab in 1079. Fierce battle lasted for weeks and both sides suffered great slaughter. At length, his army gained victory and captured much wealth and 100,000 slaves, whom he drove away to Ghazni, record *Tarikh-i-Alfi* and *Tabakat-I Akbari.*[699]

By Ghaurivid invaders: Sultan Muhammad Ghauri, an Afghan, launched the third wave of Islamic invasion of India in the late twelfth century establishing Muslim rule in Delhi (1206). In the attack of Benaras in 1194, '*The slaughter of the Hindus was immense; none were spared except women and children and the carnage of the men went on until the earth was weary,*' records Ibn Asir.[700] The "women and children" were normally spared for enslaving. His illustrious general Qutbuddin Aibak attacked Raja Bhim of Gujarat in 1195 capturing 20,000 slaves;[701] in his attack of Kalinjar in 1202, records Hasan Nizami, '*Fifty thousand men came under the collar of slavery, and the plain became black as pitch with Hindus.*'[702] In 1206, Muhammad Ghauri marched to exterminate the recalcitrant Khokhar rebels who had established their sway in regions of Multan. The slaughter of the rebels was so thorough that none survived to light a fire. '*Much spoils in slaves and weapons, beyond all enumerations, fell into the possession of the victors,*' adds Nizami.[703] In summarizing the feat of slave-taking of Sultan Ghauri and Aibak, says *Fakhr-i-Mudabbir*, '*even poor (Muslim) householders became owner of numerous slaves.*'[704] According to Ferishtah, '*three to four hundred thousand Khokhars were converted to Islam*' by Muhammad Ghauri.[705] These conversions came mostly through enslavement.

Having become the first sultan of India in 1206, Aibak conquered Hansi, Meerut, Delhi, Ranthambor and Kol. During his reign (1206–10), Aibak undertook many expeditions capturing much of the areas from Delhi to Gujarat, from Lakhnauti to Lahore. Every victory yielded slaves, but their number is not recorded. The fact that Aibak generally captured slaves in his wars can be gauged from Ibn Asir's assertion that he made '*war against the provinces of Hind... He killed many, and returned with prisoners and booty.*'[706]

Simultaneously, Bakhtiyar Khilji unleashed extensive conquest, involving massacre and enslavement, in Bengal and Bihar in Eastern India. The number of slaves captured by Bakhtiyar is not recorded either. About Bakhtiyar, Ibn Asir said, bold and enterprising, he made incursions into Munghir and

697. *History of Punjab: Ghanznivide Dynasty,*
http://www.punjabonline.com/servlet/library.history?Action=Page&Param=13

698. Elliot & Dawson, Vol. II, p. 135,139–40

699. Ibid, Vol. V, p. 559–60; Lal (1994), p. 23

700. Elliot & Dawson, Vol. II, p. 251

701. Ferishtah, Vol. I, p. 111

702. Elliot & Dawson, Vol. II, p. 232; also Lal (1994), p. 42

703 Elliot & Dawson, Vol. II, p. 234–35

704. Lal (1994), p. 44

705. Ibid, p. 43

706. Elliot & Dawson, Vol. II, p. 251

Bihar, brought away much plunder and obtained plenty of horses, arms and *men* (i.e., slaves).[707] In Bakhtiyar's attack of Lakhmansena of Bengal in 1205, records Ibn Asir, *'his whole treasure, and all his wives, maid servants, attendants, and women fell into the hands of the invader.'*[708]

After Aibak settled in Delhi, slaves were not transported overseas anymore like in earlier raids of Sultan Mahmud and Muhammad Ghauri, who used to come from Ghazni. Captives were, thereafter, engaged in various activities of royal courts, and by the generals, nobles and soldiers. The excess of slaves were sold in the markets of India for the first time in her history.

During Sultan Iltutmish to Balban (1210–1285): Next, Sultan Iltutmish (r. 1210–36) spent his early years in suppressing the Turkish opponents. He was also in fear of invasion by Genghis Khan. In 1226, he attacked Ranthambhor. Minhaj Siraj records that 'much plunder fell into the hands of his followers;'[709] the plunder obviously included slaves. In the 1234–35 attack of Ujjain, he made captives of the *'women and children of the recalcitrant,'* according to Shiraj and Ferishtah.[710]

After the death of Iltutmish, there was a brief lull in enslavement because of the weakened power of the sultans. In 1244, Sultan Nasiruddin Mahmud, commanded by Ulugh Khan Balban, attacked the Gukkar rebels of the Jud Mountain in Multan and carried away *'several thousand Gukkars of all ages and of each sex,'* records Ferishtah.[711] Ulugh Khan Balban attacked Karra in 1248; there, records Siraj, his *'taking of captives and his capture of the dependents of the great Ranas (Hindu princes) cannot be counted.'* In attacking the Rana *Dalaki wa Malaki,* *'He took prisoners the wives, sons, and dependents of that accursed one, and secured great booty.'*[712] In 1252, Balban attacked and defeated the great Rana, Jahir Deo, of Malwa; *'many captives fell into the hands of the victors,'* records Siraj.[713]

In the attack of Ranthambhor in 1253, Balban captured many slaves, while in the attack of Haryana in 1259, many women and children were enslaved. Balban led expeditions twice against Kampil, Patiali and Bhojpur enslaving large numbers of women and children each time. In Katehar, he captured the women and children after a general massacre of the men above eight years in age, notes Ferishtah. In 1260, Balban attacked Ranthambhor, Mewat and Siwalik—proclaiming that those who brought a live captive would receive two silver *tankahs* and one *tankah* for the head of a slain infidel. Soon three to four hundred living persons and heads of the slain were brought to his presence, records Ferishtah. While serving under Sultan Nasiruddin (d. 1266), Balban made many attacks against the infidels, but the number of the captives taken by him are not mentioned. However, a guess can be made from the fact that, slaves were so abundant that Sultan Nasiruddin had presented author Minhaj Siraj with forty of them for sending to his sister in Khurasan.[714]

Balban became the sultan in 1265 assuming the title of Ghiyasuddin Balban. As the commander of the previous sultan, Balban showed great military prowess, leading numerous expeditions against the infidels. After assuming power, his first job was, as noted already, to exterminate hundreds of thousands of recalcitrant Hindu rebels, the *Muwattis* etc. He ordered to *'destroy the villages of the marauders, to slay the men, **to make prisoners of the women and children**.'*[715]

---

707. Ibid, p. 306

708. Ibid, p. 308–09

709. Ibid, p. 325

710. Lal (1994), p. 44–45

711. Ferishtah, Vol. I, p. 130

712 Elliot & Dawson, Vol. II, p. 348; also Ferishtah, Vol. I, p. 131

713 Elliot & Dawson, Vol. II, p. 351

714. Lal (1994), p. 46–48

715. Elliot & Dawson, Vol. III, p. 105

During Khilji dynasty: Under the Khilji (1290–1320) and Tughlaq (1320–1413) dynasties, the hold of the Muslim rule in India had been firmly established with the expanded army and territory. The sultan's power was so overwhelming that '*no one dared to make an outcry,*' noted Afif. Apart from campaigns to suppress many Hindu rebellions, many expeditions against infidel-held territories were undertaken with an ever-increasing zeal to bring them under the Muslim control. Rich booty was plundered, which obviously contained slaves, but their recording is sketchy, probably because, it had become too common. However, a few available testimonies left by contemporary chroniclers give a general idea of the extent of enslavement. Jalaluddin Khilji (r. 1290–96), the founder of Khilji dynasty, undertook ruthless campaigns to suppress Hindu revolts and to extend the boundary of the sultanate. He led expeditions to Katehar, Ranthambhor, Jhain, Malwa, and Gwalior. In the campaigns to Ranthambhor and Jhain, he sacked temples, plundered, and took captives making "a hell of paradise", writes Amir Khasrau. From the Malwa campaign, large quantities of booty (which always included slaves) was brought to Delhi, adds Khasrau.[716]

Next, Sultan Alauddin Khilji (r. 1296–1316) beat all earlier sultans in the capture of slaves. He sent a large expedition to Gujarat in 1299 sacking all major cities and towns: Naharwala, Asaval, Vanmanthali, Surat, Cambay and Somnath. According to the records of Muslim chroniclers Isami and Barani, he acquired great plunders and a large number of captives of both sexes. In the sack and plunder of Somnath alone, testifies Wassaf, the Muslim army '*took captive a great number of handsome and elegant maidens, amounting to 20,000*', as well as '*the children of both sexes.*' Ranthambhor was attacked in 1301 and Chittor in 1303. In the Chittor invasion, 30,000 people were massacred; and as a standard practice, their women and children were enslaved although some of the Rajput women had committed *Jauhar*. Large numbers of slaves were captured in the expeditions to Malwa, Sevana and Jalor between 1305 and 1311. Sultan Alauddin also captured slaves in his expedition to Rajasthan. During his reign, capturing slaves became like a child's play as Amir Khasrau puts it, '*the Turks whenever they please, can seize, buy or sell any Hindu.*' So stupendous was his slave-taking that he had '*50,000 slave boys in his personal service*' and '*70,000 slaves worked on his buildings,*' record Afif and Barani, respectively. Barani testifies that '*fresh batches of captives were constantly arriving*' in the slave-markets of Delhi during Alauddin's reign.'[717]

During Tughlaq dynasty: In 1320, the Tughlaqs captured power. Muhammad Shah Tughlaq (r. 1325–51), the most learned amongst Muslim rulers of India, was the most powerful rulers of the Sultanate period (1206–1526). His notorious zeal for capturing slaves had even outstripped the feats of Alauddin Khilji. Shihabuddin Ahmad Abbas wrote of his capture of slaves that '*The Sultan never ceases to show the greatest zeal in making war upon the infidels... Everyday thousand of slaves are sold at a very low price, so great is the number of prisoners.*' During his notorious reign, he undertook numerous expeditions to put down revolts and to bring far-off regions of India under his sway, reaching deep into South India and Bengal. He also brutally put down sixteen major rebellions. Many of these expeditions brought great booty, which invariably included slaves in large numbers. Slaves were so abundant that the sultan had sent ten female slaves to traveler Ibn Battutah on his arrival in Delhi.[718] The sultan sent a diplomatic mission to the Chinese emperor, led by Battutah, with a caravan of gifts, which included '*a hundred white slaves, a hundred Hindu dancing- and singing-girls...*'[719] Sending slaves as gifts to the caliphs and rulers overseas was also a common practice during Sultan Iltutmish and Feroz Tughlaq (d. 1388). Ibn Battutah testifies that the sultan used to accumulate slaves round the year

---

716. Lal (1994), p. 48

717. Ibid, p. 49–51

718. Ibid, p. 51

719. Gibb, p. 214

and marry them off during the celebration of two major Islamic festivals, the *Eid*.[720] This was obviously aimed at swelling the Muslim population in India.

Next, Sultan Firoz Shah Tughlaq (r. 1351–88) was a kind-hearted toward the infidels, for he first allowed drafting some non-Muslims into his army, defying Muslim opposition. Even under his rule, enslaving the infidels went on with great vigor. He had acquired a mind-blowing 180,000 young slave boys in his court, testifies Afif.[721] He, like his predecessor, used to capture thousands of male and female slaves round the year and marry them off on the days of *Eid* celebration. According to Afif, '*slaves became too numerous*' under Firoz Tughlaq and '*the institution (of slavery) took root in every centre of the land.*' Soon afterwards, the sultanate broke into several independent kingdoms, but the enslavement of the infidels continued as usual in every "centre of the land", writes Afif.[722]

In Amir Timur's invasion: Amir Timur from Central Asia, waged Jihad against India (1398–99) to become a *ghazi* or a martyr, had accumulated over 100,000 captives when he reached Delhi. On the eve of his attack on Delhi, he killed them all. From his assault on Delhi onward to his return to his capital, he has left a tragic trail of barbaric slaughter, destruction, pillage and enslavement, which he recorded in his memoir, *Malfuzat-I-Timuri*.[723]

Of his assault on Delhi on 16 December 1398, records Timur, '*15,000 Turks were engaged in slaying, plundering and destroying... The spoil was so great that each man secured fifty to a hundred prisoners—men, women and children. There was no man who took less than twenty.*' If each soldier, on an average, had taken 60 captives, the total yield of slaves was about 1000,000 (1.0 million)[724].

On the way back to his capital in Central Asia, narrates Timur, he instructed his commanders '*to take every fort and town and village*' they came across, and '*to put all the infidels of the country to the sword... My brave fellows pursued and killed many of them, made their wives and children prisoners.*' After reaching Kutila, he attacked the infidels; '*After a slight resistance, the enemy took flight, but many of them fell under the swords of my soldiers. All the wives and children of the infidels were made prisoners.*'

Moving forward, upon arriving at the bank of the Ganges during the bathing festival, his soldiers '*slaughtered many of the infidels and pursued those who fled to the mountains.*' The spoil, adds Timur, '*which exceeds all computations... fell into the hands of my victorious soldiers.*' Spoils of course included slaves.

When he reached Siwalik, notes Timur, '*the infidel gabrs were dismayed at the slight and took flight. The Holy warriors pursued them, and made heaps of slain... Immense spoil beyond all compute*' was obtained; '*All the Hindu women and children in the valley were made prisoners.*'

On the other side of the river, Raja Ratan Sen, hearing of Timur's approach, had drawn his force at the fortress of Trisarta (Kangra). When attacked the fortress, records Timur, '*the Hindus broke and fled, and my victorious soldiers pursued*' them with only a few escaping; '*...they secured great plunders,*' exceeding all calculations and each with '*ten to twenty slaves.*' This means that the assault yielded 200,000 to 300,000 slaves.

---

720. Lal (1994), p. 51–52

721. Elliot & Dawson, III, p. 297

722. Ibid, p. 53

723. Elliot & Dawson, Vol. III, p. 436–71; Bostom, p. 648–50

724. By mistake, the number of prisoners captured by Timur was cited to be 10 times less in previous editions.

On the other side of the Siwalik Valley was the large and important town of Hindustan, called Nagarkot. In the attack, '*The Holy warriors... made heaps of corpses,*' and '*a vast booty,*' including '*prisoners... fell into the hands of the victors, who returned triumphant and loaded with spoil,*' concluded Timur.

On his way back from Delhi, Timur had made five major assaults on the Hindu fortresses, towns and villages, besides other smaller incursions and captured slaves in each. The rough number of captives—some 200,000 to 300,000—is available only for the assault in Kangra. If similar number of slaves were captured in the other assaults, he must have acquired 1.0 to 1.5 million slaves in the course of his return. Combined with the captives taken at Delhi, he had driven away some 2.0 to 2.5 milion slaves from India. At Delhi, he also had selected thousands of artisans and craftsmen, whom he brought to his capital.[725]

During the Sayyid and Lodi dynasties (1400–1525): In the period, subsequent to Timur's invasion, the numbers of slaves taken in wars are not properly recorded; only abstract references are found in various documents.[726] Following Timur's departure after devastating the power in Delhi, the Tughlaqs, followed by the Sayyids, while consolidating their authority, made many expeditions. Many of these campaign yielded slaves in large numbers. As recorded by Ferishtah, in the reign of Sultan Sayyid Mubarak (r. 1431–35), the Muslim army plundered Katehar and enslaved many of the Rahtore Rajputs (1422), enslaved many in Malwa in 1423, carried away the surrendered *Muwatti* rebels in Alwar in 1425 and the subjects of Raja of Hulkant (in Gwalior, in 1430) were carried away as prisoners and slaves.[727]

In 1430, Amir Shaikh Ali from Kabul attacked Sirhind and Lahore in Punjab. In Lahore, records Ferishtah, '*40,000 Hindus were computed to have been massacred, besides a great number carried away prisoners*'; in Toolumba (Multan), his army '*plundered the place, and put to death all the men able to bear arms... and carried the wives and children of the inhabitants into captivity.*'[728]

Following the Sayyids, the Lodi dynasty (1451–1526) re-established the authority of the sultanate and continued the practice of enslavement as usual. Sultan Bahlul, founder of the dynasty, '*turned a free-booter and with his gains from plunder built up a strong force.*' In his assault against Nimsar (in Hardoi district), he '*depopulated it by killing and enslaving its people.*' His successor Sikandar Lodi produced the same spectacle in Rewa and Gwalior regions.[729]

During Mughal rule (1526...): By defeating Sikandar Lodi in 1526, Jahiruddin Shah Babur, proud descendent of Amir Timur, established the Mughal rule in India. In his autobiographical memoir *Babur Nama*, he describes his campaigns against the Hindus as Jihad, punctuated with verse and references from the Quran. The records of capturing slaves during Babur's reign are not documented systematically. However, in his attack of the small Hindu principality of Bajaur in present-day Pakistan's North-West Frontier Province, records Babur: '*they were put to general massacre and their wives and children made captives. At a guess, more than 3,000 men went to their death... [I] ordered that a tower of heads should be set up on the rising ground.*'[730] Similarly, he made pillars with the heads of slain Hindus at Agra. In 1528, he attacked and defeated the enemy in Kanauj and '*their families and followers were made prisoners.*'[731] These examples

---

725. Lal (1994), p. 86

726. Ibid, p. 70–71

727. Freishtah, Vol. I, p. 299–303

728. Ibid, p. 303,306

729. Lal (1994), p. 86

730. Babur JS (1975) *Baburnama*, trs. AS Beveridge, Sange-Meel Publications, Lahore, p. 370–71

731. Ferishtah, Vol. II, p. 38–39

suggest that the enslavement of women and children was a general policy in Babur's Jihad campaigns. *Babur Nama* also mentions that there were two major trade-marts between Hindustan and Khurasan, namely at Kabul and Qandahar, where caravans came from India carrying slaves (*barda*) and other commodities to sell at great profits.

Following Babur's death (1530), a period of turmoil followed over the rivalry between his son Humayun and Sher Shah Suri, an Afghan. In 1562, Emperor Akbar the Great, Babur's grandson and an apostate of Islam, prohibited wholesale enslavement of women and children in wars.[732] In Akbar's reign notes Moreland, '*it became a fashion to raid a village or a group of villages without any obvious justification, and carry off the inhabitants as slaves*'; this prompted Akbar to enact a ban on enslavement.[733] However, the deeply engrained tradition hardly stopped. Despite the ban, Akbar's generals and provincial rulers went on their own to plunder and enslave non-Muslims. As noted already, Akbar's small-time general Abdulla Khan Uzbeg boasted of enslaving and selling 500,000 men and women. Even Akbar, disregarding his earlier decree, ordered to enslave the women of the slain Rajputs in Chittor (1568), who committed *jauhar*. Enslavement had continued across the provinces despite the ban. In ordinary time in Akbar's reign, notes Moreland, children were stolen or kidnapped as well as purchased; Bengal was notorious for this practice in the most repulsive form (i.e., slaves were castrated).[734] This forced Akbar to reissue the ban on enslavement in 1576. In his reign, witnessed della Valle, '*servant and slaves were so numerous and cheap that 'everybody, even of mean fortune, keeps a great family, and is splendidly attended.*''[735] These examples give a clear idea about the scale at which enslavement was taking place even in enlightened Akbar's reign.

Enslavement undoubtedly worsened during Akbar's successors Jahangir (1605–27) and Shah Jahan (1628–58), under whose reigns, orthodoxy and Islamization was gradually revived. Emperor Jahangir in his memoir testifies of children in Bengal being castrated by helpless parents for giving '*them to the governors as slaves in place of revenue.*' '*This practice has become common,*' he adds. Said Khan Chaghtai, a noble of Jahangir, had '*possessed 1,200 eunuch slaves alone,*' according to multiple testimonies.[736] Jahangir had sent some 200,000 Indian captives to Iran for sale in 1619–20 alone.[737]

Under next Emperor Shah Jahan, the condition of the Hindu peasants had become unbearable. European traveler Manrique witnessed in Mughal India that the tax-collectors were carrying away destitute peasants along with their children and wives '*to various markets and fairs*' for selling them to realize the tax. French physician and traveler Francois Bernier, who spend twelve years in India and was Emperor Aurangzeb's personal doctor, affirms the same. He wrote of unfortunate peasants, who were incapable of paying taxes, that their children '*were carried away as slave.*'[738] During Aurangzeb's reign (1658–1707), considered devastating to the Hindus, some 22,000 young boys were emasculated in 1659 alone in the city of Golkunda (Hyderabad).[739] They were to be given to Muslim rulers and governors, or sold in slave-markets.

Nadir Shah of Iran invaded India in 1738–39. After committing great massacre and devastation, he captured a large number of slaves and drove them away along with a huge plunder. Ahmad Shah Abdali from Afghanistan invaded India thrice in the mid-eighteenth century. In his victory in the *Third Battle of Panipat*

732. Nizami, p. 106

733. Moreland, p. 92

734. Ibid, p. 92–93

735. Ibid, p. 88–89

736. Lal (1994), p. 116–117

737. Levi (2002), p. 283–84

738. Lal (1994), p. 58-59

739. Lal (1994), p. 117

(1761), some 22,000 women and children of the slain Maratha soldiers were driven away as slaves.[740] As already cited, the last independent Muslim ruler, Tipu Sultan, had enslaved some 7,000 people in Travancore. They were driven away and forcibly converted to Islam.[741] Enslavement of the infidels in India went on as long as Muslims were ruling with authority. The consolidation of power by the British mercenaries in the nineteenth century eventually ended enslavement in India. Even during the Partition (1947), Muslims kidnapped tens of thousands of Hindu and Sikh women and married them to Muslims: a form of age-old enslavement (discussed already). In November 1947, as already noted, Muslim Pathan raiders carried away Hindu and Sikh girls from Kashmir and sold in the markets of Jhelum (in Pakistan).[742]

These are accounts of enslavement by Muslim invaders and rulers mainly in Northern India. Enslavement was going on in earnest in far-off provinces across India, including Gujarat, Malwa, Jaunpur, Khandesh, Bengal and the Deccan, which were either under the control of Delhi or were independent Muslim sultanates. The records of enslavement in those regions were not always recorded systematically.

ENSLAVEMENT BY MUSLIMS ELSEWHERE

Muslim invaders and rulers engaged in enslaving the vanquished infidels in large numbers in their raids and wars everywhere. Prophet Muhammad's inauguration of wholesale enslavement of non-Muslims for selling them or engaging in household work and concubinage was progressively expanded after his death as the Muslim power progressively increased through the reigns of the Rightly Guided Caliphs (632–60), the Umayyads (661–750) and the Abbasids (751–1250).

When Muslim General Amr, directed by Caliph Omar, conquered Tripoli in 643, he took away the women and children from both the Jews and Christians. Caliph Othman, records ninth-century historian Abu Khalif al-Bhuturi, imposed a treaty on the Nubia (Sudan) in 652, requiring its rulers to send an annual tribute of slaves—360 for the caliph and forty for the Egyptian governor,[743] which continued until 1276. Similar treaties were concluded during the Umayyad and Abbasid rules with the towns of Transoxiana, Sijistan, Armenia and Fezzan (modern Northwest Africa), who had to send a stipulated annual tribute of slaves of both sexes.[744] During the Umayyad rule, Musa bin Nusair, an illustrious Yemeni General, was made governor of North Africa (Ifrikiya, 698–712) to put down a renewed Berber rebellion and to spread the domain of Islam. Musa put down the revolts and enslaved 300,000 infidels. The Caliph's one-fifth share, numbering 60,000, was sold into slavery and the proceeds were deposited into the caliphal treasury. Musa engaged 30,000 of the captives into military service.[745]

In his four-year campaign in Spain (711–15), Musa had captured 30,000 virgins from the families of Gothic nobility alone.[746] This excludes the enslaved women from other backgrounds, and of course, the children. In the sack of Ephesus in 781, 7,000 Greeks were driven away as slaves. In the capture of Amorium in 838, slaves were so numerous that Caliph al-Mutasim ordered them to be auctioned in batches of five and

740. Ibid, p. 155

741. Hasan M (1971) *The History of Tipu Sultan*, Aakar Books, Delhi, p. 362–63

742. Talib, SGS (1991), *Muslim League Attack on Sikhs and Hindus in the Punjab 1947*, Voice of India, New Delhi, p. 201

743. Vantini G (1981) *Christianity in the Sudan*, EMI, Bologna, p. 65–67

744. Ibn Warraq, p. 231

745. *Umayyad Conquest of North Africa*, Wikipedia, http://en.wikipedia.org/wiki/Umayyad_conquest_of_North_Africa

746. Lal (1999), p103; Hitti (1961), p. 229-30

ten. In the assault of Thessalonia in 903, 22,000 Christians were divided among the Arab chieftains or sold into slavery. In Sultan Alp Arsalan's devastation of Georgia and Armenia in 1064, there was immense slaughter and all the survivors were enslaved. Almohad Caliph Yaqub al-Mansur of Spain raided Lisbon in 1189, enslaving some 3,000 women and children. His governor of Cordoba attacked Silves in 1191, making 3,000 Christians captive.[747]

Having captured Jerusalem from the Crusaders in 1187, Sultan Saladin enslaved the Christian population and sold them. In the capture of Antioch in 1268, Mamluk Sultan al-Zahir Baybars (r. 1260–77) enslaved 100,000 people after putting 16,000 defenders of the garrison to the sword. '*The salve market became so gutted that a boy would fetch only twelve dirhams and a girl five,*' notes Hitti.[748]

It is already noted that, after Muslims assumed power in Southeast Asia, they had promoted slavery to such an extent that the Portuguese—arriving after a century—found that almost all the people belonged to slave-masters and the Arabs were prominent among the masters. It is also noted that Muslim rulers in Southeast Asia often enslaved the entire population after capturing a territory and carry them away. In Java, Muslim rulers reduced the entire hill people, a substantial part of the population, to slavery through raids and purchase. Sultan Iskandar Muda (r. 1607–36) of Aceh brought thousands of slaves to his capital as a result of the conquests in Malaya. Java was the largest exporter of slaves in around 1500; these slaves were captured in '*decisive wars of Islamization*'.[749] The Sulu Sultanate, despite being under constant threat of being overtaken by the Spanish, brought as many as 2.3 million Filipinos as slaves from the Spanish-controlled Philippines through Moro Jihad raids between 1665 and 1870. Late in the 1860s to 1880s, slaves constituted 6 percent to two-thirds of the population in the Muslim-ruled regions of the Malay Peninsula and Indonesian Archipelago.

Late in the eighteenth century, Moroccan Sultan Moulay Ismail (r. 1672–1727) '*had an army of black slaves, said to number 250,000.*'[750] In 1721, Moulay Ismail ordered an expedition against a rebel territory in the Atlas Mountains, where the rebels had resolved against sending tributes to the sultan. Upon defeating the rebels, '*All the men were put to the sword, while the women and children... were carried back*' to the capital. Soon afterwards, he ordered another expedition of 40,000-strong force under the command of his son Moulay as-Sharif against the rebel town of Guzlan that had withdrawn tribute. Upon seeing no hope of winning the battle, the rebels surrendered and sued for mercy. But Moulay as-Sharif '*ordered every man to be killed and decapitated.*'[751] Their women and children were obviously carried away as slaves.

Guinea (Africa, currently 85 percept Muslim) came under the Muslim rule in the eighteenth century. During the latter part of this century, the '*Upper Guinea Coast had "slave town" with as many as 1,000 inhabitants*' under a chief. Traveling in Islamic Sierra Leone in 1823, Major Laing witnessed "slave town" in Falaba, the capital of Salima Susu.[752] These slaves worked in agricultural projects of the chief. The East African Empire of famed Sultan Sayyid Sa'id with its capital in Zanzibar (1806–56) '*was founded upon

---

747. Brodman JW (1986) *Ransoming Captives in Crusader Spain: The Order of Merced on the Christian-Islamic Frontier*, University of Pennsylvania Press, Philadelphia, p. 2-3

748. Hitti (1961), p. 316

749. Reid (1988), p. 133

750. Lewis B (1994) *Race and Slavery in the Middle East*, Oxford University Press, Chapter 8, http://www.fordham.edu/halsall/med/lewis1.html

751. Milton, p. 143,169–71

752. Rodney W (1972) In MA Klein & GW Johnson eds., *Perspectives on the African Past*, Little Brown Company, Boston, p. 158

slavery... Slaves were shipped to the markets of Southern Arabia and Persia as domestic retainers and concubines.'[753]

Ronald Segal, who is sympathetic to Islam,[754] informs that African children of the age-group of ten to eleven years were captured in large numbers for military training to serve in the Muslim army. From Persia to Egypt to Morocco, slave armies consisting of 50,000 to 250,000 soldiers became commonplace.[755] Similar to the rearing of the Ottoman Janissary soldiers (discussed below), Sultan Moulay Ismail used to pick up ten-year-olds from the black slave-breeding farms and nurseries, castrate them and train them into loyal and fierce fighters, called *bukhari*, because, they pledged allegiance to the sultan swearing by *Sahih Bukhari*. The best of these *bukharis* served as the sultan's personal and palace guards; the rest served in maintaining orders in the provinces. He had 25,000 *bukharis* guarding his capital at Meknes, while 75,000 were stationed in the garrison town of Mahalla.[756]

According to estimates of Paul Lovejoy (*Transformations in Slavery*, 1983), about two million slaves were transported from Africa and the Red Sea coast to the Islamic world in the nineteenth century alone, with at least eight million (estimated mortality rate 80–90 percent) likely perished in process. In the eighteenth century, estimated 1,300,000 black Africans were enslaved. Lovejoy estimates that a total of some 11,512,000 slaves were dispatched from Africa to the Islamic world by the nineteenth century, while the estimate of Raymond Mauvy (cited in *The African Slave Trade from the Fifteenth to the Nineteenth Century*, UNESCO, 1979) puts the total number at fourteen million, which also include some 300,000 enslaved in the first half of twentieth century.[757] Murray Gordon's *Slavery in the Arab World* put the total number of black slaves harvested by Muslim slave-raiders at eleven million—roughly equal to the number taken by European traders to their colonies of the New World. At the end of the eighteenth century, caravans from Darfur used to transport 18,000–20,000 slaves in a single trip to Cairo. Even after Europe banned slavery in 1815 and pressured Muslim governments to stop the practice, '*In 1830, the Sultan of Zanzibar claimed dues on 37,000 slaves a year; in 1872, 10,000 to 20,000 slaves a year left Suakin (Africa) for Arabia.*'[758]

THE OTTOMAN *DEWSHIRME*

One severely condemned practice of Islamic slavery is the institution of *Dewshirme*, introduced by Ottoman Sultan Orkhan in 1330. This scheme consisted of collecting a part of the boys of the age-group of seven to twenty years from Christian and other non-Muslim families of the Ottoman Empire. About the introduction of this policy, Bernard Lewis quotes sixteenth-century Ottoman historian Sadeddin (aka Hoca Efendi) as thus:

---

753. Gann L (1972) In Ibid, p. 182

754. Segal emphasizes that anti-Semitism is in complete conflict with the amicable relationship Prophet Muhammad had established with Judaism and Christianity. He asserts that there is no historical conflict between Jews and Muslims, although some conflict arose only after the crusades. Such assertionsl go directly against Prophet's exterminating or exiling the Jews of Medina and Khaybar and his final instruction, while in death-bed, to cleanse Arabia of the Jews and Christians. He also urged his followers to kill the Jews to the last one [Sahih Muslim, 41:6985]

755. Segal R (2002) *Islam's Black Slaves*, Farrar, Straus and Giroux, New York, p. 55

756. Milton, p. 147–150

757. Segal, p. 56–57

758. Braudel, p. 131

'The renowned king... entering into consultation with his ministers of State, the result hereof was, that for the time to come, there should be choice made, of valiant and industrious youths, out of the children of the unbelievers, fit for the service, whom they should likewise innoblize, by the faith of Islam; which being a means to make them rich and religious, might be also a way to subdue the strongholds of the unbelievers.'[759]

Under the scheme, non-Muslim children, mainly Christian, were "culled" from Greece, Serbia, Bulgaria, Georgia, Macedonia, Bosnia and Herzegovina, Armenia and Albania that had come under the Ottoman rule. On a fixed date, non-Muslim fathers (mostly Christian) were to bring their children to a designated public square. The Muslim recruiting agents used to choose the healthy, strong and handsome ones of them. After Sultan Mehmet II conquered Constantinople in 1453, *Dewshirme* received a boost as notes Stephen O'Shea: '*...following the conquest, Fatih (the Conqueror) expanded the heartless devshirme or 'gathering' system, whereby young Christians were abducted and moved to the capital... Once every few years roving Ottoman talent scouts, accompanied by soldiers, descended on the villages... and culled the most promising peasant boys from their playmates and siblings.*'[760] The number of children collected as part of *Dewshirme* varies: '*Some scholars place it as high as 12,000 a year, others at 8,000...*'[761]

These lots of the best of Christian, Jewish and Gypsy children were circumcised and converted to Islam, and were indoctrinated with the ideology of Jihad from this impressionable early age. They were meticulously trained solely for Jihadi warfare and served in a special unit of the Ottoman army, the Janissary Regiment. Barred from marriage and confined to their barracks, the Janissary soldiers single-mindedly focused on becoming deadly soldiers for waging Jihad against the infidels, their coreligionists of the yesteryear.

The policy proved a boon for the Ottomans. Muslim rulers had remained frustrated in their repeated failures to capture Constantinople—the greatest centre of Christianity, since the time of Caliph Mu'awiyah (d. 680). In their many early attempts to capture Constantinople, they often suffered disastrous reverses. Finally, the Janissaries launched a devastating assault on Constantinople in 1453 and overran it, winning the greatest prize for Islam. The reigning Ottoman Sultan, Mehmet II, allowed the Janissaries to pillage the city and slaughter their erstwhile coreligionists, mainly Christians, for three days. Those who survived were enslaved. Later on, soldiers were recruited into the Janissary Regiment indiscriminately, including Muslims and many Sufis alongside those collected as part of *Dewshirme*. Discipline and resolve gradually declined in the Regiment, which, incidentally, also marked the decline of Ottoman power.

The institution of *Dewshirme* obviates the fact as to how the Islamic world expanded by exploiting the muscles of the infidels for conquering infidel territories further. Following the Ottoman institution of *Dewshirme*, Sultan Firoz Tughlaq in India (r. 1351–88) instituted the recruitment of Hindu children in similar fashion. He commanded his provincial officers and generals to capture slaves and pick out the young and best ones for sending to the services of his court. In this fashion, he accumulated 180,000 young boys as slaves.[762]

Criticism of Dewshirme: The Ottoman scheme of *Dewshirme*, abolished in 1656, has been severely criticized because of the way slaves were culled. However, the orthodox Ottomans, who were codifying their laws in accordance with the Sunni Sharia law, had their justification for the *Dewshirme* in the Quran and Islamic laws. The Quran 8:42 says, '*And know that whatever thing you gain (spoils of war), a fifth of it is for Allah and for the Messenger...*'

---

759. Lewis (2000), p. 109

760. O'Shea, p. 279

761. Ibn Warraq, p. 231

762. Lal (1994), p. 57–58

The one-fifth of the plunder obtained from the infidels in wars, allotted to Allah and his messenger, initially went to Prophet Muhammad, the head and treasury of the nascent Islamic state. After his death, this share was acquired by the caliphal treasury. A minimum one-fifth of all produce from *Dhimmi* subjects was collected as *kharaj* under a taxation policy promulgated by Caliph Omar, although this share was often raised higher under special circumstances or by whimsical Muslim rulers. Since, newly born children of the infidels were also a kind of produce of the state, the institution of *Dewshirme* became justified in Islamic holy laws. The Prophet himself had set an example of acquiring Christian children when he forbade the tribe of Taghlib not to baptize their children. Later on, Caliph Omar ordered another Taghlib tribe '*not to mark their children (with cross on their arm or wrist) and not to force their religion on them (i.e., not to baptize them).*'[763] As a result, those children entered the house of Islam. The only difference is that the Prophet and Caliph Omar had acquired all the children of the Taghlib tribes, while the Ottomans acquired only a part of them through *Dewshirme*.

With such Quranic sanction and prophetic example, the Rightly Guided Caliph Othman had enacted a *Dewshirme*-like scheme by forcing the Nubian Christians to send a yearly tribute of slaves to Cairo (652–1276). Similar agreements were enacted by the Umayyad and Abbasid caliphs as already cited. The *Dewshirme* policy was, therefore, not an Ottoman invention. Moreover, this policy was obviously much more humane than Prophet Muhammad's protocol of capturing slaves as applied to the Jews of Banu Qurayza and Khaybar etc., whereby he slew all the grown-up men and enslaved the women and children: a divine protocol approved by Allah [Quran 33:26–27]. During the centuries of Islamic conquest and rule, Prophet Muhammad's protocol of enslavement, much more cruel and barbaric than the *Dewshirme*, was commonly applied.

STATUS OF SLAVES

According to Ibn Warraq:

> Under Islam, slaves have no legal rights whatsoever, they are considered mere "things"—the property of their master, who may dispose them in any way he chooses—sale, gifts etc. Slaves cannot be guardians or testamentary executors, and what they earned belongs to their owner. A slave cannot give evidence in a court of law. Even conversion to Islam by a non-Muslim slave does not mean that he is automatically liberated. There is no obligation on the part of the owner to free him (and her).[764]

It will be seen below that Sharia law lists slaves amongst common properties and commodities, and stipulates rules and guidelines for their sale as applies to an article of trade. After buying a slave, if the master finds any defect in him, he may beat and torture him without leaving visible wounds or scars. According to *Fatwa-i-Alamgiri*, the master may return the slave to the seller with full compensation as long as the beating and torture cause no permanent injuries. The *Hedayah*, a twelfth-century compendium of Hanafi laws, informs us that '*amputation of a slave for theft was a common practice recognized by the law.*' Although Islam recommends good treatment of slaves, it is considered a natural death if a master kills his slave.[765]

In their victorious assaults on the infidels, the Muslim holy warriors often used to slaughter all male captives of weapon-bearing age (who could pose security threats by regrouping later) and enslaved the

---

763. Al-Biladhuri AY (1865) *Kitab Futuh al-Buldan*, Ed. MJ De Geoje, Leiden, p. 181

764. Warraq, p. 203

765. Lal (1994), p. 148

women and children, who normally had to embrace Islam. Concerning slaying of captives, the *Hedayah* says, '*The Imam (ruler), with respect to captives, has it in his choice to slay them, because the Prophet put captives to death, and also because, slaying them terminates their wickedness.*' The non-threatening women and children were generally enslaved, says the *Hedayah*, '*because by enslaving them (for conversion to Islam), the wickedness is remedied; and at the same time, Muslims reap an advantage (by exploiting their labor and growing in number)...*'[766] Famous Islamic thinker Ibn Khaldun (d. 1406), eulogized even by many Western scholars,[767] describes the profession of slavery with religious pride: '*...[captives] were brought from the House of War to the House of Islam under the rule of slavery, which hides in itself a divine providence; cured by slavery, they entered the Muslim religion with the firm resolve of true believers...*'[768] In Bakhtiyar Khilji's sack of Kol in 1194, the "wise and cute" ones among the besieged, as already noted, were converted to Islam, but those who stood by their religion were slaughtered. Here "wise and cute" ones meant those who were quick to accept Islam to avoid the sword and become slaves. The *Hedayah* stipulates that even if a captive becomes Muslim, '*he (the Imam) may lawfully make them slaves, because the reason for making slaves (i.e., being infidel) had been in existence pervious to their embracing the faith. It is otherwise where infidels become Muslims before their capture...*'[769]

SUFFERING OF SLAVES

Undoubtedly, reducing human beings into something like deaf and dumb domestic animals causes great psychological and mental pains, plus the loss of dignity, honor and self-respect, to victims. Moreover, Muslim captors generally subjected the captives to ridicule and degradation by parading them in public squares. Those of noble birth and dignity were normally singled out for subjecting to heightened indignity and ridicule. For example, Sultan Mahmud brought enslaved Hindu King Jaipal of Kabul to Ghazni and subjected him to extreme humiliation. In a slave-market, where he was auctioned like an ordinary slave, he '*was paraded about so that his sons and chieftains might see him in that condition of shame, bonds and disgrace... inflicting upon him the public indignity of 'commingling him in one common servitude.*''[770] Choosing death rather than living with such extreme humiliation, Jaipal committed suicide by jumping into fire.

The fate of slaves was the same or worse everywhere even during the late period. Late in the reign of Sultan Moulay Ismail of Moroccan (d. 1727), the white captives, caught in the sea, were put in chains upon their capture and ceremoniously marched through the town on their arrival at the coast or the capital. Large numbers of roughish people used to assemble to curse and ridicule them and to subject them to all kinds of degrading, hostile treatments. According to English captive George Elliot caught on a ship, when brought to the shore, he and his crewmates were surrounded by "*several hundred idle, rascally people and roughish boys*" who made barbarous shouts at them and they were "*forced like a drove of sheep through several streets.*"[771]

---

766. Hughes TP (1998) *Dictionary of Islam*, Adam Publishers and Distributors, New Delhi, p. 597

767. British historian Toynbee termed his *Muqaddimah* as "undoubtedly the greatest work of its kind that has ever been created by any mind in time or place. Bernard Lewis in his *The Arabs in History* called him "the greatest historian of the Arabs and perhaps the greatest historical thinker of the Middle Ages."

768. Lal (1994), p. 41

769. Hughes, p. 597

770. Lal (1994), p. 22

771. Milton, p. 65–66

The greatest pain and sufferings that slaves endured were the physical ones: hunger, thirst and disease. Physical pain and sufferings started immediately after the capture and continued until they arrived at the destination. The destinations were often situated thousands of miles away in foreign lands, where they were herded like common animals through difficult terrains. The captives used to be kept in chains until sold to their ultimate masters. Sometimes, a slave changed handed up to twenty times.

An example of how the journey began for slaves can be found in the description of King Jaipal's enslavement by Sultan Mahmud. According to al-Utbi, '*his (Jaipal's) children and grand children, his nephews and the chief men of his tribe, and his relatives, were taken prisoners, and being strongly bounded with ropes, were carried before the Sultan like common evil-doers... Some had their arms forcibly tied behind their backs, some were seized by the neck, some were driven by blows on their neck.*'[772]

It should be understood that Sultan Mahmud sometimes spent months on his campaigns in India capturing slaves in tens to hundreds of thousands along the way. These captives, tied together in an uncomfortable and agonizing condition, were then driven away to his capital in Ghazni, hundreds to thousands of miles away. The majority of these slaves used to be feeble women and children, who had to travel bare-footed under such uncomfortable conditions through rugged terrain and jungles, sometimes for months. When Timur embarked on his expedition to India, it lasted four–five months (Sept. 1398 to Jan. 1399). Along the way, he had accumulated 100,000 slaves before reaching Delhi; they were intended to be driven back to his capital Samarkhand in Central Asia. On his way back from Delhi, he captured another 200,000 or more slaves and drove them to Samarkhand, thousands of miles away.

These examples clearly point to the enormous physical strain, pain and sufferings endured by captives. Those who failed to keep up the pace, because of physical weakness and fatigue, received beating of the worst kind in order to keep them walking. There was little guarantee that such large numbers of captives got enough food and water along the way. Those who fell ill certainly did not receive required medical treatment. If they failed to carry on, they were abandoned half-alive to die on their own in the wilderness in agonizing pain or to be devoured by wild animals.

The suffering of captives has been vividly recounted in an eyewitness account of Ulugh Khan Balban's attack of King Kanhardeva of Jalor (Rajasthan), documented by Prabandha, a fifteenth-century Indian author. Referring to the large number of women and children taken slaves, tied and huddled together, the author wrote:

> "During the day, they bore the heat of the scorching sun, without shade or shelter as they were (in sandy Rajasthan deserts) and shivering cold during the night under the open sky. Children, torn away from their mother's breasts and homes, were crying. Each one of the captives seems as miserable as the other. Already writhing in agony due to thirst, the pangs of hunger... added to their distress. Some of the captives were sick, some unable to sit up. Some had no shoes to put on and no clothes to wear..."

He added:

> "Some had iron shackles on their feet. Separated from each other, they were huddled together and tied with straps of hide. Children were separated from their parents, wives from their husbands, thrown apart by this cruel raid. Young and old were seen writhing in agony, as loud wailings arose from that part of the camp where they were all huddled up... Weeping and wailing, they were hoping that some miracle might save them even now."[773]

---

772. Lal (1994), p. 22
773. Ibid, p. 54–55

This is only an account of the early few days of sufferings. It will not be difficult to guess how terribly the captives suffered when they had to travel thousands of miles over months to reach foreign capitals: those of Sultan Mahmud, Muhammad Ghauri and Amir Timur. Similar was the case with the black slaves of Africa, who had to travel long distance in such agonizing condition to reach the markets in the Middle East and even India. The terrible sufferings that European captives, caught in the sea by Barbary pirates, endured will give a general idea of their horrifying treatments and sufferings. When Sultan Moulay Ismail captured the fortified town of Taroudant, a French outpost, in 1687 and put the inhabitants to the sword, 120 French citizens found there were enslaved, a treasured gift for the sultan. Upon their capture, they were poked and prodded and declared overfed and denied food for a week. When they started crying for food, the sultan ordered them on a long march to his capital at Meknes. One of the slaves, Jean Ladire, later recounted the dreadful 300-mile journey to French padre, Dominique Busnot. Chained and shackled as they were herded along, they suffered from debilitating sickness and fatigue; several of them dropped dead. The heads of the dead were cut off and the survivors had to carry those heads, because their guards feared that the dreaded sultan will accuse them of having sold the missing captives or let them escape.[774]

Upon their capture, slaves were accommodated in miserable conditions in infamous underground dungeons, called *matamores* in Africa. Each *matamore* accommodated fifteen to twenty slaves; into these, the only light and ventilation came through a small iron-grate in the roof. In winter, rain poured through the grate flooding the floor. On weekly market-days, they were put on auction. The captives had to climb through this grate with the help of a suspended rope. They often had to spend weeks in these dungeons. Captive Germain Mouette wrote of the horrifying living conditions in *matamores* that '*the water and sewage frequently bubbled up from the mud floor in the wet winter months.*' There used to be knee-deep water on the floor for six month of the year, making sleeping difficult. For sleeping, they used to make some sort of hammocks or beds of ropes hanged by nails, one above another, the lowest ones almost touching the water. Often times, the uppermost hammock would come down crashing bringing all others below down into the water; they would spend the rest of the night standing in the chilly water.

The dungeons used to be so small and crammed that they were forced to lie in a circle with feet meeting in the middle. "*There is no more space left than to hold an earthen vessel to ease themselves in,*" wrote Mouette. During humid summer days, the *matamores*, with so many people crammed inside, became "*filthy, stinking and full of vermin*" and "*the place becomes intolerable when all the slaves are in and it grows warm,*" continued Mouette, adding that death was a blessed relief for the inmates.[775] This was a general living condition of slaves in North Africa over the ages. About a century earlier, British captive Robert Adams, captured in the 1620s, was able to relay a letter to his parent in England, narrating the living condition in the slave-pen of Sultan Moulay Zidan (1603–27); it was "*a dungeon underground, where some 150 to 200 of us lay altogether, having no comfort of the light, but a little hole.*" His hair and rugged clothes, added Adams, "*were full of vermin and not being allowed time to pick myself... I am almost eaten up by them.*"[776]

The captives, shut up in over-crowed *matamores*, received very little food, often "*nothing but bread and water.*" On the auction day, they were driven like wild beasts, whipped and put through their paces, to the market. At the auction bazaar, they were jostled through the crowd from one dealer to another. They were made to jump and skip to demonstrate their strength and agility, and fingers were poked into their ears and mouths causing a humiliating spectacle to the wretched captives,[777] who were honorable free men a few days earlier.

---

774. Milton, p. 34

775. Ibid, p. 66–67

776. Ibid, p. 20

777. Ibid, p. 68–69

The suffering of slaves was not over after their arrival at their master's abode. Thomas Pellow, a twelve-year-old British captive, caught onboard a ship, was bought by Sultan Moulay Ismail and ended up in the imperial palace. When Pellow and his comrades, trekking 120 miles through the desert, reached the capital, they were greeted by jeering and hostile Muslim crowds assembled outside the palace to mock and insult the hated Christians. The unruly crowd shouted, mocked and tried to attack them as they were led through to the palace. Despite guarding by the sultan's soldiers, many in the crowd were able to punch and lash them and pull their hair.[778]

In the imperial palace, Pellow initially worked, alongside hundreds of European slaves, in the sultan's huge armory, toiling for fifteen hours daily to repair and keep the arms in immaculate condition. He was soon given to his son, Prince Moulay es-Sfa. The prince had extreme contempt for Christian slaves and subjected Pellow to beating and harrowing torment by making him perform the useless task of running "*from morning to night after his horse's heels,*" wrote Pellow. Later on, the prince, as was his custom, pressed Pellow to convert to Islam, saying: "*if I would, I should have a very fine horse to ride on and I should live like one of his esteemed friends.*" When Pellow firmly refused to convert and requested the prince not to press for his conversion, an enraged es-Sfa said, "*then prepare yourself for such torture as shall be inflicted on you, and the nature of your obstinacy deserves.*" Thereupon, es-Sfa locked Pellow in a room for several months and subjected him to terrible torture, "*every day severely bastinading me,*" wrote Pellow.[779]

Such was a general punishment for European slaves. The captives were suspended with ropes upside down and bastinaded, normally on the soles of their feet. On one occasion, according to Father Busnot, Sultan Moulay Ismail ordered two slaves to be given 500 bastinadoes, which dislocated the hip of one of them. The dislocated hip was put in place by another round of bastinadoes at a later date.[780]

Es-Sfa personally beat Pellow while uttering "*Shehed, shehed! Cunmoora, Cunmoora! In English, Turn Moor (Muslim)! Turn Moor,*" wrote Pellow. Daily beating had become unbearable for him as the intensity of beating increased by the day. He was denied food for days and when food was offered, it was only bread and water. After months of sufferance, wrote Pellow: "*My tortures were now exceedingly increased..., burning my flesh off my bones by fire, which the tyrant did, by frequent repetitions, after a most cruel manner.*" Tortures and pain of half-starved young Pellow reaching beyond endurance, he finally gave in one day as es-Sfa came in for another round of beating, "*calling upon God to forgive me, who knows that I never gave up the consent of the heart,*" added Pellow.[781] Decades earlier, John Harrison, who had made eight diplomatic voyages to Morocco (1610–32), wrote: "*He (sultan) did cause some English boys perforce turn Moores.*"[782]

Torturing the European slaves for converting to Islam was not limited to the male captives alone; it equally applied to the female ones. The Barbary corsairs once plundered a British ship headed for Barbados; they took the crew captive and brought to Moulay Ismail's palace. Among the captives were four women, one of them virgin. This delighted the sultan, who tempted her to give up her Christian faith "*with promises of great rewards if she would turn Moor and lie with him,*" noted British captive, Francis Brooks. Her refusal enraged the sultan, who "*caused her to be stript and whipt [sic] by his eunuchs with small cords, so long till she lay for dead.*" He then instructed to take her away and feed her nothing but rotten bread. Eventually, the poor girl had no option but to "*resign her body to him, though her heart was otherwise inclined.*" The sultan

---

778. Ibid, p. 71–72

779. Ibid, p. 79–80

780. Ibid, p. 81

781. Ibid, p. 82

782. Ibid, p. 21

"had her washed and clothed... and lay with her." Once his desire was sated, *"he inhumanly, in great haste, forced her away out of his presence,"* added Brooks.[783]

On another occasion, Anthony Hatfeild, a British consul to Morocco, narrated the fate of an Irish woman, taken captive aboard a ship in 1717. She was brutally tortured for refusing to convert. Failing to endure the torture, she gave in and became a Muslim and entered the sultan's seraglio.[784] In 1723, father Jean de la Faye and his brother went to Morocco hoping to free the French captives from Moulay Ismail's palace. He narrated the story of a female captive, who—upon her refusal to convert to Islam—was tortured so barbarically that she died of her injuries. *"The blacks (guards) burnt her breasts with candles; and with the utmost cruelty they had thrown melted lead in those areas of her body which, out of decency, cannot be named,"* wrote father Jean.[785]

Let us return to Pellow's conversion to Islam. A ceremonial peasantry was thrown for his circumcision formally confirming his conversion to Islam. Whilst recovering from the painful wounds of circumcision, es-Sfa continued beating Pellow because of his refusal to wear Muslim garbs. Pellow finally gave in and donned the Muslim dress. Es-Sfa now continued punishing Pellow for his obstinate persistence to remain a Christian. The news of Pellow conversion reached the pious sultan; delighted, he ordered es-Sfa to release Pellow from his custody and send him to a madrasa for learning Arabic. The prince ignored the sultan's instruction and continued torturing Pellow. This defiance infuriated the sultan, who summoned es-Sfa to his presence and at the sultan's beaconing, his bodyguards dispatched es-Sfa instantly—a treatment, neither first nor the last, meted out to his offspring.[786]

The sultan was, however, no kind guardian of his captives. The slaves of the imperial palace lived a horrid life. They were accommodated in a military prison-like compound surrounded by high ramparts. Although the compound was large, the large number of inmates made living very uncomfortable. It was the most barbarous place in the world, said British captive John Willdon of the living condition and treatment of the slaves in the imperial palace. Willdon and his slave-mates were *"forced to draw carts of lead with ropes about our shoulders, all one as horses,"* he wrote. They were beaten and whipped until their skin was raw, and made them to carry *"great bars of iron upon our shoulders, as long as we could well get up, and up to our knees in dart, and as slippery that we could hardly go without the load,"* added Willdon.[787]

British ship Captain John Stocker, captured in the sea and brought to the sultan's palace, left an account of the horrible diet served to slaves. They were given *"nothing but one small cake and water for 24 hours after hard work"* and *"I am in a most deplorable condition,"* he wrote to a friend in England. Of the living condition in the slave-pen, he wrote, *"[I] live upon the bare ground, and [have] nothing to cover me, and [am] as lousy (louse-infested) as possible."* Thomas Pellow's crewmates in the slave-pen were given an old straw mat and they slept bare on the cold ground. The compound was infested with fleas and cockroaches. In midsummer days, the slave-pen used to get oppressively hot, humid and airless. In the open slave-barrack, *"they are exposed to the scorching heat of the sun in summer, and the violence of frost, snow, excessive rain and stormy winds in winter,"* wrote Simon Ockley.[788]

The daily food ration was fourteen ounces of black bread and an ounce of oil, badly inadequate for the overworked slaves. The bread was made from stinking barley dough, which sometimes gave *"such a nauseous smell that a man could not endure it at his nose,"* wrote captive John Whitehead. Moreover, when

---

783. Ibid, p. 121
784. Ibid, p. 173
785. Ibid, p. 219
786. Ibid, p. 83–84
787. Ibid, p. 91–92
788. Ibid, p. 92,94

the stock of barley ran low, they were given nothing at all. Willdon wrote, *"we have not had a bit of bread allowed us for eight days..."*[789]

More terrifying was the unbearable load of hard work and torture, which the slaves endured at the hands of the black guards appointed to oversee them. These slave-drivers drove them at daybreak to respective works, where they continued toiling until it got dark in the evening. They played the master over their charge of captives and used to take sadistic delight at torturing and beating the poor slaves and making their life as miserable as possible. They would often torture or torment the white slaves to amuse themselves by making the exhausted souls walk at night or do filthy works. They would punish them for the most negligible lapses in work or other mistakes, by denying them food or beating them with a heavy cudgel that they always carried while on duty. In beating, they chose those parts of the body, where it would hurt most, wrote Pellow. If a slave was beaten so hard that he could not work, the slave-drivers enabled him for work by *"redoubling the stripes, so that the new ones made him forget the old,"* wrote Mouette.[790]

Sickness of the slaves was no excuse for missing work. They were not allowed to rest *"till they (black guards) see they are not able to wag hand or foot...,"* wrote Mouette. As for treatment of sick slaves, *"If the slaves complained of any pains in their body..., they have iron rods, with buttons of the same metal at the end, as big as walnuts, which they made red hot and burn the wretched patient in several parts,"* added Mouette. The sultan had no mercy for those, who fell ill. Instead, he used to beat them for not working hard enough. When the building program was once delayed because of illness of a large number of slaves, the slave-guards, upon the sultan's order, dragged the sick slaves out of the infirmary to the sultan's presence. Seeing that the sick slaves could not stand on their feet, the infuriated sultan, *"instantly killed seven of them, making their resting place a slaughter house,"* wrote Brooks.[791]

On his daily visit to the construction sites, Sultan Moulay Ismail was merciless with those, who were slack in work or if their quality of work was not to his satisfaction. While inspecting bricks on one occasion, he found them too thin. The angry sultan ordered his black guards to break fifty bricks on the head of the master mason. After the punishment, the blood-soaked slave was thrown into prison. On another occasion, the sultan accused a number of slaves for producing mortar of inferior quality. The enraged sultan struck their heads one by one *"with his own hands and broke their heads so miserably that the place was all bloody like a butcher's stall."*[792]

There were other endless kinds of punishment, slaves suffered in the sultan's palace. Once, a Spanish slave walked past the sultan, forgetting to remove his hat. The angry sultan threw his spear at the poor slave, which pierced deep into the flesh. The poor slaved took it out of his skin and returned to the sultan to be repeatedly stricken by it into his stomach. There was another punishment, frequently meted out to a slave, called "tossing"; three or four black guards, upon the sultan's order, *"taking hold of his hams (thighs), throw him up with all their strength and, at the same time, turning him round, pitch him down head foremost,"* wrote Pellow. The horrible punishment often broke their neck or dislocated shoulders. This spectacle continued until the sultan ordered them to stop.[793]

Underfed, malnourished, overworked and living in horribly unhygienic condition in the slave-pen, disease and sickness was daily companion of the slaves. Plagues were a frequent visitor. With little medical

---

789. Ibid, p. 93

790 Ibid, p. 105

791. Ibid, p. 96–97

792. Ibid, p. 106

793. Ibid, p. 107

attention, it killed large number of them, especially those who were already very weak or suffering from diarrhoea or dysentery. On one occasion, wrote Mouette, it killed one in four of the French slaves.[794]

At the imperial palace, a most insignificant mistake could earn death to Moulay Ismail's slaves. The sultan's son Moulay Zidan once "killed *his favorite black slave with his own hand*" for accidentally disturbing pigeons the prince was feeding. The sultan "*was of so fickle, cruel and sanguine a nature that none could be even for an hour secure of life,*" wrote Pellow.[795]

Nine decades earlier, John Harrison had made repeated diplomatic visits to the court of Sultan Moulay Abdallah Malek (r. 1627–31) for releasing British captives. While on these failed missions, Harrison observed the torture and suffering of slaves, of which, he wrote: "*He (sultan) would cause men to be drubbed, or beaten almost to death in his presence... cause some to be beaten on the soles of their feet, and after, make them run up and down among the stones and thorns.*" Harrison added that the sultan ordered some of his slaves be dragged by horses until they were torn to shreds, while a few had been dismembered while alive, with "*their fingers and toes cut off by every joint; arms and legs and so head and all.*" A few years earlier, captive Robert Adams wrote to his parents from his miserable captivity in the Barbary corsair town of Salé that "*He (owner) made me work at a mill like a horse from morning until night, with chains upon my legs, of 36 pounds weights apiece.*"[796]

These instances should give one a rough idea of the sufferings that the enslaved endured in Muslim hands at different stages of the captive life. It is widely accepted that 80 to 90 percent of those captured by Muslim slave-hunters and traders in Africa died before reaching the slave-markets. A great many of these died in the process of castration—a procedure, universally performed upon male black slaves to be sent to the Muslim world. What an enormous suffering and loss of human life that was! The pain, strain and agony—both mental and physical—they endured, is simply indescribable, probably even unimaginable.

FATE OF SLAVES

When Prophet Muhammad died in 632, he had left behind a few thousand dedicated Muslim converts, who mainly engaged in raiding and plundering for making a living as well as for expanding the Muslim territory. This rather small band of Muslim warriors embarked on a stunning mission of conquest bringing vast territories of the world under their sway within a short time. In the process, they enslaved great multitude of the vanquished infidels, a large majority of whom involuntarily became Muslim.

Upon entering Sindh with only 6,000 Arab soldiers, Qasim had enslaved approximately 300,000 Indian infidels in three years. Similarly, Musa (698–712) had enslaved 300,000 Blacks and Berbers in North Africa. The early community of Muslims in Sindh consisted of a larger number of slave Muslims and a much smaller number of their Arab masters. Combined together, they formed the administrative machinery of the new Islamic state. Running such an enterprise needed a large amount of manpower in that non-technological era. Consequently, large numbers of these infidels, turned Muslims through enslavement, had to be engaged in many kinds of activities—as sex-slaves to the expansion of the military. In India, '*There was no occupation in which the slaves of Firoz Shah were not employed,*' noted medieval chronicle *Masalik.*[797] This was the case under all Muslim rulers, not only in India, but also everywhere else. In Southeast Asia under the Muslim rule,

794. Ibid, p. 99

795. Ibid, p. 124–25

796. Ibid, p. 16,20–21

797. Lal (1994), p. 97

slaves were also engaged in '*almost every conceivable function.*'[798] Indeed, almost entire work-force in Islamic Southeast Asia consisted of slaves as already noted.

Employment in building and construction: One major task Muslim invaders and rulers undertook in conquered lands was the construction of outstanding buildings for mosques, minarets, monuments and palaces. These were intended for declaring the might and glory of Islam, overshadowing the achievements of the native infidels. According to *Chachnama*, Qasim, informing of the building initiatives undertaken by him in Sindh, wrote to Hajjaj, '*...the infidels converted to Islam or destroyed. Instead of idol temples, mosques and other places of worships have been built, pulpits have been erected...*'[799] Qutbuddin Aibak had started construction of the impressive *Qwat-ul-Islam* (might of Islam) mosque in Delhi as early as 1192, more than a decade before establishing Muslim rule in India (1206). According to Ibn Battutah, the site of the *Qwat-ul-Islam* mosque '*was formerly occupied by an idol temple, and was converted into a mosque on the conquest of the city.*'[800] Aibak started the construction of the magnificent *Qutb Minar*—a minaret for announcing the Islamic call to prayers—in Delhi in 1199. The *Qutb Minar* '*has no parallel in the land of Islam,*' wrote eyewitness Battutah.[801]

The undertaking of these huge ventures in India, ahead of establishing a firm foothold for Islam, affirms that the declaration of the might and glory of Islam was an urgent and focal mission of the conquest. To undermine and degrade the achievements of the infidels further, materials from destroyed temples, churches, synagogues etc. were used in the construction of Islamic structures. A Persian inscription on the *Qwat-ul-Islam* mosque testifies that materials from twenty-seven destroyed Hindu and Jain temples were used in its construction.[802] Similar materials were used in the construction of *Qutb Minar*, about which, writes Prof. Habibullah, '*the sculptured figures (of Hindu gods, goddesses etc.) on the stones being either defaced or concealed by turning them upside down.*'[803]

Muslim invaders of India started with the building of such magnificent mosques, minarets, citadels, and mausoleums of their religious significance; to these, they later added outstanding palaces and other buildings across India. Their constructions were often completed in double-quick time. In excessive enthusiasm, Barani informs us that a palace could be built in two to three days and a citadel in two weeks during Sultan Alauddin Khilji. Although an exaggeration, it nonetheless tells us that a large number of people, invariably slaves, were employed in these works of great endeavor; and they had to work under tremendous pressure to complete those ventures in the quickest of time in that non-technological era. It is little wonder then that Sultan Alauddin had accumulated 70,000 slaves, who worked continuously in buildings. *Qwat-ul-Islam* mosque and *Qutb Minar* were projects of great endeavor, since materials from destroyed temples had to be dismantled with great care for reusing them. Nizami records that the temples were demolished using elephants, each of which could haul a stone, for which 500 men would be needed. Much of the delicate work, however, was done by human hands and a large number of slaves must have been employed.[804]

Furthermore, there was little respite in building new cities, palaces and religious structures. Many often, after a new Sultan ascended the throne—happened frequently because of ceaseless uprisings and intrigues, which so characterized the Islamic rule in India—he would construct a new city and palace in order to leave an enduring legacy of his own. Abandoning Iltutmish's old city, Sultan Ghiysuddin Balban (r. 1265–

---

798. Reid A (1993) *The Decline of Slavery in Nineteenth-Century Indonesia*, In Klein MA ed., *Breaking the Chains: Slavery, Bondage and Emancipation in Modern Africa and Asia*, University of Wisconsin Press, Madison, p. 68

799. Sharma, p. 95

800. Gibb, p. 195

801. Ibid

802. Watson and Hero, p. 96

803. Lal (1994), p. 84

804. Ibid, p. 84–85

85) built the famous Qasr-i-Lal (Red Fort) in Delhi. Likewise, Kaiqubab built the city of Kilughari. Battutah testifies that '*It is their custom that the king's palace is deserted on his death... and his successor builds a new palace for himself.*'[805] He noted of Delhi that it was '*the largest city in the entire Muslim Orient,*' made up of four contiguous cities, built by different sultans.[806]

Moreover, congested cities, with no modern sewage and garbage management systems, used to get dirty and uninhabitable quickly and a new city used to be built to replace it. Battutah and Babur recorded the destruction of old cities because of moisture, which necessitated shifting to a new city where everything was clean and tidy. Hindus, enslaved in large numbers, were engaged in cleaning up the dirt and in constructing new cities for the largely city-dwelling Muslims. As already cited, Sultan Firoz Tughlaq had assembled 180,000 slaves for his services. Of these, a contingent of masons and builders with 12,000 slaves may have been engaged in stone-cutting alone, estimates Lal. Emperor Babur recorded that '*[only] 680 men worked daily on my buildings in Agra...; while 1491 stone-cutters worked daily on my building in Agra, Sikri, Biana, Dulpur, Gwalior and Kuli (Aligarh). In the same way there were numberless artisans and workmen of every sort in Hindustan.*'[807]

Throughout Islamic rule, Muslim rulers of India built great mosques, monuments, mausoleums, citadels, palaces and cities as well as repaired them. Indisputably, the greatest Muslim achievements in India were the great architectural monuments; their glares draw numerous visitors to India from around world even today. And it is the great multitude of enslaved Indians, who supplied unconditional labor as well as skills at all levels of their construction, with Muslim masters on watch with whips (*Korrah*) in their hands.

A similar pattern in building palaces, monuments and cities of exquisite stature existed in other parts of the Islamic world. In Morocco, previous rulers had built great capital cities in Fez, Rabat and Marrakesh with stunning palaces and monuments. When Sultan Moulay Ismail captured power in 1672, he decided to build a new imperial city at Meknes, which was to surpass the scale and grandeur of all great cities in the world. He ordered to pull down all houses and edifices clearing a huge area for building a stunning palace, whose walls stretched many miles. The palace compound was to feature '*various interlocking palaces and chambers*' extending in '*endless succession across the hills and valleys around Meknes. There were to be vast courtyards and colonnaded galleries, green-tiled mosques and pleasure gardens. He (the sultan) ordered the building of a huge Moorish harem, as well as stables and armories, fountains, pools and follies.*'[808]

Sultan Moulay Ismail had wished to build a palatial city greater than that of King Louis XIV at Versailles, the greatest palace in Europe. In reality, he much outdid the Versailles palace. A British entourage, led by Commodore Charles Stewart, on a diplomatic mission to sign a peace treaty with Sultan Moulay Ismail and to free the English captives, visited the palace; they found it far larger than any building in Europe. Even the greatest and most opulent palace of King Louis XIV was much tinier. The most stunning edifice was the al-Mansur palace, which stood 150-feet high and was '*surmounted by twenty pavilions decorated with glazed green tiles.*'[809]

The sultan's palace was built exclusively by European slaves, aided by bands of local criminals. The palace was four miles in circumference and its walls were twenty-five feet thick. According to Windus, "*30,000 men and 10,000 mules were employed everyday in the building of the palace.*" Every morning the sultan would appear to oversee the construction and give idea for the days work. Slaves would work meticulously to finish the allotted work in time. As soon as he finished one project, he would start another.

---

805. Ibid, p. 86,88
806. Gibb, p. 194–95
807. Lal (1994), p. 88
808. Milton, p. 100–01
809. Ibid, p. 102

The scale of the building project was so huge that *"Never had such a similar palace been seen under any government, Arab or foreign, pagan or Muslim,"* wrote Moroccan historian ez-Zayyani. Some 12,000 soldiers were needed to guard the ramparts alone.[810]

There was no respite in the building activity in Sultan Moulay Ismail's palace. Rarely satisfied with finished buildings, he would order their demolition for rebuilding all over. In order to keep his slaves busy, he would order them to demolish twelve miles of the palace wall for their reconstruction at the same place. When inquired about this, the sultan replied, *"I have a bag full of rats (slaves); unless I keep that bag stirring, they would eat their way through."*[811]

Sultan Moulay Ismail's successor Moulay Abdallah was as cruel as his father. In order to subject his slaves to hard labor and keep them busy, he ordered the stunning palace buildings built by his father—"the pride and joys of Meknes"—be razed down and reconstructed by his European slaves. And he took sadistic joy at the suffering and even death of his slaves while they worked. *"While the slaves were working,"* wrote Frenchman Adrian de Manault, *"one of his pleasures was to put a great number of them at the foot of the wall which were about to collapse, and watch them be buried alive under the rubble."* He treated his slaves in *"a most grievous and cruel manner,"* wrote Pellow.[812]

Engagement in the army: Another major enterprise, in which, slaves were employed in large numbers was the Muslim army. Musa in North Africa had drafted 30,000 slaves into the military service. Late in the eighteenth century, Sultan Moulay Ismaili had a 250,000-strong army of black slaves. Muslim slave armies, 50,000 to 250,000 strong, were normal in Morocco, Egypt and Persia. The dreaded Ottoman Janissary Regiment that brought down Constantinople in 1453 consisted exclusively of slave soldiers. Qutbuddin Aibak, the first sultan of Delhi, was a slave of Sultan Muhammad Ghauri. The sultans of Delhi until 1290 were all slaves. Their army also consisted mostly of slaves, imported from foreign lands.

Many Muslim and non-Muslim historians and commentators have sought to sell this policy of employing the slaves in the armed forces as an ennobling and liberating act on the part of Muslim rulers. This noble exercise, they argue, enabled slaves to reach the highest rank in the military; they even became rulers. It is true that many slaves rose to the top in the military; and some, through cliques and intrigues, even rose to the position of rulers. But this, for Muslim rulers, was never a gesture of their generosity. Instead, it was, for them, a necessity to continue the conquest for their own interest: for expanding their kingdoms and for acquiring more plunder, slaves and revenues from the vanquished. It also became a tool for continued brutality, mass-slaughter and enslavement of the infidels. Every slave, who happened to reach the height of power, paved the way for the brutalization and destruction of tens to hundreds of thousands of innocent lives. Every slave, who became a normal soldier, destroyed a few to many innocent lives.

After capturing Debal in 712 with 6,000 Arab warriors, Qasim could not take his conquest further without expanding the army. Hence, after taking a city, he had to take time to consolidate power and expand the military, for which, some of the enslaved were unconditionally drafted in.[813] Once the military power improved, he could send forward a new expedition while keeping the already-conquered territories secure. He made about half-a-dozen major expeditions after arriving in Sindh and gradually his army swelled to 50,000 soldiers. A part of the new recruits came from enslaved Indians. *'Kingship is the army and the army is the kingship,'* wrote Barani, implying the central importance of a powerful army in the plunderous Muslim rule and conquest. The engagement of slaves in the army, therefore, was not a favor by Muslim rulers to the

---

810. Ibid, p. 104–05

811. Ibid

812. Ibid, p. 240–41

813. Large numbers of volunteer Jihadists from the Islamic world, seeing new opportunities for engaging in holy war against the infidels, also poured into Sindh to join Qasim's army.

enslaved, but quite the opposite. It was not a generous act of liberation and elevation of slaves by Muslim rulers; it was a compulsion for their own good fortune. Most of all, joining the Muslim army was not a free choice for slaves, but a compulsion. And every slave drafted into the army paved the way for the destruction and brutalization of the lives of scores of innocent non-Muslims, normally their coreligionists of the yesteryear.

After suffering reverses in the battle of Tours (France) in 732, Islamic conquests became somewhat subdued. The Jihadi spirit of the Muslim army was probably dwindling. With vast territories conquered and huge wealth accumulated, the Arab and Persian soldiers had probably lost their zest for engaging in further bloodletting wars, which risked their lives. This time, the North African black and Berber slaves formed the bulk of the Muslim army that continued Jihadi expeditions in Europe. On the eastern borders of the Islamdom, Muslim rulers found another people, the Turks, with an unceasing zeal for wars and bloodbath. The Abbasid caliphs, especially Caliph al-Mutasim (833–42), started drafting the Turks in the army in large numbers, replacing the lackadaisical Arabs and Persians. Most of these Turks were enslaved in wars. They were also imported at young age as *Dewshirme*-style tributes and trained for serving in the army. This trend continued under subsequent caliphs, making Turks the major force in the army; the supremacy of the Arabs and Persians in the military was dismantled.

Some of these powerful Turk commanders later revolted against the caliphs and declared their independence. The first independent Turk dynasty was established in Egypt in 868. On the eastern front of Islamdom, there arose a Turk slave ruler, named Alptigin—a purchased slave of Persian (Samanid dynasty) King Ahmad bin Ismail (d. 907) of Transoxiana, Khurasan and Bukhara. For his military excellence, Alptigin was appointed in the charge of 500 villages and about 2000 slaves by the Samanid governor Abdul Malik (954–61). Alptigin later became an independent chief in Ghazni. He purchased another Turkish slave, named Subuktigin, who, after Alptigin's death, prevailed in acquiring power. Subuktigin '*made frequent raids into Hind in the prosecution of holy wars,*' wrote al-Utbi. However, it was the son of Subuktigin, Sultan Mahmud Ghazni, who launched devastating holy wars against the infidels of India. About one-and-half centuries later, another band of slave sultans, the Afghan Ghaurivids, launched the final blow to India's sovereignty, establishing the Muslim sultanate in Delhi. Qutbuddin Aibak, Sultan Ghauri's Turkish slave turned military commander, became the first sultan of Delhi. The Delhi sultans used to maintain an army, consisting mainly of slaves of foreign origin during the early period. Slaves from various foreign nationalities—Turks, Persians, Seljuqs, Oghus (Iraqi Turkmen), Afghans and Khiljis—were purchased in large number and drafted into the Ghaznivid and Ghaurid army. Black slaves, purchased from Abyssinia, became the dominant force in the army of Sultana Raziyah (r. 1236–40), the daughter of Sultan Iltutmish.

When the Khilji dynasty (1290–1320), the first non-slave rulers in India, came to power—the Indians, enslaved and forcibly converted to Islam, started appearing in the army, much to the annoyance of orthodox Muslims, who detested the inclusion of the lowly Indians into the armed forces. But the Mongols had been attacking India's northwest frontier at this time. The Sultan needed a powerful army, which necessitated the inclusion of slave Muslims of Indian origin. Moreover, the Khiljis had captured power by ousting the Turks, who had been raising constant revolts. Hence, the Khiljis could not employ the Turks heavily in the army because of the loyalty issue. Later on, Sultan Firoz Tughlaq (r. 1351–88), sensing an impending invasion by the Islamized Mongols (which, indeed, came in 1398 with Timur's barbaric assaults), needed to assemble a large army. As a result, the Hindus were allowed to be drafted into the Muslim army for the first time in India. Similar Muslim opposition against the employment of the conquered infidels turned Muslims into the army also existed elsewhere. In Egypt, the native Coptic Christians, who converted to Islam, were not included into the army for a long time.

Role of Indian soldiers: In the army, the Indian soldiers (mostly converted slaves), known as *paiks*, were normally engaged in lower ranks. They belonged to the infantry. They were drawn from slaves captured in expeditions or obtained as tributes; some Hindus also joined the army at later stages to secure a livelihood.

The *paiks* performed all kinds of sundry jobs, such as looking after the horses and elephants; they were engaged in personal services of the higher-ranked cavalrymen. Muslim sultans and emperors in India kept a huge army; and in the reign of Akbar, '*A Mogul army in the field had on the average two or three servants for each fighting man,*' notes Moreland.[814] Naturally, numerous slaves were engaged in the army in different capacities during later periods. When on a military campaign, the *paiks* cleared jungles and prepared roads for the marching army. When halted or arrived at the destination, they set up camps and fixed tents—sometimes on lands, as much as 12,546 yards in circumference, records Amir Khasrau.[815]

In the battle-field, the *paiks* were stationed at the frontline on foot to absorb the initial assaults. They could not escape from the frontal onslaught, because, '*horses were on their left and right... and behind (them), were the elephants so that not one of them can run away,*' writes Alqalqashindi in *Subh-ul-Asha.* Portuguese official Duarte Barbosa (1518) records in his eyewitness account, ''(*paiks*) *carry swords and daggers, bows and arrows. They are right good archers and their bows are long like those of England... They are mostly Hindus.*'' Some Indian-origin slave soldiers (converted Muslims)—such as Malik Kafur, Malik Naik, Sarang Khan, Bahadur Nahar, Shaikha Khokhar, and Mallu Khans *et al.*—also rose to positions of power through their military valor and loyalty to the sultans.[816]

In general, Indian slaves in the army did all kinds of sundry jobs, including acting as servants to soldiers, caretakers of the stable of horses and elephants, in clearing jungles and setting up tents and camps. In battle-fields, they stood in the frontline on foot with daggers and swords, bows and arrows and bore the brunt of enemy attacks.

A similar trend existed in the employment of native soldiers elsewhere. When the Egyptian Coptic converts to Islam had to be drafted into the army after the initial resistance, '*they were enrolled in the foot-soldier brigades, which meant that, in case of the army's victory, they were entitled to receive only half the horsemen's share of the war spoils.*'[817] The European captives turned Muslims in Morocco, the most hated ones among the slaves, were employed in the army to do difficult battles against deadly rebels. They had to lead the first wave of attack against the enemy; and they had no way to escape but take the enemy assaults on their bodies. In the battle, if they tried to betray or give way, they were cut up in pieces.[818]

Employment in royal factories: Another major enterprise for employing slaves in large numbers was the royal *karkhana* (factory/workhouse), which existed throughout the Sultanate and Mughal periods in India. These workhouses used to produce and manufacture goods of every conceivable royal usage: articles of gold, silver, brass and other metals, textiles, perfumes, armors, weapons, leather goods and clothes, saddles for horses and camels, and covers for elephants.[819] Thousands of slaves trained as artisans and craftsmen worked in running these factories, watched by senior *Amirs* or Khans. Firoz Shah Tughlaq had 12,000 slaves working in his *karkhanas.* They produced articles of excellent quality for every need of the sultans and emperors, and their generals, soldiers and nobles—including weapons for warfare, and gifts for sending to overseas kings and overlords. Commodore Steward and his entourage, visiting Sultan Moulay Ismail's workhouses in Morocco, found them ''*full of men and boys at work... making saddles, stocks for guns, scabbards for cymiters [sic] and other things.*''[820]

---

814. Moreland, p. 88
815. Lal (1994), p. 89–93
816. Ibid
817. Tagher, p. 18
818. Milton, p. 135–36
819. Lal (1994), p. 96–99
820. Milton, p. 186

Employment in palaces and royal courts: Following is a summary of Lal's account of the employment of slaves in royal palaces and court.[821] Slaves were used in large numbers in various departments of the royal courts. Large numbers of them acted as spies; thousands were needed in the Revenue and Postal Departments for collecting revenues and carrying official communications, respectively. At the palace, slaves were also needed in very large numbers. Emperor Akbar, Jahangir and Shah Jahan had 5,000 to 6,000 women (wives and concubines) in their harems; and each one of them had a few to many *bandis* (slave women) to care for them. They lived in separate apartments and were guarded by female guards, eunuchs, and porters in successive circles.

There were also large bands of slaves playing trumpets, drums, and pipes etc. Slaves were engaged in fanning the royal persons and driving away mosquitoes. In the services of Sultan Muhammad Shah Tughlaq (d. 1351), wrote Shihabuddin al-Omari:

> '...there are 1,200 physicians; 10,000 falconers who ride on horseback and carry birds trained for hawking; 300 beaters go in front and put up the game; 3,000 dealers in articles required for hawking accompany him when he goes out hunting; 500 table companions dine with him. He supports 1,200 musicians excluding about 1,000 slave musicians who are in charge of teaching music, and 1,000 poets of Arabic, Persian and Indian languages. About 2,500 oxen, 2,000 sheep, and other animals were slaughtered daily for the supplies of the royal kitchen.'

The number of slaves needed for these huge undertakings on a daily basis and all other chores of the royal palaces are not available, but not impossible to guess. Numerous staffs were employed for amusements and sports: hunting, shooting, pigeon-flying and so on. Sultan Alauddin Khilji had 50,000 pigeon-boys in his collection. Slaves were engaged even to train the fighting instinct of a variety of animals '*down to frogs and spiders,*' recorded Moreland. Emperor Humayun's rival Sher Shah, a not-so-powerful and well-established ruler, had employed 3,400 horses in postal communications and maintained about 5,000 elephants in his stable. Seven slaves were engaged to look after each elephant. Emperor Jahangir records in his memoir that four slaves looked after each of his dogs brought as presents from England. According to Moroccan chronicler Ahmed ben Nasiri, Sultan Moulay Ismail had about 12,000 horses in his stable and two slaves were employed to look after every ten stallions.[822] According to Pellow, who briefly acted as a harem-guard, Sultan Moulay Ismail's huge harem had 4,000 concubines and wives.[823] Obviously a large number of slaves were engaged in guarding the harems.

Employment in household and agricultural works: In royal palaces, slaves were employed in tens of thousands. The nobles, provincial governors and high-ranking generals employed slaves in hundreds to thousands in activities of the courts and household chores. One official of Emperor Jahangir had 1,200 eunuch slaves alone. From expeditions, Muslim soldiers used to get many slaves as their share. Some of them used to be sold away, while the rest were employed in the household and outdoor chores and activities to provide the masters every comfort.

According to Islamic laws as enshrined in the *Pact of Omar*, non-Muslims could not purchase slaves belonging to Muslims. Therefore, only Muslims could legally buy slaves in the markets of Islamdom. This restriction was likely implemented strictly in the early periods of Islam. The Muslim population was small during the early decades and centuries of Islam, while the yield of slaves for sale was very large because of the rapid success in conquests. This oversupply of slaves enabled even ordinary Muslim households to own many slaves as already noted. The yield of captives in certain campaigns was so large that they had to be sold in batches as did Caliph al-Mutasim in 838.

---

821. Lal (1994), p. 99–102
822. Milton, p. 132
823. Ibid, p. 120

What were these slaves, from a few to many, doing in the household of the ordinary, even poor, Muslim owners? Obviously, they were employed in every conceivable type of labor and chores possible: household works of every kind and anything that required physical exertion, such as herding the animals and working in the backyards and farms. The slaves, thus, enabled their owners to lead a life of comfort, ease and indulgence free of labor. According to Lewis, '*Slaves, most of them black Africans, appeared in large number in economic projects. From early Islamic times, large numbers of black slaves were employed in draining the salt flats of southern Iraq. Poor conditions led to a series of uprisings. Other black slaves were employed in the gold mines of Upper Egypt and Sudan, and in the salt mines of Sahara.*'[824] Segal adds: '*(They) dug ditches, drained marshland, cleared salt flats of their crust; they cultivated sugar, and cotton in plantations; and they were accommodated in camps that contained five hundred to five thousand each.*'[825] Because of these deadly uprisings, Muslim rulers, later on, were cautious about employing slaves in large congregations on specific projects.

In Islamic Guinea and Sierra Leone, the masters of "slave town" employed their slaves in agricultural farms in the nineteenth century.[826] The slaves of Sultan Sayyid Sa'id (d. 1856) in East Africa '*labored in the great clove plantations on Zanzibar and Pemba islands...*'[827] Segal quotes Nehemia Levtzion that "*In the fifteenth century, slaves were in great demand for expanding plantation agriculture in Southern Morocco.*' In the nineteenth century, adds Segal, '*when the demand for cotton was high and supply of slaves from Sudan was plentiful, they were used to increase production of crop in Egypt, while large numbers of slaves... were used for grain production on the East African coast and in the clove plantation on the islands of Zanzibar and Pemba.*"[828] In the nineteenth century, some 769,000 black slaves were engaged in the Arab plantations of Zanzibar and Pemba, while 95,000 of them were shipped to the Arab plantations in the Mascareme Islands from East Africa alone.[829]

SEX-SLAVERY & CONCUBINAGE

The female slaves worked as domestic maids and in the backyards, while the young and pretty ones also had to provide sex to their masters. Thus, they not only provided menial services and pleasure to masters, but also helped swell the Muslim populace through procreation. Sex-slavery is not a negligible institution in Islam; Allah has shown utmost seriousness about its practice by repeatedly reminding Muslims about it in the Quran. Prophet Muhammad himself had taken at least three slave-girls as his concubines, namely Juwairiya of Banu Mustaliq [Bukhari 3:46:717], Rayhana of Banu Qurayza, and Maria, sent by the Egyptian governor to pacify Muhammad after receiving his threatening letter. From his large share of captives, he also distributed slave-girls amongst his companions for keeping as concubines. In one instance, he gave Ali (his son-in-law and the fourth caliph), Uthman b. Affan (his son-in-law and the third caliph) and Omar ibn Khattab (his father-in-law and the second caliph) a slave-girl each.[830] In explaining the institution of slavery on the basis of Quranic verses 23:5–6, brilliant Islamic scholar Sayyid Abul Ala Maududi (d. 1979) wrote:

824. Lewis (2000), p. 209

825. Segal, p. 42

826. Rodney W (1972) In MA Klein & GW Johnson eds., p. 158

827. Gann L (1972), In Ibid, p. 182

828. Ibid, p. 44–45

829. Ibid, p. 60–61

830. Ibn Ishaq, p. 592–93; Al-Tabari, Vol. IX, p. 29

Two categories of women have been excluded from the general command of guarding the private parts: (a) wives, (b) women who are legally in one's possession, i.e. slave-girls. Thus the verse [Quran 23:5–6] clearly lays down the law that one is allowed to have sexual relation with one's slave-girl as with one's wife, the basis being possession and not marriage. If marriage had been the condition, the slave-girl also would have been included among the wives, and there was no need to mention them separately.[831]

In agreement with the institution of sex-slavery in Islam and its above-mentioned purpose, the *Hedayah* states that the object of owning female slaves is '*cohabitation and generation of children.*'[832] Accordingly, physical fitness, regular menstruation and absence of disabilities became major considerations in purchasing a female slave. According to *Hedayah*, odor in the mouth and armpit of a female slave is a defect—obviously because, she is meant for kissing, caressing and sleeping with; but the same does not matter in case of male slaves. The *Hedayah* further stipulates that when a female slave is shared by two masters, she becomes property of the one, who establishes sexual relationship with her with the consent of the other.[833] *Fatwa-i-Alamgiri* stipulates that if a purchased female slave has too large breasts, or too loose or wide vagina, the purchaser has the right to return her for a refund—obviously because, the owner cannot get maximum pleasure from sex with such a woman, as she is intended for. Similarly, the purchaser can return a slave on the basis of whether she is a virgin.[834]

These criteria for chosing or judging female slaves come from the time of Prophet Muhammad himself. He was in the habit of choosing the prettiest of captive women for himself. In Khaybar, he chose Safiyah, wife of Kinana, for himself, hearing that she was of exquisite beauty and worthy of himself only. He, thereby, deprived another Jihadi, who had obtained her initially.[835] In another example, after the Prophet had distributed the captured women of the Hawazin tribe among his Jihadi comrades, a deputation from the tribe came to him seeking the release of their women. He agreed to release them for six camels apiece. His disciple Uyayna bin Hisn refused to release a woman of some nobility, fallen in his share, expecting a higher price. To this, Zubayr Abu Surad, another companion of Muhammad, convinced Uyayna to let her go, because '*her mouth was cold and her breast was flat; she could not concieve... and her milk was not rich.*' When Uyayna complained about this to Al-Aqra, another comrade of the Prophet, he persuaded Uyayna by saying: '*By God, you did not take her as virgin in her prime nor even full-figured in her middle age!*'[836]

Using the female slaves for sex—a norm and a widespread practice throughout the history of Islam—is clearly sanctioned in the Quran, the *Sunnah* and the Sharia. It has, therefore, received unabashed and overt approval of Islamic jurists, imams and scholars well into the modern age. Apart from the lure of booty, the greed for capturing the women for using as sex-slaves became a significant motivating factor for Muslim Jihadis to take part in holy wars since Muhammad's time. According to Islamic laws, the slayer becomes the owner of the victim's wife, children and properties. Sir William Muir thought that the sanction of the sex-slavery in Islam acted '*as an inducement to fight in the hope of capturing the females who would then be lawful concubines as 'that their right hand possessed.*''[837]

---

831. Maududi SAA, *The Meaning of the Quran*, Islamic Publications, Lahore, Vol. III, p. 241, note 7

832. Lal (1994), p. 142

833. Ibid, p. 145,147

834. Ibid, p. 145

835. Ibn Ishaq, p. 511; Muir, p. 377

836. Ibn Ishaq, p. 593

837. Muir, p. 74, notes; also Quran 4:3

From Muhammad's own practice of slave-concubinage, it flourished into a widely practised institution in later periods as captives became numerous. Islam puts no limit on the number of sex-slaves Muslim men can keep; '*there is absolutely no limit to the number of slave girls with whom a Mohammedan may cohabit, and it is the consecration of this illimitable indulgence which so popularizes the Mohammedan religion amongst the uncivilized nations and so popularizes slavery in the Muslim religion,*' writes Thomas Hughes.[838] Accordingly, writes Lewis, '*The slave women of every ethnic origin were acquired in great numbers to staff the harems of the Islamic world—as concubines or menials, the two functions not always clearly differentiated... Some were trained as performers—singers, dancers, and musicians.*'[839] Ronald Segal also affirms this in saying: '*Female slaves were required in considerable numbers for musicians, singers and dancers—many more were bought as domestic workers and many were in demand as concubines. The harems of rulers could be enormous. The harem of Abd al-Rahman III (d. 961) in Cordoba contained over 6,000 concubines; and the one in the Fatimid palace in Cairo had twice as many.*'[840] Muslim rulers of India did not lag behind either; even enlightened Akbar had 5,000 women in his harem, while Jahangir and Shah Jahan had 5,000 to 6,000 each. In the eighteenth century, Sultan Moulay Ismail had 4,000 concubines in his harem.

Clearly, Muslim rulers—from Africa to Europe, from the Middle East to India—had accumulated sex-slaves in their thousands. In the heyday of Islam, court officials, nobles, high-ranking generals and provincial governors had dozens to hundreds and even thousands of slaves. Even the poor Muslim households or common shopkeepers used to have many slaves, as recorded by Muslim chroniclers. In general, the young female slaves in all households had to provide sex to their masters as demanded. It appears that capturing the women for keeping as concubines was a major focus of Islamic slave-hunting; because, for every male slave, two females were captured in Africa for transporting to the Muslim world. And for those transported by Europeans to the new world, there were two males for every female.

Niccolao Manucci, who lived in India during Emperor Aurangzeb's reign, observed of the Muslim infatuation with women and sex that '*all Mohammedans are fond of women, who are their principal relaxation and almost their only pleasure.*'[841] Dutchman Francisco Pelsaert, who visited India during Emperor Jahagir's reign (1605-27), wrote of the sexual indulgence of Muslim rulers and noblemen in the harems that:

'...each night the Amir visits a particular wife or *mahal* (quarter), receives a very warm welcome from his wife and from the slaves [girls], who dressed especially for the occasion... If it is the hot weather, they... rub his body with pounded sandalwood and rosewater. Fans are kept going steadily. Some of the slaves chafe the master's hand and feet, some sit and sing, or play music and dance, or provide other recreation, the wife sitting near him all the time. Then if one of the pretty slave girls takes his fancy, he calls her and enjoys her, his wife not daring to show any signs of displeasure, but dissembling, though she will take it out on the slave girl later on.'[842]

However, the wife could never get rid of such beautiful slave-girls from the harem, because it was only in the power of the master to free her (Muslim women cannot own slaves).

Similarly Maria Ter Meetelen, a Dutch slave-girl of Moulay Ismail's palace in Morocco, left an eyewitness account of the sultan's sensual indulgence with his wives and concubines in the harem. She wrote:

---

838. Huges, p. 600

839. Lewis (2000), p. 209

840. Segal, p. 39

841. Manucci N (1906) *Storia do Mogor*, trs. Irvine W, Hohn Murray, London, Vol. II, p. 240

842. Lal (1994), p. 169–70

''I found myself in front of the sultan in his room, where he was lying with at least fifty women,'' who ''were painted on their faces and clothed like goddesses, extraordinarily beautiful, and each with her instrument.'' Maria added: ''...they played and sang, for it was a melody more lovely than anything I'd ever heard before.''[843]

In sum, slave-concubinage—the most degrading and dehumanizing form of prostitution—became a prominent hallmark of Islamic tradition well into modern age. The Ottoman sultans maintained a harem full of women until the empire was dissolved in 1921. In the princely state of Bahawalpur in Sindh, first to be conquered by Muslim invaders—the last Nawab, who ruled until 1954 before its incorporation into Pakistan, *'had more than three hundred and ninety women'* in his harem. The Nawab had become impotent early and used all kinds of tools to satisfy his great multitude of concubines and wives. When Pakistani army took over his palace, *'they found a whole collection of dildos. About six hundred, some made of clays, some bought in England and battery-operated. The army dug a pit and buried these dildos.'*[844] The Arab kings till today maintain sizable harems of some kind.

EUNUCHS AND *GHILMAN*

Another extremely cruel, dehumanizing and degrading aspect of Islamic slavery was the large-scale castration of male captives. It has received little attention of critics and historians. Historically, castration did receive little opposition in the Muslim world well into the modern age. But Muslims normally engaged Jews or other non-Muslims to perform the operation on the argument that mutilation of human bodies was prohibited in Islam. (This is hypocritical in the least, since beheading of totally innocent people in large numbers has been a common practice right from the days of the Prophet, while amputation of hands and legs are divine Islamic punishment for certain crimes.) Yet, the employment of eunuchs is clearly sanctioned by Allah, as the Quran instructs Muslim women to cover their body and ornaments with cloaks except *'to their husbands or their fathers, or the fathers of their husbands, or their sons, or the sons of their husbands, or their brothers, or their brothers' sons, or their sisters' sons, or their women, or those whom their right hands possess, or **the male servants not having need (of women)**...'* [Quran 24:31]. Prophet Muhammad had himself accepted a eunuch as gift, says a hadith, which has been excluded from canonical collections.[845]

Castrated males, normally young handsome boys, were in great demands amongst Muslim rulers and elites mainly for three reasons. First, Muslim harems and households used to have a few to thousands of wives and concubines. Naturally, most of these women were left sexually unsatisfied as well as jealous and indignant about sharing their husbands and masters with so many women. Keeping male slaves in such palaces and households was a cause of concern for the husband and master, because those sexually unsatisfied and often indignant women could be tempted into sexual contact with the male-slaves. Attraction of harem women to other men was rather common. For example, when Pellow, not a eunuch, was surprisingly placed as a harem-guard by Moulay Ismail upon a request from one of his favourite wives, his wives showed amorous interest in him. Aware of the consequence of such a tango if the sultan found out, ''*I thought it highly prudent to keep a very strict guard upon all my actions,*'' wrote Pellow.[846]

---

843. Milton, p. 120

844. Naipaul (1998), p. 332

845. Pellat Ch, Lambton AKS and Orhonlu C (1978) *Khasi,* In *The Encyclopaedia of Islam,* E J Brill ed., Leiden, Vol. IV, p. 1089

846. Milton, p. 126

It was, therefore, safer for masters—particularly the rulers and high officials, who kept large harem—to keep eunuchs, instead of virile men, in their households and palaces. It is no wonder that the term *harem* originated from *haram*, meaning prohibited—more specifically, "out of bounds" (to unrelated men).

According to John Laffin, black slaves were generally castrated *'based on the assumption that the blacks had an ungovernable sexual appetite.'*[847] From India to Africa, eunuchs were specifically engaged in guarding the royal harems. They kept tab on the passage of men and women in and out of the seraglio and spied for the ruler on the harem women about their behaviour, infidelity in particular. Eunuchs were needed in their thousands to look after huge harems, probably the largest royal department in medieval Islamic kingdoms.

Secondly, the castrated men, with no hope of a family or offspring to look forward to in their old age, were likely to show greater fidelity and devotion to the master in order to earn their favor and support when they grew old. The castrated slaves, devoid of sexual distractions, could also devote themselves exclusively to work relatively easily in the usually sexually-charged Islamic culture.

The third reason for the high demand for eunuchs was homosexual infatuation of many Muslim rulers, generals and nobles. Eunuchs, kept for carnal indulgence, also called *ghilman*, used to be handsome young boys. They used to wear *'rich and attractive uniforms and often beautified and perfumed their bodies in effeminate fashion.'* The concept of *ghilman* comes from the following verses of the Quran, which describes heavenly male attendants (*ghilman*) in paradise:

- 'Round about them will serve, (devoted) to them, young male servants (handsome) as Pearls well-guarded.' [Quran 52:24]

- 'There wait on them immortal youths, with bowls and ewers and a cup from a pure spring.' [Quran 56:17–18]

Anwar Shaikh in his essay *Islamic Morality* describes *ghilman* as follows: *'Paradise is the description of the luxurious surroundings dwelt in by Houris and Ghilman. Houris are the most beautiful ever-young virgins with wide, flexing eyes and swelling bosoms. Ghilman are the immortal young boys, pretty like pearls, clothed in green silk and brocade and embellished with bracelets of silver.'*[848] The concept of *ghilman* in Islam may have been prompted by the dominant culture of sodomy that existed amongst Arabs during Muhammad's time as discussed already (see p. 131–32). Sodomy was also prevalent in Persia. According Hitti, *'We read of ghilman in the reign of al-Rashid; but it was evidently the Caliph al-Amin, who, following Persian precedent, established in the Arab world the ghilman institution for the practice of sexual relations. A judge of whom there is record used four hundred such youths. Poets did not disdain to give public expression to their perverted passions and to address amorous pieces of their compositions to beardless young boys.'*[849]

Castration was not performed on the black captives alone, but on captives of all shades and races: be it the blacks of Africa, the browns of India, the yellows of Central Asia or the whites of Europe. In the Middle Ages, notes Segal, Prague and Verdun became castration centers for white eunuchs, while Kharazon near the Caspian Sea for Central Asian eunuchs. Islamic Spain was another center for producing white eunuchs. At the beginning of the tenth century, Caliph al-Muqtadir (r. 908–937) had assembled in the Baghdad palace some 11,000 eunuchs: 7,000 Blacks and 4,000 Whites (Greek).[850]

---

847. Segal, p. 52

848. Shaikh A, *Islamic Morality*, http://iranpoliticsclub.net/islam/islamic-morality/index.htm

849. Hitti PK (1948) *The Arabs : A Short History*, Macmillan, London, p. 99

850. Segal, p. 40–41; Hitti (1961), p. 276

It is noted already that there was widespread castration of slaves in Bengal during Mughal Emperor Jahangir, which had become a widespread practice across India. It appears that since Bakhtiyar Khilji's conquest of Bengal in 1205, it had become a leading source of enslavement and castration for supplying eunuchs. On his way back to Venice from Kublai Khan's Court, Marco Polo visited India in the late thirteenth century; he found Bengal as a major source of eunuchs. Duarte Barbosa in the late sultanate period (1206–1526) and Francois Pyrard in the Mughal period (1526–1799) also found Bengal as the leading supplier of castrated slaves. *Ain-i-Akbari* (compiled 1590s) also affirms the same.[851] Some 22,000 individuals were emasculated in 1659 in Golkunda during Aurangzeb. Said Khan Chaghtai of Jahangir's reign owned 1,200 eunuchs. Even kind-hearted Akbar employed eunuchs in large numbers. According to *Ain-i-Akbari*, Akbar's harem '*contained 5,000 ladies, each of whom had separate apartments... watched in successive circles by female guards, eunuchs, Rajputs and the porters at the gates...*'[852]

Sultan Alauddin Khilji had engaged 50,000 young boys in his personal services, while Muhammad Tughlaq had 20,000 and Firoz Tughlaq 40,000. Many, if not most, of these slave-boys were likely castrated. Even Malik Kafur, Alauddin's famous commander, was a eunuch. Khusrau Khan, Sultan Kutbuddin Mubarak Khilji's favorite commander, who killed the sultan in 1320 and occupied the throne briefly, was a eunuch too. Medieval Muslim historians—namely Muhammad Ferishtah, Khondamir, Minhaj Siraj and Ziauddin Barani *et al.*, have recorded stories of infatuation of other illustrious sultans, namely Mahmud Ghazni, Qutbuddin Aibak and Sikandar Lodi—for handsome young boys. Sikandar Lodi had once boasted, '*If I order one of my slaves to be seated in a palanquin,*[853] *the entire body of nobility would carry him on their shoulders at my bidding.*'[854] Sultan Mahmud had infatuation toward charming Tilak the Hindu, his favorite commander.[855]

Castration of male captives was performed on an unprecedented scale in order to meet the demand of eunuchs in the Muslim world. It was Muslims, who inaugurated the practice of castrating male slaves on a grand scale. Most of the male slaves of the Muslim world—particularly, those captured in Africa—were castrated. While eleven million African slaves were transported to the New World (West Indies and Americas) during the 350-year trans-Atlantic slave-trade, a larger number of them ended up in the Middle East, North Africa, Central Asia, India, Islamic Spain and Ottoman Europe during the thirteen centuries of Islamic domination. However, if compared the Diaspora left by black slaves in the New World with that in the Islamic world, it becomes evident that the overwhelming majority of the black slaves of the Islamic world were castrated; therefore, they failed to leave a notable Diaspora behind.

The fate of the millions of European, Indian, Central Asian and Middle Eastern infidels—reduced to wearing the shackles of Islamic slavery—might not have been much different. Marco Polo (1280s) and Duarte Barbosa (1500s) witnessed large-scale castrations in India; the same was occurring in the reign of Abkar (d. 1605), Jahangir (d. 1628) and Aurangzeb (d. 1707). Castration, therefore, was a common practice in India throughout the Muslim rule. It might have contributed to some extent to the decrease in India's population from about 200 million in 1000 CE to 170 million in 1500 CE (discussed earlier).

---

851. Moreland, p. 93, note 1

852. Ibid, p. 87–88

853. Palanquins were used for carrying the women, especially the newly married brides, in medieval India.

854. Lal (1994), p. 106–09

855. Elliot & Dawson, Vol. II, p. 127–29

ISLAMIC SLAVE-TRADE

The advent of Islam raised the institution of slavery to an unprecedented scale: slaves became like a normal commodity and slave-trade a normal business enterprise all over the Islamic world. As noted already, Sharia laws place slaves in the category of common property or commodity and specify prices of slaves based on their physical fitness, sexual attraction, and so on. *Fatwa-i-Alamgiri* specifies regulation of purchase of a female slave on the basis of her having a too large breasts, too wide vagina or being a virgin or not. Traditions of the Prophet and his honourable companions support these regulations.

The origin of Islamic slave-trade: Slave-trade in Islam started with Prophet Muhammad's selling some of the enslaved Banu Qurayza women to Najd for acquiring weapons and horses. The Prophet and his nascent Muslim community in Medina, dedicating themselves exclusively in the cause of Allah, engaged in raiding and plundering trade-caravans and infidel communities, which also became their means of making a living. In these campaigns, they frequently captured slaves, mostly the women and children. However, slave-trade was then not a flourishing trade vocation in Arabia. It was also not safe for the nascent Muslim community to sell the enslaved in open markets. In this situation, the Prophet used to demand ransom from captives' families to earn revenues as an alternative to selling them. Revenues were raised through ransoming the captives taken in the attack of Nakhla, the battle of Badr and other campaigns. Muhammad's ransoming the captured women of the Hawazin tribe, six camels apiece, has been cited already. Later on, Caliph Omar declared that non-Muslims could not buy slaves belonging to Muslims. This means that captives taken thereafter were not ransomed anymore, not to return them to non-Muslim hands. They could be bought by Muslims only. This ensured that they remained within the fold of Islam; it helped swell the Muslim populace faster.

Capturing slaves for sale: From the 300,000 slaves captured in North Africa, Musa sold caliph's share of 60,000 into slavery. Having engaged 30,000 into military service, he distributed the rest amongst his soldiers—who, in turn, might have sold a part of them. Ibn Khaldun (d. 1406) notes of his eyewitness account of the slave-trade in Egypt that *'the slave merchants bring them to Egypt in batches... and government buyers have them displayed for the inspection and bid for them, raising the price above their value.'*[856] Of the approximately 300,000 Indians enslaved by Qasim in his three-year campaign in Sindh, he forwarded one-fifth portion to the caliph in Damascus. The caliph used to add the young and pretty female slaves of noble or royal birth to his harem, give some of them to his nobles as gifts, engage many in various services of the royal court and sell the rest for generating revenues.

Caliph al-Mutasim (d. 842), an enlightened progenitor of the Islamic "Golden Age", sold slaves in batches of five and ten after the campaign of Amorium. Sultan Mahmud used to capture slaves in tens to hundreds of thousands in India and drive them to the markets in Ghazni. As mentioned already, he drove away 500,000 slaves from Waihind (1002), 200,000 from Thanesar (1015) and 53,000 from his expedition in 1019. Of the two million people, reduced as a result of his campaigns in India as estimated by Lal, a large part of them were carried away as captives and the rest slaughtered. It is also noted that Muhammad Ghauri had converted 300,000 to 400,000 Khokhars to Islam through enslavement. Both Sultan Mahmud and Muhammad Ghauri drove the captives to Ghazni, where they were sold in markets. During Sultan Mahmud, Ghazni had become a prominent slave-trading centre, where *'merchants came from different cities to purchase them so that the countries of Mawarau-n-nahr, Iraq and Khurasan were filled with them,'* wrote al-Utbi.[857] The revenue from the first-round of sale of slaves went to the state treasury. The slave merchants continued the trade in markets of the Islamic world.

---

856. Lal (1994), p. 124

857. Ibid, p. 121

After direct Muslim rule began in Delhi (1206), the power and opportunity for making expeditions against non-Muslim communities in the vast landscape of India greatly increased. The scale of enslavement and yield of slaves naturally increased during subsequent centuries, until apostate Akbar officially banned the divinely sanctioned institution, but with only limited success. Enslavement was slowly revived after Akbar's death in 1605; it peaked in the reign of orthodox Aurangzeb (d. 1707). It tapered down quickly after the British consolidation of power in India beginning in 1757.

Once the sultanate was founded in Delhi, slaves were mainly supplied to domestic markets, instead of transporting them to overseas market. Naturally, slave-markets mushroomed across India for the first time in history. Amir Khasrau wrote about the time of Sultan Alauddin Khilji (r. 1296–1316) that '*the Turks, whenever they please, can seize, buy, or sell any Hindu.*' The buying and selling of slaves obviously occurred in slave-markets. It is already noted that '*fresh batches of captives were constantly arriving*' in the slave-markets of Delhi during Sultan Alauddin. During Sultan Muhammad Tughlaq (d. 1351), Ibn Battutah found an excessive supply of slaves in the markets of Delhi, making them very cheap. Shihabuddin Ahmad Abbas also records, '*Everyday thousands of slaves are sold at a very low price*' during his reign.[858] Manrique and Bernier witnessed during Emperor Shahjahan and Aurangzeb (1628–1707) that destitute peasants and their women and children were carried away by tax-collectors for selling them to exact revenues (noted already).

Price of slaves: The price at which the slaves were sold is not given in most instances. KS Lal has summarized available information on the prices of Indian slaves as discussed below.[859] Sultan Mahmud had ransomed King Jaipal's release at '*200,000 golden dinars and 250 elephants*', plus '*the necklace taken from Jaipal was valued at another 200,000 golden dinars.*' Al-Utbi informs us that the 53,000 captives brought by Sultan Mahmud in 1019 were sold at two to ten *dirhams* apiece. The combined assault of Muhammad Ghauri and Qutbuddin Aibak on the Hindus of the Salt Range yielded so large a number of captives that '*five Hindu captives could be bought for a dinar,*' wrote Hasan Nizami.

Slave-trade in India had become such a prominent trade vocation that some rulers even took the onus of regulating slave-markets by fixing prices. During Sultan Alauddin Khilji, Indian markets were teeming with slaves. He fixed the price for a good-looking girl suitable for concubinage from twenty to thirty and even forty *tankhas* (ten *tankhas* = one gold coin), while male slaves were priced at 100 to 200 *tankhas*. Handsome boys were to be sold at twenty to forty *tankhas*, while those in poor demand could be sold at seven to eight *tankhas*. The price of a child slave was fixed at seventy to eighty *tankhas*.[860] Special arrangement was there for setting wholesale prices. However, in times of huge catches of slaves, the law of supply and demand prevailed; and the prices could not be kept at the fixed higher rates. On the contrary, when the supply was low, the prices went up. Captives of special significance—such as of royal or noble birth, young age, outstanding beauty, or of exceptional military capability—could be sold as high as 1,000 to 2,000 *tankhas*. Poet Badr Shah had allegedly bought a slave, named *Gul-Chehra* (Rose Face), for 900 *tankhas*, while famous commander Malik Kafur was called *Hazardinari*, meaning that he was purchased for one thousand (*hazar*) *dinars*.

After Sultan Alauddin's death, the later sultans had done away with price-control of slaves. During Sultan Muhammad Shah Tughlaq's reign (1325–51), the capture of slaves was huge and their prices came down so low that "*the value at Delhi of a young slave girl for domestic service does not exceed eight tankhas. Those, deemed fit for the dual role of domestic maid and concubine, were sold for about fifteen tankhas.*" Ibn

---

858. Ibid, p. 51

859. Ibid, p. 120–27

860. Child slaves brought such high prices, because they could serve the master for their whole life and that they could be handled easily and moulded into whatever the master wanted, particularly to groom them to be ruthless soldiers for waging Jihad against the infidels (like Janissaries).

Battutah had bought one beautiful slave girl for one gold coin (ten *tankhas*) in Bengal, while his friend had bought a young slave for two gold coins.

As Muslim sultans started indulging in the life of debauchery and created huge harems by accumulating concubines in their thousands, plus numerous *ghilmans*, "*demands for beautiful girls and beardless boys made them a scarce commodity, and their prices rose to 500 tankhas and sometimes even to one thousand and two thousand tankhas*," records Barani. Al-Omari testifies that "*in spite of low price of slaves, 2,000 tankhas, and even more, are paid for young Indian girls.*" When asked for the reason, he was told that "*these young girls are remarkable for their beauty and the grace of their manner.*"

Slaves from foreign lands, considered talented and articles of luxury, were in high demand and flowed into Indian markets. Both male and female slaves of foreign origin were bought at higher prices for engaging them in special duties: in important position in the army, in concubinage or for keeping watch on the harem women. Aurangzeb had bought Tartar and Uzbek women as harem-guards because of their war-like nature and skills, while an eastern European woman was his sex-slave. Sultan Qutbuddin Aibak had purchased two accomplished Turkish slaves for 100,000 *jitals* (2,000 *tankhas*), while Sultan Iltutmish purchased one Qamaruddin Timur Khan for 50,000 *jitals*.[861]

Over in Morocco, Sultan Moulay Ismail bought Thomas Pellow and his crewmates in 1715 from their corsair captor at £15 apiece. However, in open markets, common white slaves were priced between £30 and £35, while young boys were sold at £40 apiece. The older and weaker men were sold at lower prices. Jewish traders sometimes raised the price, from £15 to £75 for a captive on one occasion.[862] Some seven decades earlier (1646), when the British government sent merchant Edmund Cason to Algiers to buy back British captives held at the sultan's palace, he paid £38 per male slave.[863] But releasing the female slaves proved extremely expensive. He paid £800 for Sarah Ripley, £1,100 for Alice Hayes and £1,392 for Mary Bruster.[864] The prices of black slaves, always abundant in supply, were much lower. Around 1680, European slave-traders at the Gambian coast bought young black slaves at £3.4 apiece, while the inland slave-dealers bought them for between £1 and £3 each, depending on the distance from the coast.[865]

Cross-border slave-trade: Slave-trade was a prominent business enterprise all over the Islamic world. Apart from India, North Africa, the Middle East (Baghdad and Damascus) as well as Khurasan, Ghazni and Samarkhand in Central Asia were prominent centres of slave-trade. Emperor Babur (d. 1530) noted of two major trade-marts in Kabul and Qandahar, where caravans from India brought slaves. To Kabul, similar caravans came from Khurasan, Rum (Istanbul), Iraq and China.

Merchants from Islamic Turkey, Syria, Persia and Transoxiana used to offer consignments of slaves to Muslim rulers of India. Indian Muslim rulers also sent merchants overseas for purchasing foreign slaves, a treasured commodity. Sultan Iltutmish once sent merchants to Samarkhand, Bukhara and Tirmiz to buy foreign slaves. They brought 100 slaves for the sultan, including famous Balban, who seized power in 1265. Slaves were coming to India from Uzbekistan and Tataristan. The Muslim rulers of India used to purchase foreign slaves in large numbers for their placement in important positions, including in the army, likely to avert indigenous uprisings. Even Akbar's Court, first to open doors to the employment of Hindus, was predominantly foreign. His Minister Abul Fazl records that nearly 70 percent of the royal appointments by

861. Lal (1994), p. 130–35

862. Milton, p. 69–70, 77

863. At this time, an ordinary London shopkeeper earned £10 a year, while wealthy merchants made £40 at best.

864. Milton, p. 27

865. Curtin PD (1993) *The Tropical Atlantic of the Slave Trade* in *Islamic & European Expansion*, in Adas M Ed., p. 174

Akbar were men of foreign origin. Of the remaining 30 percent, more than half were Muslims and the rest Hindus.[866]

About the expanse and diversity of the slave-trade in the Muslim world, writes Lewis:[867]

The slave population of the Islamic world was recruited from many lands. In the earliest days, slaves came principally from the newly conquered countries—from the Fertile Crescent and Egypt, from Iran and North Africa, from Central Asia, India, and Spain... As the supply of slaves by conquest and capture diminished, the needs of the slave market were met, more and more, by importation from beyond the frontier. Small numbers of slaves were brought from India, China, Southeast Asia, and the Byzantine Empire, most of them specialists and technicians of one kind or another. The vast majority of unskilled slaves, however, came from the lands immediately north and south of the Islamic world—whites from Europe and the Eurasian steppes, blacks from Africa south of the Sahara.

Black slaves were brought into the Islamic world by a number of routes—from West Africa across the Sahara to Morocco and Tunisia, from Chad across the desert to Libya, from East Africa down the Nile to Egypt, and across the Red Sea and Indian Ocean to Arabia and the Persian Gulf. Turkish slaves from the steppe-lands were marketed in Samarkand and other Muslim Central Asian cities and from there exported to Iran, the Fertile Crescent, and beyond. Caucasians, of increasing importance in the later centuries, were brought from the land bridge between the Black Sea and the Caspian and were marketed mainly in Aleppo and Mosul.

According to Segal, Muslim traders brought slaves from the Red Sea Coast to the Middle East across the Sahara Desert along six major routes. Slaves from East Africa were herded across the Indian Ocean. As already cited, in the nineteenth century alone, some 1,200,000 slaves came across the Sahara to the Middle East markets, while 450,000 down the Red Sea and 442,000 from the East African coastal ports. Segal records a number of eyewitness accounts of slave-trading in African markets as follows:

In the 1570s, a Frenchman visiting Egypt found many thousands of blacks on sale in Cairo on market days. In 1665–66, Father Antonios Gonzalis, a Spanish/Belgian traveler, reported 800 to 1,000 slaves on sale in the Cairo market on a single day. In 1796, a British traveler reported a caravan of 5,000 slaves departing from Darfur. In 1849, the British vice consul reported the arrival of 2,384 slaves at Murzuq in the Fezzan (Northwest Africa).[868]

EUROPEAN SLAVES

About slaves coming from Europe to the Muslim world, Lewis adds:

In Europe there was also an important trade in slaves, Muslim, Jewish, pagan, and even Orthodox Christian... Central and East European slaves, generally known as *Saqaliba* (i.e. Slavs), were imported by three main routes: overland via France and Spain, from Eastern Europe via the Crimea, and by sea across the Mediterranean. They were mostly but not exclusively Slavs. Some were captured by Muslim naval raids on European coasts, particularly the Dalmatian. Most were supplied by European, especially Venetian, slave merchants, who delivered cargoes of them to the Muslim markets in Spain and North Africa.

---

866. Moreland (1995), p. 69–70

867. Lewis (1994), op cit

868. Segal, p. 59

European slaves were in special demand for serving as concubines, in the royal army and palaces, and in establishments of the rich in Morocco, Tunisia, Algeria and Libya. According to Giles Milton's *White Gold* and Robert Davis' *Christian Slaves, Muslim Masters*, since the 1530s, North African Muslim pirates raided European coastal towns and villages from Sicily to Cornwall as well as European ships for some three centuries and enslaved over one million Europeans (including many American seamen). British humanist author Christopher Hitchens queries on this enslavement: '*How many know that perhaps 1.5 million Europeans and Americans were enslaved in Islamic North Africa between 1530 and 1780? ...what of the people of the town of Baltimore in Ireland, all carried off by 'corsair' raiders in a single night?*'[869]

The Barbary Muslim pirates kidnapped Europeans from ships in North Africa's coastal waters (Barbary Coast). They also attacked and pillaged the Atlantic coastal fishing villages and town in Europe, enslaving the inhabitants. Villages and towns on the coast of Italy, Spain, Portugal and France were the hardest hit. Muslim slave-raiders also seized people as far afield as Britain, Ireland and Iceland.

In 1544, the island of Ischia off Naples was ransacked, taking 4,000 inhabitants prisoners, while some 9,000 inhabitants of Lipari Island off the north coast of Sicily were enslaved.[870] Turgut Reis, a Turkish pirate chief, ransacked the coastal settlements of Granada (Spain) in 1663 and carried away 4,000 people as slaves. In 1625, Barbary pirates captured the Lund Island in the Bristol Channel and planted the standard of Islam. From this base, they went ransacking and pillaging surrounding villages and towns, causing a stunning spectacle of mayhem, slaughter and plunder. According to Milton, '*Day after day, they struck at unarmed fishing communities, seizing the inhabitants, and burning their homes. By the end of the dreadful summer of 1625, the mayor of Plymouth reckoned that 1,000 skiffs had been destroyed and similar number of villagers carried off into slavery.*'[871] Between 1609 and 1616, the Barbary pirates '*captured a staggering 466 English trading ships.*'

Murad Rais, a European convert to Islam, became a leader of the Barbary pirates at the coastal Corsair town of Salé off Morocco. In 1627, he went on a pillaging and enslaving campaign to Iceland. After dropping anchor at Reykjavik, his forces ransacked the town and returned with 400 men, women and children and sold them in Algiers. In 1631, he made a voyage with a brigand of 200 pirates to the coast of Southern Ireland and ransacked and pillaged the village of Baltimore, carrying away 237 men, women and children to Algiers.[872]

The barbaric slave-raiding activities of the Muslim pirates had a telling effect on Europe. France, England, and Spain lost thousands of ships, devastating to their sea-borne trade. Long stretches of the coast in Spain and Italy were almost completely abandoned by their inhabitants until the nineteenth century. The finishing industry was virtually devastated.

Paul Baepler's *White Slaves, African Masters: An Anthology of American Barbary Captivity Narratives* lists a collection of essays by nine American captives held in North Africa. According to his book, there were more than 20,000 white Christian slaves by 1620 in Algiers alone; their number swelled to more than 30,000 men and 2,000 women by the 1630s. There were a minimum of 25,000 white slaves at any time in Sultan Moulay Ismail's palace, records Ahmed ez-Zayyani; Algiers maintained a population of 25,000 white slaves between 1550 and 1730, and their numbers could double at certain times. During the same period, Tunis and Tripoli each maintained a white slave population of about 7,500. The Barbary pirates enslaved some 5,000 Europeans annually over a period of nearly three centuries.[873]

869. Hitchens C (2007) *Jefferson Versus the Muslim Pirates*, City Journal, Spring Issue

870. Povoledo E (2003) *The mysteries and majesties of the Aeolian Islands*, International Herald Tribune, 26 September.

871. Milton, p. 11

872 Milton, p. 13–14; Lewis B (1993) *Islam and the West*, Oxford University Press, New York, p. 74

873. Milton, p. 99,271–72

The most famous European Christian to serve as a slave in Barbary Muslim Africa was Miguel de Cervantes, the famous Spanish author of the *Don Quixote* epic. He was taken captive in 1575 by Barbary pirates and was later released upon payment of ransom.

The Ottoman penetration into Europe in the 1350s and their capture of Constantinople later in 1453 opened new floodgates for slave-trade from the European front. In their last attempt to overrun Europe in 1683, the Ottoman army, although defeated, returned from the Gates of Vienna with 80,000 captives.[874] An immense number of slaves flowed from the Crimea, the Balkans and the steppes of West Asia to Islamic markets. BD Davis laments that the *"Tartars and other Black Sea peoples had sold millions of Ukrainians, Georgians, Circassians, Armenians, Bulgarians, Slavs and Turks,"* which received little notice.[875] Crimean Tatars enslaved and sold some 1,750,000 Ukrainians, Poles and Russian between 1468 and 1694.[876] According to another estimate, between 1450 and 1700, the Crimean Tatars exported some 10,000 slaves, including some Circassians, annually—that is, some 2,500,000 slaves in all, to the Ottoman Empire.[877] The Tatar slave-raiding Khans returned with 18,000 slaves from Poland (1463), 100,000 from Lvov (1498), 60,000 from South Russia (1515), 50,000–100,000 from Galicia (1516), 800,000 from Moscow (1521), 200,000 from South Russia (1555), 100,000 from Moscow (1571), 50,000 from Poland (1612), 60,000 from South Russia (1646), 100,000 from Poland (1648), 300,000 from Ukraine (1654), 400,000 from Valynia (1676) and thousands from Poland (1694). Besides these major catches, they made countless more Jihad raids during the same period, which yielded a few to tens of thousands of slaves.[878] These figures of enslavement must be considered in the context that the population of the Tatar Khanate was only about 400,000 at the time.[879]

THE VIKING SLAVE-TRADE & MUSLIM CONNECTION

In the seventh and eighth centuries after Islam's birth, Muslim invaders and rulers enslaved the infidels in immense numbers, promoting slave-trade into a flourishing business venture in the Muslim world. Late in the eighth century, there arose a band of non-Muslim slave hunters, the Vikings, in Europe. Vikings were a North European people, originating in Scandinavia (Sweden, Denmark), who turned brutal raiding brigands between the eighth and eleventh centuries. Belonging to the so-called *barbarian* Germanic race, they engaged in raiding and pirate attacks along the coasts of the British Isles and mainland Europe as far east as the Volga River in Russia. *'Famed for their long ships—the Vikings had established settlements along the coasts and rivers of mainland Europe, Ireland, Normandy, the Shetland, Orkney, and Faroe Islands, Iceland, Greenland, and Newfoundland over three centuries. They reached south to North Africa and east to Russia and Constantinople as looters, traders, or mercenaries. Vikings under Leif Ericson, heir to Erik the Red, reached North America, with putative expeditions to present-day Canada in the 10th century. Viking raiding voyages decreased with the introduction of Christianity to Scandinavia in the late 10th and 11th century.'*[880] The period of the rise and domance of the Vikings between 793 and 1066 CE became known as the Viking Age.

874. Erdem YH (1996) *Slavery in the Ottoman Empire and Its Demise, 1800-1909*, Macmillan, London, p. 30

875. Lal (1994), p. 132

876. Fisher AW (1972) *Muscovy and the Black Sea Slave Trade*, in *Canadian-American Slavic Studies*, 6(4), p577–83,592–93

877. Inalcik H (1997) *An Economic and Social History of the Ottoman empire, 1300-1600*, Cambridge University Press, Vol. 1, p. 285; Fisher, p. 583–84

878. Bostom, p. 679-81

879. Williams BG (2001) *The Crimean Tatars: The Diaspora Experience and the Forging of a Nation*, E J Brill, Lieden, p. 69–72

880. Viking, Wikipedia, http://en.wikipedia.org/wiki/Vikings

The Vikings have been severely condemned for their vocation of savage raids on innocent and peaceful families and communities along the coasts of Europe, killing the adults and capturing the children and young women for selling into slavery. The major reasons for the rise and spread of the Vikings, think historians, were overpopulation, technological innovations, and climate change, plus the interruption of trade and flow of goods from Central Europe to Scandinavia after the destruction of the Frisian fleet by Roman Emperor Charlemagne in 785.

Little attention is, however, given to the positive influence that Islam played in their engagement in slave-trade. The defeat of the Muslim army in the Battle of Tours in 732 dramatically subdued Islamic conquest on the European front. They even had to withdraw from some of the territories they had already captured. Thereafter, the enslavement of the prized white women from Europe for keeping as concubines in Muslim harems of the Islamic world had greatly reduced.

As capturing of white sex-slaves through wars and raids reduced, purchasing them became the alternative for meeting their unceasing and obsessive demand in the Muslim world. At the rise of the berserk Viking raiders, the Scandinavian fur-traders reached the Europe-Arab trading center of Bulgar Volga (in Russia), where they met traders from the Muslim world with huge demand of white women for Islamic harems. The savage Vikings, thereafter, embarked on capturing young white women for selling to traders from the Muslim world. This first opened the Eastern European route of slave-trade with the Muslim world. The supply route of white slaves via Spain also soon opened. With the spread of Christianity to Northern Europe, Viking slave-trade tapered down and eventually ceased.

Viking slave-trade has been thoroughly condemned, but little has been said of the role, Islam played, in seducing the Vikings into this abhorrent profession. There is no excuse for the crime the Vikings had committed. It is also impossible to disconnect Islam from the Viking slave-trade, because the supply was absolutely meant for meeting Islamic world's unceasing demand for the prized white slaves.

The supply of white slaves to the Islamic world did not cease with the end of the Viking Age. Once Viking slave-trade ended, Muslim slave-hunters themselves slowly expanded the capture of white slaves in Europe to meet the Muslim world's demand for them, thus replacing the Viking suppliers. In 1353, the Ottoman Turks, having crossed over to Europe bypassing Constantinople, launched a new wave of raging Jihad expeditions against Europe overrunning Bulgaria and Serbia. This marked a new beginning for the capture of white slaves by Muslims in great multitudes. The Turks enslaved 7,000 whites in the attack of Thessaloniko (Greece) in 1430; while, in the sacked of Methone (Greece) in 1499, Ottoman Sultan Bayezid II slaughtered all those (males) aged over ten years and "seized women and children".[881] Persian rulers Shah Tahmasp (d. 1576) attacked Georgia in 1553, enslaving more than 30,000 women and children. In his expedition to Georgia in 1551, the Ghazis *slew the men and took captive their wives and children.* The sultan had earlier made another two successful expeditions against Georgia in 1540 and 1546, but the numbers enslaved are not available.[882] The Ottomans and Safavids made numerous raids into European territories until the late seventeenth century. Despite suffering defeat and heavy loss in the siege of Vienna in 1683, the Ottoman Turks returned with 80,000 captives. This clearly suggests that slaves were captured in large numbers in all their campaigns.

Meanwhile the Tatar Khans embarked on numerous holy war expeditions (*Razzia*) into Eastern Europe and Russia in the mid-fifteenth century, capturing white slaves in tens to hundreds of thousands as noted above. The North African Barbary pirates also continued raiding and capturing white slaves along the European coastal towns from Sicily to Cornwall and from ships in the sea, enslaving more than one million white men and women between 1530 and 1780. The hunting of white slaves by Barbary pirates continued until the 1820s.

---

881. Bostom, p. 613,619

882. Ibid, p. 620–21

EUROPEAN SLAVE-TRADE & ISLAMIC COMPLICITY

The trans-Atlantic slave-trade, conducted by European slave-traders, in which millions of African slaves were shipped to the New World, has received intense condemnations from Muslims and non-Muslims alike from everywhere, the West included. The issue of the Islamic slave-trade, however, remains largely untouched, unspoken and somewhat forgotten.

The European supply of slaves to the New World started when the Holy Roman Emperor Charles V first authorized the involvement of Europe in slave-trade in 1519. The Portuguese and Spaniards, notorious amongst Europeans as slavers, first jumped into this lucrative venture followed by the Dutch, and then, the French. Britain's King Charles I first authorized slave-trade in 1631 and his son Charles II reintroduced it by a Royal Charter in 1672.

It is estimated that about eleven million African slaves were transported to the New World. Of these, approximately 4.0 million (35.4 percent) went to Portuguese controlled Brazil, 2.5 million (22.1 percent) to the Spanish colonies of South and Central America, 2.0 million (17.7 percent) to the British West Indies— mostly Jamaica, 1.6 million (14.1 percent) to the French West Indies, 0.5 million (4.4 percent) to the Dutch West Indies, and another 0.5 million to North America.[883]

Abolition: The French revolution was organized for wrestling the "rights of man", although without giving any serious thought to the rights of slaves. It, nonetheless, later on prompted the legal emancipation of slaves of the French Empire in 1794. In the 1790s, Denmark and Netherlands took measures to abolish their own slave-trade. Meanwhile in Britain, parliamentarian William Wilberforce started a campaign in 1787 for the suppression of slave-trade, which soon transformed into a vigorous movement for the abolition of slavery in the British Empire. Twenty years later in 1807, the British House of Commons passed a bill for abolishing slave-trade by an overwhelming majority of 283 to sixteen votes, a decisive blow to slavery. Later in 1809, the British government took further steps to stop slave-trading by mobilizing its Navy to search ships, including foreign vessels, suspected of carrying slaves. It also used diplomatic cards with Muslim governments—in Persia, Turkey, Egypt, and so on—for the abolition of slavery in the Muslim world.

In 1810, the British Parliament made engagement in slave-trade punishable by fourteen years of hard labor. In 1814, Britain started lobbying for the inclusion of the abolition of slave-trade in the *International Treaty of Europe*, which led to the signing of such a Treaty by all the European powers on 9 June 1815. In 1825, Britain made complicity in slave-trade punishable by death. The greatest moment for the anti-slavery movement came in 1833: the British Parliament abolished the institution of slavery altogether and freed all slaves, about 700,000, of the British Empire. France followed the British example of emancipating slaves in 1848, prompting the same in Dutch colonies. The United States emancipated its slaves in 1865.

Islamic complicity: The European slave-trade must be condemned for the very dehumanizing and cruel nature of this grotesque crime against humanity. Muslims are very forthcoming in doing this laudable exercise in *holier than thou* pious tones as though their history is clean of slavery. In truth, even in the European slave-trade, Muslims played—both directly and indirectly—an essential and financially rewarding role. But there exists a peculiar silence about it amongst Muslims. Even non-Muslim scholars, including those of the West, are largely silent about Islam's contributory roles in the trans-Atlantic slave-trade.

The "indirect" role of Islam in the trans-Atlantic slave-trade lies in the fact that Muslims had created an example of sustained and vibrant slave-trade across the vast Muslim world many centuries before the Europeans embarked on it. More importantly, the Europeans were a sustained and brutal victim of the Islamic enslavement and slave-trade: it started with the Muslim attack on Spain in 711 and continued until the early nineteenth century. The Vikings also were Muslims' proxy-partners in raiding and abducting the white women and children to meet the Islamic world's demand for white slaves, particularly concubines. The last

---

883. Hammond P (2004) *The Scourge of Slavery*, in Christian Action Magazine, Vol. 4

Ottoman Sultan had a British captive in his harem. She was rescued and brought to Britain after the sultan's ouster from Turkey. The psychological impact of this sustained and brutal subjection of Europeans to enslavement and sale for so many centuries can not be underestimated. It must have convinced them that slavery, which had become a brutal part and parcel of their life, was something not quite abnormal. The Europeans, having suffered violent subjection to Islamic slavery and slave-trade for nine centuries, finally embarked on the trade themselves.

Concerning the "direct" role of Islam in the trans-Atlantic slave-trade, it was mostly the Muslim raiders and traders, who did the inhuman part of capturing the slaves in Africa. European traders bought slaves mainly from these Muslim slave-catchers and transported to the New World. When the Europeans embarked on the slave-trade, Muslims were the masters of large parts of Africa with centuries of experience in the art of slave-hunting. They became the ready supplier of slaves for European traders. The European merchants were stationed in trading centers along the African coast. Muslim slave hunters and traders brought black captives from inland locations to these coastal centers and sold to Europeans.

The European traders obtained some slaves, as high as 20 percent, directly forgoing the hands of Muslim traders. This direct procurement took place, not through violent raids and abductions, but through willing sale by non-Muslim owners, or possibly by some parents and relatives. (Some of them might have been supplied by non-Muslim slave-hunters, who following Muslims, had taken to the profession.) The Sahel region of West Africa, just south of Sahara and the regions of Angola were notorious for the lack of rainfall, occasionally for two to three years in succession. When that happened causing devastating drought and famines, people—faced with starvation and death—fled and '*sold themselves or family members in order to survive at all.*' Senegal experienced a series of drought and poor harvest between 1746 and 1754, which dramatically increased the volume of slave-trade. '*French exports from Senegal in 1754 were the highest ever,*' writes Curtin.[884]

The European traders acquired greater than 80 percent of slaves in Africa from Muslim slave-hunters and traders. Muslim warriors had turned Africa into a slave-catching and -breeding ground to meet the demand of slaves in the Muslim world, which later on also became a supply-house for European merchants. Sayyid Sa'id, a prince of Oman, moved to East Africa with the pirates of the port of Masqat, who had been put out of business by the British. Having established himself in Zanzibar (1806), his Arab raiders from the East Coast penetrated deep inland, reaching as far as Uganda and Congo for capturing slave.[885] This way he founded his famed slave-empire in East Africa. In Africa, writes Curtin, there were *slave-raiding chiefs* or *gangs* of forty to fifty men. They went out in groups to nearby villages '*stealing cattle and kidnapping people, trying to pick individuals or small groups, like women on the way to the village well or others unlikely to be able to defend themselves.*' Although these gangs could fight if needed, '*they depended on stealth and speed to make their capture and sell them at a distance...*'[886] The opening of new markets in the New World proved very lucrative for the Muslim slave hunters and traders of Africa.

DENIALS OF ISLAMIC SLAVERY

To most Muslims, the only slave-trade that existed in the world was the trans-Atlantic one, which they are very forthcoming to condemn. To them, the more extensive and barbarous practice of slavery of the Muslim

---

884. Curtin, p. 172–73

885. Gavin, R J (1972) In MA Klein & GW Johnson eds., p. 178

886. Curtin, p. 177–79

world that continued well into the late twentieth century (indeed, continues today) never existed. This perception amongst them is undoubtedly the result of their ignorance about the history of Islam. Some Muslims—knowledgeable about it, or when presented with undeniable evidence—take recourse of the much familiar denials. They offer two common arguments to counter the undeniable facts about the widespread practice of slavery in the Muslim world. Firstly, slavery is not at all approved in Islam; its practice in the Muslim world resulted from the abuse or disregard of Islam. The second type of response comes from the more knowledgeable Muslims, who—failing to deny the approval of slavery in Islam and its widespread practice in the Muslim world—would agree that slavery was accepted in Islam, albeit reluctantly and on a limited scale, because of its overwhelming practice in Arabia at the time. They then come with a set of Quranic verses and prophetic traditions to claim that '*Islam actually set the first example for the abolition of slavery.*'

The first type of response definitely comes from the group of Muslims, the overwhelming majority, who are thoroughly ignorant of the theological content of Islam regarding the sanction of slavery and Prophet Muhammad's engagement in enslavement, slave-trade and concubinage. The second group, deliberately using deceptive ploys, comes up with a set of arguments from the Quran and the *Sunnah*, which need addressing here. The commonly cited set of Quranic references are:

1. Quran 4:36 urges Muslims to show kindness to orphans, parents, travelers and *slaves.*

2. Quran 9:60 directs part of obligatory charity toward freeing of slaves.

3. Quran 24:33 advises owners of well-behaved slaves to set terms for their release in writing.

4. Quran 5:92 and 18:3 propose freeing of slaves as a means of expiation for sins.

5. Quran 4:92 states that a Muslim should free a *believing* slave as expiation for involuntary manslaughter.

Based on such references, Ahmad Alawad Sikainga, Professor of History at the Ohio State University, explains away the Quranic recognition of slavery as '*broad and general propositions of an **ethical nature** rather than specific legal formulations.*'[887] In a similar vein, famous Pakistani scholar and poet Muhammad Iqbal (d. 1938) held slavery in Islam as a benign institution, completely devoid of true servitude. According to him,[888]

> [Prophet Muhammad] declared the principle of equality and though, like every wise reformer, he slightly conceded to the social conditions around him in retaining the name of slavery, he quietly took away the whole institution of slavery. The truth is that the institution of slavery is a mere name in Islam.

Other more emphatic apologists come up with such lofty claims that Islam has clearly and categorically forbidden the primitive practice of capturing a free man, to make him a slave, or to sell him into slavery. They affirm their position by quoting Prophet Muhammad: "*There are three categories of people against whom I shall myself be a plaintiff on the Day of Judgment. Of these three: he, who enslaves a free man, then sells him, and eats this money.*"[889] Muslim scholar Syed Ameer Ali (d. 1928), widely read in the West, argued that Muslims should efface the dark page of slavery from the world '*to show the falseness of the aspersions cast*

---

887. *Islam and slavery*, Wikipedia, http://en.wikipedia.org/wiki/Islam_and_Slavery

888. Iqbal M (2002) *Islam as a Moral and Political Ideal, in Modernist Islam, 1840-1940: A Sourcebook*, C Kurzman ed., Oxford University Press, London, p. 307–8

889. Muhammad S (2004) *Social Justice in Islam*, Anmol Publications Pvt Ltd, New Delhi, p. 40

on the memory of the noble Prophet, by proclaiming in explicit terms that slavery is reprobated by their faith and discountenanced by their code.'[890] Joining the tune of these Muslim apologists, Lewis argues: '*The Islamic law and practice, from an early stage, severely restricted the enslavement of free persons... limiting it in effect to the non-Muslims captured or conquered in a war.*'[891]

Those scholars, who claim that Islam categorically forbid the primitive practice of slavery, should pay attention to the words of Allah in Quranic verses 16:71, 16:76 and 30:28, which unequivocally and categorically state the division of human race into masters and slaves as natural, as His grace, and as part of His design. Iqbal and Ali should take note of the fact that Prophet Muhammad had owned no slaves prior to taking up the Islamic mission; and at the time of his death, he owned dozens of slaves and a few concubines, the majority of whom were obtained through brutal raids and attacks on innocent communities. Sikainga should not forget that, in Islamic thought, the Quran is the final words of the Creator of the Universe in all matters; and therefore, whatever the Quran sanctions becomes the eternal law for the Islamic society. This fundamental position of Islam contradicts Sikainga's assertion that slavery is no "specific legal formulations" in Islam. In reality, slavery in Islam is a fundamental institution, repeatedly reiterated by Allah and widely practiced by Prophet Muhammad, which would stand unaltered until the end of the world. Furthermore, it is equally nonsensical and inexcusable to term the division of *fundamentally equal* human beings into masters and slaves as a formulation of "ethical nature" as Sikainga puts it. More so is the repeated Quranic sanction of violent enslavement of women for reducing them into sex-slaves.

Gulam Ahmad Parwez (d. 1983), another Muslim scholar and activist of the subcontinent, uses a deceptive ploy of different kind. He argues that '*those whom your right hand possesses*' in Quran 47:4, referring to slaves, should be read in the past tense; that is, as '*those whom your right hand **possessed**.*' This way, he argues, slavery belonged to the past and the Quran closed '*the door to future slavery.*'[892] Muslims should probably follow this crooked ploy and read the instructions of the Quran regarding prayers, fasting, pilgrimage and everything else in the past tense and relegate Islam to the dustbin of history.

Prophet Muhammad relocated from Mecca to Medina in 622, when he had only about 200–250 converts: from Mecca and Medina combined. With this small group of followers, he formed a raiding brigand expressly for the purpose of attacking caravans from Mecca to plunder them for booty. As his power grew, he scaled up his adventures by attacking the Pagan, Jewish and Christian communities that came within his reach and power for the purpose of plundering and capture of slaves. After Muhammad's death in 632, this unconditional war on the infidels continued with greater vigor as Muslim power grew in leaps and bounds. They started undertaking campaigns of massive scales eventually bringing down world's great powers: Persia, Byzantium and India. They often enslaved in tens to hundreds of thousands in a single campaign, besides putting large numbers of the vanquished non-Muslims to the sword.

At the advent of Islam, Prophet Muhammad's raiding and warring brigand, consisting of just a few hundred neo-Muslim Bedouins of Arabia, declared an aggressive, unconditional and relentless holy war on the rest of humanity with the intention to subjugate and enslave them. Those like Lewis, who think that Islam "categorically forbade" or "severely restricted" the enslavement of a free man, should realize that Islam called for the unrestrained subjugation and enslavement of all free men and women of the globe at the hands of a few hundred Bedouin Arab raiders and plunderers. The Islamic legislation of enslavement is not of "severely restricted" nature, but of the highest scale imaginable, unprecedented in the history of mankind. The soldiers of Islam have executed this divine command with aplomb; the history of Islam has been the witness to that. By any standard, the sanction of slavery in Islam was the most devastating blow to the spirit and dignity of the free human being.

---

890. Ali SA (1891) *The Life and Teachings of Muhammed*, WH Allen, London, p. 380

891. Lal (1994), p. 206

892. Parwez GA (1989) *Islam, a Challenge to Religion*, Islamic Book Service, New Delhi, p. 345–46

Humane treatment of slaves in Islam

It is true that Islam urges Muslims to treat slaves humanely. Verses of the Quran listed above encourage Muslims to set slaves free (manumission) for various reasons, including for the redemption of involuntarily killing a Muslim (not an infidel). In Islam, manumission is seen as an act of benevolence or expiation of sins. On the basis of these arguments, apologists of Islam would claim that '*It is not true to say that Islam instituted, or was responsible for the institution of slavery; it is more correct to say that it was the first religion, which put the first steps necessary for its extinction*' (personal communication). Joining this camp of Muslims, Prof. Jonathan Brockopp of Pensylvania State Univerity writes:

> Other cultures limit a master's right to harm a slave but few exhort masters to treat their slaves kindly, and the placement of slaves in the same category as other weak members of society who deserve protection is unknown outside the Quran. The unique contribution of the Quran, then, is to be found in its emphasis on the place of slaves in society and society's responsibility toward the slave, perhaps the *most progressive legislation* on slavery in its time.[893]

Concerning Islamic injunctions for good treatment of slaves and their manumission, there was nothing new in it. We have noted that, nearly a thousand years before the advent of Islam, Buddha had urged his followers to treat slaves well and not to overwork them. In Athens, the Greek statesman and political reformer Solon (c. 638–558 BCE) had enacted a decree abolishing enslavement for debts, a major cause of enslavement at the time.

The tradition of manumission of slaves existed in Greece about a millennium before the advent of Islam. Inscriptions in stones, belonging to the fourth century BCE and later, document emancipation of slaves in Greece, likely as voluntary acts of masters (predominantly male and also female from the Hellenistic period). To buy their freedom, slaves could either use their savings or take loan from friends or masters.[894]

The sense justice toward slaves in Greek Society can be guaged from Socrates' encounter with Euthyphro outside a law-court. Euthyphro's father had killed one of his slaves (accidentally, probably while discipling him), who had killed another slave. And Euthyphro took his father to court for his crime of killing the slave. On Euthyphro's way to the court, Socrates stopped him so as to inquire about his motivation or the righteousness that inspired him to prosecute his own father. Euthyphro told Socrates that '*although his family think it impious for a son to prosecute his father as a murderer, he knows what he is about. His family is ignorant about what is **holy**, whereas he has 'an accurate knowledge of all that.' He therefore had no doubt about the rightness of his action.*'[895] While this case, undoubtedly, was an exception to norm, it nonetheless informs us of the sense of justice toward slaves that had penetraded into the then Greek Society (a housands years before Muhammad)—something impossible even today in any Muslim soceity.

The Islamic exhortation for treating slaves well and for freeing them was thus nothing new. Such benevolent practice existed in Greece nearly a millennium earlier. Solon had even enacted a ban on the major form of enslavement in Athens nearly twelve centuries before the birth of Islam. Neither the practice of emancipation of slaves was absent in Arabia during Muhammad's life or prior to that; evidence for it comes from the following Islamic text [Bukhari 3:46:715]:

> Narrated Hisham: My father told me that Hakim bin Hizam manumitted one-hundred slaves in the pre-Islamic period of ignorance and slaughtered one-hundred camels (and distributed them in charity). When he embraced Islam he again slaughtered one-hundred camels and manumitted

893. Brockopp JE (2005) *Slaves and Slavery*, in *The Encyclopedia of the Qur'ān*, McAuliffe JD *et al.* ed., EJ Brill, Leiden, Vol. 5, p. 56–60.

894. Slavery in Ancient Greece, Wikipedia, http://en.wikipedia.org/wiki/Slavery_in_Ancient_Greece

895. Gottlieb, A (2001) *Socrates: Philosophy's Martyr*, in *The Great Philosopher* (Monk R & Raphael F eds.), Phoenix, London, p. 28-29

one-hundred slaves. Hakim said, 'I asked Allah's Apostle, 'O Allah's Apostle! What do you think about some good deeds I used to practice in the pre-Islamic period of ignorance (jahiliyah) regarding them as deeds of righteousness?' Allah's Apostle said, 'You have embraced Islam along with all those good deeds you did.'

Good treatment and freeing of slaves definitely existed in the seventh-century Arab society, prior to the founding of Islam. Muhammad himself had freed his only slave Zayd when he was a Pagan, some fifteen years before undertaking the Islamic mission. He even adopted Zayd as his son. These generous and humane gestures of Pagan Muhammad clearly reflected the existing benevolent pre-Islamic tradition and culture of the Arab society. Hence, Islam and Prophet Muhammad added nothing new to the humane aspect of slavery.

Islam aggravated slavery

Islam did not institute slavery, but embraced the age-old practice with open arms and gave it a divine validation to last for the eternity and promoted it to a hitherto unprecedented scale. It is groundless to claim that Islam closed the door to slavery or took the first step toward its abolition. In the Quran, Allah repeatedly gave approval of slavery as part of His divine plan, which must stand until the end of the world. Not only that, Islam aggravated the practice of slavery at its very inception, which worsened further over the centuries. Prophet Muhammad enslaved the children and women of Banu Qurayza, Khaybar and Banu Mustaliq [Bukhari 3:46:717], after slaughtering the men. This ideal protocol of the Prophet became the *modus operandi* for Muslim warriors through the ages until the West abolished its own engagement in slavery and enforced its ban in the Muslim world—much to the anger, disappointment and even violent opposition of Muslims.

One must take note of the way the Banu Qurayza, Banu Mustaliq and Khaybar Jews were slaughtered and enslaved by the Prophet. Nothing as barbaric and cruel, and on such large-scales, as these took place in the Arabian Peninsula during Muhammad's life. Islamic history tells us that Muhammad's father had only one Abyssinian slave-girl, named Barakat. The leading men of Mecca are not recorded to have possessed slaves in their dozens. The Prophet's first wife Khadijah, despite owning a big business, possessed only one slave, Zayd, whom she presented to Muhammad after their marriage. Muhammad, a Pagan at the time, freed Zayd and adopted him as his son.

During the next fifteen years of his life as a Pagan, Muhammad owned no slave. Over the next twenty-three years of his life as a Muslim and the Prophet of Islam, he accumulated fifty-nine slaves and thirty-eight servants as listed by Ghayasuddin Muhammad Khondmir in *Rauzat-us-Safa*. Zubair, Muhammad's close companion, had a massive 1,000 slaves at the time of his death.[896]

As a Pagan, Muhammad, and also possibly Zubair, owned no slaves. But after embracing the Islamic faith, they amassed slaves in dozens to a thousand. These examples make it clear that, instead of taking any step toward its abolition, the Prophet of Islam and his closest companions themselves had elevated the institution of slavery to a much higher scale, compared to what pre-existed in Arabia. Islam also introduced a most barbaric and cruel means, albeit with divine sanctions, for capturing slaves on a scale not seen in the then Arabia.

Slavery, theologically & historically, an integral part of Islam

Despite widespread denials about the existence of slavery in Islam and the claim that Islam took the first step toward its abolition, slavery is indisputably a divinely sanctioned institution in Islam, which will stand valid

---

896. Lal (1994), p. 13

until the end of the human race. In Islamic doctrine, slavery is integral in Allah's eternal plan; it's a part of His divine grace to humankind. All Schools of Islamic jurisprudence, the Sharia, and the religious doctors of Islam throughout history have unequivocally and proudly accepted and preached slavery as an integral part of Islam. The great Islamic thinker Ibn Khaldun recognized mass enslavement of non-Muslims in gloating religious pride when Muslims had transformed Africa into a slave-hunting and -breeding ground. In practicing slavery, writes Lewis, *"(Muslims) were upholding an institution sanctioned by scripture, law (Sharia), and tradition (Sunnah) and one which in their eyes was necessary to the maintenance of the social structure of Muslim life."*[897] Hughes correctly asserts that in Islam, *'slavery is interwoven with the Law of marriage, the Law of sale, and the Law of inheritance... And its abolition would strike at the very foundation of the code of Mohammedanism.'*[898]

Ibn Khaldun thought the extensive enslavement of Blacks in Africa by Muslims was justified, *'because they have attributes that are quite similar to dumb animals.'*[899] In the annals of Muslim historians, enslavement in general, especially of the allegedly barbarian Blacks, became a matter of pride. It was also deemed as an act of generosity toward curing them of their barbaric nature and sinful religions by bringing them into the true faith and civilized world of Islam. About this line of thinking of the devout Islamic thinkers, writes Arnold, *'devout minds have even recognized in enslavement God's guidance to the true faith...'*[900]

The Negroes from the Upper Nile countries were violently enslaved in massive numbers and converted to Islam. They were summarily castrated and transported across great distances; in the course of this, the majority of them (80–90 percent) perished. Of those, transported across the Atlantic to the new world, some 30–50 percent perished *'in transit to the coast, in confinement awaiting shipment and at sea on the way to Americas.'* The mortality of slaves on board ships in their passage to the New World is estimated at 10 percent.[901]

This tragic doom of captives of mammoth proportion was also seen as a generosity and *'God's grace'* in Islamic mindset of which, writes Arnold, *'God has visited them in their mishap; they can say 'it was His grace', since they are thereby entered into the saving religion.'*[902] Even many religious-minded Western historians, echoed this tune of Muslim thinkers about the massive enterprise of enslavement of Blacks in Africa. Bernard Lewis summarizes the general sentiment in this regard as thus: *'...slavery is a divine boon to mankind, by means of which pagan and barbarous people are brought to Islam and civilization... Slavery in the East has an elevating influence over thousands of human beings, and but for it hundreds of thousands of souls must pass their existence in this world as wild savages, little better than animals; it, at least, makes men of them, useful men too...'*[903]

This divine justification, indeed inspiration, for the enslavement of Blacks was so strong amongst Muslims in Africa that they had *'given up wholly to the pursuit of commerce or to slave hunting'*; and as a result, they were hated and feared by the people as slave-dealers, notes Arnold.[904] Sultan Moulay Ismail (d. 1727), as noted already, had slave-breeding nurseries in Morocco. In the Sudan region of Africa, there were firms that specialized in the breeding of Black slaves for sale like cattle and sheep even in the nineteenth

---

897. Lal (1994), p. 175

898. Hughes, p. 600

899. Lal (1994), p. 80

900. Ibid

901. Curtin, p. 182

902. Arnold TW (1999) *The Preaching of Islam*, Kitab Bhavan, Delhi, p. 416–17

903. Lal (1994), p. 60

904. Arnold, p. 172–73,345–46

century. *Hudud al-Alam*—a Persian geographical manuscript written in 982 for the Ghaurivid ruler Abu al-Harith Muhammad ibn Ahmad, records of the Sudan that, '*no region is more populated than this. The merchants steal the children there and take them away. They castrate them and take them to Egypt, where they sell them.*' Slavery reached such a level that '*Among them there are people who steal each others children to sell them to the merchants when they come,*' adds the document.[905]

Muslims had integrated the institution of slavery into the African society so thoroughly that when the Europeans, particularly their missionaries, tried to liberate them, the slaves felt it preferable to remain under their masters than embrace the challenging free life of taking their destiny into their own hands. A report on the first three years of British administration in Central Africa noted that slave-trade stood as "*a rival kind of civilization to that of white man which it is of a much easier notion for the Negro mind to accept.*"[906] Enslavement became so widespread in Africa that as '*Africa became almost synonymous with slavery, the world forgot the eagerness with which the Tartars and other Black Sea peoples had sold millions of Ukrainians, Georgians, Circassians, Armenians, Bulgarians, Slavs, and Turks,*' laments BD Davis.[907] The most precious commodity that Muslim traders brought from the trading centre of Volga in the tenth century was white slaves, normally sold by the Vikings.

SPECIAL CRUELTY AND CASUALTY OF ISLAMIC SLAVERY

Possibly the most devastating aspect of Islamic slavery was the castration of male captives. The majority of the enslaved African males were emasculated before selling them in the Muslim world. In India, we have noted of large-scale castration of male captives from the beginning to the end of the Islamic rule. Even top generals, namely Malik Kafur and Khusrau Khan, were castrated, which suggest that the castration of male captives was widespread in India, too. There was also widespread castration of European slaves.

The worst casualty of castration was obviously the robbing of man's most fundamental identity and treasure—his manhood, which he is born with. The greatest tragedy of castration was, however, the massive mortality in the operation. According to Koenraad Elst, '*Islamic civilization did indeed practice castration of slaves on an unprecedented scale. Several cities in Africa were real factories of eunuchs; they were an expensive commodity as only 25 percent of the victims survived the operation.*'[908] Furthermore, a large number of captives perished during their passages to markets of the Muslim world, often thousands of miles away; this constituted another huge tragedy of Islamic slavery. The casualties in the raids for harvesting slaves could also be enormous. In Central Africa, recorded Commander VL Cameron, Islamic slave-raiders left the trails of

> burnt villages, of slaughter and the devastation of crops. The loss of life caused by these raids must have been enormous, though it is of course impossible to give any exact figures. Burton, a British explorer, estimated that in order to capture fifty-five women, the merchandise of one of the caravan he observed, at least ten villages had been destroyed, each having a population

---

905. Lal (1994), p. 133

906. Gann, p.196

907. Lal (1994), p. 61

908. Elst K (1993) *Indigenous Indians: Agastya to Ambedkar*, Voice of India, New Delhi, p. 375

between one and two hundred souls. The greater part of these were exterminated or died of starvation.[909]

On the magnitude of the mortality of slaves, writes Segal,

'The arithmetic of the Islamic black slave trade must also not ignore the lives of those men, women and children taken or lost during the procurement, storage and transport. One late nineteenth century writer held that the sale of a single captive for slavery might represent a loss of ten in the population—from defenders killed in attacks on villages, the deaths of women and children from related famine and the loss of children, the old and the sick, unable to keep up with their captors or killed along the way in hostile encounters, or dying of sheer misery.'[910]

Segal collates a number of incidents of slaves being perished in their transportation.[911] Explorer Heinrich Barth recorded that a slave caravan of his friend Bashir, *wazir* of Bornu, on the way to Mecca during pilgrimage season lost forty slaves in the course of a single night, killed by severe cold in the mountain. One British explorer came across over 100 human skeletons from a slave caravan *en route* to Tripoli. The British explorer Richard Lander came across a group of thirty slaves in West Africa, all of them stricken with smallpox, all bound neck to neck with twisted strips of bullock hide. One caravan from the East African coast with 3,000 slaves lost two-thirds of its number from starvation, disease and murder. In the Nubian Desert, one slave caravan of 2,000 slaves literally vanished as every slave had died.

Various estimates put the number of black Africans reduced to slavery in the Islamic world from eleven to thirty-two million. Since 80–90 percent of the captives had perished before reaching their destination, it is not difficult to imagine the quantum of human lives lost as a result of the cruel and barbaric institution of Islamic slavery. Ronald Segal, despite being sympathetic to Islam, puts the number of enslaved black Africans at eleven million and admits that well over thirty million of people might have died at the hands of Muslim slave hunters and traders or ended up as slaves in the Muslim world. From the data presented so far, the institution of Islamic slavery, undoubtedly, has been one of the greatest tragedies to befall humankind.

ABOLITION OF SLAVERY & ISLAMIC RESISTANCE

Slavery is evidently a divinely-sanctioned institution of Islam; its practice is theoretically binding on the Muslim community at all times. Hence, the campaign for its abolition, quite expectedly, faced staunch resistance in the Muslim world and has not achieved complete success to this day. Slavery still exists in Mauritania, Sudan, and Saudi Arabia etc. in one form or another.

European nations banned slave-trade in 1815 and Britain abolished slavery altogether and freed all slaves in 1833. During the same century, the Islamic world continued the profession, enslaving two million Blacks in Africa; another eight million likely perished in the process. This happened despite active efforts by Western nations to stop slavery in the Muslim world. When India slowly came under the British control beginning in 1757, the enslavement of Indian infidels by Muslims eventually ended. In 1843, the East India Company passed a bill, *Indian Slavery Act V*, banning slavery, which led to its eventual disappearance. A

---

909. Cameron CVL (1877) *Across Africa*, Dalty, Isbister & Co., London, Vol. II, p. 137–38

910. Segal, p. 62

911. Ibid, p. 63–64

study at the time of passing the bill found that individual proprietors owned bodies of 2,000 slaves in Bengal, Madras and Bombay.[912]

In Afghanistan, which remained outside European control, violent enslavement of non-Muslims continued. Alexander Gardner, who extensively traveled across Central Asia between 1819 and 1823, left an eyewitness account of slave-hunting and slave-trade still ongoing in Kafiristan, a province in Afghanistan inhabited by non-Muslims. He observed that the sultan of Kunduz had reduced Kafiristan to "*the lowest state of poverty and wretchedness*" through regular raids for plunder and catching slaves for supplying to the markets in Balkh and Buhkara. Gardner added: "*All this misery was caused by the oppression of the Kunduz chief, who, not content with plundering his wretched subjects, made an annual raid into the country south of Oxus; and by chappaos (night attacks), carried off all the inhabitants on whom his troops could lay hands. These, after the best had been chosen by the chief and his courtiers, were publicly sold in the bazaars of Turkestan.*"[913]

In the nineteenth century, there were hardly any families in the Islamic heartland of Mecca that did not possess slaves, including concubines. It is already noted that slaves constituted 6 percent to two-thirds of the population in the 1870–80s in the Muslim-controlled regions of Indonesia and Malaysia.

EUROPEAN STRUGGLE AGAINST ISLAMIC SLAVERY IN NORTH AFRICA

Starting in the 1530s, Muslim pirates in Barbary North Africa continued catching white slaves until the 1830s from onboard European ships, and from the islands and coastal villages of Europe. The worst-hit were Spain, Italy, France and the United Kingdom. Following independence from Britain in 1776, the U.S. ships and their crews also became victims of Barbary piracy and enslavement. This section will highlight the British and US struggle against enslavement of their citizens in North Africa.

The British struggle

In the 1620s, the wives of enslaved British mariners—some 2,000 of them—joined hands to raise a campaign to force the government to act on releasing their enslaved husbands, who "*for a long time continued in most woeful, miserable and lamentable captivity and slavery...*" in North Africa. They further added that the misery they have suffered, caused by the absence of their husbands, to the extent that their poor children and infants were almost ready to perish from starvation for the lack of means and food.[914]

Having suffered depredations of their trade-ships and coastal villages and ports for nearly a century, British King Charles I, after assuming power in 1625, was already acting on the issue. He sent young adventurer John Harrison to North Africa for securing the release of British captives and for signing a treaty against attacks on British ships. The King wrote a letter addressing the hard-headed Sultan Moulay Zidan, while suggesting Harrison that he might have a better prospect of success in direct negotiations with the corsairs of Salé, who often acted in defiance of the sultan.

John Harrison, deciding for a direct negotiation with the pirates of Salé, set off on a hazardous and arduous journey in the summer of 1625 in the guise of a Muslim penitent—bare-legged and in a pilgrim-like garb. After arriving at Salé, he tried to contact Sidi Mohammed el-Ayyachi, the spiritual leader of the slave-hunters of the city. Sidi Mohammed was a wily holy man (*marabout* or Sufi master), who boasted of causing

---

912. Moreland, p. 90

913. Lal (1994), p. 8

914. Milton, p17

257

the death of 7,600 Christians. He showed inclination toward freeing the slaves only if Britain offered him assistance in attacking the Spanish. He also demanded a supply of heavy weaponry, including fourteen brass pieces of ordnance and a proportion of powder and shot. He also asked for taking some of his damaged cannons to England for their repair. Harrison returned to London to discuss the terms with the King and Privy Council. He returned to Salé with a reduced cache of weapons and the promise to assist in his attack of the Spanish. Sidi Mohammed released some 190 captives from his dungeons, although Harrison was expecting some 2,000 of them. At length, he realized that a great many of them had died from plagues, while others were sold to the sultan or elsewhere in North Africa.[915]

John Harrison landed with the freed slaves in England in the summer of 1627. In his eight diplomatic voyages to North Africa, he made repeated visits to the court of Sultan Moulay Abdalla Malek (r.1627–31), but failed to secure the release of British slaves held there. Sidi Mohammed also broke the truce after some time as his men—dependent on slave-hunting for making a living—pressurized him on the ground that the British government gave them a smaller cache of weapons and was not forthcoming in attacking the Spanish. They executed a number of spectacular raids on British ships and soon they had captured 1,200 British sailors, including twenty-seven women.

The British King ran out of patience. In 1637, he sent a fleet of six warships under the command of Captain William Rainsborough toward the corsair stronghold of Salé for bombarding it into rubbles. He reached Salé after a month's voyage, when the pirates had just made all their ships ready to go on the hunt to the coast of England. The English fleet was surprised by the huge number of ships under their command. The new governor of Salé had ordered the corsairs *"that they should go for the coasts of England... [and] fetch the men, women and children out of their bed."*[916]

Having realized that a deadly and likely disastrous confrontation lie ahead, Rainsborough took stock of the situation in Salé and found out that there was a power-struggle between two groups. One was led by Sidi Mohammed, another by a rebel named Abdallah ben Ali el-Kasri, who had seized control of a part of Salé and was holding 328 English captives. Instead of going on a likely disastrous offensive, Rainsborough decided to exploit the rivalry between the two warlords. He proposed to Sidi Mohammed to launch a joint attack against el-Kasri, hoping that this will enable him secure the release of all British captives and a peace treaty with Sidi Mohammed. Sidi Mohammed, anxious of getting rid of el-Kasri, agreed to the proposal. Rainsborough showered el-Kasri's stronghold with heavy bombardments, causing total carnage and killing many. Rainsborough then directed his heavy cannon at the corsair ships belonging to el-Kasri, destroying many of them. Meanwhile Sidi Mohammed attacked the rebel stronghold with 20,000 soldiers, wreaking havoc. After three weeks of intense bombardment, the rebels capitulated. They were forced to release the British captives. Rainsborough, having thus completely crushed the rebels and securing a solemn assurance from Sidi Mohammed that he would refrain from attacking the English vessels and villages, sailed back to England in the autumn of 1637 with 230 British slaves.

Rainsborough received a hero's welcome back to England. There was a widespread feeling that the menace of the Salé corsairs was over once and for all. This belief was reinforced by the signing of a treaty with Moroccan Sultan Mohammed esh-Sheikh es-Seghir (r. 1636–55); he agreed to prohibit and restrain all his subjects from taking, buying or receiving British subjects to use as slaves or bondsmen. But the illusion was soon over as the sultan threw away the treaty within a few months, because of the British government's failure to stop English merchants from trading with Moroccan rebels. The corsairs of Salé also resumed their attacks. By 1643, a great many British ships were plundered and their crews enslaved. By the 1640s, some 3,000 British citizens were in the hands of Barbary slave-hunters.[917]

In 1646, merchant Edmund Cason was sent to Algiers with a large sum of money to free the British slaves. He was able to locate 750 English captives, while many more were forced to turn Muslim (who were

---

915. Ibid, p. 17–20

916. Ibid, p. 22–23

917. Ibid, p. 23–6

never released; neither the British government desired so because of their apostasy). Cason paid £38 apiece for each male captive, while a hopping £800, £1,100 and £1,392 for three females. Having run out of cash, he returned to England with only 244 captives, leaving many more behind.

Hereafter, the Barbary corsairs intensified slave-hunting in the sea; they also widened their sphere, attacking ships from far away Norway and Newfoundland. The Russians and Greeks were also enslaved along with merchants and noblemen from the Holy Roman Empire. Spain and Italy were the worst-hit, while Britain, France and Portugal continued to be major victims. In 1672, famous Sultan Moulay Ismail consolidated power and intended to expand the slave-hunting venture to hold the European rulers to ransom for extracting large sums of tribute.

In 1661, Portugal had handed over Tangier to Britain, when King Charles II was betrothed to Catherine of Portugal. The British government had planned to use Tangier, which stood across the straits of Gibraltar, to attack and eradicate the Barbary pirates. In 1677, Sultan Moulay Ismail ordered the capture of Tangier to clear the way for his slave-hunters. Sultan's General Kaid Omar laid a siege on the garrison city of 2,000 British occupants for five years but failed to overrun it. In 1678, Kaid Omar was able to capture eight defenders and another fifty-seven in a new wave of attacks that followed. In 1680, Kaid Omar's forces were poised to overrun the garrison, but a British reinforcement arrived in time and beat back Kaid Omar's forces, forcing the latter to abandon the offensive.[918]

King Charles II soon afterwards (December 1680) sent an ambassadorial delegation, headed by Sir James Leslie, to secure the release of the British soldiers, captured during the siege of Tangier. The arrival of the gifts for the sultan from London was delayed. So, Sir Leslie sent forth Colonel Percy Kirke to inform the sultan about the delay. A timid and drunkard with no diplomatic experience, Colonel Kirke was overwhelmed by the sight and charm of the dreaded sultan. Overawed by the extravagant welcome, hospitality and flattery shown by wily Moulay Ismail, who had kept Europe at ransom, Colonel Kirke forgot his role and started a negotiation himself. When raised the issue of a peace treaty, the sultan offered a four-year truce, but asked for ten big guns in return. The naïve Colonel not only obliged but also promised to "*help him with everything he lacked.*" Colonel Kirke not only breached his role as an emissary, not a diplomat, he also totally forgot about the captives, some 300 of them, held at the sultan's palace. Overjoyed by his diplomatic success, he wrote to England, "*I must tell the whole world, I have met with a kind prince and a just general.*"[919]

At length the presents intended for the sultan arrived at Gibraltar and Sir Leslie left for the sultan's court. When he raised the issue of British prisoners, the sultan, not interested in the negotiation, withdrew and asked his General Kaid Omar to sign a truce. Unwilling to release the captives, the sultan reluctantly agreed to release the seventy soldiers captured during the siege of the Tangier garrison, but asked for so high a price that Sir Leslie had to return to London empty handed.

However, the sultan sent an ambassador, Kaid Muhammad ben Haddu Ottur, to London giving him all powers to negotiate the terms for the release of the English captives. The Sultan's ambassadorial team was given excellent hospitality for months in London. After intense negotiations behind closed doors, a truce was eventually signed: the British captives would be released at 200 Spanish dollars apiece and that the sultan's corsairs would spare England's coastal villages. No mention was made of the attack on British ships. But the whimsical sultan disapproved the treaty and replied to the British King's letter promising to rest only after "*I have sat down before Tangier and filled it with Moors.*" On the request for a negotiation about attacks on British ships, he wrote, "*we have no need of it*" and that the corsairs would continue their attacks.

---

918. Ibid, p. 28,37–38

919. Ibid, p. 39–41

Disheartened by the failure of the negotiation, the King lost interest in the Tangier garrison, which had failed to stop the depredations of the corsairs, and evacuated the post in the following year.[920]

British citizens continued to be captured and suffer in Sultan Moulay Ismail's dungeons through the rest of the King's reign. King Charles III, who ascended the throne in 1685, was very concerned and eager to have the captives released. After a protracted bargain lasting five years, the sultan agreed to free the captives at the exorbitant price of £15,000 and 1,200 barrels of gunpowder. "*The ship was so full of powder that we were in continual fear of her blowing up,*" wrote Captain George Delaval, who transported the ransom to Morocco. But the sultan started disputing the terms of the treaty after Delaval's arrival. Delaval refused to handover the money until he was sure that the captives would be released. At length, the sultan released 194 British slaves, keeping thirty of them in his custody. Later on, when Queen Anne ascended the throne in 1702 and hinted at joining a Moroccan attack on the Spanish enclave at Ceuta, the remaining captives were suddenly released. Moroccan palace was empty of British captives for the first time in 150 years. Soon afterwards, the corsairs of Salé went on the offensive, when Queen Anne showed reluctance to join the sultan's offensive against the Spaniards; British captives started streaming in.[921]

Another truce was signed between Sultan Moulay Ismail and Queen Anne in 1714 on the promise of huge gifts. As the Queen's death in the summer of the same year delayed the delivery of the gift, the sultan sent his slave-hunters back into the sea. King George I, the German-born ruler of Hanover, was given the throne after the death of childless Queen Anne. He showed little interest in the miserable plight of British captives held in Morocco. In 1717, the wives and widows of the enslaved mariners wrote a desperate and emotionally-charged petition to the King, pleading for securing the release of their enslaved husbands. The King remained unmoved by it and the Secretary of State, Joseph Addison, took up the difficult cause. Just a few months earlier, Admiral Charles Cornwall had returned from the sultan's palace empty-handed as the sultan was reluctant to sign a lasting peace-treaty and release the captives.

After a long deliberation in a crisis meeting in May 1717, a high level delegation, led by Captain Coninsby Norbury, was sent to Morocco. Angered by the continued illegal capture of British mariners and breach of every peace-treaty signed, Norbury was too haughty for such a delicate negotiation and showed an air of defiance and disdain of the sultan. When Sultan Moulay Ismail first met him rather courteously hoping to receive the huge gift from England, Norbury "*demanded the slave, saying that without them, he'd make no peace, and would blockade all their sea-ports and destroy their commerce, with other threats of that kind.*"[922] In the habit of treating foreign dignitaries with contempt, the sultan was obviously unprepared for the snub and nothing came out of Norbury's mission. But the sultan agreed to the posting of a British consul in Morocco. Merchant Anthony Hatfeild, chosen for the post, made diligent efforts over the years to release the captives, but failed to achieve anything.

Hatfeild gathered intelligence about the activities of the corsairs, which had increased since 1717, and kept London informed about it. Alarmed by the intelligence, another diplomatic mission, led by Commodore Charles Stewart, was sent in 1720. Stewart possessed all the diplomatic niceties and skills for negotiation with the unpredictable and haughty ruler of Morocco. He signed a treaty first with Basha Hamet, the sultan's governor of Tetouan in Northern Morocco. Thereafter, he proceeded to the sultan's court, where his delegation was received with great hospitality. After protracted negotiations, a treaty was eventually signed in exchange of large gifts for the sultan. The slaves, 293 of them, from both England and colonial America, were released.[923]

---

920. Ibid, p. 39–41
921. Ibid, p. 49–50
922. Ibid, p. 116
923. Ibid, p. 172–95

The sultan and his pirates could hardly be restrained for long. By 1726, the corsairs had arraigned more British ships; the captives were sent to the sultan's palace in Meknes. The next year (1727), Sultan Moulay Ismail died, which followed a period of deadly chaos and turmoil. During such chaotic periods, rogue elements, including the slave-hunters, normally increased their criminal activities. As a result, large numbers of European captives streamed into the slave-pens of North Africa. In 1746, the British ship, *Inspector*, was wrecked by the corsairs and eighty-seven survivors were captured. "*Large chains were locked around our necks and twenty of us were linked together in one chain,*" wrote Thomas Troughton, one of the ship's crew. The British government once again secured the release of the captives from the palace at Meknes in 1751. The sultans of Morocco rarely released slaves of other nationalities: French, Spanish, Portuguese, Italian and Dutch etc. Finally, a more humane and level-headed man, Sidi Mohammed, seized the throne in 1757. He was an enlightened man and believed that the shattered economy of Morocco could be repaired better by promoting international trade than by piracy and slavery. He, therefore, declared war against the pirates of Salé and decimated them. He signed peace treaties, first with Denmark in 1757 and, eventually, with all European nations that had fallen victim to Barbary piracy, including the United States.[924]

The deadly piracy in seas off the Moroccan Coast was dead for many years, although corsairs in Algiers and Tunis continued the depredation of European and American ships. After the death of Sultan Sidi Mohammed in 1790, his successor and son Moulay Sulaiman, despite ratifying his father's treaty, encouraged the corsairs of Salé to attack European ships. However, the heydays of the Barbary slave-hunters in Salé and elsewhere in North Africa were becoming numbered. Britain and the United States—seeing no end to the scourge after centuries of inaction, appeasement and ransom payment—finally decided to hit back with military might to put an end to the piracy in North Africa forever.

One must bear in mind that the British struggle against the Barbary piracy and enslavement recount above is only a part of whole struggle in North Africa; similar struggles also took place in Tripoli and Algiers.

The U.S. struggle and strike-back

U.S. trade-ships also fell victim to Barbary piracy in North Africa. In 1646, the first U.S. ship and its crew were captured by the pirates of Salé. Until the U.S. independence in 1776, American ships in North Africa were under the British protection. The release of British captives from North African dungeons also included the American captives. British protection to American ships was withdrawn after the U.S. achieved in 1776. The U.S. ships from then on became the direct target of Barbary pirate attack. In 1784, Muslim pirates in Morocco and Algiers captured three American merchant ships, enslaving the crew. After protracted negotiations, $60,000 ransom was paid to release the hostages from Moroccan. Those captured by the Algerian pirates suffered a worse fate; they were sold into slavery.

To discuss about this issue, the exasperated U.S. diplomats Thomas Jefferson and John Adams met Abd al-Rahman, the Tripolian Ambassador to London, in 1785. When they enquired by what right the Barbary States justified their raids on American ships, enslaving the crew and passengers, al-Rahman informed them that "*it was written in the Quran that all Nations who should not have acknowledged their (Islamic) authority were sinners; that it was their right and duty to make war upon whoever they could find and to make slaves of all they could take as prisoners; and that every Mussulman who should be slain in battle was sure to go to Paradise.*"[925] The ambassador demanded tribute as protection against the attack and also asked for his own commission.

Right from that moment, Thomas Jefferson promised to wage war against the Barbary States for putting an end to the barbaric practice of slavery as well as to make the sea-ways secure for trade. While on

---

924. Ibid, p. 269–70
925. Berube CG and Rodgaard JA (2005) *A Call to the Sea: Captain Charles Stewart of the USS Constitution*, Potomac Books Inc., Dulles, p. 22

diplomatic duty in Paris, he unsuccessfully tried to build a coalition of American-European naval powers for putting an end to the Barbary depredations of European and American trading ships. He faced opposition even back from home; even John Adams opposed his idea. Adams, amongst many others, preferred the payment of tribute than engaging in a protracted war against a doggedly warrior people. When asked for Adams' opinion about organizing *"an international taskforce comprised of all European nations whose shipping was being victimized,"* he wrote to Jefferson that although his idea was *"bold and wholly honourable..., We ought not to fight them at all unless we determine to fight them forever."*[926]

Meanwhile the depredation of American ships and enslavement of their crews continued; 130 seamen had been captured between 1785 and 1793. The U.S. Government dispatched diplomats Joel Barlow, Joseph Donaldson, and Richard O'Brien to North Africa in 1795, who successfully concluded treaties with Algiers, Tunis and Tripoli agreeing to pay tribute for the safe passage of American ships. Algiers also freed 83 American sailors, it had enslaved. During the presidency of John Adams (1797–1801), America continued paying tribute, which gradually reached as high as 10 percent of the national budget.

The humiliating exercise of paying tribute, combined with stories of appalling sufferings of white slaves in North African dungeons, gradually changed the public sentiment against ransom-payment and in favor of military actions. When Thomas Jefferson became the President in 1801, the Pasha of Tripoli, Yusuf Qaramanli, citing late payment of tribute declared war on the United States, seizing two American brigs, and demanded additional tributes. This followed demands for larger tributes from other Barbary States as well. Jefferson was all along totally against the humiliating exercise of paying tribute to the Barbary States. As early as in 1784, he had told Congressman James Monroe (later U.S. President, 1817–25): *"Would it not be better to offer then an equal treaty? If they refuse, why not go to war with them... We ought to begin a naval power if we mean to carry on our own commerce."*[927]

Not forgotten of his encounter with the Tripolian ambassador sixteen years earlier, the new President, without informing the Congress, sent forth a naval fleet to Barbary North Africa. In retaliation, Tripoli declared war on the United States in May 1801 and Morocco soon followed suit. America soon suffered a setback when Tripoli captured the U.S. frigate *Philadelphia*, but Edward Preble and Stephen Decatur soon mounted a heroic raid on the Tripolian harbor, destroying the captured ship and inflicting heavy damage on the city's defences. This news created great excitement in the U.S. and Europe: a new power has arrived on the world-stage.

Meanwhile William Eaton, American consul in Tunis, allied with Hamid, the exiled brother of Tripolian pasha Yusuf Karamanli, offering him to make the American nominee for Tripoli's crown. The ploy did not receive appreciation back home, but Eaton pursued it anyway. In 1805, he made a daring journey with a small detachment of marines and a force of irregulars across the desert from Egypt to Tripoli. They made a surprise attack and the city of Darna with its huge garrison surrendered. As Eaton had engaged pasha's forces, Jefferson and Karamanli reached an understanding to end the war. The terms of truce included the release of the *Philadelphia* crew upon payment of a tribute, but America would pay no more tribute in future. In this, stressed Jefferson, Eaton's derring-do had played a part. Daring and uncompromising, Eaton denounced the deal as a sellout.

New hostilities began between Britain and the United States in 1812. Exploiting this Anglo-American hostility, the new pasha of Algiers, Hajji Ali, rejected the American tribute negotiated in the 1795 treaty as insufficient. Algerian corsairs resumed the capture of American ships. Once the *Treaty of Ghent* ended the war with Britain, President James Madison requested the Congress to declare war on Algiers. On 3 March 1815, the war was declared and Madison dispatched the battle-hardened naval force under the command of Stephen Decatur to North Africa again to put a complete end to the piracy problem. The U.S.

---

926. Ibid
927. Ibid

navy destroyed the fleets of reigning Dey Omar Pasha, filled his grand harbor with heavily armed American ships and took hundreds prisoner. Dey Omar capitulated and reluctantly accepted the treaty dictated by Decatur, which called for an exchange of U.S. and Algerian prisoners and an end to the practice of tribute and ransom. Having defeated Algiers—the most powerful Barbary State, Decatur sailed to Tunis and Tripoli, and dictated the signing of similar treaties. Decatur also secured the release of all European captives from Pasha Qaramanli's dungeons in Tripoli. President Madison's words on this occasion—"*It is a settled policy of America, that as peace is better than war, war is better than tribute; the United States, while they wish for war with no nation, will buy peace with none*"—inaugurated a new U.S. foreign policy paradigm.[928]

The British-led European strike-back

The United States settled her accounts with the Barbary States in 1815: the year, all European nations jointly declared a ban on slave-trade. But the depredation of European ships continued. The U.S. derring-do actions in Barbary North Africa (1801–05, 1815) had elicited calls for similar actions in Europe, particularly in Britain. When the crown heads and ministers of Europe gathered for the *Congress of Vienna* in 1814 to discuss a peace treaty following the end of the Napoleonic war, Sir Sydney Smith, a staunch proponent of military settlement of the Barbary piracy crisis, petitioned for a military showdown with the rulers of North Africa. "*This shameful slavery is not only revolting to humanity, but it fetters commerce in the most disastrous manner,*" he told the Congress.

Sir Smith's plea drew attention to a dehumanizing and commercially crippling problem that had lasted centuries. Britain pushed for the inclusion of a ban on slave-trade in the European treaty. The Vienna Congress passed a resolution condemning all forms of slavery, but took no steps against the Barbary States. However, the support for Sir Smith's battle-cry for military actions was soon forthcoming from all corners Europe; they had all suffered terribly from this obnoxious enemy. They were taking cues and encouragement from the U.S. success in Algiers a few months earlier. Because Britain was not as bad a sufferer, who intermittently concluded truce and secured release of English captives, other nations criticized Britain for '*turning a blind eye to the ravages of the corsairs, since Britain stood to benefit whenever her trading rivals were attacked.*'[929]

Stricken by the criticism, Britain, a proponent for the abolition of black slavery, now resolved to end the white slavery as well. In 1815, the British government dispatched a large fleet, commanded by Sir Edward Pellow, to the North African coastal waters, aiming to compel the rulers of Barbary States to abstain from seizing ships and slaves from anywhere in Europe. The British government resolved against the payment of tributes, stating: "*If force must be resorted to, we have the consolation of knowing that we fight in the sacred cause of humanity.*"[930]

Having arrived with an impressive fleet in the waters off Algiers in late 1815, Sir Pellow sent an uncompromising message to Omar Pasha demanding his unconditional surrender within one hour, release of all European slaves and abandonment of capturing European ships and slaves forever. After the earlier U.S. attacks, Omar Pasha had fortified his defences and recruited battle-hardened soldiers to ward off likely European attacks. When no response from him came, Sir Pellow declared war. The British fleet was bolstered by a squadron of six Dutch vessels. The battle began with heavy bombardment of Algiers destroying the city to rubbles. The forces of Omar Pasha showed stiff resistance and counterattacked, causing significant damage and casualties to the British side. Having reduced the city to rubbles, Sir Pellow directed his attention to the fleet of corsair ships docked in the harbor firebombing and shelling them, which set them all in flames. By the

---

928. Hitchens, op cit

929. Milton, p. 272

930. Ibid

next morning, the city and the corsair fleets were in total ruin. The British side had 141 men dead and 78 wounded, while 2,000 were dead on the enemy side. After surveying the devastation the next morning, Omar Pasha, swallowing his pride, surrendered unconditionally, agreeing to all demands of the British commander. The terms for the truce included releasing of all European captives and complete stoppage to enslaving Europeans.

Having suffered the shocking battering by the United States and Britain, the Barbary States stopped attacking the British and U.S. ships, but continued ravaging ships from other nations. For example, the French ships continued to suffer. The French government then stepped up its own military action. A joint Anglo-French naval fleet was sent to the Barbary Coast again in 1819 to batter the Barbary ports. In order to put a complete end to the depredation of Barbary corsairs and to liberate Christians who suffered terrible subjection in North Africa, France conquered Algiers in 1830, ending the Barbary slave-hunting forever.

MUSLIM RESISTANCE AGAINST THE OTTOMAN BAN ON SLAVERY

Under pressure from the West, the Ottoman government declared a ban on slave-trade in the empire in 1855. This ban of the divine institution sometimes faced fierce popular resistance, prominently in the Hejaz and Sudan. Armed with the argument that this was a West-dictated ban on a God-sanctioned institution, Muslims in the Islamic heartland of Hejaz (Saudi region) rose in revolt against the Ottomans. Sheikh Jamal, the chief of the *Ulema* in Hejaz, issued a *fatwa* against the ban on slave-trade and other Christian-inspired anti-Islamic reforms undertaken by the Ottomans. It read: *'The ban on slave is contrary to the Holy Shari'a... With such proposals, the Turks have become infidels. Their blood is forfeit and it is lawful to make their children slaves.'*[931]

The Ottomans were able to put down the renewed Jihad in the Hejaz within a year. However, the revolt and the *fatwa* had their desired effect. Fearful of long-term fallout from this ban on a divine institution in the Islamic heartland, the Ottomans declared a concession, exempting Hejaz from the ban on slavery. In this connection, the Ottoman sultan had the Chief Mufti of Istanbul, Aref Efendi, written a letter to the *Qadi, Mufti, Ulema, Sharifs, Imams* and preachers of Mecca, calling the ban on slavery and other Ottoman reforms as "slanderous rumors". The letter read: *"It has come to our hearing and has been confirmed to us that certain impudent persons lustful for the goods of this world have fabricated strange lies and invented repulsive vanities to the effect that the Lofty Ottoman state was perpetrating—almighty God preserve us— such things as prohibition of male and female slaves... all of which is nothing but libelous lies..."*[932]

The Ottoman-Egyptian effort to disband slave-trade also faced strong resistance in Sudan, the most fertile ground for Muslim slave hunters and traders through the ages. According to Rudolph Peters, *'Discontent amongst the Sudanese increased when the European Powers compelled the Egyptian government to suppress the slave trade.'* The discontent was not only for material reasons, notes Peters, *'but also for religious considerations.'* He adds: *'As Islam permits slavery, most Muslims did not see any harm in it. Suppression of it, especially as it was actually carried out by Europeans employed by the Egyptian government, was seen as an affront against Islam.'*[933] As a result, Muhammad Ahmad (d. 1885), a Sufi leader, rose in Jihad against the Ottoman-Egyptian administration and their Western allies. The aggrieved slave-traders and Sufi masters, with their private armies, joined the Jihad movement.[934]

---

931. Lewis, p. 102–3
932. Ibid, p. 103
933. Peters, p. 64
934. Ibid, p. 64–65

Following the Ottoman failure to disband slavery in the Hejaz (Saudi region), slave-trade remained legal in Saudi Arabia for another 107 years. Lord Shackleton reported to the House of Lords in 1960 that African Muslims going for the Hajj pilgrimage carried slaves with them for selling in Mecca, *"using them as living travelers cheques."*[935] Saudi Arabia and Yemen banned slave-trade in 1962, nearly 155 years after its ban in Britain; Mauritania banned it only in 1980. This ban was, of course, enacted by virtue of intense international pressure, mainly from the West, but with only partial success.

CONTINUATION & REVIVAL OF SLAVERY IN MUSLIM COUNTRIES

Slavery continues in Saudi Arabia, Sudan and Mauritania in various forms to this day. Reuters recently published a report, entitled *Slavery Still Exist in Mauritania*, which said:

> They do not wear chains, nor are they branded with the mark of their masters, but slaves still exist in Mauritania... Herding camels or goats out in the sun-blasted dunes of the Sahara, or serving hot mint tea to guests in the richly carpeted villas of Nouakchott, Mauritanian slaves serve their masters and are passed on as family chattels from generation to generation... They may number thousands, anti-slavery activists say.' Boubacar Messaoud, a born slave and now an anti-slavery activist told Reuters that *'It's like having sheep or goats. If a woman is a slave, her descendants are slaves.'*[936]

Slavery also continues in Saudi Arabia; but because of the secretive nature of the holy Islamic kingdom, very little information comes out of it. The hundreds of thousands of young women from poor countries like Bangladesh, Indonesia, Philippines, Sri Lanka and so on, who go to Saudi Arabia to work as maids at the homes of Saudi Sheikhs, live a life of virtual slavery in domestic confinement. A majority of them likely end up providing sexual service to their masters to comply with the Quranic sanction of concubinage. Homaidan Al-Turki, a former Ph.D. student at the University of Colorado from Saudi Arabia, who was sentenced in 2006 to twenty-year imprisonment for sexually assaulting his Indonesian maid, denied that it was a sexual assault; it is a *'traditional Muslim behaviour,'* he claimed.[937] Human Rights Watch reports on the exploitation and abuse of foreign maids in Saudi that,

> Some women workers that we interviewed were still *traumatized from rape and sexual abuse at the hands of Saudi male employers*, and could not narrate their accounts without anger or tears. Accustomed to unrestricted freedom of movement in their home countries, these and other women described to us locked doors and gates in Riyadh, Jeddah, Medina, and Dammam that kept them virtual prisoners in workshops, private homes, and the dormitory-style housing that labor subcontracting companies provided to them. Living in forced confinement and extreme isolation made it difficult or impossible for these women to call for help, escape situations of exploitation and abuse, and seek legal redress.[938]

The Times of India wrote on 10 December 1993 that *'There is no doubt that many thousands of slaves are still serving in the wealthy palaces of Arabia.'* The old and rich Saudi Sheikhs frequently travel to Malaysia, India,

---

935. Lal (1994), p. 176

936. Fletcher P, *Slavery still exists in Mauritania*, Reuters, 21 March 2007

937. *US Urged to Review Saudi Student's Case*, Arab News, Riyadh, 28 March 2008

938. Human Rights Watch, *Exploitation and Abuse of Migrant Workers in Saudi Arabia*, http://hrw.org/mideast/saudi/labor/

Sri Lanka, Egypt and other poor countries to marry young girls from poor families paying handsome amount of money to their parents and take the girls to Saudi Arabia, where they naturally live as nothing but slaves.

Revival of slavery in Sudan: Sudan (Nubia) has been the worst victim of Islamic slavery, which struck Sudan very early: it was forced to send an annual tribute of 400 slaves between 652 and 1276. Since the early days of Islam, suggests the tenth-century document *Hudud al-Alam*, Sudan had become a fertile ground for the Muslim slave-hunters and continues to be so till today. John Eibner, who worked on a project for freeing slaves in Sudan in the 1990s, reports the enslavement of black Sudanese women and children—Christian, Animist and even Muslim—by Arab militias and the government-sponsored Popular Defence Force (PDF). The enslaved women were forced to become Muslim and generally used as concubines, while the young boys were trained to become Jihadis for fighting their coreligionists. He freed 1,783 slaves in 1999, while his organization, the Christian Solidarity International, freed 15,447 slaves between 1945 and 1999.[939] Even the colonial British government (1899–1956) had failed to stop enslavement and slave-trade effectively in Sudan. A 1947 memorandum prepared by the British civil servants noted that, in the late 1920s, '*an extensive trade in slaves from Ethiopia was unmasked and even today there are occasional kidnappings, and the victims are hurried into the hands of the desert nomads of the far north.*'[940]

Worse still is the fact that, with the government-sponsored resurgence of Islamism since the 1980s, there has been a revival of violent enslavement in Sudan. In 1983, the Islamist Sudanese government headed by President Jaafar Nimeiry, prodded by the Islamist leader Dr. Hasan al-Turabi, declared unification of the black Christian- and Animist-dominated Southern Sudan with the Arab-dominated North, abrogating former's long-standing autonomy. The government also enacted Sharia laws uniformly all over Sudan. The purpose of the government was to transform multireligious and multiethnic Sudan into an Arab dominated Muslim state through the process of Jihad.

In protest, rebels in the dominantly non-Muslim south formed a resistance movement, Sudan People's Liberation Army (SPLA), headed by Colonel John Garang. In response, the Islamist government started arming tribal Arab militias (Baqqara). Armed with automatic weapons, these Arab brigands spearheaded the government's war effort against the rebels and their sympathizers. They attacked villages killing the adult men, abducting the women and children, looting and plundering cows, goats and grain, and burning the rest. There was a brief respite after the Islamist government was overthrown in 1985. The Jihad resumed again after Sadiq al-Mahdi, an Islamist and brother-in-law of al-Turabi, became the Prime Minister in the 1986 election. The Arab militia raids returned with '*deliberate killing of tens of thousands of civilians*' and '*the abduction of women and children, who were forced into slavery.*'[941]

After the coup in 1989, led by al-Turabi and General Umar al-Bashir of the National Islamic Front (NIF), slave-raids by Arab militias became widespread and institutionalized. The authoritarian Islamist regime of President al-Bashir formed an irregular force, the PDF, for spearheading Jihad against the rebels, and the communities sympathetic to them. The worst victim of the PDF raids and slave-hunting has been the Dinka people in the Southwest Bahr al-Ghazal states and the Nuba tribes of southern Kordofan region. The Blacks of the southern Nuba Mountains, despite being Muslims, were declared apostates in an Islamic *fatwa* on the account of their sympathy for the rebels. The *fatwa*, according to U.N. special rapporteur Gaspar Biro, read:[942]

---

939. Eibner J (1999), *My Career Redeeming Slaves*, Middle East Quarterly, December Issue

940. Henderson KDD (1965) *Sudan Republic*, Ernest Benn, London, p. 197

941. Metz HC ed. (1992) *Sudan: A Country Study*, Library of Congress, Washington DC, 4th ed., p. 257

942. David Littman (1996) *The U.N. Finds Slavery in the Sudan*, Middle East Quarterly, September Issue

An insurgent who was previously a Muslim is now an apostate; and a non-Muslim is a nonbeliever standing as a bulwark against the spread of Islam, and Islam has granted the freedom of killing both of them.

In 1998, the PDF, supported by the regular army, waged a harrowing slave-raiding campaign against the Dinkas in Bahr al-Ghazal, displacing over 300,000 and enslaving and slaughtering unknown numbers. Following these raids, claimed Santino Deng, an advisor to the provincial government, that the Islamic militia were holding 50,000 Dinka children captives in Babanusa (Western Kordofan). A UNICEF report claimed that the PDF enslaved 2,064 people and killed 181 between December 1998 and February 1999.[943] Based on the ongoing slave-raiding in Sudan, estimates John Eibner, there were some 100,000 chattel slaves in 1999.[944] Between 1986 and 2003, notes an Anti-Slavery document, an estimated 14,000 people have been abducted and forced into slavery in Sudan.[945]

The worse was yet to come, this time in Darfur. In 2004, Arab militias (Janjaweed), patronized by the Sudan government, launched a harrowing wave of Jihad against the rebels and their sympathizers. The government-sponsored Jihad in Sudan killed some two million people between 1983 and 2003. In the renewed Jihad in Darfur since 2004, the U.N. puts the death toll at roughly 300,000; the former U.N. undersecretary-general puts the number at no less than 400,000.[946] In Darfur, an estimated two-and-a-half million people have been displaced and an unknown number likely enslaved. In July 2008, the International Criminal Court charged President al-Bashir of sponsoring war-crime and crime against humanity in Darfur.[947]

Trimingham observed in 1949 that the Baqqara Arabs, who had lived on slave-raiding for ages and whose life was made difficult by the colonial British administration's ban on slavery, '*still hanker after the practice.*'[948] After the infidel British rulers were kicked out in 1956, the Arabs in Sudan slowly got back what they had lost and hankered after: their God-sanctioned age-old profession of slavery.

MUSLIMS BRING SLAVERY TO THE WEST

It is a disturbing fact that Muslims, especially those from some Middle East countries, have been importing the imprints of slavery to the West. In recent years, there have been a number of reports of Saudi and Sudanese families in the United States and United Kingdom, who have reduced their maids to slavery, leading to legal processes. According to the Anti-Slavery document cited above, a former slave named Mende Nazer—who recently published her autobiography, *Slave: My True Story*—was captured in 1992 from the Nuba Mountains in Sudan. She was a slave first in a rich Arab family in Khartoum, and then, to a Sudanese diplomat in London, from where she escaped in 2002 and sought political asylum in Britain. According to a 2003 report in *National Reviews*,[949]

943. Inter Press Service (Khartoum), July 24, 1998.

944. Eibner, op cit

945. Anti-Slavery, *Mende Nazer—From Slavery to Freedom*, October 2003

946. Lederer, EM, *UN Says Darfur Conflict Worsening, with Perhaps 300,000 Dead*, Associated Press, 22 April 2008.

947. Walker P and Sturcke J, *Darfur genocide charges for Sudanese president Omar al-Bashir*, Guardian, 14 July 2008

948. Trimingham JS (1949) *Islam in the Sudan*, Oxford University Press, London, p. 29

949. Joel Mowbray, *Maids, Slaves, and Prisoners: To be employed in a Saudi home—forced servitude of women in Saudi Arabia and in homes of Saudis in US*, National Review, 24 Feb. 2003

Three members of the Saudi royal family, including a sister of King Fahd, were caught up in a scandal five years ago in London for their treatment of three Filipina women. The women sued the Saudi royals, alleging that they had been physically abused, starved, and held against their will in the Saudis' mansion in London. The Filipinas said they were often locked in the attic, were fed mere scraps of food, and were denied medical attention when they became gravely ill.

About the treatment of domestic workers in Saudi homes in the United States, it reported:

> …most situations involving domestics working for Saudis have seven hallmarks: confiscation of passports, contract terms unilaterally changed, overlong working hours, denial of medical attention, verbal and often physical abuse, a prison-like atmosphere... All of the women with whom we spoke worked in the U.S., although some first worked inside Saudi Arabia; the women who worked in both countries said their conditions did not improve once in the U.S.

CONCLUSION

Whatever residues of slavery that exist in the Muslim world today are insignificant to what existed throughout the history of Islam: right from the days of Prophet Muhammad to the mid-twentieth century. Undoubtedly, external pressures, namely from Western countries and the U.N. etc., has played a *decisive* role in limiting slavery in Muslim countries. But the rise of orthodox Islamic militants globally, who aim to conquer the world for establishing Islamic rule, styled after the medieval Islamic caliphate, is a worrying sign. In a London demonstration against the publication of Prophet Muhammad's cartoons in a Danish newspaper in 2006, a Muslim protester shouted that let us invade Denmark and 'take their women as war booty,' while another called out: 'take lessons of the Jews of Khaybar.'[950] However shameful the institution of slavery is and those historical incidents are, the pious Muslim minds, often highly educated ones, feel inspired by them even today.

In 1999, the Sudanese government even took the justification of its supports for the ongoing slavery in Sudan to the U.N. On 23 March 1999, Sudanese rebel leader John Garang complained to Mary Robinson, the U.N. High Commissioner for Human Rights, about the Government-sponsored violent Jihad and enslavement. In response, the former PM Sadiq al-Mahdi (r. 1986–89) wrote to Robinson defending the Sudanese Government's complicity in the harrowing activities on a religious basis. He wrote,[951]

> The traditional concept of Jihad ...is based upon a division of the world into two zones: one the zone of Peace, the other the zone of War. It requires initiating hostilities for religious purposes... It is true that the (NIF) regime has not enacted a law to realize slavery in Sudan. But the traditional concept of Jihad does allow slavery as a by-product (of jihad).

Therefore, if the radical Islamist movements worldwide succeed in achieving their goals, the revival of the sacred institution of Islamic slavery on the world stage with its past glory remains quite a possibility.

---

950. *Chilling Islamic Demonstration of Cartoons, London,*
http://video.google.com/videoplay?docid=574545628662575243, accessed on 20 July 2008.

951. *Letter from Sadiq Al-Mahdi to Mary Robinson, U.N. High Commissioner for Human Rights* (Section III: War Crimes), Mar. 24, 1999.

Chapter VIII

The Last Word

This book has clearly demonstrated that the doctrine of Jihad as revealed by Allah in the Quran calls for forced conversion, particularly of idolaters, for establishing an imperial rule on a global scale with an integral purpose of economic exploitation of non-Muslim subjects and for engaging in slavery, including slave-trade and sex-slavery. These divine commands of Allah were meticulously acted upon by the Prophet of Islam. With sword, he forcibly converted the Polytheists of Arabia to Islam, created the first imperial state in Arabia by expelling and slaughtering the unyielding Jews *en masse* and enslaved the women and children of Jewish and Polytheist tribes in large numbers. Prophet Muhammad and his comrades kept the young beautiful women as sex-slaves and concubines; he also sold some of the enslaved women. The Muslim caliphs and sultans, thereafter, embraced and expanded these ideal models of prophetic actions, creating an Islamdom of vast expanse.

All commands of the Quran, including for Jihad, must stand for all times. Therefore, the Islamic institutions of forced conversion, imperialism and slavery—if Allah's commands are to be obeyed—must persist for eternity. As for forced conversion, it must continue until such times that there remain no more infidels to be converted. However, even if all peoples of the earth are converted to Islam, some rebellious Muslims will always turn infidels through apostasy. Therefore, technically the Islamic institution of forced conversion would not cease until the end of the world. As to the institution of slavery, it cannot cease to exist either, even if the whole world converts to Islam. Those who leave Islam through apostasy will always be legitimate target for slaughter or enslavement. Additionally, Islamic law stipulates that, those infidels, converted to Islam after their capture in the battle-field, would remain slaves. The offspring of slaves will be slaves. Thus, slavery, the divine institution of Allah, would remain an integral part of humanity through the ages. Regarding Islamic imperialism, the perpetuation of a global Islamic rule for eternity is the ultimate goal of Allah.

Allah's command of Jihad—embraced by a lone person, Prophet Muhammad—has indeed achieved stunning success in the course of the last fourteen centuries. Prophet Muhammad and his successors converted tens of millions of infidels to Islam at the pain of death, through enslavement as well as by coercing them to embrace Islam by subjecting to severe economic exploitation. Muslims now constitute a staggering 1.4 billion, greater than 20 percent, of the world population. It has been made abundantly clear that Muslims have practised the institution of slavery—slave-trade and sex-slavery included—on a grand scale well into the twentieth century. And of course, Islamic imperialism, established in the Middle East, Central Asia, North Africa, Bangladesh and Pakistan amongst other places since the early times of Islam, would remain under perpetual Islamic rule.

Beginning at the time of *Renaissance*, the gradual ascendancy of Christian Europe over the Islamic world has played a spoiler in Allah's stratagem of Jihad for establishing an imperial Islamic state on a global scale for blessing all humankind with His perfected final creed of Islam. Europe, indeed, played spoiler to Allah's mission thrice: first at the *Battle of Tours* (732) and twice at the *Gates of Vienna* against the Ottomans (1527 & 1683). Europe dealt even a bigger blow to Allah's divine mission by capturing most of the lands, which Muslims had captured through resplendent Jihad over the centuries. In places like Turkey and Iran, where Europeans did not or could not capture power directly, they made the rulers of those countries their surrogate.

The usurpation of Islamic imperialism by later European imperialism dealt a severe blow to the Godly profession of Jihad in more ways than one. The European imperialists did not only terminate Islamic political domination and further expansion, they almost completely wiped out the vital Jihadi professions: forced conversions as well as enslavement, slave-trade and sex-slavery. Jihad, the central creed of Islam, to a great extent, was dead. When the European imperialists eventually withdrew, a good part of the land previously captured by the heroism and blood of Allah's anointed Jihadis came under the control of the infidels: India being a prime example. This was a great loss for Islam.

However, the designs of almighty Allah could hardly be kept under control or abolished by some mortal earthly powers. Allah's anointed ones kept aloft the zeal of Jihad against European occupiers until they withdraw in the twentieth century. But those former imperialists have created other kinds of stratagems and regimes, such as international law, human rights, abolition of slavery and many such things—all hampering the implementation of the ideals of Jihad for the fast progress of Islam. In the nineteenth and early twentieth century, the Europeans also opened doors to many Muslim students, often from elite families, to their universities for gaining knowledge. It was a good thing, if they learned the sciences and crafts of creating powerful weapons to confront Western powers. But most often, they came back indoctrinated with un-Islamic ideas—secularism, human rights, feminism and many such things that contravene the central doctrines of Jihad. Iran and Turkey, the two biggest Muslim powers, became the slaves of those non-Islamic foreign ideas and embraced secularism, wholly abandoning the divine profession of Jihad.

But Allah is the greatest plotter says the Quran; He has the power and craft of undoing all human stratagems to flounder His mission. '*Surely they (infidels) will make a scheme. And I (too) will make a scheme,*' says Allah [Quran 86:15–16]. '*In all things the master-planning is Allah's,*' warns the Quran to those, who devise plots against Him [Quran 13:42]. The West-infatuated regime of Iran has been ousted by the great Ayatollahs. The Kemalist secularists in Turkey are on their way to be ousted soon. Jihad has been active in Iran in full measure over the last three decades, while it is slowly taking hold in Turkey.

In the subcontinent, the Jihadi zeal of its sizeable Muslim population, effectively suppressed by the British for so long, were let loose in the course of the Partition (1946–48). A few million Hindus and Sikhs were converted to Islam on the pain of death, and tens of thousands of their young women were enslaved and carried away. Even today, the same practice continues in one form or another. In Pakistan for example, hundreds of Hindus, Sikhs and Christians are forcibly converted to Islam and dozens of their young girls are enslaved through kidnapping every year. If they offer resistance, they are driven out through violent outbursts or other forms of social compulsions, causing their rapid decline in number. These oppressive measures are in force in countries like Bangladesh, Pakistan, Egypt, Lebanon, Palestine, and in almost every Islamic country.

As to slavery, it has been noted that slavery is alive and well in Saudi Arabia in one form or another. Slavery is widespread in Mauritania, while there has been a revival of it in Sudan since the mid-1980s after the Islamists took control of the country. Islamic imperialism is also being expanded in various ways: through the creation of new Muslim states, Kosovo for example. Similar expansion is likely to follow in Kashmir, Mindanao and Southern Thailand amongst other places. The doctrine of Jihad, with its integral components—

forced conversion, imperialism and slavery—is perpetual in nature. Till today, it has maintained its timeless character.

In sum, Allah's divine institution of Jihad with all its integral components is alive and well today. However, the future of the whole gamut of resplendent Jihad looks even brighter. In the early days and through the period of past domination of Islam, Allah gave succor to his anointed Jihadis by flushing them with the wealth and treasures of the infidels by making them victorious in difficult, even improbable, battles with the help of numerous angels. Now that the power of angels has become ineffective against super powerful weapons invented by the infidels, Allah has come with a new succour: the black gold, preserved underground in huge quantities in many Islamic lands—Saudi Arabia, Kuwait, Iraq and Iran being most endowed. The need for the black gold for driving the wheels of the world is so strong that the whole world, including the powerful West, is held hostage by the producers of this vital product, led by Islamic countries. Sky-rocketing price of this liquid gold since the 1970s has made those Muslim countries, Saudi Arabia in particular, flush with wealth, which they could never attain through plunderous Jihad of the old days.

Saudi Arabia, the blessed custodian of the birthplace of Islam, has generously poured in the succor of Allah, billions of dollars annually, to promote the purity of Islam globally. Mosques and *madrasas* have mushroomed across the world, the West included, for training the Muslim mind with the true doctrines of Islam. Based on the crucial part of Prophet Muhammad's career in Medina, it has been emphasized that Jihad is the central doctrine, the heart, of Islam. Muslims have consumed this cardinal essence of Islam very well. Osama bin Laden has invested most generously his share of his father's windfall of the Saudi oil business. Through the founding of al-Qaeda and unleashing acts of Jihad in the most courageous image of the Prophet, he has truly inspired the slumberous Muslim mind with what it means to be real Muslim. Numerous al-Qaeda-minded Jihadi groups have mushroomed across the globe, including in infidel-dominated countries: India, China, Russia and the West.

Jihad is on a spectacular march once again. It will only gain in strength over the coming decades. Jihad has been launched in two forms—violent and soft—with the same end goal: establishing the laws of Allah, the Sharia, with dhimmitude, slavery, forced conversion embedded in it. The violent Jihad can be manageable, but the soft form, particularly through limitless procreation to flood the population in infidel-dominated countries, will be the hardest to beat. Over the next few decades, India, Russia and Europe will most likely become the real playgrounds for the Jihadis, whether of violent or soft kind.

Howsoever ludicrous and unjust it may appear to rational minds, Jihad, in one form or another, will play a vigorous role on the world-stage in the coming decades. In the course of the creation of Pakistan in 1947, Jahan Khan, an M. P. of the Provincial Legislative Assembly, leading a violent Muslim mob, told the Hindus and Sikhs that '*It is Muslim Raj now. Pakistan has been created. We are the rulers and Hindus are the ryot (peasants). The Sikhs will have to fly the Pakistan flag... pay land revenues (kharaj) and other dues (jiziyah etc.).*'[952] Pakistani scholar, Dr. Israr Ahmed,[953] the founder of *Tanzeem-e-Islami Party*, says on the issue of non-Muslims in Islamic states:[954]

---

952. Khosla, p. 159

953. Dr Israr Amhed is a well-known figure in Pakistan, India, the Middle East, and North America for his efforts in drawing the attention of Muslims toward the teachings and wisdom of the Holy Quran. He host a daily show on the Mumbai-based *Peace TV*, a platform for moderate preachers of Islam, which reaches hundreds of millions of people in Asia, Europe, Africa, Australia and North America.

954. Dr Israr Ahmed; http://in.youtube.com/watch?v=ZJ7B-VG71Pc&feature=related; accessed 14 October 2008

We said (to non-Muslims): either become Muslim and enjoy equal rights, or they have to live as second grade citizens under our rule. Otherwise come to the open field and let the sword resolve the issue.

In Palestine, Hassan El-Masalmeh, a member of the Bethlehem City Council and Hamas leader, advocated for the imposition of discriminatory tax, the *jiziyah*, on non-Muslim residents in 2006. It was abandoned but El-Masalmeh promised, '*We in Hamas intend to implement this tax some day.*'[955]

Even Malaysia, a modern Muslim state, has set up economic, educational and social privileges for Muslim citizens, a form of modern-day institution of *dhimmitude* and *jiziyah*. The non-Muslim minority in 2006 called for the removal of this state-sponsored apartheid that had been in force for three-and-a-half decades. In response, the ruling party activists and leaders, in the annual convention of the party in December 2006, raised a fever-pitch outcry demanding that the privileged rights of Muslims over non-Muslim subjects be maintained. In emotive speeches, some delegates even offered to shed blood to defend the higher rights of Muslims; the youth chief of the party even unsheathed a sword (*keris*) to warn the non-Muslim subjects against demanding eqaulity.

The radical Islamic movements have been gaining fast ascendancy in the Muslim world, while the Sharia laws creeping into the legal system bit by bit even in the West. It remains to be seen whether or not the central professions of Jihad—forced conversion, imperialism and slavery along with economic exploitations and social disabilities of non-Muslims—return to the world-stage with its medieval glories.

---

955. Weiner, op cit

Bibliography

- *Abu Dawud, Sunan*; trans. A Hasan, Kitab Bhavan, New Delhi, 2007, Vols. 1–3
- Adas M ed. (1993) *Islam & European Expansion*, Temple University Press, Philadelphia
- Ahmed A (1964) *Studies in Islamic Culture in the Indian Environment*, Clarendon Press, Oxford
- Al-Attas SN (1963) *Some Aspects of Sufism as Understood and Practice Among the Malays*, S Gordon ed., Malaysian Sociological Research Institute Ltd., Singapore
- Ali SA (1891) *The Life and Teachings of Muhammed*, WH Allen, London
- Al-Tabari (1988) *The History of Al-Tabari*, State University of New York Press, New York, Vols. 6–10
- Al-Thaalibi I (1968) *Lata'if Al-Ma'arif. The Book of Curious and Entertaining Information*, ed. CE Bosworth, Edinburgh University Press
- Ambedkar BR (1979–98) *Writings and Speeches* , Government of Maharashtra, Mumbai
- Armstrong K (1991) *Muhammad: A Attempt to Understand Islam*, Gollanz, London
- Arnold T and Guillaume A eds. (1965) *The Legacies of Islam*, Oxford University Press, London
- Arnold TW (1896) *The Preaching of Islam*, A. Constable & Co., London
- Ashraf KM (1935) *Life and Conditions of the People of Hindustan*, Calcutta
- Banninga JJ (1923) *The Moplah Rebellion of 1921*, in *Moslem World* 13
- Basham AL (2000) *The Wonder That Was India*, South Asia Books, Columbia
- Batabyal R (2005) *Communalism in Bengal: From Famine to Noakhali*, 1943–47, SAGE Publications
- Bernier F (1934) *Travels in the Mogul Empire (1656-1668)*, Revised Smith VA, Oxford
- Berube CG & Rodgaard JA (2005) *A Call to the Sea: Captain Charles Stewart of the USS Constitution*, Potomac Books Inc., Dulles
- Bodley RVC (1970) *The Messenger: The Life of Muhammad*, Greenwood Press Reprint
- Bostom AG (2005) *The Legacy of Jihad*, Prometheus Books, New York
- Braudel F (1995) *A History of Civilizations*, Translated by Mayne R, Penguin Books, New York
- Brockopp JE (2005) *Slaves and Slavery, in The Encyclopedia of the Qur'ān*, McAuliffe JD et al. ed., EJ Brill, Leiden
- Brodman JW (1986) *Ransoming Captives in Crusader Spain: The Order of Merced on the Christian-Islamic Frontier*, University of Pennsylvania Press, Philadelphia
- *Bukhari, Sahih*; trans. MM Khan, Kitab Bhavan, New Delhi, 1987, Vols. 1–9
- Chadurah HM (1991) *Tarikh-Kashmir*, ed. and trans. R Bano, Bhavna Prakashan, Delhi
- Clarence-Smith WG (2006) *Islam and the Abolition of Slavery*, Oxford University Press, New York
- Collins L & Lapierre D (1975) *Freedom at Midnight*, Avon, New York
- Copland I (1998) *The Further Shore of Partition: Ethnic Cleansing in Rajasthan 1947, Past and Present*, Oxford, 160
- Crone P and Cook M (1977) *Hagarism: The Making of the Islamic World*, Cambridge University Press, Cambridge
- Durant W (1999) *The Story of Civilization: Our Oriental Heritage*, MJF Books, New York
- Eaton RM (1978) *Sufis of Bijapur 1300–1700*, Princeton University Press, Princeton
- Eaton RM (2000) *Essays on Islam and Indian History*, Oxford University Press, New Delhi
- Eliot HM & Dawson J, *The History of India As Told By Its Own Historians*, Low Price Publications, New Delhi, Vols. 1–8

- Elst K (1993) *Negationism in India*, Voice of India, New Delhi
- Endress G (1988) *An Introduction to Islam*, trs. C Hillenbrand, Columbia University Press, New York
- Erdem YH (1996) *Slavery in the Ottoman Empire and Its Demise, 1800–1909*, Macmillan, London
- Esin E (1963) *Mecca the Blessed, Medina the Radiant*, Elek, London
- Ferishta MK (1997) *History of the Rise of the Mahomedan Power in India*, translated by John Briggs, Low Price Publication, New Delhi, Vols. I–IV
- Fisher AW (1972) *Muscovy and the Black Sea Slave Trade, in Canadian-American Slavic Studies*, 6(4)
- Fregosi P (1998) *Jihad in the West*, Prometheus Books, New York
- Ghosh SC (2000) *The History of Education in Medieval India 1192-1757*, Originals, New Delhi
- Gibb HAR (2004) *Ibn Battutah: Travels in Asia and Africa*, D K Publishers, New Delhi
- Goel SR (1996) *Story of Islamic Imperialism in India*, South Asia Books, Columbia (MO)
- Goldziher I (1967) *Muslim Studies*, trs. CR Barber and SM Stern, London
- Goldziher I (1981) *Introduction to Islamic Theology and Law*, Trs. Andras & Ruth Hamori, Princeton
- Habibullah, ABM (1976) *The Foundations of Muslim Rule in India*, Central Book Depot, Allahabad
- Haig W (1958) *Cambridge History of India*, Cambridge University Press, Delhi
- Hasan M (1971) *The History of Tipu Sultan*, Aakar Books, New Delhi
- Hitti PK (1961) *The Near East in History*, D. Van Nostrand Company Inc., New York
- Hitti, PK (1948) *The Arabs : A Short History*, Macmillan, London
- Hughes TP (1998) *Dictionary of Islam*, Adam Publishers and Distributors, New Delhi
- Ibn Ishaq, *The Life of Muhammad*, (trs. A Guillaume), Oxford University Press, Karachi, 2004 imprint
- Ibn Sa'd AAM, *Kitab al-Tabaqat*, Trans. S. Moinul Haq, Kitab Bhavan, New Delhi, 1972 print
- Ibn Warraq (1995) *Why I am not a Muslim*, Prometheus Books, New York
- Inalcik H (1997) *An Economic and Social History of the Ottoman empire, 1300-1600*, Cambridge University Press
- Iqbal M (2002) *Islam as a Moral and Political Ideal, in Modernist Islam, 1840-1940: A Sourcebook*, C Kurzman ed., Oxford University Press, London
- Johnson L (2001) *Complete Idiot Guide Hinduism*, Alpha Books, New York
- Jones JP (1915) *India: Its Life and Thought*, The Macmillan Company, New York
- Kamra AJ (2000) *The Prolonged Partition and Its Pogroms*, Voice of India, New Delhi
- Khan Y (2007) *The Great Partition: The Making of India and Pakistan*, Yale University Press, Yale
- Khosla GD (1989) *Stern Reckoning: A Survey of Events Leading Up To and Following the Partition of India*, Oxford University Press, New Delhi
- Lahiri PC (1964) *India Partitioned and Minorities in Pakistan*, Writers' Forum, Calcutta
- Lal KS (1973) *Growth of Muslim Population in Medieval India*, Aditya Prakashan, New Delhi
- Lal KS (1992) *The Legacy of Muslim Rule in India*, Aditya Prakashan, New Delhi
- Lal KS (1994) *Muslim Slave System in Medieval India*, Aditya Prakashan, New Delhi
- Lal KS (1995) *Growth of Scheduled Tribes and Castes in Medieval India*, Aditya Prakashan, New Delhi
- Lal KS (1999) *Theory and Practice of Muslim State in India*, Aditya Prakashan, New Delhi
- Levi (2002) *Hindus Beyond the Hindu Kush: Indian in the Central Asian Slave Trades*, Journal of the Royal Asiatic Society, 12(3)
- Lewis (1994) *Race and Slavery in the Middle East*, Oxford University Press, New York
- Lewis B (1966) *The Arabs in History*, Oxford University Press, New York
- Lewis B (1993) *Islam and the West*, Oxford University Press, New York
- Lewis B (2000) *The Middle East*, Phoenix, London
- Lewis B (2002) *What Went Wrong:Impact and Middle Eastern Response*, Phoenix, London

- Lundström J (2006) *Rape as Genocide under International Criminal Law, The Case of Bangladesh*, Global Human Rights Defence, Lund University
- MA Klein & GW Johnson eds. (1972) *Perspectives on the African Past*, Little Brown Company, Boston
- Maimonides M (1952) *Moses Maimonides' Epistle to Yemen: The Arabic Original and the Three Hebrew Versions*, ed. AS Halkin and trans. B Cohen, American Academy for Jewish Research, New York.
- Majumdar RC ed. (1973) *The Mughal Empire*, in *The History and Culture of the Indian People*, Bombay
- Manucci N (1906) *Storia do Mogor*, trs. Irvine W, Hohn Murray, London
- Maududi AA (1993) *Towards Understanding the Quran*, trs. Ansari ZI, Markazi Maktaba ʻIslamic Publishers, New Delhi
- Maududi SAA, *The Meaning of the Quran*, Islamic Publications, Lahore
- Menon VP (1957) *The Transfer of Power*, Orient Longman, New Delhi
- Milton G (2004) *White Gold*, Hodder & Stoughton, London
- Moreland WH (1923) *From Akbar to Aurangzeb*, Macmillan, London
- Moreland WH (1995) *India at the Death of Akbar*, Low Price Publications, New Delhi
- Muhammad S (2004) *Social Justice in Islam*, Anmol Publications Pvt Ltd, New Delhi
- Muir W (1894) *The Life of Mahomet*, Voice of India, New Delhi
- *Muslim, Sahih*; trans. AH Siddiqi, Kitab Bhavan, New Delhi, 2004 imprint, Vols. 1–4
- Naipaul VS (1977) *India: A Wounded Civilization*, Alfred A Knopf Inc., New York
- Naipaul VS (1981) *Among the Believers: An Islamic Journey*, Alfred A Knopf, New York
- Naipaul VS (1998) *Beyond Belief: The Islamic Incursions among the Converted Peoples*, Random House, New York
- Nehru J (1989) *Glimpses of World History*, Oxford University Press, New Delhi
- Nehru J (1995) *The Discovery of India*, Oxford University Press, New Delhi
- Nizami KA (1989) *Akbar and Religion*, Idarah-i-Adabiyat-i-Delhi, New Delhi
- Nizami KA (1991a) *The Life and Times of Shaikh Nizamuddin Auliya*, New Delhi
- Nizami KA (1991b) *The Life and Times of Shaikh Nasiruddin Chiragh-I Delhi*, New Delhi
- O'Leary DL (1923) *Islam at the Cross Roads*, E. P. Dutton and Co, New York
- O'Shea S (2006) *Sea of Faith: Islam and Christianity in the Medieval Mediterranean World*, Walker & Company, New York
- Owen S (1987) *From Mahmud Ghazni to the Disintegration of Mughal Empire*, Kanishka Publishing House, New Delhi
- Ozcan A (1977) *Pan Islamism, Indian Muslims, the Ottomans & Britain (1877-1924)*, Brill, Leiden
- Parwez GA (1989) *Islam, a Challenge to Religion*, Islamic Book Service, New Delhi
- Pellat Ch, Lambton AKS and Orhonlu C (1978) *'Khasi,' The Encyclopaedia of Islam*, E J Brill ed., Leiden
- Pipes D (1983) *In the Path of God*, Basic Books, New York
- Pipes D (2003) *Militant Islam Reaches America*, WW Norton, New York
- Prasad RC (1980) *Early Travels in India*, Motilal Banarsidass, India
- Pundit KN trs. (1991) *A Chronicle of Medieval Kashmir*, Firma KLM Pvt Ltd, Calcutta
- Rabbi KF (1895) *The Origins of the Musalmans of Bengal*, Calcutta
- Reid A (1983) *Introduction: Slavery and Bondage in Southeast Asian History, in Slavery Bondage and Dependency in Southeast Asia*, Anthony Reid ed., University of Queensland Press, St. Lucia
- Reid A (1988) *Southeast Asia in the Age of Commerce 1450–1680*, Yale University Press, New Haven
- Reid A (1993) *The Decline of Slavery in Nineteenth-Century Indonesia, in Breaking the Chains: Slavery, Bondage and Emancipation in Modern Africa and Asia*, Klein MA ed., University of Wisconsin Press, Madison

- Rizvi SAA (1978) *A History of Sufism in India*, Munshiram Manoharlal Publishers, New Delhi
- Rizvi SAA (1993) *The Wonder That Was India*, Rupa & Co., New Delhi
- Robinson F (2000) *Islam and Muslim History in South Asia*, Oxford University Press, New Delhi
- Rodinson M (1976) *Muhammad*, trs. Anne Carter, Penguin, Harmondsworth
- Roy Choudhury ML (1951) *The State and Religion in Mughal India*, Indian Publicity Society, Calcutta
- Rudolph P (1979) *Islam and Colonialism: The Doctrine of Jihad in Modern History*, Mouton Publishers, The Hague
- Runciman S (1990) *The Fall of Constantinople, 1453*, Cambridge University Press, London
- Russell B (1957) *Why I Am Not a Christian*, Simon & Schuster, New York
- Sachau EC (1993) *Alberuni's India*, Low Price Publications, New Delhi
- Said EW (1997) *Islam and the West In Covering Islam: How the Media and Experts Determine How We See the Rest of the World*, Vintage, London
- Sarkar J (1992) *Shivaji and His Times*, Orient Longham, Mumbai
- Saunders TB (1997) *The Essays of Arthur Schopenhauer: Book I : Wisdom of Life*, De Young Press
- Segal R (2002) *Islam's Black Slaves*, Farrar, Straus and Giroux, New York
- Shaikh A (1998) *Islam: The Arab Imperialism*, The Principality Publishers, Cardiff
- Sharma SS (2004) *Caliphs and Sultans: Religious Ideology and Political Praxis*, Rupa & Co, New Delhi
- Sherwani LA ed. (1977) *Speeches, Writings, and Statements of Iqbal*, Iqbal Academy, Lahore
- Smith VA (1958) *The Oxford History of India*, Oxford University Press, London
- Sobhy as-Saleh (1983) *Mabaheth Fi 'Ulum al- Qur'an*, Dar al-'Ilm Lel-Malayeen, Beirut
- Swarup R (2000) *On Hinduism Reviews and Reflections*, Voice of India, New Delhi
- Tagher J (1998) *Christians in Muslim Egypt: A Historical Study of the Relations between Copts and Muslims from 640 to 1922*, trs. Makar RN, Oros Verlag, Altenberge
- Talib SGS (1991) *Muslim League Attack on Sikhs and Hindus in the Punjab 1947* (compilation), Voice of India, New Delhi
- *The Quran*, Translations by Yusuf Ali A, Pickthal M and Shakir MH; available at http://www.usc.edu/dept/MSA/quran/
- Triton AS (1970) *The Caliphs and Their Non-Muslim Subjects*, Frank Cass & Co Ltd, London
- Umaruddin M (2003) *The Ethical Philosophy of Al-Ghazzali*, Adam Publishers & Distributors, New Delhi
- Van Nieuwenhuijze CAO (1958) *Aspects of Islam in Post-Colonial Indonesia*, W. van Hoeve Ltd, The Hague
- Waddy C (1976) *The Muslim Mind*, Longman Group Ltd., London
- Walker B (2002) *Foundations of Islam*, Rupa & Co, New Delhi
- Warren JF (1981) *The Sulu Zone 1768-1898: The Dynamics of the External Slave Trade, Slavery and Ethnicity in the Transformation of a Southeast Asian Maritime State*, Singapore University Press, Singapore
- Watt WM (1961) *Islam and the Integration of Society*, Routledge & Kegan Paul; London
- Watt WM (2004) *Muhammad in Medina*, Oxford University Press, Karachi
- Widjojoatmodjo RA (1942) *Islam in the Netherlands East Indies*, In *The Far Eastern Quarterly*, 2 (1), November
- Williams BG (2001) *The Crimean Tatars: The Diaspora Experience and the Forging of a Nation*, E J Brill, Lieden
- Zwemer SM (1907) *Islam: A Challenge to Faith*, Student Volunteer Movement, New York

Index

www.ingramcontent.com/pod-product-compliance
Lightning Source LLC
Chambersburg PA
CBHW080526090426
42733CB00015B/2504